Java™ Web Services For Experienced Programmers

Deitel™ Developer Series

Deitel™ Books, Cyber Classrooms, Complete Tra
published by

DEITEL™ *Developer* Series

C#: A Programmer's Introduction

C# for Experienced Programmers

Java™ Web Services for Experienced Programmers

Visual Basic® .NET for Experienced Programmers

Visual C++® .NET: A Managed Code Approach For Experienced Programmers

Web Services: A Technical Introduction

Java 2 Micro Edition for Experienced Programmers (Spring 2003)

Java 2 Enterprise Edition for Experienced Programmers (Spring 2003)

ASP .NET and Web Services with Visual Basic® .NET for Experienced Programmers (Fall 2002)

ASP .NET and Web Services with C# for Experienced Programmers (Spring 2003)

How to Program Series

Advanced Java™ 2 Platform How to Program

C How to Program, 3/E

C++ How to Program, 3/E

C# How to Program

e-Business and e-Commerce How to Program

Internet and World Wide Web How to Program, 2/E

Java™ How to Program, 4/E

Perl How to Program

Python How to Program

Visual Basic® 6 How to Program

Visual Basic® .NET How to Program, 2/E

Wireless Internet & Mobile Business How to Program

XML How to Program

.NET How to Program Series

C# How to Program
Visual Basic® .NET How to Program, 2/E

Visual Studio® Series

C# How to Program
Visual Basic® .NET How to Program, 2/E
Getting Started with Microsoft® Visual C++™ 6 with an Introduction to MFC
Visual Basic® 6 How to Program

For Managers Series

e-Business and e-Commerce for Managers

Coming Soon

e-books and e-whitepapers
Premium CourseCompass, WebCT and Blackboard Multimedia Cyber Classroom versions

ining Courses and Web-Based Training Courses
Prentice Hall

Multimedia Cyber Classroom and *Web-Based Training* Series

(For information regarding Deitel™ Web-based training visit **www.ptgtraining.com**)

C++ Multimedia Cyber Classroom, 3/E

C# Multimedia Cyber Classroom

e-Business and e-Commerce Multimedia Cyber Classroom

Internet and World Wide Web Multimedia Cyber Classroom, 2/E

Java™ 2 Multimedia Cyber Classroom, 4/E

Perl Multimedia Cyber Classroom

Python Multimedia Cyber Classroom

Visual Basic® 6 Multimedia Cyber Classroom

Visual Basic® .NET Multimedia Cyber Classroom, 2/E

Wireless Internet & Mobile Business Programming Multimedia Cyber Classroom

XML Multimedia Cyber Classroom

The Complete Training Course Series

The Complete C++ Training Course, 3/E

The Complete C# Training Course

The Complete e-Business and e-Commerce Programming Training Course

The Complete Internet and World Wide Web Programming Training Course, 2/E

The Complete Java™ 2 Training Course, 4/E

The Complete Perl Training Course

The Complete Python Training Course

The Complete Visual Basic® 6 Training Course

The Complete Visual Basic® .NET Training Course, 2/E

The Complete Wireless Internet & Mobile Business Programming Training Course

The Complete XML Programming Training Course

To follow the Deitel publishing program, please register at

www.deitel.com/newsletter/subscribe.html

for the *DEITEL™ BUZZ ONLINE* e-mail newsletter.

To communicate with the authors, send e-mail to:

deitel@deitel.com

For information on corporate on-site seminars offered by Deitel & Associates, Inc. worldwide, visit:

www.deitel.com

For continuing updates on Prentice Hall and Deitel publications visit:

www.deitel.com,
www.prenhall.com/deitel or
www.InformIT.com/deitel

Library of Congress Cataloging-in-Publication Data

On file

Acquisitions Editor: *Karen McLean*
Project Manager: *Mike Ruel*
Executive Managing Editor: *Vince O'Brien*
Formatters: *Chirag Thakkar, John Lovell*
Director of Creative Services: *Paul Belfanti*
Art Editor: *Xiaohong Zhu*
Creative Director: *Carole Anson*
Design Technical Support: *John Christiana*
Chapter Opener and Cover Designers: *Laura Treibick, Dr. Harvey M. Deitel and Tamara L. Newnam*
Manufacturing Manager: *Trudy Pisciotti*
Manufacturing Buyer: *Lisa McDowell*
Marketing Manager: *Kate Hargett*
Marketing Assistant: *Corrine Mitchell*

© 2003 Pearson Education, Inc.
Upper Saddle River, New Jersey 07458

Cover photo: *Peter Adams/Index Stock Imagery, Inc.*

10 9 8 7 6 5 4 3 2 1

ISBN 0-13-046134-2

Pearson Education Ltd., *London*
Pearson Education Australia Pty. Ltd., *Sydney*
Pearson Education Singapore, Pte. Ltd.
Pearson Education North Asia Ltd., *Hong Kong*
Pearson Education Canada, Inc., *Toronto*
Pearson Educacion de Mexico, S.A. de C.V.
Pearson Education–Japan, *Tokyo*
Pearson Education Malaysia, Pte. Ltd.
Pearson Education, Inc., *Upper Saddle River, New Jersey*

JAVA™ WEB SERVICES FOR EXPERIENCED PROGRAMMERS
DEITEL™ DEVELOPER SERIES

H. M. Deitel
Deitel & Associates, Inc.

P. J. Deitel
Deitel & Associates, Inc.

J. P. Gadzik
Deitel & Associates, Inc.

K. Lomelí
Deitel & Associates, Inc.

S. E. Santry
Deitel & Associates, Inc.

S. Zhang
Deitel & Associates, Inc.

Prentice Hall

PRENTICE HALL, Upper Saddle River, New Jersey 07458

Trademarks

In loving memory of Morris and Lena Deitel.

Harvey and Paul Deitel

To my sister, Lindsay, whose infinite spunkiness has always made me smile.

Jon Gadzik

To Jessica and my family:

Thank you for being there for me when I needed you most.

Kyle Lomelí

To my parents, for the boundless love and support they have given me.

Sean Santry

To my parents and Justin, from the heart, for their inspiration and consistent support.

Su Zhang

Contents

Illustrations

7   Web Services Description Language   158

16 Case Study Part II: Client Applications   517

Preface

Live in fragments no longer. Only connect.
Edward Morgan Forster

We wove a web in childhood,
A web of sunny air.
Charlotte Brontë

Welcome to Web services and the world of interoperable, distributed programming with XML, SOAP, WSDL, UDDI and the Java™ platform! This book is one of the first in the new *Deitel™ Developer Series*, which presents leading-edge computing technologies to software developers and IT professionals.

Web-services technology has gained much attention from the information-technology press and from companies that employ Internet-based applications to conduct business. The term Web services refers to a specific class of applications that use platform and programming-language-neutral data representations and communications protocols to achieve interoperability. By using Web services, companies can ensure that their applications will communicate with those of their business partners and customers.

The primary technologies that enable Web services include the eXtensible Markup Language (XML), the Simple Object Access Protocol (SOAP), the HyperText Transfer Protocol (HTTP), the Web Services Description Language (WSDL), and Universal Description, Discovery and Integration (UDDI) registries.

The World Wide Web Consortium (W3C) developed XML in response to the Web developer community's growing need for a platform-independent language capable of describing data. Web developers wanted a simple language like the HyperText Markup Language (HTML) but with the added flexibility that would allow them to create customized language elements to describe data. XML provides this capability by defining a markup-language syntax with which developers can create element vocabularies. Developers then can use these elements to mark up individual pieces of data, forming XML documents. Since XML documents are text based and use a standard character encoding, they can be processed on any platform. The portability of XML and its rapid adoption throughout the information-technology industry made it an obvious choice for enabling cross-platform data communication in Web services.

Though the W3C now oversees the development of SOAP, a number of industry leaders, including IBM Microsoft and DevelopMentor, originally developed SOAP as a general means for building distributed computing systems. SOAP is an XML vocabulary of elements that enables programs on separate computers to interact across a network, such as the Internet or a company intranet. SOAP messages are XML documents whose contents describe a particular action to invoke on a remote application. For example, a client could send a SOAP message to a credit-card-verification Web service. After performing the verification, the Web service could respond with a SOAP message that contains credit-card authorization information. Any application that supports XML can process SOAP messages.

SOAP defines the structure of these messages, not how the messages are transferred between computers. SOAP relies on an underlying transport protocol such as HTTP—the fundamental protocol of the Web—to transfer messages across the network. HTTP is a simple, text-based protocol already familiar to most Web developers. Also, most networks allow HTTP communications to pass through their firewalls uninhibited. This ensures that communication between Web-services based applications will not be hindered by firewall security restrictions. To ensure that Web-services-based applications are secure, the W3C and other organizations are developing a number of technologies, including XML Encryption, XML Signature, XML Key Management Specification (XKMS), Security Assertions Markup Language (SAML) and eXtensible Access Control Markup Language (XACML), each of which we discuss in Chapter 13, Web Services Security.

WSDL is an XML vocabulary that enables Web-services developers to describe their Web services in a standardized format. WSDL documents provide information for programs to determine how to use the functionalities that Web services provide. By processing a WSDL document, an application can determine exactly what data is required for requests to a Web service and what data the Web service will return.

With the popularity of Web services comes the need for organizing published services so that developers and applications can locate appropriate Web services and obtain their WSDL descriptions. UDDI registries follow the model of the telephone book to organize Web services. Web-services providers can publish their Web services—with WSDL descriptions—in public UDDI registries. Developers and applications then can query these registries to locate desired Web services, along with their complete WSDL descriptions and information about the companies that provide the Web services.

While developers can build Web services in any programming language and on any platform that supports these technologies, Sun Microsystems' Java 2 Platform and Microsoft's .NET Framework stand out as the primary, most complete environments for building, deploying and accessing Web services. The Java 2 Platform has an established community of developers and industry support for enhancing the platform with new technologies through the Java Community Process (JCP). The .NET Framework has pervasive Web services support and enables developers to build applications in many programming languages. Web services were designed with interoperability in mind, so Web-services-based applications built on either of these platforms, and many others can work together.

In *Java Web Services for Experienced Programmers*, we introduce the fundamental technologies that enable Web services, and concentrate on the APIs available for building Web services on the Java platform. Using the Java Web Services Developer Pack from Sun Microsystems, and Web-services platforms from vendors such as the Apache Foundation, Systinet, The Mind Electric, Cape Clear and others, we demonstrate the interoperability that SOAP and WSDL provide. The Java Web Services Developer Pack (JWSDP) was released as a product by Sun Microsystems three weeks before this book went to the presses. This fortuitous event enabled us to ensure that the discussions and code examples throughout the book are fully compliant with the JWSDP.

Who Should Read This Book

Deitel & Associates, Inc. has several Java and Web-services publications, intended for various audiences. We provide information on **www.deitel.com**, here, inside this book's back cover and in the *Deitel™ Buzz Online* e-mail newsletter (**www.deitel.com/ newsletter/subscribe.html**) to help you determine which publication is best for you.

Our Java book, *Java How to Program, 4/e* is part of our *How to Program Series* for college students and professionals. It provides a comprehensive treatment of Java and includes learning aids and extensive ancillary support. *Java How to Program* assumes that the reader has little or no programming experience, but it gets up to speed quickly and offers a solid treatment of Java programming through the intermediate level. Early chapters focus on fundamental programming principles. The book builds on these to create increasingly complex and sophisticated programs that demonstrate how to use Java technologies to create graphical user interfaces, networking applications, multithreaded applications, Web-based applications, graphics, multimedia and more. We encourage professors and professionals to consider the *Java Complete Training Course, 4/e*. This package includes *Java How to Program, 4/e* as well as the *Java Multimedia Cyber Classroom, 4/e*, an interactive multimedia Windows®-based CD-ROM that provides extensive e-Learning features. The *Java Complete Training Course, 4/e* and *Java Multimedia Cyber Classroom, 4/ e* are discussed in detail later in this Preface.

Our book, *Advanced Java 2 Platform How to Program*, is intended for advanced college courses and for professional developers. With *Java How to Program, 4/e* as a launching point, *Advanced Java 2 Platform How to Program* provides in-depth treatments of several groupings of advanced topics—advanced GUI and graphics, distributed systems, introductory Web services, Enterprise Java and XML technologies. Specific technologies include Swing, the Model-View-Controller architecture, graphics with Java 2D™ and Java 3D™, JavaBeans, Security, JDBC, servlets, JavaServer Pages™ (JSP), Java 2 Micro Edition™ (J2ME), Enterprise JavaBeans™ (EJB), Java Message Service (JMS), Jini™, Jiro™, JavaSpaces™, Java Management Extensions (JMX), CORBA®, Peer-to-Peer, JXTA and Apache SOAP.

This book, *Java Web Services for Experienced Programmers*, is part of the new *Deitel™ Developer Series*, intended for professional software developers—from novices through experienced programmers. *Java Web Services for Experienced Programmers* is part of the *For Experienced Programmers* subseries, designed for the experienced programmer who wants a deep treatment of a new technology. *Java Web Services for Experienced Programmers* begins with an overview of XML, which provides a foundation for

Web-services technologies. The book continues by delving deeply into more sophisticated topics, such as Simple Object Access Protocol (SOAP), Web Services Description Language (WSDL), the Java API for XML-based RPC (JAX-RPC), the Java API for XML Messaging (JAXM) and more. Unlike the *How to Program Series* books, the *Deitel*™ *Developer Series* books do not include the extensive pedagogic features, such as chapter exercises and ancillary support materials (for college professors) required for academic courses.

Web Services A Technical Introduction is the first publication in our *A Technical Introduction* subseries, which offers broad overviews of new technologies. We designed this publication to be a "literacy" book that explains Web services, explores the benefits they provide to businesses and discusses key concepts related to the technology. We believe that the information we present will be useful both to programmers, who must learn to incorporate Web services in their applications and networks, and to IT managers, who must decide when and how to adopt this important new technology. For programmers, this book does include programming-intensive appendices on building Web services in Java and in Visual Basic® .NET (with ASP .NET).

Each of our Java books presents many complete, working Java programs and depicts their inputs and outputs in actual screen shots of running programs. This is our signature *LIVE-CODE*™ *approach.* Each book's source code is available free for download at **www.deitel.com**.

For a detailed listing of Deitel™ products and services, please see the "advertorial" pages at the back of this book and visit **www.deitel.com**. Readers may also want to register for our new *Deitel*™ *Buzz Online* e-mail newsletter (**www.deitel.net/news-letter/subscribe.html**), which provides information about our publications, company announcements, links to informative technical articles, programming tips, teaching tips, challenges, anecdotes and more.

As you proceed, if you would like to communicate with us, please send an e-mail to **deitel@deitel.com**—we always respond promptly. Please check our Web sites, **www.deitel.com**, **www.prenhall.com/deitel** and **www.InformIT.com/deitel** for frequent updates, errata, FAQs, etc. When sending an e-mail, please include the book's title and edition number. We sincerely hope that you enjoy learning Web services technologies with our publications.

Features of *Java Web Services: For Experienced Programmers*

This edition contains many features, including:

- *Syntax Highlighting.* This book uses five-way syntax highlighting to emphasize XML and Java programming elements in a manner similar to that of many development tools. Our syntax-highlighting conventions are as follows:

```
comments
keywords
literal values
errors and JSP directives
text, class, method and variable names
```

- *"Code Washing."* This is our term for the process we use to format the book's programs so that they have a carefully commented, open layout. The code is grouped into small, well-documented pieces. This greatly improves code readability—an especially important goal for us, considering that this book contains approximately 13,321 lines of code in 103 complete LIVE-CODE™ programs.

- ***XML.*** Use of Extensible Markup Language (XML) is exploding in the software-development industry, in the e-business and e-commerce communities, and is foundational to Web services. Because XML is a platform-independent technology for describing data and for creating markup languages, XML's data portability integrates well with Java-based portable applications and services. Chapters 2–5 introduce XML, Document Type Definitions, the Document Object Model (DOM™) and Extensible Stylesheet Language (XSL and XSLT).

- ***Simple Object Access Protocol (SOAP).*** The Simple Object Access Protocol is the *lingua franca* that enables Web-services interoperability. SOAP is a simple markup language for describing messages between applications. Built using XML, SOAP provides the true platform and programming-language independence that modern applications require for integrating business processes and transactions across the Web. We discuss SOAP and Web-services platforms for deploying SOAP-based Java Web services in Chapter 6.

- ***Web Services Description Language (WSDL).*** The Web Services Description Language provides developers with an XML-based language for describing Web services and exposing those Web services for public access. Chapter 7, Web Services Description Language discusses WSDL.

- ***XML Registries and Universal Description, Discovery and Integration (UDDI).*** Businesses and consumers need to be able to locate organizations that provide Web services. XML registries, including those based on Universal Description, Discovery and Integration (UDDI), provide common repositories for business information and WSDL descriptions of Web services. Chapter 8, UDDI, Discovery and Web Services Registries, introduces the fundamentals of XML registries. Chapter 10, Java API for XML Registries, presents the Java technology that enables programmatic access to UDDI and other XML registries.

- ***Java API for XML-based Remote Procedure Calls (JAX-RPC).*** SOAP is an important protocol for Web services, but not all developers need to work with SOAP messages directly. JAX-RPC provides developers with a powerful API for building RPC-oriented Web services and Web-services clients without requiring developers to manipulate SOAP messages. This enables developers to concentrate on the Web services and clients, instead of on the underlying messaging protocol. Based in part on Java's Remote Method Invocation (RMI) API, JAX-RPC enables developers to define remote interfaces for their Web services, and provides tools for generating WSDL documents, stubs and ties from those interfaces. JAX-RPC also enables client developers to generate client-side classes for interacting with a Web service based on that service's WSDL document. Chapter 9, Java API for XML-Based RPC, discusses the details of using JAX-RPC for building Web services and for building clients, including those that use the Dynamic Invocation Interface (DII), dynamic proxies and static stubs. We also demonstrate a JAX-RPC client that interacts with a Web service implemented in Visual Basic® .NET.

- *Java API for XML Messaging (JAXM) and SOAP with Attachments API for Java (SAAJ).* SAAJ provides a robust API for developers who require access to the detailed structures of SOAP messages. Using JAXM, developers can create Web services based on various profiles, which enable the use of messaging frameworks such as ebXML. JAXM also enables developers to build asynchronous Web services and clients through the use of message providers. Chapter 11, JAXM and SAAJ, presents these foundational Java-Web-services technologies.

- *Java API for XML Registries (JAXR).* XML registries based on UDDI, ebXML and other technologies enable businesses to publish and discover Web services. JAXR provides a Java API with which developers can manipulate these registries. Through JAXR, developers can build applications for searching XML registries, for publishing new Web services and for manipulating existing registry entries. Chapter 10, Java API for XML Registries, discusses JAXR for querying, publishing and manipulating XML registry entries.

- *Computer, Internet and Web-Services Security.* The ease with which businesses can integrate transactions and processes across the Internet by using Web-services technologies raises numerous security concerns. The World Wide Web Consortium (W3C) and other industry leaders are developing security technologies for Web services, such as XML Encryption, Security Assertions Markup Language (SAML), and others. Chapter 12, Computer and Internet Security, and Chapter 13, Web Services Security, discuss general security concerns and specific technologies for securing Web services.

- *Wireless Web Services.* By some estimates, about a billion people worldwide are using mobile devices, such as wireless phones and PDAs, and this number is increasing rapidly. Enabling access to Web services from mobile devices is crucial to these technologies. The Java 2 Micro Edition provides a Java platform for building mobile applications, and various third parties have developed APIs and implementations for accessing Web services from J2ME-enabled devices. Chapter 14, Wireless Web Services and J2ME, discusses the integration of mobile devices into the Web-services infrastructure and presents J2ME MIDlets that access Web services.

Pedagogic Approach

Java Web Services for Experienced Programmers contains a rich collection of examples. The book concentrates on the principles of good software engineering and stresses program clarity. We are educators who teach edge-of-the-practice topics in industry classrooms worldwide. We avoid arcane terminology and syntax specifications in favor of teaching by example.

We use fonts to distinguish between features such as menu names and menu items and other elements that appear in graphical user interfaces (GUIs). Our convention is to emphasize GUI features in a sans-serif bold Helvetica font (e.g., **File** menu) and to emphasize program text in a serif bold Courier font (e.g., `boolean x = true;`).

LIVE-CODE™ Teaching Approach

Java Web Services for Experienced Programmers includes 103 LIVE-CODE™ examples. This presentation style exemplifies the way we teach and write about programming and is the focus of our multimedia *Cyber Classrooms* and Web-based training courses as well. Each new concept is presented in the context of a complete, working example that is followed by one or more windows showing the program's input/output dialog. Reading the examples in the text is much like entering and running them on a computer. Readers have the option of downloading all of the book's code examples from **www.deitel.com**, under the **Downloads/Resources** link. Other links provide errata and answers to frequently asked questions.

World Wide Web Access

All of the source code for the program examples in *Java Web Services: For Experienced Programmers* (and our other publications) is available on the Internet as downloads from the following Web sites:

```
www.deitel.com
www.prenhall.com/deitel
```

Registration is quick and easy and these downloads are free. We suggest downloading all the examples, then running each program as you read the corresponding portion of the book. Make changes to the examples and immediately see the effects of those changes—this is a great way to improve your programming skills. Setup instructions for required software can be found in Chapter 1, Introduction, and at our Web sites, along with the examples. [*Note:* This is copyrighted material. Feel free to use it as you study, but you may not republish any portion of it in any form without explicit permission from Prentice Hall and the authors.]

Objectives

Each chapter begins with objectives that inform readers of what to expect and give them an opportunity, after reading the chapter, to determine whether they have met the intended goals.

Quotations

The chapter objectives are followed by sets of quotations. Some are humorous, some are philosophical and some offer interesting insights. We have found that readers enjoy relating the quotations to the chapter material. Many of the quotations are worth a "second look" *after* you read each chapter.

Outline

The chapter outline enables readers to approach the material in top-down fashion. Along with the chapter objectives, the outline helps users anticipate topics and set a comfortable and effective learning pace.

13,321 Lines of Code in 103 Example Programs (with Program Outputs)

We present Java Web services features in the context of complete, working Web services and client programs. All examples are available as downloads from our Web site, **www.deitel.com**.

Summary

Each chapter ends with a summary that helps readers review and reinforce key concepts.

Approximately 1,818 Index Entries (with approximately 2,682 Page References)

We have included an extensive Index. This resource enables readers to search for any term or concept by keyword. The Index is especially useful to practicing programmers who use the book as a reference.

"Double Indexing" of All LIVE-CODE™ Examples

Java Web Services for Experienced Programmers has 103 LIVE-CODE™ examples, which we have "double indexed." For every program in the book, we took the figure caption, and indexed it both alphabetically and as a subindex item under "Examples." This makes it easier to find examples using particular features.

Java Multimedia Cyber Classroom and The Complete Java Training Course

For readers who want to learn Java or reinforce their Java skills before reading this book, we have prepared an interactive, CD-ROM-based, software version of *Java How to Program, 4/e* called the *Java Multimedia Cyber Classroom, 4/e*. This resource, ideal for corporate training and college courses, is loaded with interactive e-learning features. The *Cyber Classroom* is packaged with the *Java How to Program, 4/e* book at a discount in the boxed product called *The Complete Java Training Course, 4/e*. If you already have the book and would like to purchase the *Java Multimedia Cyber Classroom, 4/e* separately, please visit **www.InformIT.com/cyberclassrooms**. The ISBN number for the *Java Multimedia Cyber Classroom, 4/e* is 0-13-064935-X. Many Deitel™ *Cyber Classrooms* are available in CD-ROM and Web-based training formats.

The CD-ROM provides an introduction in which the authors overview the *Cyber Classroom*'s features. The textbook's 197 LIVE-CODE™ example Java programs truly "come alive" in the *Cyber Classroom*. If you are viewing a program and want to execute it, you simply click the lightning-bolt icon, and the program will run. You immediately will see—and hear, when working with audio-based multimedia programs—the program's output. Click the audio icon, and one of the authors will discuss the program and "walk you through" the code.

The *Cyber Classroom* also provides navigational aids, including extensive hyperlinking. The *Cyber Classroom* is browser based, so it remembers sections that you have visited recently and allows you to move forward or backward among those sections. The thousands of index entries are hyperlinked to their text occurrences. Furthermore, when you key in a term using the "find" feature, the *Cyber Classroom* will locate occurrences of that term throughout the text. The Table of Contents entries are "hot," so clicking a chapter name takes you immediately to that chapter.

Readers like the fact that solutions to approximately half the exercises in *Java How to Program, 4/e* are included with the *Cyber Classroom*. Studying and running these extra programs is a great way for readers to enhance their learning experience.

Professionals and student users of our *Cyber Classrooms* tell us that they like the interactivity and that the *Cyber Classroom* is an effective reference due to its extensive hyperlinking and other navigational features. We received an e-mail from a reader who said he lives "in the boonies" and cannot attend a live course at a university, so the *Cyber Classroom* provided an ideal solution to his educational needs.

Professors tell us that their students enjoy using the *Cyber Classroom*, spend more time on the courses and master more of the material than in textbook-only courses. For a complete list of the available and forthcoming *Cyber Classrooms* and *Complete Training Courses*, see the *Deitel™ Series* page at the beginning of this book, the product listing and ordering information at the end of this book or visit **www.deitel.com**, **www.pren-hall.com/deitel** or **www.InformIT.com/deitel**.

Deitel e-Learning Initiatives

e-Books and Support for Wireless Devices

Wireless devices will play an enormous role in the future of the Internet. Given recent bandwidth enhancements and the emergence of 3G wireless technologies, it is projected that, within two years, more people will access the Internet through wireless devices than through desktop computers. Deitel & Associates is committed to wireless accessibility and has published *Wireless Internet & Mobile Business How to Program*. To fulfill the needs of a wide range of customers, we are developing our content in traditional print formats and in new electronic formats, such as e-books, so that readers can access content virtually anytime, anywhere. Subscribe to the *Deitel™ Buzz Online* newsletter (**www.deitel.com/newsletter/subscribe.html**) for periodic updates on all Deitel technology initiatives.

e-Matter

Deitel & Associates is partnering with Prentice Hall's parent company, Pearson PLC, and its information technology Web site, **InformIT.com**, to launch the Deitel e-Matter series at **www.InformIT.com/deitel** in Spring 2003. The Deitel e-Matter series will provide professionals with an additional source of information on specific programming topics at modest prices. e-Matter consists of stand-alone sections taken from published texts, forthcoming texts or pieces written during the Deitel research-and-development process. Developing e-Matter based on pre-publication manuscripts allows us to offer significant amounts of the material well before our books are published.

Learning Management Systems

We are working with many corporate e-Learning providers to make our electronic products available in popular, AICC-compliant, SCORM-compliant learning management systems.

Course Management Systems: WebCT, Blackboard, CourseCompass and Premium CourseCompass

We are working with Prentice Hall to integrate our *How to Program Series* courseware into four series of Course Management Systems-based products: WebCT, Blackboard™, CourseCompass and Premium CourseCompass. These enable college instructors to create, manage and use sophisticated Web-based educational programs. Course Management Systems feature course customization (such as posting contact information, policies, syllabi, announcements, assignments, grades, performance evaluations and progress tracking), class and student-management tools, a grade book, reporting tools, communication tools (such as chat rooms), a whiteboard, document sharing, bulletin boards and more. Instructors can use these products to communicate with their students, create online quizzes and exams from questions directly linked to the text and efficiently grade and track test results. For more information about these upcoming products, visit **www.prenhall.com/cms**. For demonstrations of existing WebCT, Blackboard and CourseCompass course materials, visit **cms.prenhall.com/webct**, **cms.prenhall.com/blackboard** and **cms.prenhall.com/coursecompass**, respectively.

Deitel and InformIT Newsletters

Deitel Column in the InformIT Newsletters

Deitel & Associates contributes articles to the free *InformIT* weekly e-mail newsletter, sub-scribed to by more than 750,000 IT professionals worldwide. To subscribe, visit **www.In-formIT.com** and click the **MyInformIT** tab.

Deitel™ Buzz Online Newsletter

Our own free newsletter, the *Deitel™ Buzz Online*, includes commentary on industry trends and developments, links to articles and resources from our published books and upcoming publications, product-release schedules, challenges, anecdotes and more. To subscribe, vis-it **www.deitel.com/newsletter/subscribe.html**.

The Deitel™ Developer Series

Deitel & Associates, Inc., is making a major commitment to Web services through the launch of our *Deitel™ Developer Series. Java Web Services for Experienced Programmers* and *Web Services A Technical Introduction* are the first Web-services books in this new se-ries. These will be followed by additional titles on Web-services technologies.

   The *Deitel™ Developer Series* is divided into three subseries. The *A Technical Intro-duction* subseries provides IT managers and developers with detailed overviews of emerging technologies. The *A Programmer's Introduction* subseries is designed to teach the fundamentals of new languages and software technologies to developers from the ground up. These books discuss programming fundamentals, followed by brief introduc-tions to more sophisticated topics. Finally, the For *Experienced Programmers* subseries is designed for seasoned developers seeking to learn new programming languages and tech-nologies. The books in this subseries move quickly to in-depth coverage of the program-ming languages and software technologies being covered.

Acknowledgments

One of the great pleasures of writing a book is acknowledging the efforts of many people whose names may not appear on the cover, but whose hard work, cooperation, friendship and understanding were crucial to the production of the book.

   Many other people at Deitel & Associates, Inc., devoted long hours to this project. Below is a list of our full-time employees who contributed to this publication:

- Tem R. Nieto, a graduate of the Massachusetts Institute of Technology, is Director of Product Development at Deitel & Associates, Inc. He is co-author of *C#: A Pro-grammer's Introduction, C# for Experienced Programmers, Visual Basic .NET for Experienced Programmers* and numerous texts in the *How to Program* series. Tem co-authored Chapters 2–5 on XML technologies.

- Lauren Trees, a graduate of Brown University with a concentration in Literatures in English contributed to the Preface, Chapter 1, Introduction, Chapter 8, UDDI, Discovery and Web Services Registries, Chapter 12, Computer and Internet Secu-rity and Chapter 13, Web Services Security.

- Rashmi Jayaprakash, a graduate of Boston University with a degree in Computer Science, co-authored Chapter 8, UDDI, Discovery and Web Services Registries.

- Laura Treibick, a graduate of the University of Colorado at Boulder with a degree in Photography and Multimedia, is Director of Multimedia at Deitel & Associates, Inc. She created and enhanced many of the graphics throughout the text.

- Barbara Deitel applied copy edits to the manuscript and compiled the quotations for all the chapters.

- Abbey Deitel, a graduate of Carnegie Mellon University's Industrial Management Program and President of Deitel & Associates, Inc., co-authored Chapter 12, Computer and Internet Security, and Chapter 13, Web Services Security.

We would also like to thank the participants in the Deitel & Associates, Inc., College Internship Program who contributed to this publication.[1]

- A. James O'Leary, a senior in Computer Science and Psychology at Rensselaer Polytechnic Institute, co-authored Chapter 11 and Chapter 12.

- Christina Carney, a senior in Psychology and Business at Framingham State College, researched the Internet and Web Resources URLs.

We are fortunate to have been able to work with the talented and dedicated team of publishing professionals at Prentice Hall. We especially appreciate the extraordinary efforts of our editor, Karen McLean of PH/PTR and her assistant, Michael Ruel, who manages the extraordinary review processes for our *Deitel™ Developer Series* publications. We would also like to thank Mark L. Taub, Editor-in-Chief of computer publications at PH/PTR, for conceptualizing the *Deitel™ Developer Series* and providing the necessary resources and encouragement to help us generate the many books in this series. A special note of appreciation goes to Marcia Horton, Editor-in-Chief of Engineering and Computer Science at Prentice Hall. Marcia has been our mentor in publishing and our friend for 18 years at Prentice Hall. She is responsible for all aspects of Deitel publications at all Pearson divisions including Prentice Hall, PH/PTR and Pearson International.

Laura Treibick, the Director of Multimedia at Deitel & Associates, Inc., and Dr. Harvey M. Deitel designed the cover. Tamara Newnam (**smart_art@earthlink.net**) carried the cover through to completion, and inserted five of our Deitel bug characters in the cover art (can you find them?).

We wish to acknowledge the efforts of our reviewers, who, adhering to a tight time schedule, scrutinized the text and the programs, providing countless suggestions for

---

1. The *Deitel & Associates, Inc. College Internship Program* offers a limited number of salaried positions to Boston-area college students majoring in Computer Science, Information Technology, Marketing, Management and English. Students work at our corporate headquarters in Maynard, Massachusetts full-time in the summers and (for those attending college in the Boston area) part-time during the academic year. We also offer full-time internship positions for students interested in taking a semester off from school to gain industry experience. Regular full-time positions are available to college graduates. For more information about this competitive program, please contact Abbey Deitel at **deitel@deitel.com** and visit **www.deitel.com**.

improving the accuracy and completeness of the presentation. We sincerely appreciate the time these people took from their busy professional schedules to help us ensure the quality, accuracy and timeliness of this book.

Dibyendu Baksi (Sun Microsystems)
Arun Gupta (Sun Microsystems)
Christian Hessler (Sun Microsystems, Inc.)
Doug Kohlert (Sun Microsystems)
Debra Scott, Ph.D. (Sun Microsystems)
Saleem Arif (Data Concepts)
Kevin Curley (Cape Clear)
Christopher Fry (Clear Methods)
Kyle Gabhart (Objective Solutions, Inc.)
Ari Goldberg (Alphawolf)
Adam C. Gross (Grand Central Communications, Inc.)
Mason Ham (Zambit Technologies)
Michael Hudson (Blueprint Technologies, Inc.)
Anne Thomas Manes (Systinet)
George McKevitt (Comcast)
Paul Monday (J. D. Edwards & Co.)
JP Morganthal (iKimbo)
Clifton Nock (J. D. Edwards & Co.)
Neal Patel (Microsoft Corporation)
Mike Plusch (Clear Methods)
Teri Radichel (Radical Software)
Rani Sandoy-Brown (AT&T Wireless)
Chris Trevino (AT&T Wireless)
Sazi Temel (BEA Systems)
Priscilla Walmsley (Consultant)
David Weller (Valtech Technologies, Inc.)
Justin Whitney (Writer and Web Services Game Designer)
Ilan Zolar (Pacific Bell)

We would sincerely appreciate your comments, criticisms, corrections and suggestions for improving the book. Please address all correspondence to:

deitel@deitel.com

We will respond promptly.

Well, that's it for now. Welcome to the exciting world of Web services. Good luck!

Dr. Harvey M. Deitel
Paul J. Deitel
Jonathan Gadzik
Kyle Lomelí
Sean E. Santry
Su Zhang

About the Authors

Dr. Harvey M. Deitel, Chairman and Chief Strategy Officer of Deitel & Associates, Inc., has 41 years experience in the computing field, including extensive industry and academic experience. Dr. Deitel earned B.S. and M.S. degrees from the Massachusetts Institute of Technology and a Ph.D. from Boston University. He worked on the pioneering virtual-memory operating-systems projects at IBM and MIT that developed techniques now widely implemented in systems such as UNIX®, Linux™ and Windows XP. He has 20 years of college teaching experience, including earning tenure and serving as the Chairman of the Computer Science Department at Boston College before founding Deitel & Associates, Inc., with his son, Paul J. Deitel. He is the author or co-author of several dozen books and multimedia packages and is writing many more. With translations published in Japanese, Russian, Spanish, Traditional Chinese, Simplified Chinese, Korean, French, Polish, Italian, Portuguese and Greek, Dr. Deitel's texts have earned international recognition. Dr. Deitel has delivered professional seminars to major corporations, and to government organizations and the military.

Paul J. Deitel, CEO and Chief Technical Officer of Deitel & Associates, Inc., is a graduate of the Massachusetts Institute of Technology's Sloan School of Management, where he studied Information Technology. Through Deitel & Associates, Inc., he has delivered Java, C, C++ and Internet and World Wide Web programming courses to industry clients including Compaq, Hewlett-Packard, Sun Microsystems, White Sands Missile Range, Rogue Wave Software, Boeing, Dell, Stratus, Fidelity, Cambridge Technology Partners, Open Environment Corporation, One Wave, Hyperion Software, Lucent Technologies, Adra Systems, Entergy, CableData Systems, NASA at the Kennedy Space Center, the National Severe Storms Laboratory, IBM and many other organizations. He has lectured on C++ and Java for the Boston Chapter of the Association for Computing Machinery and has taught satellite-based Java courses through a cooperative venture of Deitel & Associates, Inc., Prentice Hall and the Technology Education Network. He and his father, Dr. Harvey M. Deitel, are the world's best-selling programming-language textbook authors.

Jonathan Gadzik is a graduate of the Columbia University School of Engineering and Applied Science, where he received a Bachelor of Science in Computer Science. He is a Sun-Certified Programmer and Developer for the Java 2 Platform, and is a Sun-Certified Web-Component Developer for the J2EE Platform. He has contributed to several Deitel publications, including *Java How to Program, 4/e*, *Advanced Java 2 Platform How to Program*, *Visual Basic .NET How to Program* and *C# How to Program*.

Kyle Lomelí is a graduate of Oberlin College where he majored in Computer Science and minored in East Asian Studies. At Oberlin College he researched, designed and developed agent-based distributed systems. He is a Sun Certified Developer for the Java 2 Platform, and has contributed to several Deitel publications, including *Advanced Java 2 Platform How to Program*, *Visual Basic .NET How to Program* and *C# How to Program*.

Sean E. Santry, Director of Software Development with Deitel & Associates, Inc., and co-author of *Advanced Java 2 Platform How to Program*, is a graduate of Boston College where he studied Computer Science and Philosophy. At Boston College he performed original research on the application of metaphysical systems to object-oriented software design. Through Deitel & Associates, Inc. he has delivered advanced-level industry courses in Java, C++, object-oriented programming, Enterprise JavaBeans, Web services, design patterns and other technologies for clients including Sun Microsystems, Computer Associates, EMC, Dell, Compaq, HP, Boeing, Washingtonpost.Newsweek Interactive and others. He has contributed to numerous Deitel publications, including various editions of *Java How to Program*; *XML How to Program*; *C++ How to Program*; *C# How to Program*; *C How to Program*; *e-Business and e-Commerce How to Program* and *e-Business and e-Commerce for Managers*. Before joining Deitel & Associates, he developed e-business applications with BiT Group, a Boston-area consulting firm.

Su Zhang holds B.Sc and a M.Sc degrees in Computer Science from McGill University. Her graduate research included modeling and simulation, real-time systems and Java technology. She worked on Java and Web-technologies-related projects prior to joining Deitel. She has contributed to other Deitel publications, including *Advanced Java 2 Platform How to Program* and *Python How to Program*.

About Deitel & Associates, Inc.

Deitel & Associates is an internationally recognized corporate instructor-led training and content-creation organization specializing in Internet/World Wide Web software technology, e-business/e-commerce software technology, object technology and programming-languages education. The company provides courses in Internet and World Wide Web programming, wireless Internet programming, Web services (in both Java and .NET languages), object technology, and major programming languages and platforms, such as Visual Basic® .NET, C#, Visual C++ .NET, Java™, Advanced Java™, C, C++, XML, Perl, Python, ASP .NET, ADO .NET and more. Deitel & Associates, Inc., was founded by Dr. Harvey M. Deitel and Paul J. Deitel, the world's leading programming-language textbook authors. The company's clients include many of the world's largest computer companies, government agencies, branches of the military and business organizations. Through its 27-year publishing partnership with Prentice Hall, Deitel & Associates, Inc., publishes leading-edge programming textbooks, professional books, interactive CD-ROM-based multimedia *Cyber Classrooms*, *Complete Training Courses*, e-books, e-matter, Web-based training courses and course-management-systems e-content. Deitel & Associates and the authors can be reached via e-mail at:

> `deitel@deitel.com`

To learn more about Deitel & Associates, its publications and its worldwide corporate on-site curriculum, see the last few pages of this book or visit:

> `www.deitel.com`

Individuals wishing to purchase Deitel books, *Cyber Classrooms*, *Complete Training Courses* and Web-based training courses can do so through bookstores, online booksellers and:

> `www.deitel.com`
> `www.prenhall.com/deitel`
> `www.InformIT.com/deitel`
> `www.InformIT.com/cyberclassrooms`

Bulk orders by corporations and academic institutions should be placed directly with Prentice Hall. See the last few pages of this book for worldwide ordering details. To follow the Deitel publishing program, please register for the *Deitel*™ *Buzz Online* newsletter at

www.deitel.com/newsletter/subscribe.html

The World Wide Web Consortium (W3C)

Deitel & Associates, Inc., is a member of the *World Wide Web Consortium (W3C)*. The W3C was founded in 1994 "to develop common protocols for the evolution of the World Wide Web." As a W3C member, Deitel & Associates, Inc., holds a seat on the W3C Advisory Committee (the company's representative is our CEO and Chief Technology Officer, Paul Deitel). Advisory Committee members help provide "strategic direction" to the W3C through meetings held around the world. Member organizations also help develop standards recommendations for Web technologies (such as XHTML, XML and many others) through participation in W3C activities and groups. Membership in the W3C is intended for companies and large organizations. To obtain information on becoming a member of the W3C visit **www.w3.org/Consortium/Prospectus/Joining**.

1

Introduction

Objectives

- To review the history of the Internet, distributed computing and object technology.
- To explain enterprise communications requirements that have led to computing innovations.
- To understand the evolution of Web services.
- To discuss the potential of Web services and challenges to their adoption.
- To provide examples of companies benefiting from Web services.
- To introduce the software needed for building Java Web services.
- To tour the book.

Before beginning, plan carefully.
Marcus Tullius Cicero

Look with favor upon a bold beginning.
Virgil

I think I'm beginning to learn something about it.
Auguste Renoir

Outline

1.1 Introduction

Welcome to the world of Web services! Over the past several decades, computing has evolved at an unprecedented pace. This progress affects organizations in significant ways, forcing information-technology (IT) managers and developers to adjust rapidly to new computing paradigms. Innovations in programming and hardware have led to more powerful and useful technologies, including object-oriented programming, distributed computing, Internet protocols and Extensible Markup Language (XML). Organizations have learned to leverage the power of their networks and the Internet to gain competitive advantage.

Web-services technology—which represents the next stage in distributed computing—will profoundly affect organizations in 2002 and beyond. Web services encompass a set of related standards that can enable computer applications to communicate and exchange data via the Internet. Although the true impact of Web services is not yet known, many factors—including software vendors' widespread support for underlying standards—indicate that Web services will radically change IT architectures and partner relationships. Companies are already implementing Web services to facilitate a wide variety of business processes, such as application integration and business-to-business transactions.

Since its public introduction in 1995, Java™ has evolved from a language for building interactive animations for Web pages into a complete suite of software platforms. With its three editions—Java 2 Standard Edition (J2SE™), Java 2 Enterprise Edition (J2EE™) and Java 2 Micro Edition (J2ME™)—developers can use Java to build virtually any type of application. The vast majority of application-server vendors support J2EE for building enterprise applications. J2SE's Swing user-interface libraries and deep support for networking, databases, graphics and multimedia enable developers to build rich desktop applications. J2ME extends the Java platform to small devices, such as cell phones and set-top boxes. With its support for industry-standard protocols, including Web-services protocols, Java is ready for the next generation of interoperable distributed systems.

When the topic of Web services began to appear in magazines, trade papers and industry conferences, we began to anticipate the extraordinary effect Web services would have on the future of interoperable distributed systems. At the 2002 JavaOne™ conference, there was an entire track with over 140 technical and "birds-of-a-feather" sessions devoted to Web services. For two of this book's authors who attended the conference (PJD and SES), it was clear that Web services would be a primary focus for the future of Java. We hope to provide you with insight into the technologies and standards available to Java developers. These insights, along with practical examples throughout the book, will prepare you for developing truly interoperable distributed systems with Java.

As you proceed through *Java Web Services for Experienced Programmers*, if you would like to communicate with us, send an e-mail to **deitel@deitel.com**, or browse our Web sites at **www.deitel.com**, **www.prenhall.com/deitel** and **www.InformIT.com/deitel**. To learn about the latest developments in Web services and other leading-edge software technologies, register at **www.deitel.com/newsletter/subscribe.html** for the new *Deitel™ Buzz Online* e-mail newsletter. We hope that you find *Java Web Services for Experienced Programmers* both informative and enjoyable.[1]

1.2 Computing Advancements and Web Services

Computer technology is constantly evolving to better serve the needs of programmers and users. Advances in programming and networking have improved software-development and communications capabilities, paving the way for Web services. This section overviews key developments in computing technology that have led to the creation of Web services.

1.2.1 Structured Programming to Object Technology

One of this book's authors, HMD, remembers the great frustration felt in the 1960s by software-development organizations, especially those creating large-scale projects. During the summers of his undergraduate years, HMD had the privilege of working at a leading computer vendor on the teams developing time-sharing, virtual-memory operating systems. It was a great experience for a college student, but, in the summer of 1967, reality set in: The company "decommitted" from commercially producing the particular system that hundreds of people had been working on for several years. Software development is a complicated process, and it was difficult to get software right.

During the 1960s, many large software-development projects encountered severe difficulties. Development efforts typically ran behind schedule, costs often greatly exceeded budgets, and the finished products were unreliable. People began to realize that software development was a far more complex activity than they had imagined. Research intended

---

1. The *Deitel Developer Series* book *Web Services: A Technical Introduction* provides a more business-oriented discussion of Web services, with appendices on implementing both Java-based and .NET-based Web services.

to address these issues led to *structured programming*—a disciplined approach to creating programs that are clear, demonstrably correct and easy to modify.

As the benefits of structured programming and of the related disciplines of structured systems analysis and design were realized in the 1970s, improved software technology did begin to appear. However, it was not until *object-oriented programming* became widely used in the 1980s and 1990s that software developers finally felt they had the necessary tools to improve the software-development process dramatically.

What are objects, and why are they special? Object technology is a packaging scheme that enables programmers to create meaningful software units. These units can be large and are focused on particular applications areas. There are date objects, time objects, paycheck objects, invoice objects, audio objects, video objects, file objects, record objects and so on. In fact, almost any noun can be reasonably represented as a software object. Objects have *properties* (i.e., *attributes*, such as color, size and weight) and perform *actions* (i.e., *behaviors*, such as moving, sleeping and drawing). *Classes* represent groups of related objects. A class is to an object as a blueprint is to a house. A class specifies the general format of its objects; the properties and actions available to an object depend on its class.

We live in a world of objects. Just look around you—there are cars, planes, people, animals, buildings, traffic lights, elevators and so on. Before object-oriented languages appeared, procedural programming languages (such as Fortran, Pascal, Basic and C) focused on actions (verbs) rather than objects (nouns). This paradigm shift made program writing a bit awkward. However, with the advent of popular object-oriented languages, such as C++, Java, C# and Visual Basic .NET, programmers can write code more naturally in an object-oriented manner that reflects the way in which they perceive the world. This process has resulted in significant productivity gains.

One of the key problems with procedural programming is that the software units created do not mirror real-world entities effectively and therefore are not particularly reusable. Programmers often write software for one project then rewrite similar software for other projects. This wastes time and money as developers repeatedly "reinvent the wheel." By contrast, object-oriented programming allows for code to be organized and encapsulated as classes, which facilitates the reuse of software components. Developers can group classes into *class libraries*, which they can then make available to developers working on other projects.

Web services extend the object-oriented paradigm, in that objects can represent Web services. Every Web service is, potentially, a self-contained object that can be reused by, or incorporated into, other applications. In this manner, the technology encourages a modular approach to programming, transforming a network such as the Internet into an enormous library of programmatic components available to developers. This can greatly reduce the effort required to implement certain kinds of systems—especially compared with the effort involved in reinventing these capabilities for every new project.

1.2.2 Distributed Computing

When developers create substantial applications, often it is more efficient, or even necessary, for concurrent tasks to be performed on different computers. The emergence of more powerful computers and networks led to the *distributed computing* phenomenon, in which an organization's computing is distributed over networks, instead of being performed only at a central computer installation. *N-tier applications* split up applications over numerous computers. For example, a *three-tier application* might have a user interface on one computer, business-logic processing on a second and a database on a third—all interacting as the application runs.

For a distributed system to function correctly, application components (often encapsulated as programming objects) executing on different computers throughout a network must be able to communicate. In the early 1990s, many companies and organizations—including the Object Management Group (OMG), Microsoft, Sun Microsystems and IBM—realized the need for such functionality and began developing their own technologies to enable communication among distributed components. Each of the main technologies—OMG's *Common Object Request Broker Architecture* (*CORBA*), Microsoft's *Distributed Component Object Model* (*DCOM*), Sun Microsystem's *Remote Method Invocation over Internet Inter-Orb Protocol* (*RMI/IIOP*) and IBM's *Distributed System Object Model* (*DSOM*)—allows programs written in various languages, with varying implementations and running in disparate locations, to communicate as if they were on the same computer. This was a significant development, because businesses could use these technologies to integrate applications with business partners' computing systems.

Unfortunately, *interoperability* (the ability to communicate and share data with software from different vendors and platforms) is limited among these technologies. For example, the two most popular technologies, DCOM and CORBA, cannot communicate easily. DCOM and CORBA components often communicate via a *COM/CORBA bridge*. If DCOM's and CORBA's underlying protocols change, programmers must modify the bridge to reflect the changes. Such problems have impeded distributed computing's ability to facilitate business-process integration and automation.

Web services improve distributed-computing capabilities by addressing the issue of limited interoperability. Unlike DCOM and CORBA, Web services operate using *open* (i.e., nonproprietary) *standards*. This means that Web services can, theoretically, enable any two software components to communicate—regardless of the technologies used to create the components or the platforms on which the components reside. Also, Web services-based applications are often easier to debug, because Web services use a text-based communications protocol, rather than the binary (i.e, consisting of ones and zeros) communications protocols employed by DCOM and CORBA. Organizations are implementing Web services to improve communication between DCOM and CORBA components and to create standards-based distributed-computing systems. Thus, Web services will help organizations to finally achieve the goals of distributed computing.

1.2.3 World Wide Web

Although the Internet was created more than three decades ago, the *World Wide Web* (*WWW*) is a relatively recent development. The Web allows computer users to locate and view multimedia-based documents (i.e., documents with any combination of text, graphics, animations, audios and videos) on almost any subject. In 1989, Tim Berners-Lee of CERN (the European Organization for Nuclear Research) began to develop a technology for sharing information via hyperlinked text documents. Basing the new language on the well-established *Standard Generalized Markup Language* (*SGML*)—a standard for business data interchange—Berners-Lee called his invention the *Hypertext Markup Language* (*HTML*). He also wrote communication protocols to form the backbone of his new hypertext information system, which he referred to as the World Wide Web.

The Internet and Web will surely be listed among the most important and profound creations of the 20th century. In the past, most applications ran on standalone computers. Today's applications can be written to communicate among the world's hundreds of millions of computers. The Internet and Web expedite and simplify our work, changing the way we do business and how we conduct our personal lives. Web services—which typically operate over Internet and Web protocols—extend the Web's capabilities to include direct communication between computer programs, even those written in different languages and running on disparate platforms.

1.2.4 Electronic Data Interchange (EDI)

As computers became integral to business, organizations wanted to use electronic capabilities to reach their markets faster and more efficiently. By shortening *lead time* (the time it takes to receive a product from a supplier after an order has been placed) businesses can lower their inventory costs and gain competitive advantage.[1] Many organizations have invested in *Electronic Data Interchange* (*EDI*) technology to link business partners and help manage supply chains.

Conventional EDI systems combine computers and communications equipment to enable businesses to conduct secure, reliable electronic transactions. Every supplier, manufacturer and distributor in a supply chain is linked to the EDI system through a *value-added network (VAN)*—a closed network that includes all members of a production process. EDI systems track and document a business's daily accounting and inventory data, including information on purchase orders, invoices and other transactions. For example, operations personnel at a manufacturing plant might use an EDI system to buy supplies, track shipments and maintain accurate inventories. The EDI system transfers electronic documentation that verifies each party in a transaction, records the terms and conditions of the transaction and processes the order.[2]

Although EDI systems improve efficiency and promote better accounting practices, they can be expensive to operate. Also, many suppliers and distributors are small machine shops and shipping companies that do not have the technology to link into EDI systems. Worse, EDI systems are not standardized, so a supplier or distributor that conducts business with multiple customers or partners might require separate EDI connections for each relationship. Finally, EDI systems can be difficult to maintain, because they are *tightly coupled*: If a developer changes one component of a tightly coupled system, the developer must reprogram all components in the system that rely on the altered component.[3] However, EDI traffic can now be carried over the Internet, which reduces costs and makes EDI accessible to more organizations. Nevertheless, EDI remains prohibitively expensive for many companies.[4]

Web services provide capabilities similar to those offered by EDI, but are simpler and less expensive to implement. Since Web services are built on open standards, fewer incompatibility problems arise. Also, Web services are more conducive to constructing *loosely coupled* systems—systems in which a developer can alter a programming component without having to modify other components to reflect the original change.[5] Web services can be configured to work with EDI systems, which allows organizations to use the two technologies together or to phase out EDI while adopting Web services. Some companies are using Web services and EDI to implement more affordable business-process management systems.[6]

1.3 Emergence of Web Services

Although organizations are just beginning to implement Web services, the basic standards and ideas have existed for several years. In 1999, Hewlett-Packard became the first software vendor to introduce the concept of Web services. HP's product, *e-Speak*, was a platform that enabled developers to build and implement "e-services," program units similar to Web services. However, the proprietary nature of e-Speak's underlying technologies prevented the platform from gaining widespread industry support.

Microsoft coined the actual term "Web services" in June 2000, when the company introduced Web services as a key component of its *.NET initiative*, a broad new vision for embracing the Internet in the development, engineering and use of software. Microsoft announced that it was "betting the company" on Web services and almost immediately, Web services became the "next big thing." Now, nearly every major software vendor is marketing Web services tools and applications.[7]

With the announcement of Web services, many realized that the technology could revolutionize distributed computing. Previously, both CORBA and DCOM had been submitted to standards organizations, with the expectation that companies would choose one or the other as a universal distributed-computing standard. However, this did not occur, because organizations had already made significant investments in either Windows or Java platforms and their corresponding distributed technologies. Migration to a different platform costs businesses time, money and employee productivity.[8]

The industry's experience with interoperability problems led to the development of open standards for Web services technologies, in an effort to enable cross-platform communication. The primary standard used in Web services is XML, a language for marking up data so that information can be exchanged between applications and platforms. Microsoft and DevelopMentor built the *Simple Object Access Protocol* (*SOAP*) as a messaging protocol for transporting information and instructions between Web services, using XML as a foundation for the protocol. Two other Web services specifications—*Web Services Description Language* (*WSDL*) and *Universal Description, Discovery and Integration* (*UDDI*)—are also based on XML. WSDL provides a standard method of describing Web services and their specific capabilities; UDDI defines XML-based rules for building directories in which companies advertise themselves and their Web services.

As a programming platform that "grew up" on the Internet, Java is well suited for developing distributed systems with Web services. Java has rich support for XML and provides extensive libraries for networking with standard Internet protocols. As Web services technologies have developed, the Java Community Process (JCP)—an organization that enables organizations and individuals to extend the Java platform with new APIs and technologies—has kept pace with the emerging standards. Through the JCP, Sun Microsystems and its partners have developed numerous APIs for building and integrating Web services with the Java platform. The Java APIs for XML Messaging (JAXM) and XML-Based Remote Procedure Calls (JAX-RPC) enable developers to work at a high level of abstraction in building standards-compliant Web services. The Java API for XML Registries enables integration through XML registries based on UDDI, ebXML and other technologies. Sun has worked closely with the open-source community to ensure that these technologies remain open. Coupled with broad support from application-server vendors, Java has become a primary platform for building and delivering Web services.

1.4 Web Services Advantages

After the dot-com crash, businesses are more hesitant to invest significantly in new technologies. Readers might be wondering, "Why, then, is the computing industry so enthusiastic about Web services, given that many other promising technologies have failed?" To understand the answer to this question, let us consider some advantages associated with Web services:

- Web services operate using open standards, which enable components written in different languages and for different platforms to communicate.

- Web services promote a modular approach to programming, so companies can re-use the same Web services to communicate with multiple organizations.

- Web services are comparatively easy and inexpensive to implement, because they employ an existing infrastructure (a network, such as the Web) to exchange information.

- Web services can significantly reduce the costs of enterprise application integration (EAI) and business-to-business (B2B) communications, thus offering companies tangible returns on their investments.[9]

- Web services can be implemented incrementally, rather than all at once. This lessens the cost of adopting Web services and can reduce organizational disruption resulting from an abrupt switch in technologies.

The most important advantage of Web services over previous distributed-computing technologies is that Web services employ open standards. Because Web services must facilitate communication among disparate applications and platforms, standardization and interoperability are crucial. The *World Wide Web Consortium* (*W3C*)—an organization that defines Web technologies—and other standards bodies are committed to ensuring that Web services protocols and specifications remain open, royalty free and interoperable across vendor implementations. For example, the W3C established a *Web Services Activity*[2] to oversee the continued development of Web services technologies and to guarantee their compatibility with other W3C standards.[10]

Major software vendors, such as Microsoft and IBM, are also promoting interoperability among Web services implementations. The two companies are founding members of the *Web Services Interoperability Organization* (*WS-I*), a vendor consortium encompassing over a hundred companies from various industries (**www.ws-i.org**). The WS-I's goals include (1) developing guidelines and testing procedures for creating interoperable Web services, (2) establishing best practices for implementing Web services using SOAP, XML and UDDI, and (3) providing developers with sample Web services that conform to WS-I guidelines. Although not a standards organization, the WS-I plans to help the W3C refine and improve Web services specifications.[11]

---

2. A W3C Working Group is a unit of technical experts developing and improving a particular technology. *Activity* is the term that the W3C uses to represent an area of development around which one or more working groups are formed.

1.5 Real Web Services

Although Web services have yet to reach their full potential, they are already reshaping business communications. Companies are recognizing the benefits of Web services, and many have already deployed such services to address specific business needs. This section describes Web services implementations in industries such as education, manufacturing, financial services and travel.

Organizations are employing Web services to integrate and improve communications systems. For example, the University of California at Berkeley is using Web services to unify the school's e-mail, voice mail and facsimile service into individual in-boxes that are accessible from cell phones, PDAs, telephones and e-mail clients. With this new architecture, a single number can provide access to a cell phone, telephone, a fax and a pager, and users can customize their personal settings. The set of Web services (called the *Unified Communications Technical Project*) will connect existing communications channels, allowing the school to integrate the channels while preserving legacy systems. The communications project also offers the flexibility to add new technologies or change vendors if necessary. At the time of this writing, the project was under development. If successful, the system will serve 50,000 students, faculty and staff by 2003.[12]

Manufacturing companies are implementing Web services to improve supply chains and inventory and customer-management systems. For example, Eastman Chemical allows customers to access information about the company's numerous products via Web services. Eastman's distributors used to retrieve product information via the company's Web site or e-mail and, in turn, pass the information on to customers. Because Eastman updates its product information frequently, this system caused distributors to supply customers with dated information. In response, Eastman implemented a Web services solution that allows customers to access the company's product catalog directly. Without Web services, this would have required that each Eastman distributor install a complex proprietary application. However, Web services enable Eastman to provide distributors with a standard application (i.e., a Web services client) that facilitates communication with Eastman's servers.[13]

Financial services companies require the most current market statistics to make effective decisions. The consulting firm Accenture has developed Web services products, called *Live Information Models*, that enable stock traders to access real-time quotes and market information. Prior to Web services, brokerages had to install new terminals to access market information from subscription services. This situation often forced brokers to look at multiple screens to gather information. Accenture's Web services product allows brokers to receive real-time updates and to access different information sources from a single terminal.[14]

The travel industry also is benefitting from Web services' integration capabilities. Airlines, travel agencies, rental-car companies and hotels all provide travel-related services. However, most of these organizations cannot integrate their computing systems because they do not use the same software or platforms. With Web services, companies in the travel business can streamline the reservation process. For example, consider the Web service implemented by business partners Dollar Rent a Car and Southwest Airlines. When Southwest approached Dollar about enabling customers to make rental-car reservations from the airline's site, it was obvious that connecting the reservation system and the Web site would benefit both businesses. However, integration would be difficult due to the companies' different operating systems—Southwest uses UNIX systems and Dollar uses Microsoft Windows. Dollar knew it could create a one-time solution to connect its electronic reservation system to Southwest's site, but it would not be able to reuse a customized system with other partners. Instead, Dollar turned its reservation system into a Web service. Since Web services communicate via the Internet using open standards, Dollar can connect additional businesses to its reservation system without creating a customized solution for each relationship.[15]

These examples illustrate ways that Web services can facilitate communication within an organization or between trusted business partners. Other organizations are developing public Web services, which are accessible to any interested party. Many public Web services are listed by Web services broker sites, such as **www.xmethods.net** and **www.salcentral.com**. At this time, XMethods lists approximately 175 Web services, and Salcentral lists approximately 400. The majority of these services are free, but some are fee-based. Figure 1.1 lists some public Web services and their capabilities.

Web Services Can...

Offer updates on local traffic conditions or the status of an eBay auction.
(**alerts.microsoft.com/alerts/UserHome.asp**)

Provide computer and network security
(**www.McAfee.com**)

Return the distance in miles between two locations.
(**www.codebump.com**)

Locate entertainment, restaurants and lodging in a given area.
(**www.zagat.com**)

Return the name and postal address associated with a phone number
(**www.serviceobject.com/products/dots_geophone.asp**)

Find information about ski resorts in a given city or zip code.
(**www.skiwhere.com**)

Locate trademark-status information from the U.S. Patent and Trademark Office's Web site.
(**www.serviceobjects.com/products/dots_tradetrack.asp**)

Conjugate verbs in over a hundred languages.
(**www.verbix.com**)

Find ATM locations in a given zip code.
(**www.serviceobjects.com/products/dots_atm_demo.asp**)

Return the position of the sun, moon and planets at a specific time.
(**www.orbitarium.com**)

Find the current price of any book at **BarnesandNoble.com**.
(**www.esynaps.com/eSynaps_home.aspx**)

Communicate with e-mail servers to validate e-mail addresses.
(**www.cdyne.com/service.aspx**)

Find the current conversion rate between two currencies.
(**www.esynaps.com/eSynaps_home.aspx**)

Fig. 1.1   Examples of existing Web services and their capabilities.[16] (Part 1 of 2.)

Web Services Can...

Translate text between two languages.
(**babelfish.altavista.com**)

Process electronic payments—including credit cards, debit cards and e-checks.
(**www.richsolutions.com**).

Check and correct postal addresses.
(**www.cdynecom/services.aspx**)

Track the current location and status of a FedEx package.
(**fedex.com/us/tracking**)

Perform financial calculations—including APR, tax and mortgage rates.
(**www.xmlbus.com/docs/5.2/demos**)

Report current weather conditions at airports and airfields.
(**capescience.capeclear.com/webservices/airportweather**)

Return stock quotes (with a fifteen-minute delay).
(**www.cdynecom/services.aspx**)

Send SMS messages and ring-tones to Internet-enabled wireless devices.
(**www.webservicebuy.com/x/smsreg.asp**)

Fig. 1.1   Examples of existing Web services and their capabilities.[16] (Part 2 of 2.)

1.6 Web Services Challenges

Web services offer many benefits, but also create significant challenges for application developers and IT staffs. A key problem is that SOAP, WSDL and UDDI—the standards that drive Web services—are still in draft form. SOAP and WSDL are under development by the W3C, and UDDI has not yet been submitted to a standards organization. This means that the protocols and specifications are likely to change in the near term.[17] Many businesses want to wait until the underlying technologies are stable before adopting Web services. Others are concerned that the current cooperation among software vendors such as Microsoft, IBM and Sun to create interoperable implementations might fail, resulting in splinter standards and incompatible Web services implementations.[18]

Another impediment to Web services adoption is the absence of standard security procedures. Web services typically allow direct access to a company's applications, which can expose corporate networks to security threats such as hackers and viruses. The core standards used in Web services, such as SOAP, are not designed to provide security. New Web services–specific security technologies are under development, but many companies are hesitant to deploy Web services outside corporate firewalls until security mechanisms are standardized.[19] This book provides an in-depth treatment of general computer and network security issues in Chapter 12, Computer and Internet Security, and examines Web services-specific security issues in Chapter 13, Web Services Security.

Other Web services challenges involve defining and guaranteeing *Quality of Service* (*QoS*). Before invoking a Web service, customers often want to verify that the service will meet their expectations. Possible QoS problems with Web services include slow response times, infrequent updates and an inability to handle large numbers of requests. Some businesses have developed *service-level agreements* (*SLAs*)—contracts between service providers and users that guarantee certain amounts of uptime, performance, security and so on. Also, independent companies have begun to provide third-party evaluations of Web services.

1.7 Java Web Services Software[3]

Throughout *Java Web Services for Experienced Programmers*, we rely on a number of software packages. In the following subsections, we discuss these software packages, provide URLs for obtaining the software and refer you to complete installation instructions.

1.7.1 Java 2 Standard Edition

We developed the Java-based Web services in this book using the Java 2 Standard Edition Software Development Kit, version 1.4.0 from Sun Microsystems. The J2SE SDK and documentation are available for download from the Sun Web site at

> `java.sun.com/j2se/1.4/download.html`

Complete installation instructions also are available at

> `java.sun.com/j2se/1.4/install.html`

In particular, be sure to update your operating system's **PATH** environment variable as instructed. This will facilitate the use of the J2SE SDK's command-line utilities. Also, we recommend that you do not set the **CLASSPATH** environment variable. For each example in this book, we provide complete compilation and execution instructions, which include setting the appropriate **CLASSPATH**. You also should set the **JAVA_HOME** environment variable to the location at which you installed the J2SE SDK. For example, if you installed the SDK to the **C:\j2sdk1.4.0** directory on a Windows system, you would set the **JAVA_HOME** environment variable to the value **C:\j2sdk1.4.0**.

If you choose to use an integrated development environment (IDE), such as NetBeans (**www.netbeans.org**), Sun™ ONE Studio (formerly Sun's Forte for Java, **wwws.sun.com/software/sundev/jde/index.html**) or Borland's JBuilder (**www.borland.com/jbuilder**), you will need to refer to the IDE vendor's documentation for instructions on compiling and executing programs.

1.7.2 JWSDP Download and Installation

In June 2002, Sun released the Java Web Services Developer Pack (JWSDP), version 1.0, which includes the primary APIs and reference implementations for building Java-based Web services and clients. JWSDP includes the following items:

- Java API for XML Messaging (JAXM), v1.1
- Java API for XML Processing (JAXP), v1.2
- Java API for XML Registries (JAXR), v1.0_01

---

3. We assume an audience of experienced programmers who are aware that software is constantly changing. We also assume that this may cause programs in this book to require adjustment. We will post known problems and fixes at **www.deitel.com**.

- Java API for XML-based RPC (JAX-RPC), v1.0

- SOAP with Attachments API for Java (SAAJ), v1.1

- JavaServer Pages Standard Tag Library (JSTL), v1.0

- Java WSDP Registry Server, v1.0_01

- Web Application Deployment Tool

- Ant Build Tool v1.4.1

- Apache Tomcat v4.1.2 servlet container

Examples throughout *Java Web Services for experienced Programmers* demonstrate the use of these APIs. JWSDP can be downloaded from

java.sun.com/webservices/downloads/webservicespack.html

Complete installation instructions for UNIX and Windows systems are available at

java.sun.com/webservices/downloads/install-unix.html
java.sun.com/webservices/downloads/install-windows.html

In particular, be sure to set the **PATH** environment variable as instructed. You also should set the **JWSDP_HOME** environment variable to the directory in which you installed JWSDP. For example, if you installed JWSDP to the **C:\jwsdp-1_0** directory on a Windows system, you would set the **JWSDP_HOME** environment variable to the value **C:\jwsdp-1_0**.

1.7.3 Cloudscape Installation

Several examples in this book use the Cloudscape database, which is included in the Java 2 Enterprise Edition Software Development Kit, version 1.3.1. This is available for download at

java.sun.com/j2ee/sdk_1.3

After installing the J2EE SDK, make sure to set the **%J2EE_HOME%** environment variable to the directory in which J2EE is installed. Also, make sure to include **%J2EE_HOME%/bin** in the path.

Cloudscape represents each database as a directory with the same name as the database. For example, Cloudscape will store a database named **books** in a directory called **books**. The scripts needed to create all the databases used in examples in this book are available to download from our Web site **www.deitel.com**. Each script has extension **sql**, and the script's name is identical to the name of the database that the script creates— for example, **books.sql** is needed to create the **books** database. Place each script in the **%J2EE_HOME%/cloudscape** directory. On our Web site we also provide **createDatabase.bat**, which is a batch file that creates a database from a script. To create a database, type

createDatabase *script*

For example, to create the books database, type

createDatabase books.sql

Each Web application that accesses a Cloudscape database must have **RmiJdbc.jar** and **cloudclient.jar** in the **lib** directory of the Web application directory. Figure 1.2 shows this directory structure. **RmiJdbc.jar** and **cloudclient.jar** are located in the **%J2EE_HOME%\lib\cloudscape** directory.

To start Cloudscape (assuming that **%J2EE_HOME%\bin** is included in the path), type in the command shell

```
cloudscape -start
```

To stop Cloudscape, type in the command shell

```
cloudscape -stop
```

Also, always make sure to start Cloudscape before starting Tomcat. When Tomcat starts, the Web applications that use Cloudscape will attempt to load the database drivers. If Cloudscape is not operational, Tomcat will report an error.

In the next section, we take a detailed tour of *Java Web Services for Experienced Programmers*. This book is divided into several sections. Chapters 2–5 introduce XML, which is a foundational technology for Web services. We explore the basics of creating XML and manipulating documents using the Java API for XML Processing (JAXP). Chapters 6–8 describe the core technologies and standards associated with Web services, including the Simple Object Access Protocol (SOAP), SOAP-Based Web-Services Platforms, Web Services Description Language (WSDL) and Universal Description Discovery and Integration (UDDI). Chapters 9–11 present the primary Java technologies for implementing Web services and Web services clients and for manipulating XML registries. Reflecting on the need for securing Web services, Chapters 12 and 13 introduce the fundamentals of computer security and discuss the various technologies for securing Web services. Chapter 14 presents the available APIs and technologies for integrating wireless devices, such as cell phones, into Web-services infrastructures. Chapters 15–17 present a capstone case study that integrates many of the technologies discussed in Java Web Services for Experienced Programmers, to build a significant Web-services-based application. The book concludes with appendices that introduce Java servlets and JavaServer Pages, two technologies supporting Java Web services.

Web application directory and file structure

```
webapps
    WEB-INF
        web.xml
        classes
            Web-application classes (some of which use Cloudscape)
        lib
            RmiJDBC.jar
            cloudclient.jar
```

Fig. 1.2   Directory and file structure for a Web application that uses the Cloudscape database.

1.8 Tour of the Book

In this section, we take a detailed tour of *Java Web Services for Experienced Programmers*. This book is divided into several sections. Chapters 2–5 introduce XML, which is a foundational technology for Web services. We explore the basics of creating XML and manipulating documents using the Java API for XML Processing (JAXP). Chapters 6–8 describe the core technologies and standards associated with Web services, including the Simple Object Access Protocol (SOAP), SOAP-Based Web-Services Platforms, Web Services Description Language (WSDL) and Universal Description Discovery and Integration (UDDI). Chapters 9–11 present the primary Java technologies for implementing Web services and Web services clients and for manipulating XML registries, such as the Java API for XML-based Remote Procedure Calls (JAX-RPC), the Java API for XML Messaging (JAXM), and the Java API for XML Registries (JAXR).

Reflecting on the enormous importance of Web-services security, Chapters 12 and 13 introduce the fundamentals of computer security and discuss the various technologies for securing Web services, such as XML Encryption, XML Key Management Specification (XKMS), Security Assertions Markup Language (SAML) and Extensible Access Control Markup Language (XACML). Chapter 14 presents the available APIs and technologies for integrating wireless devices, such as cell phones, into Web-services infrastructures.

Chapters 15–17 present a capstone case study that integrates many of the technologies discussed in Java Web Services for Experienced Programmers, to build a significant Web-services-based application. This application integrates Web services across several businesses to enable customers to search for the best prices on Deitel books. In the case study, three fictitious book stores provide Web services that enable business partners to obtain pricing information and place book orders. A consumer-oriented service called the Price Finder Web service retrieves the best prices from the book stores and enables consumers to place orders directly through the Price Finder. In addition, we integrate the Deitel Book Information Web service to enable online stores and other businesses to get up-to-date information on Deitel publications, including titles, descriptions, cover images and more. To demonstrate the interoperability that Web services facilitate, we deploy the various Web services on disparate service platforms. We also implement three different client applications for interacting with the Price Finder Web service, including a Web-based client using servlets, a J2ME client for cell phones and a Swing-based desktop application. The book concludes with appendices that introduce Java servlets and JavaServer Pages, two key technologies that support Java Web services. We use these technologies throughout the book and in the Price Finder case study.

In the walkthrough of each chapter, there will be terms that are unfamiliar to you—they will be defined in the chapters of the book. Many chapters end with an Internet and World Wide Web Resources section that provides a listing of Web sites you should visit to enhance your knowledge of the technologies discussed in those chapters. You may also want to visit **www.deitel.com** and **www.prenhall.com/deitel** to keep informed of updates on Java Web services technologies, book errata and additional teaching and learning resources.

Chapter 1—Introduction
This chapter overviewed the technologies presented in *Java Web Service for Experienced Programmers*. We presented a tour of the book with a brief overview of each chapter. We provided installation and execution instructions for the software required in the book.

Chapter 2—Creating Markup with XML

XML is the fundamental enabling technology for Web services. We include a substantial introduction to XML in Chapters 2–5. Chapter 2 introduces the fundamentals of XML. We discuss the properties of the XML character set, called *Unicode*—the standard aimed at providing a flexible character set for most of the world's languages. We provide a brief overview of *parsers*—programs that process XML documents and their data. We also overview the requirements for a *well-formed document* (i.e., a document that is syntactically correct). We discuss *elements*, which hold data in XML documents. Several elements can have the same name, resulting in *naming collisions*; we introduce *namespaces*, which differentiate these elements to avoid such collisions.

Chapter 3—XML Document Type Definitions

A *Document Type Definition (DTD)* is a structural definition for an XML document, specifying the type, order, number and attributes of the elements in the document as well as other information. By defining the structure of an XML document, a DTD reduces the validation and error-checking work of the application using the document. We discuss well-formed and valid documents (i.e., documents that conform to a DTD). This chapter shows how to specify different element and attribute types, values and defaults that describe the structure of an XML document.

Chapter 4—XML Document Object Model (DOM)

The W3C *Document Object Model (DOM)* is an API for XML that is platform and language independent. The DOM is a standard API for manipulating the contents of XML documents. The *Java API for XML Processing* (*JAXP*) provides DOM support for Java programs. XML documents are hierarchically structured, so the DOM represents XML documents as tree structures. Using DOM, programs can modify the content, structure and formatting of documents dynamically. This chapter examines several important DOM capabilities, including the ability to retrieve data, insert data and replace data. We also demonstrate how to create and traverse documents using the DOM.

Chapter 5—XSLT: Extensible Stylesheet Language Transformations

XSL was designed to manipulate the rich and sophisticated data contained in an XML document. XSL has two major functions: formatting XML documents and transforming them into other data formats such as XHTML and Rich Text Format (RTF). In this chapter, we discuss the subset of XSL called XSLT. XSLT uses XPath—a language of expressions for accessing portions of XML documents—to match nodes for transforming an XML document into another text document. We use JAXP—which includes XSLT support—in our examples. An XSL stylesheet contains *templates* with which elements and attributes can be matched. New elements and attributes can be created to facilitate a transformation.

Chapter 6—SOAP-Based Web Services Platforms

Web services are built using a variety of technologies, such as SOAP, WSDL, UDDI and ebXML. One of the greatest problems facing Web services developers is trying to understand how implementations of these protocols work together to create Web-services environments. This chapter overviews the general operation of Web services platforms. The chapter provides the reader with detailed instructions on how to deploy a simple Web service called the Book Title Service in a variety Web services platforms, such as Apache's

Axis, CapeClear's CapeConnect, The Mind Electric's GLUE, Systinet's Web Applications and Services Platform (WASP) and IBM's Web Services Took Kit (WSTK). The chapter demonstrates how to create a simple client that connects to the Book Title Web service running on any of these Web-services platforms. The chapter also provides a detailed look at the process of sending and receiving SOAP messages to and from a Web service.

Chapter 7—Web Services Description Language (WSDL)
Clients that wish to access Web services generally have no prior knowledge either of the specific Web services that an application has made available or of the addresses (URLs) of these services. To publicize this information, a Web service developer uses an XML-based language called *Web Service Description Language* (*WSDL*) to specify the information in a *WSDL document*. The developer places the document in the Web-services environment and clients of the service download the WSDL document to access information about the available services. In this chapter, we discuss how developers use WSDL to provide this information to clients. We discuss the WSDL syntax, and how to generate WSDL documents. To conclude the chapter, we build clients that use WSDL documents to invoke Web services and we discuss the importance of these documents in this process.

Chapter 8—UDDI, Discovery and Web Services Registries
For Web services to achieve widespread adoption, a unified system must enable developers and applications to locate specific Web services. Several organizations have developed Web services registry systems, but the leading registry is based on the Universal Description, Discovery and Integration (UDDI) specification. This chapter details aspects of UDDI, including dynamic discovery, the public UDDI Business Registry (UBR) and private registries. We describe the UDDI information model, which is composed of business information, business-service information, bind information, service specification information and publisher-assertion information. We then discuss the UDDI publishing and querying APIs. We also explain key limitations of UDDI and introduce alternative discovery methods provided by ebXML, WS-Inspection and Discovery of Web Services (DISCO).

Chapter 9—Java API for XML-Based Remote Procedure Calls (JAX-RPC)
This chapter introduces the Java API for XML-based Remote Procedure Calls (JAX-RPC), which is a protocol-independent API for building Java-based Web services and Web-services clients. With JAX-RPC, Web services and their clients use XML-based protocols, such as SOAP, and common transport protocols, such as HTTP, to communicate. JAX-RPC abstracts away the complexities of working with SOAP and HTTP directly, yet maintains interoperability. In this chapter, we introduce the JAX-RPC architecture and present three examples that use JAX-RPC APIs to build and access Web services.

Chapter 10—Java API for XML Registries (JAXR)
The Java XML for Registries (JAXR) is an API that enables developers to register business information in UDDI and ebXML registries. This chapter discusses JAXR API features by registering the Deitel Book Title Service (introduced in Chapter 6) with a UDDI registry. The chapter discusses how to register, modify and delete a business entry in a UDDI-compliant registry and explains the process of categorizing a business under various classification schemes.

Chapter 11—Java API for XML Messaging (JAXM)

The *Java API for XML Messaging* (*JAXM*) is Sun Microsystem's latest API for sending messages between components. Unlike Sun's other messaging technologies (*JavaMail* and *Java Messaging Service*), JAXM packages messages in SOAP XML format and is used by developers to build applications that both access and provide Web services. Using the JAXM API, developers can program two types of applications: *standalone* applications that use JAXM to access Web services, and applications that use a *JAXM message provider* to provide and access Web services. We discuss the JAXM API, which we then use to build a standalone application. Later in the chapter, we explain the importance and efficiency of a JAXM message provider and use the provider to construct a JAXM application that can both send and receive SOAP requests and responses.

Chapter 12—Computer and Internet Security

Security breaches and network attacks cause immense damage, costing organizations billions of dollars and affecting their productivity and credibility. To minimize these problems, it is essential that companies protect their data and ensure secure transactions. Effective security involves authenticating the identities of senders and receivers, verifying data integrity, ensuring that sensitive information remains private and proving that information was sent and properly received. This chapter defines basic security terminology and explores the history of cryptography. We examine and illustrate several cryptographic techniques used to encode information, including secret-key cryptography and public-key cryptography. We explore user authentication methods, such as digital signatures, digital certificates, digital watermarks and Kerberos. We also analyze the strengths and weaknesses of popular security standards and mechanisms, including Secure Sockets Layer (SSL), Internet Protocol Security (IPSec) and Virtual Private Networks (VPNs). Finally, we consider network security options, such as firewalls and intrusion-detection systems.

Chapter 13—Web Services Security

Web services can move transactions beyond corporate firewalls and enable outside entities to access corporate applications. This offers many benefits to organizations, but also increases the potential for security breaches and data corruption. This chapter addresses security—one of the main obstacles to widespread Web services adoption. We describe why existing security technologies such as HTTP and SSL are insufficient to protect Web services transmissions. We then present several evolving Web-services security specifications, including XML Signature and XML Encryption; the XML Key Management Specification (XKMS) for registering and distributing encryption keys can be used with these techniques to authenticate each party in a transaction and to set up Public Key Infrastructure (PKI) for Web services. We also examine authorization and policy standards, such as Security Assertion Markup Language (SAML) and Extensible Access Control Markup Language (XACML). The chapter concludes by discussing the effects of Web-services security on firewalls and networks.

Chapter 14—Wireless Web Services and Java 2 Micro Edition (J2ME)

Accessing Web services via wireless mobile devices continues to emerge throughout industry as Web-service–based applications become more predominant. The advantage of wireless Web services is that wireless devices enable users to access Web services at any time and from virtually anywhere. This is especially convenient for services such as checking stock quotes and discovering local activities. In this chapter, we introduce *Java 2 Micro Edition (J2ME™)*, which is Sun Microsystem's most recent Java platform for developing applications for various consumer devices, such as Web terminals, mobile phones and cell pagers. We discuss the J2ME API and use it to program J2ME applications. We then show how to enable a J2ME client to access Web services that have been deployed in Web-services environments (e.g., WASP servers). We also discuss Enhydra's *kSOAP* and *kXML* packages, which enable a J2ME client to make SOAP requests to Web-service environments.

Chapters 15, 16 and 17—Case Study

At this point, we have introduced the technologies and services that enable developers to build, publish and access Web services. In these final chapters, we integrate many of those technologies into a substantial case study that demonstrates an application built with Web services. The Price Finder Web service enables clients to find and purchase Deitel books at the best available prices. The Price Finder Web service itself uses Web services provided by several fictitious online bookstores to obtain price information and to place orders. The Price Finder Web service also communicates with the Deitel Book Information Web service to obtain book descriptions, titles, authors, cover images, etc. In addition to the Web-service implementations, we present several applications that consume the Price Finder Web Service, including a servlet-based Web site, a J2ME application for wireless devices and a Swing-based desktop application.

Appendix A—Servlets

Servlets extend the functionality of servers—typically Web servers. Servlets are effective for developing Web-based solutions that interact with databases on behalf of clients, dynamically generate custom content to be displayed by browsers, and maintain unique session information for each client. Many developers feel that servlets are the right solution for database-intensive applications that communicate with so-called *thin clients*—applications that require minimal client-side processing capability. Clients connect to the server using standard protocols, such as *HyperText Transfer Protocol (HTTP)*, available on most client platforms through Web browsers (and other applications). Thus, the application logic can be written once and reside on the server for access by clients. The *Java Servlet API* allows developers to add functionality to Web servers for handling client requests. Unlike the *Common Gateway Interface (CGI)*, in which a separate process may be started for each client request, servlets typically are threads in a single JVM process. Servlets also are reusable across Web servers and across platforms. This appendix demonstrates the Web's request–response mechanism (primarily with HTTP **get** and **post** requests), session-tracking capabilities, redirecting requests to other resources and interacting with databases through JDBC. We provide this appendix as a tutorial and reference, since several of the Web-services platforms and reference implementations use servlets to provide Web-services endpoints. Also, in several examples throughout the book, including the case study of Chapters 15–17, we implement servlets as Web-services clients.

Appendix B—JavaServer Pages

This appendix introduces an extension of servlet technology called *JavaServer Pages (JSP)*. JSPs enable delivery of dynamically generated Web content and are used primarily for developing presentation logic in Enterprise Java applications. JSPs may contain Java code in the form of *scriptlets* and may also use JavaBeans components. *Custom tag librar-ies* enable Web-page designers unfamiliar with Java to enhance Web pages with powerful dynamic content and processing capabilities created by Java developers. To enhance per-formance, each JSP is compiled into a Java servlet—this normally occurs the first time each JSP is requested by a client. Subsequent client requests are fulfilled by the compiled servlet. We provide this appendix as a tutorial and reference, since we use JSP technology in the Price Finder case study of Chapters 15–17.

1.9 Summary

Web services technology—which represents the next stage in distributed computing—will profoundly affect organizations in 2002 and beyond. Web services encompass a set of re-lated standards that can enable computer applications to communicate and exchange data via the Internet.

With its three editions—Java 2 Standard Edition (J2SE), Java 2 Enterprise Edition (J2EE) and Java 2 Micro Edition (J2ME)—developers can use Java to build virtually any type of application. With its support for industry-standard protocols, including Web-ser-vices protocols, Java is ready for the next generation of interoperable distributed systems.

Web services extend the object-oriented paradigm, in that every Web service is, poten-tially, a self-contained object that can be reused by, or incorporated into, other applications. Web services encourage a modular approach to programming, transforming a network such as the Internet into an enormous library of programmatic components available to developers.

For a distributed system to function correctly, application components (often encapsu-lated as programming objects) executing on different computers throughout a network must be able to communicate. In the early 1990s, many companies and organizations realized the need for such functionality and began developing their own technologies to enable commu-nication among distributed components. Each of the main technologies allows programs written in various languages, with varying implementations and running in disparate loca-tions, to communicate as if they were on the same computer.

Unfortunately, interoperability (the ability to communicate and share data with soft-ware from different vendors and platforms) is limited among these technologies. Such problems have impeded distributed computing's ability to facilitate business-process inte-gration and automation. Web services improve distributed-computing capabilities by addressing the issue of limited interoperability. Unlike DCOM and CORBA, Web services operate using open (i.e., nonproprietary) standards. Organizations are implementing Web services to improve communication between DCOM and CORBA components and to create standards-based distributed-computing systems.

Web services—which typically operate over Internet and Web protocols—extend the Web's capabilities to include direct communication between computer programs, even those written in different languages and running on disparate platforms.

Many organizations have invested in Electronic Data Interchange (EDI) technology to link business partners and help manage supply chains. Although EDI systems improve effi-ciency and promote better accounting practices, they can be expensive to operate. EDI remains prohibitively expensive for many companies.

Web services provide capabilities similar to those offered by EDI, but are simpler and less expensive to implement. Web services are built on open standards and are more con-ducive to constructing loosely coupled systems. Web services can be configured to work with EDI systems, which allows organizations to use the two technologies together or to phase out EDI while adopting Web services.

With the announcement of Web services, many realized that the technology could revolutionize distributed computing. The industry's experience with interoperability problems led to the development of open standards for Web services technologies. The primary standard used in Web services is XML, a language for marking up data so that information can be exchanged between applications and platforms. The Simple Object Access Protocol (SOAP) is a messaging protocol for transporting information and instructions between Web services, using XML as a foundation. WSDL provides a standard method of describing Web services and their specific capabilities; UDDI defines XML-based rules for building directories in which companies advertise themselves and their Web services.

Java has rich support for XML and provides extensive libraries for networking with standard Internet protocols. Through the Java Community Process (JCP), Sun Microsystems and its partners have developed numerous APIs for building and integrating Web services with the Java platform. The Java APIs for XML Messaging (JAXM) and XML-Based Remote Procedure Calls (JAX-RPC) enable developers to work at a high level of abstraction in building standards-compliant Web services. The Java API for XML Registries enables integration through XML registries based on UDDI, ebXML and other technologies.

An impediment to Web services adoption is the absence of standard security procedures. New Web-services-specific security technologies are under development, but many companies are hesitant to deploy Web services outside corporate firewalls until security mechanisms are standardized.

WORKS CITED

1. R. F. Bruner, et. al., *The Portable MBA* (New York: John Wiley & Sons, Inc., 1998) 146.

2. K. Kaplan, "New Competitors for Dot-com," 10 July 2000 `<www.latimes.com>`.

3. T. Clements, "Overview of SOAP," 17 August 2001 `<dcb.sun.com/practices/webservices/overviews/overview_soap.jsp>`.

4. M. McGarr, "Transforming Business Processes with EDI," *Electronic Commerce World* May 2002: 23.

5. T. Clements, "Overview of SOAP," 17 August 2001 `<dcb.sun.com/practices/webservices/overviews/overview_soap.jsp>` .

6. M. McGarr, "Transforming Business Processes with EDI," *Electronic Commerce World* May 2002: 25.

7. F. Harvey, "The Internet Reaches the Age of the Living Page," *Financial Times* 15 May 2002: 9.

8. D. Gisolfi, "Web Services Architect, Part 3—Is Web Services the Reincarnation of CORBA?" July 2001 `<www-106.ibm.com/developerworks/webservices/library/ws-arc3/>`.

9. J. Borck, "InfoWorld Technology of the Year: Web Services," *InfoWorld* 4 February 2002: 48.

10. J. Rapoza, "Web Services Standards Can't Be Rigged," *eWeek* 11 February 2002: 54.

11. C. Purpi, "Web Services Organization Gets Down to Business," *Software Development Times* 15 May 2002: 1, 10.

12. J. Fontana, "XML the Glue for Unified Messaging," *Network World* 22 April 2002: 14-16.

13. J. Fontana, "New Formula for Apps Access," *Network World* 15 April 2002: 18, 74.

14. M. Vernon, "Transparency is the Key to Early Appearance on Trading Floors," *Financial Times* 1 May 2002: FT-IT 5.

15. "Dollar Rent A Car E-Commerce Case Study on Microsoft Business," Microsoft Case Study 1 July 2001 <www.microsoft.com/BUSINESS/casestudies/b2c/dollarrentacar.asp>.

16. `<www.xmethods.net>`, `<www.salcentral.com>`.

17. S. Vaughan-Nichols, "WS-I: Another Standards Battle Begins," *Software Development Times* 15 May 2002: 27.

18. J. McCarthy, "The Standards Body Politic," *InfoWorld* 20 May 2002: 44.

19. M. Vernon, "Why IT Managers Remain Cautious," *Financial Times* 1 May 2002: FT-IT 3.

2

Creating Markup with XML

Objectives

- To learn how to use XML to create custom markup.
- To understand the concept of an XML parser.
- To use elements and attributes to mark up data.
- To understand the difference between markup text and character data.
- To use **CDATA** sections and processing instructions.
- To understand the concept of an XML namespace.

The chief merit of language is clearness, and we know that nothing detracts so much from this as do unfamiliar terms.
Galen

Every country has its own language, yet the subjects of which the untutored soul speaks are the same everywhere.
Tertullian

The historian, essentially, wants more documents than he can really use; the dramatist only wants more liberties than he can really take.
Henry James

Entities should not be multiplied unnecessarily.
William of Occam

Outline

2.1 Introduction

Web services are based on the Extensible Markup Language (XML), a technology for structuring data. Java and XML share a similar goal: Interoperability. Java's platform independence, the separation of an application from the platform on which it runs, allows executable code to run in any programming environment for which there is a Java Virtual Machine (JVM). XML's data independence, the separation of content from its presentation, allows structured data to be portable across applications. When used together, Java and XML allow applications and their associated data to be deployed on a wide range of platforms; this interoperability and portability are crucial to Web services.

In this chapter, we demonstrate how to output an XML document's contents, using a Java application we created, named **ParserTest**.[1] This application is included with the book's examples at **www.deitel.com**.

2.2 Introduction to XML Markup

In this section, we begin to use XML to mark up data. Consider a simple XML document (**first.xml**) that marks up a message (Fig. 2.1). We output the entire XML document to the command line.

```
1    <?xml version = "1.0" encoding = "UTF-8"?>
2
3    <!-- Fig. 2.1 : first.xml                 -->
4    <!-- Simple introduction to XML markup -->
5
6    <myMessage id = "643070">
7       <message>Welcome to XML!</message>
8    </myMessage>
```

Fig. 2.1   Simple XML document containing a message. (Part 1 of 2.)

1. Before running the examples in this chapter, execute the batch file (**jws1_xml.bat**) provided with the book's examples.

```
c:\>java -classpath %CLASSPATH% com.deitel.jws1.xml.ParserTest
chapter2/fig02_1/first.xml
<?xml version="1.0" encoding="UTF-8"?>
<!-- Fig. 2.1 : first.xml                     -->
<!-- Simple introduction to XML markup -->
<myMessage id="643070">
    <message>Welcome to XML!</message>
</myMessage>
```

Fig. 2.1 Simple XML document containing a message. (Part 2 of 2.)

The document begins with the optional *XML declaration* (line 1), which identifies the document as an XML document. The **version** *information parameter* specifies the version of XML used in the document. Currently, there is only one version of XML—version 1.0.

The optional **encoding** declaration specifies the method used to represent characters electronically. **UTF-8** is a character encoding typically used for Latin-alphabet characters (e.g., English) that can be stored in one byte. When present, this declaration allows authors to specify a character encoding explicitly. When omitted, either UTF-8 or *UTF-16* (a format for encoding and storing characters in two bytes) is the default. We discuss character encoding in Section 2.4.

Portability Tip 2.1

*The **encoding** declaration allows XML documents to be authored in a wide variety of human languages.*

Portability Tip 2.2

Although the XML declaration is optional, it should be included to identify the version of XML used in the document. Otherwise, in the future, a document without an XML declaration might be assumed to conform to the latest version of XML. Errors or other serious problems may result.

Common Programming Error 2.1

Placing anything, including whitespace (i.e., spaces, tabs, carriage returns and line feeds), before an XML declaration is an error.

Good Programming Practice 2.1

*By convention, XML documents use the file extension **.xml**.*

Lines 3–4 are comments, which begin with **<!--** and end with **-->**. Comments can be placed almost anywhere in an XML document and can span multiple lines. For example, we could have written lines 3–4 as

```
<!-- Fig. 2.1 : first.xml
     Simple introduction to XML markup -->
```

Common Programming Error 2.2

Placing -- between <!-- and --> is an error.

In XML, data are marked up using *tags*, which are names enclosed in *angle brackets* (**< >**). Tags are used in pairs to delimit the beginning and end of markup. A tag that begins markup is called a *start tag*, and a tag that terminates markup is called an *end tag*. Examples of start tags include **<myMessage>** and **<message>** (lines 6–7). End tags differ from start tags in that the former contain a *forward slash* (**/**) character. Examples of end tags include **</message>** and **</myMessage>** in lines 7–8.

Individual units of markup (i.e., everything from a start tag to an end tag, inclusive) are called *elements*, which are the most fundamental building blocks of an XML document. XML documents contain exactly one element—called a *root element* (e.g., **myMessage** in lines 6–8)—that contains all other elements in the document. Elements are embedded or nested within each other to form hierarchies—with the root element at the top of the hierarchy. Nesting allows document authors to create explicit relationships between data. XML documents can contain any number of elements.

Common Programming Error 2.3
Improperly nesting XML tags is an error. For example, **<x><y>hello</x></y>** *is an error; the nested* **<y>** *tag must end before the* **</x>** *tag.*

Good Programming Practice 2.2
When creating an XML document, add whitespace to emphasize the document's hierarchical structure. This practice makes documents more readable to humans.

Common Programming Error 2.4
Providing more than one root element in an XML document is an error.

Elements, such as the root element, that contain other elements are called *parent elements*. Elements nested within a parent element are called *children*. Parent elements can have any number of children, but an individual child element can have only one parent. As we will see momentarily, it is possible for an element to be both a parent element and a child element. Element **message** is an example of a child element, and element **myMessage** is an example of a parent element.

Common Programming Error 2.5
XML is case sensitive. Using the wrong mixture of case is an error. For example, pairing the start tag **<message>** *with the end tag* **</Message>** *is an error.*

In addition to being placed between tags, data can be placed in *attributes*, which are name–value pairs in start tags. Elements can have any number of attributes. In Fig. 2.1, attribute **id** is assigned the value **"643070"**. XML element and attribute names can be of any length and may contain letters, digits, underscores, hyphens and periods; they must begin with a letter or an underscore.

Good Programming Practice 2.3
XML elements and attribute names should be meaningful. For example, use **<address>** *instead of* **<adr>**.

Common Programming Error 2.6
Using spaces in an XML element name or attribute name is an error.

Common Programming Error 2.7

Not placing an attribute's value in either single or double quotes is an error.

2.3 Parsers and Well-Formed XML Documents

A software program called an *XML parser*[2] (or an *XML processor*) is required to process an XML document. XML parsers read the XML document, check its syntax, report any errors and allow programmatic access to the document's contents. An XML document is considered *well formed* if it is syntactically correct (i.e., errors are not reported by the parser when the document is processed). Figure 2.1 is an example of a well-formed XML document.

If an XML document is not well formed, the parser reports errors. For example, if the end tag (line 8) in Fig. 2.1 is omitted, the error message shown in Fig. 2.2 is generated by the parser.

Parsers can support the *Document Object Model (DOM)* and/or the *Simple API for XML (SAX)* for accessing a document's content programmatically, using languages such as Java™, Python and C. A DOM-based parser builds a tree structure in memory that contains the XML document's data. A SAX-based parser processes the document and generates *events* (i.e., notifications to the application) when tags, text, comments, etc., are encountered. These events return data from the XML document. Software programs can "listen" for the events to obtain data from the XML document.

```
1   <?xml version = "1.0" encoding = "UTF-8"?>
2
3   <!-- Fig. 2.2 : error.xml              -->
4   <!-- XML document missing an end tag -->
5
6   <myMessage id = "643070">
7       <message>Welcome to XML!</message>
```

```
c:\>java -classpath %CLASSPATH% com.deitel.jws1.xml.ParserTest
chapter2/fig02_2/error.xml
[Fatal Error] error.xml:24:4: XML document structures must start and
end within the same entity.
Exception in thread "main" org.xml.sax.SAXParseException: XML docu-
ment structures must start and end within the same entity.
        at org.apache.xerces.parsers.DOMParser.parse(
DOMParser.java:235)
        at org.apache.xerces.jaxp.DocumentBuilderImpl.parse(
DocumentBuilderImpl.java:201)
        at javax.xml.parsers.DocumentBuilder.parse(Unknown Source)
        at com.deitel.jws1.xml.ParserTest.main(ParserTest.java:43)
```

Fig. 2.2   XML document missing an end tag.

---

2. In this chapter, we use the reference implementation for the Java API for XML Processing 1.2 (JAXP), which is part of the Java Web Services Pack 1.0.

The examples we present use DOM-based parsing.[3] In Chapter 7, we provide a detailed discussion of the DOM. We do not discuss SAX-based parsing in this book.

2.4 Characters

In this section, we discuss the collection of characters—called a *character set*—permitted in an XML document. XML documents may contain carriage returns, line feeds and *Unicode*® characters. Unicode is a character set created by the *Unicode Consortium* (**www.unicode.org**). The Unicode Consortium encodes the vast majority of the world's commercially vable languages.

2.4.1 Characters vs. Markup

Once a parser determines that all characters in a document are legal, it must differentiate between markup text and character data. Markup text is enclosed in angle brackets (**<** and **>**). Character data (sometimes called *element content*) are the *text* delimited by the start tag and end tag. Child elements are considered markup—not character data. Lines 1, 3–4 and 6–8 in Fig. 2.1 contain markup text. In line 7, the tags **<message>** and **</message>** are the markup text, and the text **Welcome to XML!** is character data.

2.4.2 Whitespace, Entity References and Built-In Entities

Spaces, tabs, line feeds and carriage returns are characters commonly called *whitespace characters*. An XML parser is required to pass all character data in a document, including whitespace characters, to the application (e.g., a Java application) consuming the XML document's data.

Figure 2.3 demonstrates that whitespace characters are passed by the parser to the application consuming the XML document's data. In this case, we simply print the data returned by the parser.

```
1   <?xml version = "1.0" encoding = "UTF-8"?>
2
3   <!-- Fig. 2.3 : whitespace.xml              -->
4   <!-- Demonstrating whitespace, entities -->
5   <!-- and empty elements                     -->
6
7   <information>
8
9      <!-- empty element whose attribute value -->
10     <!-- contains significant whitespace      -->
11     <company name = "Deitel   &amp; Associates, Inc." />
12
13     <!-- start tag contains insignificant whitespace -->
14     <city      >  Sudbury       </city>
15
```

Fig. 2.3   Whitespace characters in an XML document. (Part 1 of 2.)

---

3. Some DOM-based parsers may internally use SAX-based parsing to create the initial tree structure.

```
16
17      <state>Massachusetts</state>
18  </information>
```

```
c:\>java -classpath %CLASSPATH% com.deitel.jws1.xml.ParserTest
chapter2/fig02_3/whitespace.xml
<?xml version="1.0" encoding="UTF-8"?>
<!-- Fig. 2.3 : whitespace.xml          -->
<!-- Demonstrating whitespace, entities -->
<!-- and empty elements                 -->
<information>

    <!-- empty element whose attribute value -->
    <!-- contains significant whitespace       -->
    <company name="Deitel   &amp; Associates, Inc."/>

    <!-- start tag contains insignificant whitespace -->
    <city>   Sudbury     </city>


    <state>Massachusetts</state>
</information>
```

Fig. 2.3   Whitespace characters in an XML document. (Part 2 of 2.)

A parser can inform an application as to whether individual whitespace characters are *significant* (i.e., need to be preserved) or *insignificant* (i.e., need not be preserved). The output window illustrates that the majority of whitespace characters in the document are considered significant. Lines 2 and 6 were considered insignificant by the application, as were the extra space characters in the start tag on line 14. Lines 8, 12 and 15–16 were considered significant, because they are part of the character data. We will explore the subtleties of whitespace interpretation in greater detail in Chapter 6.

The element in line 11 is called an *empty element*, because it does not contain character data between its start and end tags. The forward-slash character closes the tag. Alternatively, this empty element can be written as

```
<company name = "Deitel   &amp; Associates, Inc."></company>
```

Both forms are equivalent.

Almost any character can be used in an XML document, but the characters *ampersand* (**&**) and *left angle bracket* (**<**) are reserved in XML and may not be used in character data or in attribute values. To use these symbols in character data or in attribute values, *entity references* must be used. Entity references are special names that begin with an ampersand (**&**) and end with a *semicolon* (**;**). XML provides entity references (or *built-in entities*) for the ampersand (**&**), left angle bracket (**<**), right angle bracket (**>**), apostrophe (**'**) and quotation-mark (**"**) characters. XML parsers replace these entity references with their corresponding characters.

Common Programming Error 2.8

*Using the left-angle bracket (**<**) in character data or in attribute values is an error.*

Common Programming Error 2.9

Using the ampersand (&)—other than in an entity reference—in character data or in attribute values is an error.

2.5 CDATA Sections and Processing Instructions

In this section, we introduce **CDATA** *sections*, which can contain text, reserved characters (e.g., <) and whitespace characters, and *processing instructions*, which allow document authors to embed application-specific data within an XML document.

Character data in a **CDATA** section are not processed by the XML parser. A common use of a **CDATA** section is for delimiting programming code (e.g., Java, JavaScript and C++), which often includes characters such as **&** and **<**. Character data in a **CDATA** section are passed to the application consuming the XML document's data. Figure 2.4 presents an XML document that compares text in a **CDATA** section with character data.

 Common Programming Error 2.10

Placing one or more spaces inside the string <![CDATA[or the string]]> is an error.

The first **sample** element (lines 8–12) contains C++ code as character data. Each occurrence of **<**, **>** and **&** is replaced by an entity reference. Lines 15–20 use a **CDATA** section to indicate a block of text that the parser should not treat as character data or markup. **CDATA** sections begin with **<![CDATA[** and terminate with **]]>**. Notice that the **<** and **&** characters (lines 18–19) do not need to be replaced by entity references.

```
 1    <?xml version = "1.0" encoding = "UTF-8"?>
 2
 3    <!-- Fig. 2.4 : cdata.xml              -->
 4    <!-- CDATA section containing C++ code -->
 5
 6    <book title = "Russ Tick&apos;s C++ Programming" edition = "8">
 7
 8       <sample>
 9             // sample code
10             if ( this-&gt;getX() &lt; 5 &amp;&amp; value[ 0 ] != 3 )
11                cerr &lt;&lt; this-&gt;displayError();
12       </sample>
13
14       <sample>
15          <![CDATA[
16
17             // sample code
18             if ( this->getX() < 5 && value[ 0 ] != 3 )
19                cerr << this->displayError();
20          ]]>
21       </sample>
22
23       Russ Tick&apos;s C++ programming
24
```

Fig. 2.4   Using a **CDATA** section. (Part 1 of 2.)

```
25        <?button cpp = "sample.cpp" ansi = "yes"?>
26    </book>
```

```
c:\>java -classpath %CLASSPATH% com.deitel.jws1.xml.ParserTest
chapter2/fig02_4/cdata.xml
<?xml version="1.0" encoding="UTF-8"?>
<!-- Fig. 2.4 : cdata.xml                    -->
<!-- CDATA section containing C++ code -->
<book edition="8" title="Russ Tick's C++ Programming">

    <sample>
         // Sample code
         if ( this-&gt;getX() &lt; 5 &amp;&amp; value[ 0 ] != 3 )
            cerr &lt;&lt; this-&gt;displayError();
    </sample>

    <sample>
       <![CDATA[

         // Sample code
         if ( this->getX() < 5 && value[ 0 ] != 3 )
            cerr << this->displayError();
       ]]>
    </sample>

    Russ Tick's C++ programming

    <?button cpp = "sample.cpp" ansi = "yes"?>
</book>
```

Fig. 2.4   Using a **CDATA** section. (Part 2 of 2.)

Because a **CDATA** section is not parsed, it can contain almost any text, including characters normally reserved for XML syntax, such as **<** and **&**. However, **CDATA** sections cannot contain the string **]]>**, because this string is used to terminate a **CDATA** section. For example,

```
<![CDATA[
   The following characters cause an error: ]]>
]]>
```

is an error.

Line 25 is an example of a processing instruction (or *PI*). Processing instructions have no effect on a document if the application processing the document does not use them. The information contained in a PI is passed to the application that is consuming the XML document's data.

Processing instructions are delimited by **<?** and **?>** and consist of a *PI target* and a *PI value*. Almost any name may be used for a PI target, except the reserved word **xml** (in any mixture of case). In the current example, the PI target is named **button**, and the PI value is **cpp = "sample.cpp" ansi = "yes"**. This PI might be used by an application to create a button that, when clicked, displays the entire code listing for a file named

sample.cpp. The **ansi = "yes"** portion of the PI value might be used to indicate that the C++ code is standard C++ compliant.

Software Engineering Observation 2.1

Processing instructions provide a means for programmers to insert application-specific information into an XML document without affecting the document's portability.

2.6 XML Namespaces

Object-oriented programming languages, such as Java and standard C++, provide class libraries that group their indentifiers (i.e., classes, methods, etc.) into packages and namespaces. These packages and namespaces prevent *naming collisions* between programmer-defined identifiers, third-party identifiers and class-library identifiers. For example, a class named **Transaction** might represent a monetary transaction between two large companies; however, a bank might use class **Transaction** to represent a monetary transaction with a Federal Reserve Bank. A naming collision would occur if these two classes were used in the same Java application without their fully qualified package names.

Like Java and standard C++, XML supports *namespaces*,[4] which provide a means of uniquely identifying XML elements. Because document authors create their own markup languages or *vocabularies*, namespaces are needed to group a vocabulary's elements logically.

Elements are qualified with *namespace prefixes*, which identify the namespaces to which elements belong. For example,

<deitel:book>Java Web Services</deitel:book>

qualifies element **book** with the namespace prefix **deitel**. This indicates that element **book** is part of namespace **deitel**.

Common Programming Error 2.11

*Creating a namespace prefix named **xml** in any mixture of case is an error.*

The markup in Fig. 2.5 demonstrates the use of namespaces. This XML document contains two **file** elements that are differentiated by using namespaces.

```
1   <?xml version = "1.0" encoding = "UTF-8"?>
2
3   <!-- Fig. 2.5: namespace.xml   -->
4   <!-- Demonstrating namespaces -->
5
6   <text:directory xmlns:text = "urn:deitel:textInfo"
7      xmlns:image = "urn:deitel:imageInfo">
8
9      <text:file filename = "book.xml">
10        <text:description>A book list</text:description>
11     </text:file>
12
```

Fig. 2.5   XML namespaces demonstration. (Part 1 of 2.)

4. XML Namespaces is a W3C Recommendation (**www.w3.org/TR/REC-xml-names**).

```
13        <image:file filename = "funny.jpg">
14            <image:description>A funny picture</image:description>
15            <image:size width = "200" height = "100" />
16        </image:file>
17
18    </text:directory>
```

```
c:\>java -classpath %CLASSPATH% com.deitel.jws1.xml.ParserTest
chapter2/fig02_5/namespace.xml
<?xml version="1.0" encoding="UTF-8"?>
<!-- Fig. 2.5: namespace.xml   -->
<!-- Demonstrating namespaces -->
<text:directory xmlns:image="urn:deitel:imageInfo"
xmlns:text="urn:deitel:textInfo">

    <text:file filename="book.xml">
        <text:description>A book list</text:description>
    </text:file>

    <image:file filename="funny.jpg">
        <image:description>A funny picture</image:description>
        <image:size height="100" width="200"/>
    </image:file>

</text:directory>
```

Fig. 2.5   XML namespaces demonstration. (Part 2 of 2.)

Lines 6–7 use attribute **xmlns** to declare two namespace prefixes: **text** and **image**. Each namespace prefix is bound (or mapped) to a series of characters called a *uniform resource identifier* (*URI*) that uniquely identifies the namespace. Document authors create their own namespace prefixes and URIs.

To ensure that namespaces are unique, document authors must provide unique URIs. Here, we use the text **urn:deitel:textInfo** and **urn:deitel:imageInfo** as URIs. A common practice is to use *Universal Resource Locators* (*URLs*) for URIs, because the domain names (such as **www.deitel.com**) used in URLs are guaranteed to be unique. For example, lines 6–7 could have been written as

```
<text:directory xmlns:text =
    "http://www.deitel.com/xmlns-text"
    xmlns:image = "http://www.deitel.com/xmlns-image">
```

These URLs relate to the Deitel & Associates, Inc., domain name. The parser never visits these URLs—they simply represent a series of characters used to differentiate names. The URLs need not refer to actual Web pages or be formed properly.

Lines 9–11 qualify elements **file** and **description** with namespace prefix **text**. Lines 13–16 qualify elements **file**, **description** and **size** with namespace prefix **image**. Notice that namespace prefixes are applied to end tags as well.

To eliminate the need to qualify every element of a particular vocabulary with a namespace prefix, document authors can specify a *default namespace* (i.e., a namespace

that does not have a namespace prefix bound to it). Figure 2.6 demonstrates the creation
and use of default namespaces.

Line 6 declares a default namespace, using attribute **xmlns** with a URI as its value.
Once this default namespace is declared, child elements belonging to the namespace are not
qualified by namespace prefixes. Element **file** (line 9–11) is in the namespace corresponding to the URI **urn:deitel:textInfo**. Compare this example with Fig. 2.5,
where we qualified **file** and **description** with **text** (lines 9–11).

The default namespace applies to the **directory** element and all elements that are
not qualified with namespace prefixes. However, namespace prefixes can be used to
qualify other elements as belonging to different namespaces. For example, the **file** element in line 13 is qualified with **image** to indicate that it is in the namespace corresponding to the URI **urn:deitel:imageInfo**, rather than the default namespace.

```xml
1    <?xml version = "1.0" encoding = "UTF-8"?>
2
3    <!-- Fig. 2.6: defaultnamespace.xml -->
4    <!-- Using a default namespace        -->
5
6    <directory xmlns = "urn:deitel:textInfo"
7       xmlns:image = "urn:deitel:imageInfo">
8
9       <file filename = "book.xml">
10          <description>A book list</description>
11       </file>
12
13       <image:file filename = "funny.jpg">
14          <image:description>A funny picture</image:description>
15          <image:size width = "200" height = "100" />
16       </image:file>
17
18    </directory>
```

```
c:\>java -classpath %CLASSPATH% com.deitel.jws1.xml.ParserTest
chapter2/fig02_6/defaultnamespace.xml
<?xml version="1.0" encoding="UTF-8"?>
<!-- Fig. 2.6: defaultnamespace.xml -->
<!-- Using a default namespaces      -->
<directory xmlns="urn:deitel:textInfo" xmlns:image="urn:deitel:image-
Info">

   <file filename="book.xml">
      <description>A book list</description>
   </file>

   <image:file filename="funny.jpg">
      <image:description>A funny picture</image:description>
      <image:size height="100" width="200"/>
   </image:file>

</directory>
```

Fig. 2.6   Default namespace demonstration.

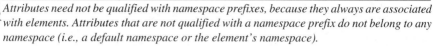

Software Engineering Observation 2.2

Attributes need not be qualified with namespace prefixes, because they always are associated with elements. Attributes that are not qualified with a namespace prefix do not belong to any namespace (i.e., a default namespace or the element's namespace).

In this chapter, we have introduced XML. In Chapter 5, we introduce Document Type Definition files (DTDs), which describe an XML document's structure. DTDs allow programmers to confirm that the XML documents being processed are complete and use the correct markup.

2.7 Summary

XML is a technology for creating vocabularies to describe data of virtually any type in a structured manner. To process an XML document, a software program called an XML parser is required. The XML parser reads the XML document, checks its syntax, reports any errors and allows access to the document's data. An XML document is considered well formed if it is syntactically correct (i.e., if the parser did not report any errors due to missing tags, overlapping tags, etc.). Every XML document must be well formed. XML documents may contain carriage-return, line-feed and Unicode characters.

All XML start tags must have a corresponding end tag, and all start and end tags must be properly nested. Elements define a structure. An element may contain content (i.e., child elements and/or character data). An element may have zero, one or more attributes associated with it that describe the element.

CDATA sections allow the document author to include data that are not intended to be parsed and may contain text, reserved characters (e.g., **<**) and whitespace characters. Processing instructions allow document authors to embed application-specific data within an XML document.

Because document authors can create their own vocabularies, naming collisions (i.e., conflicts that arise when document authors use the same names for elements) can occur. Namespaces provide a means for document authors to prevent naming collisions.

2.8 Internet and World Wide Web Resources

www.w3.org/XML
Worldwide Web Consortium Extensible Markup Language home page. Contains links to related XML technologies, recommended books, a time line for publications, developer discussions, translations, software, etc.

www.w3.org/Addressing
Worldwide Web Consortium addressing home page. Contains information on URIs and links to other resources.

www.xml.com
This is one of the most popular XML sites on the Web. It has resources and links relating to all aspects of XML, including articles, news, seminar information, tools and Frequently Asked Questions (FAQs).

www.xml.org
"The XML Industry Portal" is another popular XML site that includes links to many different XML resources, such as news, FAQs and descriptions of XML-derived markup languages.

www.coverpages.org
Oasis XML Cover Pages home page is a comprehensive XML reference. The site includes links to news, articles, software and information about events.

html.about.com/compute/html/cs/xmlandjava/index.htm
This site contains articles about XML and Java and is updated regularly.

www.w3schools.com/xml
This site contains a tutorial that introduces the reader to XML. The tutorial contains many examples.

java.sun.com/xml/jaxp
Home page of Sun's JAXP and parser technology.

xml.apache.org
Home page of Apache Software Foundation. This site contains news, links to Apache projects, Foundation information and downloads.

3

Document Type Definition (DTD)

Objectives

- To understand what a Document Type Definition (DTD) is.
- To write DTDs.
- To declare elements and attributes in a DTD.
- To understand the difference between general entities and parameter entities.
- To use conditional sections with entities.
- To use **NOTATION**s.
- To understand how an XML document's whitespace is processed.

To whom nothing is given, of him can nothing be required.
Henry Fielding

Like everything metaphysical, the harmony between thought and reality is to be found in the grammar of the language.
Ludwig Wittgenstein

Grammar, which knows how to control even kings.
Molière

Outline

3.1 Introduction

In this chapter, we introduce *Document Type Definitions* (*DTDs*),[1] which define an XML document's structure (e.g., what elements, attributes, etc., are permitted in the document). An XML document is not required to have a corresponding DTD. However, DTDs are often recommended to ensure document conformity, especially in business-to-business (B2B) transactions, where XML documents are exchanged. DTDs specify an XML document's structure and are themselves defined using *EBNF* (*Extended Backus-Naur Form*) grammar—not the XML syntax introduced in Chapter 2.

3.2 Parsers and Well-Formed and Valid XML Documents

Parsers are classified as *validating* or *nonvalidating*. A validating parser is able to read a DTD and determine whether the XML document conforms to it. If the document conforms to the DTD, it is referred to as *valid*. If the document fails to conform to the DTD, but is syntactically correct, it is well formed, but not valid. By definition, a valid document is well formed. A non-validating parser is able to read the DTD, but cannot check the document against the DTD for conformity. Nonvalidating parsers can determine only if an XML document is well formed.

In this chapter, we use a Java program[2] we created to validate XML documents. This program, named **Validator**, is located with the book's examples at **www.deitel.com**.

---

1. DTDs are part of the W3C XML 1.0 Recommendation.
2. Before running the examples in this chapter, execute the batch file (**jws1_xml.bat**) provided with the book's examples.

3.3 Document Type Declaration

DTDs are introduced into XML documents via the *document type declaration* (i.e., **DOC-TYPE**). A document type declaration is placed in the XML document's *prolog* (the area that precedes the root element), begins with **<!DOCTYPE** and ends with **>**. The document type declaration can point to declarations that are outside the XML document (called the *external subset*) and/or can contain the declaration inside the document (called the *internal subset*). For example, an internal subset might look like

```
<!DOCTYPE myMessage [
    <!ELEMENT myMessage ( #PCDATA )>
]>
```

The first **myMessage** is the name of the document type declaration. Anything inside the *square brackets* (**[ ]**) constitutes the internal subset. As we will see momentarily, **ELEMENT** and **#PCDATA** are used in element type declarations.

 Good Programming Practice 3.1

By convention, DTD files have a **.dtd** *extension.*

External subsets physically exist in a different file. External subsets are specified using either the keyword **SYSTEM** or the keyword **PUBLIC**. For example, the reference to the **DOCTYPE** external subset might look like

```
<!DOCTYPE myMessage SYSTEM "dot032201.dtd">
```

which points to the **dot032201.dtd** document. The **PUBLIC** keyword indicates that the DTD is used widely. The DTD may be made available in well-known locations for more efficient downloading. For example, the **DOCTYPE**

```
<!DOCTYPE html PUBLIC "-//W3C//DTD XHTML 1.0 Strict//EN"
    "http://www.w3.org/TR/xhtml1/DTD/xhtml1-strict.dtd">
```

uses the **PUBLIC** keyword to reference the well-known DTD for the *Extensible HyperText Markup Language* (*XHTML*)[3] version 1.0. XML parsers that do not have a local copy of the DTD may use the URL provided to download the DTD in order to perform validation.

Both the internal and external subset may be specified at the same time. For example, the **DOCTYPE**

```
<!DOCTYPE myMessage SYSTEM "dot032201.dtd" [
    <!ELEMENT myElement ( #PCDATA )>
]>
```

contains declarations from the **dot032201.dtd** document, as well as an internal declaration.

---

3. XHTML has replaced the *HyperText Markup Language* (*HTML*) as the primary means of describing Web content. XHTML provides more robust, extensible and richer features than does HTML. For more on XHTML/HTML, visit **www.w3.org/markup**.

Software Engineering Observation 3.1

The document type declaration's internal and external subsets form the DTD.

Software Engineering Observation 3.2

The internal subset is visible only within the document in which it resides. Other external documents cannot be validated against it. DTDs that are used by many documents should be placed in the external subset.

3.4 Element Type Declarations

Elements are the primary building blocks used in XML documents and are declared in a DTD with *element type declarations* (**ELEMENT**s). For example, to declare element **my-Element**, we might write

```
<!ELEMENT myElement ( #PCDATA )>
```

The element name (e.g., **myElement**) that follows keyword **ELEMENT** is often called a *generic identifier*. The set of parentheses that follows the element name specifies the element's allowed content and is called the *content specification*. Keyword **PCDATA** specifies that the element must contain *parsable character data*. These data will be processed by the XML parser; therefore, any markup text (e.g., **<** and **&**) will be treated as markup. We will discuss the content specification in detail momentarily.

Common Programming Error 3.1

Attempting to use the same element name in multiple element type declarations is an error.

Figure 3.1 presents an XML document that contains a reference to an external DTD in the **DOCTYPE**. We use **Validator** to check the document's conformity against its DTD.

The document type declaration (line 6) specifies the name of the root element as **myMessage** and references the external subset contained in the file **welcome.dtd** (Fig. 3.2). The element **myMessage** (lines 8–10) contains a single child element named **message** (line 9).

In Fig. 3.2, we present the DTD referenced by Fig. 3.1. Line 3 of the DTD declares element **myMessage**. Notice that the content specification contains the name **message**. This syntax indicates that element **myMessage** contains exactly one child element, which is named **message**. Because **myMessage** can have only an element as its content (i.e., it is not permitted to have character data), it is said to have *element content*. Line 4 declares element **message**, whose content is of type **PCDATA**.

```
1   <?xml version = "1.0" encoding = "UTF-8"?>
2
3   <!-- Fig. 3.1: welcome.xml     -->
4   <!-- Using an external subset -->
5
6   <!DOCTYPE myMessage SYSTEM "welcome.dtd">
7
```

Fig. 3.1   XML document referencing its associated DTD. (Part 1 of 2.)

```
8   <myMessage>
9      <message>Welcome to XML!</message>
10  </myMessage>
```

Fig. 3.1   XML document referencing its associated DTD. (Part 2 of 2.)

```
1   <!-- Fig. 3.2: welcome.dtd -->
2   <!-- External declarations -->
3   <!ELEMENT myMessage ( message )>
4   <!ELEMENT message ( #PCDATA )>
```

```
c:\examples>java -classpath %CLASSPATH% com.deitel.jws1.xml.Valida-
tor chapter3/fig03_1_2/welcome.xml
Document is valid.
```

Fig. 3.2   Validation by using an external DTD.

Common Programming Error 3.2

*Having a root-element name other than the name specified in the document type declaration (i.e., **DOCTYPE**) is an error.*

If an XML document's structure is inconsistent with its corresponding DTD, but is syntactically correct, the document is only well formed—not valid. Figure 3.3 shows the errors generated when the required **message** element is omitted.

```
1   <?xml version = "1.0" encoding = "UTF-8"?>
2
3   <!-- Fig. 3.3 : welcome-invalid.xml     -->
4   <!-- well-formed, but invalid document -->
5
6   <!DOCTYPE myMessage SYSTEM "welcome.dtd">
7
8   <!-- root element missing child element message -->
9   <myMessage>
10  </myMessage>
```

```
c:\examples>java -classpath %CLASSPATH% com.deitel.jws1.xml.Valida-
tor chapter3/fig03_3/welcome-invalid.xml
Error parsing Document:
org.xml.sax.SAXParseException: The content of element type "myMes-
sage" is incomplete, it must match "(message)".
        at org.apache.xerces.parsers.DOMParser.parse(
DOMParser.java:235)
        at org.apache.xerces.jaxp.DocumentBuilderImpl.parse(
DocumentBuilderImpl.java:201)
        at javax.xml.parsers.DocumentBuilder.parse(Unknown Source)
        at com.deitel.jws1.xml.Validator.main(Validator.java:46)
```

Fig. 3.3   Invalid XML document.

3.4.1 Sequences, Pipe Characters and Occurrence Indicators

DTDs allow the document author to define the order and frequency of child elements. The *comma* (**,**)—called a *sequence*—specifies the order in which the elements must occur. For example,

```
<!ELEMENT classroom ( teacher, student )>
```

specifies that element **classroom** must contain exactly one **teacher** element followed by exactly one **student** element. The content specification can contain any number of items in sequence.

Similarly, choices are specified using the *pipe character* (**|**), as in

```
<!ELEMENT dessert ( iceCream | pastry )>
```

which specifies that element **dessert** must contain either one **iceCream** element or one **pastry** element, but not both. The content specification may contain any number of pipe-character-separated choices.

An element's frequency (i.e., number of occurrences) is specified by using either the *plus-sign* (**+**), the *asterisk* (*****) or the *question-mark* (**?**) *occurrence indicator* (Fig. 3.4).

A plus sign indicates one or more occurrences. For example,

```
<!ELEMENT album ( song+ )>
```

specifies that element **album** contains one or more **song** elements.

The frequency of an *element group* (i.e., two or more elements that occur in some combination) is specified by enclosing the element names inside the content specification with parentheses, followed by either the plus sign, the asterisk or the question mark. For example,

```
<!ELEMENT album ( title, ( songTitle, duration )+ )>
```

indicates that element **album** contains one **title** element followed by any number of **songTitle**/**duration** element groups. At least one **songTitle**/**duration** group must follow **title**, and in each of these element groups, the **songTitle** must precede the **duration**. An example of markup that conforms to this specification is

```
<album>
   <title>XML Classical Hits</title>

   <songTitle>XML Overture</songTitle>
   <duration>10</duration>

   <songTitle>XML Symphony 1.0</songTitle>
   <duration>54</duration>
</album>
```

which contains one **title** element followed by two **songTitle**/**duration** groups.

The asterisk (*****) character indicates an optional element that, if used, can occur any number of times. For example,

```
<!ELEMENT library ( book* )>
```

Occurrence Indicator	Description
Plus sign (**+**)	An element can appear any number of times, but must appear at least once (i.e., the element appears one or more times).
Asterisk (*****)	An element is optional and, if used, can appear any number of times (i.e., the element appears zero or more times).
Question mark (**?**)	An element is optional and, if used, can appear only once (i.e., the element appears zero or one times).

Fig. 3.4   Occurrence indicators.

indicates that element **library** contains any number of **book** elements, including the possibility of none at all. Markup examples that conform to this specification include

```
<library>
   <book>The Wealth of Nations</book>
   <book>The Iliad</book>
   <book>The Jungle</book>
</library>
```

and

```
<library></library>
```
or `<library/>`

Optional elements that, if used, may occur only once are followed by a question mark (**?**). For example,

```
<!ELEMENT seat ( person? )>
```

indicates that element **seat** contains at most one **person** element. Examples of markup that conform to this specification include

```
<seat>
   <person>Jane Doe</person>
</seat>
```

and

```
<seat></seat>
```
or `<seat/>`

Now we consider three more element type declarations and provide an example for each. The declaration

```
<!ELEMENT class ( number, ( instructor | assistant+ ),
   ( credit | noCredit ) )>
```

specifies that a **class** element must contain a **number** element, either one **instructor** element or one or more **assistant** elements, and either one **credit** element or one **noCredit** element. Markup examples that conform to this specification include

```
<class>
   <number>123</number>
   <instructor>Dr. Ant E. Lope</instructor>
   <credit>4</credit>
</class>
```

and

```
<class>
   <number>456</number>
   <assistant>Russ Tick</assistant>
   <assistant>Ms. Quito</assistant>
   <credit>3</credit>
</class>
```

Multiple occurrence indicators can be used in the content specification to form more complex content descriptions. For example, the declaration

```
<!ELEMENT donutBox ( jelly?, lemon*,
   ( ( creme | sugar )+ | glazed ) )>
```

specifies that element **donutBox** can have zero or one **jelly** elements, followed by zero or more **lemon** elements, followed by one or more **creme** or **sugar** elements or exactly one **glazed** element. Markup examples that conform to this specification include

```
<donutBox>
   <jelly>grape</jelly>
   <lemon>half-sour</lemon>
   <lemon>sour</lemon>
   <lemon>half-sour</lemon>
   <glazed>chocolate</glazed>
</donutBox>
```

and

```
<donutBox>
   <sugar>semi-sweet</sugar>
   <creme>whipped</creme>
   <sugar>sweet</sugar>
</donutBox>
```

The declaration

```
<!ELEMENT farm ( farmer+, ( dog* | cat? ), pig*,
   ( goat | cow )?, ( chicken+ | duck* ) )>
```

indicates that element **farm** can have one or more **farmer** elements, any number of optional **dog** elements or an optional **cat** element, any number of optional **pig** elements, an optional **goat** or **cow** element, and one or more **chicken** elements or any number of optional **duck** elements. Examples of markup that conform to this specification include

```
<farm>
    <farmer>Jane Doe</farmer>
    <farmer>John Doe</farmer>
    <cat>Daisy</cat>
    <pig>Bo</pig>
    <chicken>Luke</chicken>
</farm>
```

and

```
<farm>
    <farmer>Red Green</farmer>
    <duck>Billy</duck>
    <duck>Sue</duck>
</farm>
```

3.4.2 EMPTY, Mixed Content and ANY

Child elements must be further refined by specifying the types of content they contain. In the previous section, we introduced element content and discussed how an element can contain one or more child elements as its content. In this section, we introduce *content specification types*, which are used to describe nonelement content.

In addition to element content, three other types of content exist: **EMPTY**, *mixed content* and **ANY**. Keyword **EMPTY** declares empty elements, which do not contain character data or child elements. For example,

```
<!ELEMENT oven EMPTY>
```

declares element **oven** to be an empty element. The markup for an **oven** element would appear as

```
<oven/>
```

or

```
<oven></oven>
```

in an XML document that conforms to the DTD containing this declaration.

An element also can be declared as having mixed content. Such elements may contain any combination of elements and **#PCDATA**. For example, the declaration

```
<!ELEMENT summary ( #PCDATA | technology )*>
```

indicates that element **summary** contains mixed content. Markup conforming to this declaration might look like

```
<summary>The two key software components used to build the
    application are <technology>Java</technology> and
    <technology>XML</technology>.
</summary>
```

Element **summary** contains two **technology** elements and three instances of character data. Because of the *****, element **summary** could have be written as an empty element.

Figure 3.5 specifies the DTD as an internal subset (lines 6–10). In the prolog (line 1), we use the ***standalone*** attribute with a value of **"yes"**. An XML document is *standalone* if it does not need to reference an external subset. This DTD defines three elements: One that contains mixed content and two that contain parsed character data.

Line 7 declares element **summary** as a mixed-content element. According to the declaration, the **summary** element may contain either parsed-character data (**PCDATA**), element **subject** or element **title**. The asterisk indicates that the content can occur zero or more times. Lines 8–9 specify that **subject** and **title** elements have only **PCDATA** for their content specification—they cannot contain child elements. Despite the fact that elements with a **PCDATA** content specification cannot contain child elements, they are considered to have mixed content. The comma (**,**), plus-sign (**+**) and question-mark (**?**) occurrence indicators cannot be used with mixed-content elements that contain only **PCDATA**.

Figure 3.6 shows the results of changing the second pipe character in line 7 of Fig. 3.5 to a comma and the result of removing the asterisk. Both of these changes result in illegal DTD syntax.

```
1    <?xml version = "1.0" encoding = "UTF-8" standalone = "yes"?>
2
3    <!-- Fig. 3.5 : mixed.xml          -->
4    <!-- Mixed content type elements -->
5
6    <!DOCTYPE summary [
7       <!ELEMENT summary ( #PCDATA | subject | title )*>
8       <!ELEMENT subject ( #PCDATA )>
9       <!ELEMENT title ( #PCDATA )>
10   ]>
11
12   <summary>
13      Book catalog entry:
14      <subject>XML</subject>
15      <title>XML How to Program</title>
16      This book explains XML-based systems development.
17   </summary>
```

```
c:\examples>java -classpath %CLASSPATH% com.deitel.jws1.xml.Valida-
tor chapter3/fig03_5/mixed.xml
Document is valid.
```

Fig. 3.5   Example of a mixed-content element.

```
1    <?xml version = "1.0" encoding = "UTF-8" standalone = "yes"?>
2
3    <!-- Fig. 3.6 : invalid-mixed.xml -->
4    <!-- Mixed content type elements  -->
5
6    <!DOCTYPE summary [
7       <!ELEMENT summary ( #PCDATA | subject, title )>
```

Fig. 3.6   Changing a pipe character to a comma in a DTD. (Part 1 of 2.)

```
 8        <!ELEMENT subject ( #PCDATA )>
 9        <!ELEMENT title ( #PCDATA )>
10   ]>
11
12   <summary>
13      Book catalog entry:
14      <subject>XML</subject>
15      <title>XML How to Program</title>
16      This book explains XML-based systems development.
17   </summary>
```

```
c:\examples>java -classpath %CLASSPATH% com.deitel.jws1.xml.Valida-
tor chapter3/fig03_6/invalid-mixed.xml
Error parsing Document:
org.xml.sax.SAXParseException: The mixed content model "summary" must
end with ")*" when the types of child elements are constrained.
        at org.apache.xerces.parsers.DOMParser.parse(
DOMParser.java:235)
        at org.apache.xerces.jaxp.DocumentBuilderImpl.parse(
DocumentBuilderImpl.java:201)
        at javax.xml.parsers.DocumentBuilder.parse(Unknown Source)
        at com.deitel.jws1.xml.Validator.main(Validator.java:46)
```

Fig. 3.6   Changing a pipe character to a comma in a DTD. (Part 2 of 2.)

Common Programming Error 3.3

*When declaring mixed content, not placing **#PCDATA** as the first item in the content specification is an error.*

An element declared as type **ANY** can contain any content, including **PCDATA**, elements or a combination of elements and **PCDATA**. Elements with **ANY** content also can be empty elements.

Software Engineering Observation 3.3

*Elements with **ANY** content commonly are used in the early stages of DTD development. Document authors typically replace **ANY** content with more specific content as the DTD evolves.*

3.5 Attribute Declarations

In this section, we discuss *attribute declarations*, which are used to declare an element's attributes. An attribute declaration specifies an *attribute list* for an element by using the **ATTLIST** *attribute list declaration*. For example,

```
<!ELEMENT file EMPTY>
<!ATTLIST file path CDATA #REQUIRED>
```

declares **EMPTY** element **file**. The attribute declaration specifies that **path** is an attribute of **file**. Keyword **CDATA** indicates that **path** can contain any character text except for the < and & characters. Note that the **CDATA** keyword in an attribute declaration has a different meaning than that of the **CDATA** section (introduced in Chapter 2). Recall that, in a **CDATA** section, any Unicode characters are permitted, except for the string **]]>**. Keyword

REQUIRED specifies that the attribute must be provided for element **file**; otherwise, the absence of the attribute invalidates the document. We will say more about other keywords momentarily.

Figure 3.7 demonstrates how to write attribute declarations for an element. Line 9 declares attribute **id** for element **message**. Attribute **id** contains required **CDATA**. Line 14 assigns attribute **id** the value **"6343070"**.

DTDs allow document authors to specify an attribute's default value, using *attribute defaults #IMPLIED, #REQUIRED* and *#FIXED*. Keyword **IMPLIED** specifies that if the attribute does not appear in the element, then the application consuming the XML document can use whatever value (if any) it chooses.

An attribute declaration with default value **#FIXED** specifies that the attribute value is constant and cannot be different in the XML document. For example,

> *<!ATTLIST address zip #FIXED "02115">*

indicates that the value **"02115"** is the only value that attribute **zip** can have. The XML document is not valid if attribute **zip** contains a value other than **"02115"**. If element **address** does not contain attribute **zip**, then the default value **"02115"** is passed to the application that is consuming the XML document's data.

3.6 Attribute Types

Attribute types are classified as either *string* (**CDATA**), *tokenized* or *enumerated*. String attribute types do not impose any constraints on attribute values, other than disallowing the **<** and **&** characters. Entity references (i.e., **<** and **&**) must be used for these characters. Tokenized attribute types impose constraints on attribute values, such as restrictions on which characters are permitted in an attribute name. We discuss tokenized attribute types in the Section 3.6.1. Enumerated attribute types are the most restrictive of the three types. They can take only one of several values listed in the attribute declaration. We discuss enumerated attribute types in Section 3.6.2.

```
1    <?xml version = "1.0" encoding = "UTF-8" standalone = "yes"?>
2
3    <!-- Fig. 3.7: welcome2.xml -->
4    <!-- Declaring attributes    -->
5
6    <!DOCTYPE myMessage [
7       <!ELEMENT myMessage ( message )>
8       <!ELEMENT message ( #PCDATA )>
9       <!ATTLIST message id CDATA #REQUIRED>
10   ]>
11
12   <myMessage>
13
14      <message id = "6343070">
15         Welcome to XML!
16      </message>
17
18   </myMessage>
```

Fig. 3.7   Declaring attributes. (Part 1 of 2.)

```
c:\examples>java -classpath %CLASSPATH% com.deitel.jws1.xml.Valida-
tor chapter3/fig03_7/welcome2.xml
Document is valid.
```

Fig. 3.7   Declaring attributes. (Part 2 of 2.)

3.6.1 Tokenized Attribute Type (ID, IDREF, ENTITY, and NMTOKEN)

Tokenized attribute types allow a DTD author to restrict the values used for attributes. For example, an author may want to have a unique ID for each element or to allow an attribute to have only one or two different values. Four different tokenized attribute types exist: *ID*, *IDREF*, *ENTITY* and *NMTOKEN*.

Tokenized attribute type **ID** uniquely identifies an element. Attributes with type **IDREF** point to elements with an **ID** attribute. A validating parser verifies that every **ID** attribute type referenced by **IDREF** is in the XML document.

Figure 3.8 presents an XML document that uses **ID** and **IDREF** attribute types. Element **bookstore** consists of element **shipping** and element **book**. Each **shipping** element describes who shipped the book and how long it will take for the book to arrive.

```
 1   <?xml version = "1.0" encoding = "UTF-8" standalone = "yes"?>
 2
 3   <!-- Fig. 3.8: IDExample.xml                        -->
 4   <!-- Example for ID and IDREF values of attributes -->
 5
 6   <!DOCTYPE bookstore [
 7      <!ELEMENT bookstore ( shipping+, book+ )>
 8      <!ELEMENT shipping ( duration )>
 9      <!ATTLIST shipping shipID ID #REQUIRED>
10      <!ELEMENT book ( #PCDATA )>
11      <!ATTLIST book shippedBy IDREF #IMPLIED>
12      <!ATTLIST book isbn CDATA #REQUIRED>
13      <!ELEMENT duration ( #PCDATA )>
14      <!ENTITY isbnXML "0-13-028417-3">
15      <!ENTITY isbnJava "0-13-034151-7">
16      <!ENTITY isbnCPP "0-13-0895717-3">
17   ]>
18
19   <bookstore>
20      <shipping shipID = "bug2bug">
21         <duration>2 to 4 days</duration>
22      </shipping>
23
24      <shipping shipID = "Deitel">
25         <duration>1 day</duration>
26      </shipping>
27
28      <book shippedBy = "Deitel" isbn = "&isbnJava;">
29         Java How to Program 4th edition.
30      </book>
```

Fig. 3.8   XML document with **ID** and **IDREF** attribute types. (Part 1 of 2.)

```
31
32        <book shippedBy = "Deitel" isbn = "&isbnXML;">
33           XML How to Program.
34        </book>
35
36        <book shippedBy = "bug2bug" isbn = "&isbnCPP;">
37           C++ How to Program 3rd edition.
38        </book>
39     </bookstore>
```

```
c:\examples>java -classpath %CLASSPATH% com.deitel.jws1.xml.Valida-
tor chapter3/fig03_8/idexample.xml
Document is valid.
```

```
c:\examples>java -classpath %CLASSPATH% com.deitel.jws1.xml.ParserT-
est chapter3/fig03_8/idexample.xml
<?xml version="1.0" encoding="UTF-8"?>
<!-- Fig. 3.8: IDExample.xml                              -->
<!-- Example for ID and IDREF values of attributes -->
<bookstore>
    <shipping shipID="bug2bug">
        <duration>2 to 4 days</duration>
    </shipping>

    <shipping shipID="Deitel">
        <duration>1 day</duration>
    </shipping>

    <book isbn="0-13-034151-7" shippedBy="Deitel">
        Java How to Program 4th edition.
    </book>

    <book isbn="0-13-028417-3" shippedBy="Deitel">
        XML How to Program.
    </book>

    <book isbn="0-13-0895717-3" shippedBy="bug2bug">
        C++ How to Program 3rd edition.
    </book>

</bookstore>
```

Fig. 3.8   XML document with **ID** and **IDREF** attribute types. (Part 2 of 2.)

Line 9 declares attribute **shipID** as an **ID** type attribute. Every **shipping** element in a conforming XML document must have a **shipID** attribute with a unique ID number. Lines 28–38 contain **book** elements with attribute **shippedBy** (line 11) of type **IDREF**. Attribute **shippedBy** is assigned the **shipID** attribute value of a **shipping** element.

The DTD contains an *entity declaration* for each of the entities **isbnXML, isbnJava** and **isbnCPP** in lines 14–16. The parser replaces the entity references with their values. These entities are called *general entities*.

Figure 3.9 is a variation of Fig. 3.8 that assigns **shippedBy** (line 32) the value **"bug"**. The XML document is invalid, because no **shipID** attribute has the value **"bug"**.

```
1    <?xml version = "1.0" encoding = "UTF-8" standalone = "yes"?>
2
3    <!-- Fig. 3.9: invalid-IDExample.xml              -->
4    <!-- Example for ID and IDREF values of attributes -->
5
6    <!DOCTYPE bookstore [
7       <!ELEMENT bookstore ( shipping+, book+ )>
8       <!ELEMENT shipping ( duration )>
9       <!ATTLIST shipping shipID ID #REQUIRED>
10      <!ELEMENT book ( #PCDATA )>
11      <!ATTLIST book shippedBy IDREF #IMPLIED>
12      <!ELEMENT duration ( #PCDATA )>
13   ]>
14
15   <bookstore>
16      <shipping shipID = "bug2bug">
17         <duration>2 to 4 days</duration>
18      </shipping>
19
20      <shipping shipID = "Deitel">
21         <duration>1 day</duration>
22      </shipping>
23
24      <book shippedBy = "Deitel">
25         Java How to Program 4th edition.
26      </book>
27
28      <book shippedBy = "Deitel">
29         C How to Program 3rd edition.
30      </book>
31
32      <book shippedBy = "bug">
33         C++ How to Program 3rd edition.
34      </book>
35   </bookstore>
```

```
c:\examples>java -classpath %CLASSPATH% com.deitel.jws1.xml.Valida-
tor chapter3/fig03_9/invalid-idexample.xml
Error parsing Document:
org.xml.sax.SAXParseException: An element with the identifier "bug"
must appear in the document.
        at org.apache.xerces.parsers.DOMParser.parse(
DOMParser.java:235)
        at org.apache.xerces.jaxp.DocumentBuilderImpl.parse(
DocumentBuilderImpl.java:201)
        at javax.xml.parsers.DocumentBuilder.parse(Unknown Source)
        at com.deitel.jws1.xml.Validator.main(Validator.java:46)
```

Fig. 3.9   Error displayed when an incorrect **ID** is referenced.

Common Programming Error 3.4

*Not beginning a type attribute **ID**'s value with a letter, an underscore (_) or a colon (:) is an error.*

Common Programming Error 3.5

*Providing more than one **ID** attribute type for an element is an error.*

Common Programming Error 3.6

*Declaring attributes of type **ID** as **#FIXED** is an error.*

Related to entities are *entity attributes*, which indicate that an attribute has an entity for its value. Entity attributes are specified by using tokenized attribute type **ENTITY**. The primary constraint placed on **ENTITY** attribute types is that they must refer to *external unparsed entities*. An external unparsed entity is defined in the external subset of a DTD and consists of character data that will not be parsed by the XML parser. Figure 3.10 provide an XML document that demonstrates the use of entities and entity attribute types.

Line 7 declares a *notation* named **html** that refers to a **SYSTEM** identifier named **"iexplorer"**. Notations provide information that an application consuming the XML document's data can use to handle unparsed entities. For example, the application may choose to open Internet Explorer and load the document **tour.html** (line 8).

Line 8 declares an entity named **city** that refers to an external document (**tour.html**). *Keyword **NDATA*** indicates that the content of this external entity is not XML. The name of the notation (e.g., **xhtml**) that handles this unparsed entity is placed to the right of **NDATA**.

```
1    <?xml version = "1.0" encoding = "UTF-8" standalone = "yes"?>
2
3    <!-- Fig. 3.10: entityExample.xml      -->
4    <!-- ENTITY and ENTITY attribute types -->
5
6    <!DOCTYPE database [
7       <!NOTATION xhtml SYSTEM "iexplorer">
8       <!ENTITY city SYSTEM "tour.html" NDATA xhtml>
9       <!ELEMENT database ( company+ )>
10      <!ELEMENT company ( name )>
11      <!ATTLIST company tour ENTITY #REQUIRED>
12      <!ELEMENT name ( #PCDATA )>
13   ]>
14
15   <database>
16      <company tour = "city">
17         <name>Bug2Bug International Travel</name>
18      </company>
19   </database>
```

```
c:\examples>java -classpath %CLASSPATH% com.deitel.jws1.xml.Valida-
tor chapter3/fig03_10/entityexample.xml
Document is valid.
```

Fig. 3.10   XML document that contains an **ENTITY** attribute type.

Line 11 declares attribute **tour** for element **company**. Attribute **tour** specifies a required **ENTITY** attribute type. Line 16 assigns entity **city** to attribute **tour**. If we were to replace line 16 with

```
<company tour = "country">
```

the document would fail to conform to the DTD, because entity **country** is not defined in the DTD. Figure 3.11 shows the error message generated when **tour** is assigned the value **"country"**.

 Common Programming Error 3.7

*Not assigning an unparsed external entity to an attribute with attribute type **ENTITY** results in an invalid XML document.*

Attribute type **ENTITIES** also may be used in a DTD to indicate that an attribute has multiple entities for its value. Each entity is separated by a space. For example,

```
<!ATTLIST directory file ENTITIES #REQUIRED>
```

specifies that attribute **file** is required to contain multiple entities. An example of markup that conforms to this specification might look like

```
<directory file = "animations graph1 graph2">
```

where **animations**, **graph1** and **graph2** are entities declared in a DTD.

A more restrictive attribute type is **NMTOKEN** (*name token*), whose value consists of letters, digits, periods, underscores, hyphens and colon characters. For example, consider the declaration

```
<!ATTLIST sportsClub phone NMTOKEN #REQUIRED>
```

```
1   <?xml version = "1.0" encoding = "UTF-8" standalone = "yes"?>
2
3   <!-- Fig. 3.11: invalid-entityExample.xml -->
4   <!-- ENTITY and ENTITY attribute types      -->
5
6   <!DOCTYPE database [
7      <!NOTATION xhtml SYSTEM "iexplorer">
8      <!ENTITY city SYSTEM "tour.html" NDATA xhtml>
9      <!ELEMENT database ( company+ )>
10     <!ELEMENT company ( name )>
11     <!ATTLIST company tour ENTITY #REQUIRED>
12     <!ELEMENT name ( #PCDATA )>
13  ]>
14
15  <database>
16     <company tour = "country">
17        <name>Bug2Bug International Travel</name>
18     </company>
19  </database>
```

Fig. 3.11   Error generated when a DTD contains a reference to an undefined entity. (Part 1 of 2.)

```
c:\examples>java -classpath %CLASSPATH% com.deitel.jws1.xml.Valida-
tor chapter3/fig03_11/invalid-entityexample.xml
Error parsing Document:
org.xml.sax.SAXParseException: ENTITY "country" is not valid.
        at org.apache.xerces.parsers.DOMParser.parse(
DOMParser.java:235)
        at org.apache.xerces.jaxp.DocumentBuilderImpl.parse(
DocumentBuilderImpl.java:201)
        at javax.xml.parsers.DocumentBuilder.parse(Unknown Source)
        at com.deitel.jws1.xml.Validator.main(Validator.java:46)
```

Fig. 3.11 Error generated when a DTD contains a reference to an undefined entity.
(Part 2 of 2.)

which indicates that **sportsClub** contains a required **NMTOKEN phone** attribute. An example of markup that conforms to this specification is

> *<sportsClub phone = "555-111-2222">*

An example that does not conform to this specification is

> *<sportsClub phone = "555 555 4902">*

because spaces are not allowed in an **NMTOKEN** attribute.

Similarly, when an *NMTOKENS* attribute type is declared, the attribute may contain multiple string tokens separated by spaces. For example, consider the declaration

> *<!ATTLIST sportsClub phone NMTOKENS #REQUIRED>*

which indicates that **sportsClub** contains a required **NMTOKENS phone** attribute. An example of markup that conforms to this specification is

> *<sportsClub phone = "555-111-2222 555-555-1818">*

3.6.2 Enumerated Attribute Types

Enumerated attribute types declare a list of possible values that an attribute can have. The attribute must be assigned a value from this list in order to conform to the DTD. Enumerated type values are separated by pipe characters (|). For example, the declaration

> *<!ATTLIST person gender (M | F) "F">*

contains an enumerated attribute type declaration that allows attribute **gender** to have either the value **"M"** or the value **"F"**. A default value of **"F"** is specified to the right of the element attribute type. Alternatively, a declaration such as

> *<!ATTLIST person gender (M | F) #IMPLIED>*

does not provide a default value for **gender**. This type of declaration might be used to validate a marked-up mailing list that contains first names, last names, addresses, etc. The application that uses such a mailing list may want to precede each name by either "Mr.," "Ms." or "Mrs." However, some first names are gender neutral (e.g., Chris and Sam), and

the application may not know the **person**'s gender. In this case, the application has the
flexibility to process the name in a gender-neutral way.

NOTATION is also an enumerated attribute type. For example, the declaration

```
<!ATTLIST book reference NOTATION ( JAVA | C ) "C">
```

indicates that **reference** must be assigned a value of either **JAVA** or **C**. If a value is not
assigned, **C** is specified as the default. The notation for **C** might be declared as

```
<!NOTATION C SYSTEM
       "http://www.deitel.com/books/2000/chtp3/chtp3_toc.htm">
```

3.7 Conditional Sections

DTDs provide the ability to include or exclude declarations, using conditional sections.
Keyword **INCLUDE** specifies that declarations are included, while keyword **IGNORE** specifies that declarations are excluded. For example, the conditional section

```
<![INCLUDE[
<!ELEMENT name ( #PCDATA )>
]]>
```

directs the parser to include the declaration of element **name**.

Similarly, the conditional section

```
<![IGNORE[
<!ELEMENT message ( #PCDATA )>
]]>
```

directs the parser to exclude the declaration of element **message**. Conditional sections are
often used with entities, as demonstrated in Fig. 3.12.

```
1   <!-- Fig. 3.12: conditional.dtd          -->
2   <!-- DTD for conditional section example -->
3
4   <!ENTITY % reject "IGNORE">
5   <!ENTITY % accept "INCLUDE">
6
7   <![ %accept; [
8      <!ELEMENT message ( approved, signature )>
9   ]]>
10
11  <![ %reject; [
12     <!ELEMENT message ( approved, reason, signature )>
13  ]]>
14
15  <!ELEMENT approved EMPTY>
16  <!ATTLIST approved flag ( true | false ) "false">
17
18  <!ELEMENT reason ( #PCDATA )>
19  <!ELEMENT signature ( #PCDATA )>
```

Fig. 3.12   Conditional sections in a DTD.

Lines 4–5 declare entities **reject** and **accept**, with the values **IGNORE** and **INCLUDE**, respectively. Because each of these entities is preceded by a *percent* (**%**) *character*, they can be used only inside the DTD in which they are declared. These types of entities—called *parameter entities*—allow document authors to create entities specific to a DTD—not an XML document. Recall that the DTD is the combination of the internal subset and the external subset. Parameter entities may be placed only in the external subset.

Lines 7–13 use the entities **accept** and **reject**, which represent the keywords **INCLUDE** and **IGNORE**, respectively. Notice that the parameter entity references are preceded by **%**, whereas normal entity references are preceded by **&**. Line 7 represents the start tag of an **IGNORE** section (the value of the **accept** entity is **INCLUDE**), while line 11 represents the start tag of an **INCLUDE** section. By changing the values of the entities, we easily can choose which **message** element declaration to allow. Figure 3.13 shows the XML document that conforms to the DTD in Fig. 3.12.

Software Engineering Observation 3.4

Parameter entities allow document authors to use entity names in DTDs without having them conflict with the same entity names used in an XML document.

3.8 Whitespace Characters

In Chapter 2, we briefly discussed whitespace characters. In this section, we discuss how whitespace characters relate to DTDs. Depending on the application, insignificant whitespace characters may be collapsed into a single whitespace character or even removed entirely. This process is called *normalization*. Whitespace is either preserved or normalized, depending on the context in which it is used.

Figure 3.14 demonstrates how whitespace is handled in an XML document. Line 28 assigns a value containing multiple whitespace characters to attribute **cdata**. Attribute **cdata** (declared in line 11) is required and must contain **CDATA**. As mentioned earlier, **CDATA** can contain almost any text, including whitespace. As the output illustrates, spaces in **CDATA** are preserved and passed on to the application that is consuming the XML document's data.

```
1   <?xml version = "1.0" encoding = "UTF-8"?>
2
3   <!-- Fig. 3.13: conditional.xml -->
4   <!-- Using conditional sections -->
5
6   <!DOCTYPE message SYSTEM "conditional.dtd">
7
8   <message>
9      <approved flag = "true" />
10     <signature>Chairman</signature>
11  </message>
```

```
c:\examples>java -classpath %CLASSPATH% com.deitel.jws1.xml.Valida-
tor chapter3/fig03_12_13/conditional.xml
Document is valid.
```

Fig. 3.13   XML document that conforms to **conditional.dtd**.

Line 30 assigns a value to attribute **id** that contains leading whitespace. Attribute **id** is declared on line 14 with tokenized attribute type **ID**. Because this value is not **CDATA**, it is normalized, and the leading whitespace characters are removed. Similarly, lines 32 and 34 assign values that contain leading whitespace to attributes **nmtoken** and **enumeration**, which are declared in the DTD as an **NMTOKEN** and an enumeration, respectively. Both of these attributes are normalized by the parser.

In this chapter, we have introduced DTDs. In Chapter 4, we introduce the document object model (DOM™) for manipulating an XML document's contents programmatically.

```
 1   <?xml version = "1.0" encoding = "UTF-8"?>
 2
 3   <!-- Fig. 3.14 : whitespace.xml         -->
 4   <!-- Demonstrating whitespace parsing -->
 5
 6   <!DOCTYPE whitespace [
 7      <!ELEMENT whitespace ( hasCDATA,
 8         hasID, hasNMTOKEN, hasEnumeration, hasMixed )>
 9
10      <!ELEMENT hasCDATA EMPTY>
11      <!ATTLIST hasCDATA cdata CDATA #REQUIRED>
12
13      <!ELEMENT hasID EMPTY>
14      <!ATTLIST hasID id ID #REQUIRED>
15
16      <!ELEMENT hasNMTOKEN EMPTY>
17      <!ATTLIST hasNMTOKEN nmtoken NMTOKEN #REQUIRED>
18
19      <!ELEMENT hasEnumeration EMPTY>
20      <!ATTLIST hasEnumeration enumeration ( true | false )
21              #REQUIRED>
22
23      <!ELEMENT hasMixed ( #PCDATA | hasCDATA )*>
24   ]>
25
26   <whitespace>
27
28      <hasCDATA cdata = "  simple cdata  "/>
29
30      <hasID id = "  i20"/>
31
32      <hasNMTOKEN nmtoken = "   hello"/>
33
34      <hasEnumeration enumeration = "   true"/>
35
36      <hasMixed>
37         This is text.
38         <hasCDATA cdata = " simple    cdata"/>
39         This is some additional text.
40      </hasMixed>
41
42   </whitespace>
```

Fig. 3.14 Processing whitespace in an XML document. (Part 1 of 2.)

```
c:\examples>java -classpath %CLASSPATH% com.deitel.jws1.xml.Valida-
tor chapter3/fig03_14/whitespace.xml
Document is valid.
```

```
c:\examples>java -classpath %CLASSPATH% com.deitel.jws1.xml.ParserT-
est chapter3/fig03_14/whitespace.xml
<?xml version="1.0" encoding="UTF-8"?>
<!-- Fig. 3.14 : whitespace.xml        -->
<!-- Demonstrating whitespace parsing -->
<whitespace>

   <hasCDATA cdata="  simple cdata   "/>

   <hasID id="i20"/>

   <hasNMTOKEN nmtoken="hello"/>

   <hasEnumeration enumeration="true"/>

   <hasMixed>
      This is text.
      <hasCDATA cdata=" simple     cdata"/>
      This is some additional text.
   </hasMixed>

</whitespace>
```

Fig. 3.14   Processing whitespace in an XML document. (Part 2 of 2.)

3.9 Summary

Document Type Definitions (DTDs) define an XML document's structure (e.g., what elements, attributes, etc., are permitted in the XML document). An XML document is not required to have a corresponding DTD.

Parsers are classified as validating or nonvalidating. A validating parser can read the DTD and determine whether the XML document conforms to it. If the document conforms to the DTD, it is valid. If the document fails to conform to the DTD, but is syntactically correct, it is well formed, but not valid. By definition, a valid document is well formed.

DTDs are introduced into XML documents by using the document type declaration (i.e., **DOCTYPE**). The document type declaration can point to declarations that are outside the XML document (called the external subset) or can contain the declaration inside the document (called the internal subset). Collectively, the internal and external subsets form the DTD.

Elements are the primary building blocks used in XML documents and are declared in a DTD with element type declarations. Nonempty elements can contain other elements and/or character data.

Attributes for an element are declared using attribute type declarations. Attribute types are classified as either string (**CDATA**), tokenized or enumerated. String attribute types do not impose any constraints on attribute values, other than disallowing the **<** and **&** characters.

Tokenized attributes impose constraints on attribute values, such as restrictions on which characters are permitted in an attribute name. Enumerated attributes are the most restrictive of the three types. They can take only one of the values listed in the attribute declaration.

3.10 Internet and World Wide Web Resources

www.wdvl.com/Authoring/HTML/Validation/DTD.html
This site contains a description of the historical uses of DTDs, including a description of SGML (XML's parent language) and the HTML DTD.

www.xml101.com/dtd
This page contains tutorials and explanations on writing DTDs.

www.w3schools.com/dtd
This site contains DTD tutorials and examples.

wdvl.internet.com/Authoring/Languages/XML/Tutorials/Intro/ index3.html
This site is a DTD tutorial for Web developers.

www.networking.ibm.com/xml/XmlValidatorForm.html
This page is IBM's DOMit XML Validator.

Document Object Model (DOM™)

4.1 Introduction

In previous chapters, we concentrated on basic XML markup and DTDs for validating XML documents. In this chapter, we focus on manipulating the contents of an XML document programmatically.

XML documents, when parsed, are represented as a hierarchical tree structure in memory. This tree structure contains the document's elements, attributes, character data, etc. The W3C provides a recommendation—called the *XML Document Object Model* (*DOM*)—for building these tree structures in memory. Any parser that adheres to this recommendation is called a *DOM-based parser*. Each element, attribute, **CDATA** section, etc., in an XML document is represented by a *node* in the DOM tree. For example, when the simple XML document

```
<?xml version = "1.0" encoding = "UTF-8"?>
<message from = "Ms. Quito" to = "Russ Tick">
    <body>Hi, Russ!</body>
    <attachment>Hawaii.jpg</attachment>
</message>
```

is parsed, a DOM tree with several nodes is created in memory. One node is created for the **message** element. This node has two *child nodes* (or *children*) that correspond to the **body** element and the **attachment** element. The **body** element has a child node (in this case, a text node) that corresponds to the text **Hi, Russ!**. The **from** and **to** attributes of the **message** element also have corresponding nodes in the DOM tree. A node that contains child nodes is called a *parent node* (e.g., **message**). A parent node can have many children, but a child node can have only one parent node. Nodes that are peers (e.g., **body** and **attachment**) are called *sibling nodes*. A node's *descendent nodes* include that node's children, its children's children and so on. A node's *ancestor nodes* include that node's parent, its parent's parent and so on. The DOM tree has a single *root node* that contains the root element (e.g., **message**), which contains all other nodes in the document.

Although an XML document is a text file, using traditional sequential-file access techniques to retrieve data from the document is neither practical nor efficient, especially for adding and removing elements dynamically. A DOM-based parser *exposes* (i.e., makes available) a programmatic library—called the *DOM Application Programming Interface* (*API*)—that allows data in an XML document to be accessed and modified by manipulating the nodes in a DOM tree. Each node is an object that has methods for accessing the node's names, values, child nodes, etc.

In the DOM API,[1] the primary DOM interfaces are **Node** (which represents any node in the tree), **NodeList** (which represents an ordered set of nodes), **NamedNodeMap** (which represents an unordered set of nodes), **Document** (which represents the document), **Element** (which represents an element node), **Attr** (which represents an attribute node), **Text** (which represents a text node) and **Comment** (which represents a comment node). In Section 4.3, we provide an overview of these interfaces and their key methods.

Portability Tip 4.1

The DOM interfaces for creating and manipulating XML documents are platform and language independent. DOM parsers exist for many different languages, including Java, C, C++, Python and Perl.

4.2 DOM with Java

To introduce document manipulation with the XML DOM, we begin with a simple Java example. This example takes an XML document (Fig. 4.1) and uses the JAXP API to display the document's element names and values. Figure 4.2 presents the Java code[2] that manipulates this XML document and displays its content.

```
1   <?xml version = "1.0" encoding = "UTF-8" standalone = "yes"?>
2
3   <!-- Fig. 4.1: article.xml      -->
4   <!-- Article formatted with XML  -->
5
6   <article>
7
8      <title>Simple XML</title>
9
10     <date>May 31, 2002</date>
11
12     <author>
13        <fname>Tarz</fname>
14        <lname>Ant</lname>
15     </author>
16
17     <summary>XML is easy.</summary>
18
19     <content>Once you have mastered XHTML, you can easily learn
20        XML. You must remember that XML is not for
21        displaying information but for managing information.
22     </content>
23
24   </article>
```

Fig. 4.1   XML document used in Fig. 4.2.

1. In this chapter, we use the reference implementation for the Java API for XML Processing 1.2 (JAXP), which is part of the Java Web Services Developer Pack 1.0.
2. Before running the examples in this chapter, execute the batch file (**jws1_xml.bat**) provided with the book's examples.

Lines 9, 12 and 13 **import** packages related to XML processing. Package
javax.xml.parsers provides classes related to parsing an XML document. Package
org.w3c.dom provides the DOM-API programmatic interface (i.e., classes, methods,
etc.). Package *org.xml.sax* provides classes used by the example's exception handlers.

```
1    // Fig. 4.2 : XMLInfo.java
2    // Outputs node information
3    package com.deitel.jws1.xml;
4
5    // Java core libraries
6    import java.io.*;
7
8    // Java standard extensions
9    import javax.xml.parsers.*;
10
11   // third-party libraries
12   import org.w3c.dom.*;
13   import org.xml.sax.*;
14
15   public class XMLInfo {
16
17      public static void main( String args[] )
18      {
19
20         if ( args.length != 1 ) {
21            System.err.println( "Usage: java XMLInfo input.xml" );
22            System.exit( 1 );
23         }
24
25         try {
26
27            // create DocumentBuilderFactory
28            DocumentBuilderFactory factory =
29               DocumentBuilderFactory.newInstance();
30
31            // create DocumentBuilder
32            DocumentBuilder builder = factory.newDocumentBuilder();
33
34            // obtain document object from XML document
35            Document document = builder.parse(
36               new File( args[ 0 ] ) );
37
38            // get root node
39            Node root = document.getDocumentElement();
40
41            System.out.print( "Here is the document's root node:" );
42            System.out.println( " " + root.getNodeName() );
43
44            System.out.println( "Here are its child elements: " );
45            NodeList childNodes = root.getChildNodes();
46            Node currentNode;
```

Fig. 4.2   **XMLInfo** displays an XML document's element names and character
data. (Part 1 of 3.)

```
47
48              for ( int i = 0; i < childNodes.getLength(); i++ ) {
49
50                  currentNode = childNodes.item( i );
51
52                  // print node name of each child element
53                  System.out.println( currentNode.getNodeName() );
54              }
55
56              // get first child of root element
57              currentNode = root.getFirstChild();
58
59              System.out.print( "The first child of root node is: " );
60              System.out.println( currentNode.getNodeName() );
61
62              // get next sibling of first child
63              System.out.print( "whose next sibling is: " );
64              currentNode = currentNode.getNextSibling();
65              System.out.println( currentNode.getNodeName() );
66
67              // print value of first child's next sibling
68              System.out.println( "value of " +
69                  currentNode.getNodeName() + " element is: " +
70                  currentNode.getFirstChild().getNodeValue() );
71
72              // print name of next sibling's parent
73              System.out.print( "Parent node of " +
74                  currentNode.getNodeName() + " is: " +
75                  currentNode.getParentNode().getNodeName() );
76          }
77
78          // handle exception creating DocumentBuilder
79          catch ( ParserConfigurationException parserError ) {
80              System.err.println( "Parser Configuration Error" );
81              parserError.printStackTrace();
82          }
83
84          // handle exception reading data from file
85          catch ( IOException fileException ) {
86              System.err.println( "File IO Error" );
87              fileException.printStackTrace();
88          }
89
90          // handle exception parsing XML document
91          catch ( SAXException parseException ) {
92              System.err.println( "Error Parsing Document" );
93              parseException.printStackTrace();
94          }
95      }
96  }
```

Fig. 4.2   **XMLInfo** displays an XML document's element names and character data. (Part 2 of 3.)

```
c:\examples>java -classpath %CLASSPATH% com.deitel.jws1.xml.XMLInfo
chapter4/fig04_01_02/article.xml
Here is the document's root node: article
Here are its child elements:
#text
title
#text
date
#text
author
#text
summary
#text
content
#text
The first child of root node is: #text
whose next sibling is: title
value of title element is: Simple XML
Parent node of title is: article
```

Fig. 4.2　**XMLInfo** displays an XML document's element names and character data. (Part 3 of 3.)

Lines 28–29 create a new **DocumentBuilderFactory**. The **DocumentBuilderFactory** is required to produce an appropriate **DocumentBuilder** object for the currently configured XML parser. JAXP can be configured to use many different XML parsers, such as the Apache Group's Xerces and IBM's XML4J. JAXP also has its own parser built in, which is used by default.

Line 32 uses the **DocumentBuilderFactory** class to create a **DocumentBuilder** object. Class **DocumentBuilder** provides an interface for loading and parsing XML documents. Lines 35–36 call the **DocumentBuilder** method **parse** to load and parse the XML document passed to the application as a command-line argument. The object returned contains the in-memory representation (i.e., the tree structure) of the XML document.

To access nodes in the tree structure, the root node must be retrieved. Line 39 retrieves the root node of the XML document by calling method **getDocumentElement**. Line 42 retrieves the root node's name (i.e., **article**) by calling method **getNodeName**. Line 45 calls method **getChildNodes** to obtain an ordered list (i.e., a **NodeList**) of **Element** nodes. The **NodeList** contains all the root node's child nodes. The first **Node** in the **NodeList** has an ordinal value of **0**, the next node has an ordinal value of **1** and so on. When passed as an argument to method **item**, this ordinal value (or index) allows programmers to access any **Node** in the **NodeList**.

Line 48 calls **NodeList** method **getLength** to obtain the number of nodes in the list. Lines 48–54 retrieve each **Node**'s name in the **NodeList** by calling **NodeList** method **item**. This method is passed the index of the desired **Node** in the **NodeList**.

Line 57 calls method **getFirstChild** to obtain a **Node** reference to the first child **Node** of the **Node** referenced by **root**. Line 60 displays the name of the **Node** referenced by **currentNode**. Line 64 calls **Node** method **getNextSibling** to obtain a reference to the node's next sibling (e.g., the **Node** containing **title**). Line 65 displays the sibling

Node's name. Lines 68–70 print the name of the **Node** referenced by **currentNode** and the value of the first child **Node** referenced by **currentNode**. The **Node** method *get-NodeValue* returns different values for different node types. In the tree structure created from the XML document in Fig. 4.1, the child node is of type **Text** (which represents character data), so **getNodeValue** returns the **String** contents of the **Text** node. We will explain **Node** types in greater detail in the next section.

4.3 DOM Components

In this section, we use Java, JAXP and some of the interfaces described in Fig. 4.3 to manipulate an XML document. Due to the large number of DOM interfaces and methods available, we provide only a partial list. For a complete list of DOM classes, interfaces and methods, browse the HTML documentation (**index.html** in the **api** folder) included with JAXP.

The **Document** interface represents the top-level node of an XML document in memory and provides methods for creating nodes and retrieving nodes. Figure 4.4 lists some **Document** methods. Interface **Node** represents any node type. Figure 4.5 lists some methods of interface **Node**.

Interface	Description
Document	Represents the XML document's top-level node (i.e., the *document root*), which provides access to all the document's nodes, including the root node.
Node	Represents a node in the XML document.
NodeList	Represents an ordered list of **Node**s.
Element	Represents an element node. Inherits from **Node**.
Attr	Represents an attribute node. Inherits from **Node**.
CharacterData	Represents character data. Inherits from **Node**.
Text	Represents a text node. Inherits from **CharacterData**.
Comment	Represents a comment node. Inherits from **CharacterData**.
ProcessingInstruction	Represents a processing-instruction node. Inherits from **Node**.
CDATASection	Represents a **CDATA** section. Inherits from **Text**.

Fig. 4.3   Some DOM interfaces.

Method Name	Description
createElement	Creates and returns an element node with the specified tag name.

Fig. 4.4   Some **Document** methods. (Part 1 of 2.)

Method Name	Description
createAttribute	Creates and returns an attribute node with the specified name and value.
createTextNode	Creates and returns a text node that contains the specified text.
createComment	Creates and returns a comment node that contains the specified text.
createProcessingInstruction	Creates and returns a processing-instruction node that contains the specified target and value.
createCDATASection	Creates and returns a **CDATA** section node that contains the specified text.
getDocumentElement	Returns the document's root element.
appendChild	Appends a child node.
getChildNodes	Returns a **NodeList** containing the node's child nodes.

Fig. 4.4   Some **Document** methods. (Part 2 of 2.)

Method Name	Description
appendChild	Appends a child node.
cloneNode	Duplicates the node.
getAttributes	Returns the node's attributes.
getChildNodes	Returns the node's child nodes.
getNextSibling	Returns the node's next sibling.
getNodeName	Returns the node's name.
getNodeType	Returns the node's type (e.g., element, attribute or text). Node types are described in greater detail in Fig. 4.6.
getNodeValue	Returns the node's value.
getParentNode	Returns the node's parent.
hasChildNodes	Returns **true** if the node has child nodes.
removeChild	Removes a child node from the node.
replaceChild	Replaces a child node with another node.
setNodeValue	Sets the node's value.
insertBefore	Appends a child node in front of a child node.

Fig. 4.5   **Node** methods.

Figure 4.6 lists some node types that may be returned by method **getNodeType**. Each type listed in Fig. 4.6 is a **static final** member of interface **Node**.

Node Type	Description
Node.ELEMENT_NODE	Represents an element node.
Node.ATTRIBUTE_NODE	Represents an attribute node.
Node.TEXT_NODE	Represents a text node.
Node.COMMENT_NODE	Represents a comment node.
Node.PROCESSING_INSTRUCTION_NODE	Represents a processing-instruction node.
Node.CDATA_SECTION_NODE	Represents a **CDATA** section node.

Fig. 4.6   Some **Node** types.

Element represents an element node. Figure 4.7 lists some **Element** methods. Figure 4.8 and Fig. 4.9 present a Java application that validates **introduction.xml** (Fig. 4.10) and replaces the text in its **message** element with the text **New Changed Message!!**.

Lines 27–28 create a new **DocumentBuilderFactory**. By passing the value **true** as an argument to method **setValidating**, line 31 indicates that validating parser should be used. Line 34 creates a new **DocumentBuilder**. A **CErrorHandler** (Fig. 4.9) object is created in line 37 to define methods for handling exceptions related to parsing. Line 40 calls method **parse** to load and parse the XML document stored in the file **introduction.xml**. If parsing is successful, a tree structure representing **introduction.xml** is created. If parsing fails because the document is not valid, a **SAXException** is thrown. If the document is not well formed, a **SAXParseException** is thrown.

Method Name	Description
getAttribute	Returns the value of the specified attribute.
getTagName	Returns an element's name.
removeAttribute	Removes an element's attribute.
setAttribute	Changes the value of the attribute passed as the first argument to the value passed as the second argument.

Fig. 4.7   **Element** methods.

```
1   // Fig. 4.8 : ReplaceText.java
2   // Reads introduction.xml and replaces a text node.
3   package com.deitel.jws1.xml;
4
5   // Java core packages
6   import java.io.*;
```

Fig. 4.8   Simple example that replaces an existing text node. (Part 1 of 4.)

```
 7
 8     // Java extension packages
 9     import javax.xml.parsers.*;
10     import javax.xml.transform.*;
11     import javax.xml.transform.stream.*;
12     import javax.xml.transform.dom.*;
13
14     // third-party libraries
15     import org.xml.sax.*;
16     import org.w3c.dom.*;
17
18     public class ReplaceText {
19        private Document document;
20
21        public ReplaceText( String fileName )
22        {
23           // parse document, find/replace element, output result
24           try {
25
26              // obtain default parser
27              DocumentBuilderFactory factory =
28                 DocumentBuilderFactory.newInstance();
29
30              // set parser as validating
31              factory.setValidating( true );
32
33              // obtain object that builds Documents
34              DocumentBuilder builder = factory.newDocumentBuilder();
35
36              // set error handler for validation errors
37              builder.setErrorHandler( new CErrorHandler() );
38
39              // obtain document object from XML document
40              document = builder.parse( new File( fileName ) );
41
42              // retrieve root node
43              Node root = document.getDocumentElement();
44
45              if ( root.getNodeType() == Node.ELEMENT_NODE ) {
46                 Element myMessageNode = ( Element ) root;
47                 NodeList messageNodes =
48                    myMessageNode.getElementsByTagName( "message" );
49
50                 if ( messageNodes.getLength() != 0 ) {
51                    Node message = messageNodes.item( 0 );
52
53                    // create text node
54                    Text newText = document.createTextNode(
55                       "New Changed Message!!" );
56
57                    // get old text node
58                    Text oldText =
59                       ( Text ) message.getChildNodes().item( 0 );
```

Fig. 4.8   Simple example that replaces an existing text node. (Part 2 of 4.)

```
60
61                       // replace text
62                       message.replaceChild( newText, oldText );
63                 }
64             }
65
66          // output Document object
67
68          // create DOMSource for source XML document
69          Source xmlSource = new DOMSource( document );
70
71          // create StreamResult for transformation result
72          Result result = new StreamResult( System.out );
73
74          // create TransformerFactory
75          TransformerFactory transformerFactory =
76             TransformerFactory.newInstance();
77
78          // create Transformer for transformation
79          Transformer transformer =
80             transformerFactory.newTransformer();
81
82          transformer.setOutputProperty( "indent", "yes" );
83
84          // transform and deliver content to client
85          transformer.transform( xmlSource, result );
86          System.out.println( "Output written to: " + fileName );
87       }
88
89       // handle exception creating DocumentBuilder
90       catch ( ParserConfigurationException parserException ) {
91          parserException.printStackTrace();
92       }
93
94       // handle exception parsing Document
95       catch ( SAXException saxException ) {
96          saxException.printStackTrace();
97       }
98
99       // handle exception reading/writing data
100      catch ( IOException ioException ) {
101         ioException.printStackTrace();
102         System.exit( 1 );
103      }
104
105      // handle exception creating TransformerFactory
106      catch (
107         TransformerFactoryConfigurationError factoryError ) {
108         System.err.println( "Error while creating " +
109            "TransformerFactory" );
110         factoryError.printStackTrace();
111      }
112
```

Fig. 4.8   Simple example that replaces an existing text node. (Part 3 of 4.)

```
113        // handle exception transforming document
114        catch ( TransformerException transformerError ) {
115           System.err.println( "Error transforming document" );
116           transformerError.printStackTrace();
117        }
118     }
119
120     public static void main( String args[] )
121     {
122        ReplaceText replace = new ReplaceText();
123     }
124 }
```

Fig. 4.8   Simple example that replaces an existing text node. (Part 4 of 4.)

Line 43 retrieves the **Document**'s root node. Line 45 calls method *getNodeType* to obtain the root node's type and determines whether the root node is of type **Element**.

Line 46 downcasts **root** from a superclass **Node** type to an **Element** derived type. As mentioned earlier, class **Element** inherits from class **Node**. By calling method *getElementsByTagName*, lines 47–48 retrieve a **NodeList** containing all the **Node**s that contain the name **message** in the XML document. Line 50 determines whether the **NodeList** contains at least one item. The first **Node** in the **NodeList** is retrieved in line 51.

Lines 54–55 call **createTextNode** to create a **Text** node that contains the text **New Changed Message!!**. This node exists in memory independently of the XML document referenced by **document**—i.e., it has not been inserted into the document yet.

Lines 58–59 get the first child node of the **message** element (referenced by **Node message** in line 51), which is a **Text** node containing the text **Welcome to XML!**. Method **item** returns a **Node** that we downcast to **Text**. Line 62 calls method *replaceChild* to replace the **Node** referenced by the second argument with the **Node** referenced by the first argument. The XML document has now been modified—element **message** now contains the text **New Changed Message!!**.

Lines 66–86 output the modified **Document**. Line 69 creates a new **Source** object that wraps the modified **Document** object. Line 72 creates a new **StreamResult** object that passes an **OutputStream** as an argument, which, in this case, is **System.out**. Lines 75–76 create a new **TransformerFactory** by calling **static** method **newInstance**. Lines 79–80 create a new **Transformer** by calling method **newTransformer**. The object referenced by **transformer** writes the contents of the **document** to **System.out**. We discuss both **TransformerFactory** and **Transformer** in Chapter 5.

Line 82 sets the **"indent"** output property to **"yes"**, which causes the **Transformer** to add indentation when it produces the resulting document. Lines 90–91 handle a **ParserConfigurationException**, which can be thrown by **DocumentBuilderFactory** method **newDocumentBuilder**. Line 95 begins a **catch** block for a **SAXException**. This exception contains information about errors thrown by the parser.

Figure 4.9 presents **CErrorHandler.java**, which provides the implementation for handling errors thrown by the parser in **ReplaceText.java**. The programmer can provide an error handler, which is registered using method *setErrorHandler* (line 37 in Fig. 4.8).

```
1   // Fig. 4.9 : CErrorHandler.java
2   // Error Handler for validation errors.
3   package com.deitel.jws1.xml;
4
5   import org.xml.sax.ErrorHandler;
6   import org.xml.sax.SAXException;
7   import org.xml.sax.SAXParseException;
8
9   public class CErrorHandler implements ErrorHandler
10  {
11
12     // throw SAXException for fatal errors
13     public void fatalError( SAXParseException exception )
14        throws SAXException
15     {
16        throw exception;
17     }
18
19     // throw SAXParseException for errors
20     public void error( SAXParseException errorException )
21        throws SAXParseException
22     {
23        throw errorException;
24     }
25
26     // print any warnings
27     public void warning( SAXParseException warningError )
28        throws SAXParseException
29     {
30        System.err.println( "Warning: " + warningError.getMessage() );
31     }
32  }
```

Fig. 4.9   Class definition for **MyErrorHandler**.

Lines 5–7 of Fig. 4.9 **import ErrorHandler**, **SAXException** and **SAXParseException**. Interface *ErrorHandler* provides methods *fatalError*, *error* and *warning* for *fatal errors* (i.e., errors that violate the XML 1.0 recommendation; parsing is halted), *errors* (i.e., invalid markup; parsing is not halted) and *warnings* (i.e., any problems other than fatal errors or errors; parsing is not halted), respectively. These methods are overridden in lines 13, 20 and 27, respectively. Fatal errors and errors are rethrown, and warnings are output to the standard error stream (**System.err**).

Figure 4.10 presents the XML document manipulated by the Java application in Fig. 4.8. Notice that the **message** element's text has been changed in the output.

```
1   <?xml version = "1.0" encoding = "UTF-8" standalone = "yes"?>
2
3   <!-- Fig. 4.10 : introduction.xml        -->
4   <!-- Simple introduction to XML markup -->
```

Fig. 4.10   Input document (**introduction.xml**) and output from **ReplaceText.java**. (Part 1 of 2.)

```
 5
 6   <!DOCTYPE myMessage [
 7      <!ELEMENT myMessage ( message )>
 8      <!ELEMENT message ( #PCDATA )>
 9   ]>
10
11   <myMessage>
12      <message>Welcome to XML!</message>
13   </myMessage>
```

```
c:\examples>java -classpath %CLASSPATH% com.deitel.jws1.xml.ReplaceT-
ext chapter4/fig04_08_09_10/introduction.xml
<?xml version="1.0" encoding="UTF-8"?>
<!-- Fig. 4.10 : introduction.xml      -->
<!-- Simple introduction to XML markup -->
<myMessage>
   <message>New Changed Message!!</message>
</myMessage>
Output written to: chapter4/fig04_08_09_10/introduction.xml
```

Fig. 4.10   Input document (`introduction.xml`) and output from
`ReplaceText.java`. (Part 2 of 2.)

4.4 Creating Nodes

The majority of the XML markup that has been presented up to this point has been "hand coded" (i.e., typed into an editor by a document author). By using the DOM API, XML documents can be created in an automated way through programming. Figure 4.11 lists a Java application that creates an XML document for a list of contacts.

```
 1   // Fig. 4.11 : BuildXml.java
 2   // Creates element node, attribute node, comment node,
 3   // processing instruction and a CDATA section.
 4   package com.deitel.jws1.xml;
 5
 6   // Java core packages
 7   import java.io.*;
 8
 9   // Java extension packages
10   import javax.xml.parsers.*;
11   import javax.xml.transform.*;
12   import javax.xml.transform.stream.*;
13   import javax.xml.transform.dom.*;
14
15   // third-party libraries
16   import org.xml.sax.*;
17   import org.w3c.dom.*;
18
19   public class BuildXml {
20      private Document document;
```

Fig. 4.11   Building an XML document with the DOM. (Part 1 of 4.)

```
21
22      public BuildXml( String fileName )
23      {
24          DocumentBuilderFactory factory =
25              DocumentBuilderFactory.newInstance();
26
27          // create new DOM tree
28          try {
29
30              // get DocumentBuilder
31              DocumentBuilder builder =
32                  factory.newDocumentBuilder();
33
34              // create root node
35              document = builder.newDocument();
36          }
37
38          // handle exception thrown by DocumentBuilder
39          catch ( ParserConfigurationException parserException ) {
40              parserException.printStackTrace();
41          }
42
43          Element root = document.createElement( "root" );
44          document.appendChild( root );
45
46          // add comment to XML document
47          Comment simpleComment = document.createComment(
48              "This is a simple contact list" );
49          root.appendChild( simpleComment );
50
51          // add child element
52          Node contactNode = createContactNode( document );
53          root.appendChild( contactNode );
54
55          // add processing instruction
56          ProcessingInstruction pi =
57              document.createProcessingInstruction(
58                  "myInstruction", "action silent" );
59          root.appendChild( pi );
60
61          // add CDATA section
62          CDATASection cdata = document.createCDATASection(
63              "I can add <, >, and ?" );
64          root.appendChild( cdata );
65
66          // write XML document to disk
67          try {
68
69              // create DOMSource for source XML document
70              Source xmlSource = new DOMSource( document );
71
```

Fig. 4.11 Building an XML document with the DOM. (Part 2 of 4.)

```
72          // create StreamResult for transformation result
73          Result result = new StreamResult(
74             new FileOutputStream( new File( fileName ) ) );
75
76          // create TransformerFactory
77          TransformerFactory transformerFactory =
78             TransformerFactory.newInstance();
79
80          // create Transformer for transformation
81          Transformer transformer =
82             transformerFactory.newTransformer();
83
84          transformer.setOutputProperty( "indent", "yes" );
85
86          // transform and deliver content to client
87          transformer.transform( xmlSource, result );
88       }
89
90       // handle exception creating TransformerFactory
91       catch (
92          TransformerFactoryConfigurationError factoryError ) {
93          System.err.println( "Error creating " +
94             "TransformerFactory" );
95          factoryError.printStackTrace();
96       }
97
98       // handle exception transforming document
99       catch ( TransformerException transformerError ) {
100         System.err.println( "Error transforming document" );
101         transformerError.printStackTrace();
102      }
103
104      // handle exception writing data to file
105      catch ( IOException ioException ) {
106         ioException.printStackTrace();
107      }
108   }
109
110   public Node createContactNode( Document document )
111   {
112
113      // create FirstName and LastName elements
114      Element firstName = document.createElement( "FirstName" );
115      Element lastName = document.createElement( "LastName" );
116
117      firstName.appendChild( document.createTextNode( "Sue" ) );
118      lastName.appendChild( document.createTextNode( "Green" ) );
119
120      // create contact element
121      Element contact = document.createElement( "contact" );
122
123      // create attribute
124      Attr genderAttribute = document.createAttribute( "gender" );
```

Fig. 4.11   Building an XML document with the DOM. (Part 3 of 4.)

```
125            genderAttribute.setValue( "F" );
126
127            // append attribute to contact element
128            contact.setAttributeNode( genderAttribute );
129            contact.appendChild( firstName );
130            contact.appendChild( lastName );
131
132            return contact;
133         }
134
135         public static void main( String args[] )
136         {
137            BuildXml buildXml = new BuildXml( args[ 0 ] );
138         }
139      }
```

```
c:\examples>java -classpath %CLASSPATH% com.deitel.jws1.xml.BuildXml
chapter4/fig04_11/mydocument.xml
```

Fig. 4.11   Building an XML document with the DOM. (Part 4 of 4.)

Lines 43–44 create an element named **root** (whose **Element** node is referenced by **root**) and append it to the document root (whose **Document** node is referenced by **document**). This node is the first node appended, so it is the root node of the document. Lines 47–48 create a comment node by calling method **createComment** and append the node as a child of the node referenced by **root**. Line 52 calls programmer-defined method **createContactNode** (line 110) to create a node for a **contact** element. We will discuss this method momentarily. Lines 56–58 create a processing-instruction node. The first argument passed to **createProcessingInstruction** is the target **myInstruction**, and the second argument passed is the value **action silent**. Line 59 appends the processing-instruction node to the root node. Lines 62–63 create a **CDATA** section node, which is appended to the **Node** referenced by **root** in line 64.

Line 110 defines method **createContactNode**, which returns a **Node**. This method creates a **Node** for the **contact** element. The new **Node** is returned and appended to the **Node** referenced by **root** in line 53. Lines 114–115 create **Element** nodes for elements **FirstName** and **LastName**, which have their respective child **Text** nodes created and appended on lines 117–118. Lines 124–125 create an **Attr** node for attribute **gender** by calling method **createAttribute**. The value for this **Attr** node is set by calling method **setValue**. Line 128 associates this **Attr** node with the **Element** node (i.e., **contact**) by calling method **setAttributeNode**.

The XML document is written to disk in lines 67–88. Figure 4.12 lists the XML document (**myDocument.xml**) created by **BuildXml.java** (Fig. 4.11). [*Note*: We have modified this document for presentation purposes.]

```
1    <?xml version = "1.0" encoding = "UTF-8"?>
2
```

Fig. 4.12   Output (**myDocument.xml**) created by **buildXml.java**. (Part 1 of 2.)

```
3   <root>
4      <!--This is a simple contact list-->
5      <contact gender = "F">
6         <FirstName>Sue</FirstName>
7         <LastName>Green</LastName>
8      </contact>
9      <?myInstruction action silent?>
10     <![CDATA[I can add <, >, and ?]]>
11  </root>
```

Fig. 4.12   Output (**myDocument.xml**) created by **buildXml.java**. (Part 2 of 2.)

4.5 Traversing the DOM

In this section, we demonstrate how to use the DOM to traverse an XML document. In Fig. 4.13, we present a Java application that outputs element nodes, attribute nodes and text nodes. This application takes the name of an XML document (e.g., **simpleContact.xml** in Fig. 4.14) as a command-line argument.

```
1   // Fig. 4.13 : TraverseDOM.java
2   // Traverses DOM and prints various nodes.
3   package com.deitel.jws1.xml;
4
5   // Java core packages
6   import java.io.*;
7
8   // Java extension packages
9   import javax.xml.parsers.*;
10  import javax.xml.transform.*;
11  import javax.xml.transform.stream.*;
12  import javax.xml.transform.dom.*;
13
14  // third-party libraries
15  import org.w3c.dom.*;
16  import org.xml.sax.*;
17
18  public class TraverseDOM {
19     private Document document;
20
21     public TraverseDOM( String file )
22     {
23        // parse XML, create DOM tree, call method processNode
24        try {
25
26           // obtain default parser
27           DocumentBuilderFactory factory =
28              DocumentBuilderFactory.newInstance();
29           factory.setValidating( true );
30           DocumentBuilder builder = factory.newDocumentBuilder();
31
```

Fig. 4.13   Traversing the DOM. (Part 1 of 3.)

```
32                // set error handler for validation errors
33                builder.setErrorHandler( new CErrorHandler() );
34
35                // obtain document object from XML document
36                document = builder.parse( new File( file ) );
37                processNode( document );
38             }
39
40          // handle exception thrown by DocumentBuilder
41          catch ( ParserConfigurationException parserException ) {
42             parserException.printStackTrace();
43          }
44
45          // handle exception thrown by Parser
46          catch ( SAXException saxException ) {
47             saxException.printStackTrace();
48          }
49
50          // handle exception thrown when reading data from file
51          catch ( IOException ioException ) {
52             ioException.printStackTrace();
53             System.exit( 1 );
54          }
55       }
56
57       public void processNode( Node currentNode )
58       {
59          switch ( currentNode.getNodeType() ) {
60
61             // process Document root
62             case Node.DOCUMENT_NODE:
63                Document doc = ( Document ) currentNode;
64
65                System.out.println(
66                   "Document node: " + doc.getNodeName() +
67                   "\nRoot element: " +
68                   doc.getDocumentElement().getNodeName() );
69                processChildNodes( doc.getChildNodes() );
70                break;
71
72             // process Element node
73             case Node.ELEMENT_NODE:
74                System.out.println( "\nElement node: " +
75                                    currentNode.getNodeName() );
76                NamedNodeMap attributeNodes =
77                   currentNode.getAttributes();
78
79                for ( int i = 0; i < attributeNodes.getLength(); i++ ) {
80                   Attr attribute = ( Attr ) attributeNodes.item( i );
81
```

Fig. 4.13 Traversing the DOM. (Part 2 of 3.)

```
82                      System.out.println( "\tAttribute: " +
83                         attribute.getNodeName() + " ; Value = " +
84                         attribute.getNodeValue() );
85                   }
86
87                   processChildNodes( currentNode.getChildNodes() );
88                   break;
89
90               // process text node and CDATA section
91               case Node.CDATA_SECTION_NODE:
92               case Node.TEXT_NODE:
93                  Text text = ( Text ) currentNode;
94
95                  if ( !text.getNodeValue().trim().equals( "" ) )
96                     System.out.println( "\tText: " +
97                        text.getNodeValue() );
98                  break;
99            }
100        }
101
102    public void processChildNodes( NodeList children )
103    {
104       for ( int i = 0; i < children.getLength(); i++ )
105          processNode( children.item( i ) );
106    }
107
108    public static void main( String args[] )
109    {
110       if ( args.length < 1 ) {
111          System.err.println(
112             "Usage: java TraverseDOM <filename>" );
113          System.exit( 1 );
114       }
115
116       TraverseDOM traverseDOM = new TraverseDOM( args[ 0 ] );
117    }
118 }
```

Fig. 4.13 Traversing the DOM. (Part 3 of 3.)

Lines 21–55 define the class constructor for **TraverseDOM**, which takes the name of the file specified at the command line (i.e., **simpleContact.xml**) and loads and parses the XML document before passing it to programmer-defined method **process-Node**.

Lines 57–100 define method **processNode**, which takes one **Node** parameter and outputs information about the **Node** and its child nodes. Line 59 begins a **switch** structure that determines the **Node**'s type. Line 62 matches the document's root node. This **case** outputs the document node (represented as **#document**) and processes its child nodes by calling method **processChildNodes** (lines 102–106). We will discuss method **processchildNodes** momentarily. Line 73 matches an **Element** node. This **case** outputs the element's attributes and then processes its child nodes by calling **pro-cessChildNodes**.

An element may contain any number of attributes. Lines 76–77 call method **getAttributes** to retrieve the list of **Attr** nodes for the **Element** node referenced by **currentNode**. The unordered[3] node list returned is assigned to the **NamedNodeMap** reference **attributeNodes**. If the **Element** node contains **Attr** nodes, the **for** loop (lines 79–85) outputs each **Attr** node's name and value.

Lines 91–92 match **CDATA** section nodes and **Text** nodes. These **case**s output the node's text content (lines 95–98).

Lines 102–106 define method **processChildNodes**, which takes one **NodeList** parameter and calls **processNode** on a node's child nodes. Each child node is retrieved by calling **NodeList** method **item** (line 105). Figure 4.14 lists the contents of **simpleContact.xml**, the XML document used by **TraverseDOM.java**.

```
1   <?xml version = "1.0" encoding = "UTF-8" standalone = "yes"?>
2
3   <!-- Fig. 4.14 : simpleContact.xml   -->
4   <!-- Input file for traverseDOM.java -->
5
6   <!DOCTYPE contacts [
7      <!ELEMENT contacts ( contact+ )>
8      <!ELEMENT contact ( FirstName, LastName )>
9      <!ATTLIST contact gender ( M | F ) "M">
10     <!ELEMENT FirstName ( #PCDATA )>
11     <!ELEMENT LastName ( #PCDATA )>
12  ]>
13
14  <contacts>
15     <contact gender = "M">
16        <FirstName>John</FirstName>
17        <LastName>Black</LastName>
18     </contact>
19  </contacts>
```

```
c:\examples>java -classpath %CLASSPATH% com.deitel.jws1.xml.Traverse-
DOM chapter4/fig04_13_14/simplecontact.xml
Document node: #document
Root element: contacts

Element node: contacts

Element node: contact
        Attribute: gender ; Value = M

Element node: FirstName
        Text: John

Element node: LastName
        Text: Black
```

Fig. 4.14 Sample XML document used by **TraverseDOM.java**.

---

3. By definition, an element's attributes are unordered.

In this chapter, we have introduced the DOM. In Chapter 5, we introduce the portion of the Extensible Stylesheet Language (XSL) called *XSL Transformations* (*XSLT*), which is used for converting XML data into other text-based formats, such as the Extensible HyperText Markup Language (XHTML).

4.6 Summary

XML documents, when parsed, are represented as a hierarchal tree structure in memory. This tree structure contains the document's elements, attributes, text, etc. The W3C provides a recommendation—called the XML Document Object Model (DOM)—for building tree structures in memory that represent XML documents. Any parser that adheres to this recommendation is called a DOM-based parser.

A DOM-based parser exposes (i.e., makes available) a programmatic library—called the DOM Application Programming Interface (API)—that allows data in an XML document to be accessed and manipulated.

In the DOM API, the primary DOM interfaces are **Node** (which represents any node in the tree), **NodeList** (which represents an ordered set of nodes), **NamedNodeMap** (which represents an unordered set of nodes), **Document** (which represents the document), **Element** (which represents an element node), **Attr** (which represents an attribute node), **Text** (which represents a text node) and **Comment** (which represents a comment node). Each of these interfaces provide methods for manipulating nodes.

4.7 Internet and World Wide Web Resources

www.w3.org/DOM
W3C DOM home page.

www.w3schools.com/dom/default.asp
The W3Schools DOM introduction, tutorial and links site.

www.oasis-open.org/cover/dom.html
The Oasis-Open DOM page provides an overview of the DOM.

dmoz.org/Computers/Programming/Internet/W3C_DOM
This site contains links to different locations and instructional matter on DOM.

www.w3.org/DOM/faq.html
Answers to frequently asked questions (FAQs) on DOM.

5

XSL: Extensible Stylesheet Language Transformations (XSLT)

Objectives

- To understand what the Extensible Stylesheet Language is and how it relates to XML.
- To understand what an Extensible Stylesheet Language Transformation (XSLT) is.
- To write XSLT documents.
- To write templates.
- To iterate through a node set.
- To sort data during a transformation.
- To perform conditional processing.
- To declare variables.
- To combine multiple style sheets.

Guess if you can, choose if you dare.
Pierre Corneille

A Mighty Maze! but not without a plan.
Alexander Pope

Behind the outside pattern
the dim shapes get clearer every day.
It is always the same shape, only very numerous.
Charlotte Perkins Gilman

5.1 Introduction

The *Extensible Stylesheet Language* (*XSL*) provides rules for formatting XML documents. In this chapter, we present *XSL Transformations* (*XSLT*). XSLT *transforms* an XML document into another text-based form, such as the Extensible HyperText Markup Language (XHTML).[1] In this chapter, we present many XSLT examples and show the results of transforming XML documents into XHTML and XML.

5.2 Applying XSLTs with Java

To process XSLT documents, an *XSLT processor* is required. We have created a Java program that uses the JAXP[2] library's XSLT processor to perform XSL transformations. Our program, **Transform.java**[3] (Fig. 5.1), takes as command-line arguments the name of the XML document to be transformed, the name of the XSLT document to apply and the name of the document that will contain the result of the transformation.

```
1   // Fig. 5.1 : Transform.java
2   // Performs XSL Transformations.
3   package com.deitel.jws1.xml;
4
5   // Java core libraries
6   import java.io.*;
7   import java.util.*;
8
9   // Java standard extensions
10  import javax.xml.parsers.*;
```

Fig. 5.1   Java application that performs XSL transformations. (Part 1 of 2.)

1. XHTML has replaced the HyperText Markup Language (HTML) as the primary means of describing Web content. XHTML provides more robust, richer and more extensible features than HTML. For more on XHTML/HTML, visit **www.w3.org/markup**.
2. In this chapter, we use the reference implementation for the Java API for XML Processing 1.2 (JAXP), which is part of the Java Web Services Developer Pack 1.0.
3. Before running the examples in this chapter, execute the batch file (**jws1_xml.bat**) provided with the book's examples.

```
11   import javax.xml.transform.*;
12   import javax.xml.transform.dom.*;
13   import javax.xml.transform.stream.*;
14
15   // third-party libraries
16   import org.w3c.dom.*;
17   import org.xml.sax.SAXException;
18
19   public class Transform {
20
21      // execute application
22      public static void main( String args[] ) throws Exception
23      {
24         if ( args.length != 3 ) {
25            System.err.println( "Usage: java Transform input.xml "
26               + "input.xsl output" );
27            System.exit( 1 );
28         }
29
30         // factory for creating DocumentBuilders
31         DocumentBuilderFactory builderFactory =
32            DocumentBuilderFactory.newInstance();
33
34         // factory for creating Transformers
35         TransformerFactory transformerFactory =
36            TransformerFactory.newInstance();
37
38         DocumentBuilder builder =
39            builderFactory.newDocumentBuilder();
40
41         Document document = builder.parse( new File( args[ 0 ] ) );
42
43         // create DOMSource for source XML document
44         Source xmlSource = new DOMSource( document );
45
46         // create StreamSource for XSLT document
47         Source xslSource = new StreamSource( new File( args[ 1 ] ) );
48
49         // create StreamResult for transformation result
50         Result result = new StreamResult( new File( args[ 2 ] ) );
51
52         // create Transformer for XSL transformation
53         Transformer transformer =
54            transformerFactory.newTransformer( xslSource );
55
56         // transform and deliver content to client
57         transformer.transform( xmlSource, result );
58      }
59   }
```

Fig. 5.1   Java application that performs XSL transformations. (Part 2 of 2.)

Lines 6–39 **import** the necessary classes and create a **DocumentBuilderFactory**, a **TransformerFactory** and a **DocumentBuilder**. Line 41 creates a tree structure in memory from the XML document passed as a command-line argument. Line

44 creates a new ***DOMSource***[4] object from which the **Transformer** reads the XML **Document** referenced by **document**. Line 47 creates a **StreamSource** object from which the **Transformer** reads the XSL **File** passed as the second command-line argument. Line 50 creates a **StreamResult** object to which the **Transformer** writes a **File** containing the result of the transformation. Lines 53–54 call method ***newTransformer***, passing it the object referenced by **xslSource**. Constructing a **Transformer** that references an XSLT document allows the **Transformer** to apply the rules in that file when transforming XML documents. Line 57 calls method ***transform*** to apply the XSL document referenced by the **Transformer** to the XML document referenced by **xmlSource**. The transformation results are written to the **File** referenced by **result**.

5.3 Simple Transformation Example

In an XSL transformation, there are two trees of nodes. The first node tree is the *source tree*. The nodes in this tree correspond to the original XML document to which the transformation is applied. The document used as the source tree is not modified by an XSL transformation. The second tree is the *result tree*, which contains all of the nodes produced by the XSL transformation. The result tree represents the document produced by the transformation. The XSLT document shown in Fig. 5.2 transforms **introduction.xml** (Fig. 5.3) into a simple XHTML document (Fig. 5.4).

```
1   <?xml version = "1.0" encoding = "UTF-8"?>
2
3   <!-- Fig. 5.2 : introduction.xsl              -->
4   <!-- Simple XSLT document for introduction.xml. -->
5
6   <xsl:stylesheet version = "1.0"
7      xmlns:xsl = "http://www.w3.org/1999/XSL/Transform"
8      xmlns = "http://www.w3.org/1999/xhtml">
9      <xsl:output method = "xml" omit-xml-declaration = "no"
10        doctype-system =
11           "http://www.w3.org/TR/xhtml11/DTD/xhtml11-strict.dtd"
12        doctype-public =
13           "-//W3C//DTD XHTML 1.0 Strict//EN" />
14
15     <xsl:template match = "myMessage">
16        <html>
17           <head><title>Welcome</title></head>
18           <body><p><xsl:value-of select = "message"/></p></body>
19        </html>
20     </xsl:template>
21
22  </xsl:stylesheet>
```

Fig. 5.2   Simple XSLT document for transforming **introduction.xml** into XHTML.

4. In this example, we use a **DOMSource** object to provide the XML document to the **Transformer**, although we could have used a **StreamSource** to read from the XML file directly. We chose this method because, in previous examples in the book, we have built the DOM tree in memory, while we do not have a file from which to create a **StreamSource** object.

An XSLT document is an XML document with a root element **stylesheet**.[5] XSLT elements belong to the namespace **http://www.w3.org/1999/XSL/Transform**, which typically is bound to the namespace prefix **xsl**.

Line 6 contains the **stylesheet** root element. Attribute **version** specifies the version of XSLT to which this document conforms.[6] Namespace prefix **xsl** is defined and is bound to the XSLT URI defined by the W3C. When processed, the **output** element in lines 9–13 writes a document type declaration to the result tree. Attribute **method** is assigned the value **"xml"**, which indicates that XML is being output to the result tree. Attribute **omit-xml-declaration** is assigned the value **"no"**, which causes an XML declaration to be output to the result tree. Attributes **doctype-system** and **doctype-public** write the **DOCTYPE** DTD information to the result tree.

XSLT uses *XPath* expressions to locate nodes in an XML document.[7] [*Note*: A structured complete explanation of the XPath language is beyond the scope of this book. Instead, we explain XPath expressions as we encounter them in the examples.]

XSL documents contain one or more *templates* that describe how a specific node should be transformed. Line 15 contains a **template** *element*, which matches specific XML document nodes by using an XPath pattern in attribute **match**. In this case, any **Element** nodes with the name **myMessage** are matched.

Lines 16–19 are the contents of the **template** element. When a **myMessage** element node is **match**ed in the source tree (i.e., the document being transformed), the contents of the **template** element are placed in the result tree (i.e., the document created by the transformation). By using element **value-of** and an XPath expression in attribute **select**, the text contents of the node returned by the XPath expression are placed in the result tree. In line 18, element **message**'s value is written to the result tree. Figure 5.3 lists the input XML document. Figure 5.4 lists the results of the transformation. [*Note*: Fig. 5.4 has been modified for the purpose of presentation.]

```
1    <?xml version = "1.0" encoding = "UTF-8"?>
2
3    <!-- Fig. 5.3 : introduction.xml         -->
4    <!-- Simple introduction to XML markup -->
5
6    <myMessage>
7        <message>Welcome to XSLT!</message>
8    </myMessage>
```

```
c:\examples>java -classpath %CLASSPATH% com.deitel.jws1.xml.Trans-
form chapter5/fig05_02_03/introduction.xml chapter5/fig05_02_03/in-
troduction.xsl chapter5/fig05_02_03/results.html
```

Fig. 5.3   Sample input XML document **introduction.xml**.

---

5. Although infrequently used, **transform** also may be used as the root element in an XSLT document.
6. XSLT 1.0 is a W3C Recommendation (**www.w3.org/TR/xslt**).
7. XML Path Language 1.0 is a W3C Recommendation (**www.w3.org/TR/xpath**).

```
1   <?xml version = "1.0" encoding = "UTF-8"?>
2   <!DOCTYPE html PUBLIC "-//W3C//DTD XHTML 1.0 Strict//EN"
3       "http://www.w3.org/TR/xhtml1/DTD/xhtml1-strict.dtd">
4
5   <html xmlns = "http://www.w3.org/1999/xhtml">
6       <head><title>Welcome</head></title>
7       <body>
8           <p>Welcome to XSLT!</p>
9       </body>
10   </html>
```

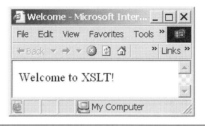

Fig. 5.4   Results of applying `introduction.xsl` to `introduction.xml`.

5.4 Creating Elements and Attributes

When transforming an XML document into another text-based format, it is often necessary to create element nodes and attribute nodes in the result tree. Figure 5.5 provides an XML document that marks up a list of various sports, and Fig. 5.6 presents the XSLT document that transforms the XML document in Fig. 5.5 into another XML document. The original XML document is transformed into a new XML document with the sport names as elements (instead of attributes, as in the original XML document).

```
1   <?xml version = "1.0" encoding = "UTF-8"?>
2
3   <!-- Fig. 5.5 : games.xml -->
4   <!-- Sports Database        -->
5
6   <sports>
7
8       <game title = "cricket">
9           <id>243</id>
10
11          <paragraph>
12              More popular among commonwealth nations.
13          </paragraph>
14      </game>
15
16      <game title = "baseball">
17          <id>431</id>
18
```

Fig. 5.5   XML document containing a list of sports. (Part 1 of 2.)

```
19            <paragraph>
20               More popular in America.
21            </paragraph>
22         </game>
23
24         <game title = "soccer">
25            <id>123</id>
26
27            <paragraph>
28               Most popular sport in the world.
29            </paragraph>
30         </game>
31
32      </sports>
```

Fig. 5.5   XML document containing a list of sports. (Part 2 of 2.)

```
1    <?xml version = "1.0" encoding = "UTF-8"?>
2
3    <!-- Fig. 5.6 : games.xsl              -->
4    <!-- Using xsl:element and xsl:attribute -->
5
6    <xsl:stylesheet version = "1.0"
7       xmlns:xsl = "http://www.w3.org/1999/XSL/Transform">
8
9       <!-- match sports elements -->
10      <xsl:template match = "/sports">
11         <sports>
12            <xsl:apply-templates select = "game"/>
13         </sports>
14      </xsl:template>
15
16      <!-- match game elements -->
17      <xsl:template match = "game">
18
19         <!-- create child element -->
20         <xsl:element name = "{@title}">
21
22            <!-- create attribute -->
23            <xsl:attribute name = "id">
24               <xsl:value-of select = "id"/>
25            </xsl:attribute>
26
27            <comment>
28               <xsl:value-of select = "paragraph"/>
29            </comment>
30
31         </xsl:element>
32      </xsl:template>
33
34   </xsl:stylesheet>
```

Fig. 5.6   Using XSLT to create elements and attributes. (Part 1 of 2.)

```
c:\examples>java -classpath %CLASSPATH% com.deitel.jws1.xml.Trans-
form chapter5/fig05_05_06/games.xml chapter5/fig05_05_06/games.xsl
chapter5/fig05_05_06/results.xml
```

Fig. 5.6   Using XSLT to create elements and attributes. (Part 2 of 2.)

The template in lines 10–14 **match** the root element **sports**. The **/** *pattern* specifies the source tree's *document root* (i.e., the parent of the root element). Element **apply-templates** (line 12) specifies that the **template** for the node corresponding to the **game** element (lines 17–32) should be applied. The **sports** element is output to the result tree.

Line 20 contains the element **element**, which creates an element in the result tree, with the name specified in attribute **name**. Therefore, the name of this XML element will be the name of the sport contained in element **game**'s **title** attribute. The **@** *pattern* specifies an attribute. *Braces*, **{ }**, enclose the pattern, because **@** is otherwise an illegal character in an element name. Attribute **name** is assigned a *literal result value* (i.e., the value assigned to **name** is the name of the element in the result tree). Braces indicate that the **@title** should not be taken literally for the element name.

Lines 23–25 contain element **attribute**, which creates an attribute for its parent element in the result tree. Attribute **name** provides the name of the attribute. The text in element **attribute** specifies the attribute's value in the result tree. In this example, the attribute **id** is created, which is assigned the **id** element's character data. Lines 27–29 create the element **comment** in the result tree. Element **paragraph**'s character data are written to the result tree's **comment** element in lines 27–29. Figure 5.7 lists the output of the transformation. [*Note*: The output has been modified for the purpose of presentation.]

```
1   <?xml version = "1.0" encoding = "UTF-8"?>
2   <sports>
3
4      <cricket id = "243">
5         <comment>
6            More popular among commonwealth nations.
7         </comment>
8      </cricket>
9
10     <baseball id = "431">
11        <comment>
12           More popular in America.
13        </comment>
14     </baseball>
15
16     <soccer id = "123">
17        <comment>
18           Most popular sport in the world.
19        </comment>
20     </soccer>
21
22  </sports>
```

Fig. 5.7   Results of applying **games.xsl** to **games.xml**.

5.5 Iteration and Sorting

XSLT allows for iteration through a *node set* (i.e., all nodes that an XPath expression matches). Node sets also can be sorted in XSLT. Figure 5.8 presents an XML document (**sorting.xml**) that contains information about a book. Figure 5.9 presents the XSLT document (**sorting.xsl**) that transforms **sorting.xml** to XHTML. Line 16 (Fig. 5.9) specifies a **template** that **match**es element **book**.

```
1   <?xml version = "1.0" encoding = "UTF-8"?>
2
3   <!-- Fig. 5.8: sorting.xml                        -->
4   <!-- XML document containing book information -->
5
6   <book isbn = "999-99999-9-X">
7      <title>Russ Tick&apos;s XML Primer</title>
8
9      <author>
10         <firstName>Russ</firstName>
11         <lastName>Tick</lastName>
12      </author>
13
14      <chapters>
15         <frontMatter>
16            <preface pages = "2" />
17            <contents pages = "5" />
18            <illustrations pages = "4" />
19         </frontMatter>
20
21         <chapter number = "3" pages = "44">
22            Advanced XML</chapter>
23
24         <chapter number = "2" pages = "35">
25            Intermediate XML</chapter>
26
27         <appendix number = "B" pages = "26">
28            Parsers and Tools</appendix>
29
30         <appendix number = "A" pages = "7">
31            Entities</appendix>
32
33         <chapter number = "1" pages = "28">
34            XML Fundamentals</chapter>
35      </chapters>
36
37      <media type = "CD" />
38   </book>
```

Fig. 5.8   XML document containing information about a book.

```
1   <?xml version = "1.0" encoding = "UTF-8"?>
2
```

Fig. 5.9   XSLT document for transforming **sorting.xml**. (Part 1 of 3.)

SPY for XML & XSL editor

```
 3   <!-- Fig. 5.9: sorting.xsl                              -->
 4   <!-- Transformation of book information into XHTML -->
 5
 6   <xsl:stylesheet version = "1.0"
 7      xmlns:xsl = "http://www.w3.org/1999/XSL/Transform"
 8      xmlns = "http://www.w3.org/1999/xhtml">
 9      <!-- write XML declaration and DOCTYPE DTD information -->
10      <xsl:output method = "xml" omit-xml-declaration = "no"
11         doctype-system =
12            "http://www.w3.org/TR/xhtml1/DTD/xhtml1-strict.dtd"
13         doctype-public = "-//W3C//DTD XHTML 1.0 Strict//EN"/>
14
15      <!-- match book -->
16      <xsl:template match = "/book">
17      <html>
18         <head>
19            <title>ISBN <xsl:value-of select = "@isbn" /> -
20               <xsl:value-of select = "title" /></title>
21         </head>
22
23         <body>
24            <h1 style = "color: blue">
25               <xsl:value-of select = "title"/></h1>
26
27            <h2 style = "color: blue">by <xsl:value-of
28               select = "author/lastName" />,
29               <xsl:value-of select = "author/firstName" /></h2>
30
31            <table style =
32               "border-style: groove; background-color: wheat">
33
34               <xsl:for-each select = "chapters/frontMatter/*">
35                  <tr>
36                     <td style = "text-align: right">
37                        <xsl:value-of select = "name()" />
38                     </td>
39
40                     <td>
41                        ( <xsl:value-of select = "@pages" /> pages )
42                     </td>
43                  </tr>
44               </xsl:for-each>
45
46               <xsl:for-each select = "chapters/chapter">
47                  <xsl:sort select = "@number" data-type = "number"
48                     order = "ascending" />
49                  <tr>
50                     <td style = "text-align: right">
51                        Chapter <xsl:value-of select = "@number" />
52                     </td>
53
54                     <td>
55                        ( <xsl:value-of select = "@pages" /> pages )
```

Fig. 5.9   XSLT document for transforming **sorting.xml**. (Part 2 of 3.)

```
56                        </td>
57                    </tr>
58                </xsl:for-each>
59
60                <xsl:for-each select = "chapters/appendix">
61                    <xsl:sort select = "@number" data-type = "text"
62                        order = "ascending" />
63                    <tr>
64                        <td style = "text-align: right">
65                            Appendix <xsl:value-of select = "@number" />
66                        </td>
67
68                        <td>
69                            ( <xsl:value-of select = "@pages" /> pages )
70                        </td>
71                    </tr>
72                </xsl:for-each>
73            </table>
74
75            <p style = "color: blue">Pages:
76                <xsl:variable name = "pagecount"
77                    select = "sum(chapters//*/@pages)" />
78                <xsl:value-of select = "$pagecount" />
79            <br />Media Type:
80                <xsl:value-of select = "media/@type" /></p>
81        </body>
82    </html>
83    </xsl:template>
84
85  </xsl:stylesheet>
```

```
c:\examples>java -classpath %CLASSPATH% com.deitel.jws1.xml.Trans-
form chapter5/fig05_08_09/sorting.xml chapter5/fig05_08_09/sort-
ing.xsl chapter5/fig05_08_09/results.html
```

Fig. 5.9   XSLT document for transforming `sorting.xml`. (Part 3 of 3.)

Lines 19–20 create the title for the XHTML document. The value of the source tree's **isbn** attribute and the contents of the source tree's **title** element are combined to create the title string **ISBN 999-99999-9-X - Russ Tick's XML Primer**.

Lines 27–29 write a header element that contains the book's author to the result tree. Because the *context node* (i.e., the current node being processed) is **book**, the XPath expression **author/lastName** selects the author's last name from the source tree, and the expression **author/firstName** selects the author's first name from the source tree.

Line 34 selects each element (indicated by an asterisk pattern) that is a child of element **frontMatter** (which is a child of **chapters**). Iteration in XSLT is performed with the *for-each* element. Line 37 calls *node-set function* **name** to retrieve the current node's element name (e.g., **preface**). The current node is the context node specified in the **for-each** (line 34).

Lines 47–48 sort **chapter**s by number in ascending order, using element *sort*. Attribute **select** selects the value of context node **chapter**'s **number** attribute. Attribute *data-type* with value **"number"** specifies a numeric sort, and attribute *order* specifies **"ascending"** order. Attribute **data-type** also can be assigned the value *"text"* (line 61), and attribute **order** may be assigned the value *"descending"*.

Lines 76–77 use an *XSL variable* to store the value of the book's page count and output it to the result tree. Attribute **name** specifies the variable's name, and attribute **select** assigns it a value. Function *sum* totals all **page** attribute values. The two slashes between **chapters** and * indicate that all descendent nodes of **chapters** are searched for elements that contain an attribute named **pages**. A variable's value is retrieved by preceding the variable name with a dollar sign (line 78).

Figure 5.10 shows the results of the transformation. Notice that the chapters and appendices appear in the correct order, even though the XML document contained their corresponding elements in a different order.

```
1   <?xml version = "1.0" encoding = "UTF-8"?>
2   <!DOCTYPE html PUBLIC "-//W3C//DTD XHTML 1.0 Strict//EN"
3      "http://www.w3.org/TR/xhtml1/DTD/xhtml1-strict.dtd">
4   <html xmlns = "http://www.w3.org/1999/xhtml">
5      <head>
6         <title>ISBN 999-99999-9-X - Russ Tick's XML Primer</title>
7      </head>
8      <body>
9         <h1 style="color: blue">Russ Tick's XML Primer</h1>
10        <h2 style="color: blue">by Tick, Russ</h2>
11        <table style="border-style: groove; background-color: wheat">
12           <tr>
13              <td style="text-align: right">preface</td>
14              <td>( 2 pages )</td>
15           </tr>
16           <tr>
17              <td style="text-align: right">contents</td>
18              <td>( 5 pages )</td>
19           </tr>
20           <tr>
21              <td style="text-align: right">illustrations</td>
22              <td>( 4 pages )</td>
23           </tr>
24           <tr>
25              <td style="text-align: right">Chapter 1</td>
26              <td>( 28 pages )</td>
27           </tr>
28           <tr>
29              <td style="text-align: right">Chapter 2</td>
30              <td>( 35 pages )</td>
31           </tr>
32           <tr>
33              <td style="text-align: right">Chapter 3</td>
34              <td>( 44 pages )</td>
35           </tr>
36           <tr>
```

Fig. 5.10   Results of applying **sorting.xsl** to **sorting.xml**. (Part 1 of 2.)

```
37                    <td style="text-align: right">Appendix A</td>
38                    <td>( 7 pages )</td>
39                </tr>
40                <tr>
41                    <td style="text-align: right">Appendix B</td>
42                    <td>( 26 pages )</td>
43                </tr>
44            </table>
45            <p style="color: blue">Pages: 151<br />Media Type:
46                CD</p>
47        </body>
48    </html>
```

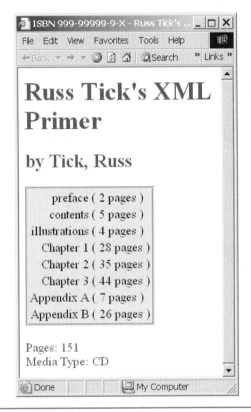

Fig. 5.10 Results of applying **sorting.xsl** to **sorting.xml**. (Part 2 of 2.)

5.6 Conditional Processing

In the previous section, we discussed iterating through a node set, using **for-each**. XSLT also provides elements for conditional processing, such as **if** elements. Figure 5.11 is an XML document that a day-planner application might use. Figure 5.12 is an XSLT document (**conditional.xsl**) for transforming the day-planner XML document (**planner.xml**) into an XHTML document. This style sheet demonstrates some of XSLT's conditional-processing capabilities.

```
1   <?xml version = "1.0" encoding = "UTF-8"?>
2
3   <!-- Fig. 5.11 : planner.xml   -->
4   <!-- Day Planner XML document -->
5
6   <planner>
7
8      <year value = "2002">
9
10        <date month = "7" day = "15">
11           <note time = "1430">Doctor&apos;s appointment</note>
12           <note time = "1620">Physics class at BH291C</note>
13        </date>
14
15        <date month = "7" day = "4">
16           <note>Independence Day</note>
17        </date>
18
19        <date month = "7" day = "20">
20           <note time = "0900">General Meeting in room 32-A</note>
21        </date>
22
23        <date month = "7" day = "20">
24           <note time = "1900">Party at Joe&apos;s</note>
25        </date>
26
27        <date month = "7" day = "20">
28           <note time = "1300">Financial Meeting in room 14-C</note>
29        </date>
30
31        <date month = "7" day = "9">
32           <note />
33        </date>
34     </year>
35
36  </planner>
```

```
c:\examples>java -classpath %CLASSPATH% com.deitel.jws1.xml.Trans-
form chapter5/fig05_11_12/planner.xml chapter5/fig05_11_12/condition-
al.xsl chapter5/fig05_11_12/results.html
```

Fig. 5.11   Day-planner XML document.

XSLT provides the ***choose*** element (lines 50–80) to allow alternative conditional statements, similar to an **if/else** structure in Java. Element ***when*** corresponds to a Java **if** statement. The ***test*** attribute of the **when** element specifies the expression that is being tested. If the expression is true, the XSLT processor evaluates the markup inside the **when** element. Lines 52–53, for instance, provide an expression that evaluates to true when the value of the source tree's **time** attribute is between **"0500"** and **"1200"**. The element **choose** serves to group all the ***when*** elements, thereby making them exclusive of one another (i.e., the first **when** element whose conditional statement is satisfied will be executed). The element **otherwise** (lines 76–78) corresponds to Java's **else** statement in an **if/else** structure and is optional.

Lines 84–86 compose the **if** element. This **if** element determines whether the current node (represented as **.**) being processed is empty. If so, **n/a** is inserted into the result tree. Unlike element **choose**, element **if** provides a single conditional test.

5.7 Combining Style Sheets

XSLT allows for modularity in style sheets. This feature enables XSLT documents to use other XSLT documents. Figure 5.13 lists an XSLT document that is imported into the XSLT document in Fig. 5.15, using element **import**.

```
1   <?xml version = "1.0" encoding = "UTF-8"?>
2
3   <!-- Fig. 5.12 : conditional.xsl              -->
4   <!-- xsl:choose, xsl:when and xsl:otherwise. -->
5
6   <xsl:stylesheet version = "1.0"
7      xmlns:xsl = "http://www.w3.org/1999/XSL/Transform"
8         xmlns = "http://www.w3.org/1999/xhtml">
9      <xsl:output method = "xml" omit-xml-declaration = "no"
10        doctype-system =
11           "http://www.w3.org/TR/xhtml11/DTD/xhtml1-strict.dtd"
12        doctype-public =
13           "-//W3C//DTD XHTML 1.0 Strict//EN" />
14
15     <xsl:template match = "/">
16        <html>
17           <head><title>Conditional Processing</title></head>
18           <body>
19              <p>Appointments
20                 <br />
21                 <xsl:apply-templates select = "planner/year" />
22              </p>
23           </body>
24        </html>
25     </xsl:template>
26
27     <xsl:template match = "year">
28        <strong>Year:</strong>
29
30        <xsl:value-of select = "@value" />
31
32        <br />
33
34        <xsl:for-each select = "date/note">
35
36           <!-- sort by date's day attribute value -->
37           <xsl:sort select = "../@day" order = "ascending"
38              data-type = "number" />
39
40           <br />
```

Fig. 5.12 Using conditional elements. (Part 1 of 3.)

```
41
42                <strong>
43                   Day:
44                   <xsl:value-of select = "../@month"/>/
45                   <xsl:value-of select = "../@day"/>
46                </strong>
47
48                <br />
49
50                <xsl:choose>
51
52                   <xsl:when test =
53                      "@time &gt; '0500' and @time &lt; '1200'">
54
55                      Morning (<xsl:value-of select = "@time" />):
56                   </xsl:when>
57
58                   <xsl:when test =
59                      "@time &gt; '1200' and @time &lt; '1700'">
60
61                      Afternoon (<xsl:value-of select = "@time" />):
62                   </xsl:when>
63
64                   <xsl:when test =
65                      "@time &gt; '1700' and @time &lt; '2200'">
66
67                      Evening (<xsl:value-of select = "@time" />):
68                   </xsl:when>
69
70                   <xsl:when test =
71                      "@time &gt; '2200' and @time &lt; '500'">
72
73                      Night (<xsl:value-of select = "@time" />):
74                   </xsl:when>
75
76                   <xsl:otherwise>
77                      Entire day:
78                   </xsl:otherwise>
79
80                </xsl:choose>
81
82                <xsl:value-of select = "." />
83
84                <xsl:if test = ". = ''">
85                   n/a
86                </xsl:if>
87
88                <br />
89          </xsl:for-each>
90
91       </xsl:template>
92
93    </xsl:stylesheet>
```

Fig. 5.12 Using conditional elements. (Part 2 of 3.)

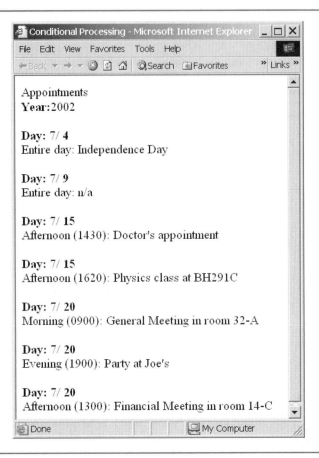

Fig. 5.12   Using conditional elements. (Part 3 of 3.)

```
1   <?xml version = "1.0" encoding = "UTF-8"?>
2
3   <!-- Fig. 5.13 : style.xsl -->
4   <!-- xsl:import example    -->
5
6   <xsl:stylesheet version = "1.0"
7      xmlns:xsl = "http://www.w3.org/1999/XSL/Transform"
8      xmlns = "http://www.w3.org/1999/xhtml">
9      <xsl:output method = "xml" omit-xml-declaration = "no"
10        doctype-system =
11           "http://www.w3.org/TR/xhtml11/DTD/xhtml11-strict.dtd"
12        doctype-public =
13           "-//W3C//DTD XHTML 1.0 Strict//EN" />
14
15     <xsl:template match = "book">
16        <html>
17           <head><title>Combining Style Sheets</title></head>
```

Fig. 5.13   XSLT document being imported. (Part 1 of 2.)

```
18              <body>
19                  <xsl:apply-templates />
20              </body>
21          </html>
22      </xsl:template>
23
24      <xsl:template match = "title">
25          <xsl:value-of select = "." />
26      </xsl:template>
27
28      <xsl:template match = "author">
29
30          <p>Author:
31              <xsl:value-of select = "lastName" />,
32              <xsl:value-of select = "firstName" />
33          </p>
34
35      </xsl:template>
36
37      <x\sl:template match = "*|text()"/>
38
39  </xsl:stylesheet>
```

Fig. 5.13 XSLT document being imported. (Part 2 of 2.)

The XSLT recommendation defines *default templates*. If a programmer does not specify a **template** that **match**es a particular element, the default XSLT template is applied. Figure 8.14 describes some default templates.

In line 19, the **apply-templates** element indicates that the default **template**s should be applied. If a more specific template for a node exists in the XSLT document, it is applied instead of the corresponding default template. For example, the **template**s on lines 15, 24 and 28 **match** specific elements, and the **template** on line 37 **match**es any element node or text node. The **template** in line 37 does not perform any action other than overriding the default **template** for element nodes and text nodes, which display the element nodes' character data. In this example, we do not want the default template to output every element's character data: We want only the book title and author name, not the chapter and appendix information.

Template / Description
| ```
<xsl:template match = "/ | *">
   <xsl:apply-templates/>
</xsl:template>
```<br>This **template match**es and applies **template**s to the child nodes of the document root (**/**) and any element nodes (**\***). |

Fig. 5.14 Some default XSLT templates. (Part 1 of 2.)
```

Template / Description

```
<xsl:template match = "text() | @*">
   <xsl:value-of select = "."/>
</xsl:template>
```
This **template match**es and outputs the values of text nodes (**text()**) and attribute nodes (**@**).

```
<xsl:template match = "processing-instruction() | comment()"/>
```
This **template match**es processing-instruction nodes (**processing-instruction()**) and comment nodes (**comment()**), but does not perform any actions with them.

Fig. 5.14 Some default XSLT templates. (Part 2 of 2.)

Line 9 in Fig. 5.15 **import**s the **template**s defined in the XSLT document (Fig. 5.13) referenced by attribute **href**. Line 13 provides a **template** for element **title**, which already has been defined in the XSLT document being **import**ed. This *local template* has higher precedence than the **import**ed **template**, so it is used instead of the **import**ed **template**. Figure 5.16 shows the results of the transformation of **sorting.xml** (Fig. 5.8) into XHTML.

Common Programming Error 5.1

*When using the **import** element, not placing it as the first child of **stylesheet** or **transform** is an error.*

```
1   <?xml version = "1.0" encoding = "UTF-8"?>
2
3   <!-- Fig. 5.15 : importer.xsl              -->
4   <!-- xsl:import example using style.xsl. -->
5
6   <xsl:stylesheet version = "1.0"
7      xmlns:xsl = "http://www.w3.org/1999/XSL/Transform">
8
9      <xsl:import href = "style.xsl" />
10
11     <!-- this template has higher precedence over the -->
12     <!-- templates being imported                     -->
13     <xsl:template match = "title">
14
15        <h2 xmlns = "http://www.w3.org/1999/xhtml">
16           <xsl:value-of select = "." />
17        </h2>
18
19     </xsl:template>
20
21  </xsl:stylesheet>
```

```
c:\examples>java -classpath %CLASSPATH% com.deitel.jws1.xml.Trans-
form chapter5/fig05_13_15/sorting.xml chapter5/fig05_13_15/import-
er.xsl chapter5/fig05_13_15/results.html
```

Fig. 5.15 Importing another XSLT document.

```
1   <?xml version="1.0" encoding="UTF-8"?>
2   <!DOCTYPE html PUBLIC "-//W3C//DTD XHTML 1.0 Strict//EN"
3       "http://www.w3.org/TR/xhtml1/DTD/xhtml1-strict.dtd">
4   <html xmlns="http://www.w3.org/1999/xhtml">
5       <head>
6           <title>Combining Style Sheets</title>
7       </head>
8       <body>
9           <h2>Russ Tick's XML Primer</h2>
10          <p>Author: Tick, Russ</p>
11      </body>
12  </html>
```

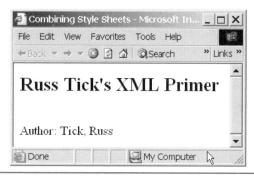

Fig. 5.16   Results of applying **importer.xsl** to **sorting.xml**.

Style sheets can include other style sheets. Figure 5.17 shows an example of the XSLT element **include**, which merges other XSLT documents in the current XSLT document. Lines 45–46 contain element **include**, which includes the style sheets referenced by attribute **href**. The difference between element **include** and element **import** is that **template**s that are **include**d have the same precedence as the local templates. Therefore, if any **template**s are duplicated, the **template** included replaces the **template** in the document that **include**s the **template**. Notice that **book.xsl** (Fig. 5.17) contains a **template** element for **chapter** in lines 36–43. Figure 5.18 and Fig. 5.19 list the XSLT documents being **include**d by Fig. 5.17. Notice that **chapters.xsl** (Fig. 5.19) contains a **template** element for **chapter** in lines 17–23.

```
1   <?xml version = "1.0" encoding = "UTF-8"?>
2
3   <!-- Fig. 5.17 : book.xsl -->
4   <!-- xsl:include example   -->
5
6   <xsl:stylesheet version = "1.0"
7       xmlns:xsl = "http://www.w3.org/1999/XSL/Transform"
8       xmlns = "http://www.w3.org/1999/xhtml">
9       <xsl:output method = "xml" omit-xml-declaration = "no"
10          doctype-system =
11              "http://www.w3.org/TR/xhtml1/DTD/xhtml1-strict.dtd"
```

Fig. 5.17   Combining style sheets using **xsl:include**. (Part 1 of 2.)

```
12              doctype-public =
13                  "-//W3C//DTD XHTML 1.0 Strict//EN" />
14
15      <xsl:template match = "/">
16
17          <html>
18              <head><title>Including Style Sheets</title></head>
19              <body>
20                  <xsl:apply-templates select = "book" />
21              </body>
22          </html>
23
24      </xsl:template>
25
26      <xsl:template match = "book">
27
28          <h2>
29              <xsl:value-of select = "title" />
30          </h2>
31
32          <xsl:apply-templates />
33      </xsl:template>
34
35
36      <xsl:template match = "chapter">
37
38          <h3>
39              <em><xsl:value-of select = "." /></em>
40          </h3>
41
42          <xsl:apply-templates />
43      </xsl:template>
44
45      <xsl:include href = "author.xsl" />
46      <xsl:include href = "chapters.xsl" />
47
48      <xsl:template match = "*|text()" />
49
50  </xsl:stylesheet>
```

```
c:\examples>java -classpath %CLASSPATH% com.deitel.jws1.xml.Trans-
form chapter5/fig05_17_18_19/sorting.xml chapter5/fig05_17_18_19/
book.xsl chapter5/fig05_17_18_19/results.html
```

Fig. 5.17   Combining style sheets using **xsl:include**. (Part 2 of 2.)

```
1   <?xml version = "1.0" encoding = "UTF-8"?>
2
3   <!-- Fig. 5.18 : author.xsl -->
4   <!-- xsl:include example      -->
5
```

Fig. 5.18   XSLT document for rendering the author's name. (Part 1 of 2.)

```
6   <xsl:stylesheet version = "1.0"
7      xmlns:xsl = "http://www.w3.org/1999/XSL/Transform">
8
9      <xsl:template match = "author">
10
11        <p xmlns = "http://www.w3.org/1999/xhtml">Author:
12           <xsl:value-of select = "lastName" />,
13           <xsl:value-of select = "firstName" />
14        </p>
15
16     </xsl:template>
17
18  </xsl:stylesheet>
```

Fig. 5.18   XSLT document for rendering the author's name. (Part 2 of 2.)

Figure 5.20 shows the results of applying the XSLT document (Fig. 5.17) to the document that describes a book (Fig. 5.8). The XHTML that is created marks up the chapter names as an unordered list and not as a series of **h3** headers containing emphasized text.

```
1   <?xml version = "1.0" encoding = "UTF-8"?>
2
3   <!-- Fig. 5.19 : chapters.xsl -->
4   <!-- xsl:include example.      -->
5
6   <xsl:stylesheet version = "1.0"
7      xmlns:xsl = "http://www.w3.org/1999/XSL/Transform"
8      xmlns = "http://www.w3.org/1999/xhtml">
9      <xsl:template match = "chapters">
10        <p>Chapters:</p>
11
12        <ul>
13           <xsl:apply-templates select = "chapter" />
14        </ul>
15     </xsl:template>
16
17     <xsl:template match = "chapter">
18
19        <li>
20           <xsl:value-of select = "." />
21        </li>
22
23     </xsl:template>
24
25  </xsl:stylesheet>
```

Fig. 5.19   XSLT document **chapters.xsl**.

```
1   <?xml version="1.0" encoding="UTF-8"?>
2   <!DOCTYPE html PUBLIC "-//W3C//DTD XHTML 1.0 Strict//EN"
```

Fig. 5.20   Result of applying **book.xsl** to **sorting.xml**. (Part 1 of 2.)

```
3        "http://www.w3.org/TR/xhtml1/DTD/xhtml1-strict.dtd">
4    <html xmlns="http://www.w3.org/1999/xhtml">
5       <head>
6          <title>Including Style Sheets</title>
7       </head>
8       <body>
9          <h2>Russ Tick's XML Primer</h2>
10         <p>Author: Tick, Russ</p>
11         <p>Chapters:</p>
12         <ul>
13            <li>Advanced XML</li>
14            <li>Intermediate XML</li>
15            <li>XML Fundamentals</li>
16         </ul>
17      </body>
18   </html>
```

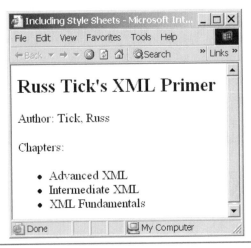

Fig. 5.20   Result of applying `book.xsl` to `sorting.xml`. (Part 2 of 2.)

In this chapter, we have discussed the applicaton of Extensible Stylesheet Language Transformations for transforming XML documents into another text-based format. In Chapter 6, we introduce an XML vocabulary called the *Simple Object Access Protocol* (*SOAP*), which is used for marking up requests and responses so that they can be transferred via protocols such as HTTP. In particular, we discuss several popular platforms for deploying Web services.

5.8 Summary

Extensible Stylesheet Language Transformation (XSLT) is a W3C recommendation for transforming XML documents into other text-based formats. XSLT uses XPath expressions to match nodes when transforming an XML document into a different document. In order to process XSLT documents, an XSLT processor is required.

XSLT documents contain one or more templates that describe how a node is transformed. XSL transformations involve two trees: The source tree, which corresponds to the XML document, and the result tree, which corresponds to the document created as a result of the transformation. XSLT documents can be reused by either including them or importing them into another XSLT document.

5.9 Internet and World Wide Web Resources

www.w3.org/Style/XSL
The W3C Extensible Stylesheet Language Web site.

www.w3.org/TR/xsl
The W3C XSL recommendation.

www.w3schools.com/xsl
This site features an XSL tutorial, along with a list of links and resources.

www.dpawson.co.uk/xsl/xslfaq.html
A comprehensive collection of FAQs on XSL.

msdn.microsoft.com/xml
Microsoft Developer Network XML home page, which provides information on XML and XML-related technologies, such as XSL/XSLT.

xml.apache.org/xalan-j/index.html
Home page for Apache's XSLT processor Xalan.

java.sun.com/xml/xml_jaxp.html
Home page for JAXP, an implementation of XSLT in Java.

SOAP-Based Web-Services Platforms

Objectives

- To understand the process of creating Web services.
- To be able to deploy a Web service on Apache's Axis.
- To be able to deploy a Web service on CapeClear's CapeConnect.
- To be able to deploy a Web service on The Mind Electric's GLUE.
- To be able to deploy a Web service on IONA's XMLBus
- To be able to deploy a Web service on Systinet's WASP.
- To be able to create a simple Web-service client.
- To understand the basic structure of a SOAP message.

Seem'd washing his hands with invisible soap
In imperceptible water.
Thomas Hood

Sometimes give your services for nothing...
Hippocrates

All the vital mechanisms, varied as they are, have only one
object, that of preserving constant the conditions of life in the
internal environment.
Claude Bernard

Anybody who doesn't know what soap tastes like never
washed a dog.
Franklin P. Jones

Outline

6.1 Introduction

Standards developed for the Web-services paradigm focus primarily on communication protocols and Web-service description. *XML messages* are used by clients and servers to define a communication protocol between two remote points. Popular protocols such as *XML-RPC* and *SOAP* are two XML messaging schemes clients can use to communicate with each other. A typical Web-service transaction is composed of at least two entities—the client and the service. A client invokes a remote Web service by creating an XML message—SOAP messages or XML-RPC invocations. The client sends the XML message by HTTP, SNMP or another network protocol to the receiving Web-service platform. The transmitted XML message contains the necessary information for the Web service platform to deserialize the request—that is, to map the XML data types defined in the message to an implementation-specific form that the targeted Web service can use. The transformed request is then delegated to the appropriate handling service. Figure 6.1 shows a typical interaction between a client and a Web service.

No standardized approaches exist for implementing Web services. In a multiplatform environment, this means that different platforms have different ways of defining the contract between a Web-services platform and its hosted Web services. Similarly, each Web-services platform has its own preferred way of handling such issues as deployment processes, custom serialization and deserialization and performance optimization. Development of Web services, in many cases, is a committed effort to adapting a service implementation to the specific requirements of the Web-services hosting platform.

There is a growing number of platforms for Java-based Web services. Each platform defines its own requirements for deployment and Web-service support. Sun's Java Web Services Developer Pack (JWSDP),[1] CapeClear's CapeConnect and IONA's XMLBus provide rich sets of features that enable administrators to deploy Web services through graphical user

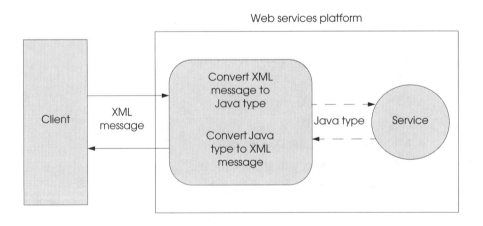

Fig. 6.1   Typical Web-service invocation process.

---

1. Development and deployment of Web services, in Sun's JWSDP, is explained in subsequent chapters.

interfaces. Other implementations, such as Apache's Axis, Systinet's Web Applications and Services Platform (WASP) and the Mind Electric's GLUE offer similar capabilities through deployment descriptors and command-line utilities.

This chapter demonstrates that developing a Web service can be as simple as deploying an existing Java class on a Web-services platform. Section 6.3.1, Section 6.4.1, Section 6.5.1, Section 6.6.1 and Section 6.7.1 explain the process that each Web-services platform uses to deliver a SOAP request to the appropriate Web service. Section 6.3.3, Section 6.4.3, Section 6.5.3, Section 6.6.3 and Section 6.7.3 explain the necessary steps to deploy a simple Web service that is defined in Section 6.2.

6.2 Developing a Web Service

Figure 6.2 shows a book-title-retrieval service that enables clients to query a hard-coded database of Deitel books. Class **BookTitleService** exposes method **getBookTitle**, which takes a **String** argument that represents the ISBN number of a recently published Deitel book. Class **BookTitleService** is a simple implementation. In a real-world scenario, class **BookTitleService** would fetch book-title information from a database or EJBs. This example is focused on showing the deployment details, so the code has been significantly simplified as a result.

```java
1   // Fig. 6.2: BookTitleService.java
2   // Class BookTitleService provides the Book Title Web
3   // service, which returns a title of a book associated with an
4   // ISBN number.
5   package com.deitel.jws1.soap.services;
6
7   import java.util.*;
8
9   public class BookTitleService {
10
11      // Map contains ISBN/Book-Title pairs
12      Map books;
13
14      // constructor to initialize books HashMap
15      public BookTitleService()
16      {
17         books = new HashMap();
18
19         // store ISBN/Book-Title pairs in HashMap
20         books.put( "0130895601",
21            "Advanced Java 2 Platform How to Program" );
22         books.put( "0130895717",
23            "C++ How to Program, Third edition" );
24         books.put( "0130293636",
25            "Visual Basic. NET How to Program" );
26         books.put( "0130284173", "XML How to Program" );
27         books.put( "0130923613", "Python How to Program" );
28
29      } // end constructor
```

Fig. 6.2   Book Title Web-service implementation. (Part 1 of 2.)

```
30
31      // service to obtain book title associated with ISBN number
32      public String getBookTitle( String ISBN )
33      {
34         return ( String ) books.get( ISBN );
35      }
36
37   } // end class BookTitleService
```

Fig. 6.2   Book Title Web-service implementation. (Part 2 of 2.)

Lines 15–29 define the default constructor that populates the **Map** by associating book titles with their respective **ISBN** numbers. Lines 32–35 define method **getBookTitle**, which is the only exposed service. Method **getBookTitle** takes a **String** parameter that represents the ISBN of the book title to return.

Class **BookTitleService** remains unaware of the XML messages that clients use to invoke its **getBookTitle** method. Web-services platforms handle service instantiation, method invocation and the response process on behalf of the service. These features are not required of a Web-services platform. However, most implementations described in this book facilitate the development of Web services by providing these capabilities.

6.3 Axis

Apache's *Axis* is a rearchitected successor to the popular Apache SOAP 2.2. Designed to offer greater flexibility than does its predecessor, Axis provides developers with a substantial set of customization options.

6.3.1 Architecture

The Axis engine is composed of a network of message-processing elements. A typical interaction with an Axis Web service starts at the *Transport Listener*. The Axis Transport Listener receives all incoming XML messages. Axis converts each XML message into a **MessageContext** object that represents the XML message. The **MessageContext** object is the internal representation that Axis uses to process incoming and outgoing messages. Each **MessageContext** object is sent through a chain of *message handlers*, which process the **MessageContext** object sequentially. The **MessageContext** object is then sent to the targeted service's *provider*, which is responsible for mapping the method calls and parameters to and instance of the Java class that implements the Web service. This sequence of events also occurs when a reply is sent back to the client: The corresponding provider obtains the results from the Java class, packages the results into a **MessageContext** object and sends the object through a response chain of message handlers. The **MessageContext** object is processed sequentially and sent to the Transport Listener, which then constructs a SOAP message out of the information contained in the **MessageContext** object and sends it to the receiving client. Figure 6.3 shows the flow of an XML message to an Axis Web service and back to the client.

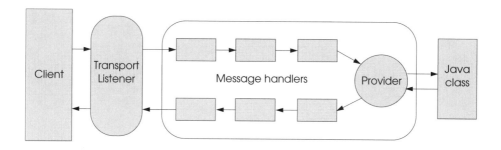

Fig. 6.3   Axis engine's architecture.

6.3.2 Installation

For the purposes of these installation instructions, we assume that Sun's Java Web Services Developer Pack (JWSDP) is installed in directory **c:\jwsdp**. Sun's JWSDP can be downloaded from

> **java.sun.com/webservices/**

only works if class does not have package structure

Axis can be downloaded from

> **xml.apache.org/axis/**

Assuming that Axis was installed into directory **c:\axis**, copy the contents of directory **c:\axis\webapps** to directory **c:\jwsdp\webapps**. Axis needs to have access to JAXP or XML Xerces distribution. Sun's JWSDP includes a version of JAXP. Copy the files located in directory **c:\jwsdp\common\endorsed** to directory **c:\jwsdp\webapps\axis\WEB-INF\lib**. Axis now can run on the Tomcat distribution that comes with Sun's JWSDP.

To verify that Axis is properly installed, start Tomcat by running the batch file **startup.bat** in directory **c:\jwsdp\bin**. Once Tomcat has started, point your browser to

> **http://localhost:8080/axis**

6.3.3 Web-Services Deployment

Axis provides two means by which system administrators can deploy Web services. System administrators can deploy a Web service effortlessly by sacrificing customization or allow for customizing a Web service through a more complex deployment process.

Simple Deployment (Instant Deployment)

Instant deployment enables system administrators to deploy a Java service easily and without having to provide a deployment file. The process consists of two simple steps: (1) copying the source file to a target directory, and (2) changing the extension of the source file from **.java** to **.jws**.

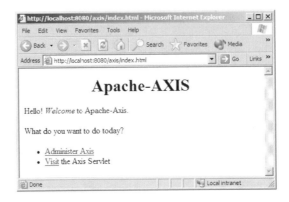

We demonstrate how to use Axis' instant-deployment features to deploy class **Book-
TitleService** (Fig. 6.2) as a Web service. We start by creating a directory structure
within directory **c:\jwsdp\webapps\axis** that corresponds to the package structure
of class **BookTitleService**. We must copy the source file **BookTitleSer-
vice.java** to

    c:\jwsdp\webapps\axis\com\deitel\jws1\soap\services

All source files for classes must be placed in a directory structure that corresponds to
their package structure. The **.java** files for classes that are in the default package must be
placed in **c:\jwsdp\axis**. Restart Tomcat. **BookTitleService** is now exposed as
a Web service. Axis will properly delegate incoming XML requests to the Book Title Web
service at endpoint

    **http://localhost:8080/axis/com/deitel/jws1/soap/services/
BookTitleService.jws**

Custom Deployment

System administrators seeking greater deployment-customization options can use Axis's
custom-deployment features. To customize the deployment of a Web service, system administrators must create a *Web Service Deployment Descriptor* (*WSDD*) file. A WSDD file
is an XML document that specifies a Web service's properties for deployment. The descriptor enables system administrators to specify the Web-service identifier, the provider
used to delegate calls to the service, the exposed methods, the serializers and deserializers
associated with the service, the request and response message handlers, and other properties. A WSDD file also determines whether the deployment tool deploys or undeploys the
Web service.

Figure 6.5 shows the WSDD file for the Book Title Web service. There are two possible root elements in a WSDD file—**deployment** or **undeployment**. The root element shown in Fig. 6.5 is element **deployment**. Element **deployment** indicates to the
Axis deployment tool that the WSDD file is a deployment file. The **service** element
(lines 4–11) describes the service being deployed.

```
1   <deployment xmlns="http://xml.apache.org/axis/wsdd/"
2      xmlns:java="http://xml.apache.org/axis/wsdd/providers/java">
3
4      <service name="BookTitle" provider="java:RPC">
5
6         <parameter name="className"
7            value="com.deitel.jws1.soap.services.BookTitleService"/>
8
9         <parameter name="methodName" value="getBookTitle"/>
10
11     </service>
12
13  </deployment>
```

Fig. 6.5   Book Title Web-service deployment descriptor.

Element **Service**'s attribute **name** identifies the service. Clients identify a Web service by its **name**. When clients access an Axis Web service, they send the Web service's **name** to an Axis routing servlet—**AxisServlet**. This servlet matches the client-supplied name to the corresponding Web service. Line 4 specifies the name **BookTitle** for the Web service that class **BookTitleService** implements. Attribute **provider** defines the provider that corresponds to the Book Title Web service. Value **java:RPC** represents Axis's standard provider, which invokes methods in the target class according to the client's XML request.

Element **service** contains two **parameter** subelements. The **name** attribute of the **parameter** element specifies the type of the information that attribute **value** defines. Attribute **name** with value **className** (line 6) indicates to the deployment tool that this **parameter** element specifies the class that contains the implementation of the Book Title Web service. Attribute **value** defines the class name. Line 9 specifies the methods that Web service **BookTitle** exposes. Attribute **value** (line 9) must contain a list of comma-separated method names. To expose all **public** methods, substitute a ***** for the list of comma-separated method names.

After creating the WSDD file, we must run the deployment tool. To deploy the Book Title Web service, start the Tomcat server. Compile class **BookTitleService**. Ensure that the classpath contains the JAR files of directories **c:\axis\lib**, **c:\jwsdp\common\lib** and **c:\jwsdp\common\endorsed**. Within the directory that contains file **BookTitleService.wsdd**, run the following command line:

> **java org.apache.axis.client.AdminClient BookTitleService.wsdd**

Ensure that the class file is in the correct package structure within directory **c:\jwsdp\webapps\axis\WEB-INF\classes**. Create directory structure **com\deitel\jws1\soap\services**, and include file **BookTitleService.class**. Restart the Tomcat server. Clients who wish to access the Web service can access it through the endpoint **http://localhost:8080/axis/services/BookTitle**.

6.3.4 Generating WSDL Documents

Axis provides two ways to generate a WSDL document. The first, and simpler, way of doing so is through a browser. After a Web service has been deployed, users can access a Web service's generated WSDL document through its endpoint URL, suffixed by **?wsdl**. To access the WSDL document of the Book Title Web service that we deployed via custom deployment in Section 6.3.3, point a browser to URL

```
http://localhost:8080/axis/services/BookTitle?wsdl
```

Axis also provides a utility that enables developers to generate WSDL documents by using the command line. Class **org.apache.axis.wsdlgen.Java2Wsdl** allows developers to generate a WSDL document tailored to command-line options. The following command generates a WSDL file for Web service **BookTitle**:

```
java org.apache.axis.wsdl.Java2WSDL
   -n http://www.deitel.com/services/
   -m getBookTitle -o BookTitleService.wsdl
   -l http://localhost:8080/axis/services/BookTitle
   com.deitel.jws1.soap.services.BookTitleService
```

Java2WSDL has numerous command-line options that enable the developer to customize the generated WSDL file. In our example, option **-n** specifies the target namespace of the Web service. Option **-m** specifies the comma-separated list of methods that the Web service exposes. Option **-o** specifies the name of the output file. Option **-l** specifies the endpoint URI of the Web service. **Java2WSDL** takes the name of the class as the argument from which to generate the WSDL file. Several additional command-line options exist. Execute **Java2WSDL** without arguments to view the complete list of command-line options.

6.4 CapeConnect 3.5

CapeClear's CapeConnect 3.5 enables developers to deploy Java services, EJBs and CORBA systems in Web-services environments. CapeConnect is a stand-alone environment that unifies legacy systems and Web-services protocols without the need for writing code.

The CapeConnect 3.5 package comprises a set of graphical deployment tools, a UDDI registry and extensive documentation that provides developers with what they need to create Web services out of existing systems. CapeConnect enables developers either to use it as a stand-alone Web-services platform or to integrate the CapeConnect framework into an application Web server.

6.4.1 Architecture

The CapeConnect system is composed of three major components—the *CapeConnect Gateway*, the *CapeConnect XML Engine* and the *Enterprise Adaptors*. The CapeConnect Gateway is a servlet that acts as the common entry point for all client requests. All SOAP requests from clients outside the network's firewall are sent first to the CapeConnect Gateway. The CapeConnect Gateway servlet forwards all client requests to the CapeConnect XML Engine servlet. Clients that reside within a firewall may send XML requests directly to the XML Engine servlet.

The CapeConnect XML Engine servlet is responsible for converting the XML request to a Java or CORBA call, using the appropriate Enterprise Adaptor and invoking the corresponding Java or CORBA service. The Java or CORBA service's response is sent back to the client through the chain that initially handled the incoming request.

The architecture of the CapeConnect system is illustrated in Fig. 6.6.

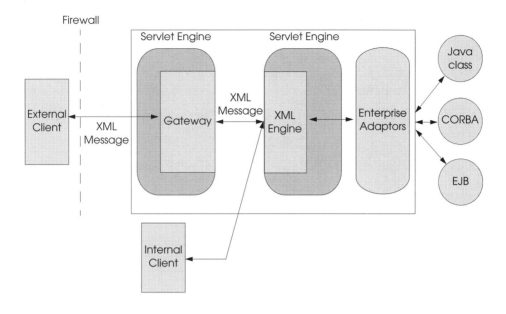

Fig. 6.6　Architecture of the CapeConnect engine.

6.4.2 Installation

CapeClear's evaluation version of CapeConnect also includes an evaluation version of their Web-service developer environment—CapeStudio. An evaluation version of CapeClear's CapeConnect 3.5 and CapeStudio is available free for download at

www.capeclear.com

Click the **Download** link and follow the download instructions. You will need to provide registration information before you have access to download an evaluation copy.

The CapeConnect and CapeStudio installation file provides a wizard that guides the installation process (Fig. 6.7). For the purposes of this section, accept all installation-specific default values. The installation process is straightforward, so it is not covered in this section. Note that CapeConnect is initially set up to use default ports that could already be in use by other applications. For example, CapeConnect's XML engine JNDI is initially set to port **1099**. This could cause conflicts with applications such as Java 2 Platform Enterprise Edition's Cloudscape database application. To change the default port numbers assigned by CapeConnect, during installation, in the **Choose Product Features** frame, click **Custom**, then click **Next**. Proceed through the installation steps until reaching the **Port Configuration** frame. Select the **Edit Port Numbers** checkbox, then click **Next**. In the **XML Engine Port Configuration** frame, edit the **XML Engine JNDI Port** textbox value to a port number not used by any application. (The CapeClear installation wizard will report if a port number is in use at the time of installation.) Continue with the installation process.

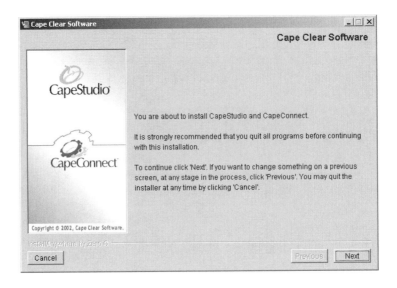

Fig. 6.7   CapeConnect installation wizard. Courtesy of Cape Clear Software, Inc.

The instructions in this section assume that CapeConnect is installed in directory **c:\CapeClear**. To verify a successful installation, go to directory **c:\Cape-Clear\CapeConnect3.5\bin**, and start the CapeConnect server by typing the following command-line instruction:

start-console-server.bat

The CapeConnect Console is a graphical tool that enables users to start and stop the Cape-Connect XML Engine. The CapeConnect Console also enables users to deploy, undeploy and manage Web services. To start the CapeConnect Console, type the following at the command line:

start-console.bat

If the installation was successful, the screen shown in Fig. 6.8 is displayed.

Fig. 6.8   Initial display of CapeConnect Console. Courtesy of Cape Clear Software, Inc.

6.4.3 Web-Services Deployment

Deploying a Java class as a Web service is a five-step process with CapeStudio. CapeStudio enables developers to deploy Java classes, Enterprise JavaBeans and CORBA components as Web services. For the purposes of this example, the deployment instructions focus on Java class deployment.

The deployment process expects JAR files to be the repositories of EJB and Java classes; developers who deploy CORBA services must provide IDL files. Using the same class from Section 6.3, package class **BookTitleService** into **BookTitleService.jar**. To create **BookTitleService.jar** with the appropriate directory structure, enter the command

```
jar cvf BookTitleService.jar
    com\deitel\jws1\soap\services\BookTitleService.class
```

To deploy class **BookTitleService** as a Web service on CapeConnect, start Cape-Studio. This executable application is located in **c:\CapeClear\CapeStudio3.0**. Create a project by selecting **Project > New**. Enter the values in the fields as shown in Fig. 6.9. The first textfield enables developers to specify the name of the project to create. Textfield **Directory** enables developers to specify the directory in which to create the project. Textfield **WSDL File** enables developers to specify a custom WSDL file to use instead of the WSDL file generated by CapeStudio. We will use CapeStudio to generate a WSDL file, so leave textfield **WSDL File** empty.

The next step in the CapeStudio Web-service deployment enables developers to generate a WSDL file by specifying the implementation classes of the Web service. To generate a WSDL file for the Book Title Web service, select **Design > Generate WSDL from Java/J2EE/CORBA...**. This will display the **Generate WSDL From Java/ J2EE/CORBA** window (Fig. 6.10), which enables developers to specify the type of Web-service implementation files. Developers have a choice of creating a Web service from EJBs, Java classes or CORBA stubs. For this example, we deploy a Web service from a Java class, so select the **Java** radio button as the **Component Type**. The **Components** pane enables developers to specify the JAR files containing the implementation class files for the Web service. A Web service may require several classes. CapeStudio enables developers to create a WSDL file that groups components into one Web service. Click **Add** to select the JAR files containing the classes for the Web service. For the purposes of this example, select **BookTitleService.jar**.

The **Settings** button enables developers to specify custom WSDL information, such as SOAP endpoint, SOAP action format, schema namespace format and method namespace format, among others. For the purposes of this example, use the default values. Click **Next >>** to advance to the next step in WSDL generation.

Figure 6.11 shows the frame that enables developers to specify support libraries, source files and the class for which to generate a WSDL file. The left pane displays the Web-service component files specified in the previous frame. The **Required Libraries** pane enables developers to include JAR files on which the Web-service implementation class files have dependencies. The **Source Files** pane enables developers to include source Java and EJB files. The **Advanced Options** button enables developers to configure CapeStudio's approach to serialization, method exposure and WSDL file generation.

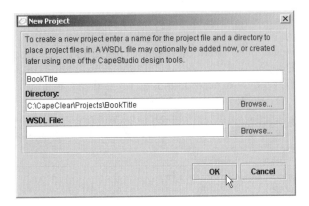

Fig. 6.9   CapeStudio project creation. Courtesy of Cape Clear Software, Inc.

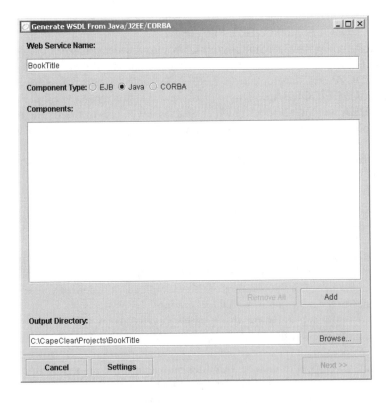

Fig. 6.10   CapeStudio WSDL generation frame (Part 1). Courtesy of Cape Clear
Software, Inc.

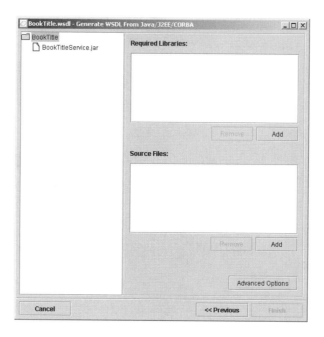

Fig. 6.11 CapeStudio WSDL generation frame (Part 2). Courtesy of Cape Clear Software, Inc.

Figure 6.12 shows the left pane after the selecting of **BookTitleService.jar** in the left pane. The right pane enables developers to select the classes for which to include methods in the WSDL file. Select checkbox **com.deitel.jws1.soap.services.BookTitleService**. Click **Finish** to generate the WSDL file.

In the next step in the deployment process, we must package the Book Title Web service's components and WSDL file. Select **Deploy > Package** to display frame **Package in a Web Service Archive (WSAR) File**. To create package **BookTitle.wsar**, click **Create** as shown in Fig. 6.13.

Deploy the Web service by selecting **Deploy > Deploy Service...** in the CapeStudio main window. This will display the **Deploy Service** window, which enables developers to specify whether a Web service belongs to a previously deployed package. In the **Deploy Service** frame, click **Deploy** to finish the deployment process.

Figure 6.14 shows the deployment-results screen that confirms the successful completion of the deployment process.

6.4.4 Generating WSDL Documents

The deployment process covered in Section 6.3.3 creates a WSDL document for each Web service deployed. The WSDL documents are accessible through the CapeConnect XML-Engine welcome screen (Fig. 6.15). Point a browser to URL

```
http://localhost:8000/index.html
```

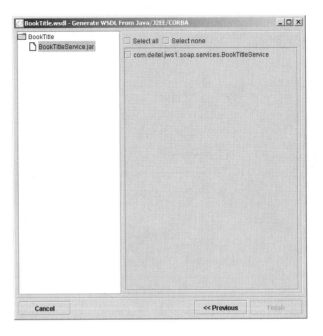

Fig. 6.12   CapeStudio WSDL generation frame (Part 3). Courtesy of Cape Clear Software, Inc.

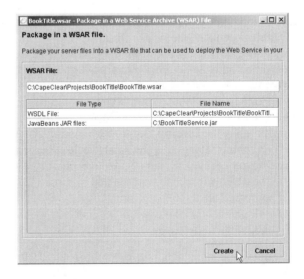

Fig. 6.13   Packaging a Web service in CapeStudio. Courtesy of Cape Clear Software, Inc.

Fig. 6.14   CapeStudio deployment-process results. Courtesy of Cape Clear Software, Inc.

Fig. 6.15   CapeConnect Gateway welcome screen. Courtesy of Cape Clear Software, Inc.

Click the **WSDL Repository** link under the **Product Links** header to access the WSDL repository (Fig. 6.16). The WSDL repository's navigation bar lists the WSDL and WSML documents that pertain to the Web services deployed in the CapeConnect Gateway. To display the WSDL document for the Book Title Web service, click the **Book-Title.wsdl** link.

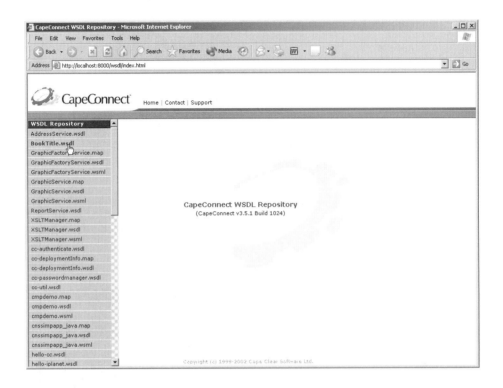

Fig. 6.16 CapeConnect WSDL repositories. Courtesy of Cape Clear Software, Inc.

Figure 6.17 shows the WSDL document for the Book Title Web service.

6.5 GLUE Standard 3.0

The MindElectric's GLUE is a small-footprint implementation of a full-featured Web-services environment. Aimed at simplifying the complex nature of Web services, GLUE provides a streamlined API that is geared toward reducing the learning curve and making the process of developing Web services less complicated. Developers also can use GLUE to create Web-services clients.

The standard release provides a Web server, servlet engine and XML parser. GLUE is capable of integrating third-party extensions that enable it to use new transport-layer protocols, registries, and WSDL bindings, among other capabilities. GLUE also enables developers to deploy a GLUE Web-services framework for deploying Web services on common application servers.

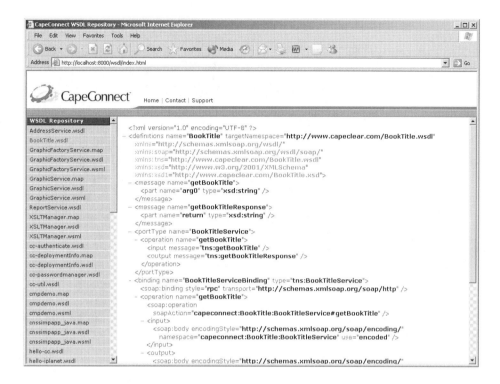

Fig. 6.17   CapeConnect-generated Book Title Web-service WSDL document.
Courtesy of Cape Clear Software, Inc.

6.5.1 Architecture

The GLUE Web-services platform is composed of several elements. The first element is the transport layer. The transport layer receives XML messages and converts them to corresponding Java objects. GLUE provides several default XML-to-Java mappings. Developers can also create mappings for custom objects. The transport layer sends each Java object corresponding to each incoming XML message to the handling **IService** *implementation*. **IService** implementations act as wrapper objects that delegate all XML invocations to instances of the appropriate Java classes. Responses are sent back to the **IService** implementation, which then sends the response to the transport layer. The transport layer creates and sends a response XML message that contains the results from the invocation on the **IService** wrapper class. GLUE enables developers to provide their own **IService** implementations. In the event that a developer deploys a service that does not implement interface **IService**, the default implementation **ObjectService** wraps the submitted service. Figure 6.18 illustrates the architecture of GLUE standard 3.0.

6.5.2 Installation

GLUE is a stand-alone Web-services platform implementation. It provides all the necessary support classes and utilities in one standard package. The standard distribution of GLUE is available free for download at **www.themindelectric.com**.

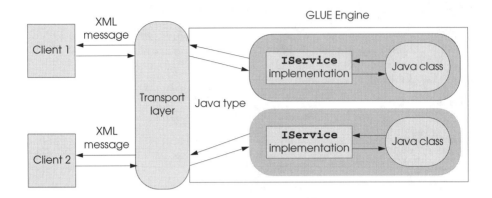

Fig. 6.18 Architecture of the GLUE engine.

For the purposes of these instructions, we have extracted the downloaded file to directory **c:\electric**. Include **GLUE-STD.jar**, **dom.jar**, **servlet.jar** and **jnet.jar** in the classpath. These files are located in directory **c:\electric\lib**. Also append directory **c:\electric\bin** to the path environment variable.

Software Engineering Observation 6.1

If you install GLUE on a directory other than /electric, set the environment variable ELECTRIC_HOME to the directory of the GLUE installation.

6.5.3 Web-Services Deployment

GLUE provides developers with two approaches through which to deploy Web services—1) starting a Web-services server with a newly-deployed Web service, and 2) deploying a Web service onto a existing Web-services server. The following subsections describe the process by which to deploy Web services when using GLUE tools.

newapp *Command-Line Tool*

To start a Web-services server for running a specified Web service, we must first use command-line tool **newapp** to create a Web-services application. A Web-services application resembles a Web application defined by the Servlets standard. A Web-services application contains the same directory structure defined by the Servlets standard—**WEB-INF**, **WEB-INF/classes** and **WEB-INF/lib**—in addition to other directory structures required by the GLUE Web-services framework. Figure 6.19 shows the directory structure of a Web-service application. [*Note*: In Fig. 6.19 we have used indentation to indicate the hierarchy of directories in the Web application.]

GLUE command-line tool **newapp** enables developers to create a Web-service application's default directory structure. The following command creates a default Web-services application directory structure in the current directory, as described in Fig. 6.19:

> **newapp** *applicationName*

Directory	Description
applicationName	Context-root of Web service application. All the JSPs, HTML documents, servlets and supporting files such as images and class files reside in this directory or its subdirectories. To provide structure in a Web application, subdirectories can be placed in the context root. For example, if your application uses many images, you might place an **images** subdirectory in this directory.
WEB-INF	This directory contains the Web application deployment descriptor (**web.xml**) and the Web services configuration file (**config.xml**). The Web application deployment descriptor specifies various configuration parameters such as the name used to invoke the servlet, a description of the servlet, and the servlet's fully qualified class name and mapping. The Web services configuration file specifies the GLUE's server settings such as connection settings, logging settings, and security settings, among others.
classes	This directory contains servlet, Web service and support class files used in the Web services application. If the classes are part of a package, the complete package directory structure would begin here.
lib	This directory contains JAR files that contain supporting class files used in a Web application.
maps	This directory contains the **map** files the GLUE Web services server uses to serialize and deserialize custom types.
services	This directory contains each Web service's XML descriptor. The GLUE Web services server uses the XML descriptor to configure a Web service's settings such as constructor to use, interface from which to create WSDL file, activation mode, among other settings.

Fig. 6.19   GLUE Web-service application directory structure.

where *applicationName* is the name of the Web-application root directory. Figure 6.20 shows **newapp**'s command-line options. To create a default Book Title Web service application, type

```
newapp booktitle
```

Option	Function
-D*property=value*	Sets the Java system property to a specified value. Use this option when a servlet or Web service requires a specific environment property/value pair.

Fig. 6.20   newapp command-line options. (Part 1 of 2.)

Option	Function
-h	Creates an application for hosting on third-party Web application severs.

Fig. 6.20 newapp command-line options. (Part 2 of 2.)

The next step in creating a Web-service application is to populate the default directory structure that **newapp** generates with the appropriate class and resource files. To deploy the Book Title Web service, add its corresponding package structure and class file to the Web-service application's **WEB-INF/classes** subdirectory.

Next, we must change the Web-services descriptor file to correspond to the Book Title Web service's settings. The Web service's descriptor file (default file name **sample.xml**) specifies the name of the Web service, the constructor to use when instantiating the Web service and the activation mode, among other settings. Figure 6.21 shows a subset of the XML elements within the Web service descriptor file and their purposes.

The name of a Web-service descriptor file determines the name by which clients access its corresponding Web service. To expose the Book Title Web service as **BookTitle**, rename file **sample.xml** to **BookTitle.xml**.

BookTitle.xml contains a set of XML elements with default values we must customize for the Book Title Web service. Change the default values of **BookTitle.xml** as shown in Fig. 6.22. Lines 3–5 specify the fully-qualified name of class **BookTitleService** as the Web service's class to instantiate. We wish to expose all methods of class **BookTitleService**, so we leave the **interface** element empty (line 9). Line 15 sets the Web-service activation mode to **application**, so that only one instance of class **BookTitleService** handles all client invocations. Line 18 notifies GLUE to activate the Web service. Line 21 sets the description the WSDL includes to **Book Title service**.

Element	Description
constructor	Specifies the fully-qualified name of the Web service class to instantiate.
interface	Specifies the fully-qualified class name of the interface that defines the Web service methods to expose.
style	Specifies the SOAP-binding style. Possible values are **rpc** (default) and **document**.
activation	Specifies the activation mode. Possible values are **application** (default), **session** and **request**. Value **application** indicates that only one instance of the Web service handles client invocations. Value **session** indicates that an instance of the Web service is created per client for the duration of the client's interaction with the server. Value **request** indicates that an instance of the Web service is created for each client request.

Fig. 6.21 Web-service descriptor's element descriptions. (Part 1 of 2.)

Element	Description
publish	Specifies whether or not the Web service is instantiated and accessible to clients. Possible values are **yes** and **no** (default).
description	Specifies a description for the Web service to be included in the Web service's WSDL file.

Fig. 6.21   Web-service descriptor's element descriptions. (Part 2 of 2.)

```
1   <service>
2     <!--name of service class-->
3     <constructor>
4       <class>com.deitel.jws1.soap.services.BookTitleService</class>
5     </constructor>
6
7     <!--name of interface(s) to publish (default is
8         all public methods)-->
9     <interface/>
10
11    <!--message style, rpc (default) or document-->
12    <style>rpc</style>
13
14    <!--activation mode, application (default), session, or request-->
15    <activation>application</activation>
16
17    <!--if yes (default), create and publish the service-->
18    <publish>yes</publish>
19
20    <!--description of service, used during WSDL generation-->
21    <description>Book Title service</description>
22
23    <!--interceptor for inbound SOAP requests-->
24    <inboundSoapRequestInterceptor/>
25
26    <!--interceptor for outbound SOAP responses-->
27    <outboundSoapResponseInterceptor/>
28
29    <!--target namespace (default is
30        http://www.themindelectric.com/wsdl/<name>/)-->
31    <targetNamespace>
32        http://www.deitel.com/webservices/booktitle
33    </targetNamespace>
34
35    <!--namespace (default is http://tempuri.org/<class name>)-->
36    <namespace>
37        http://www.deitel.com/booktitle
38    </namespace>
39
```

Fig. 6.22   Web-service descriptor file **BookTitle.xml**. Courtesy of The Mind Electric. (Part 1 of 2.)

```
40    <!--manually add named class and its closure to WSDL file-->
41    <xmlInclude/>
42
43    <!--directory for FileDataHandlers to store attachments-->
44    <dataDirectory/>
45
46    <!--handler for inbound attachments of specified content type-->
47    <dataHandler/>
48
49    <!--soapAction (default is operation name)-->
50    <soapAction/>
51  </service>
```

Fig. 6.22   Web-service descriptor file **BookTitle.xml**. Courtesy of The Mind
Electric. (Part 2 of 2.)

Lines 24 and 27 define the fully-qualified class name of the SOAP interceptors. SOAP
interceptors are implementations of interface **electric.net.soap.ISOAPInter-
ceptor** that view a SOAP message and modify its contents before and after the SOAP
messages are processed by the Web service. SOAP interceptors that are specified in the
inboundSoapRequestInterceptor element process SOAP messages before they
are processed by the Web service. SOAP interceptors that are specified in the **outbound-
SoapResponseInterceptor** element process response SOAP messages the Web service generates. Custom SOAP interceptors are beyond the scope of this discussion. For
further information on SOAP interceptors, consult the GLUE documentation. Lines 31–38
specify the namespace and target namespace that are included in the WSDL document.
Chapter 7, Web Services Description Language, discusses namespaces and target
namespaces in WSDL documents. Line 44 defines the directory in which GLUE's default
FileDataHandler temporarily stores SOAP attachments. Line 47 defines a custom
data handler for incoming SOAP messages with attachments. Line 50 defines the **SOAP-
Action** header that incoming SOAP messages must have to be routed to the Book Title
Web service. A **SOAPAction** header is an HTTP header field that specifies the purpose
or endpoint of a SOAP message. A Web-service platform's transport layer uses the **SOAP-
Action** header to identify the SOAP message's target without having to analyze the
SOAP message's contents.

Figure 6.23 shows the Book Title Web-service-application directory structure. The
final step in the Web-service deployment is to start the GLUE Web-services server. The
following command starts a Web-services server that hosts the specified Web-services
application:

   runapp *applicationName*

where *applicationName* is the Web-services application we created through the **newapp**
tool.

To start a Web-services server that hosts the Book Title Web service, execute the command

   runapp booktitle

Book Title Web service application directory and file structure

```
booktitle/
   WEB-INF/
      config.xml
      web.xml
      classes/
         com/
            deitel/
               jws/
                  soap/
                     services/
                        BookTitleService.class
      lib/
      maps/
         standard.map
      services/
         BookTitle.xml
         system/
            admin.xml
            deployment.xml
```

Fig. 6.23   Web service Book Information application directory structure.

API-Based Deployment

GLUE provides a simple API that enables developers to start a Web-service container and deploy Web services from within a Java environment. With GLUE, deployment of a Web service can be done in as little as a few lines of Java code.

Figure 6.24 shows class **WebServiceDeployment**, which starts a Web server and deploys a Web service. Line 19 uses **static** method **startup** from class **HTTP** to start an empty Web-server container. Method **startup** takes one **String** parameter—the URL of the Web server. Line 25 deploys object **webService** from line 22 with the name **BookTitle**. Class **Registry** provides numerous overloaded **static publish** methods that offer varying degrees of customization for the deployment process. The simplest of these methods (line 25) deploys a Web service on the currently instantiated Web server. In addition, the GLUE API provides other methods that can be used by developers to control the deployment process further and to administer access to Web services.

```
1   // Fig. 6.24: WebServiceDeployment.java
2   // Demonstrates the process of using GLUE APIs to
3   // deploy class BookTitleService as Web service
4   // BookTitle on Web server at http://localhost:9001/.
5   // Endpoint of Web service is http://localhost:9001/BookTitle
6
```

Fig. 6.24   **WebServiceDeployment.java** deploys a Web service from a Java class. Courtesy of The Mind Electric. (Part 1 of 2.)

```
 7   // GLUE core packages
 8   import electric.server.http.*;
 9   import electric.registry.*;
10
11   // BookTitleService package
12   import com.deitel.jws1.soap.services.*;
13
14   public class WebServiceDeployment {
15
16      public static void main( String[] args ) throws Exception
17      {
18         // start web server at port 9001
19         HTTP.startup( "http://localhost:9001/" );
20
21         // create service
22         BookTitleService webService = new BookTitleService();
23
24         // deploy service as Web service urn:BookTitleService
25         Registry.publish( "BookTitle", webService );
26      }
27   }
```

```
[STARTUP] GLUE standard beta 3.0 (c) 2001-2002 The Mind Electric
[DEPLOYMENT] deployment service started with application path C:\jws
[STARTUP] http server started on http://192.168.1.70:9001/
```

Fig. 6.24 `WebServiceDeployment.java` deploys a Web service from a Java
class. Courtesy of The Mind Electric. (Part 2 of 2.)

6.5.4 Generating WSDL Documents

The standard GLUE implementation provides developers with two simple means by which
they can generate WSDL documents. The first, and simpler, means is through a feature provided by the GLUE Web-services framework. GLUE dynamically generates a WSDL document at deployment. Clients access the Web service's WSDL document through the URL
of the Web service's target endpoint suffixed by **.wsdl**. For example, the Book Title Web
service's target endpoint is **URL http://localhost:9001/BookTitle**. Clients
can access the Book Title Web service's WSDL document through URL **http://lo-
calhost:9001/BookTitle.wsdl**.

The GLUE standard distribution also enables developers to generate a WSDL document from the command line. GLUE provides **Java2WSDL** from package **elec-
tric.wsdl.tools**. **Java2WSDL** provides numerous command-line options to
customize the generation of WSDL documents. The following command-line instruction
generates a WSDL document:

```
java electric.wsdl.tools.Java2WSDL
   com.deitel.jws1.soap.services.BookTitleService
   -e http://localhost:9001/BookTitle
   -r "Book Title service"
   -t http://www.deitel.com/webservices/booktitle
   -n http://www.deitel.com/booktitle
```

Java2WSDL generates **BooktTitleService.wsdl**. Class **Java2WSDL** accepts other command-line options as well. Figure 6.25 shows the most commonly used **Java2WSDL** options. Execute **Java2WSDL** without parameters for a complete listing of all available command-line options.

6.6 IONA Orbix E2A XMLBus 5.2

The *XMLBus 5.2 stand-alone* release is a full-featured Web-services environment aimed at simplifying the Web-service creation and deployment process. It is composed of a Web-services container and a set of tools that enable developers to test, deploy and manage Web services. The XMLBus 5.2 stand-alone package includes a Web-services container, a Web-service builder tool, a Web-services management tool, a multipurpose Web-services client console, a SOAP-Message analyzing tool and a UDDI browser.

6.6.1 Architecture

The main component of the XMLBus 5.2 stand-alone release is the XMLBus Web-services container. The XMLBus Web-services container receives XML messages, converts those XML messages to Java representations and invokes the corresponding Java services. The XMLBus Web-services container stores Web services in *XAR files*. XAR files contain all information related to a given Web service—Java classes, property files, WSDL documents and XML conversion information.

　　　Figure 6.26 illustrates the process by which a client interacts with a Web service deployed in an XMLBus container. First, a client sends an XML request to the XMLBus Web-services container. The XMLBus Web-services container finds the XAR file that corresponds to the XML request. The XAR archive contains the information corresponding to how to convert an XML message into a Java type. Given the information contained in the XAR file, the XMLBus Web-services container invokes the Java service. The Java service could be a CORBA service or an EJB that performs network communication with a back-end application. The Java service returns the results of the method invocation. The XMLBus Web-services container then converts this information into an XML response and sends it back to the client.

6.6.2 Installation

The IONA Orbix E2A XMLBus stand-alone release evaluation version can be downloaded from

　　　　　www.iona.com

Option	Purpose
-d	Specifies the output directory name.
-e	Specifies the Web service's endpoint.

Fig. 6.25 **Java2WSDL** command-line options. (Part 1 of 2.)

Option	Purpose
-n	Specifies the Web service's namespace.
-r	Specifies the Web service's description.
-t	Specifies the Web service's target namespace.

Fig. 6.25 `Java2WSDL` command-line options. (Part 2 of 2.)

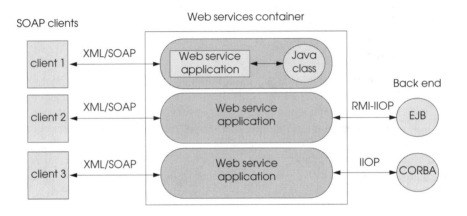

Fig. 6.26   Architecture of the XMLBus 5.2 stand-alone package.

Click the **Downloads** link. Under the section labeled **Orbix E2A Web Services Integration Platform**, click the **XMLBus Edition** link. Select the download link for **Orbix E2A Web Service Integration Platform, XMLBus Edition**. Before downloading an evaluation version of XMLBus, users must complete a registration process. During the registration process, select **Stand Alone Container** in the **Download For** checkbox.

IONA provides an installation wizard that guides the installation process (Fig. 6.27). The installation-wizard process is simple and will not be covered in this section. Follow the installation wizard's instructions to complete the installation process. For the purposes of this demonstration, install XMLBus in directory **c:\iona**.

To verify the successful installation of XMLBus Edition 5.2 in directory **C:\iona\XMLBusEdition\xmlbus\bin**, start the Web-services container by entering the following command-line instruction:

```
start_xmlbus.bat
```

Verify the proper execution of the Web-services container through the Web-services test client by pointing a browser to the following URL:

```
http://localhost:8080/WSDLClient/index.html
```

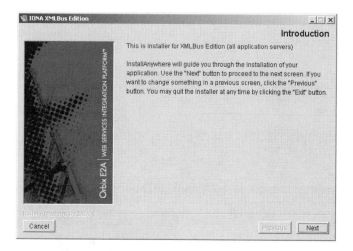

Fig. 6.27 XMLBus installation wizard. Screenshot Copyright 2002 © IONA Technologies PLC. All rights reserved.

The Web-services test client enables developers to interact with deployed Web services without needing to write code. The Web-services test-client initial display page provides links to three default Web services provided by the XMLBus package. Select Web service **Interop Test Service**, as shown in Fig. 6.28.

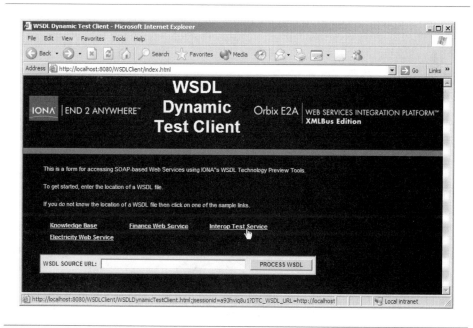

Fig. 6.28 XMLBus default Web services available after installation. Screenshot Copyright 2002 © IONA Technologies PLC. All rights reserved.

The Web-service test client enables users to select the operation to invoke from the selected Web service, as shown in Fig. 6.29. Select operation **echoString** from the list of operations. Operation **echoString** is a simple method that returns the string that was sent to it as a parameter.

We input the string **"Is anybody out there?"** as the parameter (Fig. 6.30).

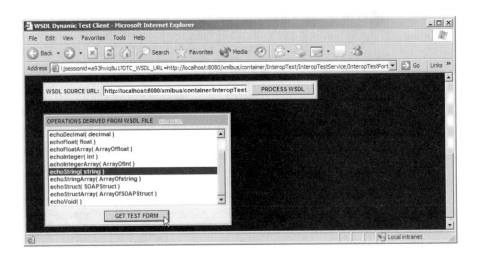

Fig. 6.29   Web-services test client enables users to invoke Web services without the need for coding. Screenshot Copyright 2002 © IONA Technologies PLC. All rights reserved.

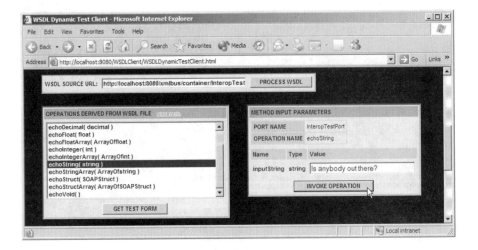

Fig. 6.30   Web-services test-client method invocation. Screenshot Copyright 2002 © IONA Technologies PLC. All rights reserved.

Figure 6.31 shows the results displayed by the Web-services test client's invocation of method **echoString**. The Web-services test client displays the Web-service response, the SOAP request and the SOAP response.

6.6.3 Web-Services Deployment

XMLBus enables developers to deploy existing Java, EJB and CORBA components as Web services. The XMLBus Web Service Builder (Fig. 6.32) enables developers to create, deploy and undeploy Web services. Web services are stored in projects under the **PROJECTS** sidebar.

To create a Web service, first create a project under which to store the Web service. From the menu bar, select **Project > New**. Enter the name of the project in the **Project Name** text box, then **OK**. Figure 6.33 shows the newly created project **DeitelServices** in the **PROJECTS** sidebar.

The project shown in Fig. 6.33 is empty. We now create a Web service and store it in project **DeitelServices**. We package class **BookTitleService** into **BookTitleService.jar** by executing the following command within the root of class **BookTitleService**'s package directory structure:

```
jar cvf BookTitleService.jar
    com\deitel\jws1\soap\services\BookTitleService.class
```

To create a Web service from **BookTitleService.jar**, select project **BookTitleService** from the **PROJECTS** sidebar. From the menu bar of the XMLBus Web Service Builder, select **Application > Create Web Service > From Class**. Figure 6.34 shows the first step of the deployment wizard.

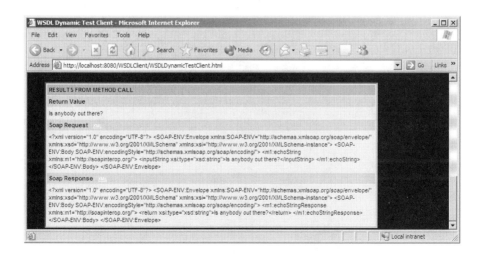

Fig. 6.31   Results of Web-services test-client method invocation. Screenshot

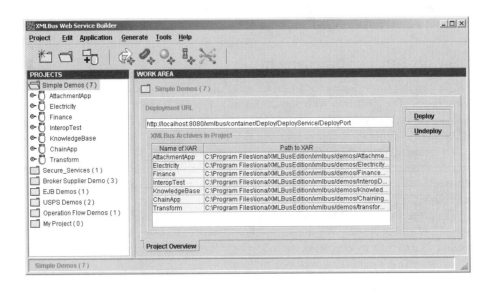

Fig. 6.32 XMLBus Web Services Builder tool. Screenshot Copyright 2002 © IONA
Technologies PLC. All rights reserved.

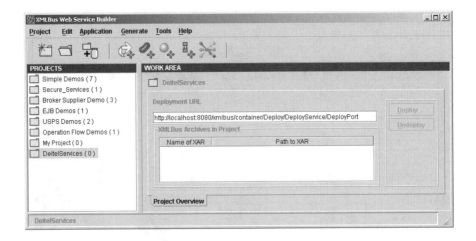

Fig. 6.33 Creating an application via the XMLBus Web Services Builder tool.
Screenshot Copyright 2002 © IONA Technologies PLC. All rights reserved.

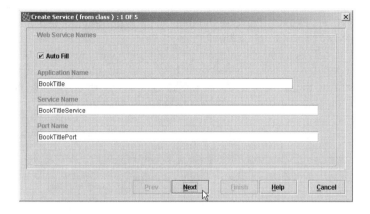

Fig. 6.34 XMLBus Web Services Builder specification for the XAR file in which information for the Book Title Web service is to be stored. Screenshot Copyright 2002 © IONA Technologies PLC. All rights reserved.

Text box **Application Name** specifies the name of the application in which the Book Title Web service is to be stored. The XMLBus container uses the application name to identify the Web service. Enter **BookTitle** as the application name. The **Service Name** text box enables developers to specify the name of the Web service as it will appear in the WSDL file. Enter **BookTitleService** in the **Service Name** text box. Finally, the **Port Name** text box enables developers to specify the name of the interface as it will appear in the WSDL document that identifies the set of operations the Book Title Web service exposes. (We recommend using the default value in the **Port Name** text box.) Click **Next**.

Step 2 of the deployment process (Fig. 6.35) enables developers to specify the Java class from which to create the Web service. Step 2 enables developers to add such resources as JAR files, ZIP files, WAR files and classes. Click **Add** to select JAR **BookTitleService.jar**; then, click **Next**.

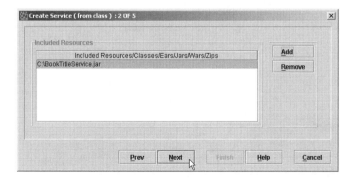

Fig. 6.35 XMLBus Web Service Builder specification of the Web service's name and port. Screenshot Copyright 2002 © IONA Technologies PLC. All rights reserved.

Step 3 (Fig. 6.36) enables developers to specify the class that implements the Web service to deploy. Click **Select**. Traverse through the package structure tree, and select class **BookTitleService**; then click **Next**.

Step 4 (Fig. 6.37) enables developers to select and configure methods to expose as Web-service operations. The left-side panel lists available methods. Select methods to expose by checking the corresponding method's check box. The right-side panel enables developers to configure the operation style and usage of each method.

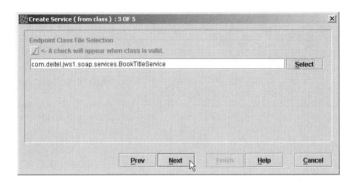

Fig. 6.36 XMLBus Web Service Builder specification of the JAR file containing class **BookTitleService**. Screenshot Copyright 2002 © IONA Technologies PLC. All rights reserved.

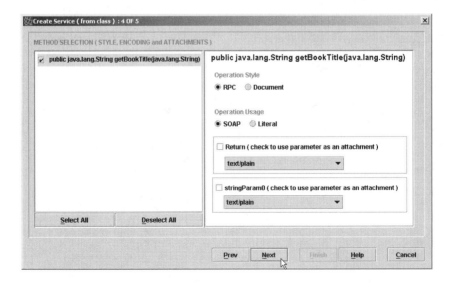

Fig. 6.37 XMLBus Web Service Builder specification of the method's operation and encoding. Screenshot Copyright 2002 © IONA Technologies PLC. All rights reserved.

In the left-side panel, select the check box that corresponds to class **BookTitleService** method **getBookTitle**. In the right-side panel, select radio buttons **RPC** and **SOAP**. Parameters can be sent as attachments in a SOAP message. When a Web service sends or receives specifically formatted data (e.g., JPEG or GIF image data), the information can be sent through the SOAP attachment part. Selecting check box **Return** and any checkboxes corresponding to method parameters will cause the parameter information to be included as an attachment to the SOAP message. Class **BookTitleService** sends only strings as parameters and return types, so we leave these check boxes unchecked. Click **Next** to proceed to the final step.

Step 5 (Fig. 6.38) enables developers to specify a name for the XAR file to create and the schema namespace and target namespace for the WSDL document. Developers can enter an existing XAR file or specify a new one. Enter **BookTitle.xar** in textbox **Output XAR File**. Chapter 7, Web Services Description Language, discusses the role of the target namespace and schema namespace in a WSDL document. For the purposes of this example, the default values in textboxes **Schema Namespace** and **Target Namespace** suffice. Click **Finish** to create the Book Title Web service's XAR file.

After creating the Book Title Web service's XAR file, we must deploy the Web service. Select project **DeitelServices** from the **PROJECTS** tree sidebar. The **WORK AREA** pane (Fig. 6.39) displays a tabbed pane that enables developers to specify the deployment URL and the XAR archive to deploy. Click **Deploy**.

Figure 6.40 shows the deployment-confirmation dialogue box. Click **Deploy** button to deploy the Book Title Web service.

6.6.4 Generating WSDL Documents

XMLBus generates a WSDL document during deployment. The auto-generated WSDL document is accessible through the XMLBus Service Manager. The XMLBus Service Manager enables developers to view a Web service's status, endpoint and WSDL document. To access the XMLBus Service Manager, point a browser to

      http://localhost:8080/xmlbus/

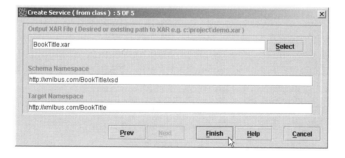

Fig. 6.38　XMLBus Web Service Builder specification of classes to include in the classpath. Screenshot Copyright 2002 © IONA Technologies PLC. All rights reserved.

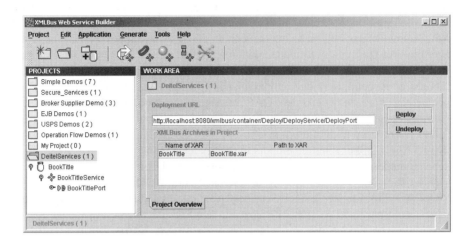

Fig. 6.39   XMLBus Web Service Builder deployment of the Book Title Web service.
Screenshot Copyright 2002 © IONA Technologies PLC. All rights reserved.

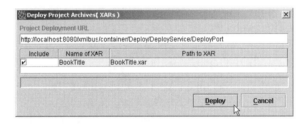

Fig. 6.40   XMLBus Web Service Builder deployment-confirmation dialog box.
Screenshot Copyright 2002 © IONA Technologies PLC. All rights reserved.

The XMLBus Service Manager screen lists the applications deployed within the XMLBus Web-services environment (Fig. 6.41). Select **BookTitleService**, which we created in the first step of the deployment process; then, click **List Services**.

Figure 6.42 lists the Web services deployed to **BookTitle**. Select **BookTitle**, and click **List Endpoints**.

Figure 6.43 shows the information specific to the Book Title Web service. The **WSDL** link displays the WSDL of the Web service. Clicking the **WSDL** link displays the WSDL document associated with the Book Title Web service.

6.7 WASP Server for Java 4.0

Web Applications and Services Platform (WASP) Server for Java 4.0 is Systinet's most current Web-services platform. WASP Server for Java 4.0 provides developers with the tools for implementing, testing, debugging and managing Web services. WASP Server for Java 4.0 enables developers to use it as a stand-alone server or to deploy it on a variety of application Web servers.

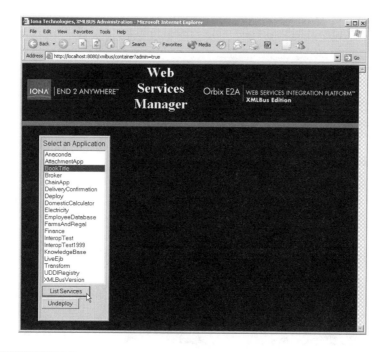

Fig. 6.41   Web Services Manager initial page. Screenshot Copyright 2002 © IONA Technologies PLC. All rights reserved.

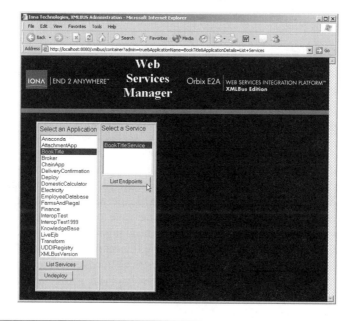

Fig. 6.42   Web Services Manager displaying exposed services for **BookTitle**. Screenshot Copyright 2002 © IONA Technologies PLC. All rights reserved.

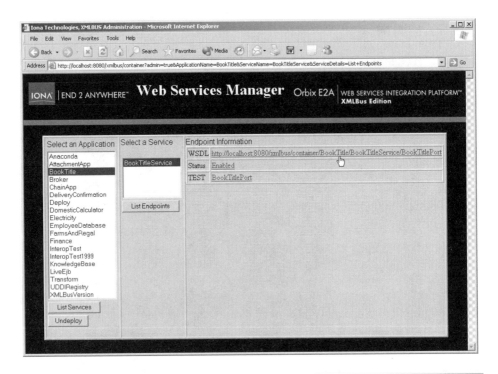

Fig. 6.43   Web Services Manager displaying the endpoint and status for the Book Title Web service. Screenshot Copyright 2002 © IONA Technologies PLC. All rights reserved.

6.7.1 Architecture

WASP's Web-services engine is composed of five levels—the transport layer, XML message-handling layer, the XML message protocol-support layer, an encoding and decoding layer, and the Java-services layer. Each layer is responsible for handling one aspect of the messaging process that delegates an XML message request to its corresponding Java service.

Each XML message that clients send to a given Java Web service is first handled by the transport layer. The transport layer is responsible for obtaining the XML message, consistent with the request's protocol. Once the transport layer receives the XML message, the XML message is sent to a system-level interceptor layer. The system-level interceptor layer handles system-level policies that are applicable to each XML message (e.g., authentication). The system-level interceptor sends the processed XML message to the dispatcher layer, which, in turn, discerns which Java service is responsible for handling the XML request.

Once the dispatcher knows the Java Web service that corresponds to the XML message request, it sends the XML message to the set of message interceptors associated with that Java Web service. These service-level message interceptors are particular to each Java Web service. Developers may configure message interceptors to provide application-specific XML conversions, among other possibilities.

The service-level interceptors send the XML message to the XML protocol-support layer. The XML protocol-support layer identifies the protocol of the XML message request—XML-RPC, SOAP, or application-specific protocols. This layer is responsible for creating a generic XML message that contains header and body parts.

The XML protocol-support layer then sends the XML message to the message-adaptation layer, which converts the processed XML message request into an implementation-specific form that the Java service can use. The Java class transmits its invocation results to the client through the chain of layers that initially processed the request.

Figure 6.44 illustrates the architecture of the WASP engine.

6.7.2 Installation

WASP Server for Java 4.0 is a Web-services server implementation that contains all the necessary software to run a Web-services server environment. WASP provides all of the required support classes and utilities in one package. The latest version of WASP is available for free download at Systinet's Web site

www.systinet.com

For the purposes of these instructions, we have extracted the installation file to directory **c:\wasp**.

Systinet simplifies the installation process for WASP by including installation files in directory **c:\wasp\bin**. To install WASP on systems running Windows 2000, execute batch file **install.bat** in directory **c:\wasp\bin**. The batch file starts the installation, which creates a **.wasp** directory within your home directory and additional batch files necessary to run WASP in directory **c:\wasp\bin**.

To complete the installation of WASP, we must configure the environment variables. Append **c:\wasp\bin** to environment variable **PATH**. Set environment variable **WASP_HOME** to **c:\wasp**. Also include **c:\wasp\lib\wasp.jar** in the classpath.

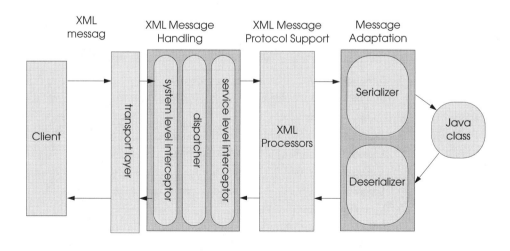

Fig. 6.44   Architecture of the WASP engine.

To confirm the successful installation of WASP Server for Java 4.0, execute batch file **serverstart.bat** within directory **c:\wasp\bin**. If the installation was successful, you will see verbose information confirming the WASP server startup.

6.7.3 Web-Services Deployment

WASP Server for Java 4.0 provides numerous means by which developers can deploy Web services. We discuss three of these methods.

Command-Line Web-Services Deployment
The process by which to deploy a Web service through the command line involves creating a WASP Web service JAR file and deploying the WASP Web service JAR file to a target WASP server.

WaspPackager enables developers to create a WASP Web-service JAR file. Web-service JAR files are WASP-specific JAR files that package such information as the Web service's classes, its support JAR files and its WSDL file. Developers generate Web service JAR files by executing **WaspPackager** and specifying command-line options. Figure 6.45 discusses **WaspPackager**'s command-line options.

The following command generates a WASP Web service JAR file that corresponds to the Book Title Web service,

```
WaspPackager -p BookTitle -o BookTitle.jar -n BookTitle
   -u /BookTitle/ --sbs rpc
   -c com.deitel.jws1.soap.services.BookTitleService
```

Testing and Debugging Tip 6.1

To generate WSDL files, **WaspPackager** *requires the classpath to include the class files and support libraries on which the Web service implementation classes have dependencies. Failing to include the class files and support libraries causes a* **NoClassDefFoundError***.*

Option	Description
-p	Specifies name that identifies package created.
-o	Specifies output JAR file name.
-n	Specifies service name.
-u	Specifies service path within Web service context.
-c	Specifies class implementation of Web service.
-w	Specifies custom WSDL file to replace that generated by **WaspPackager**.
--sbs	Specifies service binding style as either **rpc** or **document** (default).
-s	Specifies root directory that contains implementation and support classes (default local directory).
-l	Specifies library JAR files to include.

Fig. 6.45 **WaspPackager** command-line options.

The installation of WASP creates **DeployTool.bat** in directory **c:\wasp\bin**. **DeployTool** enables developers to deploy, undeploy and list Web services. Figure 6.30 discusses the most commonly used command-line options for **DeployTool**.

To deploy class **BookTitleService** as a WASP Web service, ensure that the WASP server is running and execute the following command at the command line:

```
DeployTool --deploy -t http://localhost:6060
    -j BookTitle.jar -C deitel
```

Command-line option **--deploy** instructs the **deployTool** to deploy the Java service. Option **-t** specifies the URL of the WASP server, option **-j** the WASP package to deploy. Option **-C** specifies context **deitel** at which to deploy the Book Title Web service. Command-line tool **deployTool** provides additional command-line options that enable developers to deploy a Java class as a Web service. For more information, execute **DeployTool** without command-line arguments. After the Book Title Web service has been deployed, clients can access the Book Title Web service at endpoint **http://localhost:6060/deitel/BookTitleService**.

Deployment through the WASP Server Administration Console

The WASP Server Administration Console tool enables users to deploy, undeploy and manage deployed WASP packages. To start the console, start a WASP server and point your browser to the following URL:

```
http://localhost:6060/admin/console
```

Figure 6.47 shows WASP Server Administration Console's initial screen.

To deploy the Book Title Web service through the WASP Server Administration Console, create a WASP package for the Book Title Web service, as described in the previous subsection. Select the **Web Services** tab. Within this tab, select the **New** tab, which enables developers to deploy a WASP package (Fig. 6.48).

Text field **Context name** enables developers to specify the context under which to deploy the WASP package. Specify **deitel** as the context name. The **Select package to deploy** textfield enables developers to specify the WASP package that corresponds to the Web service to deploy. Enter the path and file name of WASP package **BookTitle.jar**; then, click **Deploy**.

Option	Description
--deploy	Specifies to deploy WASP package.
--undeploy	Specifies to undeploy WASP package.
-t	Specifies URL of target WASP server.
-j	Specifies the WASP JAR file that corresponds to Web service to deploy.
-C	Specifies the context path at which to deploy the Web service.

Fig. 6.46 DeployTool command-line options.

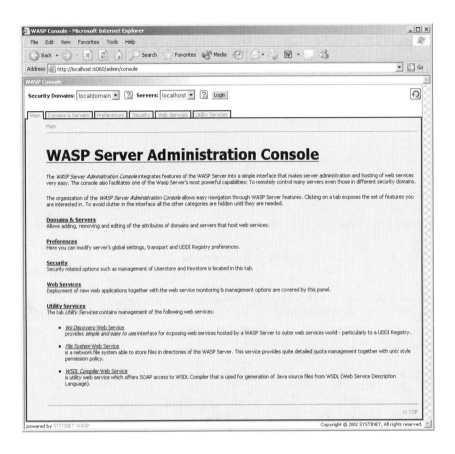

Fig. 6.47   Initial screen of the WASP Console. Courtesy of Systinet.

To verify the deployment of the Book Title Web service, select the **Deployment** tab. This displays the **Deployment view** pane, which enables developers to view a list of all deployed Web services. Click link **BookTitle** to view the Book Title Web service's information (Fig. 6.49). Clients can access the Book Title Web service at **http://local-host:6060/deitel/BookTitleService**.

6.7.4 Generating WSDL Documents

WASP enables developers to generate WSDL documents from Java class files in two ways—through the command-line tool **Java2WSDL**, and through the packaging process, using **WaspPackager**.

WSDL-Document Generation through Java2WSDL
Java2WSDL generates a WSDL document based on a Java class specified at runtime and enables developers to customize the generated WSDL document by specifying command-line options. Figure 6.50 describes commonly used command-line options for **Java2WSDL**.

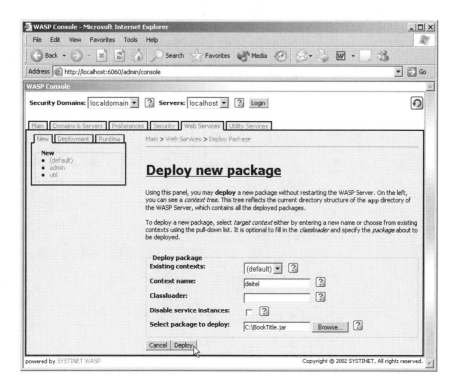

Fig. 6.48 Deployed Web service in WASP Server Administration Console. Courtesy of Systinet.

The following command generates a WSDL document for the Book Title Web service:

```
Java2WSDL
    -c com.deitel.jws1.soap.services.BookTitleService=
       http://localhost:6060/deitel/BookTitleService
    -p com.deitel.jws1.soap.services=
       http://www.deitel.com/soap/services/
    -o http://www.deitel.com/soap/services/=
       BookTitleService.wsdl
    --sbs rpc
    com.deitel.jws1.soap.services.BookTitleService
```

Option **-c** specifies the endpoint for class **BookTitleService**. Option **-p** specifies that the target namespace for Java package **com.deitel.jws1.soap.services** is **http://www.deitel.com/soap/services/**. Option **-o** specifies that the output file name for all WSDL definitions corresponding to target namespace **http://www.deitel.com/soap/services/** is **BookTitle.wsdl** in the current directory. Finally, option **--sbs** specifies the soap-binding style as **rpc**. **Java2WSDL** provides additional command-line options that further customize the WSDL file. For more information, consult **Java2WSDL**'s help menu by executing the command-line tool without parameters.

WSDL-Document Generation through *WaspPackager*

WaspPackager automatically generates a WSDL file for a package if the user does not include a custom WSDL file. To access the generated WSDL document for a given service, access the WASP server by appending **/wsdl** to the endpoint of the Web service URL. For example, to access the WSDL document file for the Book Title Web service, point a browser to URL **http://localhost:6060/deitel/BookTitle/wsdl**.

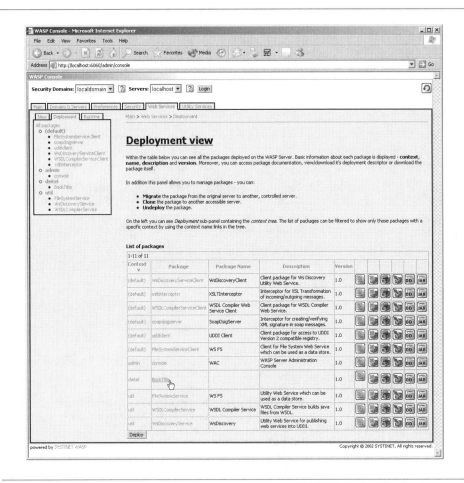

Fig. 6.49   WASP Server Administration Console **Deployment view** pane. Courtesy of Systinet.

Option	Description
-d	Specifies the output directory (default is current directory).

Fig. 6.50   **Java2WSDL** command-line options. (Part 1 of 2.)

Option	Description
-p *packageName=targetNamespace*	Maps the Java package to a target namespace (default target namespace is **http://systinet.com/wsdl/***packageStructure*)
-o *targetNamespace=fileName*	Specifies output file name for definitions that correspond to target namespace (default file name is **Definitions_***package.structure***.wsdl**)
-c *class=endpointURI*	Specifies endpoint for the specified class (default endpoint is **urn:unknown-location-uri**).
-cp	Specifies the classpath to the specified value (default classpath is the current directory) .
--sbs	Specifies the SOAP binding style. Possible values are **rpc** or **document** (default).
--verbose	Outputs processing information.

Fig. 6.50　**Java2WSDL** command-line options. (Part 2 of 2.)

6.8 Developing a Web-Services Client

Sections 6.1–6.7 have described the steps necessary to deploy a Java class as a Web service. Now that we have deployed our Web service, we can build a client capable of invoking that service.

A client is any application or software that creates and sends an XML message to a Web service. Clients can be stand-alone applications that interact with a Web service and display results to their users. Clients also can be Web services that integrate with other Web services to carry out their tasks.

As mentioned in Section 6.1, current Web-services standards focus on defining the communication protocols through which clients and Web services interact. Clients are given liberty as to how to create XML messages. As long as the XML message conforms to the established protocols, any client can interact with a Web service.[2] As a result, the Web-services environments covered in Sections 6.1–6.7 provide their own sets of APIs and implementations that enable developers to create XML messages and invoke remote Web services. These provider-specific API implementations do not limit developers to interaction with only those Web services deployed in their corresponding Web-services platforms.

6.8.1 Overview

The process of creating a Web-service client involves three steps: 1) obtaining a Web service's WSDL document from an XML registry; 2) creating a client to interact with the Web service, one based on the WSDL description; and 3) invoking the Web service. Figure 6.51 illustrates the process that must occur for a client to invoke a Web service.

---

2. Exceptions to this rule occur because of security constraints. Web services may choose to control the clients by which they are accessed.

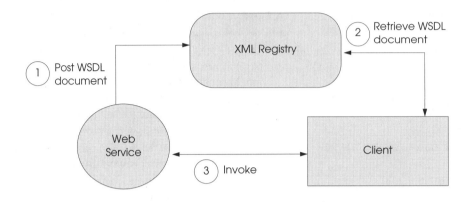

Fig. 6.51 Life cycle of a Web service.

Section 6.3.4, Section 6.4.4, Section 6.5.4, Section 6.6.4 and Section 6.7.4 described how to create a WSDL document. A Web-service administrator must publish the Web service's WSDL document in an XML registry or other WSDL repository. For example, CapeConnect provides a WSDL repository that can be accessed from any Web browser. For the purposes of this section, we assume the developer has access to the WSDL document that describes the Book Title Web service.

The WSDL document describes all the information needed by clients to interact with a Web service. Chapter 7, Web Services Description Language, discusses the process of analyzing a WSDL document for the purpose of creating a Web-service client. To simplify this section, we assume that the developer has read the Book Title Web service's WSDL document and learned that the Book Title Web service exposes one method—**getBookTitle**. Method **getBookTitle** takes one string parameter that represents an ISBN number and returns a string representing the book's title. We use this information to develop the client.

6.8.2 Implementing the Client

For the purposes of this example, we use CapeClear's CapeConnect 3.5 to host the Book Title Web service. Review the steps necessary to deploy class **BookTitleService** as a Web service, as discussed in Section 6.4. The endpoint of the Book Title Web service is **http://localhost:8000/ccx/BookTitle**.

Axis provides two means by which to invoke Web services—1) tools to generate stubs from WSDL documents or interface files, and 2) a simple API that enables developers to invoke remote Web services dynamically with few lines of code. This section discusses invoking the Book Title Web service using Axis' API. To access Axis's Web-services API, ensure that Axis' JAR files are in the class path. These files are located in the **lib** directory of the Axis installation directory. Figure 6.52 shows code that invokes method **getBookTitle** from the Book Title Web service.

```
1   // Fig. 6.52: BookTitleClient.java
2   // BookTitleClient invokes the Book Title Web service, which
```

Fig. 6.52 **BookTitleClient.java** uses the Axis API to invoke the Book Title Web service. (Part 1 of 3.)

```
3    // retrieves titles of Deitel books.
4    package com.deitel.jws1.soap.client;
5
6    // Apache core packages
7    import org.apache.axis.client.Call;
8    import org.apache.axis.client.Service;
9    import org.apache.axis.encoding.XMLType;
10
11   // Java core packages
12   import java.net.URL;
13
14   // Java extension packages
15   import javax.xml.rpc.ParameterMode;
16   import javax.xml.rpc.namespace.QName;
17
18   public class BookTitleClient {
19
20      // define ISBNs for books titles to retrieve
21      public static String[] isbn = new String[] { "0130895601",
22         "0130895717", "0130293636", "0130284173", "0130923613" };
23
24      // class entry-point
25      public static void main( String[] args )
26      {
27         // interact with Book Title Web service
28         try {
29
30            // define endpoint for Book Title Web service
31            String endPoint = "http://localhost:8000/ccx/BookTitle";
32
33            // create service instance
34            Service service = new Service();
35
36            // create call object from service
37            Call call = ( Call )service.createCall();
38
39            // set call target endpoint
40            call.setTargetEndpointAddress( new URL( endPoint ) );
41
42            // set name of operation
43            QName operationName = new QName(
44               "capeconnect:BookTitle:BookTitleService",
45               "getBookTitle" );
46
47            call.setOperationName( operationName );
48
49            // set return type for call
50            call.setReturnType( XMLType.XSD_STRING );
51
```

(handwritten annotation): `" :8000/axis/services/bookTitle`

Fig. 6.52 BookTitleClient.java uses the Axis API to invoke the Book Title
　　　　Web service. (Part 2 of 3.)

```
52              // set the SOAPAction header value
53              call.setSOAPActionURI(
54                 "capeconnect:BookTitle:" +
55                 "BookTitleService#getBookTitle" );
56
57              // set parameter name, type and mode
58              call.addParameter( "ISBN",
59                 XMLType.XSD_STRING, ParameterMode.IN );
60
61              // invoke Web service and display results
62              for ( int i = 0; i < isbn.length; i++ ) {
63
64                 // parameter list
65                 Object[] parameterList = new Object[ 1 ];
66                 parameterList[ 0 ] = isbn[ i ];
67
68                 String response =
69                    ( String ) call.invoke( parameterList );
70
71                 System.out.println( "ISBN #" + isbn[ i ] +
72                    ", Title: " + response );
73
74              } // end for block
75
76           } // end try block
77
78           catch( Exception exception ) {
79              exception.printStackTrace();
80           }
81
82        } // end method main
83
84     } // end class BookTitleClient
```

```
ISBN #0130895601, Title: Advanced Java 2 Platform How to Program
ISBN #0130895717, Title: C++ How to Program, Third edition
ISBN #0130293636, Title: Visual Basic. NET How to Program
ISBN #0130284173, Title: XML How to Program
ISBN #0130923613, Title: Python How to Program
```

Fig. 6.52 BookTitleClient.java uses the Axis API to invoke the Book Title
Web service. (Part 3 of 3.)

Line 34 creates an instance of class **Service**. Class **Service** represents a remote
Web service. It provides four additional constructors that enable developers to populate a
Service object with information contained in a specified WSDL document. We use the
default constructor, which creates an empty **Service** object, to demonstrate other features of the Axis API.

Service instances provide factory methods for creating instances of class **Call**
(line 37). A **Call** object enables developers to invoke an exposed method in a Web service. To invoke a remote Web-service method, developers must first configure a **Call**
object with settings that correspond to the Web service. Line 40 sets the end point for the

Web service. Lines 43–45 create an instance of class **QName**, the JAX-RPC class that encapsulates the namespace and element name of an XML element. The **QName** constructor takes two parameters—the namespace, and the element name. The namespace value corresponds to binding element **BookTitleServiceBinding**'s input namespace. Element name **getBookTitle** corresponds to the operation name defined in element **operation** of WSDL element **binding BookTitleServiceBinding**. Line 49 sets the **QName** of the Web-service method that object **call** represents.

Line 50 sets the return type for the Web-service response. Many SOAP servers return untyped responses. For such cases, setting the response type for the expected Web service response is beneficial. **Call** method **setResponseType** enables developers to specify the Web service's response type. Class **XMLType** defines numerous constants that define commonly used types.

Lines 53–55 set the **SOAPAction** header value for the Web-service invocation. The **SOAPAction** header value is defined in element **operation** of WSDL element **binding**. Lines 58–59 set the type and mode for parameter **ISBN** of method **getBookTitle**. Refer to the Axis API documentation for a full listing of parameter types supported by the Axis API implementation.

Lines 62–74 iterate through the array of ISBNs and invoke the Web service through an instance of class **Call**. Line 69 calls method **invoke** of class **Call** to invoke the Web service. Method **invoke** takes an array of **Object**s. Each array element corresponds to a parameter of the Web service. Array element **0** corresponds to the parameter defined in lines 58–59. Section 6.9 discusses the structure of the SOAP message sent between the **BookTitleClient** and the Book Title Web service.

6.9 Simple Object Access Protocol (SOAP)

IBM, Lotus Development Corporation, Microsoft, DevelopMentor and Userland Software developed and drafted the SOAP specification. SOAP is an XML-based protocol that enables applications to communicate over the Internet by using XML documents called *SOAP messages*. SOAP is compatible with any object model, because it includes a base set of capabilities necessary for communications frameworks. Thus, SOAP is independent of both platform and programming language. SOAP supports transport through virtually any protocol. For example, there is a SOAP binding for HTTP that follows the HTTP request–response model. However, SOAP also has bindings for SMTP and other protocols. In addition, SOAP supports any method of encoding data, to enable SOAP-based applications to send virtually any type of information (e.g., images, objects and documents) in SOAP messages.

A SOAP message has an *envelope* that describes the content, intended recipient and processing requirements of a message. An envelope consists of two distinct parts: 1) the optional **Header** *element* and 2) the **Body** *element*. The **Header** element of a SOAP message provides processing instructions for applications that receive the message. For example, for implementations that support transactions, element **Header** could specify transaction boundaries for a particular message. Element **Header** also can incorporate routing information. Through element **Header**, SOAP can be used to build more complex protocols. **Header** entries can modularly extend the message for purposes such as authentication, transaction management and payment. The **Body** element of a SOAP message contains application-specific data for the intended recipient of the message. Figure 6.53 shows the basic structure of a SOAP message.

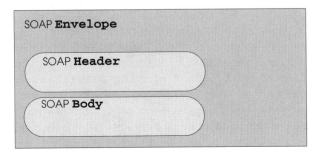

Fig. 6.53   Basic structure of a SOAP message.

Fig. 6.54 shows the actual SOAP message and HTTP **post** header that the Axis API generates for the client of Fig. 6.52. In this example, the SOAP message requests the Web service to return the book title for ISBN **0130895601**.

Lines 1–5 contain the HTTP **post** header. Lines 2–4 define common post header fields and values. Line 5 defines the **SOAPAction** header. The **SOAPAction** header specifies the intent of a SOAP message. SOAP-based Web-services platforms use this header field to obtain a brief description of the purpose or target of a SOAP message. This enables the SOAP-based Web-services platform's underlying mechanism to determine the SOAP message's destination without analyzing the message's contents.

Lines 10–28 define root element **Envelope**. Lines 11–15 contain the namespace declarations for identifying elements in the SOAP message. The SOAP message in Fig. 6.54 does not require a header element, because the SOAP request does not require special routing information or transaction processing. The SOAP header is optional, so the Axis API implementation did not generate it for this example. Lines 17–26 define child element **Body**. Element **Body** contains the elements that specify the method to invoke. Child element **getBookTitle** identifies the method to invoke. Namespace prefix **ns1** ensures that element **getBookTitle** does not conflict with other, similarly named XML elements from other namespaces. Line 22 defines the parameter method **getBookTitle** expects. The tag is named according to the parameter name. The parameter element **ISBN** defines the parameter type. Type **xsd:string** specifies that parameter **ISBN** is a string.

```
1   POST /ccx/BookTitle HTTP/1.0
2   Content-Length: 541
3   Host: localhost
4   Content-Type: text/xml; charset=utf-8
5   SOAPAction: "capeconnect:BookTitle:BookTitleService#getBookTitle"
6
7
8   <?xml version="1.0" encoding="UTF-8"?>
9
10  <SOAP-ENV:Envelope
11  SOAP-ENV:encodingStyle="http://schemas.xmlsoap.org/soap/encoding/"
12     xmlns:SOAP-ENV="http://schemas.xmlsoap.org/soap/envelope/"
```

Fig. 6.54   SOAP request message of class **BookTitleClient**. (Part 1 of 2.)

```
13      xmlns:xsd="http://www.w3.org/2001/XMLSchema"
14      xmlns:xsi="http://www.w3.org/2001/XMLSchema-instance"
15      xmlns:SOAP-ENC="http://schemas.xmlsoap.org/soap/encoding/">
16
17      <SOAP-ENV:Body>
18
19        <ns1:getBookTitle
20           xmlns:ns1="capeconnect:BookTitle:BookTitleService">
21
22           <ISBN xsi:type="xsd:string">0130895601</ISBN>
23
24        </ns1:getBookTitle>
25
26      </SOAP-ENV:Body>
27
28    </SOAP-ENV:Envelope>
```

Fig. 6.54 SOAP request message of class **BookTitleClient**. (Part 2 of 2.)

Figure 6.55 shows the SOAP response message that class **BookTitleClient** receives from the Book Title Web service. The elements of the SOAP response are similar to those shown in Fig. 6.54. The main difference is in the child elements of element **Body**. Element **getBookTitleResponse** (lines 19–27) represents the response generated from method **getBookTitle**. Common naming conventions state that a response element is identified by the name of the invoked method concatenated with the string **Response**.

```
1     HTTP/1.0 200 OK
2     Content-Type: text/xml; charset=utf-8
3     Content-Length: 580
4     Date: Mon, 20 May 2002 15:42:53 GMT
5     Servlet-Engine: CapeConnect/3.5.1.1024 (Orcas/4.4.0, Tomcat Web
Server/3.2.4)
6
7
8     <?xml version="1.0"?>
9
10    <SOAP-ENV:Envelope
11       xmlns:SOAP-ENV="http://schemas.xmlsoap.org/soap/envelope/"
12       xmlns:xsd="http://www.w3.org/2001/XMLSchema"
13       xmlns:xsi="http://www.w3.org/2001/XMLSchema-instance"
14       xmlns:SOAP-ENC="http://schemas.xmlsoap.org/soap/encoding/">
15
16      <SOAP-ENV:Body
17          SOAP-ENV:encodingStyle="http://schemas.xmlsoap.org/soap/
encoding/">
18
19        <cc1:getBookTitleResponse
20           xmlns:cc1="capeconnect:BookTitle:BookTitleService"
21           SOAP-ENC:root="1">
```

Fig. 6.55 SOAP response message of the Book Titles Web service. (Part 1 of 2.)

```
22
23                 <return  xsi:type="xsd:string">
24                     Advanced Java 2 Platform How to Program
25                 </return>
26
27             </cc1:getBookTitleResponse>
28
29         </SOAP-ENV:Body>
30
31     </SOAP-ENV:Envelope>
```

Fig. 6.55   SOAP response message of the Book Titles Web service. (Part 2 of 2.)

Element **return** (lines 23–25) contains the response data returned by the method. Attribute **xsi:type** defines the response's data type—in this case, a string. Line 24 shows the actual data in the response.

In this chapter, we have discussed the steps necessary to create Web services from Java classes using various Web services platforms—Axis, CapeConnect, GLUE, XMLBus and WASP. We have discussed how to create a simple Web-services client, using Axis's API. We have also analyzed the structure of a SOAP request and response that resulted from the interaction between our Web-services client and the Book Title Web service. Chapter 7, Web Services Description Language, discusses the structure of a WSDL document and explains the process of creating, out of the Web service's WSDL document, a client that interacts with a Web service.

6.10 Summary

Standards developed for the Web-services paradigm focus primarily on communication protocols and Web-services descriptions. XML messages are used by clients and servers to define a communication protocol between two remote points. A typical Web-service transaction is composed of the client and the service. A client invokes a remote Web service by creating an XML message. A transmitted XML message contains the necessary information for the Web-services platform to deserialize the request. No standardized approaches exist for implementing Web services. Different platforms have different ways of defining the contract between a Web-services platform and its hosted Web services.

Apache's Axis is a rearchitected successor to the popular Apache SOAP 2.2. Axis is designed to offer flexibility greater than that of its predecessor. Axis provides developers with a substantial set of customization options. CapeClear's CapeConnect 3.5 enables developers to deploy Java services, EJBs and CORBA systems in Web-services environments. CapeConnect is a stand-alone environment that unifies legacy systems and Web-services protocols without the need for writing code. The MindElectric's GLUE is a small-footprint implementation of a full-featured Web-services environment. GLUE provides a simplified API that is geared toward reducing the learning curve and making the process of developing Web services less complicated. The XMLBus 5.2 stand-alone release is a full-featured Web-services environment aimed at simplifying the Web-service creation and deployment process. The XMLBus 5.2 stand-alone release is composed of a Web-services container and a set of tools that enable developers to test, deploy and manage Web services. Web Applications and Services Platform (WASP) Server for Java 4.0 provides developers with the tools for implementing, testing, debugging and managing Web services.

SOAP is an XML-based protocol that enables applications to communicate over the Internet by using XML documents called SOAP messages. SOAP is independent of both platform and programming language. A SOAP message has an envelope that describes the content, intended recipient and processing requirements of a message. A SOAP envelope consists of two distinct parts: (1) the optional **Header** element, and (2) the **Body** element. The **Header** element of a SOAP message provides processing instructions for applications that receive the message. The **Body** element of a SOAP message contains application-specific data for the intended recipient of the message.

6.11 Internet and World Wide Web Resources

xml.apache.org/axis
Apache's Axis home page. Provides access to the most recent build of the Axis Web-services platform.

www.capeclear.com
Home page for the CapeConnect Web-services platform.

www.themindelectric.com
Home page for the GLUE Web-services platform.

www.iona.com
Home page for the XMLBus Web-services platform.

www.systinet.com
Home page for Web Applications and Service Platform (WASP).

www.w3.org/TR/SOAP
Home page for the SOAP 1.1 specification.

7

Web Services
Description Language

Objectives

- To be introduced to the Web Services Description Language.
- To learn about the association between WSDL documents and Web services.
- To understand the structure of WSDL documents.
- To learn how to generate WSDL documents.
- To be able to use WSDL documents to determine the availability of Web services.

You know more of a road by having traveled it than by all the conjectures and descriptions in the world.
William Hazlitt

No written law has ever been more binding than unwritten custom supported by popular opinion.
Carrie Chapman Catt

The beginning of wisdom is the definition of terms.
Socrates

The port is near, the bells I hear, the people all exulting.
Walt Whitman

7.1 Introduction

In this chapter, we discuss the *Web Services Description Language (WSDL)*, which is an XML vocabulary for describing the public functionality that a Web services provides. Most Web services are accompanied by *WSDL documents*, which specify information about the Web services that an application has made available, such as the functionality that Web services provide, the addresses (URLs) of the services, and how clients transfer messages to those services.

In this chapter, we discuss how to use WSDL for providing Web-service information to the client. We begin by discussing the syntax of WSDL and the features that the language provides. We then introduce methods for generating WSDL documents. The process for creating these documents is rather mechanical, so we show how to use several tools that generate WSDL documents. To conclude this chapter, we build a client that examines a WSDL document to determine information about how to invoke a Web service.

7.2 History of WSDL

Before organizations adopted WSDL as a universal method of Web services description, each Web services development environment used a proprietary method to describe available Web services. There was no standard way to access the files containing the descriptions, and service descriptions were inconsistent and incompatible. To remedy this situation, Microsoft and IBM collaborated to create a language that describes Web services in a standard, structured way. The technologies of Microsoft's *SOAP Contract Language (SCL)* and IBM's *Network Accessible Service Specification Language (NASSL)* were combined to form the basis of WSDL.[1] SCL employs XML to describe the messages exchanged between applications, and NASSL describes the interface and the implementation details of a Web service. Microsoft and IBM, with contributions from Ariba, submitted WSDL Version 1.1 to the W3C in March 2001. Although the technology still is under development, many Web services provide support for WSDL, and most development tools auto-generate WSDL documents.[2]

7.3 Role of WSDL in Web Services

Many Web services published on the Internet have associated WSDL documents, which contain the definitions (marked up as XML) that describe the Web services. The WSDL document specifies the service's capabilities, its location on the Web and instructions regarding how to access it. A WSDL document defines the structure of the messages (i.e., indicate the data that a calling application must provide for the Web service) that a Web service sends and receives. Using this information, applications searching for a Web service to fill a specific need can analyze the WSDL documents of several, comparable services and choose between the services.

Figure 7.1 illustrates the role of a WSDL document in a Web services interaction. When a Web service is published, a Web service administrator can post a link to the Web service's WSDL document in an XML registry or other WSDL repository (Step 1). The WSDL document then is available when an application, such as a SOAP client, searches a registry to locate a Web service. A client accesses the WSDL document contained in the XML registry to acquire information about the Web service and to create a SOAP message with the appropriate structure to communicate with the service (Step 2). Then, using the information in the WSDL document, the client invokes the Web service (Step 3).

7.4 WSDL Document Structure

In this section, we discuss the structure of a WSDL document. Developers do not necessarily need to understand a WSDL document's structure to be able to build and deploy a Web service associated with that WSDL document; however, developers who comprehend WSDL can more easily debug Web services that use WSDL documents, as well as customize WSDL documents when necessary. Figure 7.2 shows the WSDL document for the Book Title Web service that we created in the previous chapter. (Recall that this Web service inputs a string that represents a book's ISBN, and outputs a string that represents that book's title.) To generate this document, we used a WSDL generator that is integrated into Forte for Java 3.0. We show how to use the WSDL generator in Section 7.5. For now, we focus on the functions of the elements that the WSDL document contains.

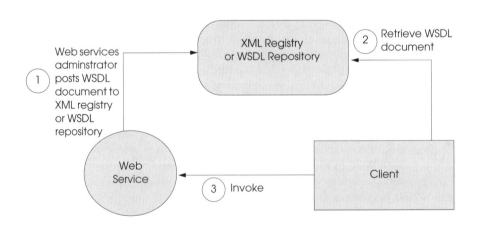

Fig. 7.1   WSDL role in Web services interactions.

```
1    <?xml version="1.0"?>
2    <wsdl:definitions
3
4      name="com.deitel.jws1.services.BookTitleService"
5      targetNamespace=
6         "urn:com.deitel.jws1.services.BookTitleService"
7      xmlns:wsdl="http://schemas.xmlsoap.org/wsdl/"
8      xmlns:xsd="http://www.w3.org/2001/XMLSchema"
9      xmlns:tns="urn:com.deitel.jws1.services.BookTitleService"
10     xmlns:http="http://schemas.xmlsoap.org/wsdl/http/"
11     xmlns:xsi="http://www.w3.org/2001/XMLSchema-instance"
12     xmlns:mime="http://schemas.xmlsoap.org/wsdl/mime/"
13     xmlns:soap="http://schemas.xmlsoap.org/wsdl/soap/"
14     xmlns:SOAP-ENC="http://schemas.xmlsoap.org/soap/encoding/">
15
16     <wsdl:message name="BookTitleService_getBookTitle_Response">
17        <wsdl:part name="response" type="xsd:string" />
18     </wsdl:message>
19
20     <wsdl:message name="BookTitleService_getBookTitle_Request">
21        <wsdl:part name="p0" type="xsd:string" />
22     </wsdl:message>
23
24     <wsdl:portType name="BookTitleService">
25
26        <wsdl:operation name="getBookTitle" parameterOrder="p0">
27           <wsdl:input name="getBookTitle"
28              message="tns:BookTitleService_getBookTitle_Request" />
29
30           <wsdl:output name="getBookTitle"
31              message="tns:BookTitleService_getBookTitle_Response" />
32        </wsdl:operation>
33
34     </wsdl:portType>
35
36     <wsdl:binding name="BookTitleServiceSOAPBinding0"
37        type="tns:BookTitleService">
38
39        <soap:binding
40           transport="http://schemas.xmlsoap.org/soap/http"
41           style="rpc" />
42
43        <wsdl:operation name="getBookTitle">
44
45           <soap:operation soapAction="" style="rpc" />
46
47           <wsdl:input name="getBookTitle">
48              <soap:body use="encoded"
49                 encodingStyle=
50                    "http://schemas.xmlsoap.org/soap/encoding/"
51                 namespace=
52                    "urn:com.deitel.jws1.services.BookTitleService"
53              />
```

Fig. 7.2   WSDL document associated with the Book Title Web service. (Part 1 of 2.)

```
54              </wsdl:input>
55
56              <wsdl:output name="getBookTitle">
57                 <soap:body use="encoded"
58                    encodingStyle=
59                       "http://schemas.xmlsoap.org/soap/encoding/"
60                    namespace=
61                       "urn:com.deitel.jws1.services.BookTitleService"
62                 />
63              </wsdl:output>
64
65           </wsdl:operation>
66
67        </wsdl:binding>
68
69        <wsdl:service name="BookTitle">
70
71           <wsdl:port name="BookTitleService"
72              binding="tns:BookTitleServiceSOAPBinding0">
73              <soap:address
74                 location="http://SCARAB:6060/BookTitleService/"/>
75           </wsdl:port>
76
77        </wsdl:service>
78
79    </wsdl:definitions>
```

Fig. 7.2   WSDL document associated with the Book Title Web service. (Part 2 of 2.)

Figure 7.2 contains all the information that a client uses to determine which operations of the Web service are available. Line 1 specifies the XML prototype, because WSDL is an XML vocabulary. Line 2 declares the **definitions** element, which is the root element of a WSDL document. This element contains all the other elements that store the information on the Web service. The **definitions** element also defines several namespaces (lines 4–14) that the WSDL document can use.

Lines 16–18 and 20–22 declare two **message** elements, which represent the variables that clients and Web services transfer between each other. Basically, these variables are either the arguments or the return types for the Web service's remote methods. A **message** element contains a **part** element, which specifies the name and data type of the message exchanged. Lines 16–18 define a **message** element named **BookTitleService_getBookTitle_Response**, which maps to a string. Similarly, lines 20–22 define a **message** element named **BookTitleService_getBookTitle_Request**, which also maps to a string.

It seems logical that the **message** elements defined in lines 16–22 should represent the messages that the client receives from, and sends to, the Web service. However, the WSDL **message** element declares only the messages that will be used, but does not specify exactly how the input and output messages associate with an operation. WSDL provides the **portType** element to accomplish this task. The **portType** element (24–34) contains **operation** elements, which map the messages defined in the WSDL **message** elements to the actual services. Each **operation** element contains an **input** and **output** element, each of which associates a **message** element to a method parameter or method return type, respectively. Lines 26–32 declare an **operation** element that corresponds to the two **message** elements defined in lines 16–22. Lines 27–28 declare the **input** element which specifies that the Book Title Web service receives the **BookTitleService_getBookTitle_Request** message as a parameter. Similarly, lines 30–31 declare the **output** element which specifies that the Book Title Web service returns the **BookTitleService_getBookTitle_Response** message to the client. Note that the message elements in lines 16–22 declared these messages as strings. Therefore, when the client sends a string as a parameter to the Book Title Web service, the client will receive another string as a return value. In "Java terms," the client will send a **String** object as a parameter to method **getBookTitle** of class **BookTitleService**, which will return a **String** object to that client.

The **binding** element (lines 36–67) specify how the client and Web service should send messages to one another. The client uses this information to access the Web service. Each **binding** element contains another **binding** element (a WSDL extension for SOAP) that specifies the protocol by which clients access the Web service. The second **binding** element is prefixed by the URI associated with that protocol. For this example, we use SOAP as the protocol that the client uses to invoke a service, as evidenced by the namespace **"http://schemas.xmlsoap.org/wsdl/soap"** prefix used on the **binding** element (line 39). A WSDL document allows us to use other protocols as well, such as MIME and HTTP (without using SOAP). If we had wanted to use either of these protocols, we would have declared the second **binding** element using the namespace prefixes associated with HTTP and MIME, respectively.

Line 40 sets the **transport** attribute of the **binding** element to **http://schemas.xmlsoap.org/soap/http**, which is a unique identifier for specifying SOAP over HTTP. Line 41 sets the **style** attribute of the **binding** element to **rpc**, which specifies that the client will make remote procedure calls via XML to access the Web service. By using this value, the Web-service environment can expect to receive a message that has a specific structure containing parameters (input) and return values (output). The other value that the **style** attribute can assume is **document**, which is the default value if the **style** attribute is omitted. This value specifies that the message contains an XML document that does not have the RPC structure (i.e., one that is not "formatted" appropriately for remote procedure calls).

Lines 45–65 define an **operation** element that contains instructions on how to access the Book Title Web service. The **operation** element proves the actual method definition for invoking the Web service—i.e., this element defines the interface for the Web service. Lines 47–54 define an **input** element, which, in turn, contains a **body** element (prefixed with the SOAP namespace) that specifies how the Web-service environment encodes SOAP requests to the Web service. This element contains attributes **use**, **encodingStyle** and **namespace**. Attribute **use** determines whether the **part** elements of the **message** elements are encoded. Attributes **encodingStyle** and **namespace** specify the encoding and namespace used for the messages, respectively. Lines 51–55 define an **output** element, which specifies how the Web-service environment encodes SOAP responses from the Web service. The attributes that an **output** element contains are identical to those of an **input** element.

The **service** element (lines 69–77) specifies the URL that clients must access to invoke the Web service. The **service** element contains several **port** elements, each of which contains a URL for a unique binding. Our example contains only one binding—

BookTitleService—so we need to use only one **port** element to reveal its location (lines 71–75). Lines 73–74 define a **address** element (prefixed with the SOAP namespace) that defines **http://SCARAB:6060/BookTitleService/** as the URL that clients can access to invoke the Book Title Web service. As we will see momentarily, the substring **SCARAB:6060** indicates that the Web service resides on a computer named **SCARAB**, and the Web-service environment listens for Web-service requests on port **6060**. The substring **BookTitleService/** is the URI that maps to the **getBookTitle** operation exposed in the Book Title Web service.

7.5 WSDL Document Generation

In the previous section, we introduced the structure of a WSDL document by discussing the document in Fig. 7.2. The manual creation of a WSDL document is often unnecessary, because most Web-service-deployment environments generate WSDL automatically. In this section, we show how the WASP Web-service-deployment tool generates the WSDL document in Fig. 7.2. In Section 7.6, we build a client that uses the WSDL document to invoke the Book Title Web service.

In this section and the next one, we use **Forte for Java, release 3.0 (Community Edition**), as the Web-service-development environment. This software is available free for download at

www.sun.com/forte/ffj/buy.html

The **WASP Developer Advanced 3.0.1—version 3.1.1** module includes a toolkit that enables developers to create and deploy Web services and a WASP server that hosts Web services. This module is free for download through the Forte **Update Center**. After installing Forte, select **Tools>Update Center**. Select and install the **WASP Developer Advanced 3.0.1** module (Fig. 7.3).

The WSDL-generation process requires three steps:

1. Starting the WASP Web-service environment to expose the Book Title Web service.

2. Generating a Web service from **BookTitleService.java** (the implementation of the Book Title Web service), which will generate a WSDL document that does not include **binding** and **service** elements.

3. Deploying the Book Title Web service, which will generate a WSDL document that contains **binding** and **service** elements.

After installing the module, the first step is to create a WASP server to act as the Web-service environment that will host our Web services. Open the **Explorer** window (**View>Explorer**, or *Ctrl-F2*), and select the **Runtime** folder. Right-click the **WASP Servers** item; then select **Add WASP Server** (Fig. 7.4). The **Adding a new WASP server** window will appear. Select **Embedded WASP server** as the **WASP server type**. The **Display name** should contain the name of the WASP server. The server is named after the machine that stores the Web service. For example, the machine on which we deploy the Book Title Web service is **SCARAB**. Use **6060** (the preferred port for WASP servers) as the **Host port**, which is where this WASP server will listen for Web-service requests. Note that we do not specify passwords for this example. After you have clicked **OK**, Forte will activate the WASP server.

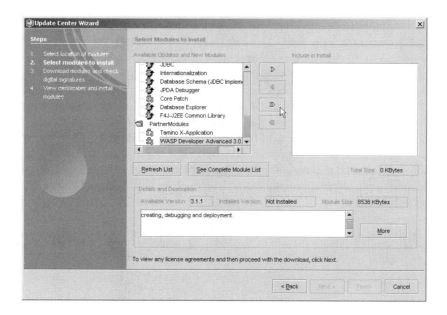

Fig. 7.3   WASP Developer Advanced 3.0.1 module installation via **Forte for Java Update Center.** Courtesy of Systinet. Reproduced with permission by Sun Microsystems, Inc.© Copyright 2002. Sun Microsystems, Inc. All Rights Reserved.

Fig. 7.4   WASP-server installation, using the **WASP Developer Advanced module. Courtesy of Systinet. Reproduced with permission by Sun Microsystems, Inc.© Copyright 2002. Sun Microsystems, Inc. All Rights Reserved.

The second step is to use the WASP toolkit to generate a Web service from a Java class (**BookTitleService.java**). From the **Explorer** window, select the **Filesystems** folder. Select **BookTitleService**—the name of the Java class for which we are generating the Web service. Then select **Tools>Generate Web Service**. A window appears that allows for specification of the methods from which the toolkit generates Web services (Fig. 7.5). Make sure that **getBookTitle** (the only method that class **BookTi-**

tleService exposes) is selected. Click **Next** to specify the properties for this Web service. We use **urn:com.deitel.jws1.services.BookTitleService** as the **Target Namespace**, **/BookTitleService/** for the **Relative URI**, and **BookTitleService** for the **Service** and **Port** names in the WSDL document that we generate in the next step. Click **Finish** to create the Web service.

After creating the Web service, note that Forte places two additional items below the **BookTitleService** item in the **Filesystems** folder in the **Explorer** window (Fig. 7.6). The first item (the item that is selected in Fig. 7.6) is **BookTitleService.wsdl**—the WSDL document for the Book Title Web service. Upon opening this document, note that it is the same WSDL document as the one in Fig. 7.2, except that it does not contain the **binding** and **service** elements (lines 32–60). Forte will include these elements when we deploy the Book Title Web service in the next step. The next item in the **Filesystems** folder is a descriptor that contains information about the Book Title Web service (e.g., Web-service location, deployment values, and properties of the Web service and WSDL compiler). We specified much of this information in the last step.

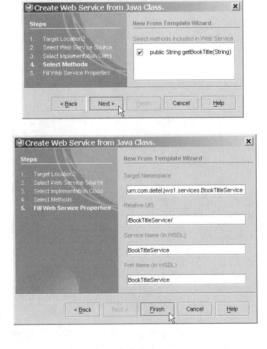

Fig. 7.5   Web-service creation from a Java class, using the **WASP Developer Advanced** module. Courtesy of Systinet. Reproduced with permission by Sun Microsystems, Inc.© Copyright 2002. Sun Microsystems, Inc. All Rights Reserved.

Fig. 7.6   Web service and WSDL document that is generated by **WASP Developer Advanced** module. Courtesy of Systinet. Reproduced with permission by Sun Microsystems, Inc.© Copyright 2002. Sun Microsystems, Inc. All Rights Reserved.

Now we can deploy the Book Title service. Right-click the descriptor item that contains the **BookTitleService** information, and select **Deploy Web Service** from the pop-up menu. The **Deploy Web Services Wizard** contains four steps:

1. The name of the Web service to deploy (**BookTitleService**) is entered in the **Package Name** screen (Fig. 7.7).

2. The WASP server on which to deploy the Web service is selected in the **WASP Server** screen (Fig. 7.8).

3. Any classes or libraries that the Web service should use are specified in the **Web Service List** screen. In our example, **BookTitleService** does not utilize any miscellaneous classes, so using the features on this screen is unnecessary (Fig. 7.9).

4. Additional information (e.g., author, version, time created) about the Web service is specified in the **Package Info** screen (Fig. 7.10).

After deploying the Web service, we can view the associated WSDL document. Essentially, the deployment tool includes the **binding** and **service** elements for the WSDL document that Forte generated after creating the Book Title Web service. To view the WSDL document, we use the administration console included by the **WASP Developer Advanced** module. To access this console, type the following in your Web browser:

```
http://localhost:6060/admin/console
```

Fig. 7.7   Web-service creation from a Java class, using the **WASP Developer Advanced** module (Step 1). Courtesy of Systinet. Reproduced with permission by Sun Microsystems, Inc.© Copyright 2002. Sun Microsystems, Inc. All Rights Reserved.

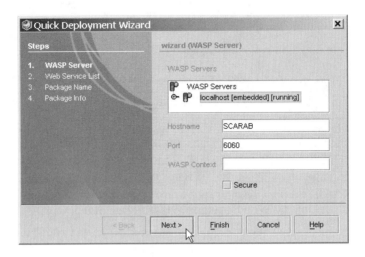

Fig. 7.8   Web-service creation from a Java class, using the **WASP Developer Advanced** module (Step 2). Courtesy of Systinet. Reproduced with permission by Sun Microsystems, Inc.© Copyright 2002. Sun Microsystems, Inc. All Rights Reserved.

Fig. 7.9   Web-service creation from a Java class, using the **WASP Developer Advanced** module (Step 3). Courtesy of Systinet. Reproduced with permission by Sun Microsystems, Inc.© Copyright 2002. Sun Microsystems, Inc. All Rights Reserved.

The administration console should appear in the browser (Fig. 7.11). Click **Refresh listing** to view the Web services that WASP deploys.

To view the methods that the Book Title Web service exposes, expand the **BookTitle** element by clicking the plus (**+**) icon. To view the complete generated WSDL document, select the link next to the **WSDL** label (highlighted in red in Fig. 7.12). Note that the WSDL document is identical to that in Fig. 7.2, because Forte added the **service** and **binding** elements.

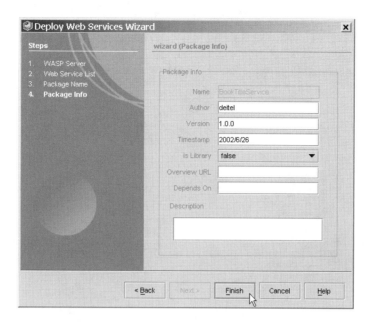

Fig. 7.10   Web-service creation from a Java class, using the **WASP Developer Advanced** module (Step 4). Courtesy of Systinet. Reproduced with permission by Sun Microsystems, Inc.© Copyright 2002. Sun Microsystems, Inc. All Rights Reserved.

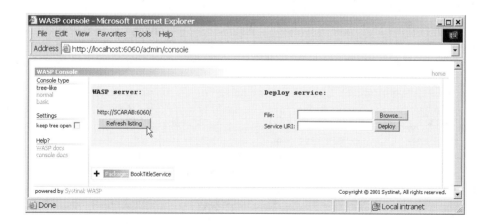

Fig. 7.11   Administration console for the **WASP Developer Advanced** module. Courtesy of Systinet. Reproduced with permission by Sun Microsystems, Inc.© Copyright 2002. Sun Microsystems, Inc. All Rights Reserved.

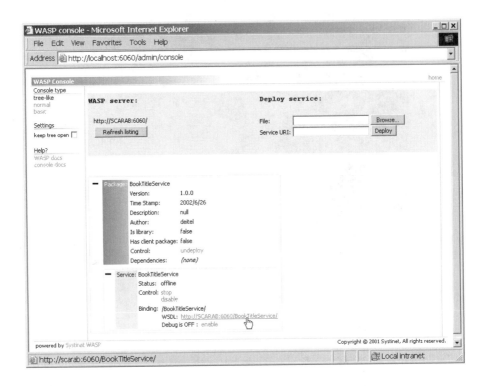

Fig. 7.12   Administration console (expanded) for the **WASP Developer Advanced** module. Courtesy of Systinet.

7.6 Using WSDL in Developing a Web-Service Client

Now that we have deployed the Book Title Web service, we can build a client to access this service. To build the client, we use the Java APIs that are included in the **WASP Developer Advanced** module. As we build the client, we discuss the importance of the WSDL document of Fig. 7.2.

Before we build the client, however, we must program the interface through which the client interacts with the Book Title Web service. The **WASP Developer Advanced** module handles generation of this interface. In the **Explorer [Filesystems]** window, right-click the descriptor item that contains the **BookTitleService** information, and select **Generate Interfaces** from the pop-up menu. In the same directory, the module will create a directory called **iface**. Inside this directory, the module will store an interface called **BookTitleService** under the file **BookTitleService.java**. We rename interface **BookTitleService** as **BookTitle** and save it under the file **BookTitle.java** (Fig. 7.13) in order to avoid ambiguity between the class and the interface, which share an identical name after the generation takes place. Also, we place interface **BookTitle** in package **com.deitel.jws1.services**. Note that interface **BookTitle** provides only one method—**getBookTitle** (line 9)—which clients will implement to invoke that Web service.

```
1    // Fig. 7.13: BookTitle.java.
2    // BookTitle is the interface through which clients can access the
3    // Book Title Web service.
4    package com.deitel.jws1.services;
5
6    public interface BookTitle {
7
8        // service to receive titles of books with matching ISBN
9        String getBookTitle( String ISBN );
10   }
```

Fig. 7.13 **BookTitle** serves as an interface for clients to access the Book Title Web service.

Figure 7.14 shows the code for **BookTitleClient**—the client that uses a WSDL document to access the Book Title Web service. We use the WASP APIs (imported in lines 14–16) to enable the client to communicate with the WASP server that hosts the Web service. Line 19 imports interface **BookTitle**, which **BookTitleClient** uses to communicate (via the WASP server) to the Book Title Web service.

BookTitleClient has three central GUI elements:

- A **JLabel** (line 43) that displays a title of a book that **BookTitleClient** receives from the Book Title Web service;

- A **JComboBox** (lines 46–51) that enables the user to select from a list of ISBN numbers, where each ISBN number specifies a distinct book for which the Book Title Web service returns an associated book title;

- A **JButton** (lines 54–87) that, when clicked, will notify the WASP server to invoke method **getBookTitle** from the Book Title service.

```
1    // Fig. 7.14: BookTitleClient.java.
2    // BookTitleClient uses the WASP API for Java to access the
3    // Book Title Web service.
4    package com.deitel.jws1.wsdl.client;
5
6    // Java core packages
7    import java.awt.*;
8    import java.awt.event.*;
9
10   // Java extension packages
11   import javax.swing.*;
12
13   // WASP packages
14   import org.idoox.webservice.client.WebServiceLookup;
15   import org.idoox.webservice.client.WebServiceLookupException;
16   import org.idoox.wasp.Context;
17
18   // Deitel packages
19   import com.deitel.jws1.services.BookTitle;
```

Fig. 7.14 **BookTitleClient** uses the WASP APIs and a WSDL document to invoke the Book Title Web service. (Part 1 of 4.)

```
20
21   public class BookTitleClient extends JFrame {
22
23      private final static int FRAME_WIDTH = 500;
24      private final static int FRAME_HEIGHT = 100;
25
26      // interface through which to invoke Book Title Web service
27      private BookTitle service;
28
29      // Web-service URL
30      private final static String SERVICE_URL =
31         "http://SCARAB:6060/BookTitleService/";
32
33      // WSDL-document URL
34      private final static String WSDL_URL =
35         "http://SCARAB:6060/BookTitleService/";
36
37      public BookTitleClient( String title )
38      {
39         super( title );
40         getContentPane().setLayout( new GridLayout( 2, 2 ) );
41
42         // JLabel to display book title from Web-service invocation
43         final JLabel resultsLabel = new JLabel();
44
45         // JComboBox for selecting ISBN to send to Web service
46         final JComboBox isbnComboBox = new JComboBox();
47         isbnComboBox.addItem( "0130895601" );
48         isbnComboBox.addItem( "0130895717" );
49         isbnComboBox.addItem( "0130293636" );
50         isbnComboBox.addItem( "0130284173" );
51         isbnComboBox.addItem( "0130923613" );
52
53         // JButton invokes remote Web Service
54         JButton serviceButton = new JButton( "Get Book Title" );
55         serviceButton.addActionListener(
56            new ActionListener() {
57
58               // invoked when user presses JButton
59               public void actionPerformed( ActionEvent event )
60               {
61                  // use WASP APIs to access Web service
62                  try {
63
64                     // get object that performs Web-service lookup
65                     WebServiceLookup serviceLookup =
66                        ( WebServiceLookup ) Context.getInstance(
67                           Context.WEBSERVICE_LOOKUP );
68
69                     // lookup Web service from registry
70                     service = ( BookTitle ) serviceLookup.lookup(
71                        WSDL_URL, BookTitle.class, SERVICE_URL );
```

Fig. 7.14 **BookTitleClient** uses the WASP APIs and a WSDL document to invoke the Book Title Web service. (Part 2 of 4.)

```
72
73                          // invoke Web service
74                          String response = service.getBookTitle(
75                              ( String ) isbnComboBox.getSelectedItem() );
76
77                          resultsLabel.setText( response );
78                      }
79
80                      // handle exception if unable to find Web service
81                      catch ( WebServiceLookupException exception ) {
82                          exception.printStackTrace();
83                      }
84
85                  } // end method actionPerformed
86              }
87          );
88
89          // store JLabel, JComboBox and JButton JFrame
90          getContentPane().add( new JLabel( "Select ISBN:" ) );
91          getContentPane().add( isbnComboBox );
92          getContentPane().add( resultsLabel );
93          getContentPane().add( serviceButton );
94
95      } // end constructor
96
97      // return size of BookTitleClient frame
98      public Dimension getPreferredSize()
99      {
100         return new Dimension( FRAME_WIDTH, FRAME_HEIGHT );
101     }
102
103     // instantiate BookTitleClient GUI
104     public static void main( String args[] )
105     {
106         BookTitleClient client =
107             new BookTitleClient( "Book Title Service" );
108         client.setDefaultCloseOperation( EXIT_ON_CLOSE );
109         client.pack();
110         client.setVisible( true );
111     }
112
113 } // end class BookTitleClient
```

Fig. 7.14 BookTitleClient uses the WASP APIs and a WSDL document to invoke the Book Title Web service. (Part 3 of 4.)

Fig. 7.14   **BookTitleClient** uses the WASP APIs and a WSDL document to invoke the Book Title Web service. (Part 4 of 4.)

When the user clicks the **JButton**, method **actionPerformed** (lines 59–85) uses the WASP APIs to invoke the Web service. The WASP API objects use the WSDL document of Fig. 7.2 to access the service. Lines 65–67 obtain a reference to a **WebService-Lookup** object. Lines 70–71 perform a lookup operation on the **WebServiceLookup** in order to obtain a remote reference to the **BookTitle** object. This lookup operation, which is handled using method **lookup** of the **WebServiceLookup** object, requires the URLs of the Book Title Web service and the WSDL document. We define these URLs in lines 30–31 and 34–35, respectively. We determine the URL of the Web service by examining the service **element** of the WSDL (line 57 in Fig. 7.2). Specifically, this value is in the **location** attribute of the **soap:address** element, which, in turn, resides in the **port** element of the WSDL document's **service** element. We determine the URL of the WSDL document by examining the URL values listed in the WASP server's administration console (Fig. 7.12).

Lines 74–75 pass the ISBN number that the user specified from the **JComboBox** to method **getBookTitle** on the remote **BookTitle** object. The WASP server handles the invocation of the remote method and ensures that the **BookTitle** object will return some value to the client. If successful, the WASP server returns a **String** that represents the book title associated with the ISBN number sent to the Web service. If unsuccessful, the WASP server returns a **String** with a **null** value. Finally, line 77 displays the **String** in the **JLabel**.

7.7 Remote Web-Service Invocation Using WSDL

So far in this chapter, we generated a WSDL document from a Java class, deployed that class as a Web service, and built a client that examined the WSDL document to gather information on the Web service. In this section, we build a client that uses an online WSDL document to invoke a Web service that provides stock quotes, based on a given company symbol.

First, we construct a client that invokes a Web service from **www.xmethods.com** (Fig. 7.15). This site provides access to several Web services, ranging from services that perform and return simple mathematical calculations to services that validate credit card numbers. **XMethods** contains a **Service List**, which categorizes each Web service by **Publisher**, **Style**, **Service Name**, **Description** and **Implementation**. The **Publisher** is the Web site of the company that promotes the Web service. The **Style** represents how each SOAP message is encoded (either as a remote-procedure call or as a document). The **Service Name** is a link to the URL of the Web service. The **Description** provides a textual description of the service. The **Implementation** is the name of the Web-service environment on which the service has been deployed. The Web service for which we construct a client is the **Delayed Stock Quote** (which, at the time of this writing, is located in the **Service List** near the bottom of the Web page). When given a company's stock symbol, this Web service returns a 20-minute delayed stock quote for the company associated with the symbol.

Select the **Delayed Stock Quote** item under the **Service Name** field in the **XMethods** Web site to view information for this Web service (Fig. 7.16). This page provides a link to the WSDL document that contains the information needed to invoke the **Delayed Stock Quote** Web service. Note that the URL of the WSDL document is

```
http://services.xmethods.net/soap/urn:xmethods-delayed-
quotes.wsdl
```

We will use this URL when we build the client that accesses this service.

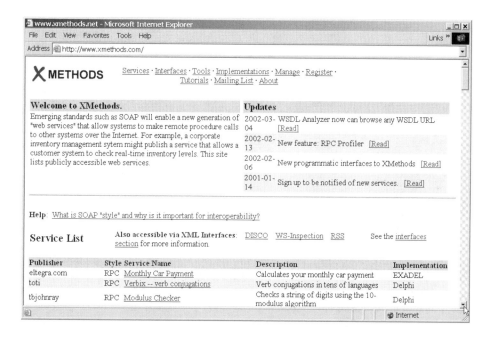

Fig. 7.15 **www.xmethods.com** exposes several Web services. (Courtesy of Xmethods, Inc.)

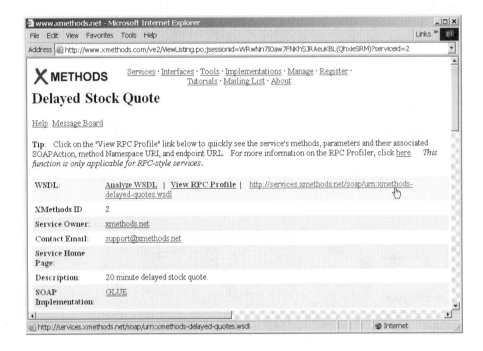

Fig. 7.16   Delayed Stock Quote Web-service information. (Courtesy of Xmethods, Inc.)

If you access this URL via Internet Explorer, the browser displays the WSDL document (Fig. 7.17). (Note that using Netscape might require downloading the WSDL document to disk, then viewing it in an appropriate editor.) Lines 12–18 define two messages called **getQuoteResponse1** and **getQuoteRequest1**, which are of Java types **float** and **String**, respectively. Lines 20–26 define a method called **getQuote**, which receives a **getQuoteRequest1** message as a parameter and must return a **getQuote-Response** message. Logically, the **getQuote** method receives as a parameter a **String** that represents a company's stock symbol and returns a **float** that represents the stock quote for the company associated with that symbol. Lines 28–47 provide the **binding** information (i.e., instructions on how that Web service is accessed), which indicates that clients can access the Web service via a remote procedure call in the form of a SOAP message over HTTP. Lines 49–58 provide the **service** element that specifies the URL of the Web service.

```
1   <?xml version="1.0" encoding="UTF-8"?>
2   <definitions name="net.xmethods.services.stockquote.StockQuote"
3      targetNamespace="http://www.themindelectric.com/wsdl/
net.xmethods.services.stockquote.StockQuote/"
4      xmlns:tns="http://www.themindelectric.com/wsdl/
net.xmethods.services.stockquote.StockQuote/"
```

Fig. 7.17   WSDL document for the Delayed Stock Quote Web service. (Part 1 of 3.) (Courtesy of Xmethods, Inc.)

```
 5      xmlns:electric="http://www.themindelectric.com/"
 6      xmlns:soap="http://schemas.xmlsoap.org/wsdl/soap/"
 7      xmlns:xsd="http://www.w3.org/2001/XMLSchema"
 8      xmlns:soapenc="http://schemas.xmlsoap.org/soap/encoding/"
 9      xmlns:wsdl="http://schemas.xmlsoap.org/wsdl/"
10      xmlns="http://schemas.xmlsoap.org/wsdl/">
11
12      <message name="getQuoteResponse1">
13          <part name="Result" type="xsd:float" />
14      </message>
15
16      <message name="getQuoteRequest1">
17          <part name="symbol" type="xsd:string" />
18      </message>
19
20      <portType
21          name="net.xmethods.services.stockquote.StockQuotePortType">
22          <operation name="getQuote" parameterOrder="symbol">
23              <input message="tns:getQuoteRequest1" />
24              <output message="tns:getQuoteResponse1" />
25          </operation>
26      </portType>
27
28      <binding
29          name="net.xmethods.services.stockquote.StockQuoteBinding"
30          type="tns:net.xmethods.services.stockquote.StockQuotePort
Type">
31          <soap:binding style="rpc"
32              transport="http://schemas.xmlsoap.org/soap/http" />
33          <operation name="getQuote">
34              <soap:operation
35                  soapAction="urn:xmethods-delayed-quotes#getQuote" />
36              <input>
37                  <soap:body use="encoded"
38                      namespace="urn:xmethods-delayed-quotes"
39                      encodingStyle="http://schemas.xmlsoap.org/soap/
encoding/" />
40              </input>
41              <output>
42                  <soap:body use="encoded"
43                      namespace="urn:xmethods-delayed-quotes"
44                      encodingStyle="http://schemas.xmlsoap.org/soap/
encoding/" />
45              </output>
46          </operation>
47      </binding>
48
49      <service
50          name="net.xmethods.services.stockquote.StockQuoteService">
51          <documentation>
52              net.xmethods.services.stockquote.StockQuote web service
53          </documentation>
```

Fig. 7.17 WSDL document for the Delayed Stock Quote Web service. (Part 2 of 3.)
(Courtesy of Xmethods, Inc.)

```
54          <port name="net.xmethods.services.stockquote.StockQuotePort"
55              binding="tns:net.xmethods.services.stockquote.StockQuote-
Binding">
56              <soap:address location="http://66.28.98.121:9090/soap" />
57          </port>
58      </service>
59  </definitions>
```

Fig. 7.17   WSDL document for the Delayed Stock Quote Web service. (Part 3 of 3.)
(Courtesy of Xmethods, Inc.)

When using a module such as the WASP Developer Advanced module for Forte to build a client that accesses Web services, it is often unnecessary to analyze the WSDL in this much detail. To use an existing WSDL document to create a Web-service client in Forte, do the following:

1. Select **File>New**. In the **Template Chooser**, select **Web Services>Create Web Service** (Fig. 7.18), then press **Next**.

2. Specify the name of the Web Service (e.g., Delayed Stock Quote) in the **Name** field, and specify the package structure (e.g., **com.deitel.jws1.servic-es**) in the **Package** field (Fig. 7.19), then press **Next**.

3. Specify **Internet** as the means by which to download the WSDL document (Fig. 7.20), then press **Next**.

4. Enter the WSDL-document URL (Fig. 7.21), then press **Next**.

5. Select the Web service to invoke (Fig. 7.22). (Only the Delayed Stock Quote Web service exists in this example.) Press **Next**.

6. We will create our own implementation class. Click **Next** when prompted to **Select Implementation Class** (Fig. 7.23).

7. The module uses the WSDL document to fill Web-service properties. Click **Finish** to accept the specified property values (Fig. 7.24).

We now program the interface through which the client interacts with the Delayed Stock Quote Web service. We create interface **Stock** and store it in the **com.deitel.jws1.services** directory (Fig. 7.25). Interface **Stock** provides only one method—**getQuote** (line 9)—which clients should use to access the Delayed Stock Quote Web service. This method should receive as an argument a **String** that indicates a company's stock symbol and should return a **float** that represents the company's current stock value (delayed by 20 minutes). Note that we could have created interface **Stock** manually by analyzing the WSDL document of Fig. 7.17; lines 22–24 specify that interface **Stock** contains only method **getQuote**, which receives a **getQuoteRequest1** (which lines 16–18 define as a **String**) and returns a **getQuoteResponse1** (which lines 12–14 define as a **float**). However, creating interfaces manually by analyzing WSDL documents is a time-consuming and error-prone process, so using a tool that provides automatic interface generation is usually preferable to, and more efficient than, coding interfaces manually.

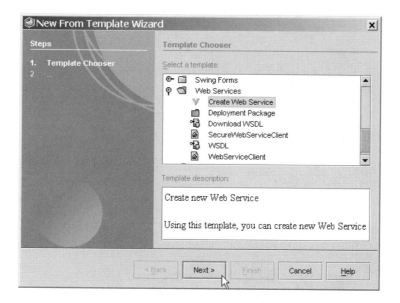

Fig. 7.18   Creating a Web service from a remote WSDL document using the **WASP Developer Advanced** module (Step 1). Courtesy of Systinet. Reproduced with permission by Sun Microsystems, Inc.© Copyright 2002. Sun Microsystems, Inc. All Rights Reserved.

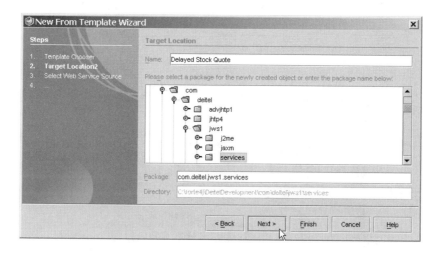

Fig. 7.19   Creating a Web service from a remote WSDL document using the **WASP Developer Advanced** module (Step 2). Courtesy of Systinet. Reproduced with permission by Sun Microsystems, Inc.© Copyright 2002. Sun Microsystems, Inc. All Rights Reserved.

Fig. 7.20   Creating a Web service from a remote WSDL document using the **WASP Developer Advanced** module (Step 3). Courtesy of Systinet. Reproduced with permission by Sun Microsystems, Inc.© Copyright 2002. Sun Microsystems, Inc. All Rights Reserved.

Fig. 7.21   Creating a Web service from a remote WSDL document using the **WASP Developer Advanced** module (Step 4). Courtesy of Systinet. Reproduced with permission by Sun Microsystems, Inc.© Copyright 2002. Sun Microsystems, Inc. All Rights Reserved.

Fig. 7.22   Creating a Web service from a remote WSDL document using the **WASP Developer Advanced** module (Step 5). Courtesy of Systinet. Reproduced with permission by Sun Microsystems, Inc.© Copyright 2002. Sun Microsystems, Inc. All Rights Reserved.

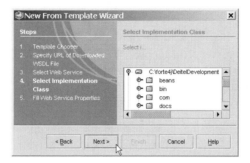

Fig. 7.23 Creating a Web service from a remote WSDL document using the **WASP Developer Advanced** module (Step 6). Courtesy of Systinet. Reproduced with permission by Sun Microsystems, Inc.© Copyright 2002. Sun Microsystems, Inc. All Rights Reserved.

Fig. 7.24 Creating a Web service from a remote WSDL document using the **WASP Developer Advanced** module (Step 7). Courtesy of Systinet. Reproduced with permission by Sun Microsystems, Inc.© Copyright 2002. Sun Microsystems, Inc. All Rights Reserved.

```
1   // Fig. 7.25: Stock.java.
2   // Stock is the interface through which clients can invoke the
3   // Delayed Stock Quote Web service.
4   package com.deitel.jws1.services;
5
6   public interface Stock {
7
8      // service to receive stock quote for associated stock symbol
9      float getQuote( String symbol );
10  }
```

Fig. 7.25 **Stock** serves as an interface for clients to access the Delayed Stock Quote Web service.

We create class **StockClient** (Fig. 7.26)—the client that uses a WSDL document to access the Delayed Stock Quote Web service—in the same manner as we created **Book-TitleClient** (Fig. 7.14). Lines 14–16 import the WASP APIs that enable the client to communicate with the server that exposes the Delayed Stock Quote service. Line 19 imports interface **Stock**, which **StockClient** uses to communicate (via the remote server) with the Delayed Stock Quote Web service.

StockClient has three central GUI elements:

- A **JLabel** (line 44) that displays the value of a company's stock that **Stock-Client** receives from the Delayed Stock Quote service;

- A **JComboBox** (lines 48–53) that enables the user to select from a list of company stock symbols.

- A **JButton** (lines 56–90) that, when clicked, notifies the remote server to invoke method **getQuote** from the Delayed Stock Quote service.

```
1   // Fig. 7.26: StockClient.java.
2   // StockClient uses the WASP API for Java and an online WSDL
3   // document to access a Web service that generates stock quotes.
4   package com.deitel.jws1.wsdl.client;
5
6   // Java core packages
7   import java.awt.*;
8   import java.awt.event.*;
9
10  // Java extension packages
11  import javax.swing.*;
12
13  // WASP packages
14  import org.idoox.webservice.client.WebServiceLookup;
15  import org.idoox.webservice.client.WebServiceLookupException;
16  import org.idoox.wasp.Context;
17
18  // Deitel packages
19  import com.deitel.jws1.services.Stock;
20
21  public class StockClient extends JFrame {
22
23     private final static int FRAME_WIDTH = 400;
24     private final static int FRAME_HEIGHT = 100;
25
26     // interface for accessing Delayed Stock Quote Web service
27     private Stock service;
28
29     // URL of Web service
30     private final static String SERVICE_URL =
31        "http://66.28.98.121:9090/soap";
32
```

Fig. 7.26 **StockClient** uses the WASP APIs and an online WSDL document to invoke the Delayed Stock Quote Web service. (Part 1 of 3.)

```
33        // WSDL-document URL
34        private final static String WSDL_URL =
35           "http://services.xmethods.net/soap/" +
36           "urn:xmethods-delayed-quotes.wsdl";
37
38        public StockClient( String title )
39        {
40           super( title );
41           getContentPane().setLayout( new GridLayout( 2, 2 ) );
42
43           // JLabel to display stock quote after invoking Web service
44           final JLabel resultsLabel = new JLabel();
45
46           // JComboBox for selecting company from which to receive
47           // associated stock quote
48           final JComboBox symbolComboBox = new JComboBox();
49           symbolComboBox.addItem( "SUNW" );
50           symbolComboBox.addItem( "MSFT" );
51           symbolComboBox.addItem( "INTL" );
52           symbolComboBox.addItem( "IBM" );
53           symbolComboBox.addItem( "CSCO" );
54
55           // JButton invokes remote Web Service
56           JButton serviceButton = new JButton( "Get Stock Quote" );
57           serviceButton.addActionListener(
58              new ActionListener() {
59
60                 // invoked when user presses JButton
61                 public void actionPerformed( ActionEvent event )
62                 {
63                    // use WASP APIs to access Web service
64                    try {
65
66                       // get object that performs Web-service lookup
67                       WebServiceLookup serviceLookup =
68                          ( WebServiceLookup ) Context.getInstance(
69                             Context.WEBSERVICE_LOOKUP );
70
71                       // lookup Web service from registry
72                       service = ( Stock ) serviceLookup.lookup(
73                          WSDL_URL, Stock.class, SERVICE_URL );
74
75                       // invoke Web service to receive stock quote
76                       float quote = service.getQuote(
77                          ( String ) symbolComboBox.getSelectedItem() );
78
79                       resultsLabel.setText( "Stock Quote: " +
80                          Float.toString( quote ) );
81                    }
82
```

Fig. 7.26 **StockClient** uses the WASP APIs and an online WSDL document to invoke the Delayed Stock Quote Web service. (Part 2 of 3.)

```
83                   // handle exception if unable to find Web service
84                   catch ( WebServiceLookupException exception ) {
85                      exception.printStackTrace();
86                   }
87
88              } // end method actionPerformed
89           }
90        );
91
92        // store JLabel, JComboBox and JButton JFrame
93        getContentPane().add( new JLabel( "Select company:" ) );
94        getContentPane().add( symbolComboBox );
95        getContentPane().add( resultsLabel );
96        getContentPane().add( serviceButton );
97
98     } // end constructor
99
100    // return StockClient frame size
101    public Dimension getPreferredSize()
102    {
103       return new Dimension( FRAME_WIDTH, FRAME_HEIGHT );
104    }
105
106    // instantiate StockClient GUI
107    public static void main( String args[] )
108    {
109       StockClient client =
110          new StockClient( "Stock Quote Service" );
111       client.setDefaultCloseOperation( EXIT_ON_CLOSE );
112       client.pack();
113       client.setVisible( true );
114    }
115
116 } // end class StockClient
```

Fig. 7.26 StockClient uses the WASP APIs and an online WSDL document to invoke the Delayed Stock Quote Web service. (Part 3 of 3.)

When the user clicks the **JButton**, method **actionPerformed** (lines 61–88) uses the WASP APIs to invoke the Web service. The WASP API objects use the WSDL document in Fig. 7.17 to invoke the service. Lines 67–73 use a **WebServiceLookup** to obtain a remote reference to the **Stock** object. The lookup operation requires the URLs of the **Stock** object and the WSDL document, which are defined in lines 30–31 and 34–36, respectively. The Delayed Stock Quote service's associated WSDL document contains the Web-service URL (Fig. 7.17, line 56), and the **Delayed Stock Quote** information page (Fig. 7.16) contains the WSDL-document URL.

Lines 76–77 pass the company stock symbol that the user specified from the **JComboBox** to method **getQuote** on the remote **Stock** object. If the Web-service invocation was successful, the Web service returns a **float** that represents the value of the stock associated with that company. Lines 79–80 display the result in the **JLabel**.

In this chapter, we introduced the Web Services Description Language by discussing the syntax and elements of the language. We showed how to generate WSDL documents via a WSDL-generation tool integrated in Forte for Java 3.0. We also built clients that invoke Web services and discussed how a WSDL document informs a client of available Web services. In Chapter 8, Universal Description, Discovery and Integration, we discuss how to publish WSDL documents to, and retrieve WSDL documents from, a *registry*, which is a lookup service for Web services.

7.8 Summary

Web Services Description Language (WSDL) enables applications to determine the capabilities of Web services. Most Web services are accompanied by a WSDL document, which contains information on a specific Web service. This document specifies information such as the Web service that an application has made available, the functionality that the Web service provides, the address (URLs) of the service, and how clients transfer messages between the service.

Before WSDL existed, Web services development environments used proprietary methods to describe available Web services. Microsoft and IBM then collaborated to create a language that describes Web services in a standard, structured way. The technologies of Microsoft's *SOAP Contract Language (SCL)* and IBM's *Network Accessible Service Specification Language (NASSL)* were combined to form the basis of WSDL.

When a Web service is published, a Web service administrator can post a link to the Web service's WSDL document in an XML registry or other WSDL repository. The WSDL document then is available when an application, such as a SOAP client, searches a registry to locate a Web service. A client accesses the WSDL document contained in the XML registry to acquire information about the Web service and to create a SOAP message with the appropriate structure to communicate with the service. Then, using the information in the WSDL document, the client invokes the Web service.

The **definitions** element is the root element of a WSDL document. This element contains all the other elements that store the information on the Web service and defines several namespaces that the WSDL document can use.

The **message** element represents the variables that clients and Web services transfer between each other. These variables are either the arguments or the return types for the Web service's remote methods. A **message** element must contain a **part** element, which specifies the name and data type of the exchanged message.

It seems logical that the **message** elements should represent the messages that the client receives from, and sends to, the Web service. However, **message** element declares only the messages that will be used, but does not specify exactly how the input and output messages associate with an operation. WSDL provides the **portType** element to accomplish this task.

The **portType** element contains **operation** elements, which map the messages defined in the WSDL **message** elements to the actual services. Each **operation** element contains an **input** and **output** element, each of which associates a **message** element to a method parameter or method return type, respectively.

The **binding** element specify how the client and Web service should send messages to one another. Each **binding** element contains another **binding** element (a WSDL extension for SOAP) that specifies the protocol by which clients access the Web service. The second **binding** element is prefixed by the URI associated with that protocol. A WSDL document allows us to use several protocols, such as SOAP, MIME and plain HTTP (i.e., without using SOAP).

The **service** element specifies the URL that clients must access to invoke the Web service. The **service** element contains several **port** elements, each of which contains a URL for a unique binding.

The manual creation of a WSDL document is often unnecessary, because most Web-service-deployment environments generate WSDL documents automatically. The **WASP Developer Advanced 3.0.1—version 3.1.1** module includes a toolkit that generates WSDL documents while creating and deploying Web services. This module also includes a server that hosts Web services.

WORKS CITED

1. "UDDI Advances with Web Services Description Language," 29 September 2000 **<www.advisor.com/Articles.nsf/aid/SMITT31>**

2. P. Cauldwell, et al. *Professional XML Web Services* (Birmingham, UK: Wrox Press, 2001) 110.

UDDI, Discovery and Web Services Registries

Objectives

- To discuss Web services discovery.
- To explain how UDDI enables client applications to locate Web services.
- To overview the relationship among SOAP, UDDI and WSDL.
- To introduce the UDDI Business Registry, how it is organized and how users can search its contents.
- To discuss how organizations or partner businesses can create private UDDI registries.
- To introduce alternative discovery technologies, such as ebXML and WS-Inspection.

The secret of all those who make discoveries is that they regard nothing as impossible.
Justus Liebig

The people who get on in this world are the people who get up and look for the circumstances they want, and, if they can't find them, make them.
George Bernard Shaw

8.1 Introduction

As the popularity of the World Wide Web surged in the 1990s, many organizations began to conduct business on the Internet. To facilitate e-commerce, companies needed a way to locate one another and exchange information electronically. Organizations responded by creating their own methods of publishing business-related data on the Web and offering third parties access to the data. However, adding new business customers and suppliers to these proprietary systems often was inefficient, difficult and time-consuming.[1] To address this problem, IBM, Microsoft and Ariba developed *Universal Description, Discovery and Integration (UDDI)*, a specification that defines registries in which businesses can publish information about themselves and the services they provide. Service consumers can use UDDI registries to locate general and technical information about various service providers. With this information, consumers can initiate business transactions, form partnerships and purchase services.

In this chapter, we overview UDDI and UDDI registries. We explain how registries operate, the kinds of data they store and how users can search their contents. We also introduce alternative registry and discovery technologies, including *electronic business XML (ebXML)* and *Web Services Inspection (WS-Inspection)*. The widespread adoption of UDDI and other discovery mechanisms will enable service requestors to find and learn about specific Web services—which is key to the ultimate success of Web service initiatives.

8.2 Discovery

Discovery is the process of locating Web services through registries. Web services registries are repositories containing documents that describe business data. Web services registries also provide features such as search capabilities and programmatic access to remote applications. By using a registry, an organization that wishes to employ a Web service to process credit-card payments, for example, can locate all publicly available services that provide the necessary functionality. The organization can compare the services, then make an educated decision as to which service best fits the organization's needs.

Discovery can be categorized into *direct discovery* and *indirect discovery*. Direct discovery is the process of obtaining data from a registry maintained by the service provider. Obtaining data through direct discovery improves the likelihood that data is accurate, because the organization providing the information also operates the Web service. With indirect discovery, an organization obtains data through a third-party registry. Such data might not be as accurate, because service providers might not update information in third-party registries as frequently. When performing indirect discovery, organizations must pose the question: How often do third-party registries interact with service providers to ensure that the data is still accurate? Although indirect discovery has its drawbacks, it allows companies to evaluate Web services from various providers before committing to use a particular service.[2]

8.3 SOAP, UDDI and WSDL

As we described in previous chapters, SOAP, WSDL and UDDI are the core technologies used in Web services interactions. These technologies enable communication among applications in a manner that is independent of specific programming languages, operating systems and hardware platforms. SOAP provides a communication mechanism between Web services and other applications, WSDL offers a uniform method of describing Web services to other programs and UDDI enables the creation of searchable Web services registries. When deployed together, these technologies allow developers to package applications as services, publish the services on the Web and advertise the services to developers and applications.

Applications typically communicate with Web services via a SOAP messaging framework. SOAP messages encapsulate programmatic instructions that are transported to a SOAP server, which processes the messages and invokes the targeted Web services. The WSDL document associated with a particular Web service informs client applications how to format a SOAP message to send to that service. For more information on SOAP and WSDL, review Chapter 6, SOAP-Based Web Services Platforms and Chapter 7, Web Services Description Language.

Figure 8.1 depicts the general architecture in which Web services operate. The UDDI registry stores the locations of WSDL documents. To publish a Web service, a service provider registers the service's WSDL document with the UDDI registry. A service consumer discovers the service from the UDDI registry. Once the service consumer knows how to access the Web service, the consumer can communicate with the Web service directly via SOAP messages.

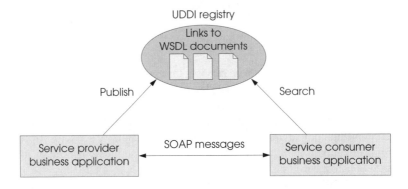

Fig. 8.1   Web services architecture.

8.4 Universal Description, Discovery and Integration (UDDI)

In September 2000, the UDDI project—led by IBM, Microsoft and Ariba—released Version 1.0 of the UDDI specification. This specification defines a framework for centralized registries that facilitate the storage, discovery and exchange of information about businesses and their Web services.[3] UDDI is used in the publicly accessible *UDDI Business Registry (UBR)* maintained by Microsoft, IBM, Hewlett-Packard and SAP. Companies also can implement UDDI in private registries, which are accessible only to authorized parties, such as a company's employees, business partners and suppliers.

In June 2001, the UDDI project released a beta specification of UDDI Version 2.0, which improves on several features of the original specification. One enhancement offers advanced searching capabilities, such as the ability to search using the wildcard character (**%**). UDDI Version 2.0 also increases the global scope of UDDI registries in that businesses can provide company and product descriptions in various languages, such as Chinese and French. Another new feature enables an organization to provide data regarding its infrastructure, such as details about departments (sales, marketing, research and development, etc.), partners and affiliates. In addition, UDDI Version 2.0 offers support for industry-specific identifiers, such as those of the *Standard Industrial Classification (SIC)* system, which assigns unique numerical identifiers to industries.[4] For example, 2621 represents Paper Mills, and 7371 represents Computer Programming Services.[5]

UDDI Version 2.0 is a beta implementation, so not all applications support it. This is because beta implementations are likely to contain bugs, which could affect the performance of some applications.[6] Furthermore, data stored using the beta implementation of a registry might be lost when the data is migrated to the final version.[7] [*Note*: The UDDI project is developing UDDI Version 3.0. After releasing Version 3.0, the UDDI project plans to submit the UDDI specification to a standards organization.][8]

At the time of this writing, more than 300 companies belong to the UDDI community.[9] These companies, known as community members, are committed to the enhancement, evolution and world-wide acceptance of the UDDI registry. Community members include many large and influential organizations, such as American Express, Boeing, Fujitsu, Hitachi and Sun Microsystems. A complete list of community members can be found at **www.uddi.org**.[10]

8.4.1 Operator Nodes and Registrars

An *operator node* is an organization that hosts an implementation of the *UDDI Business Registry (UBR)*. Four operator nodes—Hewlett-Packard, IBM, Microsoft and SAP—host beta implementations of the UBR that adhere to the UDDI Version 2.0, and two operator nodes—IBM and Microsoft—host implementations of the UBR that adhere to the UDDI Version 1.0. A company needs to register with only one operator node to be listed in the UBR. This is because the UBR is based on the "register once, publish everywhere" principle, which states that information contained in one registry is replicated in the other registries. *Replication* is the process of updating records so that all instances of those records are identical. Thus, when a company registers with one operator node (known as a *custodian*), the company's data appears in the other three registries, as well.[11] Although data is not replicated instantaneously, the operator nodes synchronize their data at least every 12 hours.[12]

At the time of this writing, only the UBR implementations that adhere to UDDI Version 1.0 support replication. However, the UBR implementations that adhere to UDDI Version 2.0 are expected to support replication by fall 2002. We list the URLs of the four operator nodes in the Internet and Web Resources section at the end of this chapter. [*Note*: The UDDI project announced that NTT Communications of Tokyo, Japan, will become an operator node in 2002.][13]

Although replication ensures that all four UBRs contain identical information, a company can update its information only through its custodian. This is because the *UDDI Version 2.0 API Specification* does not provide a protocol for reconciling disparate or duplicate data. Limiting companies to interaction with only one operator node prevents users from entering multiple versions of data in different operator nodes.[14]

Alternatively, companies can publish information in the UBR through a *registrar*—an organization that assists companies in creating data, such as business and service descriptions, to be stored in UDDI registries.[15] Note that registrars are not operator nodes, because registrars do not host implementations of the UDDI registry. A complete list of the registrars can be found at **www.uddi.org**.

8.4.2 Advantages of Registering

Registering in the UBR offers advantages to both service providers and service consumers. For service providers, the UBR is an effective method of advertising Web services. Because the UBR can be accessed from anywhere, service providers gain global visibility, enabling them to communicate and form alliances with organizations located throughout the world. This kind of worldwide exposure helps service providers expand their markets.[16]

For service consumers, the UBR saves time and simplifies the process of using Web services. The UBR stores technical details about Web services, so service consumers do not have to spend time locating service-related information, such as how to communicate with a particular Web service. By using the UBR, service consumers can integrate their applications with remote services more quickly and efficiently.[17]

The UBR also can reduce costs for service providers and service consumers. Service providers can advertise their businesses and services for free, and service consumers can locate compatible Web services for free. Without the UBR, organizations might have to pay fees to advertise and find Web services. [*Note*: Some service providers listed in the UBR charge consumers that access their Web services.][18]

8.5 Role of UDDI in Web Services

As stated previously, UDDI registries contain general and technical information about businesses and their Web services. Vendors often compare the UBR's structure to that of a phone book. In this section, we discuss the components of the UBR's phone-book structure—*white pages*, *yellow pages* and *green pages*.[19] We overview the schema for the UDDI information model, which specifies the XML elements and attributes used to describe a Web service. We also explain the UDDI publishing and inquiry APIs, which define rules for posting and searching registry content, respectively.

The UBR mainly supports indirect discovery, because it is hosted by four intermediaries. However, UDDI also can support direct discovery in private registries. This is because private registries usually are implemented by specific organizations and describe only services offered by those organizations.

8.5.1 Levels of UDDI

The UBR can be categorized into white pages, yellow pages and green pages. The white pages contain general information about a company, such as its name, address, contact information and identifiers. Identifiers are values (alphabetic or numeric) that uniquely distinguish companies. Examples of identifiers are Dun & Bradstreet's *D-U-N-S® (Data Universal Numbering System)* classifications, which are nine-digit numbers assigned to businesses.[20]

The yellow pages divide companies into various categories on the basis of their products or services. For example, a software company might be categorized under computer software or software engineering. The yellow pages allow registry users to search for companies or services that fit a particular category (such as sales, travel or books).[21]

The green pages contain technical information about a company's products, services and Web services. This data allows a service client to *bind* (i.e., establish a communication channel) to a Web service, because the information defines how to invoke the service.[22] The green pages usually include references to services' WSDL documents, which contain information on how to interact with Web services.[23]

8.5.2 Information Models in UDDI[1]

The *UDDI Version 2.0 Data Structure Reference* (available at **www.uddi.org**) stipulates that to transact business, a client company needs access to certain information about a provider's Web service. This information, known collectively as the *UDDI information model*, includes the following five components: business information, business-service information, binding information, service-specification information and publisher-assertion information. In this section, we discuss the five components of the UDDI information model.

Each component of the UDDI information model resides within a *data structure* that consists of XML elements and attributes. These XML elements and attributes describe the components of the information model. The XML representation of the UDDI information model is used when interfacing with a UDDI registry. Because there are five components, there exist five interrelated data structures. Figure 8.2 illustrates the relationships among the UDDI information model's five data-structure types.

---

1. Technical information in this section is based primarily on "UDDI Version 2.0 Data Structure Reference," 8 June 2001 <**www.uddi.org/pubs/DataStructure-V2.00-Open-20010608.pdf**>.

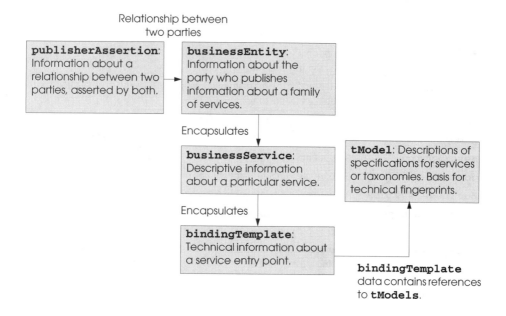

Fig. 8.2   UDDI information model. (Courtesy of UDDI.)

The **_businessEntity_** _structure_ encapsulates a business's general information, such as its name, address and contact information. This structure references the **_busi-nessService_** _structure_, which describes different types of services offered by the company. Technical information about these services resides in the **_bindingTemplate_** _structure_, which contains references to **_tModel_** _structures_. A **tModel** structure contains information on how to interact with the Web services. The **_publisherAssertions_** _structure_ describes the relationships (e.g., partnerships) between two business entities.

The _business information_ component corresponds to the UDDI white and yellow pages in that it contains general data about a business and the products and services offered by that business. The business information resides in the **businessEntity** _top-level struc-ture_, which categorizes businesses by their unique identifiers. In this context, a top-level structure encapsulates elements, attributes and other structures that describe a business and its Web services. Figure 8.3 summarizes the elements and attributes of the **businessEn-tity** structure.

Entity	Description
businessKey	A required attribute that contains a unique hexadecimal identifier for the business. The identifier is assigned by the custodian upon registration.

Fig. 8.3   **businessEntity** attributes and child elements. (Part 1 of 2.)

Entity	Description
authorizedName	An optional attribute that contains the name of the person who published the information.
operator	An optional attribute that contains the name of the operator node with which the business registered.
discoveryURLs	An optional element that contains URLs to discovery documents.
name	A required element that contains the name of the business.
description	An optional element that contains a brief description of the business.
contacts	An optional element that contains the business's contact information.
businessServices	An optional element that lists the services offered by the business.
identifierBag	An optional element that contains a list of unique identifiers (D-U-N-S® number, stock symbol, etc.) associated with the business.
categoryBag	An optional element that contains a list of industry, product or geographic classifications.

Fig. 8.3   **businessEntity** attributes and child elements. (Part 2 of 2.)

In this structure, **businessKey** is a required attribute that uniquely identifies a business. The custodian assigns a unique identifier to each **businessEntity** structure upon registration. Unique identifiers are referred to as *Universally Unique Identifiers (UUIDs)* and usually consist of hexadecimal values. The **businessServices** element contains zero or more references to the descriptions of services offered by an organization. This element references the **businessService** structure.

The *business service information* component corresponds to the UDDI green pages in that it contains technical data about the products and services offered by a particular business. The business service information resides in the ***businessService*** structure. Figure 8.4 summarizes the elements of **businessService**. Each **businessService** structure is identified uniquely by two UUIDs—**serviceKey** and **businessKey**. The required **bindingTemplates** structure contains the technical information about a Web service. The **bindingTemplates** structure includes zero or more references to the **bindingTemplate** structure, which contains the binding information.

Entity	Description
serviceKey	A required attribute that contains a unique, hexadecimal identifier for a service.
businessKey	An attribute that references the **businessKey** of the **businessEntity** structure.
name	A required element that contains the name(s) of a service.
description	An optional element that contains a brief description of a service.

Fig. 8.4   **businessService** attributes child elements. (Part 1 of 2.)

Entity	Description
bindingTemplates	A required structure that contains technical information about a service.
categoryBag	An optional element that contains a list of industry, product or geographic classifications.

Fig. 8.4 **businessService** attributes child elements. (Part 2 of 2.)

The *binding information* component also corresponds to the green pages in that it contains technical information pertaining to a Web service. This information specifies how clients can connect to a particular Web service. Figure 8.5 summarizes the elements and attributes of the **bindingTemplate** structure.

Attribute **bindingKey** is a UUID assigned to each **bindingTemplate** structure by the custodian. The **tModelInstanceDetails** structure contains references to one or more **tModelInstanceInfo** structures, which contain the elements and attributes that describe the service-specification information, or "blueprints," of a Web service. Structure **tModelInstanceInfo** references the **tModel** structure.

Entity	Description
bindingKey	A required attribute that contains a unique hexadecimal identifier. The identifier is assigned by the operator node upon registration.
serviceKey	An attribute that references the **serviceKey** of the **businessService** element. This attribute is required if the **bindingTemplate** structure is not contained in a fully qualified parent that contains another **serviceKey**.
description	An optional element that contains brief description(s) of Web service(s).
accessPoint	An element that states where to access a Web service. Valid **accessPoint** types include **mailto**, **http**, **https**, **ftp**, **fax**, **phone** and **other**. This element is required if **hostingRedirector** is not specified.
hostingRedirector	An element that contains a link to another **bindingTemplate** structure, which contains the description for a particular service. This element is required if **accessPoint** is not specified.
tModelInstanceDetails	A required structure that contains **tModelInstanceInfo** elements, which are "blueprints" of Web services. This structure specifies how to access a Web service.

Fig. 8.5 **bindingTemplate** attributes and child elements.

Whereas the binding information specifies where to access a Web service, the *service-specification information* component describes how to interact with the Web service. The service-specification information resides in the **tModel** structure, summarized in Fig. 8.6. The **tModel**, or *Service Type Registrations*, structure contains information that allows service consumers to use a service provider's Web service.[24]

In the **tModel** structure, the **tModelKey** is a UUID assigned to the structure. The custodian assigns the value to the **tModelKey**. Structure **overviewDoc** references documentation that provides information or instructions about the Web service. Usually, **overviewDoc** references WSDL documents, which contain technical ("blueprint") information about Web services. This "blueprint" information includes the parameters that a Web service receives, the data formats it accepts (**.dat**,**.txt**, etc.) and other application-specific information. This information allows programmers to determine whether a Web service is compatible with their programs.

The *publisher-assertion information* component indicates a relationship between two companies. To instantiate the relationship, both parties must agree to the relationship by declaring identical assertions (i.e., identical statements that specify a mutual relationship). A relationship is valid only when both parties reciprocate the assertions. The publisher assertion information resides in the **publisherAssertion** structure. Figure 8.7 summarizes the elements of the **publisherAssertion** structure.

Publisher-assertion information, a new feature of Version 2.0, allows organizations to acknowledge *parent-child*, *peer-peer* and *identity* relationships. A parent-child relationship indicates that one organization owns another, smaller organization (i.e., the organization identified in the **fromKey** owns the organization identified in the **toKey**). A peer-peer relationship states that the organizations identified in the **fromKey** and the **toKey** are partners or affiliates. An identity relationship states that the organization identified in the **fromKey** is the same as the organization identified in the **toKey**. Identity relationships typically are used to assert an organization's various divisions, units and departments.[25]

Entity	Descriptions
tModelKey	A required attribute that uniquely identifies the **tModel**. The identifier is assigned by the custodian upon registration.
authorizedName	An optional attribute that contains the name of the individual who published the information.
operator	An optional attribute that contains the name of the custodian.
name	A required element that contains a descriptive identifier for the **tModel**. Service consumers can use **name** to perform a search for a given **tModel**.
description	An optional element that describes the **tModel**.
overviewDoc	An optional element that redirects users to additional references, usually WSDL documents.

Fig. 8.6   **tModel** attributes and child elements. (Part 1 of 2.)

Entity	Descriptions
identifierBag	An optional element that contains a list of unique identifiers (e.g., D-U-N-S® number, stock symbol) associated with the business.
categoryBag	An optional element that contains a list of industry, product or geographic classifications.

Fig. 8.6 **tModel** attributes and child elements. (Part 2 of 2.)

Entity	Description
fromKey	A required element that uniquely identifies the business that instantiates the relationship.
toKey	A required element that uniquely identifies the business that accepts the relationship.
keyedReference	A required element that identifies the type of relationship.

Fig. 8.7 **publisherAssertion** child elements.

By providing publisher-assertion capabilities, UDDI allows large corporations to describe aspects of their businesses—such as divisions, departments, partners, affiliates and subsidiaries—to users of the UBR. This information is beneficial to service consumers who want to know how business A relates to business B before accessing the services of either business.

8.5.3 UDDI Publishing and Inquiry APIs

The UDDI Version 2.0 API Specification overviews the publishing and inquiry APIs for creating and searching registry content. The *publishing API* supports the *publish* operation, which enables companies to post and update information in the UDDI registry. Access to the publishing API is restricted, and the UDDI project requires that operator nodes implement an authentication protocol that verifies the identity of the individual or organization creating or updating the information. The publishing API consists of commands that service providers can use to create and update information. Access to the publishing API commands is available only via *HTTPS* (i.e., a variant of HTTP that uses Secure Sockets Layer to establish security).[26] For more information regarding HTTPS and Secure Sockets Layer, see Chapter 12, Computer and Internet Security, and Chapter 13, Web Services Security.

The *inquiry API* supports the *find* operation, which enables service consumers to browse the registry for service providers that offer a certain service or type of service. Anyone can use the inquiry API to perform queries on the UBR. The inquiry API supports three query patterns—browse, drill-down and invocation. The *browse pattern*, which supports the five information-model structures discussed in the previous section, allows service consumers to perform broad searches for businesses, services, templates or **tModel**s.

This query pattern returns the general, overview information (identification key, name and description) pertaining to the business, service, template or **tModel**.[27]

To obtain a more detailed description of a business, service, template or **tModel**, the inquiry API provides the *drill-down pattern*. This pattern typically is used in conjunction with the browse pattern, because it requires an identification key (obtained during the browse pattern) to retrieve the necessary information. The identification key is passed as an argument in a drill-down pattern. With the drill-down pattern, users can obtain technical information, such as integration capabilities and scalability.[28]

The *invocation pattern* queries the **bindingTemplate** structure, which contains information that programmers need to access a particular Web service. Because the location of a Web service might change, the invocation pattern searches the **bindingTemplate** structure for the service's current location. The access information always resides in the **bindingTemplate** structure; therefore, service consumers typically use automated tools that query the structure for the access information.[29]

After service consumers discover compatible Web services, the consumers must connect to, and communicate with, the computing systems of other businesses. The process of connecting to, and communicating with, a Web service is referred to as binding.[30]

8.6 UDDI Registries

As we stated previously, UDDI can be supported on both public and private registries. The UDDI Business Registry (UBR) is a free, public registry that can be accessed by individuals or businesses. Organizations that want to restrict access to their services can implement private registries, which impose additional security measures to safeguard against unauthorized access. In this section, we discuss the UBR and private registries in detail.

8.6.1 UDDI Business Registry

The UBR, which contains information about companies and their technical capabilities, allows service providers to organize and describe Web services in a central location. Service consumers can browse this registry to find information about businesses and Web services.[31] To post information in the UBR, businesses need to register with the UDDI project. However, any individual or business can perform searches on the UBR without registering.[32]

The UBR usually is referred to as a *Public Cloud*, because the "UDDI Business Registry" consists of several registries owned and maintained by public operator nodes. Although multiple organizations host implementations of the UBR, data entered in one registry is replicated in the other registries. The replication of data is guaranteed, because the operator nodes are governed by the *Operator's Council*, a committee that consists of the current operator nodes. The Operator's Council governs the UDDI specifications and quality-of-service (QoS) issues.[33] The list of companies that host public registries is provided at **www.uddi.org**.

Figure 8.8 depicts the home page for the UDDI project (**www.uddi.org**). From this Web site, users can register for, and search, the UBR. To register and publish information in the UBR, select the **Register** tab. Clicking this tab redirects the user to a page that lists the operator nodes for both Version 1.0 and Version 2.0 UDDI implementations. To register in the UBR, select an operator node and click **Go**. Then, complete the required information.

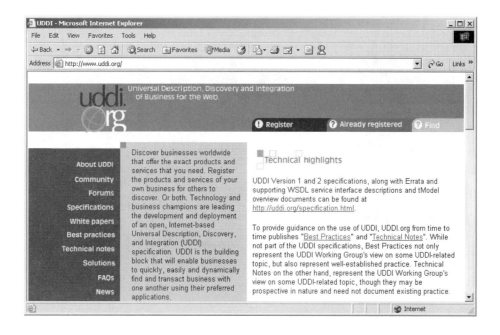

Fig. 8.8 UDDI home page. (Courtesy of UDDI.)

To search the UDDI registry for a specific Web service, select the **Find** tab. Clicking this tab redirects the user to a page that lists the operator nodes for both Version 1.0 and Version 2.0 (Fig. 8.9). To perform a search, the user selects an operator node and clicks **Go**. For demonstration purposes, we perform a search using IBM's implementation of the UBR Version 1.0 registry.

Figure 8.10 depicts the IBM **UDDI Business Registry** Web site. This site allows the user to perform searches on the basis of a **Business**, a **Service** or a **Service Type**. A search performed on a **Business** returns businesses whose names start with a particular word. Figure 8.11 demonstrates performing a **Business** search for companies whose names begin with **Books**.

Figure 8.12 illustrates the results of the search. From the results page, users can view a service provider's general information—the `businessEntity` information—by selecting a link listed under the **Business Name** column. Potential service consumers can use this information to learn about and compare service providers.

Performing a search using **Service** returns products or services that start with a specific word. In our example, we perform a search on products/services that start with the word **Books** (Fig. 8.13). From the results page, users can view the `businessService` and `bindingTemplate` information by selecting a link listed under the **Service Name** column. Potential service consumers can use this information to review descriptions of Web services.

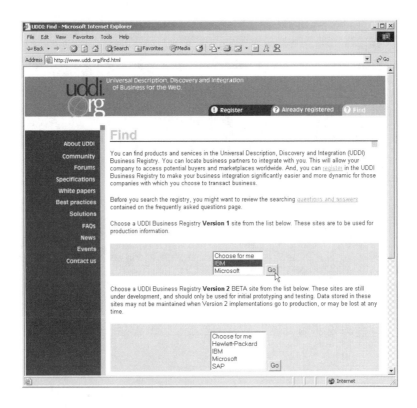

Fig. 8.9   Operator node selected. (Courtesy of UDDI.)

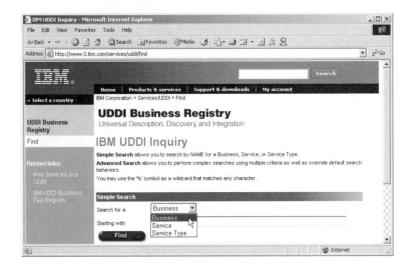

Fig. 8.10   **UDDI Business Registry** site hosted by IBM. (Courtesy of IBM Corporation.)

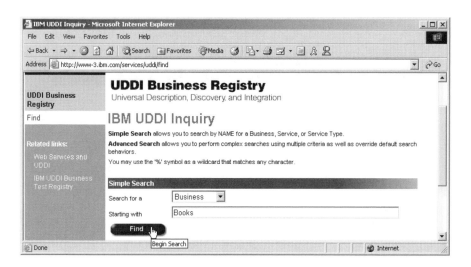

Fig. 8.11   UDDI registry used to perform a **Business** search. (Courtesy of IBM Corporation.)

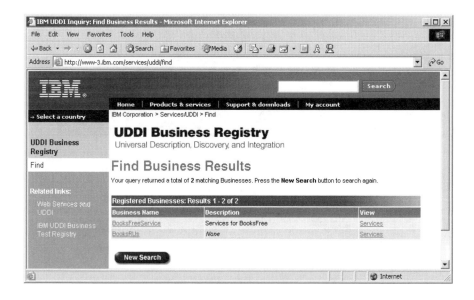

Fig. 8.12   **Business** results for search word **Books**. (Courtesy of IBM Corporation.)

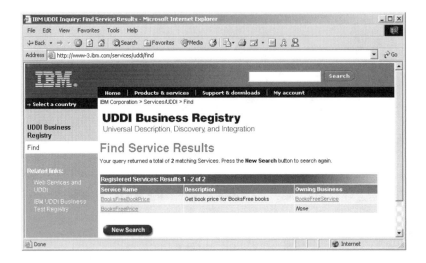

Fig. 8.13   **Service** results for search word **Books**. (Courtesy of IBM Corporation.)

Performing a search using **Service Type** returns the names of businesses that offer a service that contains a specific word. In our example, we perform a search on products/services that contain the word **Books** (Fig. 8.14). From the results page, users can view the `tModel` information by selecting a link listed under the **Service Type Name** column. This information allows users to review technical descriptions of Web services. With the information provided by the UBR, service consumers can discover, connect to and communicate with hundreds of Web services.

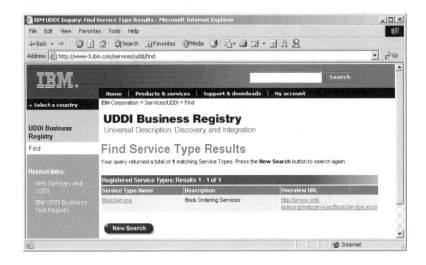

Fig. 8.14   **Service Type** results for search word **Books**. (Courtesy of IBM Corporation.)

8.6.2 Private Registries

The UBR is accessible to the general public, which means that anyone can search the UBR to discover a Web service. However, many organizations might want to limit access to their Web services. Restricting access to services can reduce concerns regarding service-level agreements and security.

Organizations that are uncomfortable exposing services in a public forum can implement *private registries*, access to which is restricted to certain parties (often the employees, partners and affiliates of a particular company). Usually, private registries contain additional security features to ensure data integrity and to safeguard against unauthorized access. Many companies develop private registries to provide personalized services for clients. To support the cost and maintenance of personalized services, most companies charge fees to use private registries.[34]

Companies are adopting private registries more quickly than public registries. This is partly because most organizations want to experiment with Web services by deploying them internally before offering publicly accessible Web services.[35] Another reason for the popularity of private registries is that organizations can use private registries to locate services offered by their own departments or by their partners. Web services accessible only within an organization or group of trusted partners can be used to expedite software-development projects and to integrate applications among departments or partners. According to Gartner, over 75 percent of Web services will reside in private registries by 2005.[36]

There are four varieties of private registries: *e-marketplace UDDI*, *portal UDDI*, *partner catalog UDDI* and *internal enterprise application integration UDDI*. An e-marketplace UDDI is a registry that is hosted by an industry and lists businesses that belong to an industry consortium. For example, an e-marketplace UDDI hosted by car manufacturers might consist of services offered by Ford, Honda and Volkswagen. The e-marketplace UDDI allows only those businesses that belong to a particular industry to publish and find information.[37]

A portal UDDI is a registry that resides on a company's firewall and contains information about a single company's Web services. The company publishes information about its services in the registry so that other companies can view the information. Usually, a portal UDDI operator enables the *find* function for external users, but disables the *publish* function. This means that only internal users (i.e., authorized employees of the company) can update and post information.[38]

The partner catalog UDDI is a registry that resides behind a company's firewall and lists Web services offered by an organization and its partners. A partner catalog UDDI is accessible only to internal users—*publish* and *find* functions are restricted to select employees of an organization and its partners.[39]

The internal enterprise application integration UDDI is a registry that resides behind a company's firewall and lists Web services offered by an organization. This type of registry is accessible only to internal users—*publish* and *find* operations are restricted to select employees of the organization.[40]

8.7 Limitations of UDDI

Although UDDI facilitates the discovery of Web services, there are certain limitations to UDDI and UDDI registries. The most significant limitation of UDDI is the immaturity of the UDDI specification. UDDI has not been submitted to a standards body, so no "official" organization is controlling its development. Also, the specification may change significantly in future versions or when it is finally submitted to a standards body.

Some UDDI registries also raise the question of data reliability. For companies to feel comfortable relying on registry data, the companies need to trust the data. However, the UBR, for instance, does not indicate when data was last updated or checked for accuracy. Because registry users do not know how often data is updated, users must question whether data, service descriptions and hyperlinks contained in registries reflect the most current information about businesses and Web services.[41]

Another limitation of UDDI is that UDDI registries describe Web services, but do not evaluate them. Before using a particular Web service, service consumers usually require information about the Web service's quality of service (QoS). For example, service consumers might want to know the following: How often can I access a certain Web service? Will the Web service "crash" if numerous companies use it simultaneously? Does the service provider offer technical support? If so, what is the turnaround time for resolving issues?[42] The answers to these types of questions would help service consumers distinguish among similar Web services. Quality-of-service information currently does not reside in UDDI registries; therefore, service consumers must perform extensive research to locate the necessary data. Although UDDI was not designed to provide quality-of-service information, registries containing such data would offer more value to service consumers.

8.8 Other Discovery Technologies

Although UDDI is the most common Web services discovery standard, other technologies also facilitate Web services discovery. It might seem redundant for the industry to support multiple discovery technologies, but different technologies are appropriate for different situations. For example, some technologies support direct discovery, whereas others support indirect discovery. In this section, we discuss two additional technologies that enable discovery—ebXML and WS-Inspection.

8.8.1 ebXML

Electronic business XML (ebXML) is a joint initiative led by the *United Nations Centre for Trade Facilitation and Electronic Business* (*UN/CEFACT*) and the *Organization for the Advancement of Structured Information Standards* (*OASIS*). UN/CEFACT, OASIS and other organizations designed the ebXML specification to standardize XML-based communication among organizations and to facilitate electronic business.[43] Currently, the ebXML initiative consists of over 1,400 organizations, including RosettaNet, Automotive Industry Action Group, Sun Microsystems and Open Travel Alliance.[44]

EbXML provides a technical framework through which companies of any size in any industry can communicate and exchange data via the Internet. Rather than supporting UDDI, ebXML defines its own registry structure through which service consumers can access XML documents that contain information about service providers. The registry includes capabilities that allow companies to initiate business agreements and perform business transactions. The ebXML registry is accessed through interfaces that expose registry services.[45]

The ebXML registry allows trading partners to share information, such as *Collaboration-Protocol Profiles* (*CPPs*), *Collaboration-Protocol Agreements* (*CPAs*), DTDs and business-process models. CPPs are XML documents that contain information about specific organizations and the services they offer.[46] A CPP includes information about a service interface and specifies the requirements to exchange documents with a particular trading partner. A CPP also contains industry classifications, contact information and a list of services offered by an organization.[47]

A CPA is a contract formed between trading partners; it defines the guidelines to which trading partners must adhere when transacting business.[48] For instance, a CPA can contain the parameters that trading partners must use to ensure that their applications are compatible. Trading partners must have identical copies of the CPA to ensure complete compatibility. It is not mandatory for trading partners to publish their CPAs in the ebXML registry.

Although UDDI and ebXML are separate technologies, organizations can combine them. For instance, organizations can use UDDI registries to advertise Web services and ebXML registries to store trading contracts/agreements. It is preferable to store contracts and agreements in ebXML registries, because ebXML provides a security model and UDDI currently does not. Thus, UDDI and ebXML can be used as complementary services.[49] EbXML registries mainly support indirect discovery, because they are supported by intermediaries. However, ebXML also can support direct discovery within private registries. This is because private registries usually are implemented by specific organizations and contain the services offered by those organizations.

8.8.2 WS-Inspection

Web Services Inspection (*WS-Inspection*) is an XML-based discovery technology developed by IBM and Microsoft. WS-Inspection defines how a client application server can locate Web services descriptions, such as WSDL documents, that reside on a particular Web server. A WS-Inspection document is maintained by a service provider and contains references to all Web service description documents on the service provider's Web server. If a developer wants to use a particular Web service and knows the Web server on which the service resides, the developer can use WS-Inspection to find WSDL documents and other data about the Web service. In such cases, using WS-Inspection is faster and more efficient than searching the entire UDDI registry for the needed information. However, if the developer does not know the Web server that contains the desired Web service, the developer would use UDDI to locate the service. Thus, WS-Inspection is designed to complement, rather than to replace, UDDI.[50] Because WS-Inspection is hosted by an individual service provider, it supports only direct discovery.

Although WS-Inspection has not been submitted to a standards organization, interested companies can obtain the specification from IBM (**www.alphaworks.ibm.com**) or from Microsoft (**msdn.microsoft.com**). The IBM Web Services Toolkit contains an implementation of the WS-Inspection specification; the most current version of Visual Studio® .NET also supports WS-Inspection.[51] WS-Inspection supersedes the Microsoft-specific *Discovery of Web Services (DISCO)* technology, which facilitates discovery of Web services in a particular directory on a server.

In the last three chapters, we examined the core technologies used in Web services—including XML, SOAP, WSDL and UDDI. For organizations to adopt Web services on a large scale, software vendors must incorporate support for these technologies into enterprise software and must provide Web services application-development tools that hide low-level programming details. Chapter 9, Java API for XML-based Remote Procedure Calls, begins our discussion of Java APIs for implementing Web services and Web services clients.

8.9 Summary

IBM, Microsoft and Ariba developed Universal Description, Discovery and Integration (UDDI), a specification that defines registries in which businesses can publish information about themselves and the services they provide. Service consumers can use the UDDI registry to locate general and technical information about various service providers. With this information, consumers can initiate business deals, form partnerships and purchase services.

Discovery is the process of locating Web services through registries. By using a registry, an organization that wishes to employ a Web service to process credit-card payments, for example, can locate all publicly available services that provide the necessary functionality. Discovery can be categorized into direct discovery and indirect discovery. Direct discovery is the process of obtaining data from registries maintained by the service provider. With indirect discovery, an organization obtains data through a third-party registry.

In September 2000, the UDDI project—led by IBM, Microsoft and Ariba—released Version 1.0 of the UDDI specification. This specification defines a framework for centralized registries that facilitate the storage, discovery and exchange of information about businesses and their Web services. In June 2001, the UDDI project released a beta specification of UDDI Version 2.0, which improves on several features of the original specification.

UDDI is used in the publicly accessible UDDI Business Registry (UBR) maintained by Microsoft, IBM, Hewlett-Packard and SAP. A company can enroll in the UBR through an operator node, an organization that hosts an implementation of the UBR. When a company registers with one operator node, the information is replicated in the other three registries. UDDI also can be implemented in private registries, which are accessible only to authorized parties. Usually, private registries enforce additional security features to ensure data integrity and to safeguard against unauthorized access.

The UDDI publishing API supports the publish operation, which enables companies to post and update information on a UDDI-based registry. Access to the publishing API is restricted. The inquiry API supports the find operation, which enables service consumers to browse the registry for service providers that offer a certain service. After service consumers discover compatible applications, they must connect to, and communicate with, the computing systems of other businesses. This process is referred to as a binding.

The UBR can be categorized into white pages, yellow pages and green pages. The UDDI white pages contain contact and general information about a company, the yellow pages divide companies into various categories, and the green pages contain technical information about a products, services and Web services.

A client company needs to know certain information about a provider's Web service. This information, known collectively as the UDDI information model, includes the following five components: business information, business service information, binding information, service-specification information and publisher assertion.

Other technologies (such as ebXML and WS-Inspection) also allow applications and developers to discover Web services. EbXML provides a technical framework through which companies can communicate and exchange data via the Internet. EbXML defines its own registry structure through which service consumers can access XML documents that contain information about service providers. Web Services Inspection (WS-Inspection) is an XML-based discovery technology that defines how a client application can locate Web services descriptions, such as WSDL documents, that reside on a particular Web server.

8.10 Internet and Web Resources

www.uddi.org
The UDDI project's site provides UDDI specifications and allows companies to register for the UDDI Business Registry. Anyone can query the UBR from this site.

www-3.ibm.com/services/uddi/find
IBM's implementation of the UDDI Version 1.0 registry can be accessed from this site. The site allows users to publish and find information. Users can perform searches on the basis of business names, service names and service types.

uddi.microsoft.com/search.aspx
This site contains Microsoft's implementation of the UDDI Version 1.0 registry. The site allows users to publish and find information. Users can perform searches on the basis of business names, business categories, business locations, **tModel** names, various taxonomic categories, URLs, etc.

uddi.hp.com/uddi/index.jsp
Hewlett-Packard's implementation of the UDDI Version 2.0 registry can be accessed from this site. The site allows users to publish and find information. It also contains links to the Hewlett-Packard home page, HP's products and services page, and a page detailing HP news and events.

www-3.ibm.com/services/uddi/v2beta/protect/registry.html
This site contains IBM's implementation of the UDDI Version 2.0 registry. The site allows users to publish and find information. Users can perform searches on the basis of business names, service names and **tModel** names. The site also contains links to Web services resources, UDDI features and UDDI specification issues.

uddi.rte.microsoft.com/search/frames.aspx
This site contains Microsoft's implementation of the UDDI Version 2.0 registry. The site allows users to publish and find information. Users can perform on the basis of service names, provider names or **tModel** names. The site also contains information about UDDI, a FAQ section and links to the Microsoft home page.

udditest.sap.com
SAP's implementation of the UDDI Version 2.0 registry can be accessed from this site. The site allows users to publish and find information; it also provides links to the SAP home page, services offered by the company, a listing of SAP partners and other resources.

www.oasis-open.org/cover/uddi.html
The XML Cover Pages provides an overview of UDDI and a brief history of the UDDI specification. The site also contains links to resources such as the UDDI technical white paper and XML Schema.

www.sun.com/software/xml/developers/uddi/
The Sun Microsystems Developer Connection site provides overviews of the UDDI Business Registry, the UDDI information model and the UDDI Programmer's API.

general.rau.ac.za/infosci/raujournal/default.asp?to=newsvol2nr4
The *South African Journal of Information Management* site discusses UDDI and the business benefits of using UDDI.

www.w3.org/2001/03/WSWS-popa/paper12
This W3C site contains information on Web services topics, such as transport and messaging protocols, security, transactions and registries. The site also contains links to references on SOAP, WSDL, UDDI and ebXML.

`www-106.ibm.com/developerworks/webservices/library/ws-wsilspec.html`
This IBM site contains the Web Services Inspection Language specification. The specification defines the document structure and services provided by WS-Inspection. The specification also explains how WS-Inspection interacts with WSDL and UDDI.

`www.perfectxml.com/WebSvc3.asp`
The Perfect XML site contains numerous links to references on WSDL, UDDI and DISCO.

WORKS CITED

1. P. Korzeniowski, "Internet Insight: A Little Slice of the UDDI Pie," *eWeek* 4 February 2002 `<www.eweek.com/print_article/0,3668,a=22053,00.asp>`.

2. W. Nagy and K. Ballinger, "The WS-Inspection and UDDI Relationship," November 2001 `<www-106.ibm.com/developerworks/webservices/library/ws-wsiluddi.html?dwzone=webservices>`.

3. "About UDDI," `<www.uddi.org/about.html>`.

4. P. Korzeniowski, "UDDI: Two Versions Down, One to Go," *eWeek* 4 February 2002 `<www.eweek.com/article/0,3658,s%253D722%2526a%253D22050,00.asp>`.

5. "SIC Division Structure," `<155.103.6.10/cgi-bin/sic/sicser5>`.

6. P. Cauldwell, et al., *Professional XML Web Services* (Birmingham: WROX 2001) 181.

7. "UDDI.org Find," `<www.uddi.org/find.html>`.

8. "UDDI Specification Index Page," `<msdn.microsoft.com/library/default.asp?url=/library/en-us/dnuddispec/html/uddispecindex.asp>`.

9. P. Korzeniowski, "Internet Insight: A Little Slice of the UDDI Pie," *eWeek* 4 February 2002 `<www.eweek.com/print_article/0,3668,a=22053,00.asp>`.

10. "UDDI.org Community," `<www.uddi.org/community.html>`.

11. "UDDI.org FAQs," `<www.uddi.org/faqs.html>`.

12. "UDDI Version 2.0 Operator's Specification," 8 June 2001 `<www.uddi.org/pubs/Operators-V2.00-Open-20010608.pdf>`.

13. W. Wong, "NTT Joins Web Services Directory Effort," 17 January 2002 `<news.com.com/2100-1001-817566.html?legacy=cnet&tag=dd.ne.dht.nl-sty.0>`.

14. "UDDI Version 2.0 API Specification," 8 June 2001 `<www.uddi.org/pubs/ProgrammersAPI-V2.00-Open-20010608.pdf>`.

15. "UDDI.org FAQs," `<www.uddi.org/faqs.html>`.

16. "UDDI.org FAQs," `<www.uddi.org/faqs.html>`.

17. "UDDI.org FAQs," `<www.uddi.org/faqs.html>`.

18. "UDDI.org FAQs," `<www.uddi.org/faqs.html>`.

19. A. Rajaram, "Overview of UDDI," 17 August 2001 `<dcb.sun.com/practices/webservices/overviews/overview_uddi.jsp>`.

20. A. Rajaram, "Overview of UDDI," 17 August 2001 `<dcb.sun.com/practices/webservices/overviews/overview_uddi.jsp>`.

21. A. Rajaram, "Overview of UDDI," 17 August 2001 `<dcb.sun.com/practices/webservices/overviews/overview_uddi.jsp>`.

22. A. Rajaram, "Overview of UDDI," 17 August 2001 `<dcb.sun.com/practices/webservices/overviews/overview_uddi.jsp>`.

23. P. Cauldwell, et al., *Professional XML Web Services* (Birmingham: WROX 2001) 191.

24. P. Cauldwell, et al., *Professional XML Web Services* (Birmingham: WROX 2001) 187.

25. D. Ehnebuske, C. Kurt and B. McKee, "UDDI tModels: Classification Schemes, Taxonomies, Identifier Systems, and Relationships," 15 November 2001 <**www.uddi.org/taxonomies/ UDDI_Taxonomy_tModels.htm**>.

26. "UDDI Version 2.0 API Specification," 8 June 2001 <**www.uddi.org/pubs/ ProgrammersAPI-V2.00-Open-20010608.pdf**>.

27. "UDDI Version 2.0 API Specification," 8 June 2001 <**www.uddi.org/pubs/ ProgrammersAPI-V2.00-Open-20010608.pdf**>.

28. "UDDI Version 2.0 API Specification," 8 June 2001 <**www.uddi.org/pubs/ ProgrammersAPI-V2.00-Open-20010608.pdf**>.

29. "UDDI Version 2.0 API Specification," 8 June 2001 <**www.uddi.org/pubs/ ProgrammersAPI-V2.00-Open-20010608.pdf**>.

30. P. Cauldwell, et al., *Professional XML Web Services* (Birmingham: WROX 2001) 181.

31. R. Cover, "The XML Cover Pages: Universal Description, Discovery and Integration," 21 December 2001 <**www.oasis-open.org/cover/uddi.html**>.

32. "**UDDI.org** FAQs," <**www.uddi.org/faqs.html**>.

33. "**UDDI.org** FAQs," <**www.uddi.org/faqs.html**>.

34. P. Cauldwell, et al., *Professional XML Web Services* (Birmingham: WROX 2001) 186.

35. P. Krill, "UDDI Seeks Its Place," *InfoWorld* 3 June 2002: 41.

36. A. Chen, "Web Directories Dial In," *eWeek* 22 April 2002: 51.

37. S. Graham, "The Role of Private UDDI Nodes in Web Services, Part 1: Six Species of UDDI," May 2001 <**www-106.ibm.com/developerworks/webservices/library/ ws-rup1.html**>.

38. S. Graham, "The Role of Private UDDI Nodes in Web Services, Part 1: Six Species of UDDI," May 2001 <**www-106.ibm.com/developerworks/webservices/library/ ws-rup1.html**>.

39. S. Graham, "The Role of Private UDDI Nodes in Web Services, Part 1: Six Species of UDDI," May 2001 <**www-106.ibm.com/developerworks/webservices/library/ ws-rup1.html**>.

40. S. Graham, "The Role of Private UDDI Nodes in Web Services, Part 1: Six Species of UDDI," May 2001 <**www-106.ibm.com/developerworks/webservices/library/ ws-rup1.html**>.

41. A. Meyer, "UDDI Registries and Reuse," 28 January 2002 <**e-serv.ebizq.net/wbs/ meyer_1.html**>.

42. A. Meyer, "UDDI Registries and Reuse," 28 January 2002 <**e-serv.ebizq.net/wbs/ meyer_1.html**>.

43. "**ebXML.org** About," <**www.ebxml.org/geninfo.htm**>.

44. "**ebXML.org** Industry Support," <**www.ebxml.org/endorsements.htm**>.

45. "**ebXML.org** FAQ," <**www.ebxml.org/faq.htm**>.

46. "Oasis ebXML CPPA," 7 May 2002 <**www.oasis-open.org/committees/ ebxml-cppa**>.

47. K. Kayl, "EbXML: The Key Components," 5 September 2001 <**java.sun.com/
features/2001/09/ebxmlkey.html**>.

48. "Oasis ebXML CPPA," 7 May 2002 <**www.oasis-open.org/committees/
ebxml-cppa**>.

49. S. Fordin, "ebXML Registry/Repository Implementation: Introducing the First J2EE™-Based ebXML Registry/Repository Implementation," August 2001 <**wwws.sun.com/software/
xml/developers/regrep/article**>.

50. R. Cover, "IBM and Microsoft Issue Specification and Software for Web Services Inspection Language," 2 November 2001 <**xml.coverpages.org/ni2001-11-02-a.html**>.

51. J. Borck, "Expressway to Discovery," *InfoWorld* 19 November 2001 <**www.infoworld.com/articles/op/xml/01/11/19/011119opborck.xml**>.

RECOMMENDED READING

Ballinger, K. and W. Nagy, "The WS-Inspection and UDDI Relationship," November 2001 <**www-106.ibm.com/developerworks/webservices/library/
ws-wsiluddi.html?dwzone=webservices**>.

Cover, R. "The XML Cover Pages: Universal Description, Discovery and Integration," 21 December 2001 <**www.oasis-open.org/cover/uddi.html**>.

Graham, S. "The Role of Private UDDI Nodes in Web Services, Part 1: Six Species of UDDI," May 2001   <**www-106.ibm.com/developerworks/webservices/library/
ws-rup1.html**>.

Kayl, K. "EbXML: The Key Components," 5 September 2001 <**java.sun.com/features/
2001/09/ebxmlkey.html**>.

Korzeniowski, P. "A Little Slice of the UDDI Pie," *eWeek* 4 February 2002 <**www.eweek.com/
print_article/0,3668,a=22053,00.asp**>.

Korzeniowski, P. "UDDI: Two Versions Down, One to Go," *eWeek* 4 February 2002 <**www.eweek.com/article/
0,3658,s%253D722%2526a%253D22050,00.asp**>.

Rajaram, A. "Overview of UDDI," 17 August 2001 <**dcb.sun.com/practices/
webservices/overviews/overview_uddi.jsp**>.

"UDDI Version 2.0 API Specification," 8 June 2001 <**www.uddi.org/pubs/
ProgrammersAPI-V2.00-Open-20010608.pdf**>.

"UDDI Version 2.0 Operator's Specification," 8 June 2001 <**www.uddi.org/pubs/
Operators-V2.00-Open-20010608.pdf**>.

Java API for XML-Based Remote Procedure Calls (JAX-RPC)

Objectives

- To understand the JAX-RPC architecture.
- To be able to write JAX-RPC-based Web services.
- To be able to deploy JAX-RPC Web services using the Java Web Services Developer Pack.
- To be able to write Web-services clients using JAX-RPC.

The service we render others is really the rent we pay for our room on earth.
Wilfred Grenfell

Just about the time you think you can make both ends meet, somebody moves the ends.
Pansy Penner

What we call results are beginnings.
Ralph Waldo Emerson

The great end of life is not knowledge but action.
Thomas Henry Huxley

9.1 Introduction

In Chapter 6, SOAP-Based Web Services Platforms, we introduced methods for creating Web services that use SOAP. This chapter and the next two discuss how to create Web services using the *Java Web Service Developer Pack* (*JWSDP*). JWSDP includes the *Java XML Pack, Tomcat Java Servlet and JavaServer Pages containers*, a registry server and the *Ant build tool*. The Java XML Pack provides the *Java API for XML-Based Remote Procedure Calls* (*JAX-RPC*). As of this writing, the current version of JWSDP is 1.0. Chapter 1, Introduction, discusses the installation of JWSDP.

RPC, which was developed in the 1980s, allows a procedural program (i.e., a program written in C or another procedural programming language) to call a function that resides on another computer as conveniently as if that function were part of the same program running on the same computer. A goal of RPC is to allow programmers to concentrate on the required tasks of an application; with RPC, the programmer can develop an application without concern for whether function calls are local or remote. RPC hides the network details that enable the application to communicate. It performs all the networking and *marshaling of data* (i.e., packaging of function arguments and return values for transmission over a network).

Web services evolved from the need to integrate applications written in many different languages with many different data formats. Whereas RPC requires the use of a single programming language and proprietary communications protocol, Web-services technology enables integration among many different languages and protocols. By relying on XML—the de facto standard for marking up data—and HTTP—the de facto standard protocol for communication over the Web—SOAP provides such integration. JAX-RPC enables Java programmers to take advantage of these advances in distributed computing by providing a clean, simple API for creating and interacting with XML-based Web services.

JAX-RPC enables developers to build interoperable Web services and clients by providing a simple, RPC-oriented API that hides the details of the underlying SOAP communications and WSDL descriptions. A developer who builds JAX-RPC Web services does not need know in what programming language clients are written, because client requests are sent as XML messages that conform to the SOAP specification. Likewise, a developer who builds Web-services clients using JAX-RPC does not need to know the details of a Web service's underlying implementation, because the service's WSDL document specifies how to interact with the service.

9.2 JAX-RPC Overview

JAX-RPC provides a generic mechanism that enables developers to create and access Web services by using XML-based remote procedure calls. While such Web services can communicate by using any transport protocol, the current release of the JAX-RPC Reference Implementation (version 1.0) uses SOAP as the application protocol and HTTP as the transport protocol. Future versions likely will support other transport protocols as they become available.

When Web-service providers publish their Web services to XML registries (e.g., UDDI registries or ebXML registries), they may provide service interfaces or WSDL definitions for these services. The JAX-RPC specification defines a mapping of Java types (e.g., **int**, **String** and classes that adhere to the JavaBean design patterns) to WSDL definitions. When a client locates a service in an XML registry, the client retrieves the WSDL definition to get the service's interface definition. To access the service using Java, the client must transform the WSDL definitions to Java types. The **xrpcc** tool included in the *replaced by wscompile* JWSDP generates Java classes from the WSDL definitions.

Figure 9.1 shows the architecture of JAX-RPC. The service side contains a *JAX-RPC service runtime environment* and a *service end point*. The client side contains a *JAX-RPC client runtime environment* and a client application. The remote procedure calls use an XML-based protocol (e.g., SOAP) as the application protocol and an appropriate transport protocol (e.g., HTTP). The JAX-RPC client and service runtime environments send and process the remote procedure call and response, respectively. The JAX-RPC client runtime system creates a SOAP message to invoke the remote method, and the JAX-RPC service runtime system transforms the SOAP message to a Java method call, then dispatches the method call to the service end point. The JAX-RPC service runtime also translates the methods call's return value into a SOAP message and delivers that SOAP message to the client.

Before JAX-RPC was introduced, *Remote Method Invocation* (*RMI*) was the predominant RPC mechanism for Java. RMI allows Java programs to transfer complete Java objects over networks, using Java's object-serialization mechanism. Since RMI can be used to make remote procedure calls over the Internet, developers may wonder why they would need to use JAX-RPC, which seems to provide similar functionality.

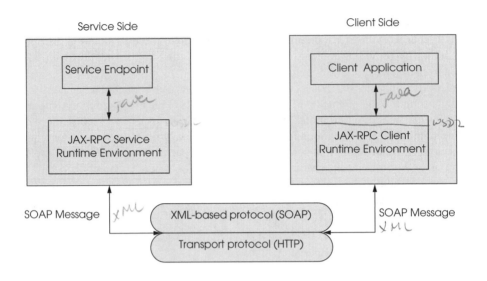

Fig. 9.1   *JAX-RPC architecture.*

As with RPC, both RMI and JAX-RPC handle the marshaling and unmarshaling of data across the network. RMI and JAX-RPC also provide APIs for transmitting and receiving data. The primary differences between RMI and JAX-RPC are as follows:

1. JAX-RPC enables applications to take advantage of SOAP's and WSDL's interoperability, which enables those applications to invoke Web services that execute on non-Java platforms, and non-Java applications to invoke Web services that execute on Java platforms. RMI supports only Java-to-Java distributed communication. The client needs only the WSDL to access the Web service. [*Note*: RMI/IIOP also provides interoperability with non-Java applications. However, JAX-RPC is easier to use. With several lines of code, the client can access Web services written in languages other than Java.]

2. RMI can transfer complete Java objects, while JAX-RPC is limited to a set of supported Java types, which we discuss in Section 9.3.1.

JAX-RPC hides the details of SOAP from the developer, because the JAX-RPC service/client runtime environments perform the mapping between remote method calls/return values and SOAP messages. The JAX-RPC runtime system also provides APIs for accessing Web services via static *stubs* (local objects that represent the remote services), dynamic proxies (objects that are generated during runtime) and for invoking Web services dynamically through the *Dynamic Invocation Interface* (*DII*). We discuss these APIs in detail in Section 9.3.5.

9.3 Simple Web Service: Vote Service

In this section, we present a simple JAX-RPC Web service that tallies votes for the users' favorite programming languages. The four major steps in this example are:

1. Defining a Web-service interface with methods that clients can invoke.

2. Writing a Java class that implements the interface [*Note*: By convention, the name of the service-implementation class is the same as that of the interface and ends with **Impl**].

3. Deploying the service using the **deploytool** included with JWSDP 1.0.

4. Generating client-side stubs and writing the client application that interacts with the service.

Fig. 9.2 shows the structure of this example.

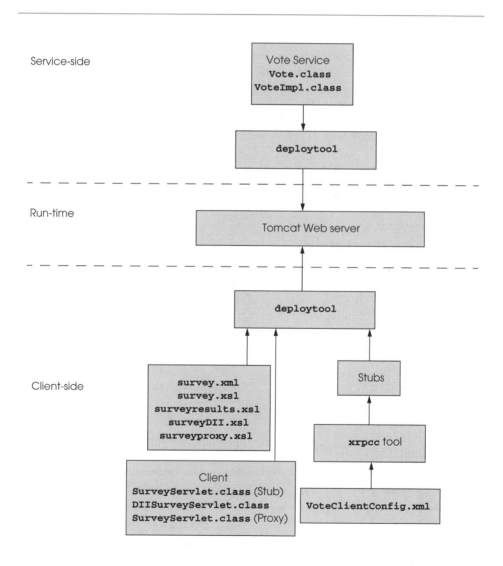

Fig. 9.2   Vote JAX-RPC Web service example structure.

Before providing the code for the example, we discuss the limited set of JAX-RPC-supported Java types.

9.3.1 JAX-RPC-Supported Java Types

JAX-RPC supports only a subset of Java types, because the data types transmitted by the remote procedure calls must map to SOAP XML data types. When a Web service receives a remote method call from a client, the JAX-RPC runtime service environment first transforms the XML representation of the call arguments to their corresponding Java types. (This process is known as *deserialization*.) The JAX-RPC runtime service environment then passes the Java representation of the call arguments to the service implementation for processing. After the call is processed, the JAX-RPC service runtime environment transforms the return object to an XML representation. (This process is known as *serialization*.) The XML representation of the return object (e.g., a SOAP message) is then sent back to the client. The serialization/deserialization process happens both at the client and at the service.

JAX-RPC supports Java primitive types and their corresponding wrapper classes. Figure 9.3 shows the mappings of Java primitive types and their wrapper classes to SOAP data types.

JAX-RPC supports a subset of standard Java classes as well. Figure 9.4 shows the mappings of this subset of standard Java classes to SOAP data types.

Java primitive types and their wrapper classes	XML elements
`boolean (Boolean)`	`xsd:boolean (soapenc:boolean)`
`byte (Byte)`	`xsd:byte (soapenc:byte)`
`double (Double)`	`xsd:double (soapenc:double)`
`float (Float)`	`xsd:float (soapenc:float)`
`int (Integer)`	`xsd:int (soapenc:int)`
`long (Long)`	`xsd:long (soapenc:long)`
`short (Short)`	`xsd:short (soapenc:short)`

Fig. 9.3   Mappings of Java primitive types and their wrapper classes to SOAP data types.

Standard Java classes	XML elements
`BigDecimal`	`xsd:decimal`
`BigInteger`	`xsd:integer`
`Calendar`	`xsd:dateTime`

Fig. 9.4   Mappings of standard Java classes to SOAP data types. (Part 1 of 2.)

Standard Java classes	XML elements
Date	xsd:dateTime
String	xsd:string

Fig. 9.4   Mappings of standard Java classes to SOAP data types. (Part 2 of 2.)

The JWSDP 1.0 final release also supports a set of classes that implement the **java.util.Collection** interface. These classes are: **Vector, ArrayList, LinkedList, Stack, HashMap, HashTable, HashSet, Properties, TreeMap** and **TreeSet**.

In addition to the aforementioned supported types, JAX-RPC supports objects of Java classes that satisfy the following conditions:

1. The class does not implement *java.rmi.Remote*.

2. The class has a *public* default constructor.

3. The class's public fields are JAX-RPC-supported Java types.

4. Java classes may follow the JavaBean's *set* and *get* method-design patterns. Bean properties must be JAX-RPC-supported Java types.

Finally, Java arrays also can be used in JAX-RPC, provided that the member type of the array is one of the aforementioned JAX-RPC-supported Java types. JAX-RPC supports multidimensional Java arrays as well.

9.3.2 Defining the Vote Service Interface

The first step in the creation of a Web service with JAX-RPC is to define the remote interface that describes the *remote methods* through which the client interacts with the service. The following restrictions apply to the service interface definition:

1. The interface must extend **java.rmi.Remote**.

2. Each public method must include **java.rmi.RemoteException** in its **throws** clause. The **throws** clause may also include application-specific exceptions.

3. No declarations of constants are allowed.

4. All method parameters and return types must be JAX-RPC-supported Java types.

To create a remote interface, define an interface that extends interface **java.rmi.Remote**. Interface **Remote** is a *tagging interface*—it does not declare any methods, but identifies the interface as supporting remote method calls. Interface **Vote** (Fig. 9.5)—which extends interface **Remote** (line 9)—is the remote interface for our first JAX-RPC-based Web-service example. Line 12 declares method **addVote**, which clients can invoke to add votes for the users' favorite programming languages. Note that, although the **Vote** remote interface defines only one method, remote interfaces can declare multiple methods. A Web service must implement all methods declared in its remote interface.

```
1   // Fig. 9.5: Vote.java
2   // VoteService interface declares a method for adding a vote and
3   // for returning vote information.
4   package com.deitel.jws1.jaxrpc.service.vote;
5
6   // Java core packages
7   import java.rmi.*;
8
9   public interface Vote extends Remote {
10
11      // obtain vote information from server
12      public String addVote( String language ) throws RemoteException;
13  }
```

Fig. 9.5   **Vote** defines the service interface for the JAX-RPC Vote Web service.

9.3.3 Defining the Vote Service Implementation

After defining the remote interface, we define the service implementation. Class **Vote-Impl** (Fig. 9.6) is the Web-service end point that implements the **Vote** interface. The client interacts with an object of class **VoteImpl** by invoking method **addVote** of interface **Vote**. Method **addVote** enables the client to add a vote to the database and obtain tallies of previously recorded votes.

Class **VoteImpl** implements remote interface **Vote** and interface *ServiceLifecycle* (line 15). Interface **ServiceLifecycle** allows service implementations to perform initialization and termination processes, such as opening and closing database connections. We use a Cloudscape database[1] in this example to store the total number of votes for each programming language.

Lines 21–74 implement method **init** of interface **ServiceLifecycle** to set up access to a Cloudscape database. The JAX-RPC runtime system invokes method **init** when the service implementation class is instantiated. Lines 29–30 cast the parameter (**context**) of method **init** to **ServletEndpointContext**. Lines 33–34 invoke method **getServletContext** of class **ServletEndpointContext** to get the associated **ServletContext**. Lines 37–42 get the database driver and database name that are specified in the servlet's deployment descriptor (**web.xml**). Line 45 loads the class definition for the database driver. Line 48 declares and initializes **Connection** reference **connection** (package **java.sql**). The program initializes **connection** with the result of a call to **static** method **getConnection** of class **DriverManager**, which attempts to connect to the database specified by its URL argument. Lines 52–62 invoke **Connection** method **prepareStatement** to create SQL **PreparedStatement**s for updating the number of votes for the client's selected programming language and getting the vote count for each programming language.

Lines 77–111 implement method **addVote** of interface **Vote**. Line 83 sets the parameter of query **sqlUpdate** to the client-specified language. After setting the parameter for the **PreparedStatement**, the program calls method **executeUpdate** of interface **PreparedStatement** to execute the **UPDATE** operation. Line 89 calls method **executeQuery** of interface **PreparedStatement** to execute the **SELECT** operation.

---

1. We discuss the installation of the Cloudscape database in Chapter 1, Introduction.

ResultSet results stores the query results. Lines 93–98 iterate through the **results** and append them to a **StringBuffer**.

Lines 114–128 implement method **destroy** of interface **ServiceLifecycle**. Lines 118–120 close the prepared statements and the database connection.

```
1   // VoteImpl.java
2   // VoteImpl implements the Vote remote interface to provide
3   // a VoteService remote object.
4   package com.deitel.jws1.jaxrpc.voteservice;
5
6   // Java core packages
7   import java.rmi.*;
8   import java.sql.*;
9
10  // Java XML packages
11  import javax.xml.rpc.server.*;
12  import javax.xml.rpc.JAXRPCException;
13  import javax.servlet.ServletContext;
14
15  public class VoteImpl implements ServiceLifecycle, Vote {
16
17      private Connection connection;
18      private PreparedStatement sqlUpdate, sqlSelect;
19
20      // set up database connection and prepare SQL statement
21      public void init( Object context )
22          throws JAXRPCException
23      {
24          // attempt database connection and
25          // create PreparedStatements
26          try {
27
28              // cast context to ServletEndpointContext
29              ServletEndpointContext endpointContext =
30                  ( ServletEndpointContext ) context;
31
32              // get ServletContext
33              ServletContext servletContext =
34                  endpointContext.getServletContext();
35
36              // get database driver from servlet context
37              String dbDriver =
38                  servletContext.getInitParameter( "dbDriver" );
39
40              // get database name from servlet context
41              String voteDB =
42                  servletContext.getInitParameter( "voteDB" );
43
44              // load database driver
45              Class.forName( dbDriver );
46
```

Fig. 9.6   **VoteImpl** defines the service implementation for the Vote JAX-RPC Web service. (Part 1 of 3.)

```
47              // connect to database
48              connection = DriverManager.getConnection( voteDB );
49
50              // PreparedStatement to increment vote total for a
51              // specific language
52              sqlUpdate =
53                 connection.prepareStatement(
54                    "UPDATE surveyresults SET vote = vote + 1 " +
55                    "WHERE name = ?"
56                 );
57
58              // PreparedStatement to obtain surveyresults table's data
59              sqlSelect =
60                 connection.prepareStatement( "SELECT name, vote " +
61                    "FROM surveyresults ORDER BY vote DESC"
62                 );
63
64           } // end try
65
66           // for any exception, throw an JAXRPCException to
67           // indicate that the servlet is not currently available
68           catch ( Exception exception ) {
69              exception.printStackTrace();
70
71              throw new JAXRPCException( exception.getMessage() );
72           }
73
74        } // end method init
75
76        // implementation for interface Vote method addVote
77        public String addVote( String name ) throws RemoteException
78        {
79           // get votes count from database and update it
80           try {
81
82              // set parameter in sqlUpdate
83              sqlUpdate.setString( 1, name );
84
85              // execute sqlUpdate statement
86              sqlUpdate.executeUpdate();
87
88              // execute sqlSelect statement
89              ResultSet results = sqlSelect.executeQuery();
90              StringBuffer voteInfo = new StringBuffer();
91
92              // iterate ResultSet and prepare return string
93              while ( results.next() ) {
94
95                 // append results to String voteInfo
96                 voteInfo.append( " " + results.getString( 1 ) );
97                 voteInfo.append( " " + results.getInt( 2 ) );
98              }
```

Fig. 9.6   **VoteImpl** defines the service implementation for the Vote JAX-RPC Web service. (Part 2 of 3.)

```
 99
100                return voteInfo.toString();
101
102        } // end try
103
104        // handle database exceptions by returning error to client
105        catch ( Exception exception ) {
106            exception.printStackTrace();
107
108            return exception.getMessage();
109        }
110
111    } // end method addVote
112
113    // close SQL statements and database when servlet terminates
114    public void destroy()
115    {
116        // attempt to close statements and database connection
117        try {
118            sqlUpdate.close();
119            sqlSelect.close();
120            connection.close();
121        }
122
123        // handle database exception
124        catch ( Exception exception ) {
125            exception.printStackTrace();
126        }
127
128    } // end method destroy
129
130 } // end class VoteImpl
```

Fig. 9.6   **VoteImpl** defines the service implementation for the Vote JAX-RPC Web service. (Part 3 of 3.)

9.3.4 Deploying the Vote Service

Once we have defined the service interface and implementation, the next step is to deploy the Web service. The JAX-RPC reference implementation provides the **deploytool** to deploy a JAX-RPC service onto Tomcat. The JAX-RPC reference implementation also provides the **xrpcc** tool to generate ties (server-side objects that represent the services), stubs and other service and client-side artifacts (such as a WSDL document). In this section, we discuss how to deploy the JAX-RPC service using the **deploytool**. Section 9.4.2 discuss how to deploy a JAX-RPC service via **xrpcc**.

The **deploytool** is a GUI utility that creates the WAR file and deploys the JAX-RPC service on Tomcat. The **deploytool** also generates the deployment descriptor (**web.xml**) and the service's WSDL document. Before starting the **deploytool**, we need to set two environment variables: **JAVA_HOME** and **JWSDP_HOME**. The **JAVA_HOME** points to the directory where the J2SE 1.3.1 or 1.4 is installed. The **JWSDP_HOME** points to the directory where the JWSDP 1.0 is installed. In our examples, the **JAVA_HOME** is set to **G:\j2sdk1.4.0** and the **JWSDP_HOME** is set to **G:\jwsdp-**

1_0. Then include the **bin** directories of the J2SE and the JWSDP to the front of the **PATH** environment variable. Before running the **deploytool**, start Tomcat. (In the command prompt terminal window, type **startup** to start Tomcat.) Type **deploytool** to start the deployment tool GUI. Once the **deploytool** is started, a **Set Tomcat Server** dialog asks for user name and password for using the Tomcat server, whose values were specified at installation time. Figure 9.7 is the **deploytool** initial window.

Click the **File** menu and select **New Web Application...** to create the Web application via the wizard. A **New Web Application Wizard - Introduction** dialog box appears. Read the instructions and click the **Next** button, which displays the **New Web Application Wizard - WAR File** dialog box. In the **WAR File Location** panel, enter the name and location where you would like to create the WAR file and enter a display name. In the **Contents** panel, click **Edit...** button to add **Vote.class**, **VoteImpl.class**, **RmiJdbc.jar** and **cloudclient.jar**. [*Note*: Compiling **Vote.java** and **VoteImpl.java** requires **jaxrpc-api.jar** and **servlet.jar**. Both JAR files are available at **%JWSDP_HOME%\common\lib** directory, where **JWSDP_HOME** is the JWSDP installation directory.] When adding the class files, be sure that the **Starting Directory** is set to the directory on your computer that contains the **com.deitel.jws1** package structure. The **deploytool** automatically places all class files into directory **classes** and all JAR files into directory **lib**. Figure 9.8 shows the result of editing the WAR file contents for this example.

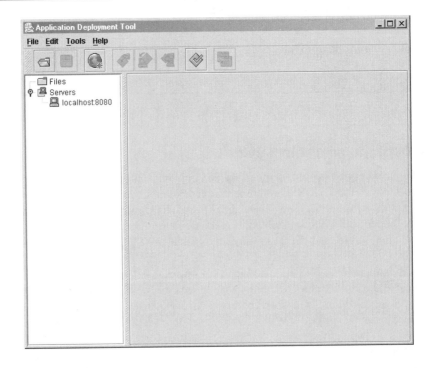

Fig. 9.7   The **deploytool** initial window.

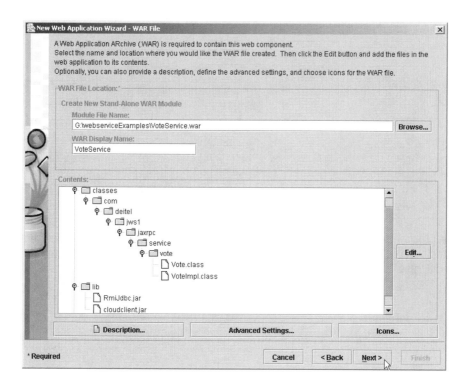

Fig. 9.8   Creating WAR file.

In the next dialog box, **New Web Application Wizard - Choose Component Type**, select the **JAX-RPC Endpoint** radio button and check the **Context Parameters** check box, then click **Next** to continue. A dialog box **New Web Application Wizard - JAXRPC Default Settings** appears. In this dialog, enter the values as shown in Figure 9.9.

The next dialog box **New Web Application Wizard - JAX-RPC Endpoint** sets the service endpoint. Figure 9.10 shows the endpoint setting for the Vote service. Click **Next** to display the **New Web Application Wizard - JAX-RPC Model** dialog box. Select the **Use Default Model Setting** radio button and click **Next** to continue.

A **New Web Application Wizard - Context Parameters** dialog box appears next. In this dialog, we set the context parameters for accessing the database. Figure 9.11 shows the parameter names and values used in the Vote service.

Click **Next** to view the setting in dialog box **New Web Application Wizard - Review Settings**, then click **Finish** to confirm the settings. Figure 9.12 shows the Vote service Web application overview.

To deploy the Vote service, select the **Tools** menu and click **Deploy...**. Enter the Web context in the **Text Input Dialog**. Figure 9.13 shows the Web context for the Vote service. Click **OK** to deploy the service. A **Deployment Console** appears to show the deployment process. Click **Close** to close the console.

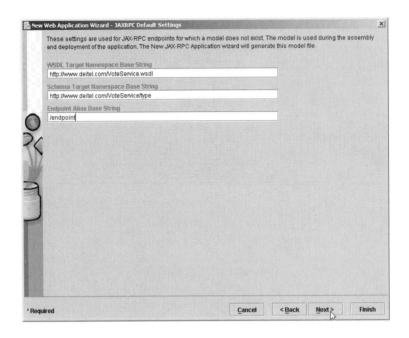

Fig. 9.9   Default setting for the Vote service.

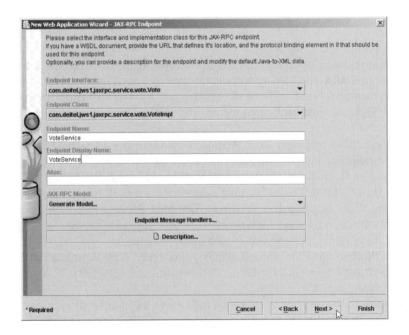

Fig. 9.10   Endpoint setting for the Vote service.

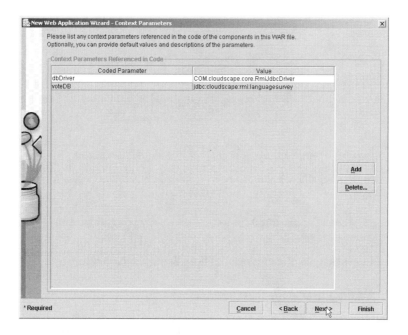

Fig. 9.11   Setting the servlet context parameters.

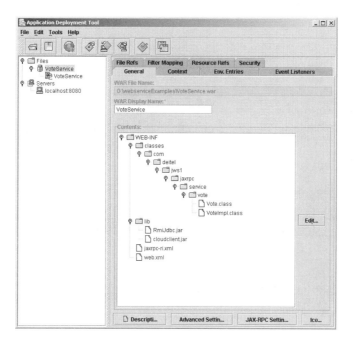

Fig. 9.12   Vote service Web application overview.

Fig. 9.13   Specifying the Web context for the Vote Web service.

To verify whether the service has been installed correctly, open a Web browser and visit:

```
http://localhost:8080/jaxrpc-VoteService/endpoint/
    VoteService
```

Figure 9.14 shows that the Vote service has been deployed successfully.

9.3.5 Accessing the Vote Service

Once a Web service is deployed, a client can access that Web service via a static stub, the dynamic invocation interface (DII) or a dynamic proxy. We discuss each of these in detail in the following sections. Before we introduce service stubs, we demonstrate how to use the **xrpcc** tool for generating the stubs.

Fig. 9.14   Service endpoint verification.

xrpcc Tool

The **xrpcc** tool generates a WSDL document or a remote-interface definition, depending on the command-line parameter. If we supply **xrpcc** with a remote-interface definition, it generates stubs, ties, a WSDL document and a server-configuration file used during deployment. If we supply **xrpcc** with a WSDL document, it generates stubs, ties, a server-configuration file and the remote-interface definition. Most users use an existing WSDL document to access a Web service. The stubs, ties, service and client-side artifacts are dictated by **xrpcc** options **-client**, **-server** and **-both**. We demonstrate the usage of all these options in the next several examples. In this example, we use **xrpcc** to generate the remote interface definition and client-side classes to access the Web service based on the WSDL document. In later examples, we use **xrpcc** to generate the WSDL document, based on the remote-interface definition.

Web service clients do not require access to the service interface and implementation classes. Clients need only the WSDL document that describes the service. The client specifies the location of the WSDL document in a configuration file and **xrpcc** generates the client-side classes that enable communication with the Web service. Figure 9.15 is the configuration file that is passed to the **xrpcc** tool to generate the client-side classes. Element **wsdl** (lines 4–5) specifies the WSDL-document URL and the fully qualified package name of the client-side classes. (The package name may differ from the package name of **SurveyServlet**.)

The command

```
xrpcc -d voteappclient -client -keep VoteClientConfig.xml
```

generates the client-side classes for the Vote service in directory **voteappclient**. **VoteClientConfig.xml** (Fig. 9.15) is the configuration file passed to **xrpcc**.

Using a Static Stub

In this section, we build a servlet-based client for the Vote Web service. Later sections introduce how to write Java applications to access Web services. Although **SurveyServlet** (Fig. 9.16) contains more than 200 lines of code, the core part that accesses the Vote service resides in lines 94–98. The remaining code uses DOM and JAXP to build and parse XML documents for interacting with the user.

SurveyServlet (Fig. 9.16) is a servlet that creates a survey form, invokes the Vote Web service to tally votes, and displays the survey results obtained from the Vote Web service.

```
1   <?xml version="1.0" encoding="UTF-8"?>
2   <configuration
3       xmlns = "http://java.sun.com/xml/ns/jax-rpc/ri/config">
4       <wsdl location="http://localhost:8080/jaxrpc-VoteService/
endpoint/VoteService?WSDL"
5           packageName = "vote">
6       </wsdl>
7   </configuration>
```

Fig. 9.15 Configuration file **VoteClientConfig.xml** to generate client-side classes from the WSDL document.

Method **doGet** (lines 28–75) displays the survey form. The **try** block (lines 37–68) performs the XML and XSL processing that results in an XHTML document containing a survey form. Creating a Document Object Model (DOM) tree from an XML document requires a **DocumentBuilder** parser object. Lines 41–42 obtain a **DocumentBuilderFactory**. Lines 45–46 obtain a **DocumentBuilder** parser object that enables the program to create a **Document** object tree in which the XML document elements are represented as **Element** objects. Line 54 invokes method **parse** of class **DocumentBuilder** to parse **survey.xml**. Lines 57–59 create an **InputStream** that will be used by the XSL transformation processor to read the XSL file. The response is created by the XSL transformation performed in method **transform** (lines 173–206).

```
1   // Fig. 9.16: SurveyServlet.java
2   // A Web-based survey that invokes a Web service
3   // from a servlet.
4   package com.deitel.jws1.jaxrpc.client.stub;
5
6   // Java core packages
7   import java.io.*;
8   import java.util.*;
9
10  // Java extension packages
11  import javax.servlet.*;
12  import javax.servlet.http.*;
13  import javax.xml.rpc.*;
14  import javax.xml.parsers.*;
15  import javax.xml.transform.*;
16  import javax.xml.transform.dom.*;
17  import javax.xml.transform.stream.*;
18
19  // third-party packages
20  import org.w3c.dom.*;
21
22  // xrpcc generated stub packages
23  import vote.*;
24
25  public class SurveyServlet extends HttpServlet {
26
27     // display survey form
28     protected void doGet( HttpServletRequest request,
29        HttpServletResponse response )
30           throws ServletException, IOException
31     {
32        // setup response to client
33        response.setContentType( "text/html" );
34        PrintWriter out = response.getWriter();
35
36        // get XML document and transform for browser client
37        try {
38
```

Fig. 9.16   SurveyServlet uses a static stub to access the Vote Web service. (Part 1 of 5.)

```
39              // get DocumentBuilderFactory for creating
40              // DocumentBuilder (i.e., an XML parser)
41              DocumentBuilderFactory factory =
42                 DocumentBuilderFactory.newInstance();
43
44              // get DocumentBuilder for building DOM tree
45              DocumentBuilder builder =
46                 factory.newDocumentBuilder();
47
48              // open InputStream for XML document
49              InputStream xmlStream =
50                 getServletContext().getResourceAsStream(
51                    "/survey.xml" );
52
53              // create Document based on input XML file
54              Document surveyDocument = builder.parse( xmlStream );
55
56              // open InputStream for XSL document
57              InputStream xslStream =
58                 getServletContext().getResourceAsStream(
59                    "/survey.xsl" );
60
61              // transform XML document using XSLT
62              transform( surveyDocument, xslStream, out );
63
64              // flush and close PrinterWriter
65              out.flush();
66              out.close();
67
68           } // end try
69
70           // catch XML parser exceptions
71           catch( Exception exception ) {
72              exception.printStackTrace();
73           }
74
75        } // end method doGet
76
77        // process survey response
78        protected void doPost( HttpServletRequest request,
79           HttpServletResponse response )
80              throws ServletException, IOException
81        {
82           // setup response to client
83           response.setContentType( "text/html" );
84           PrintWriter out = response.getWriter();
85
86           // read current survey response
87           String name = request.getParameter(
88              "favoriteLanguage" );
89
```

Fig. 9.16   **SurveyServlet** uses a static stub to access the Vote Web service.
(Part 2 of 5.)

```
90          // attempt to process vote and display current results
91          try {
92
93             // get stub and connect to Web service's endpoint
94             Vote_Stub stub = ( Vote_Stub )
95                ( new VoteService_Impl().getVotePort() );
96
97             // get vote information from server
98             String result = stub.addVote( name );
99
100            StringTokenizer voteTokens =
101               new StringTokenizer( result );
102
103            // get DocumentBuilderFactory for creating
104            // DocumentBuilder (i.e., an XML parser)
105            DocumentBuilderFactory factory =
106               DocumentBuilderFactory.newInstance();
107
108            // get DocumentBuilder for building DOM tree
109            DocumentBuilder builder =
110               factory.newDocumentBuilder();
111
112            // create Document (empty DOM tree)
113            Document resultDocument = builder.newDocument();
114
115            // generate XML from result and append to Document
116            Element resultElement = generateXML(
117               voteTokens, resultDocument );
118            resultDocument.appendChild( resultElement );
119
120            // open InputStream for XSL document
121            InputStream xslStream =
122               getServletContext().getResourceAsStream(
123                  "/surveyresults.xsl" );
124
125            // transform XML document using XSLT
126            transform( resultDocument, xslStream, out );
127
128            // flush and close PrintWriter
129            out.flush();
130            out.close();
131
132         } // end try
133
134         // catch connection and XML parser exceptions
135         catch ( Exception exception ) {
136            exception.printStackTrace();
137         }
138
139      } // end method doPost
140
```

Fig. 9.16 SurveyServlet uses a static stub to access the Vote Web service.
(Part 3 of 5.)

```
141        // generate XML representation of vote information
142        private Element generateXML( StringTokenizer voteTokens,
143           Document document )
144        {
145           // create root element
146           Element root = document.createElement( "surveyresults" );
147
148           Element language;
149           Element name;
150           Element vote;
151
152           // create language element for each language
153           while ( voteTokens.hasMoreTokens() ) {
154              language = document.createElement( "language" );
155              name = document.createElement( "name" );
156              name.appendChild( document.createTextNode(
157                 voteTokens.nextToken() ) );
158
159              language.appendChild( name );
160              vote = document.createElement( "vote" );
161              vote.appendChild( document.createTextNode(
162                 voteTokens.nextToken() ) );
163              language.appendChild( vote );
164              root.appendChild( language );
165           }
166
167           return root; // return root element
168
169        } // end method generateXML
170
171        // transform XML document using XSLT InputStream
172        // and write resulting document to PrintWriter
173        private void transform( Document document,
174           InputStream xslStream, PrintWriter output )
175        {
176           // transform XML to XHTML
177           try {
178
179              // create DOMSource for source XML document
180              Source xmlSource = new DOMSource( document );
181
182              // create StreamSource for XSLT document
183              Source xslSource = new StreamSource( xslStream );
184
185              // create StreamResult for transformation result
186              Result result = new StreamResult( output );
187
188              // create TransformerFactory to obtain Transformer
189              TransformerFactory transformerFactory =
190                 TransformerFactory.newInstance();
191
```

Fig. 9.16 SurveyServlet uses a static stub to access the Vote Web service.
(Part 4 of 5.)

```
192              // create Transformer for performing XSL transformation
193              Transformer transformer =
194                 transformerFactory.newTransformer( xslSource );
195
196              // perform transformation and deliver content to client
197              transformer.transform( xmlSource, result );
198
199           } // end try
200
201           // handle exception when transforming XML document
202           catch( TransformerException exception ) {
203              exception.printStackTrace( System.err );
204           }
205
206        } // end method transform
207
208     } // end class SurveyServlet
```

Fig. 9.16   **SurveyServlet** uses a static stub to access the Vote Web service. (Part 5 of 5.)

Method **transform** takes three arguments—the XML **Document** to which the XSL transformation will be applied, the **InputStream** that reads the XSL file and the **PrintWriter** to which the results should be written. Line 180 creates a **DOMSource** that represents the XML document. This **DOMSource** serves as the source of the XML to transform. Line 183 creates a **StreamSource** for the XSL file. Line 186 creates a **StreamResult** for the **PrintWriter** to which the results of the XSL transformation are written. Lines 189–190 create a **TransformerFactory**, which enables the program to obtain the **Transformer** object that applies the XSL transformation. Lines 193–194 invoke **TransformerFactory** method **newTransformer** to create a **Transformer**. This method receives a **StreamSource** argument that represents the XSL (e.g., **xslSource**). Line 197 invokes **Transformer** method **transform** to perform the XSL transformation on the **DOMSource** object **xmlSource** and write the result to **StreamResult** object **result**. Lines 202–204 catch a **TransformerException** if a problem occurs when creating the **TransformerFactory**, creating the **Transformer** or performing the transformation.

Method **doPost** (lines 78–139) gets the client-specified programming language (lines 87–88). Lines 94–95 then connects to the Vote Web service. Once the connection is done, line 98 invokes the **addVote** method of the Vote Web service stub. To access a Web service via a stub, we need to obtain the stub object. The **xrpcc** tool generates the client-side stub of the Vote Web service—**Vote_Stub**. When **xrpcc** generates the stub, it uses the following convention: *serviceinterface*_**Stub**. Lines 94–95 get the **Vote_Stub** by invoking method **getVotePort** of class **VoteService_Impl**. The generated **Vote_Stub** class implements the **javax.xml.rpc.Stub** interface. Class **VoteService_Impl** is the **xrpcc**-generated implementation of the **Vote** service. When **xrpcc** generates the service implementation, it uses the naming convention *servicename*_**Impl**, where *servicename* is the service name specified in the **xrpcc** configuration file.

Line 98 invokes method **addVote** of the **stub** object to process the votes. Method **addVote** places a vote for the given language and returns a tally of previously recorded votes for each language. Class **SurveyServlet** transforms the return value of method **addVote** to an XML representation. Method **generateXML** creates the XML representation of the vote information (lines 142–169). We pass two arguments to this method—the **StringTokenizer** that contains vote information and an empty **Document** tree. The complete vote information is placed in a **surveyresults** element (created at line 146). Lines 153–164 append elements for the individual votes for a programming language to the **surveyresults** element as children. Lines 154–155 use **Document** method **createElement** to create elements **language** and **name**. Lines 156–157 use **Document** method **createTextNode** to specify the language name in the **name** element, and **Element** method **appendChild** to append the text to element **name**. Line 159 appends element **name** as a child of element **language** with **Element** method **appendChild**. Similar operations are performed for the votes for a language. Line 164 appends each **language** element to the **root** element (**surveyresults**).

Once the program gets the XML representation of the vote information, line 118 appends **Element resultElement** (returned by method **generateXML**) to the **Document** object—**resultDocument**. Lines 121–123 create an **InputStream** that will be used by the XSL transformation processor to read the XSL file. Line 126 invokes method **transform** to create the response.

Class **SurveyServlet** requires one XML file that contains a list of programming languages for the survey, and two XSL files that transform XML files to XHTML responses. Method **doGet** requires **survey.xml** (Fig. 9.17) and **survey.xsl** (Fig. 9.18). Method **doPost** requires **surveyresults.xsl** (Fig. 9.19).

Figure 9.18 contains **survey.xsl**, which transforms **survey.xml** into an XHTML form. The names of the five elements in the XML document (**survey.xml**) are placed in the resulting XHTML form. Line 23 places the survey's **title** (line 1 in **survey.xml**) in the document's **title** element. Line 27 places the survey's **question** (line 2 in **survey.xml**) in a paragraph at the beginning of the document's **body** element. Lines 30–38 generate a form to be included in the document's **body** element. Line 31 uses XSLT element **for-each**, which applies the contents of the element to each of the nodes selected by attribute **select**, to include the name of each programming language in the form.

Line 32 uses XSLT element **sort** to sort the nodes by the field specified in attribute **select**, in the order specified in attribute **order** (either **ascending** or **descending**). In this example, we sort the nodes by attribute **name**, in **ascending** order. Lines 33–35 add each **language** element specified in the XML document (lines 3–7 in **survey.xml**) to the form.

```
1   <survey title = "Your Favorite Language"
2      question = "Choose your favorite programming language:">
3      <language name = "C"/>
4      <language name = "C++"/>
5      <language name = "Java"/>
6      <language name = "VB"/>
7      <language name = "Python"/>
8   </survey>
```

Fig. 9.17   survey.xml contains a list of programming languages for the survey.

```
1    <?xml version = "1.0"?>
2
3    <xsl:stylesheet xmlns:xsl = "http://www.w3.org/1999/XSL/Transform"
4       version = "1.0">
5
6    <xsl:output method = "xml" omit-xml-declaration = "no"
7       indent = "yes" doctype-system =
8       "http://www.w3.org/TR/xhtml11/DTD/xhtml11-strict.dtc"
9       doctype-public = "-//W3C//DTD XHTML 1.0 Strict//EN"/>
10
11   <!-- survey.xsl                                        -->
12   <!-- XSL document that rransforms XML into XHTML -->
13
14   <!-- specify the root of the XML document -->
15   <!-- that references this stylesheet      -->
16   <xsl:template match = "survey">
17
18      <html xmlns = "http://www.w3.org/1999/xhtml">
19
20      <head>
21
22         <!-- obtain survey title from survey element -->
23         <title><xsl:value-of select = "@title"/></title>
24      </head>
25
26      <body>
27         <p><xsl:value-of select = "@question"/></p>
28
29         <!-- create form -->
30         <form method = "post" action = "/jaxrpc-VoteClient/Survey">
31            <xsl:for-each select = "language">
32               <xsl:sort select = "@name" order = "ascending"/>
33               <input type = "radio" name = "favoriteLanguage"
34                  value = "{@name}"><xsl:value-of select = "@name"/>
35               </input><br/>
36            </xsl:for-each>
37            <br/><input type = "Submit"/>
38         </form>
39
40      </body>
41
42      </html>
43
44   </xsl:template>
45
46   </xsl:stylesheet>
```

Fig. 9.18   XSL style sheet (`survey.xsl`) that transforms `survey.xml` into an XHTML document.

Figure 9.19 contains **surveyresults.xsl**, which transforms the voting results to XHTML. Lines 30–34 use XSLT elements **for-each** to display the survey results in **ascending** order by **name**.

```
1   <?xml version = "1.0"?>
2
3   <xsl:stylesheet xmlns:xsl = "http://www.w3.org/1999/XSL/Transform"
4      version = "1.0">
5
6   <xsl:output method = "xml" omit-xml-declaration = "no"
7      indent = "yes" doctype-system =
8      "http://www.w3.org/TR/xhtml1/DTD/xhtml1-strict.dtc"
9      doctype-public = "-//W3C//DTD XHTML 1.0 Strict//EN"/>
10
11  <!-- survey.xsl                                     -->
12  <!-- XSL document that rransforms XML into XHTML -->
13
14  <!-- specify the root of the XML document -->
15  <!-- that references this stylesheet        -->
16  <xsl:template match = "surveyresults">
17
18     <html xmlns = "http://www.w3.org/1999/xhtml">
19
20     <head>
21
22        <!-- obtain survey name from survey element -->
23        <title>Survey Results</title>
24     </head>
25
26     <body>
27        <h1>Vote Information:</h1>
28
29        <!-- create result list -->
30        <xsl:for-each select = "language">
31           <p><xsl:value-of select = "name"/>:
32              <xsl:value-of select = "vote"/>
33           </p>
34        </xsl:for-each>
35
36     </body>
37
38     </html>
39
40  </xsl:template>
41
42  </xsl:stylesheet>
```

Fig. 9.19   XSL style sheet (`surveyresults.xsl`) that transforms
`surveyresults.xml` into an XHTML document.

To compile **SurveyServlet**, make sure that **jaxrpc-api.jar**; **jaxrpc-ri.jar**; **servlet.jar**; **dom.jar**; **sax.jar** and **jaxp-api.jar** are included in the classpath. These JAR files are located in directories **%JWSDP_HOME%\common\lib** and **%JWSDP_HOME%\common\endorsed**, where **JWSDP_HOME** is the home directory of the JWSDP installation.

To deploy the client using the **deploytool**, click the **File** menu and select **New Web Application....** In the **New Web Application Wizard - WAR File** dialog box, specify the **WAR File Location** and **Contents** as shown in Fig. 9.20. Directory `classes` contains `SurveyServlet.class` and client-side classes generated by `xrpcc`. The WAR contents also should include `survey.xml` (Fig. 9.17), `survey.xsl` (Fig. 9.18) and `surveyresults.xsl` (Fig. 9.19).

In the next dialog box, **New Web Application Wizard - Choose Component Type**, select the **Servlet** radio button and check the **Aliases** check box, then click **Next** to display the **New Web Application Wizard - Component General Properties** dialog box. Figure 9.21 specifies the client Web application component properties.

Click **Next** (Fig. 9.21) to display dialog box **New Web Application Wizard - Aliases**. Click **Add** to add aliases for `SurveyServlet`. Figure 9.22 shows the aliases for `SurveyServlet`.

Click **Next** to display the **New Web Application Wizard - Review Setting** window. Click **Finish** to close the review window. Figure 9.23 shoes the general information of the `VoteClient` Web application.

To deploy the client application, select the **Tools** menu and click **Deploy....** The **Text Input Dialog** (Fig. 9.24) prompts for the Web context to create for the servlet.

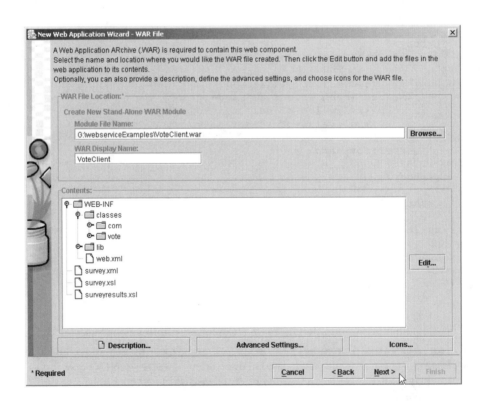

Fig. 9.20   Creating the WAR file for the Vote client Web application.

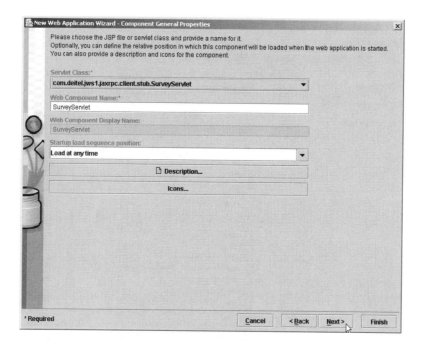

Fig. 9.21   Specifying the Vote client Web application component properties.

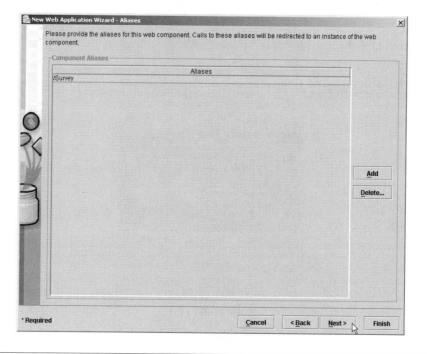

Fig. 9.22   Setting aliases for **SurveyServlet**.

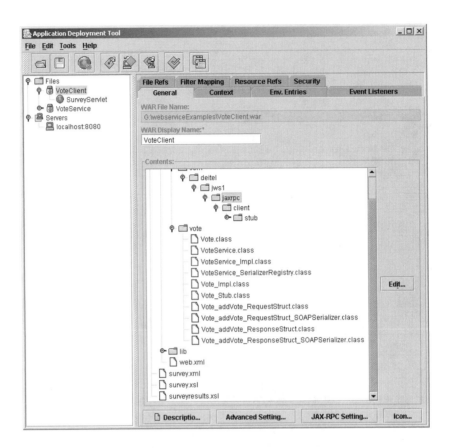

Fig. 9.23 **VoteClient** Web application general information.

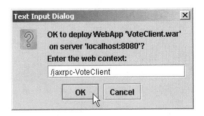

Fig. 9.24 Specifying the Web context for the Vote client.

To start the client, open a Web browser and visit:

http://localhost:8080/jaxrpc-VoteClient/Survey

Figure 9.25 shows the **VoteClient** Web application survey form and results.

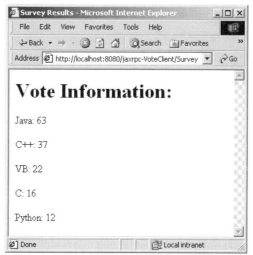

Fig. 9.25 VoteClient Web application survey form and results.

Using the Dynamic Invocation Interface

The *Dynamic Invocation Interface* (*DII*) enables Web-service clients to call methods on Web services without knowing the service's stub information. DII clients can build method calls dynamically, based on the WSDL document of the service. To use DII to invoke a Web service, clients must have the following information in advance:

1. Web-service endpoint.

2. Interface name of the Web service.

3. Name of the method call.

4. A list of the parameters.

5. Return type of the method call.

6. Service target namespace, which defines the namespaces used in the WSDL document.

7. Type namespace to register the serializers/deserializers.

8. SOAP action, which indicates the intent of the SOAP request (an empty-string value indicates that the HTTP request contains the SOAP request's intent).

9. Encoding style, which defines the serialization rules used to deserialize the SOAP message.

The Web service's WSDL document provides this information.

Next, we introduce how to invoke a Web service via DII. Using DII is more complicated than using static stubs. However, DII clients are more flexible than are static-stub clients, because DII clients can specify the remote procedure calls' properties (such as Web-service names, remote-method input parameters, and remote-method return types) at runtime.

DIISurveyServlet (Fig. 9.26) creates a survey form in method **doGet**, forwards the survey result to the Vote Web service and displays the vote information obtained from the Vote Web service in method **doPost**. Method **doGet** is almost identical to the method **doGet** of **SurveyServlet** (Fig. 9.16), except that lines 70–72 read **surveyDII.xsl** (Fig. 9.27) rather than **survey.xsl**.

```
1   // Fig. 9.26: DIISurveyServlet.java
2   // A Web-based survey that invokes the Web service
3   // from a servlet using DII.
4   package com.deitel.jws1.jaxrpc.client.dii;
5
6   // Java core packages
7   import java.io.*;
8   import java.util.*;
9
10  // Java extension packages
11  import javax.servlet.*;
12  import javax.servlet.http.*;
13  import javax.xml.parsers.*;
14  import javax.xml.transform.*;
15  import javax.xml.transform.dom.*;
16  import javax.xml.transform.stream.*;
17
18  // Java XML RPC packages
19  import javax.xml.rpc.*;
20  import javax.xml.namespace.QName;
21  import javax.xml.rpc.encoding.*;
22
23  // JWSDP reference implementation
24  import com.sun.xml.rpc.client.*;
25  import com.sun.xml.rpc.client.dii.*;
26  import com.sun.xml.rpc.encoding.*;
27  import com.sun.xml.rpc.encoding.soap.*;
28  import com.sun.xml.rpc.soap.streaming.*;
29
```

Fig. 9.26 DIISurveyServlet invokes the Web service via DII. (Part 1 of 6.)

```
30    // third-party packages
31    import org.w3c.dom.*;
32
33    public class DIISurveyServlet extends HttpServlet {
34
35        // servlet attributes
36        private String surveyText;
37        private String pageTitle;
38        private String submissionIdentifier;
39
40        // display survey form
41        protected void doGet( HttpServletRequest request,
42            HttpServletResponse response )
43                throws ServletException, IOException
44        {
45            // setup response to client
46            response.setContentType( "text/html" );
47            PrintWriter out = response.getWriter();
48
49            // get XML document and transform for browser client
50            try {
51
52                // get DocumentBuilderFactory for creating
53                // DocumentBuilder (i.e., an XML parser)
54                DocumentBuilderFactory factory =
55                    DocumentBuilderFactory.newInstance();
56
57                // get DocumentBuilder for building DOM tree
58                DocumentBuilder builder =
59                    factory.newDocumentBuilder();
60
61                // open InputStream for XML document
62                InputStream xmlStream =
63                    getServletContext().getResourceAsStream(
64                        "/survey.xml" );
65
66                // create Document based on input XML file
67                Document surveyDocument = builder.parse( xmlStream );
68
69                // open InputStream for XSL document
70                InputStream xslStream =
71                    getServletContext().getResourceAsStream(
72                        "/surveyDII.xsl" );
73
74                // transform XML document using XSLT
75                transform( surveyDocument, xslStream, out );
76
77                // flush and close PrinterWriter
78                out.flush();
79                out.close();
80
81            } // end try
82
```

Fig. 9.26   DIISurveyServlet invokes the Web service via DII. (Part 2 of 6.)

```
83          // catch XML parser exceptions
84          catch( Exception exception ) {
85             exception.printStackTrace();
86          }
87
88       } // end method doGet
89
90       // process survey response
91       protected void doPost( HttpServletRequest request,
92          HttpServletResponse response )
93             throws ServletException, IOException
94       {
95          // setup response to client
96          response.setContentType( "text/html" );
97          PrintWriter out = response.getWriter();
98
99          // read current survey response
100         String name = request.getParameter(
101            "favoriteLanguage" );
102
103         // read service endpoint
104         String endpoint = request.getParameter( "endpoint" );
105
106         // attempt to process vote and display current results
107         try {
108
109            // QName for "xsd:string"
110            QName xmlString = new QName(
111               "http://www.w3.org/2001/XMLSchema", "string" );
112
113            // QName for service port
114            QName servicePort = new QName(
115               "http://www.deitel.com/VoteService.wsdl/VoteService",
116               "VotePort" );
117
118            // QName for service name
119            QName serviceName = new QName( "VoteService" );
120
121            // get Service object from SUN's Service implementation
122            Service service =
123               ServiceFactory.newInstance().createService(
124                  serviceName );
125
126            // create Call object
127            Call call = service.createCall();
128            call.setPortTypeName( servicePort );
129            call.setTargetEndpointAddress( endpoint );
130
131            // set call properties
132            call.setProperty( Call.SOAPACTION_USE_PROPERTY,
133               new Boolean( true ) );
134            call.setProperty( Call.SOAPACTION_URI_PROPERTY, "" );
```

Fig. 9.26 **DIISurveyServlet** invokes the Web service via DII. (Part 3 of 6.)

```
135         String ENCODING_STYLE_PROPERTY =
136            "javax.xml.rpc.encodingstyle.namespace.uri";
137         call.setProperty( ENCODING_STYLE_PROPERTY,
138            "http://schemas.xmlsoap.org/soap/encoding/" );
139
140         // set call operation name and its input and output
141         QName addVoteOperation = new QName(
142            "http://www.deitel.com/VoteService.wsdl/VoteService",
143            "addVote" );
144         call.setOperationName( addVoteOperation );
145         call.addParameter( "String_1", xmlString,
146            ParameterMode.IN );
147         call.setReturnType( xmlString );
148         Object[] callInputs =
149            new Object[] { name };
150
151         // invoke addVote method
152         String callOutput = ( String ) call.invoke(
153            addVoteOperation, callInputs );
154
155         StringTokenizer voteTokens =
156            new StringTokenizer( callOutput );
157
158         // get DocumentBuilderFactory for creating
159         // DocumentBuilder (i.e., an XML parser)
160         DocumentBuilderFactory factory =
161            DocumentBuilderFactory.newInstance();
162
163         // get DocumentBuilder for building DOM tree
164         DocumentBuilder builder =
165            factory.newDocumentBuilder();
166
167         // create Document (empty DOM tree)
168         Document resultDocument = builder.newDocument();
169
170         // generate XML from result and append to Document
171         Element resultElement = generateXML(
172            voteTokens, resultDocument );
173         resultDocument.appendChild( resultElement );
174
175         // open InputStream for XSL document
176         InputStream xslStream =
177            getServletContext().getResourceAsStream(
178               "/surveyresults.xsl" );
179
180         // transform XML document using XSLT
181         transform( resultDocument, xslStream, out );
182
183         // flush and close PrintWriter
184         out.flush();
185         out.close();
186
187      } // end try
```

Fig. 9.26   DIISurveyServlet invokes the Web service via DII. (Part 4 of 6.)

```
188
189       // return error page on exception
190       catch ( Exception exception ) {
191          exception.printStackTrace();
192          out.println( "<title>Error</title>" );
193          out.println( "</head>" );
194          out.println( "<body><p>Error occurred: " );
195          out.println( exception.getMessage() );
196          out.println( "</p></body></html>" );
197          out.close();
198       }
199
200    } // end method doPost
201
202     // generate vote information XML representation
203    private Element generateXML( StringTokenizer voteTokens,
204       Document document )
205    {
206       // create root element
207       Element root = document.createElement( "surveyresults" );
208
209       Element language;
210       Element name;
211       Element vote;
212
213       // create language element for each language
214       while ( voteTokens.hasMoreTokens() ) {
215          language = document.createElement( "language" );
216          name = document.createElement( "name" );
217          name.appendChild( document.createTextNode(
218             voteTokens.nextToken() ) );
219
220          language.appendChild( name );
221          vote = document.createElement( "vote" );
222          vote.appendChild( document.createTextNode(
223             voteTokens.nextToken() ) );
224          language.appendChild( vote );
225          root.appendChild( language );
226       }
227
228       return root; // return root element
229
230    } // end method generateXML
231
232    // transform XML document using XSLT InputStream
233    // and write resulting document to PrintWriter
234    private void transform( Document document,
235       InputStream xslStream, PrintWriter output )
236    {
237       // transform XML to XHTML
238       try {
239
```

Fig. 9.26 DIISurveyServlet invokes the Web service via DII. (Part 5 of 6.)

```
240                 // create DOMSource for source XML document
241                 Source xmlSource = new DOMSource( document );
242
243                 // create StreamSource for XSLT document
244                 Source xslSource = new StreamSource( xslStream );
245
246                 // create StreamResult for transformation result
247                 Result result = new StreamResult( output );
248
249                 // create TransformerFactory to obtain Transformer
250                 TransformerFactory transformerFactory =
251                    TransformerFactory.newInstance();
252
253                 // create Transformer for performing XSL transformation
254                 Transformer transformer =
255                    transformerFactory.newTransformer( xslSource );
256
257                 // perform transformation and deliver content to client
258                 transformer.transform( xmlSource, result );
259
260             } // end try
261
262             // handle exception when transforming XML document
263             catch( TransformerException exception ) {
264                 exception.printStackTrace( System.err );
265             }
266
267         } // end method transform
268
269     } // end class DIISurveyServlet
```

Fig. 9.26   **DIISurveyServlet** invokes the Web service via DII. (Part 6 of 6.)

Method **doPost** (lines 91–200) implements support for DII clients. Lines 110–111 create a **QName** for the XML representation of Java **String** object. Class **QName** (in package **javax.xml.namespace**) represents a data type with a qualified namespace in XML (e.g., **xsd:string**, where **xsd** is the namespace URI for the **QName** and **string** is the data type).

Lines 114–119 create two **QName**s that specify the service port and service name. Lines 122–124 create a service with the specified service name by invoking **static** method **newInstance** of class **ServiceFactory** to get an instance of **Service-Factory** object, and by invoking method **createService** of class **ServiceFactory** to create a **Service** instance.

To invoke a method dynamically, line 127 creates a **Call** object, which enables dynamic invocation of a service port by invoking method **createCall** of interface **Service**. Line 128 invokes method **setPortTypeName** of interface **Call** to set the service port. Method **setPortTypeName** takes one argument that specifies the **QName** of the service port. Line 129 invokes method **setTargetEndpointAddress** of interface **Call** to set the URI of the service end point.

Lines 132–138 invoke method **setProperty** of interface **Call** to set the properties of the call. Lines 132–133 indicate that the **SOAPAction** HTTP header is used in this method call. The **SOAPAction** HTTP header indicates the intent of the SOAP request. An empty-string value indicates that the HTTP request contains the SOAP request's intent. Line 134 sets the **SOAPAction** value to an empty string. Lines 137–138 set the encoding style as a namespace URI, which specifies serialization rules in the SOAP message.

Lines 141–149 define the call's operation name, input and output. Lines 141–143 create a **QName** for the operation. Line 144 invokes method **setOperationName** of interface **Call** to set the operation name. Lines 145–146 add a parameter for the operation by invoking method **addParameter** of interface **Call**. Method **addParameter** takes three arguments—a **String** that specifies the parameter's name (i.e., **"String_1"**, as in the WSDL document generated by **xrpcc**), a **QName** that specifies the XML data type of the parameter and a **ParameterMode** object that indicates the parameter's mode (**IN**, a **static** field of class **ParameterMode**). Line 147 invokes method **setReturnType** of interface **Call** to set the return type of the call operation. Method **setReturnType** takes a **QName** argument that specifies the XML representation of the return type.

To invoke the method call, lines 152–153 call method **invoke** of interface **Call** to make the remote procedure call, using the synchronous request-response interaction mode. Method **invoke** takes a **QName** that specifies the operation name and an array of **Object**s that contains all input parameters, and returns an **Object** that contains the output. The remaining part of method **doPost** (lines 155–185) is similar to that in **SurveyServlet** (Fig. 9.16).

Figure 9.27 contains **surveyDII.xsl**, which the XSL transformation uses. Most of the content is identical to that of **survey.xls** (Fig. 9.18) except that **surveyDII.xsl** changes the form action to **/jaxrpc-VoteDIIClient/Survey** and adds the text field (line 70) for the client to specify the service endpoint.

```
1   <?xml version = "1.0"?>
2
3   <xsl:stylesheet xmlns:xsl = "http://www.w3.org/1999/XSL/Transform"
4      version = "1.0">
5
6   <xsl:output method = "xml" omit-xml-declaration = "no"
7      indent = "yes" doctype-system =
8      "http://www.w3.org/TR/xhtml1/DTD/xhtml1-strict.dtc"
9      doctype-public = "-//W3C//DTD XHTML 1.0 Strict//EN"/>
10
11  <!-- surveyDII.xsl                              -->
12  <!-- XSL document that transforms XML into XHTML -->
13
14  <!-- specify the root of the XML document -->
15  <!-- that references this stylesheet       -->
16  <xsl:template match = "survey">
17
18     <html xmlns = "http://www.w3.org/1999/xhtml">
19
```

Fig. 9.27   XSL style sheet (**surveyDII.xsl**) that transforms **survey.xml** into an XHTML document. (Part 1 of 2.)

```
20      <head>
21
22          <!-- obtain survey title from survey element -->
23          <title><xsl:value-of select = "@title"/></title>
24      </head>
25
26      <body>
27          <p><xsl:value-of select = "@question"/></p>
28
29          <!-- create form -->
30          <form method = "post" action = "/jaxrpc-VoteDIIClient/Survey">
31              <xsl:for-each select = "language">
32                  <xsl:sort select = "@name" order = "ascending"/>
33                  <input type = "radio" name = "favoriteLanguage"
34                      value = "{@name}"><xsl:value-of select = "@name"/>
35                  </input><br/>
36              </xsl:for-each>
37              <br/><p>Type in the service endpoint:</p>
38              <input type = "text" name = "endpoint" size = "70"/>
39              <br/><br/><input type = "Submit"/>
40          </form>
41
42      </body>
43
44      </html>
45
46  </xsl:template>
47
48  </xsl:stylesheet>
```

Fig. 9.27 XSL style sheet (`surveyDII.xsl`) that transforms `survey.xml` into an XHTML document. (Part 2 of 2.)

To deploy the DII client, we use the same procedure that we used to deploy the stub client. Figure 9.28 shows dialog box **New Web Application Wizard - WAR File** and Figure 9.29 shows the `VoteDIIClient` Web application. The Web contents for the DII clients include `DIISurveyServlet.class` (Fig. 9.26), `survey.xml` (Fig. 9.17), `surveyDII.xsl` (Fig. 9.27) and `surveyresults.xsl` (Fig. 9.19).

To deploy the `VoteDIIClient` Web application, we use the same approach as the one we used to deploy the `VoteClient`. In the **Text Input Dialog**, enter `/jaxrpc-Vote-DIIClient` as the Web context. To run the DII client, open a Web browser and visit:

    http://localhost:8080/jaxrpc-VoteDIIClient/Survey

Figure 9.30 shows the `VoteDIIClient` Web application survey form and results.

Using a Dynamic Proxy

In the previous examples, we used static stubs and DII to invoke the Web service. Using static stubs requires the programmer to generate the stubs using `xrpcc`. Using DII requires the programmer to do more coding. In this section, we introduce how to invoke a Web service using a dynamic proxy (a class that is generated at run time), which does not require the stubs and extra coding. To use the dynamic proxy, the clients must have access to the WSDL document and be able to extract service information from the WSDL document.

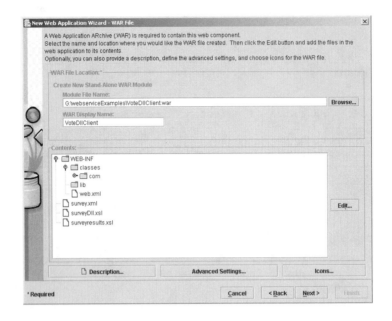

Fig. 9.28   Creating the WAR file for the DII Vote client Web application.

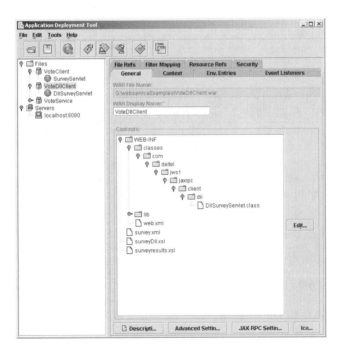

Fig. 9.29   VoteDIIClient Web application.

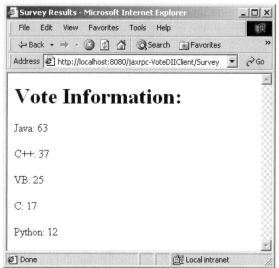

Fig. 9.30 VoteDIIClient Web application survey form and results.

SurveyServlet (Fig. 9.31) creates a survey form in method **doGet**, forwards the survey result to the Vote Web service and displays the vote information obtained from the Vote Web service in method **doPost**. Method **doGet** is almost identical to the method **doGet** of **DIISurveyServlet** (Fig. 9.26), except that lines 59–61 read **surveyProxy.xsl** (Fig. 9.32) rather than read **surveyDII.xsl** (Fig. 9.27).

```
1    // SurveyServlet.java
2    // A Web-based survey that invokes the Vote Web service
3    // from a servlet.
4    package com.deitel.jws1.jaxrpc.client.proxy;
5
6    // Java core packages
7    import java.io.*;
8    import java.util.*;
9    import java.net.URL;
10
11   // Java extension packages
12   import javax.servlet.*;
13   import javax.servlet.http.*;
14   import javax.xml.rpc.*;
15   import javax.xml.namespace.*;
16   import javax.xml.parsers.*;
17   import javax.xml.transform.*;
18   import javax.xml.transform.dom.*;
19   import javax.xml.transform.stream.*;
20
21   // third-party packages
22   import org.w3c.dom.*;
23
24   // xrpcc generated stub packages
25   import vote.Vote;
26
27   public class SurveyServlet extends HttpServlet {
28
29      // display survey form
30      protected void doGet( HttpServletRequest request,
31         HttpServletResponse response )
32            throws ServletException, IOException
33      {
34         // setup response to client
35         response.setContentType( "text/html" );
36         PrintWriter out = response.getWriter();
37
38         // get XML document and transform for browser client
39         try {
40
41            // get DocumentBuilderFactory for creating
42            // DocumentBuilder (i.e., an XML parser)
43            DocumentBuilderFactory factory =
44               DocumentBuilderFactory.newInstance();
45
46            // get DocumentBuilder for building DOM tree
47            DocumentBuilder builder =
48               factory.newDocumentBuilder();
49
```

Fig. 9.31 **SurveyServlet** invokes the Web service via a dynamic proxy.
(Part 1 of 5.)

```
50              // open InputStream for XML document
51              InputStream xmlStream =
52                 getServletContext().getResourceAsStream(
53                    "/survey.xml" );
54
55              // create Document based on input XML file
56              Document surveyDocument = builder.parse( xmlStream );
57
58              // open InputStream for XSL document
59              InputStream xslStream =
60                 getServletContext().getResourceAsStream(
61                    "/surveyProxy.xsl" );
62
63              // transform XML document using XSLT
64              transform( surveyDocument, xslStream, out );
65
66              // flush and close PrinterWriter
67              out.flush();
68              out.close();
69
70           } // end try
71
72           // catch XML parser exceptions
73           catch( Exception exception ) {
74              exception.printStackTrace();
75           }
76
77        } // end method doGet
78
79        // process survey response
80        protected void doPost( HttpServletRequest request,
81           HttpServletResponse response )
82              throws ServletException, IOException
83        {
84           // setup response to client
85           response.setContentType( "text/html" );
86           PrintWriter out = response.getWriter();
87
88           // read current survey response
89           String name = request.getParameter(
90              "favoriteLanguage" );
91
92           // attempt to process vote and display current results
93           try {
94
95              // specify service WSDL URL
96              URL serviceWSDLURL = new URL( "http://localhost:8080/" +
97                 "jaxrpc-VoteService/endpoint/VoteService?WSDL" );
98
```

Fig. 9.31   **SurveyServlet** invokes the Web service via a dynamic proxy.
(Part 2 of 5.)

```
99              // specify service QName
100             QName serviceQName = new QName(
101                "http://www.deitel.com/VoteService.wsdl/VoteService",
102                "VoteService" );
103
104             // get Service object from SUN's Service implementation
105             Service service =
106                ServiceFactory.newInstance().createService(
107                   serviceWSDLURL, serviceQName );
108
109             // specify service port QName
110             QName portQName = new QName(
111                "http://www.deitel.com/VoteService.wsdl/VoteService",
112                "VotePort" );
113
114             // get dynamic proxy
115             Vote proxy = ( Vote ) service.getPort(
116                portQName, vote.Vote.class );
117
118             // get vote information from server
119             String result = proxy.addVote( name );
120
121             StringTokenizer voteTokens =
122                new StringTokenizer( result );
123
124             // get DocumentBuilderFactory for creating
125             // DocumentBuilder (i.e., an XML parser)
126             DocumentBuilderFactory factory =
127                DocumentBuilderFactory.newInstance();
128
129             // get DocumentBuilder for building DOM tree
130             DocumentBuilder builder =
131                factory.newDocumentBuilder();
132
133             // create Document (empty DOM tree)
134             Document resultDocument = builder.newDocument();
135
136             // generate XML from result and append to Document
137             Element resultElement = generateXML(
138                voteTokens, resultDocument );
139             resultDocument.appendChild( resultElement );
140
141             // open InputStream for XSL document
142             InputStream xslStream =
143                getServletContext().getResourceAsStream(
144                   "/surveyresults.xsl" );
145
146             // transform XML document using XSLT
147             transform( resultDocument, xslStream, out );
148
149             // flush and close PrintWriter
150             out.flush();
```

Fig. 9.31   **SurveyServlet** invokes the Web service via a dynamic proxy.
(Part 3 of 5.)

```
151            out.close();
152
153        } // end try
154
155        // catch connection and XML parser exceptions
156        catch ( Exception exception ) {
157            exception.printStackTrace();
158        }
159
160    } // end method doPost
161
162    // generate vote information XML representation
163    private Element generateXML( StringTokenizer voteTokens,
164        Document document )
165    {
166        // create root element
167        Element root = document.createElement( "surveyresults" );
168
169        Element language;
170        Element name;
171        Element vote;
172
173        // create language element for each language
174        while ( voteTokens.hasMoreTokens() ) {
175            language = document.createElement( "language" );
176            name = document.createElement( "name" );
177            name.appendChild( document.createTextNode(
178                voteTokens.nextToken() ) );
179
180            language.appendChild( name );
181            vote = document.createElement( "vote" );
182            vote.appendChild( document.createTextNode(
183                voteTokens.nextToken() ) );
184            language.appendChild( vote );
185            root.appendChild( language );
186        }
187
188        return root; // return root element
189
190    } // end method generate XML
191
192    // transform XML document using XSLT InputStream
193    // and write resulting document to PrintWriter
194    private void transform( Document document,
195        InputStream xslStream, PrintWriter output )
196    {
197        // transform XML to XHTML
198        try {
199
200            // create DOMSource for source XML document
201            Source xmlSource = new DOMSource( document );
202
```

Fig. 9.31   **SurveyServlet** invokes the Web service via a dynamic proxy. (Part 4 of 5.)

```
203        // create StreamSource for XSLT document
204        Source xslSource = new StreamSource( xslStream );
205
206        // create StreamResult for transformation result
207        Result result = new StreamResult( output );
208
209        // create TransformerFactory to obtain Transformer
210        TransformerFactory transformerFactory =
211           TransformerFactory.newInstance();
212
213        // create Transformer for performing XSL transformation
214        Transformer transformer =
215           transformerFactory.newTransformer( xslSource );
216
217        // perform transformation and deliver content to client
218        transformer.transform( xmlSource, result );
219
220     } // end try
221
222     // handle exception when transforming XML document
223     catch( TransformerException exception ) {
224        exception.printStackTrace( System.err );
225     }
226
227  } // end method transform
228
229 } // end class SurveyServlet
```

Fig. 9.31   **SurveyServlet** invokes the Web service via a dynamic proxy. (Part 5 of 5.)

Method **doPost** (lines 80–160) implements support for dynamic proxy. Lines 96–97 specify the service WSDL's URL. Lines 100–102 specify the service name with a qualified namespace. The namespace and service name are obtained by examining the WSDL document. Lines 105–107 invoke method **createService** of class **ServiceFactory** with the WSDL URL and qualified service name to create a **Service** instance. Lines 110–112 specify the service port with a qualified namespace. Such information can be extracted from the WSDL document. Lines 115–116 invoke method **getPort** of class **Service** with the qualified service port and the service interface (**vote.Vote.class**) to obtain the dynamic proxy. You can define the service interface by examining the WSDL document. For simplicity, we just use the interface generated by **xrpcc** when we introduced the static stubs. Line 119 invokes method **addVote** of the Vote Web service to obtain the vote information. The remaining code in method **doPost** (lines 121–158) is similar to that of **DIISurveyServlet** (Fig. 9.26).

Figure 9.32 contains **surveyProxy.xsl**. Most of the content is identical to that of **survey.xsl** (Fig. 9.18) except that **surveyProxy.xsl** changes the form action to **/jaxrpc-VoteProxyClient/Survey** (line 31).

To deploy the dynamic proxy client, we use the same procedure that we used to deploy the stub client. Figure 9.33 shows dialog box **New Web Application Wizard - WAR File** and Figure 9.34 shows the **VoteProxyClient** Web application. Notice that directory **vote** contains only **Vote.class** rather than contains all client-side classes generated by **xrpcc**. The Web contents for the dynamic proxy clients include **SurveyServlet.class** (Fig. 9.31), **Vote.class** (generated by **xrpcc**), **survey.xml** (Fig. 9.17), **surveyProxy.xml** (Fig. 9.32) and **surveyresults.xsl** (Fig. 9.19).

```
1    <?xml version = "1.0"?>
2
3    <xsl:stylesheet xmlns:xsl = "http://www.w3.org/1999/XSL/Transform"
4       version = "1.0">
5
6    <xsl:output method = "xml" omit-xml-declaration = "no"
7       indent = "yes" doctype-system =
8       "http://www.w3.org/TR/xhtml1/DTD/xhtml1-strict.dtc"
9       doctype-public = "-//W3C//DTD XHTML 1.0 Strict//EN"/>
10
11   <!-- surveyProxy.xsl                              -->
12   <!-- XSL document that transforms XML into XHTML -->
13
14   <!-- specify the root of the XML document -->
15   <!-- that references this stylesheet      -->
16   <xsl:template match = "survey">
17
18      <html xmlns = "http://www.w3.org/1999/xhtml">
19
20      <head>
21
22         <!-- obtain survey title from survey element -->
23         <title><xsl:value-of select = "@title"/></title>
24      </head>
25
26      <body>
27         <p><xsl:value-of select = "@question"/></p>
28
29         <!-- create form -->
30         <form method = "post"
31            action = "/jaxrpc-VoteProxyClient/Survey">
32            <xsl:for-each select = "language">
33               <xsl:sort select = "@name" order = "ascending"/>
34               <input type = "radio" name = "favoriteLanguage"
35                  value = "{@name}"><xsl:value-of select = "@name"/>
36               </input><br/>
37            </xsl:for-each>
38            <br/><input type = "Submit"/>
39         </form>
40
41      </body>
42
43      </html>
44
45   </xsl:template>
46
47   </xsl:stylesheet>
```

Fig. 9.32 XSL style sheet (**surveyProxy.xsl**) that transforms **survey.xml** into an XHTML document.

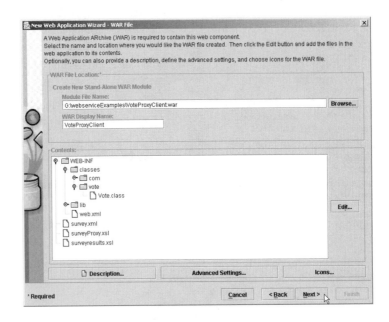

Fig. 9.33 Creating the WAR file for the dynamic proxy Vote client Web application.

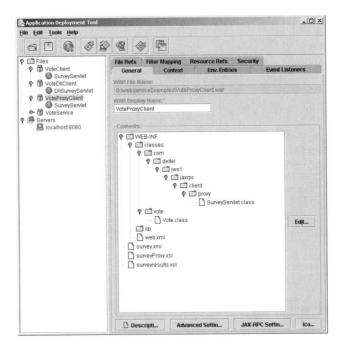

Fig. 9.34 VoteProxyClient Web application.

To deploy the **VoteProxyClient** Web application, we use the same approach we used to deploy the **VoteClient**. In the **Text Input Dialog**, enter **/jaxrpc-VoteProxyClient** as the Web context. To run the dynamic proxy client, open a Web browser and visit:

http://localhost:8080/jaxrpc-VoteProxyClient/Survey

Figure 9.35 shows the **VoteProxyClient** Web application survey form and results.

9.4 Improved Vote Service

The previous **Vote** service example takes a **String** that represents one vote for a partic-ular programming language and returns a **String** that contains votes for each program-

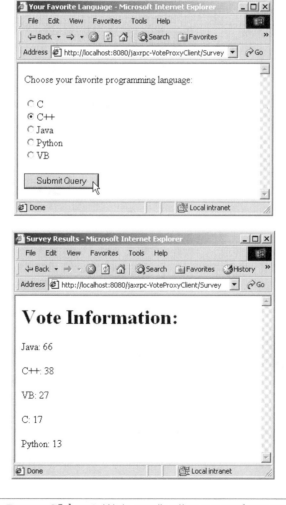

Fig. 9.35 VoteProxyClient Web application survey form and results.

ming language. Recall that vote results are separated by **" "**. In this section, we represent the **Vote** service in a more realistic way: the service returns an array of JavaBean objects, in which each JavaBean represents the vote tally for one programming language.

The three major steps in this example are as follows:

1. Defining a service interface and implementation.

2. Deploying the service to the Web server (in this example, we use the version of Tomcat distributed with the JWSDP).

3. Generating the client-side classes and writing the client application that interacts with the service.

Fig. 9.36 shows the structure of this example.

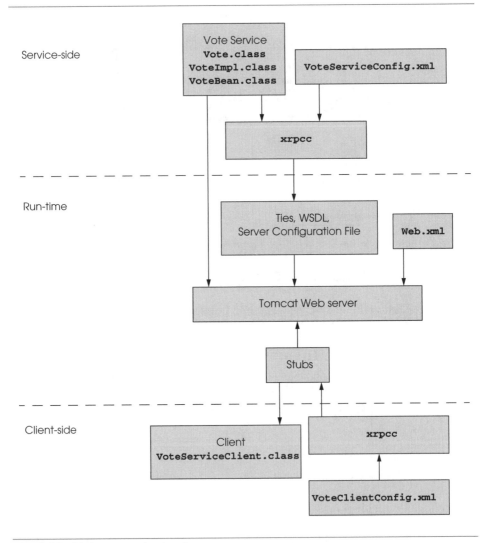

Fig. 9.36 Vote example structure.

9.4.1 Service Definition

As in the first example, the first step in the creation of a JAX-RPC Web service is to define the remote service endpoint interface. Interface **Vote** (Fig. 9.37)—which extends interface **Remote** (line 9)—is the remote interface for our second JAX-RPC Web service example. Lines 12–13 declare method **addVote**, which clients can invoke to add votes for the users' favorite programming languages. Recall that the input parameters and return values of the methods declared in a service interface must be JAX-RPC-supported types. The return value of method **addVote** is an array of **VoteBean** objects. When we implement the **VoteBean** class, we must follow the conditions listed in Section 9.3.1 to ensure compatibility with JAX-RPC.

Class **VoteImpl** implements remote interface **Vote** and interface **ServiceLifecycle** (line 18). Interface **ServiceLifecycle** allows service endpoint classes to setup access to external resources, such as databases.

Lines 24–74 implement method **init** of interface **ServiceLifecycle** to connect to a Cloudscape database. Lines 123–137 implement method **destroy** of interface **ServiceLifecycle**. These two methods are the same as in the previous example.

Lines 77–120 implement method **addVote** of interface **Vote**. Line 83 sets the parameter of **sqlUpdate** to the programming language that was selected by the user. After setting the parameter for the **PreparedStatement**, the program calls method **executeUpdate** of interface **PreparedStatement** to execute the **UPDATE** operation. Line 89 calls method **executeQuery** of interface **PreparedStatement** to execute the **SELECT** operation. **ResultSet results** stores the query results. Lines 91–107 process the **ResultSet** and store the results in an array of **VoteBean**s. Line 109 returns the **VoteBean**s to the client.

```
1   // Vote.java
2   // VoteService interface declares a method for adding votes and
3   // returning vote information.
4   package com.deitel.jws1.jaxrpc.voteservice;
5
6   // Java core packages
7   import java.rmi.*;
8
9   public interface Vote extends Remote {
10
11      // obtain vote information from server
12      public VoteBean[] addVote( String languageName )
13         throws RemoteException;
14  }
```

Fig. 9.37 **Vote** interface defines the service interface for the Vote Web service.

```
1   // VoteImpl.java
2   // VoteImpl implements the Vote remote interface to provide
3   // a VoteService remote object.
4   package com.deitel.jws1.jaxrpc.voteservice;
```

Fig. 9.38 **VoteImpl** defines the service implementation for the Vote Web service. (Part 1 of 4.)

```
 5
 6    // Java core packages
 7    import java.rmi.*;
 8    import java.sql.*;
 9    import java.util.*;
10
11    // Java extension packages
12    import javax.servlet.*;
13
14    // Java XML packages
15    import javax.xml.rpc.server.*;
16    import javax.xml.rpc.JAXRPCException;
17
18    public class VoteImpl implements ServiceLifecycle, Vote {
19
20        private Connection connection;
21        private PreparedStatement sqlUpdate, sqlSelect;
22
23        // setup database connection and prepare SQL statement
24        public void init( Object context )
25            throws JAXRPCException
26        {
27            // attempt database connection and
28            // create PreparedStatements
29            try {
30
31                // cast context to ServletEndpointContext
32                ServletEndpointContext endpointContext =
33                    ( ServletEndpointContext ) context;
34
35                // get ServletContext
36                ServletContext servletContext =
37                    endpointContext.getServletContext();
38
39                // get database driver from servlet context
40                String dbDriver =
41                    servletContext.getInitParameter( "dbDriver" );
42
43                // get database name from servlet context
44                String voteDB =
45                    servletContext.getInitParameter( "voteDB" );
46
47                Class.forName( dbDriver ); // load database driver
48
49                // connect to database
50                connection = DriverManager.getConnection( voteDB );
51
52                // PreparedStatement to add one to vote total for a
53                // specific language
54                sqlUpdate =
55                    connection.prepareStatement(
```

Fig. 9.38   **VoteImpl** defines the service implementation for the Vote Web service. (Part 2 of 4.)

```
56                          "UPDATE surveyresults SET vote = vote + 1 " +
57                          "WHERE name = ?" );
58
59              // PreparedStatement to obtain surveyresults table's data
60              sqlSelect =
61                 connection.prepareStatement( "SELECT name, vote " +
62                    "FROM surveyresults ORDER BY vote DESC" );
63
64           } // end try
65
66           // for any exception throw a JAXRPCException to
67           // indicate that the servlet is not currently available
68           catch ( Exception exception ) {
69              exception.printStackTrace();
70
71              throw new JAXRPCException( exception.getMessage() );
72           }
73
74        } // end method init
75
76        // implementation for interface Vote method addVote
77        public VoteBean[] addVote( String name ) throws RemoteException
78        {
79           // obtain votes count from database then update database
80           try {
81
82              // set parameter in sqlUpdate
83              sqlUpdate.setString( 1, name );
84
85              // execute sqlUpdate statement
86              sqlUpdate.executeUpdate();
87
88              // execute sqlSelect statement
89              ResultSet results = sqlSelect.executeQuery();
90
91              List voteInformation = new ArrayList();
92
93              // iterate ResultSet and prepare return string
94              while ( results.next() ) {
95
96                 // store results to VoteBean List
97                 VoteBean vote = new VoteBean(
98                    results.getString( 1 ), results.getInt( 2 ) );
99                 voteInformation.add( vote );
100             }
101
102             // create array of VoteBeans
103             VoteBean[] voteBeans =
104                new VoteBean[ voteInformation.size() ];
105
106             // get array from voteInformation List
107             voteInformation.toArray( voteBeans );
```

Fig. 9.38   VoteImpl defines the service implementation for the Vote Web service.
(Part 3 of 4.)

```
108
109          return voteBeans;
110
111       } // end try
112
113       // handle database exceptions by returning error to client
114       catch ( Exception exception ) {
115
116          //throw the exception back to the client
117          throw new RemoteException( exception.getMessage() );
118       }
119
120    } // end method addVote
121
122    // close SQL statements and database when servlet terminates
123    public void destroy()
124    {
125       // attempt to close statements and database connection
126       try {
127          sqlUpdate.close();
128          sqlSelect.close();
129          connection.close();
130       }
131
132       // handle database exception
133       catch ( Exception exception ) {
134          exception.printStackTrace();
135       }
136
137    } // end method destroy
138
139 } // end class VoteImpl
```

Fig. 9.38   VoteImpl defines the service implementation for the Vote Web service.
(Part 4 of 4.)

Class **VoteBean** stores data that represents the vote count for each programming language. Line 17 provides the public no-argument constructor. Lines 27–36 provide *get* methods for each piece of information. Lines 39–48 provide *set* methods for each piece of information.

```
1    // VoteBean.java
2    // VoteBean maintains vote information for one programming language.
3    package com.deitel.jws1.jaxrpc.voteservice;
4
5    // Java core packages
6    import java.io.*;
7
8    // Java extension packages
9    import javax.swing.*;
```

Fig. 9.39   VoteBean stores the vote count for one programming language.
(Part 1 of 2.).

```
10
11   public class VoteBean implements Serializable {
12
13      private String languageName; // name of language
14      private int count; // vote count
15
16      // public no-argument constructor
17      public VoteBean() {}
18
19      // VoteBean constructor
20      public VoteBean( String voteLanguage, int voteCount )
21      {
22         languageName = voteLanguage;
23         count = voteCount;
24      }
25
26      // get language name
27      public String getLanguageName()
28      {
29         return languageName;
30      }
31
32      // get vote count
33      public int getCount()
34      {
35         return count;
36      }
37
38      // set language name
39      public void setLanguageName( String voteLanguage )
40      {
41         languageName = voteLanguage;
42      }
43
44      // set vote count
45      public void setCount( int voteCount )
46      {
47         count = voteCount;
48      }
49
50   } // end class VoteBean
```

Fig. 9.39 **VoteBean** stores the vote count for one programming language. (Part 2 of 2.).

9.4.2 Service Deployment

In this section, we discuss how to generate the service-side artifacts (like ties, WSDL document) using **xrpcc** and how to deploy the service on Tomcat without using the **deploytool**. To generate a WSDL document, **xrpcc** reads an XML configuration file that lists remote interfaces. **VoteServiceConfig.xml** (Fig. 9.40) is the configuration for our **Vote** service example. **VoteServiceConfig.xml** follows the standard syntax provided by JWSDP to create the configuration file. The root element **configuration** contains one **service** element that corresponds to remote service. The **name** attribute of element **service** (line 5) indicates the service name. The **targetNamespace** attribute specifies the target namespace for the generated WSDL document (line 6). The **type-Namespace** attribute (line 7) specifies the target namespace within the **types** section of the WSDL document. The **packageName** attribute specifies the fully qualified package name of the generated stubs, ties and other classes (line 8). The value of attribute **packageName** does not need to match the package name of any of the remote interfaces. Element **interface** (lines 10–13) defines the fully qualified name of the service interface via its attribute **name**, and the fully qualified name of the service implementation via its attribute **servantName**. Element **interface** defines a service port in the WSDL file.

Using **xrpcc** requires that we include the location of the service-interface definition and implementation in the classpath. Compile the source code and place the classes in directory **voteserviceoutput**. It is necessary to create directory **voteservice-output** before executing the following **xrpcc** command

```
xrpcc -classpath voteserviceoutput -d voteserviceoutput
   -server -keep VoteServiceConfig.xml
```

to create service-side classes and the WSDL document. Option **d** specifies the directory in which to place the generated files. Option **server** specifies that only server-side files should be generated. Option **keep** instructs **xrpcc** to keep all the generated resources, including the WSDL document and the Java source code.

The **xrpcc** tool also generates server configuration file **VoteService_Config.properties**, which is used by the JAX-RPC runtime environment. We may modify **VoteService_Config.properties** (in directory **voteserviceoutput**) to make the service WSDL document available from the service end point. Open **VoteService_Config.properties** with a text editor and append the following line:

```
wsdl.location=/WEB-INF/VoteService.wsdl
```

to the end of the file. By doing so, the service WSDL document is accessible at

```
1   <?xml version="1.0" encoding="UTF-8"?>
2   <configuration
3      xmlns = "http://java.sun.com/xml/ns/jax-rpc/ri/config">
4
5      <service name = "VoteService"
6         targetNamespace = "http://www.deitel.com/VoteService.wsdl"
7         typeNamespace = "http://www.deitel.com/VoteService/type"
8         packageName = "com.deitel.jws1.jaxrpc.voteservice">
9
10        <interface
11           name = "com.deitel.jws1.jaxrpc.voteservice.Vote"
12           servantName =
13              "com.deitel.jws1.jaxrpc.voteservice.VoteImpl"/>
14     </service>
15  </configuration>
```

Fig. 9.40 **VoteServiceConfig.xml** is the configuration file for generating the Vote Web service artifacts using **xrpcc**.

```
http://localhost:8080/jaxrpc-voteapp/vote/endpoint?WSDL
```

assuming the service is deployed into the **jaxrpc-voteapp** Web context.

To deploy the Vote Web service to Tomcat, we need to:

1. Write a deployment descriptor.

2. Create a Web context, which, for this example, is **jaxrpc-voteapp**.

3. Copy required classes to directory **jaxrpc-voteapp\WEB-INFO\classes** and required libraries to directory **jaxrpc-voteapp\WEB-INFO\lib**.

Web.xml (Fig. 9.41) is the deployment descriptor for the **Vote** service. Two **context-param** elements (lines 14–19 and 21–26) specify the database name and database driver as context parameters. The URL **jdbc:cloudscape:rmi:languagesurvey** specifies the protocol for communication (**jdbc**), the subprotocol for communication (**cloudscape:rmi**) and the name of the database (**languagesurvey**). Element **servlet** (lines 28–44) describes the *JAXRPCServlet* servlet that is distributed with the JWSDP 1.0 final release. Servlet **JAXRPCServlet** is a JAX-RPC implementation for dispatching the request to the Web-service implementation. In our case, the **JAXRPCServlet** dispatches the client request to the **VoteImpl** class. When the **JAXRPCServlet** receives an HTTP request that contains a SOAP message, the servlet retrieves the data that the SOAP message contains, then dispatches the method call to the service-implementation class via the tie. Element **servlet-class** (lines 34–36) specifies the compiled servlet's fully qualified class name—**com.sun.xml.rpc.server.http.JAXRPCServlet**. The **JAXRPCServlet** obtains information about the server-configuration file, which is passed to the servlet as an initialization parameter. Element **init-param** (lines 37–42) specifies the name and value of the initialization parameter needed by the **JAXRPCServlet**. Element **param-name** (line 38) indicates the name of the initialization parameter, which is **configuration.file**. Element **param-value** (lines 39–41) specifies the value of the initialization parameter, **/WEB-INF/VoteService_Config.properties** (generated by **xrpcc**), which is the location of the server-configuration file. Element **servlet-mapping** (lines 47–50) specifies **servlet-name** and **url-pattern** elements. The URL pattern enables the server to determine which requests should be sent to the **JAXRPCServlet**.

```
1   <?xml version="1.0" encoding="UTF-8"?>
2
3   <!DOCTYPE web-app
4      PUBLIC "-//Sun Microsystems, Inc.//DTD Web Application 2.3//EN"
5      "http://java.sun.com/j2ee/dtds/web-app_2_3.dtd">
6
7   <web-app>
8      <display-name>
9         Java Web service JAX-RPC Vote service Example
10     </display-name>
11
12     <description>Vote service Application</description>
```

Fig. 9.41   **web.xml** for deploying the Vote service. (Part 1 of 2.)

```
13
14        <context-param>
15            <param-name>voteDB</param-name>
16            <param-value>
17                jdbc:cloudscape:rmi:languagesurvey
18            </param-value>
19        </context-param>
20
21        <context-param>
22            <param-name>dbDriver</param-name>
23            <param-value>
24                COM.cloudscape.core.RmiJdbcDriver
25            </param-value>
26        </context-param>
27
28        <servlet>
29            <servlet-name>JAXRPCEndpoint</servlet-name>
30            <display-name>JAXRPCEndpoint</display-name>
31            <description>
32                Endpoint for Vote Service
33            </description>
34            <servlet-class>
35                com.sun.xml.rpc.server.http.JAXRPCServlet
36            </servlet-class>
37            <init-param>
38                <param-name>configuration.file</param-name>
39                <param-value>
40                    /WEB-INF/VoteService_Config.properties
41                </param-value>
42            </init-param>
43            <load-on-startup>0</load-on-startup>
44        </servlet>
45
46        <!-- Servlet mappings -->
47        <servlet-mapping>
48            <servlet-name>JAXRPCEndpoint</servlet-name>
49            <url-pattern>/endpoint/*</url-pattern>
50        </servlet-mapping>
51
52        <session-config>
53            <session-timeout>60</session-timeout>
54        </session-config>
55    </web-app>
```

Fig. 9.41   **web.xml** for deploying the Vote service. (Part 2 of 2.)

Figure 9.42 shows the resulting **jaxrpc-voteapp** Web-application directory structure. Because the Vote Web service implementation uses a Cloudscape database, we need to include both **cloudclient.jar** and **RmiJdbc.jar** in directory **jaxrpc-voteapp\WEB-INF\lib**. These JAR files are available from directory **%J2EE_HOME%\lib\cloudscape**, where **J2EE_HOME** is the J2EE installation directory. Directory **jaxrpc-voteapp\WEB-INF\classes** contains all classes in directory **voteserviceoutput**, including **Vote.class**, **VoteImpl.class**, **VoteBean.class** and other classes generated by **xrpcc**.

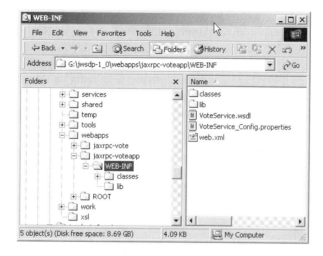

Fig. 9.42 Vote Web service Web application directory and file structure.

We may verify whether the Vote Web service is deployed successfully. To verify the deployment, start Tomcat and point your browser to

> **http://localhost:8080/jaxrpc-voteapp/endpoint**

Figure 9.43 shows the result of this action.

9.4.3 Client Invocation

Next, we demonstrate how to write a Java client of the Vote Web service using JAX-RPC. Class **VoteServiceClient** (Fig. 9.44) is the client application that invokes remote method **addVote** to add votes and obtain voting information. The **vote** package name (line 16) is specified in the configuration file (Fig. 9.45) passed to **xrpcc**.

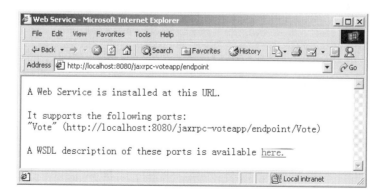

Fig. 9.43 Result of verification of the service's deployment.

In the **VoteServiceClient** constructor (lines 21–56), lines 26–49 create a **JButton voteButton** to invoke the Vote service. Lines 51–54 add the **voteButton** to the content pane. When users click **voteButton**, they must select their favorite programming language, which invokes method **showVotes** to get the vote result.

Method (lines 59–95) **showVotes** gets the service stub and casts the service stub to service interface (line 69). Line 72 invokes method **addVote** of the service interface to get an array of **VoteBean**s that contains vote information for each programming language. Lines 74–86 extract the vote information from the array and display the information in a **JOptionPane** message dialog.

Figure 9.45 is the configuration file that **xrpcc** uses to generate the client-side classes. Element **wsdl** (lines 4–6) specifies the location of the WSDL file and the fully qualified package name of the client-side classes. The package name may differ from the package name of **VoteServiceClient**.

```
1   // VoteServiceClient.java
2   // VoteServiceClient display the survey window.
3   package com.deitel.jws1.jaxrpc.voteclient;
4
5   // Java core packages
6   import java.awt.*;
7   import java.awt.event.*;
8
9   // Java extension packages
10  import javax.swing.*;
11
12  // Java XML packages
13  import javax.xml.rpc.*;
14
15  // client packages
16  import vote.*;
17
18  public class VoteServiceClient extends JFrame
19  {
20     private static String endpoint;
21
22     // VoteServiceClient constructor
23     public VoteServiceClient()
24     {
25        // create JButton for getting Vote service
26        JButton voteButton = new JButton( "Get Vote Service" );
27        voteButton.addActionListener(
28
29           new ActionListener() {
30
31              // action for the voteButton
32              public void actionPerformed( ActionEvent event )
33              {
34                 String[] languages =
35                    { "C", "C++", "Java", "VB", "Python" };
36
```

Fig. 9.44 **VoteServiceClient** is the client for the Vote Web service. (Part 1 of 3.).

```
37              String selectedLanguage = ( String )
38                 JOptionPane.showInputDialog(
39                 VoteServiceClient.this,
40                 "Select Language", "Language Selection",
41                 JOptionPane.QUESTION_MESSAGE,
42                 null, languages, "" );
43
44              showVotes( selectedLanguage );
45
46           } // end method actionPerformed
47
48        } // end ActionListener
49
50     ); // end call to addActionListener
51
52     JPanel buttonPanel = new JPanel();
53     buttonPanel.add( voteButton );
54     getContentPane().add( buttonPanel, BorderLayout.CENTER );
55
56  } // end VoteServiceClient constructor
57
58  // connect to Vote Web service and get vote information
59  public void showVotes( String languageName )
60  {
61     // connect to Web service and get vote information
62     try {
63
64        // get Web service stub
65        Stub stub = ( Stub )
66           ( new VoteService_Impl().getVotePort() );
67
68        // cast stub to service interface
69        Vote vote = ( Vote ) stub;
70
71        // get vote information from Web service
72        VoteBean[] voteBeans = vote.addVote( languageName );
73
74        StringBuffer results = new StringBuffer();
75        results.append( "Vote result: \n" );
76
77        // get vote information from voteBeans
78        for ( int i = 0; i < voteBeans.length ; i++) {
79           results.append( "   "
80              + voteBeans[ i ].getLanguageName() + ":" );
81           results.append( voteBeans[ i ].getCount() );
82           results.append( "\n" );
83        }
84
85        // display Vote information
86        JOptionPane.showMessageDialog( this, results );
87
88     } // end try
```

Fig. 9.44 **VoteServiceClient** is the client for the Vote Web service.
(Part 2 of 3.).

```
89
90          // handle exceptions communicating with remote object
91          catch ( Exception exception ) {
92             exception.printStackTrace();
93          }
94
95       } // end method showVotes
96
97       // execute VoteServiceClient
98       public static void main( String args[] )
99       {
100         // configure and display application window
101         VoteServiceClient client = new VoteServiceClient();
102
103         client.setDefaultCloseOperation( EXIT_ON_CLOSE );
104         client.pack();
105         client.setSize( 250, 65 );
106         client.setVisible( true );
107
108      } // end main
109
110   } // end class VoteServiceClient
```

Fig. 9.44   VoteServiceClient is the client for the Vote Web service.
(Part 3 of 3.).

```
1    <?xml version="1.0" encoding="UTF-8"?>
2    <configuration
3       xmlns = "http://java.sun.com/xml/ns/jax-rpc/ri/config">
4       <wsdl location =
5          "http://localhost:8080/jaxrpc-voteapp/endpoint?WSDL"
6          packageName = "vote">
7       </wsdl>
8    </configuration>
```

Fig. 9.45   VoteClientConfig.xml that **xrpcc** uses to generate client-side
classes from WSDL document.

The command

```
xrpcc -d voteclientoutput -client VoteClientConfig.xml
```

generates the client-side classes for the Vote service in directory **voteclientoutput**.
VoteClientConfig.xml (Fig. 9.45) is the configuration file passed to **xrpcc**.

Figure 9.46 shows all the JAR files that are required to compile and execute client-side
applications. Directories **%JWSDP_HOME%\common\lib** and **%JWSDP_HOME%\com
mon\endorsed** contain these JAR files, where **%JWSDP_HOME%** is the installation
directory of JWSDP.

To run the client application, type:

```
java -classpath voteclientoutput;%CLASSPATH%
     com.deitel.jws1.jaxrpc.voteclient.VoteServiceClient
```

The **%CLASSPATH%** variable contains all the JAR files listed in Fig. 9.46. Fig. 9.47 shows
the output of the client application.

JAR files required for compilation	JAR files required for execution

`jaxrpc-api.jar`
`jaxrpc-ri.jar`
	`jaxrpc-api.jar`
	`jaxrpc-ri.jar`
	`saaj-api.jar`
	`saaj-ri.jar`
	`mail.jar`
	`activation.jar`

Fig. 9.46   JAR files required to compile and execute client-side applications.

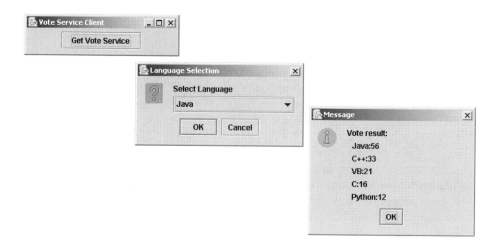

Fig. 9.47   Output of the Vote service client.

9.5 Accessing Web Services Written by a Third Party

In most B2B or B2C applications, Web service providers and Web service consumers are separate organizations. Usually, Web service consumers search for a particular Web service from a Web service registry (such as public UDDI registry or ebXML registry) or from a well-known Web site that contains a list of Web services (such as **www.xmethods.com**). This section demonstrates how to connect to and access the Unisys Weather Web Service that is available from **www.xmethods.com**. You can get the Unisys Weather Web Service information from

www.xmethods.com/ve2/ViewListing.po?serviceid=47216

which contains information such as the location of the WSDL file and the description of the service. Although the Unisys Weather Web Service was written using Microsoft's .NET Framework, we can access it easily using JAX-RPC.

9.5.1 Generating Client Stubs Using `xrpcc`

To access a Web service, JAX-RPC clients usually obtain the WSDL document of the service and use **xrpcc** to generate client stubs based on the WSDL document. This is the approach we take for our Weather Web service client. Figure 9.48 is the configuration file that **xrpcc** uses to generate client stubs. The command

```
xrpcc -client -keep -d WeatherClient XmethodsUniSys.xml
```

generates the client-side classes for the Weather service in directory **WeatherClient**. Option **-keep** specifies that **xrpcc** should generate both **.java** and **.class** files, which helps the client-side programmer understand the input and return objects of the service's methods without referring to the WSDL document directly. **XmethodsUniSys.xml** is the configuration file shown in Fig. 9.48. Line 5 specifies the location of the service's WSDL document. Line 6 defines the client package **weather**.

9.5.2 Writing the Client

Once we have the client-side classes, writing a client is straightforward. Figure 9.49 is the client that connects to the Weather Web service to get the weather forecast. Line 19 imports the client package, which is defined in line 6 of Fig. 9.48. The constructor (lines 21–87) lays out the GUI components—a **JButton** that allows clients to get the service, a **JPanel** that displays general information (such as zip code, town), and a **JPanel** that displays a seven-day weather forecast.

Method **getWeatherForecast** (lines 90–114) takes a **String** that represents the zip code, which is the required input to the service's **getWeather** method. Lines 96–97 invoke method **getWeatherServicesSoap** of **xrpcc**-generated service-implementation class **WeatherServices_Impl** to get the service interface **WeatherServicesSoap**. Lines 100–101 invoke method **getWeather** of the service interface to get the weather forecast, which is contained in an object of class **WeatherForecast**. Class **WeatherForecast** is an **xrpcc**-generated class that corresponds to the return object of method **getWeather**.

Method **createGeneralPanel** (lines 117–144) adds five **JTextField**s to the first **JPanel** to display the general information, such as zip code and town name. Method **createDailyPanel** (lines 147–153) adds a **JTextArea** to the second **JPanel** to display the seven-day weather forecast. Methods **updateGeneralContent** (lines 156–169) and **updateDailyContent** (lines 172–201) are invoked each time the user clicks the **JButton** to update the display.

```
1    <?xml version="1.0" encoding="UTF-8"?>
2    <configuration
3       xmlns="http://java.sun.com/xml/ns/jax-rpc/ri/config">
4       <wsdl name="weather"
5             location="http://hosting001.vs.k2unisys.net/Weather/
PDCWebService/WeatherServices.asmx?WSDL"
6             packageName="weather">
```

Fig. 9.48 Configuration file used by **xrpcc** to generate client stubs. (Part 1 of 2.)

```
7          <typeMappingRegistry>
8          </typeMappingRegistry>
9       </wsdl>
10   </configuration>
```

Fig. 9.48   Configuration file used by **xrpcc** to generate client stubs. (Part 2 of 2.)

```
1    // WeatherServiceClient.java
2    // WeatherServiceClient uses the Weather Web service
3    // to retrieve weather information.
4    package com.deitel.jws1.jaxrpc.weather;
5
6    // Java core packages
7    import java.rmi.*;
8    import java.awt.*;
9    import java.awt.event.*;
10
11   // Java extension packages
12   import javax.swing.*;
13   import javax.swing.border.*;
14
15   // Java XML RPC packages
16   import javax.xml.rpc.*;
17
18   // Client packages
19   import weather.*;
20
21   public class WeatherServiceClient extends JFrame
22   {
23      private JPanel generalPanel;
24      private JPanel dailyPanel;
25
26      private JTextField zipcodeField, cityField, timeField,
27         sunriseField, sunsetField;
28
29      private JTextArea dailyArea;
30
31      // WeatherServiceClient constructor
32      public WeatherServiceClient()
33      {
34         super( "Weather Forecast" );
35
36         // create JButton for invoking Weather Web service
37         JButton weatherButton =
38            new JButton( "Get Weather Service" );
39         weatherButton.addActionListener(
40
41            new ActionListener() {
42
43               public void actionPerformed( ActionEvent event )
44               {
```

Fig. 9.49   Weather Web service client. (Part 1 of 5.)

```
45               String zipcode = JOptionPane.showInputDialog(
46                  WeatherServiceClient.this, "Enter zip code" );
47
48               // if the user inputs zip code, get weather
49               // forecast according to zip code
50               if ( zipcode != null ) {
51
52                  // get weather forecast
53                  WeatherForecast weatherForecast =
54                     getWeatherForecast( zipcode );
55
56                  updateGeneralContent( weatherForecast );
57                  updateDailyContent( weatherForecast );
58               }
59
60            } // end method ActionPerformed
61
62         } // end ActionListener
63
64      ); // end call to addActionListener
65
66      // create JPanel for weatherButton
67      JPanel buttonPanel = new JPanel();
68      buttonPanel.add( weatherButton );
69
70      // create JPanel for general weather forecast
71      generalPanel = new JPanel();
72      generalPanel.setBorder( new TitledBorder( "General" ) );
73      createGeneralPanel();
74
75      // create JPanel for daily weather forecast
76      dailyPanel = new JPanel();
77      dailyPanel.setBorder(
78         new TitledBorder( "Daily Forecast" ) );
79      createDailyPanel();
80
81      // lay out components
82      Container contentPane = getContentPane();
83      contentPane.add( buttonPanel, BorderLayout.NORTH );
84      contentPane.add( generalPanel, BorderLayout.CENTER );
85      contentPane.add( dailyPanel, BorderLayout.SOUTH );
86
87   } // end WeatherServiceClient constructor
88
89   // get weather forecast from Unisys's WeatherService
90   public WeatherForecast getWeatherForecast( String zipcode )
91   {
92      // connect to Web service and get weather information
93      try {
94
95         // get Web service
96         WeatherServicesSoap weatherService = ( new
97            WeatherServices_Impl() ).getWeatherServicesSoap();
```

Fig. 9.49   Weather Web service client. (Part 2 of 5.)

```
98
99                    // get weather information from server
100                   WeatherForecast result =
101                      weatherService.getWeather( zipcode );
102
103                   return result;
104
105             } // end try
106
107             // handle exceptions communicating with remote object
108             catch ( Exception exception ) {
109                exception.printStackTrace();
110
111                return null;
112             }
113
114       } // end method getWeatherForecast
115
116       // create general panel content
117       public void createGeneralPanel()
118       {
119          generalPanel.setLayout( new GridLayout( 5, 2 ) );
120
121          zipcodeField = new JTextField( 15 );
122          cityField = new JTextField( 15 );
123          timeField = new JTextField( 15 );
124          sunriseField = new JTextField( 15 );
125          sunsetField = new JTextField( 15 );
126
127          zipcodeField.setEditable( false );
128          cityField.setEditable( false );
129          timeField.setEditable( false );
130          sunriseField.setEditable( false );
131          sunsetField.setEditable( false );
132
133          generalPanel.add( new JLabel( "ZipCode: " ) );
134          generalPanel.add( zipcodeField );
135          generalPanel.add( new JLabel( "City: " ) );
136          generalPanel.add( cityField );
137          generalPanel.add( new JLabel( "Time: " ) );
138          generalPanel.add( timeField );
139          generalPanel.add( new JLabel( "Sunrise: " ) );
140          generalPanel.add( sunriseField );
141          generalPanel.add( new JLabel( "Sunset: " ) );
142          generalPanel.add( sunsetField );
143
144       } // end method createGeneralPanel
145
146       // create daily panel content
147       public void createDailyPanel()
148       {
149          dailyArea = new JTextArea( 20, 35 );
150
```

Fig. 9.49   Weather Web service client. (Part 3 of 5.)

```
151        dailyPanel.add( new JScrollPane( dailyArea ) );
152
153     } // end method createDailyPanel
154
155     // update general forecast
156     public void updateGeneralContent(
157        WeatherForecast weatherForecast )
158     {
159        // parse WeatherForecast if not null
160        if ( weatherForecast != null ) {
161           zipcodeField.setText( weatherForecast.getZipCode() );
162           cityField.setText(
163              weatherForecast.getCityShortName() );
164           timeField.setText( weatherForecast.getTime() );
165           sunriseField.setText( weatherForecast.getSunrise() );
166           sunsetField.setText( weatherForecast.getSunset() );
167        }
168
169     } // end method updateGeneralContent
170
171     // update daily content
172     public void updateDailyContent(
173        WeatherForecast weatherForecast )
174     {
175        // get daily forecast if weatherForecast is not null
176        if ( weatherForecast != null ) {
177           ArrayOfDailyForecast dayForecast =
178              weatherForecast.getDayForecast();
179
180           // get DailyForecast array if dayForecast is not null
181           if ( dayForecast != null ) {
182              DailyForecast[] dailyForecast =
183                 dayForecast.getDailyForecast();
184
185              StringBuffer results = new StringBuffer();
186
187              // store daily forecast to results StringBuffer
188              for ( int i = 0; i < dailyForecast.length ; i++ ) {
189                 results.append( dailyForecast[ i ].getDay() );
190                 results.append( ": \n    " );
191                 results.append( dailyForecast[ i ].getForecast() );
192                 results.append( "\n" );
193              }
194
195              dailyArea.setText( results.toString() );
196
197           } // end inner if
198
199        } // end outer if
200
201     } // end method updateDailyContent
202
```

Fig. 9.49   Weather Web service client. (Part 4 of 5.)

```
203    // execute WeatherServiceClient
204    public static void main( String args[] )
205    {
206       WeatherServiceClient client =
207          new WeatherServiceClient();
208       client.setDefaultCloseOperation( EXIT_ON_CLOSE );
209       client.setSize( 425, 600 );
210       client.setVisible( true );
211
212    } // end method main
213
214 } // end class WeatherServiceClient
```

Fig. 9.49   Weather Web service client. (Part 5 of 5.)

To compile and run the client, make sure your classpath includes all the JAR files mentioned in Fig. 9.46 and in directory **unisys**, which contains **xrpcc**-generated client classes. Figure 9.50 shows the client output.

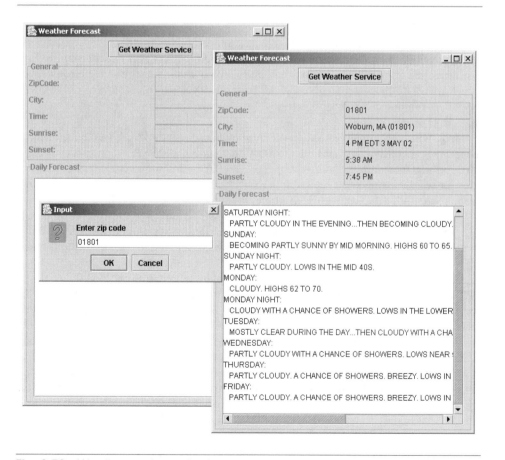

Fig. 9.50   Weather service output.

9.6 Summary

The Java Web Services Developer Pack (JWSDP) includes the Java XML Pack, Tomcat Java Servlet and JavaServer Pages containers, a Registry Server and the Ant build tool. As of this writing, the current version of JWSDP is 1.0.

RPC allows a procedural program to call a function that resides on another computer as conveniently as if that function were part of the same program running on the same computer. Whereas RPC requires the use of a single programming language and proprietary communications protocol, Web services enable integration among many different languages and protocols. As with RPC, both RMI and JAX-RPC handle the marshaling and unmarshaling of data across the network. Both RMI and JAX-RPC also provide APIs for transmitting and receiving data.

JAX-RPC provides a generic mechanism that enables developers to create Web services by using XML-based remote procedure calls. The JAX-RPC specification defines a mapping of Java types (e.g., **int**, **String** and classes that adhere to the JavaBean design pattern) to WSDL definitions. When a client locates a service in an XML registry, the client retrieves the WSDL definition to get the service-interface definition. To access the service using Java, the client must transform the WSDL definitions to Java types. The JAX-RPC client and service runtime environments send and process the remote method call and response, respectively.

JAX-RPC enables applications to take advantage of WSDL and SOAP's interoperability, which enables Java applications to invoke Web services that execute on non-Java platforms, and non-Java applications can invoke Web services that execute on Java platforms. JAX-RPC hides the details of SOAP from the developer, because the JAX-RPC service/client runtime environment performs the mapping between remote method calls and SOAP messages.

JAX-RPC supports only a subset of Java types, because the data types transmitted by the remote procedure calls must map to SOAP data types. JAX-RPC supports Java primitive types and their corresponding wrapper classes. JAX-RPC supports a subset of standard Java classes. Java arrays can be used in JAX-RPC as long as the member type of the array is one of the JAX-RPC-supported Java types.

There are some restrictions on the service-interface definition: It must implement interface **java.rmi.Remote**; all public methods must throw exception **java.rmi.RemoteException**; no constant declarations are allowed; all method parameters and return types must be JAX-RPC-supported Java types.

The JAX-RPC reference implementation provides the **deploytool** to deploy a JAX-RPC service onto Tomcat. The JAX-RPC reference implementation also provides the **xrpcc** tool to generate ties (server-side objects that represent the services), stubs and other service and client-side artifacts (such as a WSDL document).

If we supply **xrpcc** with a remote-interface definition, it generates stubs, ties, a WSDL document and a server-configuration file for use when deploying the Web service. If we supply **xrpcc** with a WSDL document, it generates stubs, ties, a server-configuration file and the remote-interface definition for use when developing a client. Most users use an existing WSDL document to access a Web service.

The stubs, ties, server and client-side artifacts are dictated by **-client**, **-server** and **-both** options of the **xrpcc** tool. The **xrpcc** tool's option **server** specifies that only server-side files should be generated. Option **client** specifies that only client-side files should be generated. Option **both** generates both of these artifacts.

Servlet **JAXRPCServlet** is a JAX-RPC implementation for dispatching the request to the Web service implementation. When the **JAXRPCServlet** receives an HTTP request that contains a SOAP message, the servlet retrieves the data that the SOAP message contains; it then dispatches the method call to the service-implementation class via the tie.

To access a Web service via a stub, we need to obtain the stub object. When **xrpcc** generates the stub, it uses the following convention: *serviceinterface*_**Stub**. When the **xrpcc** generates the service implementation, it uses the convention *servicename*_**Impl**, where *servicename* is the service name specified in the **xrpcc** configuration file.

The Dynamic Invocation Interface (DII) enables clients to call methods on Web services without knowing the service's stub information. Using DII to write clients is more complicated than using static stubs to write clients. However, DII clients are more flexible than are static-stub clients, because DII clients can specify the properties of remote procedure calls (such as Web-service names, remote-method input parameters, and remote-method return types) at runtime. To work with XML data types, DII clients must specify the mapping between Java types and XML data types. To dynamically invoke a method, DII clients need to create a **Call** object that enables dynamic invocation of a service port by invoking method **createCall** of interface **Service**.

Using static stubs requires the programmer to generate the stubs using **xrpcc**. Using DII requires the programmer to do more coding. Using dynamic proxies does not require stubs and extra coding. To use the dynamic proxy, the clients must have access to the WSDL document and be able to extract service-based information from the WSDL document.

9.7 Internet and World Wide Web Resources

java.sun.com/webservices/
Java technology and Web services at SUN.

java.sun.com/xml/jaxrpc/
This site contains links to JAX-RPC specifications, downloads, tutorials and lots more.

archives.java.sun.com/archives/jaxrpc-interest.html
Archives for people who are interested in JAX-RPC.

developer.java.sun.com/developer/technicalArticles/WebServices/getstartjaxrpc/
This site contains an article "Getting Started with JAX-RPC" that covers how to write JAX-RPC Web services and clients.

developer.java.sun.com/developer/community/chat/JavaLive/2002/j10402.html
A chat session on JAX-RPC, from Java Developer Connection.

forums.java.sun.com/forum.jsp?forum=331
A discussion forum on Java technologies for Web Services, from the Java Developer Connection.

www.fawcette.com/javapro/2002_05/magazine/features/shorrell/
An article "Introducing JAX-RPC" from JavaPro.

10

Java API for XML Registries (JAXR)

Objectives

- To understand the role of XML registries in the Web services paradigm.
- To understand the JAXR model.
- To learn how to register a business entry in an XML registry.
- To learn how to query an XML registry.
- To learn how to remove a business entry from an XML registry.

You cannot create experience. You must undergo it.
Albert Camus

I will not answer until I am addressed correctly.
Mary Hamilton

It is the mark of a good action that it appears inevitable in retrospect.
Robert Louis Stevenson

Very often it happens that a discovery is made whilst working upon quite another problem.
Thomas Alva Edison

Knowledge is of two kinds, We know a subject ourselves, or we know where we can find information upon it.
Samuel Johnson

10.1 Introduction

Typical business-to-business (B2B) and business-to-consumer (B2C) interactions require both parties to establish agreements on requested services. Before this can happen, a business in a B2B relation or a consumer in B2C relationship must be aware of the services a business provides.

Registries are independent third parties in B2B and B2C relationships that help unify businesses and clients. Registries enable businesses to post information pertaining to a company, such as contact information, available services, business classification, information on how to invoke provided services, etc. Registries are an important element in the Web services paradigm. In an environment where businesses provide interoperable services, clients and businesses need a standardized approach for exposing and discovering services within a widely accessible repository.

Figure 10.1 demonstrates the process businesses and clients conduct when establishing a business relationship through a registry. A business posts an entry in a registry (step 1). The entry contains information about the business and the services the business provides. Clients obtain this information from the registry (step 2). Clients analyze this information and determine what services the client will use (step 3). The client negotiates access rights to services the business provides (step 4). Some businesses or organizations may not require clients to establish a business relationship prior to using provided services. Once the client and business agree on payment process, access times, and other details, the client invokes the Web service (step 5).

This chapter discusses the process by which JAXR enables developers to complete steps 1 through 3. Step 4 varies among organizations and businesses. Finally, step 5 is discussed in Chapter 6, SOAP-Based Web Service Platforms.

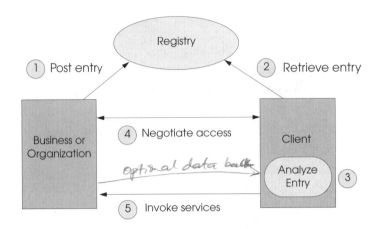

Fig. 10.1   Web services posting, discovery and invocation life cycle.

10.1.1 Java API for XML Registries (JAXR) Architecture

Currently two types of XML registries are widely available—UDDI and ebXML. Other registry types may emerge as Web services evolve. The Java API for XML Registries (JAXR) standardizes an approach by which Java programs access different XML registry types. JAXR provides developers with an abstraction of concepts common to all XML registries. JAXR is responsible for mapping general concepts to more specific entities within a target XML registry. This enables developers to write applications based on general registry concepts, which enables developers to use these applications across different types of XML registries. In this way, JAXR is much like the JDBC API, which enables developers to build Java programs that access databases in a generic fashion.

JAXR defines a pluggable architecture that enables clients to use *JAXR providers* to access different types of registries. A JAXR provider is an implementation of the JAXR API that 1) maps JAXR objects to protocol-specific entries in the target XML registry, and 2) provides implementations of generic JAXR interfaces. JAXR providers also may choose to expose specific functionality of an XML registry through provider-specific interfaces. Figure 10.2 shows the pluggable JAXR architecture.

10.1.2 Capability Profiles

UDDI and ebXML registries use different protocols to provide access to the registries' contents. Developers that wish to use both ebXML and UDDI registries must learn each registry's specific requirements. The JAXR model is a union of *capabilities* among XML registry types, so developers are not restricted to the limited set of operations common to different XML registries (Fig. 10.3).

A capability is a measure by which JAXR classifies an operation an XML registry supports. Capabilities help developers determine what methods within the JAXR interfaces to use when interacting with an XML registry. JAXR defines support for numerous XML registries, so not all registries support the same set of operations defined by the JAXR API.

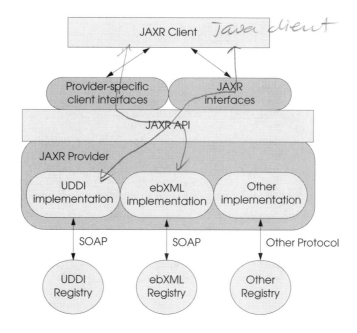

Fig. 10.2   JAXR architecture

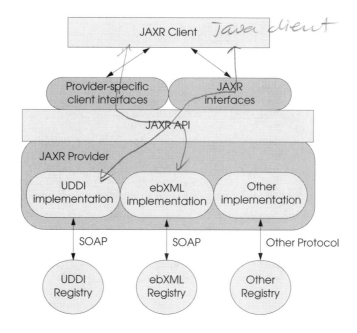

Fig. 10.3   JAXR is a union of numerous specifications as opposed to an intersection of common characteristics.

The current specification for JAXR defines support for two XML registry types or *profiles*—UDDI registries and ebXML registries. The set of capabilities a given profile supports is known as a *capability profile*. The capability profile of UDDI registries is a subset of the capability profile of ebXML registries. JAXR providers that support the capability profile for ebXML registries also support the capability profile for UDDI registries (Fig. 10.4). This means that an application that is written for a UDDI registry can operate on an ebXML registry via the use of a different JAXR provider.

JAXR capability profiles support

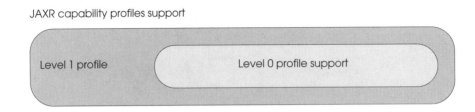

Level 1 profile   Level 0 profile support

Fig. 10.4   JAXR currently supports two capability profiles.

JAXR classifies capability profiles by levels. JAXR classifies UDDI registries as level **0**, and ebXML registries as level **1**. JAXR distinguishes which methods correspond to a capability profile by tagging each method's API documentation entry. For example, JAXR API documentation tags each method of interfaces **BusinessLifeCycleManager** and **BusinessQueryManager** as level **0**. This means that JAXR providers that provide support for UDDI registries must implement these methods. This also means that JAXR providers for ebXML registries must support these methods.

10.2 Registering for XML Registry Access

Clients that submit entries into an XML registry must obtain access rights to that XML registry. The process varies for each XML registry. Typically, users can access an XML registry's Web page to obtain information about obtaining access rights. XML registries typically validate a client's access rights based on a username and password. Two popular XML registry providers are IBM and Microsoft. The following section describes how to obtain access rights to IBM's UDDI registries.

 Software Engineering Observation 10.1

Most XML registries enable clients to perform anonymous queries, while most registries require a valid username and password to modify registry entries.

10.2.1 IBM UDDI Registries

IBM provides registries for use by businesses and developers. IBM's UDDI Business Registry is targeted at businesses that wish to publish business information in a public XML registry. IBM's UDDI Business Test Registry is targeted at developers that need to use a UDDI registry for testing purposes. To obtain access rights to IBM's XML registries, go to

www-3.ibm.com/services/uddi/

IBM provides three UDDI registries—a business registry, a test registry for developers and an UDDI version 2 beta registry. For the purposes of this chapter, select the **UDDI Business Registry V2 Beta**. Follow the instructions the IBM Web site provides to create an IBM user ID and password and activate the account. Section 10.4 discusses how to register an entry into an XML registry, so do not register an entry into the UDDI registry when the browser displays IBM's organization registration forms.

10.2.2 JAXR Reference Implementation UDDI Registry

Sun's Java Web Services Developer Pack (JWSDP) provides a reference implementation of a UDDI registry V2. The JWSDP UDDI registry is an implementation that enables developers to test the UDDI capabilities of the JAXR API reference implementation.

JWSDP's UDDI RI relies on servlet **RegistryServerServlet**, which the JWSDP includes as a pre-installed servlet in the default Tomcat installation. Start Tomcat by typing the command **startup.bat** within directory **c:\jwsdp\bin**. Next, start the Apache's XML database, Xindice (pronounced Zeen-dee-chay), by typing the command, **xindice-start.bat**. The JWSDP UDDI registry is intended for testing purposes. Users that submit or remove entries in the JWSDP UDDI registry must supply **testuser** as both username and password.

10.3 Connecting to an XML Registry

The first step for submitting an entry to an XML registry is to establish a connection to the target XML registry. Class **XMLRegistryManager** (Fig. 10.5) establishes a connection to IBM's Test UDDI registry. The constructor on lines 34–97 establishes a connection to the UDDI registry that requires a valid username and password for submitting and removing elements from the registry. The no-argument constructor (lines 100–103) establishes a connection to the UDDI registry for performing anonymous queries.

Clients connect to XML registries through subclasses of interface **Connection** from package **javax.xml.registry**. To create a **Connection** object, we must obtain a reference to the JAXR provider's **ConnectionFactory** implementation.

```
1   // Fig. 10.5: XMLRegistryManager.java
2   // Establishes connection to UDDI registry
3   // and returns references to life-cycle manager and
4   // query manager capability interfaces.
5
6   package com.deitel.jws1.jaxr;
7
8   // JAXR core packages
9   import javax.xml.registry.*;
10  import javax.xml.registry.infomodel.*;
11
12  // java core packages
13  import java.util.*;
14  import java.net.PasswordAuthentication;
15
16  public class XMLRegistryManager {
17
18      // capability interface for querying XML registry
19      private BusinessQueryManager queryManager;
20
```

Fig. 10.5 Class **XMLRegistryManager** establishes connection to XML registry. (Part 1 of 3.)

```
21    // capability interface for adding, updating, removing entries
22    private BusinessLifeCycleManager lifeCycleManager;
23
24    // UDDI registry URLs
25    private static final String queryURL =
26       "http://www-3.ibm.com:80/" +
27       "services/uddi/v2beta/inquiryapi";
28
29    private static final String lifeCycleURL =
30       "https://www-3.ibm.com:443/" +
31       "services/uddi/v2beta/protect/publishapi";
32
33    // constructor
34    public XMLRegistryManager( String userName,
35       String password ) throws JAXRException
36    {
37       // create connection instance
38       ConnectionFactory connectionFactory =
39          ConnectionFactory.newInstance();
40
41       // create Properties object that contains
42       // 1) URLs of registry service, and
43       // 2) connection factory implementation
44       Properties properties = new Properties();
45
46       // specify connection factory property
47       properties.setProperty(
48          "javax.xml.registry.factoryClass",
49          "com.sun.xml.registry.uddi.ConnectionFactoryImpl" );
50
51       // store URL of query registry service
52       // as property javax.xml.registry.queryManagerURL
53       properties.setProperty(
54          "javax.xml.registry.queryManagerURL", queryURL );
55
56       // store URL of publish registry service
57       // as property javax.xml.registry.lifeCycleManagerURL
58       properties.setProperty(
59          "javax.xml.registry.lifeCycleManagerURL", lifeCycleURL );
60
61       // set properties
62       connectionFactory.setProperties( properties );
63
64       // create connection
65       Connection connection =
66          connectionFactory.createConnection();
67
68       // set credentials iff username and password supplied
69       if ( userName != null || password != null ) {
70
```

Fig. 10.5 Class **XMLRegistryManager** establishes connection to XML registry. (Part 2 of 3.)

```
71              // create password authorization
72              PasswordAuthentication authentication =
73                 new PasswordAuthentication(
74                    userName, password.toCharArray() );
75
76              // create credentials set
77              Set credentials = new HashSet();
78
79              // populate credentials with authorization object
80              credentials.add( authentication );
81
82              // set credentials in connection instance
83              connection.setCredentials( credentials );
84           } // end if
85
86           // obtain registry service reference
87           RegistryService registryService =
88              connection.getRegistryService();
89
90           // obtain business query
91           queryManager =
92              registryService.getBusinessQueryManager();
93
94           // obtain business life cycle manager reference
95           lifeCycleManager =
96              registryService.getBusinessLifeCycleManager();
97        } // end constructor
98
99        // no-argument constructor
100       public XMLRegistryManager() throws JAXRException
101       {
102          this( null, null );
103       }
104
105       // return BusinessQueryManager
106       public BusinessQueryManager getBusinessQueryManager()
107       {
108          return queryManager;
109       }
110
111       // return BusinessLifeCycleManager
112       public BusinessLifeCycleManager getBusinessLifeCycleManager()
113       {
114          return lifeCycleManager;
115       }
116
117    } // end class XMLRegistryManager
```

Fig. 10.5 Class **XMLRegistryManager** establishes connection to XML registry. (Part 3 of 3.)

Programs obtain references to **ConnectionFactory** objects either by performing JNDI lookups or by invoking **ConnectionFactory** method **newInstance**. The JAXR reference implementation provides only one means for obtaining an instance of class **ConnectionFactory**—**ConnectionFactory** method **newInstance** (lines 38–39).

Lines 44–59 create a **Properties** object for configuring the **Connection** object class **ConnectionFactory** creates. The JAXR specification defines six standard connection properties that control the instantiation of **Connection** objects. Providers may specify additional properties. Lines 47–49 set property **javax.xml.registry.factoryClass**, which specifies the factory instance **ConnectionFactory** (lines 38–39) uses to create **Connection** objects. Lines 53–54 set property **javax.xml.registry.queryManagerURL**, which specifies the URL for the *query manager service* provider. Query manager service providers are registry-side end points to which clients submit query requests. Property **javax.xml.registry.lifeCycleManagerURL** (lines 58–59) specifies the URL for the *life cycle manager service* provider. Life cycle manager service providers are registry-side target endpoints that enable clients to add, remove and update entries in a registry. This chapter uses the query and life-cycle manager service providers for IBM's test UDDI registry. For a list of URLs for other registries' query and life-cycle manager service providers, see Section 10.7. Line 62 sets the **Connection-Factory** properties. Lines 65–66 creates an instance of interface **Connection** which represents a connection to the IBM XML registry.

Developers who modify the contents of an XML registry must provide a valid username and password. Section 10.2.1 discusses how to obtain access rights to IBM's UDDI test registry. If a user provides a username and password, lines 72–83 set the user credentials that will grant the client modification rights to content in the XML registry. Users who do not provide a username and password, will access the XML registry anonymously.

Lines 72–74 create an instance of class **PasswordAuthentication**, which is a holder class for username and password pairs. We create object **PasswordAuthentication** as a credential for authentication. **Connection** method **setCredentials** (line 83) sets the credentials that enable an XML registry to authenticate a client.

Lines 87–88 obtain a reference to an instance of interface **RegistryService**. Instances of interface **RegistryService** enable clients to obtain references to implementations of interfaces **BusinessQueryManager** and **BusinessLifeCycleManager**, which expose JAXR functionality. Implementations of interface **BusinessQueryManager** provide methods that enable developers to query an XML registry. Implementations of interface **BusinessLifeCycleManager** exposes methods that enable developers to add, remove and update entries in an XML registry. Accessor methods **getBusinessQueryManager** (lines 106–109) and **getBusinessLifeCycleManager** (lines 112–116) return instances of classes **BusinessQueryManager** and **BusinessLifeCycleManager**, respectively.

10.4 Registering Business Profile

JAXR enables developers to register business-related information, such as contact information and available services, in XML registries. Class **SubmitRegistryEntry** (Fig. 10.7) creates an **Organization** object that defines the Deitel & Associates business entry. **Organization** objects are aggregates of other objects, which represent information such as services provided by the organization and classification information. Figure 10.6 shows the structure of the business entry class **SubmitRegistryEntry** creates. The elements shown in the diagram are discussed in detail in the code explanation for class **SubmitRegistryEntry** (Fig. 10.7).

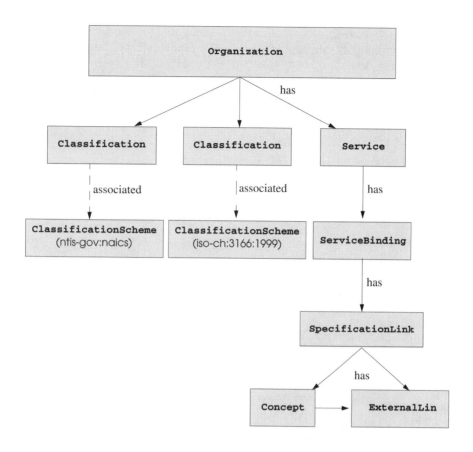

Fig. 10.6 Structure of **Deitel and Associates** XML registry entry.

The Deitel & Associates business entry contains information such as company information and contact information. The Deitel & Associates business entry contains two **Classification** objects, which categorize the business entry. Class **SubmitRegistryEntry** associates these **Classification** objects with **ClassificationScheme** objects that correspond to the taxonomies **ntis-gov:naics** and **iso-ch:3166:1999**, respectively. These taxonomies provide information about the context to which the **Classification** objects belong. For example, one of the taxonomies class **SubmitRegistryEntry** uses, **ntis-gov:naics**, describes numerous industry types such as mining, construction, and real estate industries.

The Deitel & Associates business entry contains also a **Service** object that describes a service organization Deitel & Associates provides. The **Service** object contains a **ServiceBinding** object that provides clients with information that pertains to the access point for the service. The **ServiceBinding** object contains a composition of objects **SpecificationLink**, **Concept** and **ExternalLink**. These objects represent a link to the Web service's WSDL document.

The process by which clients submit a business entry to an XML registry is composed of five steps—1) establish a connection to an XML registry, 2) create an organization entry and add business contact information to the entry, 3) add services information to the entry, 4) classify the organization, and 5) submit the entry to the XML registry.

Class **SubmitRegistryEntry** (Fig. 10.7) demonstrates steps 2–5—the process by which clients create a business entry, populate the business entry with company-related information and store the business entry in an XML registry.

```java
1   // Fig. 10.7: SubmitRegistryEntry.java
2   // Registers Deitel book title service in a UDDI registry.
3
4   package com.deitel.jws1.jaxr;
5
6   // JAXR core packages
7   import javax.xml.registry.*;
8   import javax.xml.registry.infomodel.*;
9
10  // java core packages
11  import java.util.*;
12  import java.net.PasswordAuthentication;
13
14  public class SubmitRegistryEntry {
15
16     // capability interface for querying XML registry
17     private BusinessQueryManager queryManager;
18
19     // capability interface for adding, updating, removing entries
20     private BusinessLifeCycleManager lifeCycleManager;
21
22     // default constructor
23     public SubmitRegistryEntry() throws Exception
24     {
25        // create login password pair
26        String userName = "username";
27        String password = "password";
28
29        // create XMLRegistry manager instance
30        XMLRegistryManager registryManager =
31           new XMLRegistryManager( userName, password );
32
33        // obtain business query
34        queryManager =
35           registryManager.getBusinessQueryManager();
36
37        // obtain business life cycle manager reference
38        lifeCycleManager =
39           registryManager.getBusinessLifeCycleManager();
40
41     } // end constructor
42
```

Fig. 10.7 Class **SubmitRegistryEntry** registers business entry in XML registry. (Part 1 of 7.)

```
43      // create Organization object Deitel & Associates
44      private Organization createOrganization()
45         throws JAXRException
46      {
47         // create organization
48         Organization organization =
49            lifeCycleManager.createOrganization(
50               "Deitel & Associates" );
51
52         // create description string
53         InternationalString description =
54            lifeCycleManager.createInternationalString(
55               "Content providers for Deitel(tm) " +
56               "How to Program series and the Deitel " +
57               "Developer Series" );
58
59         // set description
60         organization.setDescription( description );
61
62         // create contact information
63         User contact = lifeCycleManager.createUser();
64
65         // set contact name
66         PersonName name = lifeCycleManager.createPersonName(
67            "Kyle Lomeli" );
68
69         contact.setPersonName( name );
70
71         // set contact phone number
72         TelephoneNumber phoneNumber =
73            lifeCycleManager.createTelephoneNumber();
74
75         phoneNumber.setNumber( "(123) 456-7890" );
76
77         Collection phoneNumberList = new ArrayList();
78         phoneNumberList.add( phoneNumber );
79
80         contact.setTelephoneNumbers( phoneNumberList );
81
82         // set contact email addresses
83         EmailAddress emailAddress1 =
84            lifeCycleManager.createEmailAddress(
85               "deitel@deitel.com" );
86
87         EmailAddress emailAddress2 =
88            lifeCycleManager.createEmailAddress(
89               "Kyle.Lomeli@deitel.net" );
90
91         Collection emailAddressList = new ArrayList();
92         emailAddressList.add( emailAddress1 );
93         emailAddressList.add( emailAddress2 );
94
```

Fig. 10.7   Class **SubmitRegistryEntry** registers business entry in XML registry. (Part 2 of 7.)

```
95          contact.setEmailAddresses( emailAddressList );
96
97          // set contact information in organization
98          organization.setPrimaryContact( contact );
99
100         return organization;
101
102      } // end method createOrganization
103
104      // create service with appropriate bindings
105      private Service createService() throws JAXRException
106      {
107         // create service
108         Service service = lifeCycleManager.createService(
109            "Book Title Service" );
110
111         // create service description
112         InternationalString description =
113            lifeCycleManager.createInternationalString(
114               "Provides titles of Deitel books " +
115               "corresponding to given ISBN number." );
116
117         // set description
118         service.setDescription( description );
119
120         // create service binding
121         ServiceBinding serviceBinding =
122            lifeCycleManager.createServiceBinding();
123
124         // create service binding description
125         InternationalString bindingDescription =
126            lifeCycleManager.createInternationalString(
127               "Web service BookTitle is deployed on " +
128               "an Axis Web services platform. " +
129               "Platform set up for moderate use." );
130
131         // set description
132         serviceBinding.setDescription( bindingDescription );
133
134         // set URI for service
135         serviceBinding.setAccessURI(
136            "http://www.deitel.com:8080/axis/BookTitle" );
137
138         // contains location of WSDL document
139         SpecificationLink specificationLink =
140            lifeCycleManager.createSpecificationLink();
141
142         // create Concept for WSDL link
143         // null maps the element to tModel
144         Concept wsdlConcept =
145            lifeCycleManager.createConcept(
146               null, "wsdlSpec", "wsdlSpec" );
```

Fig. 10.7 Class **SubmitRegistryEntry** registers business entry in XML registry. (Part 3 of 7.)

```
147
148        // define key for wsdl concept
149        Key wsdlKey = lifeCycleManager.createKey(
150           "uuid:C1ACF26D-9672-4404-9D70-39B756E62AB4" );
151
152        // set concept key
153        wsdlConcept.setKey( wsdlKey );
154
155        // set Concept to specification link
156        specificationLink.setSpecificationObject(
157           wsdlConcept );
158
159        // define WSDL URL
160        String wsdlURL =
161           "http://www.deitel.com:8080/axis/BookTitle?wsdl";
162
163        String wsdlDescription =
164           "WSDL for Web service BookTitle";
165
166        // create link to wsdl document
167        ExternalLink wsdlURI =
168           lifeCycleManager.createExternalLink(
169              wsdlURL, wsdlDescription );
170
171        // add reference to WSDL file to specification link
172        specificationLink.addExternalLink( wsdlURI );
173
174        // add reference to WSDL file to concept
175        wsdlConcept.addExternalLink( wsdlURI );
176
177        // add WSDL URL to service binding
178        serviceBinding.addSpecificationLink(
179           specificationLink );
180
181        // create ArrayList of service bindings
182        Collection bindingList = new ArrayList();
183        bindingList.add( serviceBinding );
184
185        // add service binding Collection to service
186        service.addServiceBindings( bindingList );
187
188        return service;
189     } // end method createService
190
191     // create classification based on business role
192     private Classification createBusinessClassification()
193        throws JAXRException
194     {
195        // create classification scheme
196        ClassificationScheme classificationScheme =
197           queryManager.findClassificationSchemeByName(
198              null, "ntis-gov:naics" );
```

Fig. 10.7   Class **SubmitRegistryEntry** registers business entry in XML registry. (Part 4 of 7.)

```
199
200        // create classification
201        Classification classification =
202          lifeCycleManager.createClassification(
203            classificationScheme,
204            "Educational Support Services",
205            "61171" );
206
207        return classification;
208
209     } // end method createBusinessClassification
210
211     // create classification based on business location
212     private Classification createLocationClassification()
213        throws JAXRException
214     {
215        // create classification scheme
216        ClassificationScheme classificationScheme =
217          queryManager.findClassificationSchemeByName(
218            null, "iso-ch:3166:1999" );
219
220        // create concept
221        Classification classification =
222          lifeCycleManager.createClassification(
223            classificationScheme, "UNITED STATES", "US" );
224
225        return classification;
226
227     } // end method createLocationClassification
228
229     // construct and initialize an organization
230     // to submit to registry
231     public Organization getOrganization()
232        throws JAXRException
233     {
234        // create organization
235        Organization organization = createOrganization();
236
237        // create service descriptor object
238        Service service = createService();
239
240        Collection serviceList = new ArrayList();
241        serviceList.add( service );
242
243        // set service descriptor
244        organization.addServices( serviceList );
245
246        // create business classifications
247        Classification businessClassification =
248          createBusinessClassification();
249
```

Fig. 10.7   Class **SubmitRegistryEntry** registers business entry in XML registry. (Part 5 of 7.)

```
250        Classification locationClassification =
251           createLocationClassification();
252
253        Collection classificationList = new ArrayList();
254        classificationList.add( businessClassification );
255        classificationList.add( locationClassification );
256
257        // set business classification
258        organization.setClassifications( classificationList );
259
260        return organization;
261
262     } // end method getOrganization
263
264     // save organization object in registry
265     public Organization register( Organization organization )
266        throws JAXRException
267     {
268        // create Collection of organizations
269        Collection organizationList = new ArrayList();
270        organizationList.add( organization );
271
272        // submit organization
273        BulkResponse bulkResponse =
274           lifeCycleManager.saveOrganizations( organizationList );
275
276        // obtain submission keys
277        Collection keyCollection =
278           bulkResponse.getCollection();
279
280        // ensure Collection not null
281        if ( keyCollection != null ) {
282
283           Iterator keys = keyCollection.iterator();
284
285           // assign key if exists
286           if ( keys.hasNext() ) {
287              Key assignedKey = ( Key )keys.next();
288              organization.setKey( assignedKey );
289           }
290        } // end if
291
292        // ensure no exceptions occurred
293        Collection exceptionCollection =
294           bulkResponse.getExceptions();
295
296        if ( exceptionCollection != null ) {
297
298           // display exceptions
299           Iterator exceptions =
300              exceptionCollection.iterator();
301
```

Fig. 10.7   Class **SubmitRegistryEntry** registers business entry in XML registry.
(Part 6 of 7.)

```
302              while ( exceptions.hasNext() ) {
303                 JAXRException exception =
304                    ( JAXRException )exceptions.next();
305
306                 exception.printStackTrace();
307              }
308          } // end if
309
310          return organization;
311
312       } // end method register
313
314       // entry point for class ServiceRegister
315       public static void main( String[] args )
316       {
317          try {
318
319             SubmitRegistryEntry serviceRegister =
320                new SubmitRegistryEntry();
321
322             // create Deitel organization
323             Organization deitelOrganization =
324                serviceRegister.getOrganization();
325
326             // register organization
327             deitelOrganization =
328                serviceRegister.register( deitelOrganization );
329
330             // obtain key if submission successful
331             Key assignedKey = deitelOrganization.getKey();
332
333             // print results if key exists
334             if ( assignedKey != null ) {
335
336                System.out.println( "Submission successful!" );
337                System.out.println( "Service registered with key: " +
338                   assignedKey.getId() );
339             } // end if
340
341          } // end try
342
343          catch ( Exception exception ) {
344             exception.printStackTrace();
345          }
346       } // end method main
347
348   } // end class SubmitRegistryEntry
```

```
Submission successful!
Service registered with key: FC67F830-4299-11D6-9E2B-000629DC0A2B
```

Fig. 10.7 Class **SubmitRegistryEntry** registers business entry in XML registry.
(Part 7 of 7.)

Method **createOrganization** (lines 44–102) creates an organization entity and initializes the organization with contact information (step 2). Method **createOrganization** first creates an organization and sets its description (lines 48–60). Lines 48–50 call method **createOrganization** of interface **BusinessLifeCycleManager** to create an XML registry entry that represents organization Deitel & Associates. Implementations of interface **Organization** represent entries in XML registries that act as holders for an organization's information such as contact information, description of an organization and services provided by the organization.

Lines 53–57 create the description for organization Deitel & Associates. Implementations of interface **InternationalString** enable developers to store multiple **LocalizedString** instances of the specified string. Implementations of interface **InternationalString** enable clients to obtain different localized string descriptions of organizations and businesses. Developers that set the organization description must provide the string representations for the different locals. Line 60 calls method **setDescription** to set the description of the organization using the Java Virtual Machine's default locale.

Lines 63–98 set the Deitel & Associates organization entry's contact information. Line 63 uses **BusinessLifeCycleManager** method **createUser** to create **User** objects. A **User** represents a person who is associated with an organization. Instances of interface **User** contain information such as name, telephone numbers and e-mail addresses. Lines 66–69 create and set the name for the **User** to associate with organization Deitel & Associates. **BusinessLifeCycleManager** method **createPersonName** (lines 66–67) creates a **PersonName** instance initialized to the specified string. Line 69 calls **User** method **setPersonName** to set the contact name.

Lines 72–80 set the contact's telephone number. Lines 72–73 use **BusinessLifeCycleManager** method **createTelephoneNumber** to create a **TelephoneNumber**. Instances of interface **TelephoneNumber** represent a telephone number and its attributes. Line 75 sets the phone number of instance **phoneNumber** to **(123) 456-7890**. An organization's contact person can have multiple phone number entries. Lines 77–78 create a **Collection** in which to store the phone number. We specify only one phone number. Line 80 invokes **User** method **setTelephoneNumbers** to set the telephone numbers associated with the contact.

Lines 83–95 set the contact's e-mail address information. Lines 83–89 use **BusinessLifeCycleManager** method **createEmailAddress** to create an **EmailAddress** in which to store e-mail address information. Multiple e-mail addresses can be associated with a contact person, so lines 91–93 create and populate a **Collection** with the e-mail address entries. Line 95 invokes **User** method **setEmailAddresses** to associate the e-mail addresses with the contact. Line 98 calls method **setPrimaryContact** to set instance **User** as the primary contact for the organization.

Method **createService** represents step 3 (lines 105–189), which creates a service entry that provides clients with information about a service that organization Deitel & Associates offers. Deitel & Associates' service entry has three parts—1) service description, 2) access information and 3) WSDL document location.

Lines 108–118 create the service entry and its description. Lines 108–109 call method **createService** of interface implementation **BusinessLifeCycleManager** to create a **Service** with name **Book Title Service**. Instances of interface **Service**

represent a service entry in the XML registry. **Service** entries define information clients
need to access a service. Lines 112–118 define a description that qualifies the service entry.

Lines 121–136 set the information the client needs to access the server. Instances of interface **ServiceBinding** encapsulate a service's access information. A service may have
multiple access points—a **ServiceBinding** instance represents one access point. Lines
121–122 use **LifeCycleManager** method **createServiceBinding** to create a
ServiceBinding. Lines 125–132 set the description that defines information specific to
the access point object **ServiceBinding** represents. Lines 135–136 sets the access point
URI that clients use to access Web service **BookTitle** using method **setAccessURI**.

Common Programming Error 10.1

Failing to set an active access URI causes an **InvalidRequestException** *to be thrown.*

Lines 139–179 set the information clients use to access the WSDL document for the
ServiceBinding object. Lines 139–140 create a **SpecificationLink**. A **SpecificationLink** contains **ExternalLink** and **Concept** objects, which define links
to secondary technical resources that describe the service. The technical resource we reference is a WSDL document. **SpecificationLink**s use instances of interface **Concept**
to define the **SpecificationLink**'s technical resource types. Lines 144–146 invoke
method **createConcept** from interface **BusinessLifeCycleManager** to create a
Concept. Line 146 defines the **Concept**'s name and type, respectively. Note the three
parameters method **createConcept** uses to create an instance of interface **Concept**.
The first parameter represents the parent associated to the **Concept** object. JAXR defines
the **Concept** abstraction to map to different entities within the UDDI registry. When specifying **null** as the parent of **Concept**, JAXR maps object **Concept** to a specification
entity within the UDDI registry. The second two parameters define the name and value that
identify the specification the **Concept** object represents—a specification that identifies
WSDL documents.

In addition to a specification name and value, **Concept** objects that represent specifications within UDDI registries require an identification **Key**. Method **createKey** of
interface **BusinessLifeCycleManager** creates an instance of interface **Key** with the
specified ID (lines 149–150). UDDI registries do not allow clients to define their own identification **Key**, so clients must 1) register a **Concept** in the UDDI registry and obtain its
UDDI-assigned **Key**, or 2) construct a **Key** instance using the identification value of a pre-
existing **Key**.

The UDDI V2 specification defines a **Key** value that clients must use for **Concept**
instances that represent a number of pre-existing, UDDI V2 taxonomies. Examples of these
taxonomies are **xmlSpec**, **soapSpec**, and **wsdlSpec**. **Key** value **uuid:C1ACF26D-
9672-4404-9D70-39B756E62AB4** is the predefined **Key** value for **Concept**
objects that describe these specifications. For further information on pre-defined UDDI
taxonomies and other UDDI resources, see Section 10.9.

Line 153 calls method **setKey** to set the **Concept**'s **Key**. Lines 156–157 call
SpecificationLink method **setSpecificationObject** to set the **Concept**
for the WSDL document.

Lines 160–172 specify the URI for the Web service's WSDL document. Lines 167–169
invoke **BusinessLifeCycleManager** method **createExternalLink** to create an

ExternalLink. Instances of interface **ExternalLink** enable clients to specify the URI of an external resource. Clients use **ExternalLink** objects for various purposes (e.g., to specify the location of a company's homepage, location of an XML document's DTD document, etc.). Object **ExternalLink** (lines 167–169) contains the URI of the WSDL document. Line 172 adds object **ExternalLink** to object **SpecificationLink**.

A client uses the **ExternalLink** object in a **Concept** to locate the WSDL document for a service, so line 175 adds object **ExternalLink** to object **Concept**. Lines 178–179 use **ServiceBinding** method **addSpecificationLink** to add the **SpecificationLink** instance to object **ServiceBinding**. Lines 182–186 add the **ServiceBinding** instance to object **Service**.

Methods **createBusinessClassification** (lines 192–209) and **createLocationClassification** (lines 212–227) set the classification information with which registry clients find organization Deitel & Associates and its associated services (step 4). Registries enable organizations to classify their entries using *taxonomies*. A taxonomy is a system by which entries are classified based on their attributes. Several taxonomies exist that enable organizations to classify themselves based on the nature of their business, their location or other attributes.

Method **createBusinessClassification** creates a classification scheme using the taxonomy defined by the *North American Industry Classification System (NAICS)*. The NAICS provides a classification scheme that categorizes organizations based on their industry. Lines 216–217 invoke method **findClassificationScheme-ByName** of interface **BusinessQueryManager** to obtain a reference to a classification scheme that exists in the XML registry. Lines 201–205 use method **createClassification** of interface **BusinessLifeCycleManager** to create a **Classification**. **Classification** objects classify the registry entry to which they are associated. Method **createClassification** takes three parameters—the classification scheme, the name and the value. The classification scheme parameter specifies the **ClassificationScheme** from which to create the **Classification** object. Each **Classification** object corresponds to a **ClassificationScheme** object. The name and value parameters identify the element within the classification scheme. Organization Deitel & Associates is an education-services business. The NAICS taxonomy table (See Section 10.9 for information on accessing the NAICS taxonomy table) lists **Educational Support Services** as having value **61171**.

Method **createLocationClassification** (lines 212–227) creates a **Classification** object that corresponds to the ISO 3166-1-Alpha-2 taxonomy. The ISO 3166-1-Alpha-2 taxonomy categorizes elements based on their geographic locations. Lines 216–223 create a classification object that corresponds to the United States.

Method **getOrganization** (lines 231–262) outlines the process that adds the service and classification entries to the Deitel & Associates registry entry. Line 235 calls helper method **createOrganization** to create an **Organization** representing Deitel & Associates. Line 238 uses helper method **createService** to create a service entry that corresponds to service **BookTitle**. Lines 240–244 add the service entry to organization Deitel & Associates. An organization can have multiple service entries, so method **addServices** from interface **Organization** takes a **Collection** of **Service** instances. Lines 247–251 use helper methods **createBusinessClassification** and **createLocationClassification** to create two **Classification** objects for organization Deitel & Associates. Multiple **Classification** instances can qualify one **Organization** instance, so method **setClassifications** (line 258) from interface **Organization** takes a **Collection** of **Classification** instances.

Method **register** (lines 265–312) represents step 5—the submission of the organization entry to the registry. Lines 273–274 call method **saveOrganizations** of interface **BusinessLifeCycleManager** to save a **Collection** of **Organization** objects. Method **saveOrganizations** submits each **Organization** object to the registry. Method **saveOrganizations** returns a **BulkResponse** object that contains the result set for the submitted organizations. A **BulkResponse** object contains a **Collection** of **Key** objects that the registry assigned to each organization submitted and a **Collection** of **JAXRExceptions** that occurred when submitting the organizations. JAXR allows a **Collection** of **Organization** objects to be partially committed to the XML registry. Lines 277–290 obtain the **Key** instances that correspond to the **Organization** objects that lines 273–274 successfully submitted.

JAXR also enables developers to update entries in a registry. To update an entry in an XML registry, create an organization entry. Developers must set the **Key** entry for the new organization entry to match that of the old entry. Developers can obtain a **Key** value for an organization that resides within a registry by querying the registry (see Section 10.5) or by analyzing the **BulkResponse** object resulting from the original entry submission. When submitting the new entry, the new entry's information will replace the corresponding information in the old entry. Line 288 updates class **SubmitRegistryEntry**'s reference to object **Organization** by setting the **Key** that the registry assigned. Only a **Key** identifies an XML registry entry uniquely, so saving the **Key** enables us to accurately identify the entry for update and delete operations. Lines 293–308 output any exceptions that the save operation encountered.

Common Programming Error 10.2

*When updating information in an XML registry, failing to set the **Key** value for an XML entry causes the XML registry to interpret the submission as an attempt to add a new entry.*

Method **main** (lines 315–346) instantiates an instance of class **SubmitRegistryEntry** (lines 319–320) and uses the methods of class **SubmitRegistryEntry** to create an organization and submit that organization to the registry (lines 323–328). Lines 331–339 output the **Key** value assigned to organization Deitel & Associates.

10.4.1 JAXR Browser

Sun's JWSDP includes a JAXR browser, which provides a graphical user interface for querying and modifying entries in a UDDI registry. We will discuss the process by which we can verify the information class **SubmitRegistryEntry** (Fig. 10.7) submits to the IBM registry.

To start the JAXR browser, in the **c:\jwsdp\bin** directory execute the command
jaxr-browser.bat

To start the JAXR browser from a Unix-based system, execute the command
jaxr-browser.sh

From drop-down menu **Registry Location**, select **www-3.ibm.com/services/uddi/v2beta/inquiryapi**. Input **Deitel** in the **Name** textfield, then click button **Search**. The display table lists matching entries (Fig. 10.8).

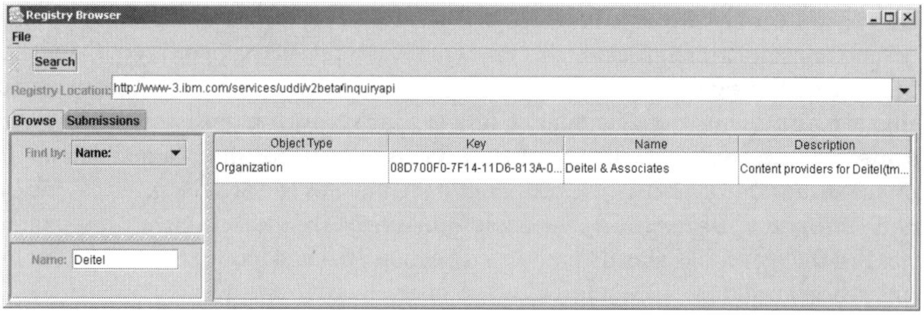

Fig. 10.8 JAXR browser displaying all organizations with **Deitel** in name.

Double-click any entry in the table to view its details (Fig. 10.9). The organization frame displays contact information and enables users to view information specific to the services associated with the entry.

10.5 Querying Registries Using JAXR

JAXR API enables developers to query XML registries. Developers can query an XML registry for any information related to any entry. Currently, JAXR exposes query-related functionality through interfaces **BusinessQueryManager** and **DeclarativeQueryManager**. As XML registry standards continue to emerge, interfaces for new capability

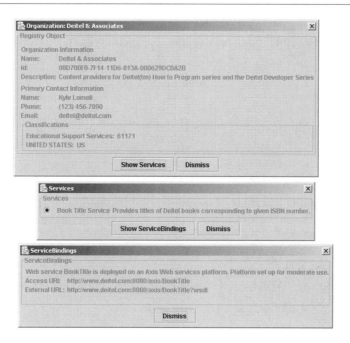

Fig. 10.9 JAXR browser description frames.

levels will replace interface **BusinessQueryManager**. This chapter discusses interface **BusinessQueryManager**, which enables developers to query XML registries for services, organizations, classification schemes the XML registry supports, etc.

Class **ObtainRegistryEntry** (Fig. 10.10) demonstrates the process by which clients query registries for organizations. Class **ObtainRegistryEntry** uses **BusinessQueryManager** method **findOrganizations** to find organizations that contain the strings **Deitel** or **Associates** in their names and are classified as **Educational Support Services** businesses in the NAICS taxonomy. This example assumes that the reader has already completed Section 10.4 and has registered the Deitel & Associates organization in IBM's test UDDI registry.

```
1   // Fig. 10.10: ObtainRegistryEntry.java
2   // Query XML registry for organizations matching "Deitel" or
3   // "Associates" in their names and classified as
4   // "Educational Support Services" in the NAICS taxonomy.
5
6   package com.deitel.jws1.jaxr;
7
8   // JAXR core packages
9   import javax.xml.registry.*;
10  import javax.xml.registry.infomodel.*;
11
12  // java core packages
13  import java.util.*;
14
15  public class ObtainRegistryEntry {
16
17     // capability interface for querying XML registry
18     private BusinessQueryManager queryManager;
19
20     // capability interface for adding, updating, removing entries
21     private BusinessLifeCycleManager lifeCycleManager;
22
23     // constructor
24     public ObtainRegistryEntry() throws Exception
25     {
26        // create XMLRegistry manager instance
27        XMLRegistryManager registryManager =
28           new XMLRegistryManager();
29
30        // obtain business query
31        queryManager =
32           registryManager.getBusinessQueryManager();
33
34        // obtain business life cycle manager reference
35        lifeCycleManager =
36           registryManager.getBusinessLifeCycleManager();
37
38     } // end constructor
39
```

Fig. 10.10 Class **ObtainRegistryEntry** queries XML registry for business entries. (Part 1 of 6.)

```
40        // queries registry with provided string
41        public BulkResponse getOrganizations() throws JAXRException
42        {
43           // define qualifiers
44           Collection qualifierList = new ArrayList();
45
46           // matches sorted in ascending order
47           qualifierList.add( FindQualifier.SORT_BY_NAME_ASC );
48
49           // matches all companies containing Deitel
50           String pattern1 = "%Deitel%";
51
52           // matches all companies containing Associates
53           String pattern2 = "%Associates%";
54
55           // matches organizations that include words
56           // "Deitel" or "Associates" in their name
57           Collection namePatternList = new ArrayList();
58           namePatternList.add( pattern1 );
59           namePatternList.add( pattern2 );
60
61           // classification for education services
62           ClassificationScheme classificationScheme =
63              queryManager.findClassificationSchemeByName(
64                 null, "ntis-gov:naics" );
65
66           // create classification
67           Classification classification =
68              lifeCycleManager.createClassification(
69                 classificationScheme,
70                 "Educational Support Services",
71                 "61171" );
72
73           Collection classificationList = new ArrayList();
74           classificationList.add( classification );
75
76           // obtain matching organizations
77           BulkResponse toReturn =
78              queryManager.findOrganizations(
79                 qualifierList, namePatternList,
80                 classificationList, null, null, null );
81
82           return toReturn;
83
84        } // end method getOrganizations
85
86        // displays Organization information
87        public static void displayOrganization(
88           Organization organization ) throws JAXRException
89        {
90           // display organization name and identifying key
91           InternationalString name = organization.getName();
```

Fig. 10.10 Class **ObtainRegistryEntry** queries XML registry for business entries. (Part 2 of 6.)

```
92          Key organizationKey = organization.getKey();
93
94          System.out.println( "\nOrganization name:   " +
95             name.getValue() );
96
97          System.out.println( "Organization key: " +
98             organizationKey.getId() );
99
100         // get organization services
101         Collection serviceCollection =
102            organization.getServices();
103
104         Iterator services = serviceCollection.iterator();
105
106         // display services information
107         while ( services.hasNext() ) {
108
109            Service service = ( Service )services.next();
110
111            // display Service information
112            displayService( service );
113         }
114
115      } // end method displayOrganization
116
117      // displays Service information
118      private static void displayService( Service service )
119         throws JAXRException
120      {
121         // display service name and description
122         InternationalString name = service.getName();
123         InternationalString description =
124            service.getDescription();
125
126         System.out.println( "Service: " + name.getValue() );
127         System.out.println( "Service description: " +
128            description.getValue() );
129
130         // get service bindings
131         Collection serviceBindingsCollection =
132            service.getServiceBindings();
133
134         Iterator serviceBindings =
135            serviceBindingsCollection.iterator();
136
137         // display Servicebindings information
138         while ( serviceBindings.hasNext() ) {
139
140            ServiceBinding serviceBinding =
141               ( ServiceBinding ) serviceBindings.next();
142
```

Fig. 10.10 Class **ObtainRegistryEntry** queries XML registry for business entries. (Part 3 of 6.)

```
143            // display ServiceBinding information
144            displayServiceBinding( serviceBinding );
145         }
146
147      } // end method displayService
148
149      // display ServiceBinding information
150      private static void displayServiceBinding(
151         ServiceBinding serviceBinding ) throws JAXRException
152      {
153         // display access URI
154         System.out.println( "Access URI: " +
155            serviceBinding.getAccessURI() );
156
157         // get specification links
158         Collection specificationLinkCollection =
159            serviceBinding.getSpecificationLinks();
160
161         Iterator specificationLinks =
162            specificationLinkCollection.iterator();
163
164         // display SpecificationLinks information
165         while ( specificationLinks.hasNext() ) {
166
167            SpecificationLink wsdlLink =
168               ( SpecificationLink )specificationLinks.next();
169
170            // display SpecificationLink information
171            displaySpecificationLink( wsdlLink );
172         }
173
174      } // end method displayServiceBinding
175
176      // display SpecificationLink information
177      private static void displaySpecificationLink(
178         SpecificationLink specificationLink ) throws JAXRException
179      {
180         // obtain external links
181         Collection externalLinksCollection =
182            specificationLink.getExternalLinks();
183
184         Iterator externalLinks =
185            externalLinksCollection.iterator();
186
187         // display ExternalLinks information
188         while ( externalLinks.hasNext() ) {
189
190            ExternalLink externalLink =
191               ( ExternalLink )externalLinks.next();
192
193            System.out.println( "External URI: " +
194               externalLink.getExternalURI() );
```

Fig. 10.10 Class **ObtainRegistryEntry** queries XML registry for business entries. (Part 4 of 6.)

```
195            }
196
197     } // end method displaySpecificationLink
198
199     // entry point for class ServiceRegister
200     public static void main( String[] args )
201     {
202
203         // query registry
204         try {
205
206             ObtainRegistryEntry registryQuery =
207                 new ObtainRegistryEntry();
208
209             // get matching orgainizations
210             BulkResponse bulkResponse =
211                 registryQuery.getOrganizations();
212
213             // ensure no exceptions occurred
214             Collection exceptionCollection =
215                 bulkResponse.getExceptions();
216
217             // exceptions during submission
218             if ( exceptionCollection != null ) {
219
220                 // get iterator of exceptions
221                 Iterator exceptions =
222                     exceptionCollection.iterator();
223
224                 // display exceptions
225                 while ( exceptions.hasNext() ) {
226
227                     JAXRException exception =
228                         ( JAXRException )exceptions.next();
229
230                     exception.printStackTrace();
231                 }
232
233             } // end if
234
235             // no exceptions during submission
236             else {
237
238                 // obtain submission keys
239                 Collection organizationCollection =
240                     bulkResponse.getCollection();
241
242                 // ensure organization found
243                 if ( organizationCollection == null ) {
244                     System.out.println(
245                         "No matching organization found!" );
246
```

Fig. 10.10 Class **ObtainRegistryEntry** queries XML registry for business entries. (Part 5 of 6.)

```
247              return;
248           }
249
250           // obtain organizations
251           Iterator organizations =
252              organizationCollection.iterator();
253
254           while ( organizations.hasNext() ) {
255
256              Organization organization =
257                 ( Organization )organizations.next();
258
259              // display Organization information
260              displayOrganization( organization );
261           }
262
263        } // end else
264
265     } // end try
266
267     catch ( Exception exception ) {
268        exception.printStackTrace();
269     }
270
271  } // end method main
272
273 } // end class ObtainRegistryEntry
```

```
Organization name:  Deitel & Associates
Organization key: FC67F830-4299-11D6-9E2B-000629DC0A2B
Service: Book Title Service
Service description: Provides titles of Deitel books corresponding to
given ISBN number.
Access URI: http://www.deitel.com:8080/axis/BookTitle
External URI: http://www.deitel.com:8080/axis/BookTitle?wsdl
```

Fig. 10.10 Class **ObtainRegistryEntry** queries XML registry for business entries. (Part 6 of 6.)

Class **ObtainRegistryEntry** has three components—1) a constructor (lines 24–38) that establishes a connection to the XML registry, 2) method **getOrganizations** (lines 41–84), which queries the XML registry, and 3) methods **displayOrganization** (lines 87–115), **displayService** (lines 118–147), **displayServiceBinding** (lines 150–174) and **displaySpecificationLink** (lines 177–197), which display information that corresponds to the matching organizations.

The constructor on lines 24–38 is similar to the constructor of class **SubmitRegistryEntry** (Fig. 10.7). The difference is that constructor **ObtainRegistryEntry** does not provide user credentials. Unlike life cycle managers, query managers typically do not require user authentication.[1] Clients interact with query managers anonymously. Lines

---

1. This applies to most public registries. However, businesses can provide private registries that require authentication for performing queries as well as modifications.

27–28 create an instance of class **XMLRegistryManager**. Lines 31–36 obtain references to instances of interfaces **BusinessQueryManager** and **BusinessLife-CycleManager**. **BusinessQueryManager** methods require instances of interfaces such as **Organization, ClassificationScheme, Concept, Service** and **ServiceBinding** to create queries. Implementations of interface **BusinessLife-Cycle-Manager** provide the factory methods by which we obtain references to instances of these objects.

Method **getOrganizations** (lines 41–84) returns the organizations that contain strings **"Deitel"** or **"Associates"** in their name and that are classified as **Educational Support Services** within the NAICS taxonomy. Lines 44–47 define the optional parameter **qualifierList** with which method **findOrganizations** qualifies the search results. Parameter **qualifierList** is a **Collection** of **String**s that affects the return value of method **findOrganizations**. Parameter **findQualifiers** can set the sort order for organizations that match the query, the precision by which method **findOrganizations** matches organizations, etc. Interface **FindQualifier** (line 47) provides string constants as qualifiers interface **BusinessQueryManager** supports. Line 47 specifies a qualifier **SORT_BY_NAME_ASC**, which sorts the returned values by name in ascending order.

Lines 50–59 define the parameter **namePattern** method that **findOrganization** uses. Parameter **namePattern** is a **Collection** of **String**s that specify name values with which method **findOrganizations** matches organizations. Parameter **namePatternList** represents a logical OR relationship for the elements in the **Collection** (i.e., organizations matching any element in the **Collection** are valid matches). Each string in the **Collection** must follow the SQL-92 LIKE specification. The SQL-92 LIKE specification determines that a pattern matches a string if, and only if, each character in the pattern is the lexicographical equivalent of its corresponding character in the string to match. The SQL-92 LIKE specification defines two wildcard characters (**%** and **_**) and an escape character (**/**). Figure 10.11 lists the wildcard characters and their meanings.

For example, the name pattern **%Deitel%** matches strings such as **Deitel, Harvey Deitel, Paul Deitel, Deitel and Associates** and **Deitel and Associates, Inc.**. The name pattern **_Deitel_** matches strings such as **aDeitel, ADeitelB** and **DeitelC**. Lines 50–53 specify the name patterns **%Deitel%** and **%Associates%** that method **findOrganizations** uses to match organizations with either **Deitel** or **Associates** in their names.

Lines 62–71 create a **Classification** object that classifies the organizations that method **findOrganization** returns. Section 10.4 discusses the purposes **ClassificationScheme** and **Classification**.

Character	Purpose
%	Matches any character zero or more times.
_	Matches any character zero or one times.

Fig. 10.11 SQL-92 LIKE wildcard specification.

Lines 72–80 call **BusinessQueryManager** method **findOrganizations** to obtain a set of organizations that match the name pattern and classification criteria. Method **findOrganizations** takes six parameters. The six parameters enable developers to find organizations based on individual or combinations of criteria—name patterns that match organization's names, classifications, service specifications, external identifiers and external links. Method **findOrganizations** matches only organizations that meet all given criteria. To indicate to method **findOrganizations** that a parameter must not be used to match organizations, developers must use **null** as the corresponding parameter. Method **findOrganizations** returns a **BulkResponse** object that contains a **Collection** of matching organizations.

Class **ObtainRegistryEntry** uses methods **displayOrganization** (lines 87–115), **displayService** (lines 118–147), **displayServiceBinding** (lines 150–174) and **displaySpecificationLink** (lines 177–197) to display the content of organizations that method **findOrganizations** returns.

Method **displayOrganization** (lines 87–115) displays the organization name and **Key** value, and calls method **displayService** to display associated **Service**s information. Lines 91–98 obtain and display the organization name and **Key** value. Lines 101–102 call **Organization** method **getServices**, which returns a **Collection** of **Service** instances. Lines 107–113 display information on each **Service** instance the organization provides by calling method **displayService** (line 158).

Method **displayService** (lines 118–147) displays the service name and calls method **displayServiceBinding** to display associated **ServiceBinding**s information. Lines 122–124 call **Service** methods **getName** and **getDescription** to obtain **InternationalString** instances for the name and description of the service, respectively. Lines 126–128 call **InternationalString** method **getValue** to get the localized string representations of the service name and description. Lines 131–132 call **Service** method **getServiceBindings** to obtain a **Collection** of **Service-Binding** instances. Lines 134–145 iterate through the **Collection** of **Service-Binding**s and call method **displayServiceBinding** to display **ServiceBinding** information.

Method **displayServiceBinding** (lines 150–174) displays the service binding's access URI and calls method **displaySpecificationLink**. Line 155 calls **ServiceBinding** method **getAccessURI** to obtain the URI of the access point for the service. Lines 158–159 call **ServiceBinding** method **getSpecificationLink**s to obtain the **Collection** of associated **SpecificationLink** instances. Lines 161–172 iterate through the **Collection** of **SpecificationLink**s display each **SpecificationLink**.

Method **displaySpecificationLink** (lines 177–197) displays the **SpecificationLink**'s external link URI. Lines 181–182 call **SpecificationLink** method **getExternalLinks** to obtain a **Collection** of **ExternalLink** instances. Lines 184–195 iterate through the **Collection** of **ExternalLink**s and call **ExternalLink** method **getExternalURI** to obtain a string representation of each WSDL document URI.

Method **main** (lines 200–271) creates an instance of class **ObtainRegistry-Entry** to query a registry. Lines 206–207 create an instance of class **ObtainRegistryEntry**. Lines 210–211 calls **ObtainRegistryEntry** method **getOrganizations** to obtain a **BulkResponse** that contains matching organizations. Lines 214–215 call **BulkResponse** method **getExceptions** to obtain a **Collection** of **JAXRException**s the registry raised. Lines 218–233 display the **JAXRException** messages. Lines 236–263 display the information for **Organization** instances that matched by calling method **displayOrganization**.

10.6 Removing Business Profile

JAXR enables developers to remove entries from a registry. Interface **BusinessLifeCycleManager** provides developers with methods that modify entries in a registry. Among those methods, interface **BusinessLifeCycleManager** exposes methods that enable developers to delete organization entries, service entries, service bindings, classifications and classification schemes.

Software Engineering Observation 10.2

Developers must provide credentials before invoking any operation that modifies or removes information from an XML registry.

Class **RemoveRegistryEntry** (Fig. 10.12) demonstrates the process by which developers use JAXR to remove entries in an XML registry 1) establish a connection to the XML registry, 2) obtain matching organizations, 3) obtain matching organizations' keys, and 3) remove corresponding organizations.

Class **RemoveRegistryEntry**'s default constructor (lines 23–41) establishes a connection to the IBM test registry. Class **RemoveRegistryEntry** removes entries from the XML registry, so lines 30–31 create an instance of class **XMLRegistryManager** that uses the specified username and password to request modification-rights to the XML registry. Lines 34–39 obtain references to implementations of interfaces **BusinessQueryManager** and **LifeCycleManager**.

Method **getOrganizations** (lines 44–87) queries the XML registry for organizations. Lines 47–50 specify a qualifier that sorts matching organizations by name in ascending order. Lines 53–62 create a name pattern parameter that matches organizations with strings **"Deitel"** or **"Associates"** in their name. Lines 65–74 create the classification that qualifies matching entries. Lines 80–83 call **BusinessQueryManager** method **findOrganizations** to find organizations that match the specified criteria.

Method **getOrganizations** uses a query that can return entries to which we do not have modification rights. When obtaining organization keys from an XML registry, ensure that your credentials enable you to have modification rights to all entries you attempt to delete. We use this inexact query to demonstrate the results of attempting to remove an organization for which we do not have modification rights.

Common Programming Error 10.3

*Ensure that your credentials enable you to have modification rights to organizations that your application attempts to delete. Attempting to delete an XML entry for which you do not have modification rights results in **JAXRException** subclass **DeleteException**.*

Method **createKeyList** (lines 90–133) obtains the **Key** values for organizations that method **getOrganizations** returns. Lines 95–96 obtain a **Collection** of **Organization** instances, which may be empty but not **null**. Lines 115–117 display the name of the organization that class **RemoveRegistryEntry** attempts to remove. Line

120 calls **Organization** method **getKey** to obtain the **Key** for the organization. Line 123 adds the **Key** to the list of **Key**s to remove. Lines 125–126 display the **Key** value.

Method **remove** (lines 136–145) attempts to remove the organizations from the registry. Lines 140–141 call **BusinessLifeCycleManager** method **deleteOrganizations** to attempt to delete organizations whose **Key**s are in **Collection keyList**. Method **deleteOrganizations** returns a **BulkReponse** object that contains a **Collection** of **Key** instances that represent the organizations that the XML registry successfully deleted and a **Collection** of **JAXRException**s that the XML registry raised.

```
1   // Fig. 10.12: RemoveRegistryEntry.java
2   // Removes previously registered entry from XML registry.
3
4   package com.deitel.jws1.jaxr;
5
6   // JAXR core packages
7   import javax.xml.registry.*;
8   import javax.xml.registry.infomodel.*;
9
10  // java core packages
11  import java.util.*;
12  import java.net.PasswordAuthentication;
13
14  public class RemoveRegistryEntry {
15
16     // capability interface for querying XML registry
17     private BusinessQueryManager queryManager;
18
19     // capability interface for adding, updating, removing entries
20     private BusinessLifeCycleManager lifeCycleManager;
21
22     // default constructor
23     public RemoveRegistryEntry() throws Exception
24     {
25        // create login password pair
26        String userName = "username";
27        String password = "password";
28
29        // create XMLRegistry manager instance
30        XMLRegistryManager registryManager =
31           new XMLRegistryManager( userName, password );
32
33        // obtain business query
34        queryManager =
35           registryManager.getBusinessQueryManager();
36
37        // obtain business life cycle manager reference
38        lifeCycleManager =
39           registryManager.getBusinessLifeCycleManager();
40
41     } // end constructor
```

Fig. 10.12 Class **RemoveRegistryEntry** removes organization entry from XML registry. (Part 1 of 6.)

```
42
43     // queries registry with provided string
44     public BulkResponse getOrganizations() throws JAXRException
45     {
46        // define qualifiers
47        Collection qualifierList = new ArrayList();
48
49        // matches sorted in ascending order
50        qualifierList.add( FindQualifier.SORT_BY_NAME_ASC );
51
52        // matches all companies containing Deitel
53        String pattern1 = "%Deitel%";
54
55        // matches all companies containing Associates
56        String pattern2 = "%Associates%";
57
58        // matches organizations that include words
59        // "Deitel" or "Associates" in their name
60        Collection namePatternList = new ArrayList();
61        namePatternList.add( pattern1 );
62        namePatternList.add( pattern2 );
63
64        // classification for education services
65        ClassificationScheme classificationScheme =
66           queryManager.findClassificationSchemeByName(
67              null, "ntis-gov:naics" );
68
69        // create classification
70        Classification classification =
71           lifeCycleManager.createClassification(
72              classificationScheme,
73              "Educational Support Services",
74              "61171" );
75
76        Collection classificationList = new ArrayList();
77        classificationList.add( classification );
78
79        // obtain matching organizations
80        BulkResponse toReturn =
81           queryManager.findOrganizations(
82              qualifierList, namePatternList,
83              classificationList, null, null, null );
84
85        return toReturn;
86
87     } // end method getOrganizations
88
89     // create Collection of organization Keys
90     public static Collection createKeyList(
91        BulkResponse bulkResponse )
92        throws JAXRException
93     {
```

Fig. 10.12 Class **RemoveRegistryEntry** removes organization entry from XML registry. (Part 2 of 6.)

```
94              // obtain organizations
95              Collection organizationCollection =
96                 bulkResponse.getCollection();
97
98              // create iterator of collection elements
99              Iterator organizations =
100                organizationCollection.iterator();
101
102             // contain organizations to remove
103             Collection keyList = new ArrayList();
104
105             // remove each organization
106             while ( organizations.hasNext() ) {
107
108                // obtain reference to Organization instance
109                Organization organization =
110                   ( Organization )organizations.next();
111
112                // obtain and display organization name
113                InternationalString name = organization.getName();
114
115                System.out.println(
116                   "\nOrganization to remove:   " +
117                   name.getValue() );
118
119                // obtain identifying key
120                Key organizationKey = organization.getKey();
121
122                // add key to Collection
123                keyList.add( organizationKey );
124
125                System.out.println( "Key: " +
126                   organizationKey.getId() );
127
128             } // end while
129
130             // return Collection
131             return keyList;
132
133          } // end method createKeyList
134
135          // remove specified organization
136          public BulkResponse remove( Collection keyList )
137             throws JAXRException
138          {
139             // remove organization
140             BulkResponse bulkResponse =
141                lifeCycleManager.deleteOrganizations( keyList );
142
143             return bulkResponse;
144
145          } // end method remove
```

Fig. 10.12 Class **RemoveRegistryEntry** removes organization entry from XML registry. (Part 3 of 6.)

```
146
147    // display exceptions contained in BulkResponse
148    public static void displayRemovedEntries(
149       BulkResponse bulkResponse )
150       throws JAXRException
151    {
152       // get removed entries
153       Collection removedCollection =
154          bulkResponse.getCollection();
155
156       // organizations successfully removed
157       Iterator removedOrganizations =
158          removedCollection.iterator();
159
160       // display removed organization keys
161       while ( removedOrganizations.hasNext() ) {
162
163          Key removedKey =
164             ( Key )removedOrganizations.next();
165
166          System.out.println( "Removed organization with key " +
167             removedKey.getId() );
168
169       } // end while
170
171    } // end method displayRemovedEntries
172
173    // display exceptions contained in BulkResponse
174    public static void displayExceptions(
175       BulkResponse bulkResponse ) throws JAXRException
176    {
177       // get exceptions Collection
178       Collection exceptionCollection =
179          bulkResponse.getExceptions();
180
181       // ensure exceptions occurred
182       if ( exceptionCollection != null ) {
183
184          // exceptions raised
185          Iterator exceptionsRaised =
186             exceptionCollection.iterator();
187
188          // display exceptions raised
189          while ( exceptionsRaised.hasNext() ) {
190
191             Exception exception =
192                ( Exception )exceptionsRaised.next();
193
194             exception.printStackTrace();
195          } // end while
196
197       } // end if
```

Fig. 10.12 Class **RemoveRegistryEntry** removes organization entry from XML registry. (Part 4 of 6.)

```
198
199      } // end method displayExceptions
200
201      // entry point for class RemoveRegistryEntry
202      public static void main( String[] args )
203      {
204         // find and remove matching organizations
205         try {
206
207            RemoveRegistryEntry entryRemoval =
208               new RemoveRegistryEntry();
209
210            // get matching organizations
211            BulkResponse bulkResponse =
212               entryRemoval.getOrganizations();
213
214            // obtain exception collection
215            Collection exceptionCollection =
216               bulkResponse.getExceptions();
217
218            // display exception information
219            if ( exceptionCollection != null ) {
220
221               // display exceptions
222               Iterator exceptions =
223                  exceptionCollection.iterator();
224
225               // display exception stack trace
226               while ( exceptions.hasNext() ) {
227                  JAXRException exception =
228                     ( JAXRException )exceptions.next();
229
230                  exception.printStackTrace();
231               }
232
233               // exit application
234               return;
235
236            } // end if
237
238            // create Collection of keys
239            Collection keyList = createKeyList( bulkResponse );
240
241            // remove organizations
242            BulkResponse removalResults =
243               entryRemoval.remove( keyList );
244
245            // display removed entries
246            displayRemovedEntries( removalResults );
247
```

Fig. 10.12 Class **RemoveRegistryEntry** removes organization entry from XML registry. (Part 5 of 6.)

```
248              // display exceptions
249              displayExceptions( removalResults );
250
251         } // end try
252
253         // catch all exceptions
254         catch ( Exception exception ) {
255            exception.printStackTrace();
256         }
257
258      } // end method main
259
260   } // end class RemoveRegistryEntry
```

```
Organization to remove:  Deitel & Associates
Key: FC67F830-4299-11D6-9E2B-000629DC0A2B

Organization to remove:  Make-Belief Associates
Key: 9D281DBD-AF25-461E-AEF5-632110ED2FBA

Removed organization with key FC67F830-4299-11D6-9E2B-000629DC0A2B
Removed organization with key 9D281DBD-AF25-461E-AEF5-632110ED2FBA

javax.xml.registry.DeleteException: UDDI DispositionReport:
Error Code = E_operatorMismatch;
Error Message = E_operatorMismatch (10130)
Cannot change data that was mastered at another Operator site.
businessEntity = 9D281DBD-AF25-461E-AEF5-632110ED2FBA;
Error Number = 10130; UDDI keyType = null
        at com.sun.xml.registry.uddi.UDDIMapper.results2BulkResponse
          (Unknown Source)
        at com.sun.xml.registry.uddi.UDDIMapper.transformResponse
          (Unknown Source)
        at java.lang.reflect.Method.invoke
          (Native Method)
        at com.sun.xml.registry.uddi.UDDIMapper.invoke
          (Unknown Source)
        at com.sun.xml.registry.uddi.UDDIMapper.processResponse
          (Unknown Source)
        at com.sun.xml.registry.uddi.UDDIMapper.processRequest
          (Unknown Source)
        at com.sun.xml.registry.uddi.UDDIMapper.deleteOrganizations
          (Unknown Source)
        at com.sun.xml.registry.uddi.BusinessLifeCycleManagerIm-
pl.deleteOrganizations
          (Unknown Source)
      at com.deitel.jws1.jaxr.RemoveRegistryEntry.remove
          (RemoveRegistryEntry.java:140)
      at com.deitel.jws1.jaxr.RemoveRegistryEntry.main
          (RemoveRegistryEntry.java:242)
```

Fig. 10.12 Class **RemoveRegistryEntry** removes organization entry from XML registry. (Part 6 of 6.)

Methods **displayRemovedEntries** (lines 148–171) and **displayExceptions** (lines 174–199) verify the deletion results. Method **displayRemovedEntries** displays **Key** values for organization entries that the XML registry successfully deleted. Lines 153–154 obtain the **Collection** of **Key** instances. If the XML registry did not remove any organization entries, method **getCollection** from class **BulkResponse** returns an empty **Collection**. Lines 157–169 display the **Key** values for organizations successfully removed.

Method **displayExceptions** (lines 174–199) displays the stack trace for **JAXRException**s the XML registry raised. Lines 178–179 obtain a **Collection** of **JAXRException** instances. Unlike method **getCollection** from class **BulkResponse**, method **getExceptions** returns **null** if the XML registry did not raise exceptions. Lines 182–197 display the **JAXRException** stack traces.

Method main (lines 202–258) conducts the steps outlined for class **RemoveRegistryEntry**. Lines 207–208 instantiate class **RemoveRegistryEntry**. Lines 211–212 call **RemoveRegistryEntry** method **getOrganizations** to query the XML registry. Lines 215–236 ensure that the XML registry does not raise exceptions when method **getOrganizations** queries the XML registry. Line 239 calls helper method **createKeyList** to create a **Collection** of **Key** instances that correspond to **Organization** instances method **getOrganizations** returns. Lines 242–243 calls **RemoveRegistryEntry** method to attempt to remove the entries from the XML registry. Line 246 calls helper method **displayRemovedEntries** to display organizations that the method successfully removed. Line 249 calls helper method **displayExceptions** to display exceptions the XML registry raised.

10.7 Query Manager and Life Cycle Manager Providers' URLs

The process by which developers obtain modification rights to a UDDI registry is different for each UDDI registry. A UDDI registry's URL provides information clients need to obtain modification rights to the registry. In addition to obtaining modification rights to a given UDDI registry, JAXR client developers must know the URLs for the query manager and life cycle manager providers of UDDI registries with which their JAXR clients will interact. Figure 10.13 lists the URLs for four commonly-used UDDI registries.

Figure 10.14 and Figure 10.15 list the URLs for the query manager providers and life cycle manager providers, respectively, that correspond to each UDDI registry.

Host	URL
HP	`uddi.hp.com`
IBM	`www-3.ibm.com/services/uddi/v2beta/protect/` `    registry.html`
Microsoft	`uddi.rte.microsoft.com`
Systinet (Standard)	`www.systinet.com:80/web/uddi`

Fig. 10.13 UDDI URLs commonly used by UDDI clients.

Host	Query Manager Provider URL
HP	`http://uddi.hp.com:80/inquire`
IBM	`http://www-3.ibm.com:80/services/uddi/v2beta/` `inquiryapi`
Microsoft	`http://uddi.rte.microsoft.com:80/inquire`
Systinet (Standard)	`http://www.systinet.com:80/wasp/uddi/inquiry`

Fig. 10.14 Query Manager Provider URLs.

Host	Life Cycle Manager Provider URL
HP	`https://uddi.hp.com:443/publish`
IBM	`https://www-3.ibm.com:443/services/uddi/v2beta/` `protect/publishapi`
Microsoft	`http://uddi.rte.microsoft.com:80/publish`
Systinet (Standard)	`http://www.systinet.com:443/wasp/uddi/publishing`

Fig. 10.15 Life Cycle Manager Provider URLs.

This chapter has presented many JAXR capabilities. However, there are additional features that are beyond the scope of this book. For a complete description of the Java API for XML Registries, see the JAXR specification, which can be downloaded from **java.sun.com/xml/jaxr/index.html**. Other resources are listed in Section 10.9. The next chapter discusses how to create Web services enabled applications using JAXM.

10.8 Summary

Typical business-to-business (B2B) and business-to-consumer (B2C) interactions require both parties to establish an agreement on requested services. Registries are independent third parties in B2B and B2C relationships that help unify businesses and clients. Registries enable businesses to post information pertaining to a company. Java API for XML Registries (JAXR) is an API that standardizes a way by which Java developers access XML registries.

The JAXR design defines a standardized pluggable architecture that enables clients to use different JAXR providers to communicate with an XML registry. JAXR provides developers with an abstraction of concepts common to all XML registries. JAXR providers are responsible for mapping these general concepts to more specific entities within a target XML registry.

Currently two types of XML registries exist—UDDI and ebXML. The JAXR model was designed to enable developers to use different registry types. For the purposes of not restricting developers to use a limited set of operations common to different XML registries, the JAXR model comprises a union of capabilities between different XML registries.

JAXR enables developers to register business-related information in XML registries. JAXR API defines sets of methods that enable developers to query an XML registry. Developers can query an XML registry for any information related to any entry. JAXR enables developers to remove entries from a registry.

10.9 Internet and World Wide Web Resources

java.sun.com/webservices
This site is the home page for the Sun's Java Web Services Developer Pack (JWSDP).

www.iso.ch
The *International Organization for Standardization (ISO)* provides a central location from which to access numerous international standards.

www.census.gov/epcd/www/naics.html
The *North American Industry Classification System (NAICS)* homepage enables users to access the NAICS codes used by UDDI registries.

www.uddi.org
The *Universal Description. Discovery and Integration of Business (UDDI)* for the Web homepage enables users to access UDDI registry types information.

www.soapclient.com/UDDIAdv.html
This site is a Web-based UDDI client that enables users to query any UDDI registry.

java.sun.com/xml/jaxr/index.html
The JAXR homepage provides resources for the current release of JAXR.

11

JAXM and SAAJ

Objectives

- To introduce the Java API for XML Messaging (JAXM).
- To introduce the SOAP with Attachments API for Java (SAAJ).
- To discuss the types of messaging APIs that Java provides.
- To understand the role of a JAXM message provider in a JAXM application.
- To deploy a Web service using JAXM.
- To build a standalone JAXM client.
- To build a JAXM application that uses a message provider.

...And many a message from the skies, ...
Robert Burns

Attachment is the great fabricator of illusions; reality can be attained only by someone who is detached.
Simon Wei

There can be no true response without responsibility; there can be no responsibility without response.
Arthur Vogel

Of a good beginning cometh a good end.
John Heywood

Outline

11.1 Introduction

In this chapter, we introduce the *Java API for XML Messaging* (*JAXM*), which enables applications to communicate using XML-based messaging protocols, such as SOAP. We begin with an overview of other Java messaging technologies—Java Messaging Service (JMS) and JavaMail—and discuss how JAXM differs from them. We then discuss how to build JAXM applications that use the *SOAP with Attachments API for Java* (*SAAJ*), which enables applications to create and manipulate SOAP messages. We then discuss *JAXM applications*, which use JAXM to send and receive XML-based messages to and from Web services. When creating a JAXM application, a developer must determine whether it should use a *message provider*—a separate component that sends and receives messages on behalf of the application. Essentially, a message provider acts as a listener for messages. When the provider receives a message, the provider forwards the message to various endpoints. As we will see, using a provider enables a JAXM application to send and receive messages asynchronously. A developer can build two types of JAXM applications—those that use a message provider and those that do not (referred to as *standalone JAXM clients*). In this section, we discuss each type of JAXM client, their advantages, disadvantages and the situations in which using one client type is more beneficial than using the other.

11.2 Java Messaging APIs

The Java platform provides three different types of messaging APIs: the Java Messaging Service (JMS), JavaMail and JAXM. These technologies share the common goal of enabling components to send and receive messages. These technologies differ in that each provides support for a distinct messaging infrastructure. Developers use JMS to build applications for Message-Oriented-Middleware (MOM) infrastructures, JavaMail to build email applications and JAXM to build applications that produce and consume Web services (or to build any application that supports XML-based messaging). These messaging infrastructures are not mutually exclusive—for example, it is common for JAXM applications to use JavaMail to send email notifications to users (as we demonstrate in Chapter 15, Case Study Part I).

JMS enables components to transfer messages via the *point-to-point* and *publish/subscribe messaging models*. In the point-to-point model, the sending component sends a message to a *message queue*, which "forwards" that message to the target component. This model requires that only one target component can consume messages from a message queue. By contrast, the publish/subscribe model allows zero or more *subscribers* to consume messages that other components *publish*. The publish/subscribe model uses the notion of *topics*. Publishers send messages to a topic on a server. Clients with active subscriptions to the topic then receive those messages.

JavaMail enables components to send messages via email. JavaMail provides APIs for creating and sending mail, determining the mailing protocols through which to send the mail, and storing and retrieving mail from servers. A message in JavaMail contains a header and a body. The header contains information such as a **From** address, the **To**, **CC** and **BCC** addresses, and the date on which the mail was sent. The body contains the actual message content. JavaMail supports several Internet-mail protocols, such as IMAP, SMTP and POP3.

JAXM enables components to transfer XML-formatted messages (e.g., SOAP messages) and, as we will see throughout this chapter, is often useful when building Business-to-Business (B2B) applications. JAXM supports both *synchronous* and *asynchronous messaging*. In synchronous messaging, a JAXM application sends a message request to a Web service and waits for a message response. From the perspective of the JAXM application that sends the request, synchronous messaging appears to be identical to JAX-RPC's remote method calls. Unlike JAX-RPC, JAXM supports asynchronous messaging, in which a JAXM application that sends a request does not wait for a response from the Web service. The asynchronous approach is ideal in situations where the response from a Web-service invocation depends on a "human factor." For example, a JAXM application might invoke a Web service to place an order for a product; however, before the receiving application can notify the sending application that the order has been shipped, workers physically must transport the merchandise from a warehouse to a delivery vehicle. This process could take an indeterminate amount of time, so it is not feasible in the sending application to wait for a response.

11.3 JAXM and SAAJ

The Java API for XML Messaging (JAXM) and the SOAP with Attachments API for Java (SAAJ) enable a *JAXM application* to send and receive SOAP messages to and from Web services. In addition, developers can use JAXM and SAAJ to create and expose Web services. Essentially, JAXM contains only one package, ***javax.xml.messaging***, which provides classes and interfaces for creating a special type of servlets (called a ***JAXMServlet***) that can send and receive SOAP messages. This package also enables **JAXMServlet**s to connect to *message providers*—separate components that act as proxies for sending and receiving SOAP messages. (We discuss the roles of message providers and their importance in Section 11.5.) SAAJ also contains only one package, ***javax.xml.soap***, which provides classes and interfaces for creating and manipulating SOAP messages. Specifically, these messages must conform to the SOAP 1.1 specification (**www.w3.org/TR/SOAP**) and the SOAP with Attachments W3C Note (**www.w3.org/TR/SOAP-attachments**). The Java Web Service Developer Pack Early-Access releases integrated SAAJ with JAXM—that is, JAXM contained both packages **javax.xml.messaging** and **javax.xml.soap**. The JWSDP current release (version 1.0) separated SAAJ from JAXM, so that other applications (e.g., JAX-RPC applications) could produce and consume SOAP messages without depending on the JAXM specification.

Figure 11.1 lists the JAR files provided by JAXM and SAAJ. Include these files, which are located in **%JWSDP_HOME%/common/lib**, in the classpath when compiling and running all JAXM applications that we show in this chapter. Also include the JAXP classes, which are located in **%JWSDP_HOME%/common/lib** and **%JWSDP_HOME%/common/endorsed**.

API	Associated JAR files	Location

JAXM	`jaxm-api.jar`
	`jaxm-runtime.jar`
	`jaxm-provider`
	`jaxm-provideradmin`
		`%JWSDP_HOME%/common/lib`

SAAJ	`saaj-api.jar`
	`saaj-ri.jar`
	`dom4j.jar`
	`activation.jar`
	`mail.jar`
	`commons-logging.jar`
		`%JWSDP_HOME%/common/lib`

JAXP	`jaxp-api.jar`
	`dom.jar`
	`sax.jar`
	`xalan.jar`
	`xercesImpl.jar`
	`xsltc.jar`
		`%JWSDP_HOME%/common/lib`
		`%JWSDP_HOME%/common/endorsed`

Fig. 11.1   JAXM, SAAJ and JAXP associated JAR files.

11.4 Standalone JAXM Clients and JAXM Web Services

A *standalone JAXM client* invokes Web services synchronously (i.e., the client must wait for a response from that service). In this respect, a standalone JAXM client acts similar to a JAX-RPC client. A standalone JAXM client does not use a message provider to forward requests to, or listen for requests from, a Web service. In Section 11.5, we will show how a message provider also enables a JAXM client to provide Web services, in addition to consuming them. A standalone JAXM client generally is not suited for providing Web services and thus is used commonly for invoking Web services.

In this section, we build a standalone JAXM client to invoke a JAXM-based Web service that returns a list of Deitel book titles. Specifically, our example shows how a standalone client sends a SOAP request to the Book Titles Web service (deployed using JAXM), which returns a list of available book titles as a SOAP response to the client.

Figure 11.2 models the flow of execution between the client and the Web service. The execution begins when **StandaloneClient** creates and sends a SOAP request to **BookTitlesServlet** via **BookTitlesProxy** (Steps 1 and 2). In our implementation, the **StandaloneClient** and **BookTitlesProxy** represent the client, and **BookTitlesServlet** and **BookTitlesImpl** (when deployed in Tomcat) represent the JAXM-based Web service. Upon receiving a SOAP request, **BookTitlesServlet** extracts the ISBN from the request (Step 3) and passes the ISBN to method **getBookTitles** of the **BookTitlesImpl** object (Step 4). Method **getBookTitles** returns an array of **String**s that represent the list of available book titles (Step 5). **BookTitlesServlet** uses this array to create a SOAP response (Step 6) and sends the response to the client (Step 7). **StandaloneClient** uses the **BookTitlesProxy** to extract the list contents from the SOAP response (Step 8) and displays the list for the user.

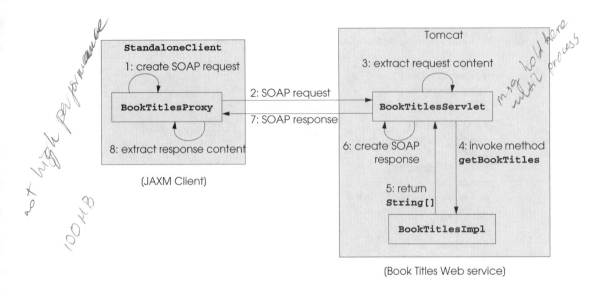

Fig. 11.2 Flowchart for a JAXM standalone client invoking the Book Titles Web service via **BookTitlesServlet**.

Note that we use JAXM to create both the standalone JAXM client and the Book Titles Web service. However, JAXM clients are not limited to transferring messages with only JAXM-based Web services, nor are JAXM-based Web services limited to transferring messages with only JAXM clients. Since the client and the Web service communicate using a common XML-based messaging protocol (e.g., SOAP), the implementation of each component is completely transparent to the other component, thus promoting interoperability. For example, a standalone JAXM client can send a message to a Web service deployed via JAX-RPC, just as easily as that client can send a message to a Web service deployed via JAXM. As another example, a JAXM-based Web service may receive a message created by a JAX-RPC client.

Web-Service Implementation

Class **BookTitlesImpl** (Fig. 11.3) is the class that **BookTitlesServlet** uses to provide the Book Titles Web service. The constructor (lines 17–55) uses **Database.properties** (Fig. 11.4) to obtain the name of the JDBC driver and URI of the database that contains the book titles. Lines 32–37 load the JDBC driver and establish a connection to the database.

Class **BookTitlesImpl** makes available method **getBookTitles** (lines 58–98), which returns a **String** array, in which each **String** represents a distinct title of a Deitel product. Lines 65–71 query the database to extract all book titles. Lines 78–84 convert the returned **ResultSet** to the **String** array of book titles, and line 89 returns this array to the client. Lastly, method **finalize** (lines 101–113) closes the connection to the database.

We deploy the Book Titles Web service using JAXM. JAXM provides class ***JAXM-Servlet***, which, when deployed in Apache Tomcat, exposes a Web service. To expose the Book Titles Web service, we create class **BookTitlesServlet** (Fig. 11.5) as a subclass of **JAXMServlet**, which extends class **javax.servlet.http.Http-**

Servlet. Method **init** (lines 26–42) overrides method **init** of class **HttpServlet**. Lines 33 instantiates a **BookTitlesImpl** object, which handles the logic for the Book Titles Web service. Using this object, **BookTitlesServlet** returns to clients the list of available book titles. Line 34 creates a *MessageFactory* object, which SAAJ provides for creating SOAP messages that conform to the SOAP 1.1 specification. Class **Message-Factory** provides **static** method **newInstance**, which returns a reference to the default **MessageFactory** object. Method **newInstance** throws a **SOAPException** if it cannot return the default **MessageFactory** instance.

```
1   // Fig. 11.3: BookTitlesImpl.java.
2   // Class BookTitlesImpl handles the logic for the Book Titles
3   // Web service, which returns a list of book titles that are
4   // stored in a database.
5   package com.deitel.jws1.services;
6
7   // Java core packages
8   import java.io.*;
9   import java.util.*;
10  import java.sql.*;
11
12  public class BookTitlesImpl {
13
14     private Connection connection; // connection to database
15
16     // constructor to initialize database connection
17     public BookTitlesImpl()
18     {
19        // load JDBC driver and establish connection to database
20        try {
21
22           // obtain URL of properties file
23           java.net.URL propertyURL = getClass().getResource(
24              "BookTitles.properties" );
25
26           // load properties file
27           Properties databaseProperties = new Properties();
28           databaseProperties.load( new FileInputStream(
29              propertyURL.getPath() ) );
30
31           // load JDBC driver
32           Class.forName( databaseProperties.getProperty(
33              "jdbcDriver" ) );
34
35           // establish database connection
36           connection = DriverManager.getConnection(
37              databaseProperties.getProperty( "databaseURI" ) );
38        }
39
```

Fig. 11.3 BookTitlesImpl handles the logic for the Book Titles Web service. (Part 1 of 3.)

```
40          // handle exception if database driver does not exist
41          catch ( ClassNotFoundException classNotFoundException ) {
42             classNotFoundException.printStackTrace();
43          }
44
45          // handle exception in making Connection
46          catch ( SQLException sqlException ) {
47             sqlException.printStackTrace();
48          }
49
50          // handle exception in loading properties file
51          catch ( IOException ioException ) {
52             ioException.printStackTrace();
53          }
54
55       } // end constructor
56
57       // service to obtain titles of books listed in database
58       public String[] getBookTitles()
59       {
60          // obtain book titles from database and return title list
61          try {
62             String[] bookTitles = null;
63
64             // SQL query to database
65             Statement statement = connection.createStatement(
66                ResultSet.TYPE_SCROLL_INSENSITIVE,
67                ResultSet.CONCUR_READ_ONLY );
68
69             // use SQL query to obtain book titles from database
70             ResultSet resultSet =
71                statement.executeQuery( "SELECT title FROM titles" );
72
73             // use ResultSet to create book-title list
74             if ( resultSet != null ) {
75
76                // instantiate book-title list according to number
77                // of titles stored in ResultSet
78                List list = new ArrayList();
79
80                // store each ResultSet item in book-title list
81                for ( int i = 0; resultSet.next(); i++ )
82                   list.add( resultSet.getObject( "title" ) );
83                bookTitles =
84                   ( String[] ) list.toArray( new String[ 0 ] );
85             }
86
87             statement.close();
88
89             return bookTitles;
90          }
91
```

Fig. 11.3 **BookTitlesImpl** handles the logic for the Book Titles Web service.
(Part 2 of 3.)

```
92          // handle exception in executing Statement
93          catch ( Exception sqlException ) {
94             sqlException.printStackTrace();          ⟵ statement. close();
95             return null;
96          }
97
98       } // end method getBookTitles
99
100      // terminate connection to database
101      protected void finalize()
102      {
103         // close database connection
104         try {
105            connection.close();
106         }
107
108         // handle if connection cannot be closed
109         catch ( SQLException sqlException ) {
110            sqlException.printStackTrace();
111         }
112
113      } // end method finalize
114
115 } // end class BookTitlesImpl
```

Fig. 11.3 **BookTitlesImpl** handles the logic for the Book Titles Web service.
(Part 3 of 3.)

```
1   # Fig. 11.4: BookTitles.properties
2   # Properties file for the Book Titles Web service.
3
4   # property for database URI
5   databaseURI=jdbc:cloudscape:rmi:books
6
7   # property for database JDBC driver
8   jdbcDriver=COM.cloudscape.core.RmiJdbcDriver
```

Fig. 11.4 Properties file used by class **BookTitlesImpl**.

```
1   // Fig. 11.5: BookTitlesServlet.java.
2   // Class BookTitlesServlet exposes the Book Titles Web service.
3   package com.deitel.jws1.jaxm.servlet;
4
5   // Java core packages
6   import java.sql.*;
7
8   // Java extension packages
9   import javax.servlet.*;
10  import javax.xml.messaging.*;
11  import javax.xml.soap.*;
```

Fig. 11.5 **BookTitlesServlet** is a **JAXMServlet** that, when deployed in
Tomcat, exposes the Book Titles Web service. (Part 1 of 3.)

```
12
13    // Deitel packages
14    import com.deitel.jws1.services.BookTitlesImpl;
15
16    public class BookTitlesServlet extends JAXMServlet
17       implements ReqRespListener {
18
19       // factory used to create SOAPMessages
20       private MessageFactory messageFactory;
21
22       // reference to object that provides Web service
23       private BookTitlesImpl service;
24
25       // initialize BookTitlesServlet
26       public void init( ServletConfig config )
27          throws ServletException
28       {
29          super.init( config );
30
31          // instantiate Web-service object and obtain MessageFactory
32          try {
33             service = new BookTitlesImpl();
34             messageFactory = MessageFactory.newInstance();
35          }
36
37          // handle exception in creating MessageFactory
38          catch ( SOAPException soapException ) {
39             soapException.printStackTrace();
40          }
41
42       } // end method init
43
44       // container invokes this method upon receiving SOAP message
45       public SOAPMessage onMessage( SOAPMessage soapMessage )
46       {
47          // invoke Web service and return results as SOAP message
48          try {
49             String bookTitles[] = null;
50
51             // invoke Book Titles Web service to obtain titles
52             if ( service != null )
53                bookTitles = service.getBookTitles();
54
55             // store results as SOAP message and return to client
56             if ( bookTitles != null ) {
57
58                // create empty SOAP message
59                SOAPMessage message = messageFactory.createMessage();
60
61                // obtain references to envelope and body of message
62                SOAPPart soapPart = message.getSOAPPart();
63                SOAPEnvelope soapEnvelope = soapPart.getEnvelope();
```

Fig. 11.5   BookTitlesServlet is a **JAXMServlet** that, when deployed in Tomcat, exposes the Book Titles Web service. (Part 2 of 3.)

```
64              SOAPBody soapBody = soapEnvelope.getBody();
65
66              // create titles element to store book titles
67              SOAPBodyElement titlesElement =
68                  soapBody.addBodyElement(
69                      soapEnvelope.createName( "titles" ) );
70
71              // store number of book titles as attribute
72              titlesElement.addAttribute(
73                  soapEnvelope.createName( "bookCount" ),
74                      Integer.toString( bookTitles.length ) );
75
76              // store each book title in title element
77              for ( int i = 0; i < bookTitles.length; i++ )
78                  titlesElement.addChildElement(
79                      soapEnvelope.createName(
80                          "title" ) ).addTextNode( bookTitles[ i ] );
81
82              return message;
83          }
84          else
85              return null;   ← crash system suggest "titles bookcount = φ"
86      }
87
88      // handle exception if unable to create SOAP message
89      catch ( SOAPException soapException ) {
90          return null;
91      }
92
93   } // end method onMessage
94
95 } // end class BookTitlesServlet
```

Fig. 11.5 `BookTitlesServlet` is a `JAXMServlet` that, when deployed in Tomcat, exposes the Book Titles Web service. (Part 3 of 3.)

A **JAXMServlet** can implement two types of messaging architectures: *request-response* and *one-way*. The request-response messaging architecture requires the **JAXM-Servlet** to send some response to the client that sent the request. The client cannot perform other operations while waiting for a response. This form of communication is called *synchronous messaging*. The one-way messaging architecture does not require the **JAXMServlet** to send a response message. This form of communication is called *asynchronous messaging*. JAXM provides interfaces ***ReqRespListener*** and ***OnewayListener*** for **JAXM-Servlet**s to implement request-response and one-way messaging, respectively. **BookTitlesServlet** implements interface **ReqRespListener** (line 17) and assumes the behavior of a request-response listener. We build a **JAXMServlet** that implements interface **OnewayListener** in Section 11.5.

Interface **ReqRespListener** declares method **onMessage**, which class **Book-TitlesServlet** implements in lines 45–93. A **ReqRespListener** invokes this method whenever it receives a SOAP request via a *post* request. In our implementation, method **onMessage** invokes method **getBookTitles** of the **BookTitlesImpl** object (line 53), stores the resulting book titles in a SOAP response (lines 59–80) and returns the message to the client (line 82).

Method **onMessage** receives as an argument a *SOAPMessage* object that represents the incoming SOAP request. Method **onMessage** returns to the client a **SOAPMessage** object that represents the SOAP response. SAAJ provides class **SOAPMessage** as the base class for all classes that represent SOAP messages. As we discussed in Chapter 6, SOAP-based Web Services Platforms, a SOAP message contains a SOAP part and optional SOAP attachments. The SOAP part contains a SOAP envelope, which contains a header and a body. The header specifies information about the SOAP message, and the body contains the message's data. After retrieving the list of book titles (line 53), **BookTitlesServlet** creates an empty SOAP message (line 59) in which to store the book-titles information. This message serves as the SOAP response message that **BookTitlesServlet** returns to the client. JAXM allows the creation of **SOAPMessage** objects via **MessageFactory** method **createMessage**. Invoking method **createMessage** returns a **SOAPMessage** object that contains a header (with content specified by the messaging profile) and an empty body. Line 62 obtains a reference to the message's **SOAPPart** by invoking **SOAPMessage** method **getSOAPPart**. Line 63 obtains the **SOAPEnvelope** from the **SOAPPart** by invoking **SOAPPart** method **getEnvelope**. Line 64 obtains the **SOAPBody** from the **SOAPEnvelope** by invoking **SOAPEnvelope** method **getBody**. We use the **SOAPBody** object to populate the message's SOAP body with the book titles. Class **SOAPEnvelope** also provides **getHeader** to return the message's **SOAPHeader**. However, because the **MessageFactory**'s method **createMessage** populates the SOAP header with content specified by the messaging profile, **BookTitlesServlet** does not require a reference to the response message's **SOAPHeader**. The header in the message that **BookTitlesServlet** creates is empty, because **BookTitlesServlet** used the default implementation of **MessageFactory**.

The SOAP response that **BookTitlesServlet** sends contains a **titles** element that stores the book titles. The **titles** element contains attribute **bookCount**, which stores the number of available book titles. The **titles** element also contains several **title** elements, in which the number of title elements is exactly the number specified by attribute **bookCount**. Each **title** element contains text that represents a distinct book title. Figure 11.6 is an example of the SOAP response that **BookTitlesServlet** would return to clients if the database contained three books.

```
1   <soap-env:Envelope
2      xmlns:soap-env="http://schemas.xmlsoap.org/soap/envelope/">
3
4      <soap-env:Header/>
5
6      <soap-env:Body>
7
8         <titles bookCount="3">
9
```

Fig. 11.6   SOAP response message from a **JAXMServlet** that exposes the Book Titles Web service. (Part 1 of 2.)

```
10              <title>
11                  Java How to Program, Fourth Edition
12              </title>
13
14              <title>
15                  XML How to Program, First edition
16              </title>
17
18              <title>
19                  Advanced Java How to Program, First edition
20              </title>
21
22          </titles>
23
24      </soap-env:Body>
25
26  </soap-env:Envelope>
```

Fig. 11.6   SOAP response message from a **JAXMServlet** that exposes the Book Titles Web service. (Part 2 of 2.)

Now, **BookTitlesServlet** populates the SOAP response. Lines 67–69 of Fig. 11.5 create an object of SAAJ class ***SOAPBodyElement***, which represents an element in the body of a SOAP message. **BookTitlesServlet** invokes method **addBodyElement** of class **SOAPBody** to include element **titles** as a child element of element **body**. Method **addBodyElement** takes as an argument an object of SAAJ class ***Name***, which represents an element's name and namespace. Method **createName** of class **SOAPEnvelope** takes as an argument a **String** that represents the name of the element, and returns a **Name**. Lines 67–69 create a **Name** called **titles**, then assign it as the name of the first element to include in the **SOAPBody**. Method **addBodyElement** returns the newly created **SOAPBodyElement**, which line 67 assigns to reference **titlesElement**. Lines 72–74 invoke method **createAttribute** of **titlesElement** to create the **bookCount** attribute and assign to it the number of available book titles. Method **createAttribute** takes two arguments: the **Name** of the attribute and a **String** that represents the attribute's value. Lines 77–80 create the **title** elements as child elements of element **titles**. This is accomplished by invoking method **addChildElement** of **titlesElement**. Each invocation of method **addChildElement** returns a **SOAPElement** object, on which line 80 invokes method **addTextNode** to store the book title in that **title** element. Lastly, line 82 returns the **SOAPMessage** to the client.

JAXM Client

We now discuss the standalone JAXM client, which uses JAXM to invoke the Book Titles Web service. Note that, although we use JAXM to implement both the client and the Web service, the client has no knowledge of the environment on which the Book Titles Web service has been deployed. We divide the standalone client into two classes—**StandaloneClient** (Fig. 11.7) and **BookTitlesProxy** (Fig. 11.9). Class **BookTitlesProxy** implements interface **BookTitles** (Fig. 11.8), which provides method **getBookTitles**, to invoke the Book Titles Web service. **StandaloneClient** provides a GUI and uses a **BookTitlesProxy** object to access the service.

Class **StandaloneClient** (Fig. 11.7) provides the GUI. The **Stand-aloneClient** constructor (lines 19–64) initializes the GUI controls for the client. Lines 24–26 create the **JList** that displays the available book titles after **StandaloneClient** invokes the Book Titles Web service. Lines 29–54 create a **JButton** that, when pressed, uses a **BookTitlesProxy** object (via a **BookTitles** reference) to invoke the Book Titles Web service (lines 40–42), then displays the results in the **JList** (line 45).

Class **BookTitlesProxy** (Fig. 11.9) is responsible for sending the SOAP request to the **BookTitlesServlet**. The **BookTitlesProxy** constructor (lines 22–56) instantiates the objects necessary for sending the request to the **JAXMServlet**. Lines 28–29 instantiate an object of JAXM class *SOAPConnectionFactory*, which **BookTitlesProxy** uses to create a *SOAPConnection*. A **SOAPConnection** establishes a point-to-point connection to a **JAXMServlet**. A JAXM application that uses a **SOAPConnection** object does not use any message provider to send and receive SOAP messages. Essentially, the **SOAPConnection** represents a point-to-point connection that a client can use to send a SOAP message directly to a Web service. Line 32 creates the **MessageFactory** that **BookTitlesProxy** uses to create SOAP requests to **BookTitlesServlet**. Lines 35–45 use **JAXMWebService.properties** (Fig. 11.10) to obtain the Web-service URL (i.e., the **BookTitlesServlet** URL). Line 48 uses this URL to create an object of JAXM class *Endpoint*. A **SOAPConnection** uses an **Endpoint** to specify the URL to which the **SOAPConnection** establishes the connection.

```
1   // Fig. 11.7: StandaloneClient.java
2   // StandaloneClient is a standalone JAXM application that
3   // uses BookTitlesProxy to invoke the Book Titles Web service.
4   package com.deitel.jws1.jaxm.client;
5
6   // Java core packages
7   import java.awt.*;
8   import java.awt.event.*;
9
10  // Java extension packages
11  import javax.swing.*;
12
13  // initialize GUI for StandaloneClient
14  public class StandaloneClient extends JFrame {
15
16      private final static int FRAME_WIDTH = 450;
17      private final static int FRAME_HEIGHT = 300;
18
19      public StandaloneClient( String title )
20      {
21          super( title );
22
23          // JList to display results from Web-service invocation
24          final JList resultsList = new JList();
25          resultsList.setSelectionMode(
26              ListSelectionModel.SINGLE_SELECTION );
```

Fig. 11.7 **StandaloneClient** is a standalone JAXM client that invokes the Book Titles Web service. (Part 1 of 3.)

```
27
28          // JButton invokes remote Web service
29          JButton serviceButton = new JButton( "Invoke Service" );
30          serviceButton.addActionListener(
31             new ActionListener() {
32
33                // invoked when user presses JButton
34                public void actionPerformed( ActionEvent event )
35                {
36                   // invoke Web service and store results in JList
37                   try {
38
39                      // invoke Web service via BookTitlesProxy
40                      BookTitlesProxy service =
41                         new BookTitlesProxy();
42                      String response[] = service.getBookTitles();
43
44                      // store results in JList
45                      resultsList.setListData( response );
46                   }
47
48                   // handle exception in Web-service invocation
49                   catch ( java.io.IOException exception ) {
50                      exception.printStackTrace();
51                   }
52                }
53             }
54          );
55
56          // store JButton on JPanel
57          JPanel userPanel = new JPanel();
58          userPanel.add( serviceButton );
59
60          // add JList and JPanel to GUI
61          getContentPane().add( new JScrollPane( resultsList ) );
62          getContentPane().add( userPanel, BorderLayout.SOUTH );
63
64       } // end constructor
65
66       // return size of StandaloneClient frame
67       public Dimension getPreferredSize()
68       {
69          return new Dimension( FRAME_WIDTH, FRAME_HEIGHT );
70       }
71
72       // instantiate StandaloneClient GUI
73       public static void main( String args[] )
74       {
75          StandaloneClient client =
76             new StandaloneClient( "Book Title Service" );
77          client.setDefaultCloseOperation( EXIT_ON_CLOSE );
78          client.pack();
```

Fig. 11.7   StandaloneClient is a standalone JAXM client that invokes the Book
Titles Web service. (Part 2 of 3.)

```
79          client.setVisible( true );
80      }
81
82  } // end class StandaloneClient
```

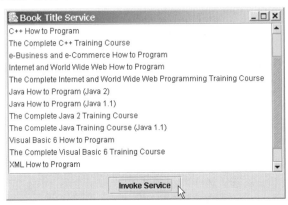

Fig. 11.7 **StandaloneClient** is a standalone JAXM client that invokes the Book
Titles Web service. (Part 3 of 3.)

```
1   // Fig. 11.8: BookTitles.java.
2   // Interface BookTitles enables clients to invoke the Book
3   // Titles Web service.
4   package com.deitel.jws1.services;
5
6   public interface BookTitles {
7
8       // return titles of books available in database
9       public String[] getBookTitles();
10  }
```

Fig. 11.8 **BookTitles** is the interface for the Book Titles Web service.

```
1   // Fig. 11.9: BookTitlesProxy.java.
2   // Class BookTitlesProxy uses JAXM to invoke the Book Titles
3   // Web service, which returns a list of available book titles.
4   package com.deitel.jws1.jaxm.client;
5
6   // Java core packages
7   import java.io.*;
8   import java.util.Iterator;
9   import java.util.Properties;
10
11  // Java extension packages
12  import javax.xml.soap.*;
13  import javax.xml.messaging.*;
14
```

Fig. 11.9 **BookTitlesProxy** uses JAXM to invoke the Book Titles Web service.
(Part 1 of 4.)

SOAP Input
< body >
</body>

```
15   public class BookTitlesProxy {
16
17      private SOAPConnectionFactory soapConnectionFactory;
18      private URLEndpoint urlEndpoint;
19      private MessageFactory messageFactory;
20
21      // initialize BookTitlesProxy
22      public BookTitlesProxy() throws java.io.IOException
23      {
24         // create factory objects
25         try {
26
27            // factory for establishing point-to-point connections
28            soapConnectionFactory =
29               SOAPConnectionFactory.newInstance();
30
31            // factory for building SOAP messages
32            messageFactory = MessageFactory.newInstance();
33
34            // obtain URL of properties file
35            java.net.URL propertyURL = getClass().getResource(
36               "JAXMWebService.properties" );
37
38            // load properties file
39            Properties serviceProperties = new Properties();
40            serviceProperties.load( new FileInputStream(
41               propertyURL.getPath() ) );
42
43            // create endpoint using properties file
44            String endpoint = serviceProperties.getProperty(
45               "bookTitlesServiceURL" );
46
47            // define URL of Web-service provider
48            urlEndpoint = new URLEndpoint( endpoint );
49         }
50
51         // handle exception in initializing factory objects
52         catch ( SOAPException exception ) {
53            throw new IOException( exception.getMessage() );
54         }
55
56      } // end constructor
57
58      // use JAXM to invoke remote Web service
59      public String[] getBookTitles()
60      {
61         // invoke Web service and convert result to String array
62         try {
63            SOAPMessage response = sendSoapRequest();
64
65            // return SOAP response
66            return handleSoapResponse( response );
```

SOAP Input
< body >
<titles count #>
<title> ... </title>
</titles>
</body>

Fig. 11.9 **BookTitlesProxy** uses JAXM to invoke the Book Titles Web service. (Part 2 of 4.)

```
67          }
68
69          // handle exception in sending or receiving SOAP message
70          catch ( SOAPException exception ) {
71             return null;
72          }
73
74       } // end method getBookTitles
75
76       // invoke remote Web service by sending SOAP request
77       private SOAPMessage sendSoapRequest() throws SOAPException
78       {
79          // use SOAPConnectionFactory to create SOAP connection
80          SOAPConnection soapConnection =
81             soapConnectionFactory.createConnection();
82
83          // use MessageFactory to create SOAP message
84          SOAPMessage soapRequest = messageFactory.createMessage();
85
86          // send SOAP message to Web-service provider
87          SOAPMessage soapResponse = soapConnection.call(
88             soapRequest, urlEndpoint );
89
90          soapConnection.close();
91
92          return soapResponse; // return Web-service response
93
94       } // end method sendSoapRequest
95
96       // convert SOAP message returned by Web service to array of
97       // Strings, in which each String represents a book title
98       private String[] handleSoapResponse( SOAPMessage soapResponse )
99          throws SOAPException
100      {
101         // obtain references to response message elements
102         SOAPPart responsePart = soapResponse.getSOAPPart();
103         SOAPEnvelope responseEnvelope = responsePart.getEnvelope();
104         SOAPBody responseBody = responseEnvelope.getBody();
105
106         // obtain Iterator of all child elements of element Body
107         Iterator responseBodyChildElements =
108            responseBody.getChildElements();
109
110         // extract element titles from SOAP message element Body
111         SOAPBodyElement titlesElement =
112            ( SOAPBodyElement ) responseBodyChildElements.next();
113
114         // extract number of book titles from element Titles
115         int bookCount = Integer.parseInt(
116            titlesElement.getAttributeValue(
117               responseEnvelope.createName( "bookCount" ) ) );
118
```

Fig. 11.9   **BookTitlesProxy** uses JAXM to invoke the Book Titles Web service.
(Part 3 of 4.)

```
119       // create array of Strings that represent book titles
120       String bookTitles[] = new String[ bookCount ];
121
122       // use Iterator to obtain child elements of element titles
123       Iterator titleIterator =
124          titlesElement.getChildElements(
125             responseEnvelope.createName( "title" ));
126
127       // store each book title in bookTitles String array
128       int i = 0;
129       while ( titleIterator.hasNext() ) {
130          SOAPElement titleElement =
131             ( SOAPElement ) titleIterator.next();
132          bookTitles[ i++ ] = titleElement.getValue();
133       }
134
135       return bookTitles;
136
137    } // end method handleSoapResponse
138
139 } // end class BookTitlesProxy
```

(handwritten annotations: "return string", "Need exception handler & data validation")

Fig. 11.9   BookTitlesProxy uses JAXM to invoke the Book Titles Web service. (Part 4 of 4.)

```
1  # Fig. 11.10: JAXMWebService.properties
2  # Properties file for specifying the location of the Book Titles
3  # Web service.
4
5  bookTitlesServiceURL=http://localhost:8080/jws1/BookTitles
```

Fig. 11.10 Properties file used by **BookTitlesProxy**.

Class **BookTitlesProxy** provides method **getBookTitles** (lines 59–74) to invoke the BookTitles Web service. Line 63 calls method **sendSoapRequest** (lines 77–94) to send the SOAP request to the Book Titles Web service. Lines 80–81 invoke method **createConnection** of the **SOAPConnectionFactory** to create a **SOAPConnection**, through which **BookTitlesProxy** transfers messages between **BookTitlesServlet**. Line 84 creates a **SOAPMessage** object by invoking method **createMessage** of the **MessageFactory**. Lines 87–88 invoke method **call** on the **SOAPConnection** object to send this message to the Book Titles Web service. Method **call** receives two arguments: the **SOAPMessage** that represents the SOAP request, and the **Endpoint** that specifies the URL of the Web service. To ensure synchronous communication, method **call** blocks until it receives a **SOAPMessage** response from **BookTitlesServlet**. We discussed earlier that, upon receiving a **SOAPMessage**, a **ReqRespListener** invokes its method **onMessage**. Our implementation of this method returns a **SOAPMessage** that contains the book-titles information. Therefore, line 87 returns the **SOAPMessage** that method **onMessage** of **BookTitlesServlet**, (which implements interface **ReqRespListener**) returns.

Line 66 passes this message to method **handleSoapResponse** (lines 98–137), which extracts the **SOAPMessage** contents to a **String** array. Lines 102–103 obtain references to the message's **SOAPPart**, **SOAPEnvelope** and **SOAPBody**. Lines 107–108 invoke method **getChildElements** of the **SOAPBody** to obtain an **Iterator** of all child elements of the SOAP body. The response that the Book Titles Web service returns has only one child—element **titles** (Fig. 11.6). Lines 111–112 assign the first object in the **Iterator** (the **titles** element) to reference **titlesElement** of type **SOAPBodyElement**. Lines 115–117 invoke **titlesElement**'s method **getAttributeValue** to obtain the value of attribute **bookCount**, which stores the number of available book titles (i.e., the number of **title** elements in the message). Using the **bookCount** attribute's value, line 120 instantiates an array of **String**s to store the book titles. Lines 123–125 invoke **titlesElement** method **getChildElements** to obtain an **Iterator** of all children elements of element **titles**. Each object in the **Iterator** corresponds to a **title** element in the SOAP message.[1] For each object in the **Iterator**, lines 130–131 cast each object from the **Iterator** to a **SOAPElement**. Line 132 invokes **SOAPElement** method **getValue** to retrieve a **String** that contains a book title. Line 132 then stores this title in a unique position in the **String** array. Line 135 returns to method **getBookTitles** the **String** array, which line 66 returns to **StandaloneClient**.

Web-Service Deployment

We deploy JAXM applications in servlet containers, so we first discuss how to deploy a JAXM-based Web service in Tomcat. First, download and install the JWSDP from

java.sun.com/webservices/downloads/webservicespack.html

Make sure to map environment variables **%CATALINA_HOME%** and **%TOMCAT_HOME%** to the directory in which the Tomcat is installed (**%JWSDP_HOME%/bin**). JWSDP also provides concrete installation instructions for JAXM in **%JWSDP_HOME%/docs/jaxm/tomcat.html**. The **Setting up Tomcat 4** section lists steps to ensure that JAXM-based applications run properly when deployed in Tomcat.

Figure 11.11 shows the files and associated directory structure needed to deploy the Book Titles Web service in Tomcat. Because we expose this service as a **JAXMServlet**, the process for deploying the Web service is as identical to that of deploying a servlet. Note that **BookTitlesImpl** uses the **books** database—the script (**books.sql**) that build this database is available on our Web site **www.deitel.com**. Instructions to build this database are in Chapter 1, Introduction.

StandaloneClient execution

Make sure that Tomcat is running before executing **StandaloneClient**. To execute **StandaloneClient**, first run **setJaxmClasspath.bat** to set the classpath to include JAR files for JAXM, SAAJ and JAXP, then type in a command shell:

---

1. Note that attribute **title** is unnecessary—we can determine this value merely by counting the number of elements in the **Iterator**. We use this attribute only to demonstrate how to integrate and extract values from attributes in SOAP messages

BookTitlesServlet Web application directory and file structure

```
booktitles
    WEB-INF
        web.xml
        classes
            com
                deitel
                    jws1
                        jaxm
                            servlet
                                BookTitlesServlet.class
                            services
                                BookTitles.class
                                BookTitlesImpl.class
                                BookTitles.properties
        lib
            cloudclient.jar
            RmiJDBC.jar
```

Fig. 11.11 Web application directory and file structure for deploying the Book Titles Web service.

```
javac -classpath %CLASSPATH% -d .
com/deitel/jws1/jaxm/client/StandaloneClient.java

java -classpath %CLASSPATH%
com.deitel.jws1.jaxm.client.StandaloneClient
```

11.5 JAXM Application with Message Provider

In the previous section, we used JAXM to build a standalone client and to expose a Web service that supported synchronous messaging. We mentioned that a standalone client uses a **SOAPConnection** to transfer messages. **SOAPConnection** method **call** sends a **SOAPMessage** request to the **JAXMServlet**, but blocks until it receives a **SOAPMessage** response. The client resumes activity only upon receiving a SOAP response from the Web service. To circumvent this problem, JAXM applications can use a *message provider*, which sends and receives messages, thus enabling a JAXM application to perform other functions after sending a SOAP request. Rather than enable the JAXM application to send a SOAP request directly to the Web service, we require the JAXM application to send the SOAP request to the message provider, which in turn sends the request directly to the Web service. Upon receiving a SOAP request from the JAXM application, the message provider informs the JAXM application that it will, at some point, send the request to the Web service. Eventually, the Web service sends a SOAP response back to the message provider, which then forwards the response to a separate component (e.g., a **JAXMServlet**) in the JAXM application, which then processes the SOAP response accordingly. This form of communication is an example of asynchronous messaging.

We now create a B2B system that involves two JAXM applications used for placing book orders. One JAXM application belongs to a company that orders books (which we call Book Buyer); the other belongs to a company that sells books (which we call Book Seller). Each JAXM application uses a message provider to send and receive SOAP messages. Figure 11.12 shows the architecture for our program. Suppose a Book Buyer employee wishes to order a book from Book Seller. From an HTML page, the employee selects the ISBN of a book and quantity to order. Clicking the **Submit** button sends the ISBN and quantity as parts of a *get* request to servlet **BookBuyerServlet** (Step 1). The servlet uses SAAJ to build a **SOAPMessage** that contains the ISBN and quantity values, then sends the **SOAPMessage** to the message provider **BuyerProvider** (Step 2). Note that both **Book-BuyerServlet** and **BuyerProvider** are located on the Book Buyer server. The **Buyer-Provider** sends the **SOAPMessage** over the network to another message provider, **SellerProvider** (Step 3), which is located on the Book Seller server. **SellerProvider** forwards the message to **BookOrderServlet** (Step 4)—a **JAXMServlet** that exposes the Book Order Web service. **BookOrderServlet** uses a **BookOrderImpl** object (Step 5) to obtain the total cost from the database and update the book quantity (Steps 6–7). **Book-OrderServlet** stores this value in a **SOAPMessage**, then sends the **SOAPMessage** to **SellerProvider** (Step 8). This provider returns this **SOAPMessage** to **Buyer-Provider** (Step 9), which forwards the **SOAPMessage** to a **ConfirmationServlet** (Step 10)—a **JAXMServlet** that confirms the book order. **ConfirmationServlet** updates the database that contains the company's book stock and inserts an order into the database that contains the company's orders (Step 11). A Book Buyer employee, at any time, can use **ViewOrderServlet** to view the orders (Steps 12–13) made in the transactions between the JAXM applications.

Before we examine the code for our JAXM applications, we must initialize the **Buyer-Provider** and **SellerProvider** message providers that each application uses. As you read the provider-initialization process, remember that neither **BuyerProvider** nor **SellerPro-vider** are actual classes that we will write; rather, they are values (URIs) that will eventually map to the default message provider that the JAXM Reference Implementation supplies. (We explain this process in detail momentarily.) The default message provider is a Web application that Tomcat will deploy automatically when you start Tomcat.

The JAXM Reference Implementation contains a **Provider Administration** tool that allows developers to initialize the default message provider. Accessing this tool requires a user name and password, which **tomcat-users.xml** specifies (located in **%JWSDP_HOME%/conf**). Edit this file to create a user name and password, in the manner shown in Fig. 11.13. For example, lines 9–10 specify that user name **deitel** has password **admin** and assumes the roles **admin**, **manager** and **provider**.

Use the user name and password specified in line 9 of Fig. 11.13 to access the **Provider Administration** tool, which is located at **http://localhost:8081/jaxm-provideradmin/index.jsp**. (Fig. 11.14).

JAXM providers must support SOAP. However, SOAP does not specify any message-addressing scheme that determines how providers are to send and receive SOAP messages. For this reason, JAXM providers often use *message profiles*, which are specifications for how providers should route their messages. The **Provider Administration** tool enables a developer to specify and customize the available profiles. A JAXM client then sends to the provider a SOAP message that adheres to a particular profile. The provider determines the profile to which the message adheres, then acts according to the values set in the **Provider Administration** tool.

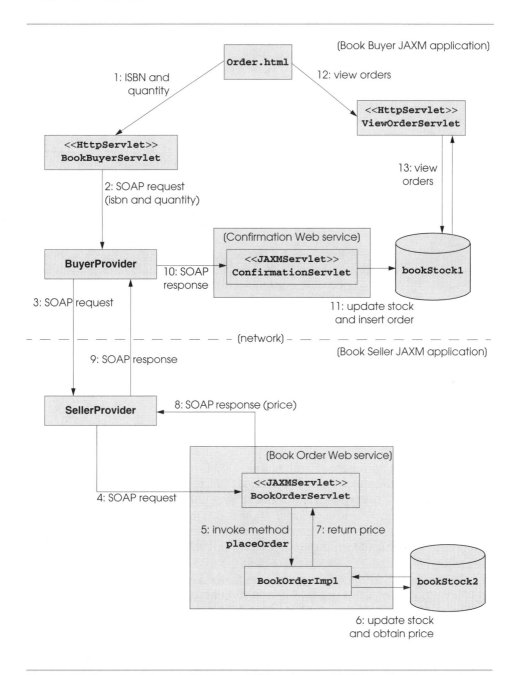

Fig. 11.12 Flowchart for a JAXM-based B2B system: a JAXM application (Book Buyer) uses a message provider to order books from another JAXM application (Book Seller).

```
1    <?xml version='1.0'?>
2
3    <!-- Fig. 11.13: Tomcat-users.xml -->
4    <tomcat-users>
5
6        <role rolename="admin"/>
7        <role rolename="manager"/>
8        <role rolename="provider"/>
9        <user username="deitel" password="admin"
10           roles="admin,manager,provider"/>
11
12   </tomcat-users>
```

Fig. 11.13 Deployment descriptor for JAXM **Provider Administration** tool.

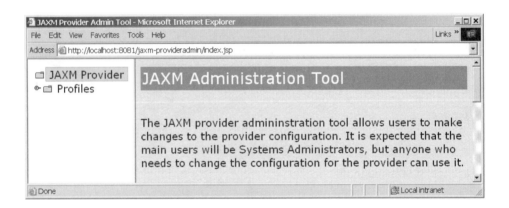

Fig. 11.14 JAXM **Provider Administration** tool. Reproduced with permission by Sun Microsystems, Inc.© Copyright 2002. Sun Microsystems, Inc. All Rights Reserved.

In our example, we use the ebXML profile to send and receive messages. In the **Provider Administration** tool, select **Profiles>ebXML>HTTP** (Fig. 11.15). The browser displays **Provider Properties** and **Endpoint Mapping** fields. **Provider Properties** specifies such information as the number of times that the provider will send a message upon failure (called a *retry*), the delay between retries and the directory in which to log information. **Endpoint Mapping** provides a list of URI-to-URL mappings. The URI is used as a string with which a JAXM client identifies the URL of a particular provider.

We create two URI-to-URL mappings: one for the Book Buyer message provider and one for the Book Seller message provider. In **Available Actions**, select **Create New Endpoint Mapping**. Figure 11.16 shows the URI-to-URL mapping for **BuyerProvider**—URI **urn:com.deitel.jaxm.BuyerProvider** maps to URL **http://localhost:8081/jaxm-provider/receiver/ebxml**. This URL points to the provider included in the JAXM Reference Implementation. Create another URI-to-URL mapping for **SellerProvider**—URI **urn:com.deitel.jaxm.SellerProvider** should map to URL **http://localhost:8081/jaxm-provider/receiver/ebxml**. For simplicity, note that the Book Buyer and Book Seller JAXM applications both use the same message provider. In a real-world application, each company would have access to its own provider, which would reside on a separate system, thus enabling each provider to have a unique URL. However, each JAXM application identifies the providers via the URIs, which have different values. Therefore, the JAXM applications are unaware of the providers' URLs. From the perspectives of the JAXM applications, both are using two separate providers. Figure 11.17 shows the final endpoint mappings for our JAXM applications.[2]

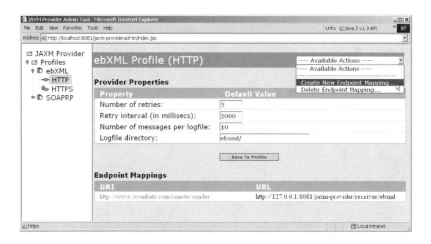

Fig. 11.15 JAXM **Provider Administration** tool **ebXML Profile**. Reproduced with permission by Sun Microsystems, Inc.© Copyright 2002. Sun Microsystems, Inc. All Rights Reserved.

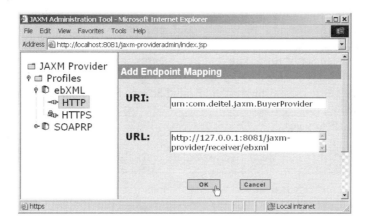

Fig. 11.16 Creating an endpoint mapping in the JAXM **Provider Administration** tool. Reproduced with permission by Sun Microsystems, Inc.© Copyright 2002. Sun Microsystems, Inc. All Rights Reserved.

2. Disregard the `http://www.wombats.com/remote/sender` endpoint mapping—this belongs to an application in the JAXM tutorial, and we do not use it in our applications.

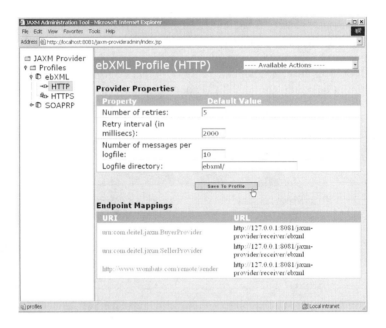

Fig. 11.17 Final endpoint mappings in the JAXM **Provider Administration** tool. Reproduced with permission by Sun Microsystems, Inc.© Copyright 2002. Sun Microsystems, Inc. All Rights Reserved.

Developers must configure each JAXM application to run in a servlet container, such as Tomcat. In addition to configuring the **web.xml** deployment descriptor, developers also must configure another deployment descriptor, called **client.xml**, for each JAXM application. Figure 11.18 is the **client.xml** for the JAXM application that sends the ISBN and quantity values and receives the price. Each **client.xml** document must have element **ClientConfig** (lines 10–29) as its root element. Element **ClientConfig** must contain elements **Endpoint**, **CallbackURL** and **Provider**. Element **Endpoint** (lines 13–15) defines a URI that the JAXM application uses to identify itself. Note that this value must be consistent with the value that the **Provider Administration** tool defines. When a provider receives a message, the provider "forwards" the message to a receiving **JAXMServlet**. **CallbackURL** (lines 19–21) specifies the URL of the **JAXMServlet** that receives these messages. In our example, line 20 specifies that **ConfirmationServlet**, which we discuss toward the end of this chapter, receives the messages sent to this message provider. Element **Provider** (lines 24–27) defines the URI-to-URL mapping of the message provider to identify the location of the provider. Line 26 specifies that the Book Buyer JAXM application uses the message provider included in the JAXM Reference Implementation.

Deployment
Now that we configured the JAXM providers, we explain how to deploy both JAXM applications. Figure 11.19 and Figure 11.19 show the files and associated directory structures needed to deploy Book Buyer and Book Seller via the JWSDP. Book Buyer and Book Seller use the **bookStock1** and **bookStock2** databases, respectively. The

scripts (**bookStock1.sql** and **bookStock2.sql**) that build these databases are available on our Web site **www.deitel.com**. Chapter 1, Introduction, provides instructions on using scripts to build databases.

Code Walkthrough

Now we examine the code for our applications. When the user presses the **Submit** button on the HTML page (Fig. 11.21 output), the Web browser sends the ISBN and quantity values via a *get* request to **BookBuyerServlet** (Fig. 11.21). Class **BookBuyerServlet** is an **HttpServlet** that uses JAXM to send these values as a **SOAPMessage** to its message provider. Lines 29–91 define method **init**, which initializes a connection to **Buyer-Provider**. A JAXM *ProviderConnection* object represents this connection. Lines 36–37 obtain a default *ProviderConnectionFactory* (i.e., the one that the JAXM Reference Implementation supplies) by invoking **static** method **newInstance** of class **ProviderConnectionFactory**. Line 38 calls method **createConnection** of the **ProviderConnectionFactory** to create a **ProviderConnection**, which represents a connection to the message provider. Using this connection, **BookBuyerServlet** sends **SOAPMessage**s to **BuyerProvider**, which in turn can send them to another JAXM provider (in this case, to **SellerProvider**). Each provider requires the developer to specify endpoints in the form of URIs that determine the URLs of the two message providers (i.e., the sender and the receiver). Lines 41–51 obtain the URIs from **endpoints.properties** (Fig. 11.22). Note that the **from** and **to** values (Fig. 11.22, lines 5–6), which **BookBuyerServlet** uses to specify the destination and source providers, match the URI values that we defined via the **Provider Administration** tool. Recall that we also used this tool to customize the ebXML-profile settings. Before **BookBuyerServlet** can create **SOAPMessage**s that use ebXML, **BookBuyerServlet** must determine whether ebXML is available as a profile for **BuyerProvider**. Line 54 calls method **getMetaData** of the **ProviderConnection** to obtain a *ProviderMetaData* object, which contains such information as whether the provider supports ebXML. Line 55 calls method **getSupportedProfiles** of the **Provider-MetaData** object to obtain an array of **String**s, in which each **String** corresponds to a profile that the provider supports. Lines 58–61 determine whether **"ebxml"** is one of these **String**s. If so, then the provider supports ebXML, and lines 65–66 create a **Mes-sageFactory** capable of building **SOAPMessage**s that use ebXML. If not, lines 68–69 throw a **ServletException** to indicate that the provider does not support ebXML.

```
1   <?xml version="1.0" encoding="ISO-8859-1"?>
2
3   <!-- Fig. 11.18: Client.xml -->
4   <!-- Deployment descriptor for Book Buyer JAXM client -->
5
6   <!DOCTYPE ClientConfig
7      PUBLIC "-//Sun Microsystems, Inc.//DTD JAXM Client//EN"
8      "http://java.sun.com/xml/dtds/jaxm_client_1_0.dtd">
9
10  <ClientConfig>
11
```

Fig. 11.18 Deployment descriptor for the JAXM client, which uses **BuyerProvider** to send ISBN and quantity values to the Book Order Web service. (Part 1 of 2.)

```
12      <!-- URI of BuyerProvider Endpoint -->
13      <Endpoint>
14         urn:com.deitel.jaxm.BuyerProvider
15      </Endpoint>
16
17      <!-- URL of JAXMServlet that BuyerProvider calls upon -->
18      <!-- receiving SOAPMessages                          -->
19      <CallbackURL>
20         http://127.0.0.1:8080/bookbuyer/confirmOrder
21      </CallbackURL>
22
23      <!-- BuyerProvider URL -->
24      <Provider>
25         <URI>http://java.sun.com/xml/jaxm/provider</URI>
26         <URL>http://127.0.0.1:8081/jaxm-provider/sender</URL>
27      </Provider>
28
29   </ClientConfig>
```

Fig. 11.18 Deployment descriptor for the JAXM client, which uses **BuyerProvider** to send ISBN and quantity values to the Book Order Web service. (Part 2 of 2.)

Book Buyer Web application directory and file structure

```
bookbuyer/
   WEB-INF/
      web.xml
      classes/
         client.xml
         com/
            deitel/
               jws1/
                  jaxm/
                     bookbuyer/
                        sender/
                           BookBuyerServlet.class
                           ViewOrderServlet.class
                           bookStock.properties
                           Endpoint.properties
                        receiver/
                           ConfirmationServlet.class
                           bookStock.properties
      lib/
         cloudclient.jar
         RmiJDBC.jar
   XSL/
      viewOrder_XHTML.xsl
```

Fig. 11.19 Web application directory and file structure for deploying Book Buyer.

Book Seller Web application directory and file structure

```
bookseller/
   order.html
   WEB-INF/
      web.xml
      classes/
         client.xml
         com/
            deitel/
               jws1/
                  jaxm/
                     bookseller/
                        receiver/
                           BookOrderServlet.class
                           Endpoint.properties
                  services/
                     BookOrder.class
                     BookOrderImpl.class
                     bookStock.properties
      lib/
         cloudclient.jar
         RmiJDBC.jar
```

Fig. 11.20 Web application directory and file structure for deploying Book Seller.

When the user presses the **Submit** button on the HTML page, the Web browser sends the ISBN and quantity values via a *get* request to **BookBuyerServlet**, which in turn invokes method **doGet** (lines 94–164). Lines 101–102 use the **MessageFactory** to create an ***EbXMLMessageImpl***, which represents a SOAP message that uses ebXML. Class **EbXMLMessageImpl** extends class **SOAPMessage** and belongs to package **com.sun.xml.messaging.ebxml**. This package does not belong to either JAXM or SAAJ—rather, this package comprises the *EbXML API* that is included in the JWSDP. (Of course, some of the EbXML classes, such as **EbXMLMessageImpl**, are subclasses of SAAJ classes). Note that method **createMessage** of the **MessageFactory** returns a **SOAPMessage** object. However, because lines 65–66 allow the **MessageFactory** to create SOAP messages that use ebXML, line 102 can cast the returned **SOAPMessage** to an **EbXMLMessageImpl**, without resulting in a **ClassCastException**. Line 105 calls method **setSender** of the **EbXMLMessageImpl** to include the URI of the provider that sends the message. Similarly, line 106 calls method **setReceiver** of the **EbXMLMessageImpl** to include the URI of the provider that will receive the message. Both methods require as arguments ***Party*** objects (of the EbXML API), which act as wrappers for the URI values. We obtain these URI values from **endpoint.properties** (Fig. 11.22); recall that the URI values must match those values defined in the **Provider Administration** tool. Methods **setSender** and **setReceiver** include the URI values in the ebXML message header. When **BookBuyerServlet** sends this message to **BuyerProvider**, **BuyerProvider** uses the header to determine the location to send the message (which in this case, is **SellerProvider**).

```
1   // Fig. 11.21: BookBuyerServlet.java
2   // BookBuyerServlet uses a message provider (BuyerProvider)
3   // to send messages to SellerProvider.
4   package com.deitel.jws1.jaxm.bookbuyer.sender;
5
6   // Java core packages
7   import java.io.*;
8   import java.util.*;
9
10  // Java extension packages
11  import javax.servlet.http.*;
12  import javax.servlet.*;
13  import javax.xml.messaging.*;
14  import javax.xml.soap.*;
15
16  // ebXML packages
17  import com.sun.xml.messaging.jaxm.ebxml.*;
18
19  public class BookBuyerServlet extends HttpServlet {
20
21     private ProviderConnection buyerProvider;
22     private MessageFactory messageFactory;
23
24     // source and destination endpoints for messages
25     private String from, to;
26     private Properties endPointProperties;
27
28     // setup connection to message provider
29     public void init( ServletConfig servletConfig )
30        throws ServletException
31     {
32        super.init( servletConfig );
33
34        // establish connection to provider
35        try {
36           ProviderConnectionFactory providerFactory =
37              ProviderConnectionFactory.newInstance();
38           buyerProvider = providerFactory.createConnection();
39
40           // obtain URL of properties file
41           java.net.URL endPointURL = getClass().getResource(
42              "endpoint.properties" );
43
44           // load properties file
45           endPointProperties = new Properties();
46           endPointProperties.load( new FileInputStream(
47              endPointURL.getPath() ) );
```

Fig. 11.21 **BookBuyerServlet** create a **SOAPMessage** that contains ISBN and quantity values, then sends the message to a JAXM message provider. (Part 1 of 4.)

```
48
49            // obtain source and destination endpoints
50            from = endPointProperties.getProperty( "from" );
51            to = endPointProperties.getProperty( "to" );
52
53            // obtain supported profiles for provider
54            ProviderMetaData metaData = buyerProvider.getMetaData();
55            String[] profiles = metaData.getSupportedProfiles();
56
57            // determine whether ebXML profile is supported
58            boolean isProfileSupported = false;
59            for ( int i = 0; i < profiles.length; i++ )
60               if ( profiles[ i ].equals( "ebxml" ) )
61                  isProfileSupported = true;
62
63            // use ebXML profile, if supported
64            if ( isProfileSupported )
65               messageFactory =
66                  buyerProvider.createMessageFactory( "ebxml" );
67            else
68               throw new ServletException( "Profile ebxml is " +
69                  "not supported." );
70         }
71
72      // handle exception in connecting to provider
73      catch ( JAXMException jaxmException ) {
74         throw new ServletException( jaxmException.getMessage() +
75            "\nUnable to connect to message provider." );
76      }
77
78      // handle exception if unable to locate Endpoint.properties
79      catch ( FileNotFoundException fileNotFoundException ) {
80         throw new ServletException(
81            fileNotFoundException.getMessage() +
82            "\nUnable to locate endpoint.properties." );
83      }
84
85      // handle exception in loading properties file
86      catch ( IOException ioException ) {
87         throw new ServletException( ioException.getMessage() +
88            "\nUnable to load endpoint.properties." );
89      }
90
91   } // end method init
92
93   // invoked when client makes get request
94   public void doGet( HttpServletRequest request,
95      HttpServletResponse response ) throws ServletException
96   {
```

Fig. 11.21 BookBuyerServlet create a **SOAPMessage** that contains ISBN and quantity values, then sends the message to a JAXM message provider. (Part 2 of 4.)

```
97          // create ebXML message for BuyerProvider
98          try {
99
100            // create ebXML message
101            EbXMLMessageImpl message =
102               ( EbXMLMessageImpl ) messageFactory.createMessage();
103
104            // set send and receive provider
105            message.setSender( new Party( from ) );
106            message.setReceiver( new Party( to ) );
107
108            // store ISBN in message attachment
109            AttachmentPart isbnAttachment =
110               message.createAttachmentPart();
111            isbnAttachment.setContent( request.getParameter(
112               "ISBN" ), "text/plain" );
113
114            // store quantity in message attachment
115            AttachmentPart quantityAttachment =
116               message.createAttachmentPart();
117            quantityAttachment.setContent( request.getParameter(
118               "Quantity" ), "text/plain" );
119
120            // add ISBN and Quantity attachments to message
121            message.addAttachmentPart( isbnAttachment );
122            message.addAttachmentPart( quantityAttachment );
123
124            // send message from BuyerProvider to Web service
125            buyerProvider.send( message );
126
127            // display HTML confirmation message to client
128            response.setContentType( "text/html" );
129            PrintWriter out = response.getWriter();
130            String viewOrderURL =
131               endPointProperties.getProperty( "viewOrderURL" );
132            out.println( "<html>" );
133            out.println( "<body>Order placed." );
134            out.println( "Visit <a href=" + viewOrderURL + ">" );
135            out.println( viewOrderURL + "</a>" );
136            out.println( "to view order status.</body>" );
137            out.println( "</html>" );
138         }
139
140         // handle exception in using message provider
141         catch ( JAXMException jaxmException ) {
142            throw new ServletException( jaxmException.getMessage() +
143               "\nError in using message provider." );
144         }
145
```

Fig. 11.21 BookBuyerServlet create a **SOAPMessage** that contains ISBN and quantity values, then sends the message to a JAXM message provider. (Part 3 of 4.)

```
146         // handle exception in creating SOAP messages
147         catch ( SOAPException soapException ) {
148            throw new ServletException( soapException.getMessage() +
149               "\nUnable to create SOAP message." );
150         }
151
152         // handle exception if servlet not initialized
153         catch ( NullPointerException nullException ) {
154            throw new ServletException( nullException.getMessage() +
155               "\nServlet not initialized properly." );
156         }
157
158         // handle exception in writing HTML to client
159         catch ( IOException ioException ) {
160            throw new ServletException( ioException.getMessage() +
161               "\nServlet not initialized properly." );
162         }
163
164      } // end method doGet
165
166   } // end class BookBuyerServlet
```

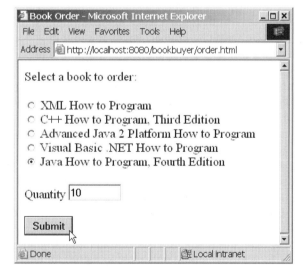

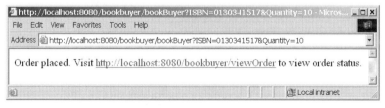

Fig. 11.21 **BookBuyerServlet** create a **SOAPMessage** that contains ISBN and quantity values, then sends the message to a JAXM message provider. (Part 4 of 4.)

```
1   # Fig. 11.22: endpoint.properties
2   # Properties file for Endpoint mappings.
3
4   # URI values for Endpoint mappings
5   from=urn:com.deitel.jaxm.BuyerProvider
6   to=urn:com.deitel.jaxm.SellerProvider
7
8   # URL of servlet to view orders
9   viewOrderURL=http://localhost:8080/bookbuyer/viewOrder
```

Fig. 11.22 Properties file that **BookBuyerServlet** uses to determine the URIs for Endpoints.

Before **BookBuyerServlet** sends the ebXML message, **BookBuyerServlet** must populate the message with the ISBN and quantity values. We can do this via *attachments*, which are additional units of information that exist outside the SOAP envelope but are included in the SOAP-message transfer. In JAXM applications, using attachments to store values is often more efficient than using XML, because JAXM applications can obtain values from attachments without having to parse entire XML documents to locate values. SAAJ provides an **AttachmentPart** to represent a SOAP attachment. Lines 109–112 create an **AttachmentPart** that stores the ISBN value. Similarly, lines 115–118 create an **AttachmentPart** that stores the quantity value. Lines 121–122 attach the **AttachmentPart**s to the ebXML message.

Line 125 sends the ebXML message to the message provider by invoking method **send** of the **ProviderConnection** and passing the **EbXMLMessageImpl** as an argument. Because **BookBuyerServlet** is using a message provider, it does not have to wait for a response from the receiving provider. Such communication is referred to as asynchronous communication. The receiving JAXM application has no obligation to return a message that contains a price. However, our architecture (Fig. 11.12) shows that the receiving JAXM application, at some point, will send this message to the original sending JAXM application. This application then updates a database that stores orders and prices. Lines 128–137 create an HTML page that confirms that **BookBuyerServlet** has placed the order, and provides a link to **ViewOrderServlet** (Fig. 11.28), which allows the user to view the contents of this database. Thus, the only way the user can confirm that the entire transaction occurred is by polling **ViewOrderServlet** repeatedly, and seeing if an additional order has been included in the database. This is one means of confirmation via asynchronous communication—an alternative architecture might send a confirmation notification via email to the client. (We use this approach in Chapter 15, Case Study Part I.)

When **BookBuyerServlet** sends the ebXML message to **BuyerProvider**, **BuyerProvider** examines the message header to determine where to send the message. Recall that line 106 declared that **BuyerProvider** should send the message to the endpoint that maps to URI **urn:com.deitel.jaxm.SellerProvider**. Using the **Provider Administration** tool, we specified that this URI maps to the **SellerProvider**'s URL (**http://localhost:8081/jaxm-provider/receiver/ebxml**), which is the URL for the message provider included in the JAXM Reference Implementation. When **SellerProvider** receives the message, **SellerProvider** must "forward" that message to a **JAXMServlet**. We specify the **JAXMServlet** that receives the message in the **client.xml** deployment descriptor of Fig. 11.23. Each JAXM application requires a unique **client.xml**, so the **client.xml** in Fig. 11.23 differs from the one in Fig. 11.18, which we created for the JAXM application that sends the ISBN and quantity values. Lines 13–15 declare an **Endpoint** element that contains the URI for **SellerProvider**. Note that this value matches the URI value that we established in the **Provider Administration** tool. Lines 19–21 declare a **CallbackURL** element, which contains the URL of the **JAXMServlet** (**BookOrderServlet**) that will receive the SOAP message from **SellerProvider**. Lines 24–27 define the URI-to-URL mapping of the message provider.

According to the deployment descriptor of Fig. 11.23, **SellerProvider** sends a SOAP message to **BookOrderServlet** (Fig. 11.24) upon receiving a message. Method **init** (lines 32–92) initializes the servlet by establishing a connection to **SellerProvider** (lines 39–41), obtaining the endpoint URI for **SellerProvider** (lines 44–52) from **endpoint.properties** (Fig. 11.25), and ensure that **SellerProvider** supports the ebXML profile (lines 55–70).

```
1    <?xml version="1.0" encoding="ISO-8859-1"?>
2
3    <!-- Fig. 11.23: Client.xml -->
4    <!-- Deployment descriptor for Book Seller JAXM client -->
5
6    <!DOCTYPE ClientConfig
7        PUBLIC "-//Sun Microsystems, Inc.//DTD JAXM Client//EN"
8        "http://java.sun.com/xml/dtds/jaxm_client_1_0.dtd">
9
10   <ClientConfig>
11
12       <!-- URI of SellerProvider Endpoint -->
13       <Endpoint>
14           urn:com.deitel.jaxm.SellerProvider
15       </Endpoint>
16
17       <!-- URL of JAXMServlet that SellerProvider calls upon -->
18       <!-- receiving SOAPMessages                           -->
19       <CallbackURL>
20           http://127.0.0.1:8080/bookseller/orderBook
21       </CallbackURL>
22
23       <!-- SellerProvider URL -->
24       <Provider>
25           <URI>http://java.sun.com/xml/jaxm/provider</URI>
26           <URL>http://127.0.0.1:8081/jaxm-provider/sender</URL>
27       </Provider>
28
29   </ClientConfig>
```

Fig. 11.23 Deployment descriptor for the Book Seller JAXM application, which uses **SellerProvider** to receive SOAP message that contain ISBN and quantity values.

In Section 11.4, we discussed that JAXM provides interfaces **ReqRespListener** and **OnewayListener** for **JAXMServlet**s to implement request-response and one-way messaging, respectively. We built standalone JAXM application **BookTitlesServlet** (Fig. 11.5), which implemented interface **ReqRespListener**, to assume the behavior of a request-response listener. We discussed how interface **ReqRespListener** provides synchronous communication via method **onMessage**, which is invoked whenever a client sends a SOAP request message via a *post* request to a **JAXMServlet**. This method promotes synchronous messaging, because a client must wait for the **JAXMServlet** to send a **SOAPMessage** object to the client. By contrast, interface **OnewayListener** promotes asynchronous messaging. Like interface **ReqRespListener**, interface **OnewayListener** also contains method **onMessage**, which the **JAXMServlet** invokes upon receiving a message from the provider. However, the return type for **OnewayListener**'s **onMessage** method is **void**, so the method implementation cannot return a **SOAPMessage**. Because the JAXM client delegates the method invocation to a message provider, the JAXM client is not required to wait for a response. This is efficient for such scenarios in which a confirmation message is dependent on a "human factor." For example, a shipping-order confirmation is dependent on human workers transporting merchandise from a warehouse to a vehicle.

```
1   // Fig. 11.24: BookOrderServlet.java
2   // Class BookOrderServlet receives an ebXML message that
3   // contains a book's ISBN and the quantity of that book to order.
4   package com.deitel.jws1.jaxm.bookseller.receiver;
5
6   // Java core packages
7   import java.io.*;
8   import java.util.*;
9
10  // Java extension packages
11  import javax.servlet.http.*;
12  import javax.servlet.*;
13  import javax.xml.messaging.*;
14  import javax.xml.soap.*;
15
16  // ebXML packages
17  import com.sun.xml.messaging.jaxm.ebxml.*;
18
19  // Deitel packages
20  import com.deitel.jws1.services.*;
21
22  public class BookOrderServlet extends JAXMServlet
23     implements OnewayListener {
24
25     private ProviderConnection sellerProvider;
26     private MessageFactory messageFactory;
27
28     // source and destination endpoints for messages
29     private String from;
30
```

Fig. 11.24 **BookOrderServlet** exposes the Book Order Web service. (Part 1 of 4.)

```
31      // setup connection to message provider
32      public void init( ServletConfig servletConfig )
33         throws ServletException
34      {
35         super.init( servletConfig );
36
37         // establish connection to provider
38         try {
39            ProviderConnectionFactory providerFactory =
40               ProviderConnectionFactory.newInstance();
41            sellerProvider = providerFactory.createConnection();
42
43             // obtain URL of properties file
44            java.net.URL endpointURL = getClass().getResource(
45               "Endpoint.properties" );
46
47            // load properties file
48            Properties endpointProperties = new Properties();
49            endpointProperties.load( new FileInputStream(
50               endpointURL.getPath() ) );
51
52            from = endpointProperties.getProperty( "from" );
53
54            // obtain supported profiles for provider
55            ProviderMetaData metaData = sellerProvider.getMetaData();
56            String[] profiles = metaData.getSupportedProfiles();
57
58            // determine whether ebXML profile is supported
59            boolean isProfileSupported = false;
60            for ( int i = 0; i < profiles.length; i++ )
61               if ( profiles[ i ].equals( "ebxml" ) )
62                  isProfileSupported = true;
63
64            // use ebXML profile, if supported
65            if ( isProfileSupported )
66               messageFactory =
67                  sellerProvider.createMessageFactory( "ebxml" );
68            else
69               throw new ServletException( "Profile ebxml is " +
70                  "not supported." );
71         }
72
73         // handle exception in connecting to provider
74         catch ( JAXMException jaxmException ) {
75            throw new ServletException( jaxmException.getMessage() +
76               "\nUnable to connect to message provider." );
77         }
78
79         // handle exception if unable to locate Endpoint.properties
80         catch ( FileNotFoundException fileNotFoundException ) {
81            throw new ServletException(
82               fileNotFoundException.getMessage() +
83               "\nUnable to locate endpoint.properties." );
```

Fig. 11.24 BookOrderServlet exposes the Book Order Web service. (Part 2 of 4.)

```
84            }
85
86        // handle exception in loading properties file
87        catch ( IOException ioException ) {
88            throw new ServletException( ioException.getMessage() +
89                "\nUnable to load endpoint.properties." );
90        }
91
92    } // end method init
93
94    // invoked when SellerProvider sends message
95    public void onMessage( SOAPMessage requestMessage )
96    {
97        // call Book Order Web service and return result to sender
98        try {
99
100           // create response message from request message
101           EbXMLMessageImpl responseMessage =
102               new EbXMLMessageImpl( requestMessage );
103
104           // specify that the message should be returned to sender
105           String to = responseMessage.getFrom().toString();
106
107           // specify sender and receiver for message
108           responseMessage.setReceiver( new Party( to ) );
109           responseMessage.setSender( new Party( from ) );
110
111           // obtain ISBN and Quantity attachments from message
112           Iterator attachments = responseMessage.getAttachments();
113           AttachmentPart isbnAttachment =
114               ( AttachmentPart ) attachments.next();
115           AttachmentPart quantityAttachment =
116               ( AttachmentPart ) attachments.next();
117
118           // obtain ISBN and Quantity from attachments
119           String isbn = ( String ) isbnAttachment.getContent();
120           Integer quantity = new Integer(
121               ( String ) quantityAttachment.getContent() );
122
123           // invoke Book Order Web service to place order
124           BookOrder service = new BookOrderImpl();
125           Double price = new Double(
126               service.orderBook( isbn, quantity.intValue() ) );
127
128           // store price in message attachment
129           AttachmentPart priceAttachment =
130               responseMessage.createAttachmentPart();
131           priceAttachment.setContent( price.toString(),
132               "text/plain" );
133
134           // add price attachments to message
135           responseMessage.addAttachmentPart( priceAttachment );
136
```

Fig. 11.24 BookOrderServlet exposes the Book Order Web service. (Part 3 of 4.)

```
137            // send message back to sending provider
138            sellerProvider.send( responseMessage );
139         }
140
141         // handle exception in invoking Book Order Web service
142         catch ( SOAPException soapException ) {
143            soapException.printStackTrace();
144         }
145
146         // handle exception in EbXMLMessageImpl creation
147         catch ( IOException ioException ) {
148            ioException.printStackTrace();
149         }
150
151     } // end method onMessage
152
153  } // end class BookOrderServlet
```

Fig. 11.24 `BookOrderServlet` exposes the Book Order Web service. (Part 4 of 4.)

```
1   # Fig. 11.25: endpoint.properties
2   # Properties file for message-provider Endpoint mapping.
3
4   # URI values for Endpoint mapping to message provider
5   from=urn:com.deitel.jaxm.SellerProvider
```

Fig. 11.25 Properties file that `BookOrderServlet` uses to determine the URI Endpoint for its provider.

Class **BookOrderServlet** implements interface **OnewayListener** (line 23) to enable asynchronous communication. **BookOrderServlet** invokes method **onMessage** (lines 95–151) upon receiving a SOAP message. Using the ebXML profile, method **onMessage** invokes the Book Order Web service to obtain a price, attaches the price to an ebXML message, then returns the message to **BuyerProvider**. Lines 101–102 create an **EbXMLMessageImpl** from the incoming **SOAPMessage**. Lines 105 retrieves from the ebXML-message header the URI of the provider that sent the message. Line 108 uses this information to set the **to** field in the ebXML response message's header. Note that this approach relies exclusively on the message sender including the correct provider URI in the **from** field. However, if a malicious client sends an erroneous value, **SellerProvider** is unable to map the URI to a valid URL and does not send the response message.

Line 112 invokes method **getAttachments** of the **EbXMLMessageImpl** to obtain an **Iterator** that contains all **AttachmentPart**s associated with the incoming message. Using the **Iterator**, lines 113–116 obtain the two **AttachmentPart**s that contain the ISBN and quantity values. Lines 119–121 extract these values from the **AttachmentPart**s by invoking method **getContent** from each **AttachmentPart**. Lines 124–126 invoke method **orderBook** on a **BookOrderImpl** object (Fig. 11.26), which handles the logic for the Book Order Web service. Lines 18–56 define the class constructor that establishes a connection to the **bookStock2** database, which holds information on price and quantity for books. Method **orderBook** (lines 59–109) takes as arguments a **String** that represents a book's ISBN and an **int** that specifies the

quantity of books to order. Using these arguments and the connection to the **bookStock2**
database, method **orderBook** calculates the cumulative price for the requested books.
Method **orderBook** returns either a **double** that represents this price or a **-1** value if
the books are unavailable. **BookOrderServlet** (Fig. 11.24) then creates an **AttachmentPart** to store the price and append the **AttachmentPart** to the **EbXMLMessageImpl** (lines 129–135). Line 138 sends the ebXML message to **SellerProvider**,
which in turn sends the message back to **BuyerProvider**.

```
1    // Fig. 11.26: BookOrderImpl.java
2    // Class BookOrderImpl handles the logic for the Book Order Web
3    // service, which determines the price of a book, based on that
4    // book's ISBN and the quantity of books to order.
5    package com.deitel.jws1.services;
6
7    // Java core packages
8    import java.io.*;
9    import java.util.*;
10   import java.sql.*;
11
12   public class BookOrderImpl
13      implements com.deitel.jws1.services.BookOrder {
14
15      private Connection connection; // connection to database
16
17      // constructor to initialize database connection
18      public BookOrderImpl()
19      {
20         // load JDBC driver and establish connection to database
21         try {
22
23            // obtain URL of properties file
24            java.net.URL propertyURL = getClass().getResource(
25               "bookStock.properties" );
26
27            // load properties file
28            Properties databaseProperties = new Properties();
29            databaseProperties.load( new FileInputStream(
30               propertyURL.getPath() ) );
31
32            // load JDBC driver
33            Class.forName( databaseProperties.getProperty(
34               "jdbcDriver" ) );
35
36            // establish database connection
37            connection = DriverManager.getConnection(
38               databaseProperties.getProperty( "databaseURI" ) );
39         }
40
```

Fig. 11.26 BookOrderImpl handles the logic for the Book Order Web service,
which uses ISBN and quantity values to obtain a price from a database.
(Part 1 of 3.)

```
41      // handle exception if database driver does not exist
42      catch ( ClassNotFoundException classNotFoundException ) {
43         classNotFoundException.printStackTrace();
44      }
45
46      // handle exception in making Connection
47      catch ( SQLException sqlException ) {
48         sqlException.printStackTrace();
49      }
50
51      // handle exception in loading properties file
52      catch ( IOException ioException ) {
53         ioException.printStackTrace();
54      }
55
56   } // end BookOrderImpl constructor
57
58   // obtain price of book based on book's ISBN and quantity
59   public double orderBook( String isbn, int quantity )
60   {
61      // detemine book availability, then determine price
62      try {
63
64         // SQL query to database
65         Statement statement = connection.createStatement(
66            ResultSet.TYPE_SCROLL_INSENSITIVE,
67            ResultSet.CONCUR_READ_ONLY );
68
69         // make query to determine number of available books
70         ResultSet resultSet = statement.executeQuery( "SELECT" +
71            " quantity, price FROM books WHERE isbn = " + isbn );
72
73         int availableBookCount = 0;
74
75         // obtain quantity associated with isbn from database
76         if ( resultSet != null ) {
77            resultSet.next();
78            availableBookCount = resultSet.getInt( "quantity" );
79         }
80
81         // determine whether quantity exceeds number of
82         // available books in database
83         if ( availableBookCount < quantity ) {
84            statement.close();
85            return -1;
86         }
87         else {
88
89            // determine price for one book
90            double pricePerBook = resultSet.getDouble( "price" );
91            int newQuantity = availableBookCount - quantity;
```

Fig. 11.26 BookOrderImpl handles the logic for the Book Order Web service, which uses ISBN and quantity values to obtain a price from a database. (Part 2 of 3.)

```
92
93              // update database to decrement number of books
94              statement.execute( "UPDATE books " +
95                 "SET quantity = " + newQuantity +
96                 " WHERE isbn = " + isbn );
97              statement.close();
98
99              return pricePerBook * quantity;
100          }
101       }
102
103       // handle exception in executing Statement
104       catch ( SQLException sqlException ) {
105          sqlException.printStackTrace();
106          return -1;
107       }
108
109    } // end method orderBook
110
111 } // end class BookOrderImpl
```

Fig. 11.26 `BookOrderImpl` handles the logic for the Book Order Web service, which uses ISBN and quantity values to obtain a price from a database. (Part 3 of 3.)

According to the **client.xml** deployment descriptor of Fig. 11.18, **BuyerProvider** sends a SOAP message to **ConfirmationServlet** (Fig. 11.27) upon receiving that message. Method **init** (lines 23–77) initializes the servlet by establishing a connection to **BuyerProvider** to receive messages (lines 30–32) and opening a connection to database **bookStock1** (lines 35–49).

```
1  // Fig. 11.27: ConfirmationServlet.java
2  // JAXMServlet that receives messages from BuyerProvider.
3  package com.deitel.jws1.jaxm.bookbuyer.receiver;
4
5  // Java core packages
6  import java.sql.*;
7  import java.io.*;
8  import java.util.*;
9
10 // Java extension packages
11 import javax.xml.messaging.*;
12 import javax.xml.soap.*;
13 import javax.servlet.*;
14 import javax.servlet.http.*;
15
16 public class ConfirmationServlet extends JAXMServlet
17    implements OnewayListener {
18
```

Fig. 11.27 `ConfirmationServlet` receives SOAP messages from `BuyerProvider` and confirms that an order has been placed. (Part 1 of 4.)

```
19      private ProviderConnection buyerProvider;
20      private Connection connection; // connection to database
21
22      // setup connection to message provider
23      public void init( ServletConfig servletConfig )
24         throws ServletException
25      {
26         super.init( servletConfig );
27
28         // establish connection to provider
29         try {
30            ProviderConnectionFactory providerFactory =
31               ProviderConnectionFactory.newInstance();
32            buyerProvider = providerFactory.createConnection();
33
34            // obtain URL of properties file
35            java.net.URL propertyURL = getClass().getResource(
36               "bookStock.properties" );
37
38            // load properties file
39            Properties databaseProperties = new Properties();
40            databaseProperties.load( new FileInputStream(
41               propertyURL.getPath() ) );
42
43            // load JDBC driver
44            Class.forName( databaseProperties.getProperty(
45               "jdbcDriver" ) );
46
47            // establish database connection
48            connection = DriverManager.getConnection(
49               databaseProperties.getProperty( "databaseURI" ) );
50         }
51
52         // handle exception in provider connection
53         catch ( JAXMException jaxmException ) {
54            throw new ServletException( jaxmException.getMessage() +
55               "\nUnable to connect to provider." );
56         }
57
58         // handle exception if database driver does not exist
59         catch ( ClassNotFoundException classNotFoundException ) {
60            throw new ServletException(
61               classNotFoundException.getMessage() +
62               "\nUnable to load database driver." );
63         }
64
65         // handle exception in making Connection
66         catch ( SQLException sqlException ) {
67            throw new ServletException( sqlException.getMessage() +
68               "\nUnable to make database connection." );
69         }
```

Fig. 11.27 ConfirmationServlet receives SOAP messages from **BuyerProvider** and confirms that an order has been placed. (Part 2 of 4.)

```
70
71          // handle exception in loading properties file
72          catch ( IOException ioException ) {
73             throw new ServletException( ioException.getMessage() +
74                "\nUnable to load bookStock.properties." );
75          }
76
77       } // end method init
78
79       // invoked upon receiving message
80       public void onMessage( SOAPMessage message )
81       {
82          // determine whether order was successful
83          try {
84
85             // obtain ISBN, Quantity and Price attachments
86             Iterator attachments = message.getAttachments();
87             AttachmentPart isbnAttachment =
88                ( AttachmentPart ) attachments.next();
89             AttachmentPart quantityAttachment =
90                ( AttachmentPart ) attachments.next();
91             AttachmentPart priceAttachment =
92                ( AttachmentPart ) attachments.next();
93
94             // obtain ISBN, Quantity and Price from attachments
95             String isbn = ( String ) isbnAttachment.getContent();
96             Integer quantity = new Integer(
97                ( String ) quantityAttachment.getContent() );
98             Double price = new Double (
99                ( String ) priceAttachment.getContent() );
100
101            // ensure book availability
102            if ( price.doubleValue() < 0 ) {
103               System.err.println( isbn + " is unavailable" );
104               return;
105            }
106
107            // SQL query to database
108            Statement statement = connection.createStatement(
109               ResultSet.TYPE_SCROLL_INSENSITIVE,
110               ResultSet.CONCUR_READ_ONLY );
111
112            // make query to determine number of available books
113            ResultSet resultSet = statement.executeQuery( "SELECT" +
114               " quantity FROM books WHERE isbn = " + isbn );
115
116            // update BookStock1 databases content
117            if ( resultSet != null ) {
118               resultSet.next();
119               int newQuantity = resultSet.getInt( "quantity" ) +
120                  quantity.intValue();
```

Fig. 11.27 ConfirmationServlet receives SOAP messages from BuyerProvider and confirms that an order has been placed. (Part 3 of 4.)

```
121
122              // update quantity of books in database
123              statement.execute( "UPDATE books SET quantity = " +
124                 newQuantity + " WHERE isbn = " + isbn );
125
126              // place order (ibsn, quantity and price) in database
127              statement.execute( "INSERT INTO orders " +
128                 "( isbn, quantity, price ) VALUES ( '" + isbn +
129                 "' , '" + quantity + "' , '" + price.toString() +
130                 "' )" );
131           }
132
133        statement.close();
134        }
135
136        // handle exception in accessing database
137        catch ( SQLException sqlException ) {
138           sqlException.printStackTrace();
139        }
140
141        // handle exception in parsing SOAP message
142        catch ( JAXMException jaxmException ) {
143           jaxmException.printStackTrace();
144        }
145
146        // handle exception in obtaining message attachments
147        catch ( SOAPException soapException ) {
148           soapException.printStackTrace();
149        }
150
151     } // end method onMessage
152
153 } // end class ConfirmationServlet
```

Fig. 11.27 **ConfirmationServlet** receives SOAP messages from
BuyerProvider and confirms that an order has been placed.
(Part 4 of 4.)

Class **ConfirmationServlet** implements interface **OnewayListener** (line
17) to enable asynchronous communication. **BookOrderServlet** invokes method
onMessage (lines 80–151) upon receiving a SOAP message. Line 86 obtains an **Iterator** that contains the **AttachmentPart**s associated with the incoming message. Lines
87–92 obtain the three **AttachmentPart**s that contain the ISBN, quantity and price
values, and lines 95–99 extract these values from the **AttachmentPart**s. If the books
were ordered successfully (i.e., the price value does not equal **-1**), lines 123–124 update
the quantity of books in the **bookStock1** database. In addition, lines 127–130 insert an
order entry in the **bookStock1** database.

At this point, the transaction between **BuyerProvider** and **SellerProvider** is complete. The Book Buyer employee should use the link to the **ViewOrderServlet** on the
HTML page that **BookBuyerServlet** generated to view the status of the orders.
ViewOrderServlet (Fig. 11.28) is an **HttpServlet** that displays as XHTML the
contents of the **bookStock1** database. Method **init** (lines 32–79) initializes the servlet

by establishing a connection to the **bookStock1** database (41–55) and creating factories for building XML documents and applying XSLT (lines 58–61). **ViewOrderServlet** stores the contents of the database as an XML document, then applies a style sheet to render the output as XHTML.

```java
1   // Fig. 11.28: ViewOrderServlet.java
2   // ViewOrderServlet enables a user to view the status of orders
3   // created by the JAXM applications.
4   package com.deitel.jws1.jaxm.bookbuyer.sender;
5
6   // Java core packages
7   import java.io.*;
8   import java.util.*;
9   import java.sql.*;
10  import java.text.NumberFormat;
11
12  // Java extension packages
13  import javax.servlet.http.*;
14  import javax.servlet.*;
15  import javax.xml.parsers.*;
16  import javax.xml.transform.*;
17  import javax.xml.transform.dom.*;
18  import javax.xml.transform.stream.*;
19
20  // W3C XML packages
21  import org.w3c.dom.*;
22
23  public class ViewOrderServlet extends HttpServlet {
24
25     private Connection connection; // connection to database
26
27     // factories for creating XML and applying XSLT
28     private DocumentBuilderFactory factory;
29     private TransformerFactory transformerFactory;
30
31     // setup database connection for servlet
32     public void init( ServletConfig servletConfig )
33        throws ServletException
34     {
35        super.init( servletConfig );
36
37        // initialize connection to database
38        try {
39
40           // obtain URL of properties file
41           java.net.URL propertyURL = getClass().getResource(
42              "bookStock.properties" );
43
44           // load properties file
45           Properties databaseProperties = new Properties();
```

Fig. 11.28 ViewOrderServlet displays the orders placed by the Book Buyer and Book Seller JAXM applications. (Part 1 of 5.)

```
46              databaseProperties.load( new FileInputStream(
47                 propertyURL.getPath() ) );
48
49              // load JDBC driver
50              Class.forName( databaseProperties.getProperty(
51                 "jdbcDriver" ) );
52
53              // establish database connection
54              connection = DriverManager.getConnection(
55                 databaseProperties.getProperty( "databaseURI" ) );
56
57              // create factory to build XML Documents
58              factory = DocumentBuilderFactory.newInstance();
59
60              // create factory to apply XSLT
61              transformerFactory = TransformerFactory.newInstance();
62           }
63
64        // handle exception if database driver does not exist
65        catch ( ClassNotFoundException classNotFoundException ) {
66              classNotFoundException.printStackTrace();
67        }
68
69        // handle exception in making Connection
70        catch ( SQLException sqlException ) {
71              sqlException.printStackTrace();
72        }
73
74        // handle exception in loading properties file
75        catch ( IOException ioException ) {
76              ioException.printStackTrace();
77        }
78
79     } // end method init
80
81     // invoked upon receiving message
82     public void doGet( HttpServletRequest request,
83        HttpServletResponse response ) throws ServletException
84     {
85        // determine whether order was successful
86        try {
87
88           // SQL query to database
89           Statement statement = connection.createStatement(
90              ResultSet.TYPE_SCROLL_INSENSITIVE,
91              ResultSet.CONCUR_READ_ONLY );
92
93           // make query to extract order information
94           ResultSet resultSet = statement.executeQuery( "SELECT" +
95              " orderID, isbn, quantity, price FROM orders" );
96
97           Document orderXmlDocument = null;
```

Fig. 11.28 ViewOrderServlet displays the orders placed by the Book Buyer and Book Seller JAXM applications. (Part 2 of 5.)

```
 98
 99             // view order information
100             if ( resultSet != null )
101                 orderXmlDocument = createXML( resultSet );
102
103             if ( orderXmlDocument != null )
104                 applyXSLT( "XSL/viewOrder_XHTML.xsl",
105                     orderXmlDocument, response );
106
107             statement.close();
108         }
109
110         // handle exception in accessing database
111         catch ( SQLException sqlException ) {
112             sqlException.printStackTrace();
113         }
114
115         // handle exception in applying XSLT
116         catch ( IOException ioException ) {
117             ioException.printStackTrace();
118         }
119
120    } // end method doGet
121
122    // create XML document from ResultSet
123    private Document createXML( ResultSet resultSet )
124       throws SQLException
125    {
126        // use ResultSet to build XML document
127        try {
128            DocumentBuilder builder = factory.newDocumentBuilder();
129            Document document = builder.newDocument();
130
131            // create orders root Element
132            Element orders = document.createElement( "orders" );
133            document.appendChild( orders );
134
135            // store ID, isbn, quantity and price in order Element
136            while ( resultSet.next() ) {
137
138                // create order Element for each order
139                Element order = document.createElement( "order" );
140
141                // obtain ID, isbn, quantity and price from resultSet
142                Integer ID =
143                    new Integer( resultSet.getInt( "orderID" ) );
144                String isbn = resultSet.getString( "isbn" );
145                Integer quantity =
146                    new Integer( resultSet.getInt( "quantity" ) );
147                Double price =
148                    new Double( resultSet.getDouble( "price" ) );
149
```

Fig. 11.28 `ViewOrderServlet` displays the orders placed by the Book Buyer and Book Seller JAXM applications. (Part 3 of 5.)

```
150              // create Elements for ID, isbn, quantity and price
151              Element orderID =
152                 document.createElement( "orderID" );
153              Element orderIsbn = document.createElement( "isbn" );
154              Element orderQuantity =
155                 document.createElement( "quantity" );
156              Element orderPrice =
157                 document.createElement( "price" );
158
159              // append elements as children to Element order
160              order.appendChild( orderID );
161              order.appendChild( orderIsbn );
162              order.appendChild( orderQuantity );
163              order.appendChild( orderPrice );
164
165              // create NumberFormat to format price to US locale
166              NumberFormat priceFormatter =
167                 NumberFormat.getCurrencyInstance( Locale.US );
168
169              // store ID, isbn, quantity and price information
170              orderID.appendChild(
171                 document.createTextNode( ID.toString() ) );
172              orderIsbn.appendChild(
173                 document.createTextNode( isbn ) );
174              orderQuantity.appendChild(
175                 document.createTextNode( quantity.toString() ) );
176              orderPrice.appendChild( document.createTextNode(
177                 priceFormatter.format( price ) ) );
178
179              // append each order Element to root Element orders
180              orders.appendChild( order );
181           }
182
183           return document;
184        }
185
186        // handle exception in parsing
187        catch ( ParserConfigurationException parserException ) {
188           parserException.printStackTrace();
189           return null;
190        }
191
192     } // end method createXML
193
194     // apply XSLT style sheet to XML document
195     private void applyXSLT( String xslFile, Document xmlDocument,
196        HttpServletResponse response ) throws IOException
197     {
198        // apply XSLT
199        try {
200
```

Fig. 11.28 `ViewOrderServlet` displays the orders placed by the Book Buyer and Book Seller JAXM applications. (Part 4 of 5.)

```
201            // open InputStream for XSL document
202            InputStream xslStream =
203               getServletContext().getResourceAsStream( xslFile );
204
205            // create StreamSource for XSLT document
206            Source xslSource = new StreamSource( xslStream );
207
208            // create DOMSource for source XML document
209            Source xmlSource = new DOMSource( xmlDocument );
210
211            // get PrintWriter for writing data to client
212            PrintWriter output = response.getWriter();
213
214            // create StreamResult for transformation result
215            Result result = new StreamResult( output );
216
217            // create Transformer for XSL transformation
218            Transformer transformer =
219               transformerFactory.newTransformer( xslSource );
220
221            // transform and deliver content to client
222            transformer.transform( xmlSource, result );
223
224         }
225
226         // handle exception transforming content
227         catch ( TransformerException transformerException ) {
228            transformerException.printStackTrace();
229         }
230
231      } // end method applyXSLT
232
233   } // end class ViewOrderServlet
```

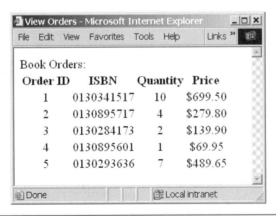

Fig. 11.28 `ViewOrderServlet` displays the orders placed by the Book Buyer and Book Seller JAXM applications. (Part 5 of 5.)

When the user accesses **ViewOrderServlet** (Fig. 11.28) via a Web browser, **ViewOrderServlet** invokes method **doGet** (lines 82–120). Lines 94–95 obtain the values for each order ID, ISBN, quantity and price from the database. Line 101 invokes method **createXML** (lines 123–192) to build the XML document from the **ResultSet** that contains these values. Lines 132–133 create root element **orders**. For each order, line 139 creates an element **order**, to which lines 151–157 append elements **orderID**, **isbn**, **quantity** and **price**. Line 180 appends each **order** element to element **orders**, and line 183 returns the XML document to method **doGet**. Lines 104–105 pass this document to method **applyXSLT** (lines 195–231), which applies **viewOrder_XHTML.xsl** (Fig. 11.29) to the XML document, then sends the content to the Web browser as XHTML.

```
1   <?xml version="1.0"?>
2
3   <!-- Fig. 11.29: viewOrder_XHTML.xsl   -->
4   <!-- XHTML stylesheet                  -->
5
6   <xsl:stylesheet version = "1.0"
7       xmlns:xsl = "http://www.w3.org/1999/XSL/Transform">
8
9       <xsl:output method = "xml" omit-xml-declaration = "no"
10          doctype-system = "DTD/xhtml1-strict.dtd"
11          doctype-public = "-//W3C//DTD XHTML 1.0 Strict//EN"/>
12
13      <!-- specify the root of the XML document -->
14      <!-- that references this stylesheet       -->
15      <xsl:template match = "orders">
16          <html xmlns="http://www.w3.org/1999/xhtml">
17
18              <head>
19                  <title>View Orders</title>
20              </head>
21
22              <body>
23                  <div class = "header">Book Orders:</div>
24
25                  <table class = "orders">
26                      <tr>
27                          <th>Order ID</th>
28                          <th>ISBN</th>
29                          <th>Quantity</th>
30                          <th>Price</th>
31                      </tr>
32
33                      <xsl:apply-templates
34                          select = "order"/>
35                  </table>
36              </body>
37          </html>
38      </xsl:template>
39
```

Fig. 11.29 XSL document that **ViewOrderServlet** uses to render **bookStock1** database contents as XHTML. (Part 1 of 2.)

```
40      <xsl:template match = "order">
41         <tr>
42            <td align = "center">
43               <xsl:value-of select = "orderID"/>
44            </td>
45
46            <td align = "center">
47               <xsl:value-of select = "isbn"/>
48            </td>
49
50            <td align = "center">
51               <xsl:value-of select = "quantity"/>
52            </td>
53
54            <td align = "center">
55               <xsl:value-of select = "price"/>
56            </td>
57         </tr>
58      </xsl:template>
59   </xsl:stylesheet>
```

Fig. 11.29 XSL document that **ViewOrderServlet** uses to render **bookStock1** database contents as XHTML. (Part 2 of 2.)

In this chapter, we discussed the Java API for XML Messaging (JAXM) and the SOAP with Attachments API for Java (SAAJ). We discussed synchronous and asynchronous messaging, then explained the role that a message provider plays in asynchronous messaging. Finally, we built Business-to-Business JAXM applications: a standalone client and two JAXM applications, each of which used a message provider to send and receive SOAP messages.

The next two chapters discuss Web-services security, which has become crucial to Web-services-based applications. Chapter 12, Security Overview, presents a detailed introduction to general computer and networking security. Chapter 13, Web Services Security, discusses Web-services-specific security issues and technologies.

11.6 Summary

The Java platform provides three messaging APIs: the Java Messaging Service (JMS), JavaMail and the Java API for XML Messaging (JAXM). JMS, JavaMail and JAXM share the common goal of enabling components to send and receive messages, but differ in that each provides support for distinct messaging infrastructures. JMS enables components to transfer messages via the point-to-point and publish/subscribe messaging models. JavaMail enables components to send messages via email to other components. JAXM enables components to transfer XML-formatted messages (e.g., SOAP messages) and is useful when building business-to-business (B2B) applications.

JAXM supports both synchronous and asynchronous messaging. In synchronous messaging, a JAXM application sends a message request to a Web service and waits for a message response. In asynchronous messaging, a JAXM application that sends a SOAP request does not wait for a response from the Web service. JAXM contains only one package, called **javax.xml.messaging**, which provides classes and interfaces for creating a special type of servlets (called a **JAXMServlet**) that can send and receive XML-based messages. JAXM also enables **JAXMServlet**s to connect to *message providers*—separate components that act as proxies for sending and receiving SOAP messages. The SOAP with Attachments API for Java (SAAJ) enables applications to create and manipulate SOAP messages that conform to the SOAP 1.1 specification and the SOAP with Attachments W3C Note. SAAJ contains only one package, called **javax.xml.soap**, which provides classes and interfaces for creating and manipulating SOAP messages. The JWSDP original releases integrated SAAJ with JAXM. The JWSDP current release (version 1.0) "extracted" SAAJ from JAXM, so that other applications could produce and consume SOAP messages without depending on the JAXM specification.

A JAXM application uses JAXM and SAAJ to send and receive SOAP messages to and from Web services. A JAXM developer can build two types of JAXM applications: one that uses a message provider, and one that does not (referred to as a standalone JAXM client). A standalone JAXM client invokes a Web service, then waits for a response from that service—in this respect, it acts like a JAX-RPC application. A standalone JAXM application does not use a message provider (a separate component that sends and receives SOAP messages) to forward requests to, or listen for requests from, a Web service.

However, JAXM clients are not limited to transferring messages with only JAXM-based Web services, nor are JAXM-based Web services limited to transferring messages with only JAXM clients. Since the client and the Web service communicate using a common XML-based messaging protocol (e.g., SOAP), the implementation of each component is completely transparent to the other component, thus promoting interoperability.

JAXM providers must support SOAP. However, SOAP does not specify any message-addressing scheme that determines how providers are to send and receive SOAP messages. For this reason, JAXM providers often use profiles, which are specifications for how providers should route their messages.

In synchronous messaging, the client blocks, or halts activity, after sending a SOAP request; the client waits until a SOAP response is received, then proceeds. In asynchronous messaging, JAXM applications use a message provider, which is responsible for sending and receiving messages, thus enabling a JAXM application to perform other functions after sending a SOAP request. Usually, a separate component in the client receives the SOAP response.

12

Computer and Internet Security

Objectives

- To understand the basic concepts of security.
- To understand public-key/private-key cryptography.
- To learn about popular security protocols, such as SSL.
- To understand digital signatures, digital certificates and certificate authorities.
- To become aware of various threats to secure computer systems, such as viruses and denial-of-service attacks.
- To learn about Virtual Private Networks and IPSec.

Three may keep a secret, if two of them are dead.
Benjamin Franklin

Attack—Repeat—Attack.
William Frederick Halsey, Jr.

Private information is practically the source of every large modern fortune.
Oscar Wilde

There must be security for all—or not one is safe.
The Day the Earth Stood Still, screenplay by Edmund H. North

No government can be long secure without formidable opposition.
Benjamin Disraeli

Outline

12.1 Introduction

As e-businesses and Web services gain widespread adoption, individuals and organizations are transmitting highly confidential information over the Internet. Consumers are submitting credit-card numbers to e-commerce sites, and businesses are exposing proprietary data on the Web. At the same time, organizations are experiencing increasing numbers of security breaches. Both individuals and companies are vulnerable to data theft and hacker attacks that can compromise data, corrupt files and crash systems. For these reasons, security is crucial to the success of e-business and Web services. In a memo to all Microsoft employees, Bill Gates stated that the company's highest priority is trustworthy computing—i.e., ensuring that Microsoft applications are reliable, available and secure. Gates's security emphasis has been echoed across the computing industry as organizations work to improve Internet and network security.[1]

There are five fundamental requirements for a successful, secure transaction: *privacy*, *integrity*, *authentication*, *authorization* and *non-repudiation*. *The privacy issue is*: How do you ensure that the information you transmit over the Internet has not been captured or passed to a third party without your knowledge? *The integrity issue is*: How do you ensure that the information you send or receive has not been compromised or altered? *The authentication issue is*: How do the sender and receiver of a message verify their identities to each other? *The authorization issue is*: How do you manage access to protected resources on the basis of user credentials? *The non-repudiation issue is*: How do you legally prove that a message was sent or received? Network security must also address the issue of *availability*. How do we ensure that the network, and the computer systems to which it connects, will operate continuously?

In this chapter, we explore the fundamentals of Internet security, including secure electronic transactions and secure networks. We discuss how to achieve e-commerce and network security using current technologies—including cryptography, Public Key Infrastructure (PKI), digital signatures, Secure Sockets Layer (SSL) and Virtual Private Networks (VPNs). We also examine authentication and authorization solutions, firewalls and intrusion detection systems. The next chapter, Web Services Security, overviews the standards and protocols used to secure Web services. XML Signature and XML Encryption provide authentication, integrity and privacy for Web services transmissions. The Security Assertions Markup Language (SAML) and Extensible Access Control Markup Language (XACML) address authentication and authorization in Web services applications. A new standard created by Microsoft, IBM and VeriSign, WS-Security, encrypts information and ensures the privacy of Web services transmissions. All these technologies are based on the security concepts described in this chapter.

12.2 Ancient Ciphers to Modern Cryptosystems

The channels through which data passes are inherently unsecure; therefore, any private information transmitted through these channels must somehow be protected. To protect information, data can be encrypted. *Cryptography* transforms data using a *cipher*, or *cryptosystem*—a mathematical algorithm for encrypting messages. A *key*—a string of digits that acts as a password—is input to the cipher. The cipher uses the key to make data incomprehensible to all but the sender and intended receivers. Unencrypted data is called *plaintext*; encrypted data is called *ciphertext*. The algorithm encrypts the data, and the key acts as a variable—using different keys results in different ciphertext. Only the intended receivers should have the corresponding key to decrypt the ciphertext into plaintext.

First used by the ancient Egyptians, cryptographic ciphers have been used throughout history to conceal and protect valuable information. Ancient cryptographers encrypted messages by hand, usually with a method based on the alphabetic letters of the message. The two main types of ciphers were *substitution ciphers* and *transposition ciphers*. In a substitution cipher, every occurrence of a given letter is replaced by a different letter; for example, if every "a" were replaced by a "b," every "b" by a "c," etc., the word "security" would encrypt to "tfdvsjuz." The first prominent substitution cipher was credited to Julius Caesar, and is referred to today as the *Caesar Cipher*. Using the Caesar Cipher, every instance of a letter is encrypted by replacing by the letter in the alphabet three places to the right. For example, using the Caesar Cipher, the word "security" would encrypt to "vhfxulwb."

In a transposition cipher, the ordering of the letters is shifted; for example, if every other letter, starting with "s," in the word "security" creates the first word in the cipher-text and the remaining letters create the second word in the ciphertext, the word "security" would encrypt to "scrt euiy." Complicated ciphers combine substitution and transposition ciphers. For example, using the substitution cipher in combination with the transposition cipher, the word "security" would encrypt to "tdsu fvjz." The problem with many historical ciphers is that their security relied on the sender and receiver to remember the encryption algorithm and keep it secret. Such algorithms are called *restricted algorithms*. Restricted algorithms are not feasible to implement among a large group of people. Imagine if the security of U.S. government communications relied on every U.S. government employee to keep a secret; the encryption algorithm could easily be compromised.

Modern cryptosystems are digital. Their algorithms are based on the individual *bits* or *blocks* (a group of bits) of a message, rather than letters of the alphabet. A computer stores data as a *binary string*, which is a sequence of ones and zeros. Each digit in the sequence is called a bit. Encryption and decryption keys are binary strings with a given *key length*. For example, 128-bit encryption systems have a key length of 128 bits. Longer keys have stronger encryption; it takes more time and computing power to break the encryption.

Until January 2000, the U.S. government placed restrictions on the strength of cryptosystems that could be exported from the United States by limiting the key length of the encryption algorithms. Today, the regulations on exporting cryptography products are less stringent. Any cryptography product may be exported as long as the end user is not a foreign government or from a country with embargo restrictions.[2]

12.3 Secret-Key Cryptography

In the past, organizations wishing to maintain a secure computing environment used *symmetric cryptography*, also known as *secret-key cryptography*. Secret-key cryptography uses the same secret key to encrypt and decrypt a message (Fig. 12.1). In this case, the sender encrypts a message using the secret key, then sends the encrypted message to the intended recipient, who decrypts the message using the same secret key. A fundamental problem with secret-key cryptography is that before two people can communicate securely, they must find a secure way to exchange the secret key. One approach is to have the key delivered by a courier, such as a mail service or FedEx. While this approach may be feasible when two individuals communicate, it is not efficient for securing communication in a large network, nor can it be considered completely secure. The privacy and the integrity of the message would be compromised if the key is intercepted as it is passed between the sender and the receiver. Also, since both parties in the transaction use the same key to encrypt and decrypt a message, one cannot authenticate which party created a message. Finally, to keep communications private with each receiver, a sender needs a different secret key for each receiver. As a result, organizations would have huge numbers of secret keys to maintain for each user.

An alternative approach to the key-exchange problem is to have a central authority, called a *key distribution center* (*KDC*). The key distribution center shares a (different) secret key with every user in the network. In this system, the key distribution center generates a *session key* to be used for a transaction (Fig. 12.2). Next, the key distribution center distributes the session key to the sender and receiver, encrypted with the secret key they each share with the key distribution center. For example, suppose a merchant and a customer want to conduct a secure transaction. The merchant and the customer each have unique secret keys that they share with the key distribution center. The key distribution center generates a session key for the merchant and customer to use in the transaction. The key distribution center then sends the session key for the transaction to the merchant, encrypted using the secret key the merchant already shares with the center. The key distribution center sends the same session key for the transaction to the customer, encrypted using the secret key the customer already shares with the key distribution center. Once the merchant and the customer have the session key for the transaction, they can communicate with each other, encrypting their messages using the shared session key.

Using a key distribution center reduces the number of courier deliveries (again, by means such as mail or FedEx) of secret keys to each user in the network. In addition, users can have a new secret key for each communication with other users in the network, which greatly increases the overall security of the network. However, if the security of the key distribution center is compromised, then the security of the entire network is compromised.

One of the most commonly used symmetric encryption algorithms is the *Data Encryption Standard* (*DES*). Horst Feistel of IBM created the *Lucifer* algorithm, which was chosen as the DES by the United States government and the National Security Agency (NSA) in the 1970s.[3] DES has a key length of 56 bits and encrypts data in 64-bit blocks. This type of encryption is known as a *block cipher*. A block cipher is an encryption method that creates groups of bits from an original message, then applies an encryption algorithm to the block as a whole, rather than as individual bits. This method reduces the amount of computer processing power and time required, while maintaining a fair level of security. For many years, DES was the encryption standard set by the U.S. government and the *American National Standards Institute* (*ANSI*). However, due to advances in technology and computing speed, DES is no longer considered secure. In the late 1990s, specialized *DES cracker machines* were built that recovered DES keys after just several hours.[4] As a result, the old standard of symmetric encryption has been replaced by *Triple DES*, or *3DES*, a variant of DES that is essentially three DES systems in a row, each with its own secret key. Though 3DES is more secure, the three passes through the DES algorithm result in slower performance. The United States government recently selected a new, more secure standard for symmetric encryption to replace DES. The new standard is called the *Advanced Encryption Standard* (*AES*). The *National Institute of Standards and Technology* (*NIST*)—which sets the cryptographic standards for the U.S. government—chose *Rijndael* as the encryption method for AES. Rijndael is a block cipher developed by Dr. Joan Daemen and Dr. Vincent Rijmen of Belgium. Rijndael can be used with key sizes and block sizes of 128, 192 or 256 bits. Rijndael was chosen over four other finalists as the AES because of its high security, performance, efficiency, flexibility and low memory requirement for computing systems.[5] For more information about AES, visit **csrc.nist.gov/encryption/aes**.

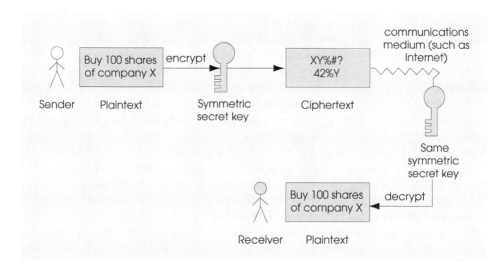

Fig. 12.1   Encrypting and decrypting a message using a secret key.

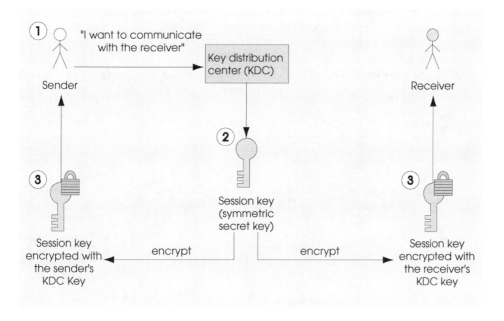

Fig. 12.2   Distributing a session key with a key distribution center.

12.4 Public-Key Cryptography

In 1976, Whitfield Diffie and Martin Hellman, researchers at Stanford University, developed *public-key cryptography* to solve the problem of exchanging keys securely. Public-key cryptography is asymmetric. It uses two inversely related keys: a *public key* and a *private key*. The private key is kept secret by its owner, whereas the public key is freely distributed. If the public key is used to encrypt a message, only the corresponding private key can decrypt it (Fig. 12.3). Each party in a transaction has both a public key and a private key. To transmit a message securely, the sender uses the receiver's public key to encrypt the message. The receiver then decrypts the message using his or her unique private key. Assuming that the private key has been kept secret, the message cannot be read by anyone other than the intended receiver. Thus the system ensures the privacy of the message. The defining property of a secure public-key algorithm is that it is "computationally infeasible" to deduce the private key from the public key. Although the two keys are mathematically related, deriving one from the other would take enormous amounts of computing power and time, enough to discourage attempts to deduce the private key. An outside party cannot participate in communication without the correct keys. The security of the entire process is based on the secrecy of the private keys. Therefore, if a third party obtains the private key used in decryption, the security of the whole system is compromised. If a system's integrity is compromised, the user can simply change the key, instead of changing the entire encryption or decryption algorithm.

Either the public key or the private key can be used to encrypt or decrypt a message. For example, if a customer uses a merchant's public key to encrypt a message, only the merchant can decrypt the message, using the merchant's private key. Thus, the merchant's identity can be authenticated, since only the merchant knows the private key. However, the merchant has no way of validating the customer's identity, since the encryption key the customer used is publicly available.

If the decryption key is the sender's public key and the encryption key is the sender's private key, the sender of the message can be authenticated. For example, suppose a customer sends a merchant a message encrypted using the customer's private key. The mer-

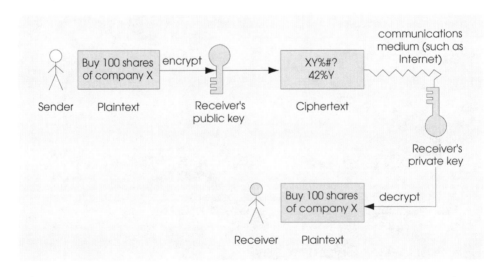

Fig. 12.3   Encrypting and decrypting a message using public-key cryptography.

chant decrypts the message using the customer's public key. Since the customer encrypted the message using his or her private key, the merchant can be confident of the customer's identity. This process authenticates the sender, but does not ensure confidentiality, as anyone could decrypt the message with the sender's public key. This systems works as long as the merchant can be sure that the public key with which the merchant decrypted the message belongs to the customer, and not a third party posing as the customer. The problem of proving ownership of a public key is discussed in Section 12.9, Public-Key Infrastructure, Certificates and Certificate Authorities.

These two methods of public-key encryption can actually be used together to authenticate both participants in a communication (Fig. 12.4). Suppose a merchant wants to send a message securely to a customer so that only the customer can read it, and suppose also that the merchant wants to provide proof to the customer that the merchant (not an unknown third party) actually sent the message. First, the merchant encrypts the message using the customer's public key. This step guarantees that only the customer can read the message. Then the merchant encrypts the result using the merchant's private key, which proves the identity of the merchant. The customer decrypts the message in reverse order. First, the customer uses the merchant's public key. Since only the merchant could have encrypted the message with the inversely related private key, this step authenticates the merchant. Then the customer uses the customer's private key to decrypt the next level of encryption. This step ensures that the content of the message was kept private in the transmission, since only the customer has the key to decrypt the message. Although this system provides extremely secure transactions, the setup cost and time required prevent widespread use.

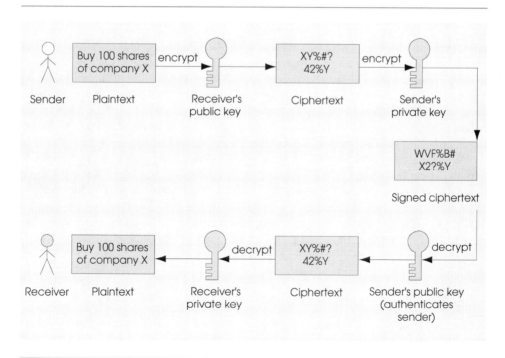

Fig. 12.4 Authentication with a public-key algorithm

The most commonly used public-key algorithm is *RSA*, an encryption system developed in 1977 by MIT professors Ron Rivest, Adi Shamir and Leonard Adleman.[6] Today, most Fortune 1000 companies and leading e-commerce businesses use their encryption and authentication technologies. With the emergence of the Internet and the World Wide Web, their security work has become even more significant and plays a crucial role in e-commerce transactions. Their encryption products are built into hundreds of millions of copies of the most popular Internet applications, including Web browsers, commerce servers and e-mail systems. Most secure e-commerce transactions and communications on the Internet use RSA products. For more information about RSA, cryptography and security, visit **www.rsasecurity.com**.

Pretty Good Privacy (*PGP*) is a public-key encryption system used for the encryption of e-mail messages and files. PGP was designed in 1991 by Phillip Zimmermann.[7] PGP can also be used to provide digital signatures (see Section 12.8, Digital Signatures) that confirm the author of an e-mail or public posting.

PGP is based on a "web of trust;" each client in a network can vouch for another client's identity to prove ownership of a public key. The "web of trust" is used to authenticate each client. If users know the identity of a public key holder, through personal contact or another secure method, they validate the key by signing it with their own key. The web grows as more users validate the keys of others. To learn more about PGP and to download a free copy of the software, go to the MIT Distribution Center for PGP at **web.mit.edu/network/pgp.html**.

12.5 Cryptanalysis

Even if keys are kept secret, it may be possible to compromise the security of a system. Trying to decrypt ciphertext without knowledge of the decryption key is known as *cryptanalysis*. Cryptologists are constantly researching commercial encryption systems to ensure that the systems are not vulnerable to a *cryptanalytic attack*. The most common form of cryptanalytic attacks are those in which the encryption algorithm is analyzed to find relations between bits of the encryption key and bits of the ciphertext. Often, these relations are only statistical in nature and incorporate an analyzer's outside knowledge about the plaintext. The goal of such an attack is to determine the key from the ciphertext.

Weak statistical trends between ciphertext and keys can be exploited to gain knowledge about the key if enough ciphertext is known. Proper key management and key expiration dates on keys help prevent cryptanalytic attacks. When a key is used for long periods of time, more ciphertext is generated that can be beneficial to an attacker trying to derive a key. If a key is unknowingly recovered by an attacker, it can be used to decrypt every message for the life of that key. Using public-key cryptography to exchange secret keys securely allows a new secret key to encrypt every message.

12.6 Key Agreement Protocols

A drawback of public-key algorithms is that they are not efficient for sending large amounts of data. They require significant computer power, which slows communication. Public-key algorithms should not be thought of as replacements for secret-key algorithms. Instead, public-key algorithms are used most often to exchange secret keys securely. The process by which two parties can exchange keys over an unsecure medium is called a *key agreement protocol*. A *protocol* sets the rules for communication—e.g., which encryption algorithm(s) to use.

The most common key agreement protocol is a *digital envelope* (Fig. 12.5). With a digital envelope, the message is encrypted using a secret key (Step 1), and the secret key is encrypted using public-key encryption (Step 2). The sender attaches the encrypted secret key to the encrypted message and sends the receiver the entire package. The sender could also digitally sign the package before sending it to prove the sender's identity to the receiver (Section 12.8, Digital Signatures). To decrypt the package, the receiver first decrypts the secret key using the receiver's private key. Then, the receiver uses the secret key to decrypt the actual message. Since only the receiver can decrypt the encrypted secret key, the sender can be sure that only the intended receiver is reading the message.

12.7 Key Management

Maintaining the secrecy of private keys is crucial for keeping cryptographic systems secure. Most compromises in security result from poor *key management* (e.g., the mishandling of private keys, resulting in key theft) rather than attacks that attempt to guess the keys.[8]

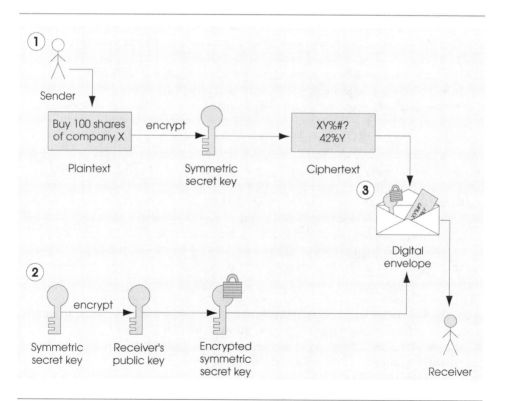

Fig. 12.5 Creating a digital envelope.

A main component of key management is *key generation*—the process by which keys are created. A malicious third party could try to decrypt a message by using every possible decryption key, a process known as *brute-force cracking*. Key-generation algorithms are sometimes unintentionally constructed to choose from only a small subset of possible keys. If the subset is too small, then the encrypted data is more susceptible to brute-force attacks. Therefore, it is important to have a key-generation program that can generate a large number of keys as randomly as possible. Keys are made more secure by choosing a key length so large that it is computationally infeasible for a malicious third party to try all combinations.

12.8 Digital Signatures

Digital signatures, the electronic equivalents of written signatures, were developed to be used in public-key cryptography to solve the problems of authentication and integrity. A digital signature authenticates the sender's identity, and, like a written signature, it is difficult to forge.

To create a digital signature, a sender first takes the original plaintext message and runs it through a *hash function*, which is a mathematical calculation that gives the message a *hash value*. A hash value identifies a message uniquely. If a malicious party changed the message, the hash value would also change, thus enabling the recipient to detect that the message was altered. The *Secure Hash Algorithm (SHA-1)* is the current standard for hashing functions. Using SHA-1, the phrase "Buy 100 shares of company X" would produce the hash value *D8 A9 B6 9F 72 65 0B D5 6D 0C 47 00 95 0D FD 31 96 0A FD B5*. An example of SHA-1 is available at **home.istar.ca/~neutron/messagedigest**. At this site, users can input text or files into a program to generate the hash value. The hash value is also known as a *message digest*. The chance that two different messages will have the same message digest is statistically insignificant. *Collision* occurs when multiple messages have the same hash value. It is computationally infeasible to compute a message from its hash value or to find two messages with the same hash value.

Next, the sender uses the sender's private key to encrypt the message digest. This step creates a digital signature and validates the sender's identity, since only the owner of that private key could encrypt the message. A message that includes the digital signature, hash function and the encrypted message is sent to the receiver. The receiver uses the sender's public key to decipher the original digital signature (this establishes the message's authenticity—i.e., it came from the sender) and reveal the message digest. The receiver then uses his or her own private key to decipher the original message. Finally, the receiver applies the hash function to the original message. If the hash value of the original message matches the message digest included in the signature, there is *message integrity*; the message has not been altered in transmission.

There is a fundamental difference between digital signatures and handwritten signatures. A handwritten signature is independent of the document being signed. Thus, if someone can forge a handwritten signature, they can use that signature to forge multiple documents. A digital signature is created using the contents of the document. Therefore, your digital signature is different for each document you sign.

Digital signatures do not provide proof that a message has been sent. Consider the following situation: A contractor sends a company a digitally signed contract, which the contractor later would like to revoke. The contractor could do so by releasing the private key and then claiming that the digitally signed contract came from an intruder who stole the contractor's private key. *Timestamping*, which binds a time and date to a digital document, can help solve the problem of non-repudiation. For example, suppose the company and the contractor are negotiating a contract. The company requires the contractor to sign the contract digitally and then have the document digitally timestamped by a third party called a *timestamping agency*. The contractor sends the digitally-signed contract to the timestamping agency. The privacy of the message is maintained since the timestamping agency sees only the encrypted, digitally-signed message (as opposed to the original plaintext message). The timestamping agency affixes the time and date of receipt to the encrypted, signed message and digitally signs the whole package with the timestamping agency's private key. The timestamp cannot be altered by anyone except the timestamping agency, since no one else possesses the timestamping agency's private key. Unless the contractor reports the private key to have been compromised before the document was timestamped, the contractor cannot legally prove that the document was signed by an unauthorized third party. The sender could also require the receiver to sign the message digitally and timestamp it as proof of receipt. To learn more about timestamping, visit **AuthentiDate.com** (**www.authentidate.com**).

The U.S. government's digital-authentication standard is called the *Digital Signature Algorithm (DSA)*. The U.S. government recently passed digital-signature legislation that makes digital signatures as legally binding as handwritten signatures. This legislation is expected to increase e-business dramatically. For the latest news about U.S. government legislation in information security, visit **www.itaa.org/infosec**. For more information about the bills, visit the following government sites:

```
thomas.loc.gov/cgi-bin/bdquery/z?d106:hr.01714:
thomas.loc.gov/cgi-bin/bdquery/z?d106:s.00761:
```

The W3C and the Internet Engineering Task Force created the XML Signature specification as a standard for encrypting XML documents. For more information on, and examples of, XML signatures, see Chapter 13, Web Services Security.

12.9 Public-Key Infrastructure, Certificates and Certificate Authorities

One problem with public-key cryptography is that anyone with a set of keys could potentially assume another party's identity. For example, a customer wants to place an order with an online merchant. How does the customer know that the Web site indeed belongs to that merchant and not to a third party that posted a site and is *masquerading* as a merchant to steal credit-card information? *Public Key Infrastructure (PKI)* provides a solution to these problems. PKI integrates public-key cryptography with *digital certificates* and *certificate authorities* to authenticate parties in a transaction. The XML Key Management Specification (XKMS) defines a set of protocols for implementing PKI in Web services. We discuss XKMS and provide an example XKMS-generated document in Chapter 13, Web Services Security.

A digital certificate is a digital document used to identify a user and issued by a *certificate authority (CA)*. A digital certificate includes the name of the subject (the company or individual being certified), the subject's public key, a serial number, an expiration date, the signature of the trusted certificate authority and any other relevant information (Fig. 12.6). A CA is a financial institution or other trusted third party, such as *VeriSign*. Once issued, the digital certificates are publicly available and are held by the certificate authority in *certificate repositories*.

The CA signs the certificate by encrypting either the subject's public key or a hash value of the public key using the CA's own private key. The CA has to verify every subject's public key. Thus, users must trust the public key of a CA. Usually, each CA is part of a *certificate authority hierarchy*. This hierarchy is similar to a chain of trust in which each link relies on another link to provide authentication information. A certificate authority hierarchy is a chain of certificate authorities, starting with the *root certificate authority*, which is the Internet Policy Registration Authority (IPRA). The IPRA signs certificates using the *root key*. The root key signs certificates only for *policy creation authorities*, which are organizations that set policies for obtaining digital certificates. In turn, policy creation authorities sign digital certificates for CAs. CAs then sign digital certificates for individuals and organizations. The CA takes responsibility for authentication, so it must check information carefully before issuing a digital certificate. In one case, human error caused VeriSign to issue two digital certificates to an imposter posing as a Microsoft employee.[9] Such an error is significant; the inappropriately issued certificates can cause users to download malicious code *unknowingly* onto their machines (see Authentication: Microsoft Authenticode feature).

Fig. 12.6 Portion of a VeriSign digital certificate. (Courtesy of VeriSign, Inc.)

VeriSign, Inc., is a leading certificate authority. For more information about VeriSign, visit **www.verisign.com**. For a listing of other digital-certificate vendors, please see Section 12.16.

Periodically changing key pairs is necessary in maintaining a secure system, as a private key may be compromised without a user's knowledge. The longer a key pair is used, the more vulnerable the keys are to attack and cryptanalysis. As a result, digital certificates are created with an expiration date, to force users to switch key pairs. If a private key is compromised before its expiration date, the digital certificate can be canceled, and the user can get a new key pair and digital certificate. Canceled and revoked certificates are placed on a *certificate revocation list* (*CRL*). CRLs are stored with the certificate authority that issued the certificates. It is essential for users to report immediately if they suspect that their private keys have been compromised, as the issue of non-repudiation makes certificate owners responsible for anything appearing with their digital signatures. In states with laws on digital signatures, certificates legally bind certificate owners to any transactions involving their certificates.

CRLs are similar to old paper lists of revoked credit-card numbers that were used at the points of sale in stores.[10] This makes for a great inconvenience when checking the validity of a certificate. An alternative to CRLs is the *Online Certificate Status Protocol* (*OCSP*), which validates certificates in real-time. OCSP technology is currently under development. For an overview of OCSP, read "X.509 Internet Public Key Infrastructure Online Certificate Status Protocol—OCSP" located at **ftp.isi.edu/in-notes/ rfc2560.txt**.

Many people still consider e-commerce unsecure. However, transactions using PKI and digital certificates can be more secure than exchanging private information over phone lines, through the mail or even than paying by credit card in person. After all, when you go to a restaurant and the waiter takes your credit card in back to process your bill, how do you know the waiter did not write down your credit-card information? In contrast, the key algorithms used in most secure online transactions are nearly impossible to compromise. By some estimates, the key algorithms used in public-key cryptography are so secure that even millions of today's computers working in parallel could not break the codes in a century. However, as computing power increases, key algorithms considered strong today could be broken in the future.

Digital-certificate capabilities are built into many e-mail packages. For example, in Microsoft Outlook, you can go to the **Tools** menu and select **Options** and the **Security** tab. At the bottom of the dialog box, you will see the option to obtain a digital ID. Selecting the option will take you to a Microsoft Web site with links to several worldwide certificate authorities. Once you have a digital certificate, you can sign your e-mail messages digitally.

To obtain a digital certificate for your personal e-mail messages, visit **www.verisign.com** or **www.thawte.com**. VeriSign offers a free 60-day trial, or you can purchase the service for a yearly fee. Thawte offers free digital certificates for personal e-mail. Web server certificates may also be purchased through VeriSign and Thawte; however, they are more expensive than e-mail certificates.

12.9.1 Smart Cards

One of the fastest growing applications of PKI is the *smart card*. A smart card generally looks like a credit card and can serve many different functions, from authentication to data storage. The most popular smart cards are *memory cards* and *microprocessor cards*. Memory cards are similar to floppy disks. Microprocessor cards are similar to small computers, with operating systems, security and storage. Smart cards also have different *interfaces* with which they interact with reading devices. One type of interface is a *contact interface*, in which smart cards are inserted into a reading device and physical contact between the device and the card is necessary. The alternative to this method is a *contactless interface*, in which data is transferred to a reader via an embedded wireless device in the card, without the card and the device having to make physical contact.[11]

Smart cards store private keys, digital certificates and other information necessary for implementing PKI. They may also store credit card numbers, personal contact information, etc. Each smart card is used in combination with a *personal identification number* (*PIN*). This application provides two levels of security by requiring the user to both possess a smart card and know the corresponding PIN to access the information stored on the card. As an added measure of security, some microprocessor cards will delete or corrupt stored data if malicious attempts at tampering with the card occur. Smart card PKI allows users to access information from multiple devices using the same smart card.

12.10 Security Protocols

Everyone using the Web for e-business and e-commerce needs to be concerned about the security of their personal information. In this section, we discuss network security protocols, such as *Internet Protocol Security (IPSec),* and transport layer security protocols such as *Secure Sockets Layer* (*SSL*). Network security protocols protect communications between networks; transport layer security protocols are used to establish secure connections for data to pass through.

12.10.1 Secure Sockets Layer (SSL)

Currently, most e-businesses use SSL for secure online transactions, although SSL is not designed specifically for securing transactions. Rather, SSL secures World Wide Web connections. The Secure Sockets Layer (SSL) protocol, developed by Netscape Communications, is a non-proprietary protocol commonly used to secure communication between two computers on the Internet and the Web.[12] SSL is built into many Web browsers, including Netscape Communicator and Microsoft Internet Explorer, as well as numerous other software products. It operates between the Internet's TCP/IP communications protocol and the application software.[13]

In a standard correspondence over the Internet, a sender's message is passed to a *socket*, which receives and transmits information from a network. The socket then interprets the message through *Transmission Control Protocol/Internet Protocol* (*TCP/IP*). TCP/IP is the standard set of protocols used for connecting computers and networks to a network of networks, known as the Internet. Most Internet transmissions are sent as sets of individual message pieces, called *packets*. At the sending side, the packets of one message are numbered sequentially, and error-control information is attached to each packet. IP is primarily responsible for routing packets to avoid traffic jams, so each packet might travel a different route over the Internet. The destination of a packet is determined by the *IP address*—an assigned number used to identify a computer on a network, similar to the address of a house in a neighborhood. At the receiving end, the TCP makes sure that all of the packets have arrived, puts them in sequential order and determines if the packets have arrived without alteration. If the packets have been accidentally altered or any data has been lost, TCP requests retransmission. However, TCP is not sophisticated enough to determine if packets have been maliciously altered during transmission, as malicious packets can be disguised as valid ones. When all of the data successfully reaches TCP/IP, the message is passed to the socket at the receiver end. The socket translates the message back into a form that can be read by the receiver's application.[14] In a transaction using SSL, the sockets are secured using public-key cryptography.

SSL implements public-key cryptography using the RSA algorithm and digital certificates to authenticate the server in a transaction and to protect private information as it passes over the Internet. SSL transactions do not require client authentication; many servers consider a valid credit-card number to be sufficient for authentication in secure purchases. To begin, a client sends a message to a server. The server responds and sends its digital certificate to the client for authentication. Using public-key cryptography to communicate securely, the client and server negotiate *session keys* to continue the transaction. Session keys are secret keys that are used for the duration of that transaction. Once the keys are established, the communication proceeds between the client and the server by using the session keys and digital certificates. Encrypted data is passed through TCP/IP, just as regular packets travel over the Internet. However, before sending a message with TCP/IP, the SSL protocol breaks the information into blocks, compresses it and encrypts it. Conversely, after the data reaches the receiver through TCP/IP, the SSL protocol decrypts the packets, then decompresses and assembles the data. These extra processes provide an extra layer of security between TCP/IP and applications. SSL is primarily used to secure *point-to-point connections*—transmissions of data from one computer to another.[15] SSL allows for authentication of the server, the client, both or neither. However, in most e-business SSL sessions, only the server is authenticated. The Transport Layer Security (TLS) protocol, designed by the Internet Engineering Task Force, is similar to SSL. For more information on TLS, visit **www.ietf.org/rfc/rfc2246.txt**.

Although SSL protects information as it is passed over the Internet, it does not protect private information, such as credit-card numbers, once the information is stored on the merchant's server. When a merchant receives credit-card information with an order, the information is often decrypted and stored on the merchant's server until the order is placed. If the server is not secure and the data is not encrypted, an unauthorized party can access the information. Hardware devices, such as *peripheral component interconnect (PCI) cards* designed for use in SSL transactions, can be installed on Web servers to process SSL transactions, thus reducing processing time and leaving the server free to perform other tasks.[16] Visit **www.sonicwall.com/products/trans.asp** for more information on these devices. For more information about the SSL protocol, check out the Netscape SSL tutorial at **developer.netscape.com/tech/security/ssl/protocol.html** and the Netscape Security Center site at **www.netscape.com/security/index.html**.

12.10.2 IPSec and Virtual Private Networks (VPN)

Networks allow organizations to link multiple computers together. *Local area networks (LANs)* connect computers that are physically close, generally in the same building. *Wide area networks (WANs)* are used to connect computers in multiple locations using private telephone lines or radio waves. Organizations are now taking advantage of the existing infrastructure of the Internet—the publicly-available wires—to create *Virtual Private Networks* (*VPNs*). VPNs connect multiple networks, wireless users and other remote users. VPNs use the Internet infrastructure that is already in place, therefore they are more economical than private networks such as WANs.[17] Encryption allows VPNs to provide the same services as private networks do—over a public network.

A VPN is created by establishing a secure *tunnel* through which data passes between multiple networks over the Internet. *IPSec* (*Internet Protocol Security*) is one of the technologies used to secure the tunnel through which the data passes, ensuring data privacy and integrity, as well authenticating users.[18] IPSec, developed by the *Internet Engineering Task Force* (*IETF*), uses public-key and symmetric-key cryptography to ensure data integrity, authentication and confidentiality. The technology takes advantage of the standard that is already in place, in which information travels between two networks over the Internet via the *Internet Protocol* (*IP*). Information sent using IP, however, can easily be intercepted. Unauthorized users can access the network by using a number of well-known techniques, such as *IP spoofing*—a method in which an attacker simulates the IP of an authorized user or host to get access to resources that would otherwise be off-limits. The SSL protocol enables secure, point-to-point connections between two applications; IPSec enables the secure connection of an entire network. The Diffie-Hellman and RSA algorithms are commonly used in the IPSec protocol for key exchange, and DES or 3DES are used for secret-key encryption (depending on system and encryption needs). An IP packet is encrypted, then sent inside a regular IP packet that creates the tunnel. The receiver discards the outer IP packet, then decrypts the inner IP packet.[19] VPN security relies on three concepts—authentication of the user, encryption of the data sent over the network and controlled access to corporate information.[20] To address these three security concepts, IPSec is composed of three pieces. The *Authentication Header* (*AH*) attaches additional information to each packet, which verifies the identity of the sender and proves that data was not modified in transit. The *Encapsulating Security Payload* (*ESP*) encrypts the data using symmetric key ciphers to protect the data from eavesdroppers while the IP packet is being sent from one computer to another. The *Internet Key Exchange* (*IKE*) is the key-exchange protocol used in IPSec to determine security restrictions and to authenticate the encryption keys.

VPNs are becoming increasingly popular in businesses. However, VPN security is difficult to manage. To establish a VPN, all of the users on the network must have similar software or hardware. Although it is convenient for a business partner to connect to another company's network via VPN, access to specific applications and files should be limited to certain authorized users versus all users on a VPN.[21] Firewalls, intrusion detection software and authorization tools can be used to secure valuable data (see Section 12.13). For more information about IPSec, visit the IETF's *IPSec Working Group* Web site (**www.ietf.org/html.charters/ipsec-charter.html**).

12.11 Authentication and Authorization

As we discussed throughout the chapter, authentication and authorization are two of the fundamental requirements for e-business and Web services security. In this section, we will discuss technologies used to authenticate users in a network, such as *Kerberos*, *biometrics* and *single sign-on*.

12.11.1 Kerberos

Firewalls do not protect users from internal security threats to their local area network. Internal attacks are common and can be extremely damaging. For example, disgruntled employees with network access can wreak havoc on an organization's network or steal valuable proprietary information. It is estimated that 70 percent to 90 percent of attacks on corporate networks are internal.[22] *Kerberos* is a freely available, open-source protocol developed at MIT. It employs secret-key cryptography to authenticate users in a network and to maintain the integrity and privacy of network communications.

Authentication in Kerberos is handled by a main Kerberos system and a secondary *Ticket Granting Service* (*TGS*). This system is similar to the key distribution centers described in Section 12.3, Secret-key Cryptography. The main Kerberos system authenticates a client's identity to the TGS; the TGS authenticates client's rights to access specific network services.

Each client in the network shares a secret key with the Kerberos system. This secret key may be used by multiple TGSs in the Kerberos system. The client starts by entering a login name and password into the Kerberos authentication server. The authentication server maintains a database of all clients in the network. The authentication server returns a *Ticket-Granting Ticket* (*TGT*) encrypted with the client's secret key that it shares with the authentication server. Since the secret key is known only by the authentication server and the client, only the client can decrypt the TGT, thus authenticating the client's identity. Next, the client sends the decrypted TGT to the Ticket Granting Service to request a *service ticket*. The service ticket authorizes the client's access to specific network services. Service tickets have a set expiration time. Tickets may be renewed by the TGS.

12.11.2 Biometrics

An innovation in security is likely to be *biometrics*. Biometrics uses unique personal information, such as fingerprints, eyeball iris scans or face scans, to identify a user. This system eliminates the need for passwords, which are much easier to steal. Have you ever written down your passwords on a piece of paper and put the paper in your desk drawer or wallet? These days, people have passwords and PIN codes for everything—Web sites, networks, e-mail, ATM cards and even for their cars. Managing all of those codes can become a burden. Recently, the cost of biometrics devices has dropped significantly. Keyboard-mounted fingerprint-scanning, face-scanning and eye-scanning devices are being used in place of passwords to log into systems, check e-mail or access secure information over a network. Each user's iris scan, face scan or fingerprint is stored in a secure database. Each time a user logs in, his or her scan is compared with the database. If a match is made, the login is successful. Two companies that specialize in biometrics devices are Iridian Technologies (**iriscan.com**) and Keytronic (**www.keytronic.com**). For additional resources, see Section 12.16.

Currently, passwords are the predominant means of authentication; however, focus is beginning to shift to smart cards and biometrics. Microsoft recently announced that it will include the *Biometric Application Programming Interface* (*BAPI*) in future versions of Windows, which will make it possible for companies to integrate biometrics into their systems.[23] *Two-factor authentication* uses two means to authenticate the user, such as biometrics or a smart card used in combination with a password. Though this system could potentially be compromised, using two methods of authentication is more secure than just using passwords alone.

Keyware Inc. has already implemented a wireless biometrics system that stores user voiceprints on a central server. Keyware also created *layered biometric verification* (*LBV*), which uses multiple physical measurements—face, finger and voice prints—simultaneously. The LBV feature enables a wireless biometrics system to combine biometrics with other authentication methods, such as PIN and PKI.[24]

Identix Inc. also provides biometrics authentication technology for wireless transactions. The Identix fingerprint scanning device is embedded in handheld devices. The Identix service offers *transaction management* and *content protection* services. Transaction management services prove that transactions took place, and content protection services control access to electronic documents, including limiting a user's ability to download or copy documents.[25]

One of the major concerns with biometrics is the issue of privacy. Implementing fingerprint scanners means that organizations will be keeping databases with each employee's fingerprint. Do people want to provide their employers with such personal information? What if that data is compromised? To date, most organizations that have implemented biometrics systems have received little, if any, resistance from employees.

 ### 12.11.3 Single Sign-On

To access multiple applications or Web services on different servers, users must provide a separate password for authentication on each. Remembering multiple passwords is cumbersome. People tend to write their passwords down, creating security threats.

Single sign-on systems allow users to login once with a single password. Users can access multiple applications. It is important to secure single sign-on passwords, because if the password becomes available to hackers, all applications can be accessed and attacked.

There are three types of single sign-on services: *workstation logon scripts*, *authentication server scripts* and *tokens*. Workstation logon scripts are the simplest form of single sign-on. Users login at their workstations, then choose applications from a menu. The workstation logon script sends the user's password to the application servers, and the user is authenticated for future access to those applications. Workstation logon scripts do not provide a sufficient amount of security since user passwords are stored on the PC in plaintext. Anyone who can access the workstation can take the user's password. Authentication server scripts authenticate users with a central server. The central server controls connections between the user and the applications the user wishes to access. Authentication server scripts are more secure than workstation logon scripts, because passwords are kept on the server, which is more secure than the individual PC.

The most advanced single sign-on systems use token-based authentication. Once a user is authenticated, a non-reusable token is issued, enabling the user to access specific applications. The logon for creating the token is secured with encryption or with a single password, which is the only password that the user needs. A key problem with token authentication is that all applications must be built to accept tokens, rather than traditional logon passwords.[26] Currently, the three leaders in the development of single sign-on technology are the Liberty Alliance Project (**www.projectliberty.org**), Microsoft and

AOL Time Warner.[27] The Liberty Alliance Project is a consortium of technology and security organizations working to create an open single sign-on solution. Microsoft's Passport and AOL Time Warner's Magic Carpet are also viable solutions, though they are proprietary. To protect the privacy of information submitted to single sign-on and other applications, the *Platform for Privacy Preferences* (*P3P*) gives users control over the personal information that sites collect (see the feature, P3P: Placing Privacy Control in the Hands of Users).

12.12 Security Attacks

Recent cyberattacks on e-businesses have made the front pages of newspapers worldwide. *Denial-of-service attacks* (*DoS*), *viruses* and *worms* have cost companies billions of dollars. In this section, we will discuss the different types of attacks and the solutions you can implement to protect your information.

P3P: Placing Privacy Control in the Hands of Users

The Platform for Privacy Preferences (P3P) (`www.w3.org/P3P`) allows users to define their own privacy preferences for browsing and shopping online. Sites specify privacy policies in XML policy files that indicate what personal information the sites collect about users and what they do with this information. Many people prefer to keep personal information—such as names, credit-card numbers and mailing addresses—private. Most sites provide written privacy policies, but these can be lengthy and full of confusing legal terms. With P3P, users set privacy preferences on their browsers. When a user reaches a site with a P3P policy, the user's computer determines what information to disclose to the site on the basis of the defined preferences. P3P saves time and helps ensure that user privacy is protected.

Microsoft is encouraging the adoption of P3P for consumer privacy protection—the company includes P3P in Internet Explorer 6.0 and Microsoft Passport technology. In Internet Explorer, users can choose between several predefined levels of security (from accepting all cookies to blocking all cookies, with intermediate settings that restrict cookies from certain kinds of sites). A user can also specify certain sites for which the privacy preferences can be overridden. When the user reaches a P3P-enabled site, the computer compares the site's privacy polices to the user's personal privacy settings. If the site provides an acceptable amount of privacy, Internet Explorer lets the user continue to browse the site without interruption and allows the site to store personal information in cookies. If the user reaches a site with a privacy policy that violates the privacy preferences, the Internet Explorer window alerts the user and allows the user to choose what personal information to disclose to the site. Any cookies that violate the user's privacy preferences are rejected. IBM's P3P Policy Editor, a visual tool for generating P3P-compliant policy files in XML, is available for download at `www.alphaworks.ibm.com/tech/p3peditor`.

12.12.1 Denial-of-Service (DoS) Attacks

A denial-of-service attack occurs when a system is forced to behave improperly. In many DoS attacks, unauthorized traffic takes up a network's resources, restricting access for legitimate users. Typically, the attack is performed by flooding servers with data packets. Denial-of-service attacks usually require the power of a network of computers working simultaneously, although some skillful attacks can be achieved with a single machine. Denial-of-service attacks can cause networked computers to crash or disconnect, disrupting service on a Web site or even shutting down critical systems such as telecommunications or flight-control centers

Another type of denial-of-service attack targets the *routing tables* of a network. Routing tables are the road map of a network, providing directions for data to get from one computer to another. This type of attack is accomplished by modifying the routing tables, thus disabling network activity. For example, the routing tables can be changed to send all data to one address in the network.

In a *distributed denial-of-service attack*, the packet flooding does not come from a single source, but from many separate computers. Actually, such an attack is rarely the concerted work of many individuals. Instead, it is the work of a single individual who has installed viruses on various computers, gaining illegitimate use of the computers to carry out the attack. Distributed denial-of-service attacks can be difficult to stop, since it is not clear which requests on a network are from legitimate users and which are part of the attack. In addition, it is particularly difficult to catch the culprit of such attacks, because the attacks are not carried out directly from the attacker's computer.

Who is responsible for viruses and denial-of-service attacks? Most often the responsible parties are referred to as *hackers* or *crackers*. Hackers and crackers are usually skilled programmers. According to some, hackers break into systems just for the thrill of it, without causing any harm to the compromised systems (except, perhaps, humbling and humiliating their owners). Either way, hackers break the law by accessing or damaging private information and computers. Crackers have malicious intent and are usually interested in breaking into a system to shut down services or steal data. In February 2000, distributed denial-of-service attacks shut down a number of high-traffic Web sites, including Yahoo!, eBay, CNN Interactive and Amazon. In this case, a cracker used a network of computers to flood the Web sites with traffic that overwhelmed the sites' computers. Although denial-of-service attacks merely shut off access to a Web site and do not affect the victim's data, they can be extremely costly. For example, when eBay's Web site went down for a 24-hour period on August 6, 1999, its stock value declined dramatically.[28]

12.12.2 Viruses and Worms

Viruses are pieces of code—often sent as attachments or hidden in audio clips, video clips and games—that attach to, or overwrite other programs to replicate themselves. Viruses can corrupt files or even wipe out a hard drive. Before the Internet was invented, viruses spread through files and programs (such as video games) transferred to computers by removable disks. Today, viruses are spread over a network simply by sharing "infected" files embedded in e-mail attachments, documents or programs. A worm is similar to a virus, except that it can spread and infect files on its own over a network; worms do not need to be attached to another program to spread. Once a virus or worm is released, it can spread rapidly, often infecting millions of computers worldwide within minutes or hours.

There are many classes of computer viruses. A *transient virus* attaches itself to a specific computer program. The virus is activated when the program is run and deactivated when the program is terminated. A more powerful type of virus is a *resident virus*, which, once loaded into the memory of a computer, operates for the duration of the computer's use. Another type of virus is the *logic bomb*, which triggers when a given condition is met, such as a *time bomb* that is activated when the clock on the computer matches a certain time or date.

A *Trojan horse* is a malicious program that hides within a friendly program or simulates the identity of a legitimate program or feature, while actually causing damage to the computer or network in the background. The Trojan horse gets its name from the story of the Trojan War in Greek history. In this story, Greek warriors hid inside a wooden horse, which the Trojans took within the walls of the city of Troy. When night fell and the Trojans were asleep, the Greek warriors came out of the horse and opened the gates to the city, letting the Greek army enter the gates and destroy the city of Troy. Trojan horse programs can be particularly difficult to detect, since they appear to be legitimate and useful applications. Also commonly associated with Trojan horses are *backdoor programs*, which are usually resident viruses that give the sender complete, undetected access to the victim's computer resources. These types of viruses are especially threatening to the victim, as they can be set up to log every keystroke (capturing all passwords, credit card numbers, etc.) No matter how secure the connection between a PC supplying private information and the server receiving the information, if a backdoor program is running on a computer, the data is intercepted before any encryption is implemented.

Two of the most famous viruses to date are *Melissa*, which struck in March 1999, and the *ILOVEYOU virus* that hit in May 2000. Both viruses cost organizations and individuals billions of dollars. The Melissa virus spread in Microsoft Word documents sent via e-mail. When the document was opened, the virus was triggered. Melissa accessed the Microsoft Outlook address book on that computer and automatically sent the infected Word attachment by e-mail to the first 50 people in the address book. Each time another person opened the attachment, the virus would send out another 50 messages. Once in a system, the virus infected any subsequently saved files.

The ILOVEYOU virus was sent as an attachment to an e-mail posing as a love letter. The message in the e-mail said "Kindly check the attached love letter coming from me." Once opened, the virus accessed the Outlook address book and sent out messages to the addresses listed, helping to spread the virus rapidly worldwide. The virus corrupted all types of files, including system files. Networks at companies and government organizations worldwide were shut down for days trying to remedy the problem and contain the virus. This virus accentuated the importance of scanning file attachments for security threats before opening them.

Why do these viruses spread so quickly? One reason is that many people are too willing to open executable files from unknown sources. Have you ever opened an audio clip or video clip from a friend? Have you ever forwarded that clip to other friends? Do you know who created the clip and if any viruses are embedded in it? Did you open the ILOVE YOU file to see what the love letter said?

Most antivirus software is reactive, going after viruses once they are discovered, rather than protecting against unknown viruses. New antivirus software, such as Finjan Software's SurfinGuard® (**www.finjan.com**), looks for executable files attached to e-mail and runs the executables in a secure area to test if they attempt to access and harm files. For more information about antivirus software, see the **McAfee.com**: Antivirus Utilities feature.

12.12.3 Software Exploitation, Web Defacing and Cybercrime

Another problem plaguing e-businesses is *software exploitation* by hackers. In addition to updating virus and firewall programs constantly, every program on a networked machine should be checked for vulnerabilities. However, with millions of software products available and vulnerabilities discovered daily, this becomes an enormous task. One common vulnerability exploitation method is a *buffer overflow*, in which a program is overwhelmed by an input of more data than it has allocated space for. Buffer overflow attacks can cause systems to crash or, more dangerously, allow arbitrary code to be run on a machine. *BugTraq* was created in 1993 to list vulnerabilities, how to exploit them and how to repair them. For more information about BugTraq, visit **www.security-focus.com**.

Web defacing is another popular form of attack, wherein the crackers illegally enter an organization's Web site and change the contents. CNN Interactive has issued a special report titled "Insurgency on the Internet," with news stories about hackers and their online attacks. Included is a gallery of defaced sites. One notable case of Web defacing occurred in 1996, when Swedish crackers changed the Central Intelligence Agency Web site to read "Central Stupidity Agency." The vandals put obscenities, political messages, notes to system administrators and links to adult-content sites on the page. Many other popular and large Web sites have been defaced. Defacing Web sites has become overwhelmingly popular amongst crackers today, causing archives of attacked sites (with records of more than 15,000 vandalized sites) to close because of the volume in which sites were being vandalized daily.[29]

Cybercrime can have significant financial implications on an organization.[30] Companies need to protect their data, intellectual property, customer information, etc. Implementing a *security policy* is key to protecting an organization's data and network. When developing a security plan, organizations must assess their vulnerabilities and the possible threats to security. What information do they need to protect? Who are the possible attackers and what is their intent—data theft or damaging the network? How will the organization respond to incidents?[31] For more information about security and security plans, visit **www.cerias.com** and **www.sans.org** (see the SANS Institute: Security Research and Education feature). Visit **www.baselinesoft.com** to check out books and CD-ROMs on security policies. Baseline Software's book, *Information Policies Made Easy: Version 7* includes over 1000 security policies. This book is used by numerous Fortune 200 companies.

The rise in cybercrimes has prompted the U. S. government to take action. Under the National Information Infrastructure Protection Act of 1996, denial-of-service attacks and distribution of viruses are federal crimes punishable by fines and jail time. For more information about the U. S. government's efforts against cybercrime or to read about recently prosecuted cases, visit the U.S. Department of Justice Web site, at **www.usdoj.gov/criminal/cybercrime/compcrime.html**. Also check out **www.cybercrime.gov**, a site maintained by the Criminal Division of the U. S. Department of Justice.

The *CERT® (Computer Emergency Response Team) Coordination Center* at Carnegie Mellon University's Software Engineering Institute responds to reports of viruses and denial-of-service attacks and provides information on network security, including how to determine if a system has been compromised. The site provides detailed incident reports of viruses and denial-of-service attacks, including descriptions of the incidents, their impact and solutions. The site also includes reports of vulnerabilities in popular operating systems and software packages. The *CERT Security Improvement Modules* are excellent tutorials on network security. These modules describe the issues and technologies used to solve network security problems. For more information, visit the CERT Web site, at **www.cert.org**.

To learn more about how you can protect yourself or your network from hacker attacks, visit AntiOnline™, at **www.antionline.com**. This site has security-related news and information, a tutorial titled "Fight-back! Against Hackers," information about hackers and an archive of hacked sites. You can find additional information about denial-of-service attacks and how to protect your site at **www.denialinfo.com**.

12.13 Network Security

The goal of network security is to allow authorized users access to information and services, while preventing unauthorized users from gaining access to, and possibly corrupting, the network. There is a trade-off between network security and network performance: Increased security often decreases the efficiency of the network.

In this section, we will discuss the various aspects of network security. We will discuss firewalls, which keep unauthorized users out of the network, and authorization servers, which allow users to access specific applications based on a set of pre-defined criteria. We will then look at intrusion detection systems that actively monitor a network for intrusions and attacks. Finally, biometric authentication will be discussed. In Chapter 13, Web Services Security, we will examine how Web services affect network security.

12.13.1 Firewalls

A basic tool in network security is the *firewall*. The purpose of a firewall is to protect a *local area network* (*LAN*) from intruders outside the network. For example, most companies have internal networks that allow employees to share files and access company information. Each LAN can be connected to the Internet through a gateway, which usually includes a firewall. For years, one of the biggest threats to security came from employees inside the firewall. Now that businesses rely heavily on access to the Internet, an increasing number of security threats are originating outside the firewall—from the hundreds of millions of people connected to the company network by the Internet.[32] A firewall acts as a safety barrier for data flowing into and out of the LAN. Firewalls can prohibit all data flow not expressly allowed, or can allow all data flow that is not expressly prohibited. The choice between these two models is up to the network security administrator and should be based on the need for security versus the need for functionality.

There are two main types of firewalls: *packet-filtering firewalls* and *application-level gateways*. A packet-filtering firewall examines all data sent from outside the LAN and automatically rejects any data packets that have local network addresses. For example, if a hacker from outside the network obtains the address of a computer inside the network and tries to sneak a harmful data packet through the firewall, the packet-filtering firewall will reject the data packet, since it has an internal address, but originated from outside the network. A problem with packet-filtering firewalls is that they consider only the source of data packets; they do not examine the actual data. As a result, malicious viruses can be installed on an authorized user's computer, giving the hacker access to the network without the authorized user's knowledge. The goal of an application-level gateway is to screen the actual data. If the message is deemed safe, then the message is sent through to the intended receiver.

Using a firewall is probably the most effective and easiest way to add security to a small network.[33] Often, small companies or home users who are connected to the Internet through permanent connections, such as DSL lines, do not employ strong security measures. As a result, their computers are prime targets for crackers to use in denial-of-service attacks or to steal information. It is important for all computers connected to the Internet to have some degree of security for their systems. Numerous firewall software products are available. Several products are listed in the Web resources in Section 12.16.

Air gap technology is a network security solution that complements the firewall. It secures private data from external traffic accessing the internal network. The *air gap* separates the internal network from the external network, and the organization decides which information will be made available to external users. *Whale Communications* created the *e-Gap System*, which is composed of two computer servers and a *memory bank*. The memory bank does not run an operating system, therefore hackers cannot take advantage of common operating system weaknesses to access network information.

Air gap technology does not allow outside users to view the network's structure, preventing hackers from searching the layout for weak spots or specific data. The e-Gap *Web Shuttle* feature allows safe external access by restricting the system's *back office*, which is where an organization's most sensitive information and IT-based business processes are controlled. Users who want to access a network hide behind the air gap, where the authentication server is located. Authorized users gain access through a single sign-on capability, allowing them to use one log-in password to access authorized areas of the network.

The e-Gap *Secure File Shuttle* feature moves files in and out of the network. Each file is inspected behind the air gap. If the file is deemed safe, it is carried by the File Shuttle into the network.[34]

Air gap technology is used by e-commerce organizations to allow their clients and partners to access information automatically, thus reducing the cost of inventory management. Military, aerospace and government industries, which store highly sensitive information, use air gap technology.

12.13.2 Intrusion Detection Systems

What happens if a hacker gets inside your firewall? How do you know if an intruder has penetrated the firewall? Also, how do you know if unauthorized employees are accessing restricted applications? *Intrusion detection systems* monitor networks and application *log files*—files containing information on files, including who accessed them and when—so if an intruder makes it into the network or an unauthorized application, the system detects the intrusion, halts the session and sets off an alarm to notify the system administrator.[35]

Host-based intrusion detection systems monitor system and application log files. They can be used to scan for Trojan horses, for example. *Network-based intrusion detection* software monitors traffic on a network for any unusual patterns that might indicate DoS attacks or attempted entry into a network by an unauthorized user. Companies can then check their log files to determine if indeed there was an intrusion and if so, they can attempt to track the offender. Check out the intrusion detection products from Cisco (**www.cisco.com/warp/public/cc/pd/sqsw/sqidsz**), Hewlett-Packard (**www.hp.com/security/home.html**) and Symantec (**www.symantec.com**).

The *OCTAVE*[SM] (*Operationally Critical Threat, Asset and Vulnerability Evaluation*) *method*, under development at the Software Engineering Institute at Carnegie Mellon University, is a process for evaluating security threats of a system. There are three phases in OCTAVE: building threat profiles, identifying vulnerabilities, and developing security solutions and plans. In the first stage, the organization identifies its important information and assets, then evaluates the levels of security required to protect them. In the second phase, the system is examined for weaknesses that could compromise the valuable data. The third phase is to develop a security strategy as advised by an analysis team of three to five security experts assigned by OCTAVE. This approach is one of the firsts of its kind, in which the owners of computer systems not only get to have professionals analyze their systems, but also participate in prioritizing the protection of crucial information.[36]

12.14 Steganography

Steganography is the practice of hiding information within other information. The term literally means "covered writing." Like cryptography, steganography has been used since ancient times. Steganography allows you to take a piece of information, such as a message or image, and hide it within another image, message or even an audio clip. Steganography takes advantage of insignificant space in digital files, in images or on removable disks.[37] Consider a simple example: If you have a message that you want to send secretly, you can hide the information within another message, so that no one but the intended receiver can read it. For example, if you want to tell your stockbroker to buy a stock and your message must be transmitted over an unsecure channel, you could send the message "BURIED UNDER YARD." If you have agreed in advance that your message is hidden in the first letters of each word, the stock broker picks these letters off and sees "BUY."

An increasingly popular application of steganography is *digital watermarks* for intellectual property protection. An example of a conventional watermark is shown in Fig. 12.7. A digital watermark can be either visible or invisible. It is usually a company logo, copyright notification or other mark or message that indicates the owner of the document. The owner of a document could show the hidden watermark in a court of law, for example, to prove that the watermarked item was stolen.

Digital watermarking could have a substantial impact on e-commerce. Consider the music industry. Music publishers are concerned that MP3 technology is allowing people to distribute illegal copies of songs and albums. As a result, many publishers are hesitant to put content online, as digital content is easy to copy. Also, since CD-ROMs are digital, people are able to upload their music and share it over the Web. Using digital watermarks, music publishers can make indistinguishable changes to a part of a song at a frequency that is not audible to humans, to show that the song was, in fact, copied. Microsoft Research is developing a watermarking system for digital audio, which would be included with default Windows media players. In this digital watermarking system, data such as licensing information is embedded into a song; the media player will not play files with invalid information.

Blue Spike's Giovanni™ digital watermarking software uses cryptographic keys to generate and embed steganographic digital watermarks into digital music and images

(Fig. 12.8). The watermarks can be used as proof of ownership to help digital publishers protect their copyrighted material. The watermarks are undetectable by anyone who is not privy to the embedding scheme, and thus the watermarks cannot be identified and removed. The watermarks are placed randomly.

Digital watermarking capabilities are built into some image-editing software applications, such as Adobe PhotoShop 7.0 (**www.adobe.com**). Digimarc (**www.digimark.com**) is an example of a company that offers digital watermarking solutions.

In the last few chapters, we discussed the technologies involved in building and running an Web services. In Chapter 13, Web Services Security, we will discuss the technologies, protocols and standards used to secure Web services.

12.15 Summary

The field of security places emphasis on privacy, integrity, authentication, authorization and non-repudiation. Cryptography transforms data by using a cipher, or cryptosystem—a mathematical procedure for encrypting messages. A key—a string of digits that acts as a password—is input to the cipher. The algorithm uses the key to make data incomprehensible to all but the sender and intended receiver. Secret-key cryptography uses the same secret key to encrypt and decrypt a message. One of the most commonly used symmetric encryption algorithms is DES. The new standard is called AES. Rijndael was chosen as the AES candidate. Public-key cryptography was designed to solve the problem of exchanging keys securely. Public-key cryptography is asymmetric and uses two inversely related keys: a public key and a private key. The most common key agreement protocol is a digital envelope. With a digital envelope, the message is encrypted using a secret key, and the secret key is encrypted using public-key encryption.

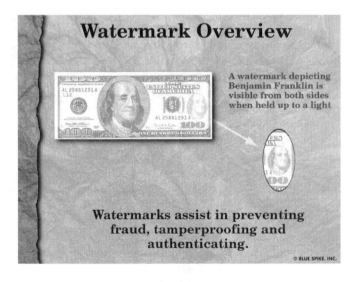

Fig. 12.7   Example of a conventional watermark. (Courtesy of Blue Spike, Inc.)

Fig. 12.8　An example of steganography: Blue Spike's Giovanni digital watermarking process. (Courtesy of Blue Spike, Inc.)

Digital signatures, the electronic equivalent of written signatures, were developed to be used in public-key cryptography to solve the problems of authentication and integrity. A digital signature authenticates the sender's identity, and, like a written signature, is difficult to forge. Timestamping, which binds a time and date to a digital document, can help solve the problem of non-repudiation. Public Key Infrastructure (PKI) integrates public-key cryptography with digital certificates and certificate authorities to authenticate parties in a transaction. A digital certificate is a digital document used to identify a user public key that is issued by a certificate authority. Trying to decrypt ciphertext without knowledge of the decryption key is known as cryptanalysis.

SSL is primarily used to secure point-to-point connections—transmissions of data from one computer to another. Virtual Private Networks (VPNs) use the Internet infrastructure that is already in place. VPNs provide the same services as private networks but use a different technique for connecting devices. IPSec uses public-key and symmetric key cryptography to ensure user authentication, data integrity and confidentiality. IPSec enables the secure connection of an entire VPN.

A denial-of-service attack occurs when a network's resources are taken up by an unauthorized individual, leaving the network unavailable for legitimate users. Viruses are computer programs that attach to, or overwrite other programs to replicate themselves. Viruses can corrupt files or even wipe out a hard drive. Software exploitation by hackers can cause systems to crash or, more dangerously, allow arbitrary code to be run on a machine.

The goal of network security is to allow authorized users access to information and services, while preventing unauthorized users from gaining access to, and possibly corrupting, the network. A basic tool in network security is the firewall. The purpose of a firewall is to protect a local area network (LAN) from intruders outside the network. Air Gap technology secures a business' data from external traffic accessing the internal network. Kerberos authenticates users in a network and maintains the integrity and privacy of network communications. Intrusion-detection systems monitor networks and alert administrators to unauthorized access of applications.

Biometrics uses unique personal information, such as fingerprints, eyeball iris scans or face scans, to identify a user and eliminate the need for passwords. Steganography is the practice of hiding information within other information. Digital watermarking could have a substantial impact on e-commerce. Using digital watermarks, music publishers can make indistinguishable changes to a part of a song at a frequency that is not audible to humans, to show that the song was, in fact, copied.

12.16 Internet and Web Resources

Security Resource Sites

www.securitysearch.com
This is a comprehensive resource for computer security, with thousands of links to products, security companies, tools and more. The site also offers a free weekly newsletter with information about vulnerabilities.

www.esecurityonline.com
This site is a great resource for information on online security. The site has links to news, tools, events, training and other valuable security information and resources.

theory.lcs.mit.edu/~rivest/crypto-security.html
The *Ronald L. Rivest: Cryptography and Security* site has an extensive list of links to security resources, including newsgroups, government agencies, FAQs, tutorials and more.

www.w3.org/Security/Overview.html
The *W3C Security Resources* site has FAQs, information about W3C security and e-commerce initiatives and links to other security related Web sites.

web.mit.edu/network/ietf/sa
The Internet Engineering Task Force (IETF), which is an organization concerned with the architecture of the Internet, has working groups dedicated to Internet Security. Visit the *IETF Security Area* to learn about the working groups, join the mailing list or read the latest drafts of the IETF's work.

dir.yahoo.com/Computers_and_Internet/Security_and_Encryption
The *Yahoo Security and Encryption* page is a great resource for security and encryption Web sites.

www.counterpane.com/hotlist.html
The Counterpane Internet Security, Inc., site includes links to downloads, source code, FAQs, tutorials, alert groups, news and more.

www.rsasecurity.com/rsalabs/faq
This site is an excellent set of FAQs about cryptography from RSA Laboratories, one of the leading makers of public key cryptosystems.

www.nsi.org/compsec.html
Visit the National Security Institute's *Security Resource Net* for the latest security alerts, government standards, and legislation, as well as security FAQs links and other helpful resources.

www.itaa.org/infosec
The Information Technology Association of America (ITAA) *InfoSec* site has information about the latest U.S. government legislation related to information security.

staff.washington.edu/dittrich/misc/ddos
The *Distributed Denial of Service Attacks* site has links to news articles, tools, advisory organizations and even a section on security humor.

www.infoworld.com/cgi-bin/displayNew.pl?/security/links/ security_corner.htm
The *Security Watch* site on **Infoword.com** has loads of links to security resources.

www.antionline.com
AntiOnline has security-related news and information, a tutorial titled "Fight-back! Against Hackers," information about hackers and an archive of hacked sites.

www.microsoft.com/security/default.asp
The Microsoft security site has links to downloads, security bulletins and tutorials.

www.grc.com
This site offers a service to test the security of your computer's Internet connection.

www.sans.org
Sans Institute presents information on security updates, along with new research and discoveries.

www.ntbugtraq.com
This site provides a list and description of various Windows NT Security Exploits/Bugs encountered by Windows NT users. One can download updated service applications.

www.securitystats.com
This computer security site provides statistics on viruses, web defacements and security spending.

Magazines, Newsletters and News sites

www.networkcomputing.com/consensus
The *Security Alert Consensus* is a free weekly newsletter with information about security threats, holes, solutions and more.

www.atstake.com/security_news
Visit this site for daily security news.

www.infosecuritymag.com
Information Security Magazine has the latest Web security news and vendor information.

www.ieee-security.org/cipher.html
Cipher is an electronic newsletter on security and privacy from the Institute of Electrical and Electronics Engineers (IEEE). You can view current and past issues online.

securityportal.com
The *Security Portal* has news and information about security, cryptography and the latest viruses.

www.scmagazine.com
SC Magazine has news, product reviews and a conference schedule for security events.

www.cnn.com/TECH/specials/hackers
Insurgency on the Internet from CNN Interactive has news on hacking, plus a gallery of hacked sites.

Government Sites for Computer Security

www.cit.nih.gov/security.html
This site has links to security organizations, resources and tutorials on PKI, SSL and other protocols.

cs-www.ncsl.nist.gov
The *Computer Security Resource Clearing House* is a resource for network administrators and others concerned with security. This site has links to incident-reporting centers, information about security standards, events, publications and other resources.

www.cdt.org/crypto
Visit the Center for Democracy and Technology for U. S. cryptography legislation and policy news.

www.epm.ornl.gov/~dunigan/security.html
This site has links organized by subject and include resources on digital signatures, PKI, smart cards, viruses, commercial providers, intrusion detection and several other topics.

www.alw.nih.gov/Security
The *Computer Security Information* page is an excellent resource, providing links to news, newsgroups, organizations, software, FAQs and an extensive number of Web links.

www.fedcirc.gov
The Federal Computer Incident Response Capability deals with the security of government and civilian agencies. This site has information about incident statistics, advisories, tools, patches and more.

axion.physics.ubc.ca/pgp.html
This site has a list of freely available cryptosystems, discussions of each system and links to FAQs and tutorials.

www.ifccfbi.gov
The Internet Fraud Complaint Center, founded by the Justice Department and the FBI, fields reports of Internet fraud.

www.disa.mil/infosec/iaweb/default.html
The Defense Information Systems Agency's *Information Assurance* page includes links to sites on vulnerability warnings, virus information and incident-reporting instructions, and other helpful links.

www.nswc.navy.mil/ISSEC/
The objective of this site is to provide information on protecting your computer systems from security hazards. Contains a page on hoax versus real viruses.

cs-www.ncsl.nist.gov/
The Computer Security Resource Center provides services for vendors and end users. The site includes information on security testing, management, technology, education and applications.

Advanced Encryption Standard (AES)

csrc.nist.gov/encryption/aes
The official site for the AES includes press releases and a discussion forum.

www.esat.kuleuven.ac.be/~rijmen/rijndael/
Visit this site for information about the Rijndael algorithm.

home.ecn.ab.ca/~jsavard/crypto/co040801.htm
This AES site includes an explanation of the algorithm with helpful diagrams and examples.

Internet Security Vendors

www.rsasecurity.com
RSA is one of the leaders in electronic security. Visit its site for more information about its current products and tools, which are used by companies worldwide.

www.checkpoint.com
Check Point™ Software Technologies is a leading provider of Internet security products and services.

www.opsec.com
The Open Platform for Security (OPSEC) has over 200 partners that develop security products and solutions using the OPSEC to allow for interoperability and increased security over a network.

www.baltimore.com
Baltimore Security is an e-commerce security solutions provider. Their UniCERT digital certificate product is used in PKI applications.

www.ncipher.com
nCipher is a vendor of hardware and software products, including an SSL accelerator that increases the speed of secure Web server transactions and a secure key management system.

www.antivirus.com
ScanMail® is an e-mail virus detection program for Microsoft Exchange.

www.zixmail.com
Zixmail™ is a secure e-mail product that allows you to encrypt and digitally sign your messages

web.mit.edu/network/pgp.html
Visit this site to download *Pretty Good Privacy®* freeware. PGP allows you to send messages and files securely.

www.certicom.com
Certicom provides security solutions for the wireless Internet.

www.raytheon.com
Raytheon Corporation's *SilentRunner* monitors network activity to find internal threats.

SSL

developer.netscape.com/tech/security/ssl/protocol.html
This Netscape page has a brief description of SSL, plus links to an SSL tutorial and FAQs.

www.netscape.com/security/index.html
The Netscape Security Center is an extensive resource for Internet and Web security. You will find news, tutorials, products and services on this site.

psych.psy.uq.oz.au/~ftp/Crypto
This FAQs page has an extensive list of questions and answers about SSL technology.

Public-key Cryptography

www.entrust.com
Entrust produces effective security software products using Public Key Infrastructure (PKI).

www.cse.dnd.ca
The Communication Security Establishment has a short tutorial on Public Key Infrastructure (PKI) that defines PKI, public-key cryptography and digital signatures.

www.magnet.state.ma.us/itd/legal/pki.htm
The Commonwealth of Massachusetts Information Technology page has loads of links to sites related to PKI that contain information about standards, vendors, trade groups and government organizations.

www.ftech.net/~monark/crypto/index.htm
The Beginner's Guide to Cryptography is an online tutorial and includes links to other sites on privacy and cryptography.

www.faqs.org/faqs/cryptography-faq
The *Cryptography FAQ* has an extensive list of questions and answers.

www.pkiforum.org
The PKI Forum promotes the use of PKI.

www.counterpane.com/pki-risks.html
Visit the Counterpane Internet Security, Inc.'s site to read the article "Ten Risks of PKI: What You're Not Being Told About Public Key Infrastructure."

Digital Signatures

www.ietf.org/html.charters/xmldsig-charter.html
The *XML Digital Signatures* site was created by a group working to develop digital signatures using XML. You can view the group's goals and drafts of their work.

www.elock.com
E-Lock Technologies is a vendor of digital-signature products used in Public Key Infrastructure. This site has an FAQs list covering cryptography, keys, certificates and signatures.

www.digsigtrust.com
The Digital Signature Trust Co. is a vendor of Digital Signature and Public Key Infrastructure products. It has a tutorial titled "Digital Signatures and Public Key Infrastructure (PKI) 101."

Digital Certificates

www.verisign.com
VeriSign creates digital IDs for individuals, small businesses and large corporations. Check out its Web site for product information, news and downloads.

www.thawte.com
Thawte Digital Certificate Services offers SSL, developer and personal certificates.

www.belsign.be
Belsign issues digital certificates in Europe. It is the European authority for digital certificates.

www.certco.com
Certco issues digital certificates to financial institutions.

www.openca.org
Set up your own CA using open-source software from The OpenCA Project.

Firewalls

www.interhack.net/pubs/fwfaq
This site provides an extensive list of FAQs on firewalls.

www.spirit.com/cgi-bin/report.pl
Visit this site to compare firewall software from a variety of vendors.

www.zeuros.co.uk/generic/resource/firewall
Zeuros is a complete resource for information about firewalls. You will find FAQs, books, articles, training and magazines on this site.

www.thegild.com/firewall
The *Firewall Product Overview* site has an extensive list of products, with links to each vendor's site.

www.watchguard.com
WatchGuard® Technologies provides security solutions for medium to large organizations.

Kerberos

www.nrl.navy.mil/CCS/people/kenh/kerberos-faq.html
This site is an extensive list of FAQs on Kerberos from the Naval Research Laboratory.

web.mit.edu/kerberos/www
Kerberos: The Network Authentication Protocol is a list of FAQs provided by MIT.

www.contrib.andrew.cmu.edu/~shadow/kerberos.html
The Kerberos Reference Page has links to several informational sites, technical sites and other helpful resources.

www.pdc.kth.se/kth-krb
Visit this site to download various Kerberos white papers and documentation.

Biometrics

www.iosoftware.com/products/integration/fiu500/index.htm
This site describes a security device that scans a user's fingerprint to verify identity.

www.identix.com
Identix specializes in fingerprinting systems for law enforcement, access control and network security. Using its fingerprint scanners, you can log on to your system, encrypt/decrypt files and more.

www.keytronic.com
Key Tronic manufactures keyboards with fingerprint recognition systems.

IPSec and VPNs

www.checkpoint.com
Check Point™ offers combined firewall and VPN solutions. Visit their resource library for links to numerous white papers, industry groups, mailing lists and other security and VPN resources.

www.ietf.org/html.charters/ipsec-charter.html
The IPSec Working Group of the Internet Engineering Task Force (IETF) is a resource for technical information related to the IPSec protocol.

www.icsalabs.com/html/communities/ipsec/certification/certified_products/index.shtml
Visit this site for a list of IPSec products, plus links to an IPSec glossary and other related resources.

www.vpnc.org
The Virtual Private Network Consortium, which has VPN standards, white papers, definitions and archives. VPNC also offers compatibility testing with current VPN standards.

Steganography and Digital Watermarking

www.bluespike.com
Blue Spike's *Giovanni* watermarks help publishers of digital content protect their copyrighted material and track their content that is distributed electronically.

www.outguess.org
Outguess is a freely available steganographic tool.

www.cl.cam.ac.uk/~fapp2/steganography/index.html
The Information Hiding Homepage has technical information, news and links related to digital watermarking and steganography.

www.demcom.com
DemCom's *Steganos Security Suite* software allows you to encrypt and hide files within audio, video, text or HTML files.

Newsgroups

news:comp.security.firewalls

news:comp.security.unix

news:comp.security.misc

news:comp.protocols.kerberos

WORKS CITED

1.   B. Gates, "Bill Gates: Trustworthy Computing," 17 January 2002 <**www.wired.com/news/business/0,1367,49826,00.html**>.

2. "RSA Laboratories' Frequently Asked Questions About Today's Cryptography, Version 4.1," 2000 **<www.rsasecurity.com/rsalabs/faq>**.

3. **<www-math.cudenver.edu/~wcherowi/courses/m5410/m5410des.html>**.

4. M. Dworkin, "Advanced Encryption Standard (AES) Fact Sheet," 5 March 2001.

5. **<www.esat.kuleuven.ac.be/~rijmen/rijndael>**.

6. **<www.rsasecurity.com/rsalabs/rsa_algorithm>**.

7. **<www.pgpi.org/doc/overview>**.

8. **<www.rsasecurity.com/rsalabs/faq>**.

9. G. Hulme, "VeriSign Gave Microsoft Certificates to Imposter," *Information Week* 3 March 2001.

10. C. Ellison and B. Schneier, "Ten Risks of PKI: What You're not Being Told about Public Key Infrastructure," *Computer Security Journal* 2000.

11. "What's So Smart About Smart Cards?" *Smart Card Forum*.

12. S. Abbot, "The Debate for Secure E-Commerce," *Performance Computing* February 1999: 37–42.

13. T. Wilson, "E-Biz Bucks Lost Under the SSL Train," *Internet Week* 24 May 1999: 1, 3.

14. H. Gilbert, "Introduction to TCP/IP," 2 February 1995 **<www.yale.edu/pclt/COMM/TCPIP.HTM>**.

15. RSA Laboratories, "Security Protocols Overview," 1999 **<www.rsasecurity.com/standards/protocols>**.

16. M. Bull, "Ensuring End-to-End Security with SSL," *Network World* 15 May 2000: 63.

17. **<www.cisco.com/warp/public/44/solutions/network/vpn.shtml>**.

18. S. Burnett and S. Paine, *RSA Security's Official Guide to Cryptography* (Berkeley: Osborne/McGraw-Hill, 2001) 210.

19. D. Naik, *Internet Standards and Protocols* Microsoft Press 1998: 79–80.

20. M. Grayson, "End the PDA Security Dilemma," *Communication News* February 2001: 38–40.

21. T. Wilson, "VPNs Don't Fly Outside Firewalls," *Internet Week* 28 May 2001.

22. S. Gaudin, "The Enemy Within," *Network World* 8 May 2000: 122–126.

23. D. Deckmyn, "Companies Push New Approaches to Authentication," *Computerworld* 15 May 2000: 6.

24. "Centralized Authentication," **<www.keyware.com>**.

25. J. Vijayan, "Biometrics Meet Wireless Internet," *Computerworld* 17 July 2000: 14.

26. F. Trickey, "Secure Single Sign-On: Fantasy or Reality," *CSI* **<www.gocsi.com>**.

27. L. Musthaler, "The Holy Grail of Single Sign-On," *Network World* 28 January 2002: 47.

28. "Securing B2B," *Global Technology Business* July 2000: 50–51.

29. T.Bridis, "U.S. Archive of Hacker Attacks To Close Because It Is Too Busy," *The Wall Street Journal* 24 May 2001: B10.

30. R. Marshland, "Hidden Cost of Technology," *Financial Times* 2 June 2000: 5.

31. F. Avolio, "Best Practices in Network Security," *Network Computing* 20 March 2000: 60–72.

32. R. Marshland, 5.

33. T. Spangler, "Home Is Where the Hack Is," *Inter@ctive Week* 10 April 2000: 28–34.

34. "Air Gap Technology," *Whale Communications* `<www.whale-com.com>`.

35. O. Azim and P. Kolwalkar, "Network Intrusion Monitoring," *Advisor.com/Security* March/April 2001: 16–19.

36. "OCTAVE Information Security Risk Evaluation," 30 January 2001 `<www.cert.org/octave/methodintro.html>`.

37. S. Katzenbeisser and F. Petitcolas, *Information Hiding: Techniques for Steganography and Digital Watermarking* (Norwood: Artech House, Inc., 2000) 1–2.

13

Web Services Security

Objectives

- To explain how traditional security methods can protect Web services transmissions.
- To discuss Web services security standards, including Security Assertion Markup Language (SAML) and XML Signature.
- To introduce XML Key Management Specification (XKMS) and XML Encryption.
- To explore emerging Web services standards, including WS-Security.
- To discuss how Web services affect network security.

Only in growth, reform, and change, paradoxically enough, is true security to be found.
Anne Morrow Lindbergh

First try and then trust.
John Clarke

Big Brother is Watching You.
George Orwell

Allies never trust each other, but that doesn't spoil their effectiveness.
Ayn Rand

Outline

13.1 Introduction

According to a Hurwitz Group study, security is the biggest obstacle to enterprise Web services adoption.[1] Web services move transactions beyond firewalls and enable outside entities to invoke applications, potentially giving outsiders access to sensitive information. As a result, Web services present new security challenges. Although existing security standards protect data as it travels over the Internet, Web services require additional measures to secure data.[2]

In Chapter 12, Computer and Internet Security, we provided a general introduction to computer and network security. This chapter builds on the foundation established in the previous chapter by focusing on Web services-specific security issues. We explore developing standards for Web services security, including Security Assertion Markup Language (SAML), XML Key Management Specification (XKMS), XML Signature and XML Encryption. We also describes how Web services affect network security and security policies.

Effective Web services security allows clients to access appropriate services while keeping sensitive information confidential. To access a secured Web service, users must provide some form of authentication, such as a login name combined with a password or digital certificate. Smart cards and biometrics provide stronger authentication. However, even when users are authenticated, login names, passwords and transmissions can be compromised if communications are not encrypted. Web services require end-to-end security for transactions that span multiple computers.

Interoperability is fundamental to Web services security, because transmissions often occur across multiple platforms and must be secured at all times. Software vendors are realizing the need for interoperable security and are cooperating to develop appropriate security standards. For example, the Web services security panel at *InfoWorld*'s *Next-Generation Web Services Conference* included representatives from Borland (**www.borland.com**), McAfee (**www.mcafee.com**) and SmartPipes (**www.smartpipes.com**). Software vendors and consortia—including the Liberty Alliance (**www.projectliberty.org**), Oblix (**www.oblix.com**) and Netegrity (**www.netegrity.com**)—are developing solutions to strengthen user authentication and to promote interoperability among Web services platforms.

Well-defined and well-documented security policies, as well as proper implementation, administration and maintenance, are crucial to any security infrastructure.[3] Thus far, organizations have been responsible for creating their own security policies, resulting in disparate security policies across organizations. The emergence of Web services is forcing industry to develop security-policy standards so that organizations can communicate effectively without compromising their security policies.[4]

Web services introduce more security and privacy concerns than previous technologies did. Standards used to implement Web services—such as XML, WSDL, UDDI and SOAP—do not directly address authorization issues such as access control and user-privilege rights.[5] The fundamental security requirements discussed in the previous chapter—privacy, integrity, authentication, authorization and non-repudiation—are essential in Web services transactions. To address Web services-specific security issues, software vendors and vendor consortia are developing new security standards. For example, SAML addresses Permissions Management Infrastructure (PMI)-related security concerns. XKMS establishes a specification for registering and distributing encryption keys for Public Key Infrastructure (PKI). XML Encryption protects data during transmissions. *XML Signature* adds authentication to files through various signature algorithms. The strong security provided by these technologies is crucial as Web services are implemented in business-critical and mission-critical systems.

13.2 Basic Security for Transmissions over HTTP

This section discusses the basic authentication and security features described in the HTTP specification (**www.w3.org/Protocols**). HTTP enables Web servers to authenticate users before allowing access to resources. A Web server might check a user's credentials (e.g., username and password) against a database before granting or denying access. HTTP security employs secret-key cryptography, message digests and other technologies discussed in the previous chapter. However, the methods outlined in the HTTP specification are weak (for example, HTTP provides no process for encrypting the body of a message). For stronger security, HTTP security should be used with other security technologies, such as SSL and Kerberos.

In *challenge-response authentication* (the method used in HTTP), users must provide specific authentication information to verify their identities. When an unauthenticated user attempts to view a protected resource over an HTTP connection, the server returns a **401 Unauthorized** response. The user must provide the server with a username and a password to access the resource. This username and password are established previously via some other method—such as an e-mail message. If the user's credentials are unacceptable, the server returns a **403 Forbidden** response and denies access to the resource. When used alone, challenge-response authentication (as defined in the HTTP specification) is a relatively weak security solution, because passwords and credentials are transmitted in plain-text. However, encryption and transport-layer security can be used with the protocol to provide stronger security.[6]

Digest authentication, part of the HTTP 1.1 specification, is a protocol in which a user's credentials are submitted to the server as a *checksum* (i.e., a message digest—discussed in Section 12.8, Digital Signatures). A message digest is a unique value derived from the message content. Checksums for digest authentication are generated using a user-name, password, the requested URI, the HTTP method and a unique value (known as a *nonce value*) generated by the server for each transmission. Digest authentication protects usernames and passwords from eavesdropping attackers, because credentials are not transmitted plain-text. MD5, the default algorithm used to create the checksum, generates a 128-bit message digest on the basis of the given input. Like message digests used in digital signatures, the generated checksums are unique to the input; therefore, no two are the same.[7] Although digest authentication is a step above basic authentication, this design does not encrypt the message content, which means that the content is vulnerable to interception. Also, both the server and the client must support digest authentication for authentication to take place. The HTTP 1.1 specification encourages using digest authentication with other authentication methods, such as public keys and Kerberos.[8]

A server also can restrict access on the basis of an IP address, password or public key. A server can disallow access to all or portions of a site for users with a certain IP address or from a specific *IP subnet* (e.g., a set of similar IP addresses, such as `123.123.45.23` and `123.123.67.89`). However, this method is vulnerable to IP spoofing (see Section 12.10.2, IPSec and Virtual Private Networks) and should be used in combination with other authorization techniques.

Password authentication also raises several concerns. Users often generate passwords using personal information (e.g., birthdays, pets' names, etc.), and crackers can compromise such passwords easily. Also, simple password authentication does not encrypt message content, so data can be compromised if a cracker intercepts transmissions. Public-key cryptography and other security methods should be used with basic HTTP security to ensure transmission security.

13.3 Web Services and Secure Sockets Layer (SSL)

Many of the Web services security technologies discussed in this chapter are still under development or are just being introduced to the market (see the WS-Security: A New Standard Protecting Web Services feature). Therefore, Web services must rely on established security standards until Web services-specific technologies mature.[9]

Secure Sockets Layer (SSL) is considered the next step beyond basic security for Web services (for introductory information on SSL, see Section 12.10.1, Secure Sockets Layer). The SSL protocol secures the channel through which data flows between a client and server and enables authentication of both parties. However, there are several problems with using SSL to secure Web services transmissions. SSL employs user credentials and certificates, which are sometimes too large to transmit efficiently between computers. This affects transaction success and disables the ability to record who initiated each step of a transaction.[10] SSL encryption calculations also use considerable processor power, which can slow down transmissions and significantly impede Web service performance. *SSL accelerators* are hardware devices or software programs that handle complex SSL-encryption calculations. Accelerators free server resources, improve performance and can be less expensive than setting up additional servers to handle SSL transactions.

In a transmission where a user provides a credit-card number to a business over an SSL connection, SSL authenticates both parties and guarantees the integrity of the data. However, in Web services interactions, information commonly passes through a third party before reaching its destination. If a user's information passes through another computer before reaching the final recipient, SSL cannot guarantee that the original data was not tampered with during the transmission, because SSL connects only two computers at a time. SSL protects data transmission, but does not provide end-to-end security.

HTTPS secures communications by sending HTTP requests and responses over an SSL connection. HTTPS connections generally take place over port 443, rather than the standard HTTP port 80. A majority of secure online transactions use HTTPS to provide end-to-end security between a client and server or consumer and vendor.

13.4 XML Signature and XML Encryption

XML-based applications raise significant security concerns, in part because XML documents are encoded in plain-text, rather than in a binary form. For example, externally referenced DTDs and stylesheets can be modified to omit, mangle or otherwise alter information. Even worse, these documents can be altered to leave large security holes, enabling anyone to access information. Digital signatures (discussed in Section 12.8, Digital Signatures) solve this problem by verifying document integrity.

WS-Security: A New Standard Protecting Web Services

In an attempt to improve Web services security, Microsoft, IBM and VeriSign have collaborated to create a new Web services security standard. The new specification, *WS-Security*, encrypts information and ensures the confidentiality of Web services transmissions.

WS-Security is the first of six Web services security specifications to be created by IBM and Microsoft. The specification is designed to secure SOAP-message transmissions.[11] Like many Web services security specifications, WS-Security is flexible and provides various security methods—including Kerberos, PKI and SSL. The specification also outlines how to use WS-Security with XML Signature and XML Encryption. According to Microsoft's director of Web services marketing, the proposed security standard will be compatible with any online authentication system, including Microsoft Passport and the Liberty Alliance Project's forthcoming single sign-on system.[12]

Six additional security specifications will be added to WS-Security in 2002–2003: WS-Policy, WS-Trust, WS-Privacy, WS-Secure Conversation, WS-Federation and WS-Authorization.[13] *WS-Policy* will define how to express a security policy's capabilities and limitations. XACML, a developing standard for representing security policies in XML, should comply with the WS-Policy standard.

WS-Trust will describe a model for establishing direct or third-party trust relationships. Trust relationships are necessary for issuing certificates used in XML Signature, Public Key Infrastructure (PKI) and the XML Key Management Specification (XKMS).

WS-Security: A New Standard Protecting Web Services (Cont.)

WS-Privacy will define how Web services express and carry out privacy practices. The Platform for Privacy Preferences (P3P) project is a W3C initiative designed to protect user privacy. Microsoft requires sites that use its Passport service to comply with P3P, and P3P will likely influence the WS-Privacy standard.

WS-Secure Conversation will describe how to manage message exchanges—including authenticating participants and establishing and deriving session keys (we discuss session keys in Chapter 12, Computer and Internet Security). *WS-Federation* will define how to manage trust relationships used in SAML, single sign-on and other B2B and authentication systems. Finally, *WS-Authorization* will define the management of authorization data and security policies.[14] To access the WS-Security specification, visit **www-106.ibm.com/developerworks/webservices/library/ws-secure**. Specifications for other WS-Security standards will be available online once the specifications are completed.

XML Trust Center—a vendor-neutral Web services security group sponsored by Verisign—created the Trust Services Integration Kit for building secure Web services using the WS-Security standard. To obtain additional information or to download this toolkit, visit **www.xmltrustcenter.org**.

The W3C's *XML Signature* specification defines an XML-based standard for representing digital signatures. XML Signature was developed by the *XML Signature Working Group*, the first formal joint project between the W3C and the Internet Engineering Task Force (IETF). The specification provides authentication, message integrity and nonrepudiation.[15] The algorithms used in the specification include the *Digital Signature Standard* (*DSS*) public-key algorithm and the *Secure Hash* (*SHA-1*) authentication algorithm (see Chapter 12, Computer and Internet Security). Developers can extend XML Signature to support their own algorithms and security models. An XML signature can sign any type of file, not just XML documents. The signed data can reside either inside or outside the XML document that contains the signature. The data object is cryptographically signed and used in generating a message digest. A *Uniform Resource Identifier* (*URI*) links the signature to the signed data object. XML Signature serves as the foundation for XKMS, SAML and other XML technologies that rely on authentication via digital signatures.[16]

As we explained in Chapter 12, Computer and Internet Security, different inputs to a hashing function produce different outputs. Hash functions verify data integrity, because it is impossible to determine the content of a message from the hash value. However, it is possible for two XML documents to contain the same data, yet differ in the way they are structured.[17] Such structure changes might break the signature between signer and verifier, even if the signed data has not changed. To prevent such problems, XML Signature puts data in *canonical form* before it is signed. If two documents have the same canonical form, they are logically equivalent. Small differences between documents—such as comments and spaces that have no impact on the meaning of an XML document—create different hash values. For this reason, XML Signature computes the hash value using the canonical form of an XML document. The *Canonical XML Specification* provides an algorithm that generates the canonical form of a document by transforming the document into a context as it would be interpreted by an application—this means that logically equivalent documents will produce the same message digest, regardless of structure.

Due to the complexity of online transactions, documents might require signatures from multiple parties. For example, when a customer purchases a book online using a credit card, an XML document containing the customer's name, address, credit-card information and order information is generated and submitted to the book seller and credit-card company (Fig. 13.1). Element **Personal** (lines 7–23) contains information, such as the credit-card number (line 18) and expiration date (line 20) in element **CreditCard** (lines 17–21) and the address information in element **Address** (lines 10–15), that must be protected as it is transmitted over the Internet.

A customer uses a signature to authenticate identity, then submits the information to the seller. The seller checks the integrity of the customer's signature and signs the document before submitting it to the credit-card company. The credit-card company receives signatures that verify the authenticity of the customer and the seller. XML Signature protects buyers against unauthorized purchases with their credit cards, increases the likelihood that retailers receive payments and prevents unauthorized businesses from using credit-card companies' services.

XML Signature provides three types of signatures. An *enveloping signature* contains the signed data as part of the signature. An *enveloped signature* resides within the data to be signed. A *detached signature* is stored separately from the signed data, but contains a reference to the signed data. If the encrypted data is not part of an XML document, a new XML document is created with **EncryptedData** as the root element. The markup in Fig. 13.2 is an example of a detached signature on the **Personal** element in the XML document **Fig12_1.xml** (Fig. 13.1).

```
1    <?xml version="1.0" encoding="UTF-8"?>
2    <!-- Fig. 13.1: Fig13_1.xml                            -->
3    <!-- XML that marks up an online bookstore purchase -->
4
5    <Purchase xmlns="http://examplebookstore.com/purchase">
6       <OrderNumber>99778866</OrderNumber>
7       <Personal>
8          <Name>Joe Smith</Name>
9
10         <Address>
11            <Street>123 Example Street</Street>
12            <City>Maynard</City>
13            <State>MA</State>
14            <Zip>01754</Zip>
15         </Address>
16
17         <CreditCard>
18            <Number>1234123412341234</Number>
19
20            <Expiration>12/04</Expiration>
21         </CreditCard>
```

Fig. 13.1 XML that marks up an online bookstore purchase. (Part 1 of 2.)

```
22
23      </Personal>
24
25      <ItemNumber quantity="1">000459</ItemNumber>
26   </Purchase>
```

Fig. 13.1   XML that marks up an online bookstore purchase. (Part 2 of 2.)

```
1    <?xml version="1.0" encoding="UTF-8"?>
2    <!-- Fig. 13.2: Fig13_2.xml                           -->
3    <!-- Detached XML Signature referencing an external element -->
4
5    <Signature Id="Purchase99778866"
6       xmlns="http://www.w3.org/TR/xmldsig-core">
7
8       <SignedInfo>
9
10         <CanonicalizationMethod Algorithm=
11            "http://www.w3.org/TR/2001/REC-xml-c14n-20010315"/>
12
13         <SignatureMethod Algorithm=
14           "http://www.w3.org/TR/2002/REC-xmldsig-core-20020212#sha1"/>
15
16         <Reference URI=
17            "http://www.example.com/purchase/Fig13_1.xml#Personal">
18
19            <Transforms>
20               <Transform Algorithm=
21                  "http://www.w3.org/TR/2001/REC-xml-c14n- 20010315"/>
22            </Transforms>
23
24            <DigestMethod Algorithm=
25            "http://www.w3.org/TR/2002/REC-xmldsig-core-20020212#sha1"/>
26
27            <DigestValue>
28            UI12389UUJFA09812JIA9123M10298REIU3JAIDHAWUYE982HA
29            </DigestValue>
30
31         </Reference>
32      </SignedInfo>
33
34      <SignatureValue>
35      FH5K17Z0IHTFR3N08Y1K5U239UFDKDN617ISDJAOWUEHAJR1UR
36      </SignatureValue>
37
38      <KeyInfo>
39         <KeyValue>
40            <X509Data>
41
```

Fig. 13.2   Detached XML Signature referencing an element in an external XML document. (Part 1 of 2.)

```
42                    <X509SubjectName>
43                        CN=Joe Smith, STREET=123 Example Street,
44                        L=Maynard, ST=MA, C=US
45                    </X509SubjectName>
46
47                    <X509Certificate>
48                        MIICWDCCAgICAQAwDQYJKoZIhvcNAQEEBQAwgbYxCzAJBgNVBAY
49                        TAlpBMRUwEwYDVQQIEwxXZXN0ZXJuIENhcGUxEjAQBgNVBAcTCUN
50                        hcGUgVG93bjEdMBsGA1UEChMUVGhhd3RlIENvbnN1bHRpbmcgY2M
51                        xHzAdBgNVBAsTFkNlcnRpZmljYXRpb24gU2VydmljZXMxFzAVBgN
52                        NVBa87421hjas2e8AYuidhuiaw471298IUAYISUYhu289yasiuy2
53                        JOiwejqwiojWEHuihqwjasndui12897ruhfjAOIQIEOU29081ifU
54                        7IUdhasun2IYEueh12e1iuYWAEAOOOidehqwunJSDNiuy12874js
55                        HH13i87ue1jhjaIUHAuhdnjweoAIJo2iJIAjhXHZBMoKkadsh813
56                        0YAuh893ieHAUhaodiuAIIA9uew8ACLetiX9usdjhds8wyeh1iu8
57                        9821yuAUSHiuhaapAMJXNBZZoiasdzkj02194yw8dyauh1o731i2
58                        D9324DIoetiksadj2q39oi14oiuOSAIDUOI2oismd6o7slau45==
59                    </X509Certificate>
60
61               </X509Data>
62           </KeyValue>
63       </KeyInfo>
64   </Signature>
```

Fig. 13.2 Detached XML Signature referencing an element in an external XML document. (Part 2 of 2.)

The **Signature Id** attribute on line 5 identifies the signature. Element **Signed-Info** (lines 8–32) contains information about the signature, including references to the algorithms used and the location of the signed data in the **Reference URI** attribute (lines 16–17). This signature uses the W3C's Canonical XML Version 1.0 Recommendation and the SHA-1 hashing algorithm. To sign an element in an XML document, the reference Uniform Resource Identifier (URI) contains the location of the document, followed by **#** and the name of the element. In our example, **#Personal** (line 17) references and signs the **Personal** element in the XML document. Lines 27–29 contain element **DigestValue**, which contains the message digest generated by the algorithm specified in the **DigestMethod**'s **Algorithm** attribute (lines 24–25). To verify that an XML digital signature is legitimate, the recipient runs the public version of the hashing algorithm on the received file and compares the result with the value in **DigestValue**. If the two values are not equivalent, then the digest might have been generated by a different file, or someone might have tampered with the data.[18] Element **SignatureValue** (lines 34–36) contains the message digest generated by the signature algorithm specified on lines 13–14 in the **SignatureMethod**'s **Algorithm** attribute. The optional **KeyInfo** element (lines 38–63) provides the key or certificate that the signature algorithm uses—in this case, an X.509 Digital Certificate (lines 48–58). Element **X509SubjectName** on lines 42–45 contains information about the key holder. XML Signature supports DSA Signatures, RSA Signatures and symmetric-key authentication codes (see Chapter 12, Computer and Internet Security).[19]

The signature verifies a sender's identity and the data's integrity, but encryption is necessary to prevent the signed data from being read en route. *XML Encryption* handles the encryption and decryption of XML documents that are secured with XML Signature. XML Encryption can protect any form of data, including an XML element and its contents.[20]

XML Encryption allows different elements of an XML document to be encrypted separately (Fig. 13.3).[21] The data to be encrypted is replaced by element **EncryptedData** in the XML document (lines 8–19). Element **CipherData** (lines 11–17) contains information about the ciphertext that is generated when the file is encrypted. The ciphertext is represented in *base-64 encoding*, which uses 64 characters (**a–z**, **A–Z**, **0–9** and the characters **/** and **+**) to represent binary data.[22] In enveloping and enveloped signatures, **CipherValue** (lines 13–15) stores the ciphertext inside the **CipherData** element. In a detached signature, **CipherReference** contains a URL that references the location of the ciphertext.[23]

Using the example of the online book seller, when a user makes a purchase, the bookstore generates an XML document containing the information submitted by the consumer (Fig. 13.1). To send this document to the seller and ensure that the personal information is protected, certain elements of the document must be encrypted.

The document in Fig. 13.3 contains the encrypted personal fields, leaving only the item and order numbers visible. Any unauthorized users attempting to view this document without the designated decryption key can access only the **ItemNumber** and **Order-Number** of the purchase.

In other cases, the bookstore might want to encrypt only the customer's credit-card information. For example, imagine that the bookstore forwards customers' personal data to a marketing database, but does not want to disclose credit-card data contained in element **CreditCard** (Fig. 13.1, lines 17–21). In Fig. 13.4, element **CreditCard** is replaced by **EncryptedData** (lines 18–28).

```
1   <?xml version="1.0" encoding="UTF-8"?>
2   <!-- Fig. 13.3: Fig13_3.xml                        -->
3   <!-- XML file with the Personal element encrypted -->
4
5   <Purchase xmlns="http://examplebookstore.com/purchase">
6      <OrderNumber>99778866</OrderNumber>
7
8      <EncryptedData xmlns="http://www.w3.org/TR/xmlenc-core"
9         Type="http://www.w3.org/TR/xmlenc-core#Element">
10
11        <CipherData>
12
13           <CipherValue>
14              H3OI2J2MOII12J4NSAKJH2UIAJWI098128321JI78293M92310CDA9
15           </CipherValue>
16
17        </CipherData>
18
19     </EncryptedData>
20
21        <ItemNumber quantity="1">000459</ItemNumber>
22  </Purchase>
```

Fig. 13.3 XML document with the **Personal** element encrypted.

```
1    <?xml version="1.0" encoding="UTF-8"?>
2    <!-- Fig. 13.4: Fig13_4.xml                                -->
3    <!-- XML document with the CreditCard element encrypted -->
4
5    <Purchase xmlns="http://examplebookstore.com/purchase">
6        <OrderNumber>99778866</OrderNumber>
7
8        <Personal>
9            <Name>Joe Smith</Name>
10
11           <Address>
12               <Street>123 Example Street</Street>
13               <City>Maynard</City>
14               <State>MA</State>
15               <Zip>01754</Zip>
16           </Address>
17
18          <EncryptedData xmlns="http://www.w3.org/TR/xmlenc-core"
19              Type="http://www.w3.org/TR/xmlenc-core#Content">
20              <CipherData>
21
22                  <CipherValue>
23                      92UIO2JFSDIOJL051N6HU872IAODMYJ71253LF819EYIYFGT87231
24                  </CipherValue>
25
26              </CipherData>
27
28          </EncryptedData>
29
30       </Personal>
31
32       <ItemNumber quantity="1">000459</ItemNumber>
33   </Purchase>
```

Fig. 13.4   XML document with the **CreditCard** element encrypted.

IBM's XML Security Suite implements XML Signature and XML Encryption. It is designed specifically for B2B transactions and provides support for digital signatures, encryption, access control, public-key cryptography and hash authentication. The XML Security Suite can be downloaded at **www.alphaworks.ibm.com/aw.nsf/ techs/xmlsecuritysuite**.

13.5 XML Key Management Specification (XKMS)

The *XML Key Management Specification (XKMS)* is a specification for registering and distributing encryption keys for Public Key Infrastructure (PKI) in Web services. XKMS was developed by Microsoft, VeriSign and webMethods, but now is a W3C initiative. Current communications and transactions using PKI are problematic, because no Web services PKI standards exist. Proprietary PKI solutions are often expensive, difficult to implement and not interoperable with other businesses' PKI products. XKMS revolutionizes PKI by establishing a platform-independent set of standards that places portions of the PKI workload on the server side, thus freeing application resources for other processes.[24] XKMS works with proprietary PKI solutions to integrate encryption, digital signatures (including revocation and processing of certificates) and authentication. XKMS simplifies the steps necessary to implement PKI (particularly key management), providing an easy and user-friendly method for secure transactions.

XKMS was designed for use with XML Signature and XML Encryption, but also will be compatible with future security technologies. XML Signature and XML Encryption provide a high level of security for XML documents, but do not address *trust management* (the handling of public and private keys), which is essential to successful PKI. XKMS provides the necessary trust management.[25] XKMS is easy to implement, which makes it an ideal solution for mobile PKI (i.e., PKI over wireless networks).

XKMS is comprised of two specifications: the *XML Key Information Service Specification* (*X-KISS*) and the *XML Key Registration Service Specification* (*X-KRSS*). X-KISS is the set of protocols that processes key information (located in an XML signature's **KeyInfo** element) associated with XML encrypted data, digital signatures and other aspects of public-key cryptography. X-KISS locates public keys and binds user information to the keys. The XML Signature specification defines **KeyInfo** as an optional element, so it might not contain enough information to ensure trust. The application that receives a signed file can use X-KISS to forward the **KeyInfo** data to an applicable *trust service*—a trusted party that validates signatures and generates and manages key pairs—for parsing and processing. This process delegates certificate processing to a trust-service server and frees the application from complex logic processing.

X-KRSS is the set of certificate-management protocols that addresses the life of a digital certificate—from registration to revocation and recovery. During registration of a certificate, the user registering the key pair submits the public key to a trusted registration server through a digitally signed request. The registration request also can contain name and attribute information. The user shows proof of ownership of the private key by signing the registration request with the private key and providing the server with the public key for decryption.

Figure 13.5 shows a register request sent to an X-KRSS server. Element **Register** (lines 5–113) of an X-KRSS request contains all of the information relevant to the certificate and owner. Element **Status** (line 7) specifies the current stage of the certificate (i.e., registration, recovery and revocation). When registering a digital certificate, character data in **Status** is **Valid**. Element **KeyID** (line 9) contains a name or location that uniquely identifies the key. In this example, **mailto:joesmith@example.com** specifies that the key is bound to the user **joesmith** at **example.com**. As in XML Signature, element **KeyInfo** (lines 11–38) contains information about the key. Element **PassPhrase** (lines 40–42) contains a generated digest of the user's password. If a user's private key is compromised, the user can revoke the key by submitting the password to the server—which generates a hash value based on the submitted password and compares it to the original digested password. Element **AuthInfo** (lines 46–106) contains elements that authenticate the registration request. Digital signatures show proof of key possession (in **ProofOfPossession**, lines 48–74) and authenticate the keybinding request (in **KeyBindingAuth**, lines 76–104). The request specifies how the server should respond; in this case, the server returns a key name (line 109) and X.509 digital certificate (line 110).

If a user decides that the previously issued assertions about a certificate are no longer valid or that the private key has been compromised, the certificate can be revoked. If **Status** contains the character data **Invalid**, the server revokes the information it previously held about the certificate. Users also can request that the server recover the assertions about any previously registered certificates. In this case, **Status** contains **Indeterminate**, and the registration server replies to the request with a confirmation response in XML. The server response states whether the registration is accepted (**Accepted**), rejected (**NotFound**) or pending (**Pending**).[26] Once a certificate is registered successfully, it is usable by X-KISS and other trust services.

```
1   <?xml version="1.0" encoding="UTF-8"?>
2   <!-- Fig. 13.5: Fig13_5.xml                      -->
3   <!-- X-KRSS Registration Request for a key pair -->
4
5   <Register>
6      <Prototype Id="keybinding">
7         <Status>Valid</Status>
8
9         <KeyID>mailto:joesmith@example.com</KeyID>
10
11        <KeyInfo>
12           <KeyName>mailto:joesmith@example.com</KeyName>
13
14           <KeyValue>
15              <X509Data>
16
17                 <X509SubjectName>
18                    CN=Joe Smith, STREET=123 Example Street,
19                    L=Maynard, ST=MA, C=US
20                 </X509SubjectName>
21
22                 <X509Certificate>
23                    CWDCCAgICAQAwDQYJKoZIhvcNAQEEBQAwgbYxCzAJBgNVBAY
24                    BMRUwEwYDVQQIEwxXZXN0ZXJuIENhcGUxEjAQBgNVBAcTCUN
25                    hgVG93bjEdMBsGA1UEChMUVGhhd3RlIENvbnN1bHRpbmcgY2M
26                    xHzgNVBAsTFkNlcnRpZmljYXRpb24gU2VydmljZXMxFzAVBgN
27                    NVBa87421hjas2e8AYuidhuiaw471298IUAYISUYhu289yasA
28                    JOiwejqwiojWEHuihqwjasndui12897ruhfjQIEOU29081ifU
29                    7IUdhasun2IYEueh12e1iuYWOOOidehqwunJSDNiuy12874js
30                    HH13i87ue1jhjaIUHAuhdnjweoAIJo2iJIAHZBMoKkadsh813
31                    0YAuh893ieHAUhaodiuAIuew8ACLetiX9usdjhds8wyeh1iu8
32                    9821yuAUSHiuhaapAMJXNBZZoiasdzkj02194yyauh1o731i2
33                    D9324DIoetiksadj2q39oi14oiuOSAIDUoismd6o7slau45==
34                 </X509Certificate>
35
36              </X509Data>
37           </KeyValue>
38        </KeyInfo>
39
40        <PassPhrase>
41           Wio923482hUSHuda389OHIA04u3jMNBZhduiWIUYTIUWYoiH3748i=
42        </PassPhrase>
43
44     </Prototype>
45
```

Fig. 13.5   X-KRSS registration request for a key pair. (Part 1 of 3.)

ask for key by name
submit

```
46      <AuthInfo>
47        <AuthUserInfo>
48          <ProofOfPossession>
49            <Signature xmlns="http://www.w3.org/TR/xmldsig-core">
50              <SignedInfo>
51                <CanonicalizationMethod Algorithm=
52            "http://www.w3.org/TR/2001/REC-xml-c14n-20010315" />
53
54                <SignatureMethod Algorithm=
55         "http://www.w3.org/TR/2002/REC-xmldsig-core-20020212#sha1" />
56
57                <Reference URI="#keybinding">
58                  <DigestMethod Algorithm=
59         "http://www.w3.org/TR/2002/REC-xmldsig-core-20020212#sha1" />
60
61                    <DigestValue>
62                      8JiSOH32zISULqWerualYR1298Lsaeu24WHE79=
63                    </DigestValue>
64
65                </Reference>
66
67              </SignedInfo>
68
69              <SignatureValue>
70                P98395u04HUSIJS586HDWHa8y98OPHEu3oUIUSu324eh
71              </SignatureValue>
72
73            </Signature>
74          </ProofOfPossession>
75
76          <KeyBindingAuth>
77            <Signature xmlns="http://www.w3.org/TR/xmldsig-core">
78
79              <SignedInfo>
80                <CanonicalizationMethod Algorithm=
81            "http://www.w3.org/TR/2001/REC-xml-c14n-20010315" />
82
83                <SignatureMethod Algorithm=
84         "http://www.w3.org/TR/2002/REC-xmldsig-core-20020212#sha1" />
85
86                <Reference URI="#keybinding">
87                  <DigestMethod Algorithm=
88         "http://www.w3.org/TR/2002/REC-xmldsig-core-20020212#sha1" />
89
90                    <DigestValue>
91                      fHdnkj394jnKJXOSDJ451RUGP932A94IHFDIohr
92                      984IHiuZXBNMBDLiIOWEIUyfhas8943uihSdho=
93                    </DigestValue>
94
95                </Reference>
96              </SignedInfo>
97
```

Fig. 13.5 X-KRSS registration request for a key pair. (Part 2 of 3.)

```
98                        <SignatureValue>
99                            Bo39udIOSijeAZjlMXioisd9u23rKLJSDPASe3fU1232u
100                           Sk0291jfhjZSIO82uiouderiyq90UAES95yyhru398d=
101                       </SignatureValue>
102
103               </Signature>
104           </KeyBindingAuth>
105       </AuthUserInfo>
106   </AuthInfo>
107
108   <Respond>
109       <string>KeyName</string>
110       <string>X509Cert</string>
111   </Respond>
112
113 </Register>
```

Fig. 13.5   X-KRSS registration request for a key pair. (Part 3 of 3.)

Many companies have already realized the benefits of XKMS and are including the framework in upcoming products. For example, Microsoft is incorporating XKMS in its .NET platform. Vordel (**www.vordel.com**), a company specializing in Web services security, supports XKMS in TalkXML—a standards-based suite for securing data transmissions through digital certificates and PKI. Baltimore Technologies developed the *XML Key Management Specification Bulk Operation (X-BULK)*, an extension to XKMS that enables bulk issuance of digital certificates for smart cards and wireless cards.[27]

13.6 Security Assertion Markup Language (SAML)

The *Security Assertion Markup Language (SAML)* is an emerging standard for transferring authentication, authorization and permissions information over the Internet. The *OASIS Security Services Technical Committee (SSTC)* is developing SAML as a standard XML specification for B2B and B2C communications. SAML is a form of *Permissions Management Infrastructure (PMI)*, a system that uses a set of policies to handle access control and authorization for computing systems.[28] Traditionally, PMI implementation has relied on complex proprietary software, which made PMI prohibitively complex and expensive for many businesses. SAML has revolutionized PMI by establishing an open standard that is accessible to more companies. Security assertions in SAML are files containing authentication credentials and other information used to authorize users.[29]

The SAML protocol was developed by combining two competing XML security standards: Securant Technologies' *AuthXML* and Netegrity's *Security Services Markup Language (S2ML)*.[30] Because SAML is designed for use in interoperable applications, businesses can exchange information securely among groups of trusted partners without demanding any security-configuration modifications.[31] SAML is vendor-neutral and is compatible with many XML communication protocols, including SOAP and ebXML.[32]

SAML also provides a method for single sign-on authentication and authorization (discussed in Chapter 12, Computer and Internet Security).[33]

Single sign-on allows users to enter authentication information once to be authenticated across multiple domains. This technology saves time and relieves users from having to remember multiple usernames and passwords. Before SAML, most single sign-on products (including Microsoft Passport) were proprietary.[34] By contrast, interoperability among SAML-based applications can provide single sign-on across disparate sites and platforms. Netegrity developed the *JSAML Toolkit* for implementing SAML-based applications in Java. For more information on this product, visit **www.netegrity.com/products**.

When a user logs into a SAML-enabled application, permission information is stored in *assertions* (Fig. 13.6).[35] A SAML assertion contains information regarding when, how and for which resources a permission was granted. An assertion has fields for an assertion ID, the subject's name, the subject's security domain and the conditions for which an assertion is valid. An assertion also contains the time that it was issued, the issuer and any other necessary information.[36] Since assertions contain the results of successful authentication, they are only as secure as the authentication process.[37] A weak authentication method can compromise the SAML security.

The subject of an assertion can be a user or a program running on behalf of a user. When the assertion containing the subject's information is generated, the authentication authority creates a *SAML token* (a unique identifier containing authentication and authorization data) that allows access to applications that accept the token (such as trusted business partners' applications or other applications within the same company). When a user reaches a site that requires authentication, the token is submitted to a SAML-equipped authority application. This application is the *Policy Enforcement Point* (*PEP*) and is responsible for requesting and enforcing authorization decisions. The PEP sends a request for an authorization decision (Step 1) to a *Policy Decision Point* (*PDP*) that is responsible for making decisions on the basis of existing security policies. The policies that the PDP uses to make decisions (Step 2) are stored in a *Policy Information Point* (*PIP*). SAML accepts several policy formats, including policies created using the Extensible Access Control Markup Language (discussed in Section 13.9). After using relevant security policies to make an authorization decision, the PDP returns an *authorization decision assertion* (Step 3). If the assertion shows an acceptable level of authorization, an attribute assertion is attached to the user's SAML token, and the user can access the protected resources (Step 4).[38] If the assertion does not provide an acceptable level of authentication, the client is redirected to log in again (Step 5) before accessing the protected content (Step 6).

For example, clients looking to remodel their kitchens and find supplies online could visit **BobsAppliances.com**, a site that supports SAML and single sign-on (Fig. 13.6). The clients would log in at this site with the necessary credentials to make an online purchase. If **BobsAppliances.com** had established a trust relationship with **JoesFlooring.com**, Joe's site would be under the same security domain and accept the token from Bob's site. When users buy flooring tiles through Bob's site, they are redirected to Joe's online store. The PEP at **JoesFlooring.com** sends an authorization request and authentication assertions to the PDP. If the credentials in the assertions are accepted by the policies in the PIP, the PDP returns an assertion that allows the user to shop at Joe's site. The user would simply log in at Bob's site and, from that point, could shop at any of the sites that accept the token as acceptable authentication.

SAML also can be used for B2B communication between Bob's Appliances and Joe's Flooring. For example, **JoesFlooring.com** might want to keep its inventory up-to-date with

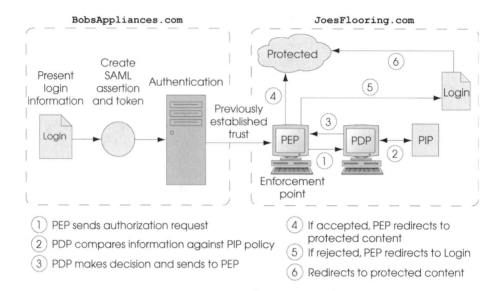

BobsAppliances.com   JoesFlooring.com

1. PEP sends authorization request
2. PDP compares information against PIP policy
3. PDP makes decision and sends to PEP
4. If accepted, PEP redirects to protected content
5. If rejected, PEP redirects to Login
6. Redirects to protected content

Fig. 13.6 Single sign-on example using SAML.

products that complement the appliances from Bob's site. To facilitate this B2B relationship, Joe would need to access Bob's database. Bob and Joe would determine an appropriate level of authentication—such as a secret password that they agree on beforehand or a certificate from a trusted third party—that would authorize access to the sales database. Assuming that the two companies agree on a secret password, the authentication assertion would resemble Fig. 13.7.

```
1   <?xml version="1.0" encoding="UTF-8"?>
2   <!-- Fig. 13.7: Fig13_7.xml            -->
3   <!-- Authentication assertion sample -->
4
5   <saml:Assertion MajorVersion="1" MinorVersion="0"
6      AssertionID="123456" Issuer="BobsAppliances.com"
7      IssueInstant="2002-05-05T10:28:00">
8
9      <saml:Conditions
10        NotBefore="2002-05-05T10:28:00"
11        NotAfter="2002-05-05T11:28:00"/>
12
13     <saml:AuthenticationStatement
14        AuthenticationMethod="password"
15        AuthenticationInstant="2002-05-05T10:28:00">
16        <saml:Subject>
17           <saml:NameIdentifier
18              SecurityDomain="BobsAppliances.com"
19              Name="Joe" />
20        </saml:Subject>
```

Fig. 13.7 Authentication assertion sample. (Part 1 of 2.)

```
21
22        </saml:AuthenticationStatement>
23     </saml:Assertion>
```

Fig. 13.7 Authentication assertion sample. (Part 2 of 2.)

This particular assertion states that the user, **Joe** (line 19), was authenticated by a password (line 14) at **10:28:00** on May 5, 2002 (line 15). Element **Conditions** (lines 9–11) states the conditions under which the assertion is valid. This assertion is valid for only one hour after the time of issuance. When Joe reaches the PEP, this assertion provides a history of how **Joe** was authenticated.[39]

In this example, another assertion (called an *attribute assertion*) provides information about the user's attributes. For instance, if the subject **Joe** is a business partner specializing in flooring, the attribute **Partner** (lines 21–29) would contain the content **Flooring**, as it does in the attribute assertion shown in Fig. 13.8.

```
1    <?xml version="1.0" encoding="UTF-8"?>
2    <!-- Fig. 13.8: Fig13_8.xml      -->
3    <!-- Attribute assertion sample -->
4
5    <saml:Assertion MajorVersion="1" MinorVersion="0"
6       AssertionID="654321" Issuer="BobsAppliances.com"
7       IssueInstant="2002-05-05T10:28:00">
8
9       <saml:Conditions
10         NotBefore="2002-05-05T10:28:00"
11         NotAfter="2002-05-05T11:28:00" />
12
13      <saml:AttributeStatement>
14
15         <saml:Subject>
16            <saml:NameIdentifier
17                 SecurityDomain="BobsAppliances.com"
18                 Name="Joe" />
19         </saml:Subject>
20
21         <saml:Attribute>
22            <saml:AttributeDesignator
23                 AttributeName="Partner"
24                 AttributeNamespace="http://BobsAppliances.com" />
25
26               <saml:AttributeValue>
27                Flooring
28               </saml:AttributeValue>
29         </saml:Attribute>
30
31      </saml:AttributeStatement>
32   </saml:Assertion>
```

Fig. 13.8 Attribute assertion sample.

After the PDP decides whether to grant permission, it returns an authorization-decision assertion. This assertion states that the user **Joe** is permitted to **read** the sales data for Bob's Appliances (Fig. 13.9).

SAML represents a significant advancement in security for B2B and B2C e-commerce transactions. Baltimore Technologies' (**www.baltimoretechnologies.com**) *SelectAccess 5.0* is the first application to incorporate SAML support.[40] For the latest updates and information on SAML's progress, visit **www.oasis-open.org/committees/security**.

13.7 Extensible Access Control Markup Language (XACML)

As we discussed in the previous chapter, it is important for companies to establish clear security policies. Organizations must communicate their security policies to various parties— including vendors, customers and clients—and the advent of Web services has increased this need. *Extensible Access Control Markup Language (XACML)*, developed by OASIS (**www.oasis-open.org**), is a markup language that allows organizations to communicate their policies for accessing online information. XACML defines which clients can access information, what information is available to clients, when clients can access the information and how clients can gain access to the information.[41]

XACML is built on the foundations of IBM's *XML Access Control Language (XACL)* and the University of Madrid's XML-AC. The OASIS technical committee overseeing the development of this new technology includes members from Baltimore Technologies, IBM, Hewlett-Packard (**www.hp.com**) and Sun Microsystems (**www.sun.com**).[42] XACML security policies can regulate information access using factors such as a client's identity, the client's method of authentication and the port through which the client is communicating.[43] For example, a policy might specify that a document can be read only by senior management authorized by a password and communicating over a secure connection.[44]

```
 1   <?xml version="1.0" encoding="UTF-8"?>
 2   <!-- Fig. 13.9: Fig13_9.xml                     -->
 3   <!-- Authorization decision assertion sample -->
 4
 5   <saml:Assertion
 6      MajorVersion="1" MinorVersion="0"
 7      AssertionID="321456" Issuer="BobsAppliances.com"
 8      IssueInstant="2002-05-05T10:28:00">
 9
10        <saml:Conditions
11           NotBefore="2002-05-05T10:28:00"
12           NotAfter="2002-05-05T11:28:00" />
13
14        <saml:AuthorizationDecisionStatement
15           Decision="Permit"
16           Resource="http://BobsAppliances.com/private/sales_data.xml">
17
18           <saml:Actions Namespace=
19   "http://www.oasis-open.org/committees/security/docs/draft-sstc-
     core-25/rwedc">
```

Fig. 13.9   Authorization decision assertion sample. (Part 1 of 2.)

```
20                <saml:Action>Read</saml:Action>
21            </saml:Actions>
22
23            <saml:Subject>
24                <saml:NameIdentifier
25                    SecurityDomain="BobsAppliances.com"
26                    Name="Joe" />
27            </saml:Subject>
28
29        </saml:AuthorizationDecisionStatement>
30    </saml:Assertion>
```

Fig. 13.9 Authorization decision assertion sample. (Part 2 of 2.)

XACML also can enforce *Digital Rights Management* (*DRM*) for content delivered over the Internet. DRM is the set of protocols designed to protect media against piracy and unauthorized access online. As DRM technologies develop, organizations such as the Secure Digital Music Initiative (**www.sdmi.org**) and the Electronic Book Exchange Working Group (**www.ebxwg.org**) oversee DRM developments and establish new technical standards. The permission policies established in XACML can support DRM by declaring that a user has certain access privileges. For instance, an electronic-book distributor can use XACML to allow anyone to view the first chapter of a certain book, but allow only registered users to read the entire work. Registered users that pay an extra fee can print the file.

Working with SAML, XACML policies can provide the basis for authoritative decision-making at a Policy Decision Point. The PEP sends an authorization decision query to the PDP, which consults established security policies. The request must contain the target resource to access and the operation to perform (read, write, etc.) The assertion may also contain optional authentication credentials. Files requiring different levels of security will have different authentication standards. The PDP will return access decisions on the basis of the security policies in place. Building on our example from Section 13.6, imagine that **BobsAppliances.com** wants to allow customers to look at their own purchase histories, but prevent customers from writing to this file or accessing other customers' files. The XACML policy in Fig. 13.10 describes the conditions necessary to view a customer's purchase history stored in **BobsAppliances.com**'s database.

Root element **rule** is comprised of elements that specify the resource protected by the rule, the actions that a user can perform on the resource and the conditions necessary for each action. Attribute **effect** (line 5) contains either the value **"permit"**—which permits the actions outlined in the rule—or **"deny"**—which prohibits the actions outlined in the rule. A description of the policy is placed within the **description** element in lines 8–10. Element **target** (lines 15–41) defines the **resources** (lines 26–35), **subjects** (lines 17–24) and **actions** (lines 37–39).[45]

```
1    <?xml version="1.0" encoding="UTF-8"?>
2    <!-- Fig. 13.10: Fig13_10.xml                                          -->
```

Fig. 13.10 XACML policy that allows customers to view their purchase history.
(Part 1 of 3.)

```
3    <!-- XACML policy that restricts access to purchase histories -->
4
5    <rule effect="permit"
6        ruleID="http://www.BobsAppliances.com/customers/policy1"
7        xmlns="http://www.oasis-open.org/committees/xacml/docs/draft-
     xacml-schema-policy-12.xsd"
8        xmlns:saml="http://www.oasis-open.org/committees/security/docs/
     draft-sstc-schema-assertion-28.xsd"
9        xmlns:xsi="http://www.w3.org/2001/XMLSchema-instance"
10       xsi:schemaLocation="http://www.oasis-open.org/committees/xacml/
     docs/draft-xacml-schema-policy-12.xsd">
11       <description>
12        Allow customers to access and read their purchase history at
     BobsAppliances.com
13       </description>
14
15       <target>
16
17          <subjects>
18
19             <saml:Attribute AttributeName="RFC822Name"
20              AttributeNameSpace="http://www.BobsAppliances.com">
21                <saml:AttributeValue>*</saml:AttributeValue>
22             </saml:Attribute>
23
24          </subjects>
25
26          <resources>
27
28             <saml:Attribute AttributeName="documentURI"
29              AttributeNamespace="http://www.BobsAppliances.com">
30                <saml:AttributeValue>
31                  http://www.BobsAppliances.com/customers/record.*
32                </saml:AttributeValue>
33             </saml:Attribute>
34
35          </resources>
36
37          <actions>
38             <saml:Action>read</saml:Action>
39          </actions>
40
41       </target>
42
43       <condition>
44
45          <equal>
46             <saml:AttribueDesignator AttributeName="requestor"
47                 AttributeNamespace=
48        "http://www.oasis-open.org/committees/xacml/docs/identifiers/" />
49             <saml:AttributeDesignator
50                 AttributeName="customerID"
```

Fig. 13.10 XACML policy that allows customers to view their purchase history.
(Part 2 of 3.)

```
51                    AttributeNamespace=
52              "http://www.BobsAppliances.com/customers/record/custID/" />
53          </equal>
54
55       </condition>
56    </rule>
```

Fig. 13.10 XACML policy that allows customers to view their purchase history.
(Part 3 of 3.)

The PDP compares the **resource**s, **subject**s and **action**s in an authorization decision request to those in the XACML policy's rules before making an authorization decision.[46] In this example, the protected resource (located at **www.BobsAppliances.com/customers/record.***) is the customer's purchase history. Element **actions** (lines 37–39) specifies that an authorized viewer can **read** the resources. The **subject** (lines 17–24) is the customer that is requesting the purchase history. The conditions under which the actions are granted to the customer are contained in element **condition** (lines 43–55). Element **equal** (lines 45–53) contains attributes that must be equal for the conditions to be true—in this case, **requestor** and **customerID** must be equal. The **condition** element also can use **and**, **or** and **not** to create more complex conditional expressions. Like SAML and many other Web service security standards, XACML is changing rapidly; to view the latest specification, visit **www.oasis-open.org/committees/xacml/#documents**.

Figure 13.11 overviews the security standards we cover in this chapter. We list each technology, then summarize its purpose and strengths.

Technology	Fundamentals Addressed	Strengths
Basic HTTP	Authentication	Challenge-response authentication—credentials required for access to protected resources.
Digest Authentication	Authentication, Authorization, Privacy	Authorization credentials are protected through generated checksums, rather than plaintext transmission of passwords and usernames.
SSL (HTTPS)	Authentication, Privacy, Integrity	Authenticates both parties in a transaction. Encrypts data for end-to-end security between a client and server.
XML Signature	Authentication, Integrity	Verifies document integrity and sender identity. Multiple parties can sign a document or parts of a document.

Fig. 13.11 Web services security solutions. (Part 1 of 2.)

Technology	Fundamentals Addressed	Strengths
XML Encryption	Integrity, Privacy	Uses public-key or secret-key cryptography to protect data during transmission. Multiple parties can encrypt a document or parts of a document.
XKMS	Authentication, Privacy, Integrity	Provides XML-based PKI for Web services. Manages key and certificate information. Controls key registration, recovery and revocation.
SAML	Authentication, Authorization Non-Repudiation, Integrity	Designed for interoperable authentication and authorization solutions, including single sign-on. Records when and how a user was authenticated.
XACML	Authorization	XML-based language for creating security policies that can be used with SAML.

Fig. 13.11 Web services security solutions. (Part 2 of 2.)

13.8 Authentication and Authorization for Web Services

As we discussed in Chapter 12, Computer and Internet Security, authentication and authorization are necessary in any security model. Basic authentication and authorization techniques—such as those we discussed in Section 13.2—are not sufficient to secure Web services transactions. The latest Web services products use a combination of security mechanisms, including Kerberos and single sign-on. Microsoft's Passport, Sun's Liberty Alliance and AOL Time Warner's *Screen Name Service* are authentication and authorization systems designed for use with Web services. Web service providers that want to reach the largest number of users should provide authentication and authorization via various popular sign-on services.

Microsoft Passport authenticates and authorizes users for .NET Web services restricted to privileged users. Passport provides single sign-on using Kerberos authentication.[47] In addition to authorizing users for .NET services, Passport has been adopted by many e-businesses, including eBay, Monster and McAfee. Almost 200 million users worldwide are registered for the Passport service, which is required to access several Windows XP applications and Microsoft Hotmail. Microsoft plans to integrate new authentication methods—including digital certificates, biometrics and smart cards—with Passport.[48] All participating Passport sites must adhere to the P3P privacy standard and must provide privacy policies indicating what information they gather from users and how they use the information. To establish a Passport account or to set up a Passport-compliant Web site, visit **www.passport.com**.

The Liberty Alliance (**www.projectliberty.org**) was formed in October 2001 by Sun Microsystems. This organization's goal is to establish non-proprietary single sign-on standards for e-business. Liberty Alliance participants include AOL Time Warner, General Motors, American Express, Mastercard International and RSA Security. The proposed standards seek to secure businesses' and users' confidential information and to establish universal single sign-on methods. Liberty Alliance's specifications are designed to support *decentralized authentication* and interoperability. In decentralized authentication, users are not required to contact a central server to receive authentication, as is necessary in Kerberos and PKI. This increases flexibility and provides an ideal authentication system for wireless communications, in which users might not have access to a central server. The Liberty Alliance will offer an alternative to Microsoft's Passport service.[49] The interfaces designed by the Liberty Alliance could be used with .NET, enabling Passport to operate with other single sign-on systems.

AOL Time Warner developed Screen Name Service (SNS) for Web services authentication and authorization using single sign-on. In January 2002, AOL informally launched SNS, based on the company's *Magic Carpet* single sign-on technology. Screen Name Service combines accounts from AOL's America Online, Compuserve 2000, AOL Instant Messenger, Netscape and NetBusiness into a unified system. Users not registered with any of the previous programs can visit **my.screenname.aol.com** for free registration. SNS was designed to compete with Microsoft .NET's Passport system. Approximately 175 million users are registered for SNS, making it one of the most popular single sign-on products. AOL Time Warner is a member of the Liberty Alliance, but it is unclear whether SNS will be compatible with the Liberty Alliance's proposed specification. Negotiations between Microsoft and AOL to enable Passport and Magic Carpet interoperability failed, because AOL felt that Microsoft operating systems should provide equal support for Magic Carpet and Passport.[50] Businesses that currently support SNS include FedEx, CNN, Time, People and **NBA.com**.

Several emerging standards also provide authentication and authorization for Web services. The XML Key Management Specification (XKMS) manages key pairs used in PKI for encryption and user authentication. SAML transmits authentication, authorization and permissions information via assertions. XACML establishes an interoperable standard for creating security policies and permissions management used in Web services authorization.

13.9 Web Services and Network Security

In Chapter 12, Computer and Internet Security, we discussed aspects of network security, including firewalls and intrusion-detection systems. Web services (and features like single sign-on) create additional network-security concerns. Networks typically authenticate users before allowing access to protected resources. However, Web services often are designed to use single sign-on, which allows access to applications on the basis of another source's authentication credentials. Web services carry transactions beyond corporate firewalls, which places internal resources at a greater risk of attack.

The biggest concern regarding Web services security is the immaturity of underlying standards.[51] As with any new technology, certain vulnerabilities are not discovered until attacks occur in a real-world setting. Most organizations that operate Web services over internal networks are restricting external access to the services until emerging Web services security standards are incorporated in security software. Developers that do offer external access to Web services must take extra steps to protect their applications and networks.[52] A combination of traditional and Web services–specific security methods can be used to protect networks while Web services security standards mature. Encrypting data and using secure channels, such as SSL, protects data integrity and prevents data interception.[53] Firewalls between Web services and internal resources prevent Web service users from accessing protected information. If a computer within a firewall is exploited, an attacker can use that machine to access protected systems on the network. In addition to internal firewalls, a separate firewall should protect Web services from unauthorized visitors and filter traffic from a denial-of-service attacks.

Web services create new security challenges, but also can protect computers on a network. Products under development by Network Associates and Symantec use Web services to search networks for signs of viruses and apply updates to infected computers.[54] As Web services security solutions develop, developers will be forced to decide between traditional security and new Web services-specific security methods. Although we certain technologies are immature, that does not make them insecure. Web services security is an ongoing process, not a one-time solution. Administrators using Web services need to stay apprised of all security developments and update their systems regularly.

13.10 Summary

Web services move transactions beyond firewalls and enable outside entities to invoke applications, potentially giving outsiders access to sensitive information. As a result, Web services present new security challenges. Although existing security standards protect data as it travels over the Internet, Web services require additional measures to secure data.

In HTTP challenge-response authentication, users must provide specific authentication information to verify their identities. When used alone, challenge-response authentication provides only weak security, because passwords and credentials are transmitted in plain-text. Digest authentication is a protocol in which a user's credentials are submitted to the server as a checksum. Digest authentication protects usernames and passwords from eavesdropping attackers, but does not encrypt the message content, which means that the content is vulnerable to interception. Secure Sockets Layer (SSL) secures the channel through which data flows between a client and server and enables authentication of both parties.

XML-based applications raise significant security concerns, in part because XML documents are encoded in plain-text, rather than in a binary form. Digital signatures solve this problem by verifying document integrity. The W3C's XML Signature specification defines an XML-based standard for representing digital signatures. A signature verifies a sender's identity and the data's integrity, but encryption is necessary to prevent the signed data from being read en route. XML Encryption handles the encryption and decryption of XML documents that are secured with XML Signature.

The XML Key Management Specification (XKMS) is a specification for registering and distributing encryption keys for Public Key Infrastructure (PKI) in Web services. XKMS improves PKI by establishing a platform-independent set of standards and by simplifying the steps necessary to implement PKI.

The Security Assertion Markup Language (SAML) is an emerging standard for transferring authentication, authorization and permissions information over the Internet. SAML is a form of Permissions Management Infrastructure (PMI), a system that uses a set of policies to handle access control and authorization. SAML has revolutionized PMI by establishing an open standard that is accessible to more companies.

Extensible Access Control Markup Language (XACML) is a markup language that allows organizations to communicate their policies for accessing online information. XACML security policies can regulate information access using factors such as a client's identity, the client's method of authentication and the port through which the client is communicating. XACML also can enforce Digital Rights Management (DRM) for content delivered over the Internet.

The biggest concern regarding Web services security is the immaturity of underlying standards. As with any new technology, certain vulnerabilities are not discovered until attacks occur in a real-world setting. Developers that offer external access to Web services must take extra steps to protect their applications and networks. As Web services security solutions develop, organizations must decide between traditional security and new Web services-specific security methods. Web services security is an ongoing process, not a one-time solution. Administrators using Web services need to stay apprised of all security developments and update their systems regularly.

13.11 Internet and Web Resources

General Web Services Security

dcb.sun.com/practices/devnotebook/webserv_security.jsp
This article, titled "Building Security into Web Services," provides an overview of Web services security.

msdn.microsoft.com/vstudio/techinfo/articles/XMLwebservices/security.asp
This Visual Studio .NET site provides an introduction to Web services security in .NET. It discusses Web services, how to restrict access to a Web service, ASP.NET security features and more.

www.infoworld.com/articles/tc/xml/02/01/14/020114tcsecure.xml
This article, titled "The Road to Secure Web Services," discusses the current state of Web services security and solutions that are under development.

msdn.microsoft.com/library/default.asp?url=/library/en-us/dnglobspec/html/wssecurspecindex.asp
The MSDN *WS-Security Specification Index Page* overviews the WS-Security specification. This site also includes links to the specification, Schema and a security road-map tutorial.

XML Signature

www.ietf.org/html.charters/xmldsig-charter.html
The IETF's *XML Digital Signatures* site discusses the goals of the XML Digital Signature Working Group and includes the latest version of the standards document.

www.w3.org/Signature
The W3C's XML Signature Working Group site includes standards drafts, sample code, tools, SDKs and tutorials.

www.w3.org/TR/xmldsig-requirements
The *XML-Signature Requirements* site lists the design principles for the specification.

www.xml.com/pub/a/2001/08/08/xmldsig.html
This article, titled "An Introduction to XML Digital Signatures," overviews XML Signature technology, including how to create and verify XML digital signatures. Markup examples are also provided.

www-106.ibm.com/developerworks/xml/library/s-xmlsec.html/index.html
This tutorial on XML Encryption and XML Signature technologies includes several markup examples and links to other helpful online tutorials.

www.w3.org/Signature/2001/04/05-xmldsig-interop.html
This site presents the requirements for XML Signature interoperability.

www.xmltrustcenter.org/xmlsig/index.htm
The XML Trust Center includes FAQs, links and resources related to XML signatures and other XML security technologies.

www.webservicesarchitect.com/content/articles/hankison03.asp
This brief tutorial discusses digital signatures and Web services that use XKMS and the XML Digital Signature Specification.

XML Key Management Specification (XKMS)

www.w3.org/TR/xkms
This W3C site provides the specification for XKMS.

www.xmltrustcenter.org/xkms/index.htm
This XKMS resource site includes links to XKMS FAQs, articles and other resources.

www.w3.org/2001/XKMS
The W3C XML Key Management Working Group site contains the specifications, XKMS toolkits from multiple vendors (for Java and .NET) and links to other resources.

www.verisign.com/developer/xml/xkms.html
This site includes an article on integrating XML Signature and XML Encryption with XKMS, as well as links to whitepapers and other free guides.

Security Assertion Markup Language (SAML)

www.oasis-open.org/committees/security
This site contains links to SAML documents, mailing lists and other resources.

www.fawcette.com/xmlmag/2002_02/magazine/columns/collaboration/edejesus
This article discusses how SAML distributes authorization and authentication information.

xml.coverpages.org/saml.html
This site includes information about SAML and links to numerous SAML articles.

XML Encryption

www.w3.org/Encryption/2001
This site includes information about the XML Encryption specification, technical documentation and links to XML Encryption tools and articles.

www.w3.org/TR/xmlenc-core
This document explains the process of encrypting data with XML Encryption.

www.w3.org/Encryption/2001/Overview.html
The W3C XML Encryption Working Group site contains a mission statement, code, meeting schedules and background information regarding XML Encryption.

www.xmlhack.com/read.php?item=1431
This site contains links to information on various XML Encryption topics.

WORKS CITED

1.   J. Fontana, "Microsoft Touts Tighter Web Services Security," *Network World* 10 June 2002:1–8.

2.   E. Schwartz, "Secure Web Services a Moving Target," *InfoWorld* 17 January 2002 **<www.infoworld.com/articles/hn/xml/02/01/17/020117hntarget.xml>**.

3. M. Andress, "The Road to Secure Web Services," *InfoWorld* 10 January 2002 `<www.infoworld.com/articles/tc/xml/02/01/14/020114tcsecure.xml>`.

4. R. Yasin, "XML Standard to Keep Web Services Secure," *Internet Week* 30 July 2001 `<www.internetweek.com/infrastructure01/infra073001-1.htm>`.

5. R. Yasin, "XML Standard to Keep Web Services Secure," *InternetWeek* 30 July 2001: 21.

6. G. Samtani and D. Sadhwani, "Security and the .NET Framework," *Web Services Journal* February 2002: 34–37.

7. R. Rivest, "The MD5 Message-Digest Algorithm," April 1992 `<theory.lcs.mit.edu/~revisit/Rivest-MD5.txt>`.

8. "HTTP Authentication: Basic and Digest Access Authentication," `<www.ietf.org/rfc/rfc2617.txt>`.

9. S. Vaughan-Nichols, "The Woes of Web Services," 11 February 2001 `<www.byte.com/documents/s=6974/byt1013212280038/0211_vaughan-nichols.html>`.

10. M. Andress, "The Road to Secure Web Services," *InfoWorld* 10 January 2002 `<www.infoworld.com/articles/tc/xml/02/01/14/020114tcsecure.xml>`.

11. "Web Services Security, Version 1.0.," 5 April 2002 `<msdn.microsoft.com/library/en-us/dnglobspec/html/ws-security.asp>`.

12. W. Wong, "Tech Giants Partner on Security Standard," 11 April 2002 `<news.zdnet.co.uk/story/0,,t281-s2108174,00.html>`.

13. J. Fontana, "Whirlwind of Web Services Work on Tap," *Network World* 20 May 2002: 12.

14. M. Milgliore, "IBM, Microsoft and Verisign Release SOAP Security Spec," 11 April 2002 `<www.esj.com/news/article.asp?EditorialsID=174>`.

15. "XML-Signature Syntax and Processing," March 2001 `<community.roxen.com/developers/idocs/rfc/rfc3075.html>`.

16. "XML Signature," `<www.xmltrustcenter.org/xmlsig/index.htm>`.

17. M. Mactaggart, "Enabling XML Security: An Introduction to XML Encryption and XML Signature," September 2001 `<www-106.ibm.com/developerworks/xml/library/s-xmlsec.html>`.

18. E. Simon, P. Madsen and C. Adams, "An Introduction to XML Digital Signatures," 8 August 2001 `<www.xml.com/lpt/a/2001/08/08/xmldsig.html>`.

19. P. Festa, "W3C Backs XML-Based Digital Signature," 14 February 2002 `<zdnet.com.com/2102-1106-838335.html>`.

20. M. Mactaggart, "Enabling XML Security: An Introduction to XML Encryption and XML Signature," September 2001 `<www-106.ibm.com/developerworks/xml/library/s-xmlsec.html>`.

21. M. Andress, "The Road to Secure Web Services," *InfoWorld* 10 January 2002 `<www.infoworld.com/articles/tc/xml/02/01/14/020114tcsecure.xml>`

22. D. Singh, "XML and Binary Data," `<www.topxml.com/xml/articles/binary>`.

23. B. Shaffner, "Protect Sensitive Data with the XML Protocol," *TechRepublic* 11 February 2002 `<www.techrepublic.com/article_guest.jhtml?id=r00820020211sch01.htm>`.

24. C. Boulton, "VeriSign Bows New XML Specs, Services," 29 November 2000 `<www.internetnews.com/dev-news/article.php/10_522211>`.

25. R. Bragg, "Locking Down Web Services," *Enterprise Systems* November 2001: 22–25.

26. "XML Key Management: XML Trust Services," <**www.verisign.com/resources/wp/xml/keyManagement.pdf**>.

27. "W3C Publishes New XKMS 2.0 and X-BULK Working Drafts," 20 March 2002 <**www.webservices.org/index.php/article/articleview/208**>.

28. G. Yost, "PMI: The Tough Sell," *Technical Support* June 2000 <**www.naspa.com/PDF/2000/0600%20TS%20PDFs/T0006014.pdf**>.

29. M. Glaser, "SAML Looks to Allay XML Security Concerns," 8 February 2002 <**dcb.sun.com/practices/webservices/overviews/overview_saml.jsp**>.

30. E. DeJesus, "SAML Brings Security to XML," *XML Magazine* February 2002: 35–37.

31. R. Cover, "The XML Cover Pages: Security Services Markup Language (S2ML)," 21 February 2001 <**xml.coverpages.org/s2ml.html**>.

32. A. Patrizio, "SAML Advances Single Sign-On Prospects," *XML Magazine* March 2002: 10–11.

33. D. Taft, "Services Security Tightens," *eWeek* 29 April 2002: 18.

34. A. Patrizio, "SAML Advances Single Sign-On Prospects," <**www.fawcette.com/xmlmag/2002_03/magazine/departments/marketscan/saml/default.asp**>.

35. "Assertions and Protocol for the OASIS Security Assertion Markup Language," <**www.oasis-open.org/committees/security/docs/draft-sstc-core-27.pdf**>.

36. M. Chanliau, "Security Assertions Markup Language (SAML)," <**www.simc-inc.org/archive0002/February02/Speakers/SAML-SIMC-short**>.

37. J. Byous, "Single Sign-On Simplicity With SAML: An Overview of Single Sign-On Capabilities Based on the Security Assertions Markup Language (SAML) Specification," <**java.sun.com/features/2002/05/single-signon.html**>.

38. J. Byous, "Single Sign-On Simplicity With SAML: An Overview of Single Sign-On Capabilities Based on the Security Assertions Markup Language (SAML) Specification," <**java.sun.com/features/2002/05/single-signon.html**>.

39. M. Glaser, "SAML Looks to Allay XML Security Concerns," 8 February 2002 <**dcb.sun.com/practices/webservices/overviews/overview_saml.jsp**>.

40. J. Fontana, "Baltimore Tech First to Add SAML," *Network World* 29 March 2002: 14.

41. "OASIS eXtensible Access Control Markup Language (XACML)," 9 May 2002 <**www.oasis-open.org/committees/xacml/repository/draft-xacml-schema-policy-13.pdf**>.

42. "XACML - Extensible Access Control Markup Language," 24 April 2001 <**xml.coverpages.org/XACML-PR20010424.html**>.

43. E. DeJesus, "Secure Your Web Services Applications," *.NET Magazine* June 2002:22–26.

44. P. Madsen and C. Adams, "Privacy and XML, Part 2," 1 May 2002 <**www.xml.com/pub/a/2002/05/01/privacy.html**>.

45. "OASIS eXtensible Access Control Markup Language (XACML)," 9 May 2002 <**www.oasis-open.org/committees/xacml/repository/draft-xacml-schema-policy-13.pdf**>.

46. P. Madsen and C. Adams, "Privacy and XML, Part 2," 1 May 2002 <**www.xml.com/pub/a/2002/05/01/privacy.html**>.

47. M. Andress, "The Road to Secure Web Services," *InfoWorld* 10 January 2002 `<www.infoworld.com/articles/tc/xml/02/01/14/020114tcsecure.xml>`.

48. ".NET Passport Overview, "`<www.microsoft.com/myservices/passport/overview.asp>`.

49. M. La Monica, "Web Services Leave a Wake of Security Worries," *InfoWorld* 18 February 2002: 18.

50. "Microsoft Accuses AOL of Net Plot," 4 April 2002 `<msn.com.com/2100-1104-876289.html>`.

51. S. Burns, "Web Services Security—An Overview," 20 November 2001 `<rr.sans.org/managed/web_services.php>`.

52. W. Rash, "Web Services Nightmare," *Software Development Times* 1 November 2001: 31.

53. T. Dyck, "Here Be Dragons: Web Services Risks," *eWeek* 25 March 2002: 42.

54. M. Denton, "Making Web Services Work," *Electronic Commerce World* May 2002: 30–33.

RECOMMENDED READING

Actaggat, A. "Enabling XML Security," September 2001 `<www-106.ibm.com/developerworks/xml/library/s-xmlsec/html>`.

Connolly, P. J. "Getting Serious About Web Services," *InfoWorld* 14 September 2001 `<www.infoworld.com/articles/tc/xml/01/09/17/010917tcsecurity.xml>`.

DeJesus, E. X. "Security Implications of Web Services," 6 June 2001 `<www.webservicesarchitect.com/content/articles/deJesus01.asp>`.

Desmond, P. "Securant, Netegrity Offer Competing Security Standard Proposals," December 2000/January 2001 `<www.softwaremag.com/archive/2000dec/SecurityStandards.html>`.

Dillaway, B. "Implementing XML Key Management Services Using ASP.NET," January 2002 `<msdn.microsoft.com/library/en-us/Dnaspp/html/Im.plementingxkms.asp>`.

Finlay, D. "XML Security Spec Solves PKI Interface Dilemma," *Software Development Times* 1 January 2001 `<www.sdtimes.com/news/021/story1.htm>`.

Fonseca, B. "Authenticating Web Services," *InfoWorld* 3 December 2001 `<www.infoworld.com/articles/fe/xml/01/12/03/011203feauthent.xml>`.

Fonseca, B. "Secure XML Standard Defined for E-Commerce," *InfoWorld* 15 November 2000 `<www.infoworld.com/articles/hn/xml/00/11/15/001115hnnetegrity.xml?p=br&s=4>`.

Lindstrom, P. "Special Report: The Language of XML Security," *Network Magazine* 5 June 2001 `<www.networkmagazine.com/article/NMG20010518S0010/3>`.

Loeb, L. "XML Signatures: Behind the Curtain," December 2001 `<www-106.ibm.com/developerworks/library/s-digsig>`.

Messmer, E. "Software Vendors Planning XML-Based Security Spec," *Network World* 15 November 2000 `<www.nwfusion.com/news/2000/1115xmlspec.html>`.

Messmer, E. "Vendors Jostling Over XML Security Specs," 20 November 2000 `<www.nwfusion.com/news/2000/1120xml.html>`.

Microsoft. "XML Web Services Security," **<msdn.microsoft.com/vstudio/technical/ articles/security.asp>**.

"Secure XML Standard Defined for E-Commerce," 15 November 2000 **<www.itworld.com/ AppDev/1503/IW001115hnnetegrity>**.

Sundsted, T. "Taking Web Service Security Beyond SSL," 15 October 2001 **<dcb.sun.com/ practices/devnotebook/beyond_ssl.jsp>**.

Vijayan, J. "Web Services, Internet Collaboration Pose Security Challenges for 2002," *Network World* 3 January 2002 **<www.nwfusion.com/news/2002/0103sec.html>**.

14

Wireless Web Services and Java 2 Micro Edition

Objectives

- To be introduced to Java 2 Micro Edition (J2ME).
- To be introduced to the J2ME user interface and networking features.
- To be able to build a J2ME client capable of receiving data from servlets.
- To be able to build a J2ME client capable of invoking Web services.
- To learn how to send SOAP requests from wireless devices.

It's all in the ear of the beholder.
Tom Hayden

Outline

14.1 Introduction

It has been forecast that by the end of 2003, more people will access the Web from wireless devices than from desktop "wireline" devices. Wireless devices enable users to access Web services at any time and from virtually any location. This flexibility is convenient for services such as checking stock quotes or discovering a list of activities in which to engage in a particular locale.

In this chapter, we introduce *Java 2 Micro Edition* (*J2ME*™), which is Sun Microsystem's Java platform for developing applications for various consumer devices, such as set-top boxes, Web terminals, embedded systems, mobile phones and pagers. We discuss the J2ME API and show how it can be used to program some simple J2ME applications. We then discuss how to enable a J2ME client to access Web services via servlets and via SOAP requests.

14.2 Java 2 Micro Edition

Sun introduced J2ME to provide the functionality that the other Java platforms—Java 2 Standard Edition (J2SE™) and Java 2 Enterprise Edition (J2EE™)—do not provide. J2SE provides an API for building desktop applications, and J2EE provides an API for building scalable enterprise business solutions. However, prior to the release of J2ME, Sun did not provide a standard, widely employed platform for building applications that operate on devices with limited resources (e.g., limited memory, means of input and display). Realizing the need to provide a platform that enables developers to create applications for this market, Sun developed J2ME.

A common misconception is that developers use J2ME to develop applications only for wireless devices. In fact, J2ME enables developers to write applications for other consumer devices, such as Web terminals and embedded systems. Our treatment of J2ME involves building applications for wireless devices—specifically, mobile phones. To run the applications that we will build, we will use the Sun MIDP-device emulator, which also will serve as a client for invoking the Price Finder Web services that we create in Chapter 15. We discuss how to install and use this emulator later in the chapter.

14.2.1 CLDC and MIDP

The J2ME platform defines two central technologies that enable developers to build J2ME applications, as well as guarantee that these applications will run on any J2ME-compatible device. The first technology is a *configuration*, which includes both a Java Virtual Machine (JVM) that enables J2ME programs to execute on a J2ME device and a set of APIs that enables developers to create applications that run on devices containing limited resources. The second technology is a *profile*, which provides a set of APIs that enables developers to create applications that run on specific devices (e.g., mobile phones), which, in turn, use a configuration. For the applications that we develop in this chapter, we will use and discuss the *Connected Limited Device Configuration* (*CLDC*) and the *Mobile Information Device Profile* (*MIDP*), which collectively offer developers a set of APIs that they can use to write J2ME applications called *MIDlet*s and deploy them across several types of mobile devices.

Connected Limited Device Configuration (CLDC)

The *Connected Limited Device Configuration* (*CLDC*) is a set of APIs that allows developers to create applications for devices that have limited resources—e.g., limited screen size, memory, power and bandwidth. The J2ME CLDC contains both a virtual machine and a set of classes with which developers can develop and run programs on resource-limited devices. The *KVM*—the virtual machine offered by the CLDC—runs J2ME applications (as the JVM runs J2SE applications). The "K" in KVM represents the word "kilo," because J2ME applications are small enough to be measured in kilobytes.

The J2ME CLDC contains packages **java.io**, **java.lang** and **java.util**, which developers use to perform such common operations as creating primitive data types, using simple data structures, and sending and receiving data from networks. These packages are subsets of the J2SE packages **java.io**, **java.lang** and **java.util**, respectively—that is, the J2ME CLDC packages do not contain every class from the J2SE packages. Figure 14.1 lists the contents of the J2ME **java.io**, **java.lang** and **java.util** packages. For the complete J2ME CLDC class list (i.e., one that includes error and exception classes), visit

> **java.sun.com/j2me/docs/pdf/cldcapi.pdf**

One challenge of J2ME programming is that the API does not contain certain data types and classes that developers often take for granted in other Java platforms. For example, J2ME does not include floating-point operations, serializable objects, thread groups or JNI (Java Native Interface). Nor does J2ME provide specific "convenience" classes, such as **java.util.StringTokenizer**. As wireless-device technology advances, it is possible that future versions of J2ME will support these features.

 Common Programming Error 14.1

Attempting to use J2SE packages in the KVM will result in a compilation error, because the KVM cannot handle the volume of classes, due to its KVM's limited resources.

Classes	java.io	java.lang	java.util
Interfaces	**DataInput** **DataOutput**	**Runnable**	**Enumeration**

Fig. 14.1   J2ME **java.io**, **java.lang** and **java.util** packages. (Part 1 of 2.)

Classes	java.io	java.lang	java.util
Classes	ByteArrayInputStream	Boolean	Calendar
	ByteArrayOutputStream	Byte	Data
	DataInputStream	Character	Hashtable
	DataOutputStream	Class	Random
	InputStream	Integer	Stack
	InputStreamReader	Long	Timer
	OutputStream	Math	TimerTask
	OutputStreamReader	Object	TimeZone
	PrintStream	Runtime	Vector
	Reader	Short	
	Writer	String	
		StringBuffer	
		System	
		Thread	
		Throwable	

Fig. 14.1   J2ME **java.io**, **java.lang** and **java.util** packages. (Part 2 of 2.)

Mobile Information Device Profile

The *Mobile Information Device Profile (MIDP)* is a set of APIs that allows developers to handle mobile-device-specific issues, such as creating user interfaces, permitting local storage and defining the life cycles of MIDP client applications (MIDlets). Devices that use the MIDP to run applications are called *MIDP devices*. Such devices include cell phones and pagers.

MIDP contains packages **javax.microedition.lcdui**, **javax.microedition.io**, **javax.microedition.rms** and **javax.microedition.midlet**. Package **javax.microedition.lcdui** contains classes that allow developers to construct user interfaces for MIDlets. Package **javax.microedition.io** enables networking between MIDlets and other systems. Package **javax.microedition.rms** contains classes that permit local storage. Package **javax.microedition.midlet** contains class **MIDlet**, which defines the *MIDlet lifecycle*—or the execution sequence of a MIDlet. Figure 14.2 lists the contents of the MIDP **javax.microedition.lcdui** and **javax.microedition.io** packages. Figure 14.3 lists the contents of the MIDP **javax.microedition.rms** and **javax.microedition.midlet** packages. For the complete J2ME MIDP class list (i.e., one that includes error and exception classes), visit

java.sun.com/products/midp/midp-wirelessapps-wp.pdf

To conform to the MIDP specification, a MIDP device requires a monochrome display of at least 96 pixels x 54 pixels, a two-way wireless network, some input device (such as a one-handed keypad or touch screen), at least 128 kilobytes for CLDC/MIDP classes and at least 32 kilobytes for the KVM. A MIDlet will run on any device that meets these requirements.

Classes	javax.microedition.lcdui	javax.microedition.io
Interfaces	Choice CommandListener ItemListener	Connection ContentConnection Datagram DatagramConnection HttpConnection InputConnection OutputConnection StreamConnection StreamConnectionNotifier
Classes	Alert AlertType Canvas ChoiceGroup Command DateField Display Displayable Font Form Gauge Graphics Image ImageItem Item List Screen ScreenItem TextBox TextField Ticker	Connector

Fig. 14.2   MIDP **javax.microedition.lcdui** and **javax.microedition.io** packages.

Classes	javax.microedition.rms	javax.microedition.midlet
Interfaces	RecordComparator RecordEnumeration RecordFilter RecordListener	
Classes	RecordStore	MIDlet

Fig. 14.3   MIDP **javax.microedition.rms** and **javax.microedition.midlet** packages.

14.2.2 MIDlets

A *MIDlet* is a Mobile Information Device application that runs on a MIDP device. The name is similar to the terms "applet" and "servlet," because these applications share similar characteristics—for example, each has a life cycle and occupies various states during program execution. Also, the developer does not invoke a constructor for objects of these classes (**Applet**, **HttpServlet** and **MIDlet**) explicitly in order to instantiate the objects. For example, a servlet container loads the servlet into memory—normally, in response to the first request that the servlet receives. MIDlets are loaded in a similar manner. MIDP developers store several MIDlets in a JAR file—called a *MIDlet suite*—on a server. The MIDP device contains a program called the *Application Management Software* (*AMS*), which downloads the MIDlet suite from the server, opens the MIDlet suite and launches the user-specified MIDlet on the MIDP device.

MIDlet Life Cycle like servlet

Figure 14.4 shows the code for our first MIDlet, called **WelcomeMIDlet**. We use this MIDlet to discuss the *life cycle*, or general execution, of a MIDlet. Every MIDlet must extend class **MIDlet** (line 10) of package **javax.microedition.midlet** (imported on line 7). The life cycle begins when the AMS calls the MIDlet's constructor (lines 16–18) to launch the MIDlet. In this state, **WelcomeMIDlet** cannot accept user input or display screens that the developer created. When the constructor finishes, the AMS calls method **startApp** (lines 22–29), which places the MIDlet in an *active state*, allowing the MIDlet to display content and accept user input. The MIDlet then waits for user input or another notification from the AMS. If the AMS calls method **pauseApp** (line 32), the MIDlet returns to the *paused state*. When a MIDlet is paused, it will not process user input, and the AMS must call method **startApp** in order to enable the MIDlet to reenter the active state. If the AMS calls method **destroyApp** (line 35), which clears the device's memory for another application, the MIDlet's execution terminates. Methods **startApp**, **pauseApp** and **destroyApp** are **abstract** methods of class **MIDlet**, so every **MIDlet** subclass must override these methods.

```
1   // Fig. 14.4: WelcomeMIDlet.java.
2   // Class WelcomeMIDlet is a MIDlet that displays "Welcome to J2ME!"
3   // to the user.
4   package com.deitel.jws1.j2me.client;
5
6   // import Java 2 Micro Edition packages
7   import javax.microedition.midlet.*;
8   import javax.microedition.lcdui.*;
9
10  public class WelcomMIDlet extends MIDlet {
11
12      private Display display; // display manager
13      private Form mainScreen; // screen to display
14
```

Fig. 14.4 WelcomeMIDlet demonstrates the **MIDlet** life cycle and displays a message to the user. Reproduced with permission by Sun Microsystems, Inc.© Copyright 2002. Sun Microsystems, Inc. All Rights Reserved. (Part 1 of 2.)

```
15      // constructor initializes display manager for MIDP device
16      public WelcomeMIDlet()
17      {
18         display = Display.getDisplay( this );
19      }
20
21      // called to start MIDlet after AMS calls constructor
22      public void startApp()
23      {
24         // create a Form to display
25         mainScreen = new Form( "WelcomeMIDlet" );
26         mainScreen.append( "Welcome to J2ME!" );
27
28         display.setCurrent( mainScreen ); // display Form
29      }
30
31      // called by AMS to pause MIDlet state
32      public void pauseApp() {}
33
34      // called by AMS to terminate MIDlet lifecycle
35      public void destroyApp( boolean unconditional ) {}
36
37   } // end class WelcomeMIDlet
```

Fig. 14.4 **WelcomeMIDlet** demonstrates the **MIDlet** life cycle and displays a message to the user. Reproduced with permission by Sun Microsystems, Inc.© Copyright 2002. Sun Microsystems, Inc. All Rights Reserved. (Part 2 of 2.)

WelcomeMIDlet also uses J2ME's MIDP user-interface package **javax.micro-edition.lcdui** (imported in line 8) to display a message to the user. Line 18 initializes an instance of class **Display**, which acts as a "display manager" for a MIDlet. A MIDlet must contain exactly one **Display** in order to display any **Displayable** object. The **static** method **getDisplay** of class **Display** returns a reference to the MIDlet's **Display** object.

The **Display** object can display at most one screen at any given time. A certain subclass of abstract class **Displayable**, which we will explain in greater detail in the next section, represents a screen. Package **javax.microedition.lcdui** provides a *Form*, which is a **Displayable** subclass that enables a MIDlet to display text and images on the screen. Line 25 creates a **Form** object with **"WelcomeMIDlet"** as its title. Line 26 invokes method **append** to include on the **Form** a message to the user. Line 28 invokes method **setCurrent** of class **Display** to display the **Form** on screen.

MIDlet Deployment
We now explain how to deploy and run a MIDlet, such as the one we created in Fig. 14.4. We use the *Java 2 Micro Edition Wireless Toolkit*, Release 1.0.3, which is available for download at the following URL:

> **java.sun.com/products/j2mewtoolkit/download.html**

This site also provides instruction on how to install the toolkit on your system. This toolkit contains several emulators for MIDP applications. Throughout this chapter, we use the Sun MIDP-device emulator, although the examples we create throughout this chapter should operate correctly on all emulators provided by the toolkit (such as RIM's Blackberry-957™ and the Motorola i85s™).

After installing the toolkit, open the Wireless Toolkit application by executing **KToolbar** in the **bin** directory where you installed the toolkit. Next, click **New Project**. In the **Project Name** text field, type

> **WelcomeMIDlet**

In the **MIDlet Class Name** text field, type

> **com.deitel.jws1.j2me.client.WelcomeMIDlet**

Then click **Create Project**. When the **Settings** frame appears, click **OK**. Next, copy **WelcomeMIDlet.java** to the **apps/WelcomeMIDlet/src** directory in the directory where you installed the toolkit. For example, **C:\J2mewtk** is the directory where we installed the toolkit on our system, so we copy **WelcomeMIDlet.java** to

> **C:\J2mewtk\apps\WelcomeMIDlet\src**

Return to the Wireless toolkit window, and click **Build**. When **WelcomeMIDlet** has finished compiling, click **Run** to execute **WelcomeMIDlet**. The **Device** menu—located on the toolkit's right side—enables you to select from among several devices on which to run **WelcomeMIDlet**.

Upon clicking **Run**, the Application Management Software uses an *application descriptor file* to load the **WelcomeMIDlet** application. This file, which has a **.jad** extension, contains information such as the names of the MIDlets present in the MIDlet suite; the MIDlet suite's size and URL; each MIDlet's name, vendor and version; and the MIDP device's profile and configuration. The AMS uses this information to ensure that the MIDlet application will run on any given MIDP device. The J2ME Wireless Toolkit generates this file when creating a MIDlet suite. The code in Fig. 14.5 shows the **WelcomeMIDlet**'s application descriptor file.

14.3 Using J2ME to Access Web Services via Servlets

We now discuss some of the features that J2ME offers by creating a J2ME client that invokes the Book Titles Web service that we deployed in Chapter 11, JAXM and SAAJ. In this section, we also discuss the high-level J2ME APIs for creating graphical user interfaces, navigating through applications and networking with other systems.

In Chapter 11, we built a stand-alone client that used the Java API for XML Messaging (JAXM) and the SOAP with Attachments API for Java (SAAJ) to send a SOAP request to a **JAXMServlet**, called **BookTitlesServlet** (Fig. 11.5), which exposed the Book Titles Web service. Now, we build a servlet called **BookTitleProxyServlet**, which will send the request to **BookTitlesServlet**. We then build a J2ME client that makes a *get* request to **BookTitleProxyServlet** (step 1 of Fig. 14.6), which uses JAXM and SAAJ to send a SOAP message to **BookTitlesServlet** (step 2) that exposes the Book Titles Web service (steps 3 and 4). **BookTitlesServlet** returns to **BookTitleProxyServlet** a SOAP response that contains a list of available book titles in a database (step 5). **BookTitlesProxyServlet** then extracts the contents of the SOAP response message to a **String**. This **String** contains a set of **String**s, where each **String** represents a distinct book title and is delimited by the newline character (**'\n'**). Finally, **BookTitleProxyServlet** returns this **String** to the J2ME client (step 6). In Section 14.4, we use Enhydra's kSOAP package to build a client that sends SOAP requests directly to the Web service, rather than use a servlet as a bridge between the J2ME client and the Web service.

Figure 14.7 contains the code for **BookTitleProxyServlet**—the servlet through which our MIDlet invokes the Book Titles Web service. **BookTitleProxyServlet** uses JAXM and SAAJ to send SOAP requests to, and receive SOAP responses from, a **JAXMServlet**. Method **init** (lines 23–47) creates a **SOAPConnectionFactory** and a **MessageFactory** for creating messages and specifies the **SERVICE_URL** (which references the **BookTitlesServlet** URL) as the **URLEndpoint**. The deployment descriptor associates the **SERVICE_URL** parameter (line 42) with the value **http://localhost:8080/booktitles/BookTitles**.

```
1   MIDlet-Jar-Size:1122
2   MIDlet-1:WelcomeMIDlet,, com.deitel.jws1.j2me.client.WelcomeMIDlet
3   MIDlet-Jar-URL:WelcomeMIDlet.jar
4   MicroEdition-Configuration:CLDC-1.0
5   MIDlet-Version:0.0.1
6   MIDlet-Vendor:Deitel and Associates, Inc.
7   MIDlet-Name:WelcomeMIDlet
8   MIDlet-Description:This midlet displays a message to the user
9   MIDlet-Data-Size:0
10  MicroEdition-Profile:MIDP-1.0
```

Fig. 14.5 Application descriptor (JAD) for **WelcomeMIDlet**.

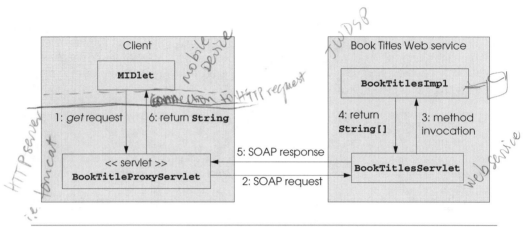

Fig. 14.6 Flowchart for a MIDP device that invokes a Web service via a servlet.

```
1    // Fig. 14.7: BookTitleProxyServlet.java.
2    // BookTitleProxyServlet uses JAXM and SAAJ to invoke the Book
3    // Titles Web service.
4    package com.deitel.jws1.j2me.servlet;
5
6    // Java core packages
7    import java.io.*;
8    import java.util.Iterator;
9
10   // Java extension packages
11   import javax.servlet.*;
12   import javax.servlet.http.*;
13   import javax.xml.soap.*;
14   import javax.xml.messaging.*;
15
16   public class BookTitleProxyServlet extends HttpServlet {
17
18      private SOAPConnectionFactory soapConnectionFactory;
19      private URLEndpoint urlEndpoint;
20      private MessageFactory messageFactory;
21
22      // initialize BookTitleProxyServlet
23      public void init() throws ServletException
24      {
25         // create factory objects
26         try {
27
28            // factory for establishing point-to-point connections
29            soapConnectionFactory =
30               SOAPConnectionFactory.newInstance();
31
32            // factory for building SOAP messages
33            messageFactory = MessageFactory.newInstance();
34         }
```

Fig. 14.7 Proxy servlet that a J2ME client can use to invoke the Book Titles Web service. (Part 1 of 4.)

```
35
36          // handle exception in initializing factory objects
37          catch ( SOAPException exception ) {
38             throw new ServletException( exception.getMessage() );
39          }
40
41          String endpoint =
42             getServletConfig().getInitParameter( "SERVICE_URL" );
43
44          // define Web-service URL
45          urlEndpoint = new URLEndpoint( endpoint );
46
47       } // end constructor
48
49       // use JAXM to invoke remote Web service
50       public void doGet( HttpServletRequest request,
51          HttpServletResponse response ) throws ServletException,
52          IOException
53       {
54          // invoke Web service and convert result to String array
55          try {
56             SOAPMessage responseMessage = sendSoapRequestMessage();
57
58             // store response message in String array
59             String titles[] =
60                handleSoapResponseMessage( responseMessage );
61
62             DataOutputStream out = new DataOutputStream(
63                new BufferedOutputStream(
64                   response.getOutputStream() ) );
65
66             // send String to client
67             for ( int i = 0; i < titles.length; i++ ) {
68                for ( int j = 0; j < titles[ i ].length(); j++ )
69                   out.writeChar( titles[ i ].charAt( j ) );
70                out.writeChar( '\n' );
71             }
72
73             out.close();
74          }
75
76          // handle exception in sending or receiving SOAP message
77          catch( SOAPException exception ) {
78             throw new IOException( exception.getMessage() );
79          }
80
81          // handle exception in populating bookTitles String array
82          catch ( ArrayIndexOutOfBoundsException exception ) {
83             throw new IOException( exception.getMessage() );
84          }
85
86       } // end method doGet
```

Fig. 14.7   Proxy servlet that a J2ME client can use to invoke the Book Titles Web service. (Part 2 of 4.)

```
87
88       // invoke remote Web service by sending SOAP request
89       private SOAPMessage sendSoapRequestMessage()
90          throws SOAPException
91       {
92          // use SOAPConnectionFactory to create SOAP connection
93          SOAPConnection soapConnection =
94             soapConnectionFactory.createConnection();
95
96          // use MessageFactory to create SOAP message
97          SOAPMessage soapRequestMessage =
98             messageFactory.createMessage();
99
100         // send SOAP message to Web service
101         SOAPMessage soapResponseMessage = soapConnection.call(
102            soapRequestMessage, urlEndpoint );
103
104         soapConnection.close();
105
106         return soapResponseMessage;
107
108      } // end method sendSoapRequestMessage
109
110      // convert SOAP message returned by Web service to array of
111      // Strings, in which each String represents a book title
112      private String[] handleSoapResponseMessage(
113         SOAPMessage soapResponseMessage ) throws SOAPException
114      {
115         // obtain references to response message elements
116         SOAPPart responsePart = soapResponseMessage.getSOAPPart();
117         SOAPEnvelope responseEnvelope = responsePart.getEnvelope();
118         SOAPBody responseBody = responseEnvelope.getBody();
119
120         // obtain Iterator of all child elements of element Body
121         Iterator responseBodyChildElements =
122            responseBody.getChildElements();
123
124         // extract element Titles from SOAP message element Body
125         SOAPBodyElement titlesElement =
126            ( SOAPBodyElement ) responseBodyChildElements.next();
127
128         // extract number of book titles from element Titles
129         int bookCount = Integer.parseInt(
130            titlesElement.getAttributeValue()
131               responseEnvelope.createName( "bookCount" ) ) );
132
133         // create array of Strings that represent book titles
134         String bookTitles[] = new String[ bookCount ];
135
136         // extract element Titles from SOAP message element Body
137         SOAPBodyElement titlesElement =
138            ( SOAPBodyElement ) responseBodyChildElements.next();
```

Fig. 14.7   Proxy servlet that a J2ME client can use to invoke the Book Titles Web service. (Part 3 of 4.)

```
139
140          // use Iterator to obtain child elements of element Titles
141          Iterator titleIterator =
142             titlesElement.getChildElements(
143                responseEnvelope.createName( "title" ) );
144
145          // store each book title in bookTitles String array
146          int i = 0;
147          while ( titleIterator.hasNext() ) {
148             SOAPElement titleElement =
149                ( SOAPElement ) titleIterator.next();
150             bookTitles[ i++ ] = titleElement.getValue();
151          }
152
153          return bookTitles;
154
155       } // end method handleSoapResponseMessage
156
157    } // end class BookTitleProxyServlet
```

Fig. 14.7   Proxy servlet that a J2ME client can use to invoke the Book Titles Web service. (Part 4 of 4.)

When a client makes a *get* request to **BookTitleProxyServlet**, method **doGet** (lines 50–86) invokes method **sendSoapRequestMessage** (lines 89–108). The latter method sends a SOAP message to **BookTitlesServlet**, requesting invocation of the Book Titles Web service. **BookTitlesServlet** returns a SOAP message that contains the available book titles. Lines 59–60 invoke method **handleSoapResponseMessage** (lines 112–155) to convert the message contents to a **String** array, in which each **String** represents a unique book title. Lines 62–64 open a **DataOutputStream** to the J2ME client, which lines 67–71 use to send the **String** array.

Figure 14.8 presents the code for **BookTitleMIDlet**, which is the J2ME client that accesses the Book Titles Web service. **BookTitleMIDlet** provides two ways to access the Web service—one via **BookTitleProxyServlet** and one via SOAP requests, using Enhydra's kSOAP package. This section discusses how **BookTitleMIDlet** invokes the Book Titles Web service by making a *get* request to **BookTitleProxyServlet**. Section 14.4 discusses how **BookTitleMIDlet** invokes the same Web service by using Enhydra's APIs.

The **BookTitleMIDlet** constructor (lines 21–47) creates a **List** that displays the available Web services that the client may access (line 24). [*Note*: For this example, the Book Titles Web service is the only service made available.] A **List** contains a set of **String**s from which the user can select by using the MIDP device's keypad. Class **List** belongs to package **javax.microedition.lcdui**, which contains classes that compose the J2ME user-interface API. J2ME divides this API into low-level and high-level APIs. The low-level API allows developers to incorporate graphics and shapes at precise pixel locations and to provide animation for applications such as games. The high-level user-interface API allows developers to incorporate text fields, lists, forms and images for programs such as e-commerce applications and basic user interfaces. The J2ME low-level user-interface API gives developers finer grained control of creating screens than does the high-level API. However, the low-level API does not guarantee layout congruity among devices with differing screen sizes, while the high-level API provides a more consistent layout among devices. Class **List** belongs to the high-level user-interface API.

Figure 14.9 shows a portion of the J2ME user-interface API. Each rectangle represents a class in the API. Each name in italics represents an abstract class, and the arrows represent inheritance relationships. (Each arrow points to the superclass.) In the J2ME user-interface API, abstract superclass **Displayable** represents content that a MIDP-device can display on screen. The abstract superclasses **Screen** and **Canvas** both inherit from class **Displayable** and represent the high-level and low-level displayable content, respectively. Classes **Alert**, **Form**, **TextBox** and **List** are concrete subclasses of class **Screen**. An **Alert** is a **Screen** that the MIDlet displays for a brief period before displaying another **Screen**. A **TextBox** enables the user to input and edit text. A **Form** aggregates text fields, images and groups of selectable items for the user. Recall that we used a **Form** in Fig. 14.4 (class **WelcomeMIDlet**) to display **"Welcome to J2ME"** to the user. Class **Canvas** does not have any subclasses. To use a **Canvas**, first create a concrete class that extends class **Canvas**; then override its **paint** method to draw graphics on the **Canvas**.

```
1   // Fig. 14.8: BookTitleMIDlet.java.
2   // BookTitleMIDlet invokes the Book Titles Web service from a
3   // servlet to receive a list of book titles.
4   package com.deitel.jws1.j2me.client;
5
6   // import J2ME packages
7   import javax.microedition.midlet.*;
8   import javax.microedition.lcdui.*;
9
10  // import Deitel packages
11  import com.deitel.jws1.services.BookTitles;
12
13  public class BookTitleMIDlet extends MIDlet {
14
15     private Display display; // display manager
16     private List mainScreen; // list of available Web services
17
18     private final static int SERVLET = 0;
19     private final static int ENHYDRA = 1;
20
21     public BookTitleMIDlet()
22     {
23        // create main screen with Web-service list
24        mainScreen = new List( "Web services", List.IMPLICIT );
25        mainScreen.append( "Get Book Titles", null );
26
27        // create soft button commands
28        Command selectCommand =
29           new Command( "Select", Command.OK, 0 );
30        mainScreen.addCommand( selectCommand );
31
```

Fig. 14.8 **BookTitleMIDlet** invokes the Book Titles Web service via a servlet or via Enhydra. Reproduced with permission by Sun Microsystems, Inc.© Copyright 2002. Sun Microsystems, Inc. All Rights Reserved. (Part 1 of 4.)

```
32            // allow soft button access for mainScreen
33            mainScreen.setCommandListener(
34               new CommandListener() {
35
36                  // invoked when user presses soft button
37                  public void commandAction(
38                     Command command, Displayable displayable )
39                  {
40                     display.setCurrent( createServiceAccessForm() );
41                  }
42               }
43            );
44
45            // get appropriate Display manager for MIDP device
46            display = Display.getDisplay( this );
47         }
48
49         // start MIDlet and enable user input
50         public void startApp()
51         {
52            // set display to main Screen
53            display.setCurrent( mainScreen );
54         }
55
56         // pause MIDlet
57         public void pauseApp() {}
58
59         // terminate MIDlet lifecycle
60         public void destroyApp( boolean unconditional ) {}
61
62         // create Form for selecting how to access Web service
63         private Screen createServiceAccessForm()
64         {
65            Form accessScreen = new Form( "Invoke Web service via:" );
66
67            // ChoiceGroup that enables user to specify means of access
68            final ChoiceGroup choices = new ChoiceGroup( "",
69               ChoiceGroup.EXCLUSIVE );
70            choices.append( "Servlet", null );
71            choices.append( "Enhydra", null );
72
73            // append ChoiceGroup to Form
74            accessScreen.append( choices );
75
76            // create soft button commands
77            Command invokeCommand =
78               new Command( "Invoke", Command.OK, 0 );
79            accessScreen.addCommand( invokeCommand );
80
81            Command backCommand =
82               new Command( "Back", Command.BACK, 1 );
```

Fig. 14.8 **BookTitleMIDlet** invokes the Book Titles Web service via a servlet or via Enhydra. Reproduced with permission by Sun Microsystems, Inc.© Copyright 2002. Sun Microsystems, Inc. All Rights Reserved. (Part 2 of 4.)

```
83              accessScreen.addCommand( backCommand );
84
85          // allow soft button access for this Screen
86          accessScreen.setCommandListener(
87             new CommandListener() {
88
89                // invoked when user presses soft button
90                public void commandAction(
91                   Command command, Displayable displayable )
92                {
93                   // invoke service if user presses SELECT button
94                   if ( command.getCommandType() == Command.OK ) {
95
96                      BookTitles service = null;
97
98                      // determine means of Web-service access
99                      int selection = choices.getSelectedIndex();
100                     if ( selection == SERVLET )
101                        service = new BookTitleServiceViaServlets();
102                     else if ( selection == ENHYDRA )
103                        service = new BookTitleServiceViaEnhydra();
104
105                     String titles[] = null;
106
107                     // invoke Web service through interface
108                     if ( service != null )
109                        titles = service.getBookTitles();
110
111                     // display book titles in List
112                     if ( titles != null ) {
113                        List titlesScreen = new List(
114                           "Book Titles", List.IMPLICIT );
115
116                        // store book titles in List
117                        for ( int i = 0; i < titles.length; i++ )
118                           titlesScreen.append( titles[ i ], null );
119
120                        // display List of book titles
121                        display.setCurrent( titlesScreen );
122                     }
123
124                     // display error page for 3 seconds if error
125                     else {
126                        Alert errorPage = new Alert( "Error",
127                           "Cannot invoke Web Service", null,
128                           AlertType.ERROR );
129                        errorPage.setTimeout( 3000 );
130                        display.setCurrent( errorPage );
131                     }
132                  }
133
```

Fig. 14.8 BookTitleMIDlet invokes the Book Titles Web service via a servlet or via Enhydra. Reproduced with permission by Sun Microsystems, Inc.© Copyright 2002. Sun Microsystems, Inc. All Rights Reserved. (Part 3 of 4.)

```
134                     // display mainScreen if user presses BACK button
135                     else if ( command.getCommandType() == Command.BACK )
136                         display.setCurrent( mainScreen );
137
138                 } // end method commandAction
139
140             } // end anonymous inner class
141         );
142
143         return accessScreen;
144
145     } // end method createServiceAccessForm
146
147 } // end class BookTitleMIDlet
```

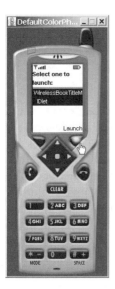  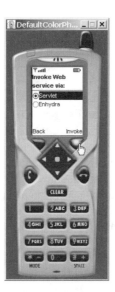 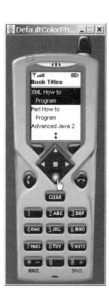

Fig. 14.8 **BookTitleMIDlet** invokes the Book Titles Web service via a servlet or via Enhydra. Reproduced with permission by Sun Microsystems, Inc.© Copyright 2002. Sun Microsystems, Inc. All Rights Reserved. (Part 4 of 4.)

Note that line 24 of Fig. 14.8 specifies that the **List** should be **IMPLICIT**. This argument determines how the user navigates the **List** with the keypad. It can accept one of three constant values: **List.IMPLICIT**, **List.EXCLUSIVE** and **List.MULTIPLE**. **List.IMPLICIT** indicates that the currently highlighted item in the **List** is the user's selection—i.e., the user changes the selection by scrolling among **List** items. **List.EXCLUSIVE** requires the user to select a **List** item by pressing a button on the MIDP keypad. The user must then finalize the selection by pressing a separate button; however, before finalizing the selection (but after having marked the selection), the user can scroll among **List** items. **List.MULTIPLE** enables the user to select several items in the **List**.

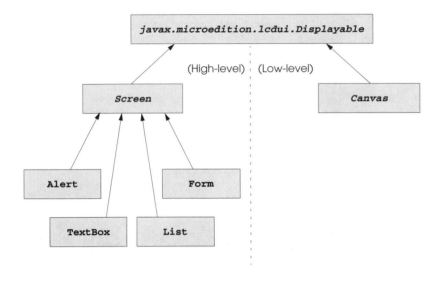

Fig. 14.9   Class hierarchy of J2ME user-interface API.

Line 25 invokes method **append** of class **List** to add item **Get Book Titles** to the **List**. By selecting this item, the user can specify how the MIDlet should access the Web service (i.e., via a proxy servlet or via Enhydra's kSOAP). The MIDlet provides this functionality through the use of *soft buttons*. Soft buttons usually are located below the display (but above the keypad) on wireless devices. For example, in the first screen in Fig. 14.8, the mouse cursor is hovering over the right soft button, which is highlighted. The word **Select** on the screen above the right soft button indicates that the user will select the highlighted **List** item (i.e., invoke the Book Titles Web service) when the user presses this soft button. The MIDlet then will perform some action, such as display a different **Screen**. J2ME provides this functionality to MIDlets through **Command** objects, which encapsulate executable actions. Lines 28–29 of **BookTitleMIDlet** create **Command** object **selectCommand**. The first argument to the **Command** constructor is the name—or label—to be displayed on the **Screen** above the soft button. The second argument is a constant that specifies how the MIDlet should respond after the user presses the soft button. For example, **Command.OK** indicates that the user has provided some input (via a text field or selection of a list item), and, accordingly, the MIDlet should perform some action (e.g., invoke a Web service). We program the logic that handles how the MIDlet behaves for each command type. The third argument indicates above which soft button the device will place the label. In a series of **Command** instantiations, the **Command** object with the lowest number has its label situated above the right soft button in the Sun MIDP-device emulator. For the object associated with the next lowest number, Sun's device places its label above the left soft button. According to lines 28–30, the device situates **Select** above the right soft button. It is important to note that the **Command** numbering scheme varies from device to device. For example, the Sun emulator's default location for **Command** text is above the right soft button. Other devices may situate the text above the left soft button.

Lines 33–43 create an anonymous **CommandListener** object that listens for events from **selectCommand** and associate the listener with **mainScreen**. When the user presses a soft button, **selectCommand** invokes method **commandAction** (lines 37–41). This method takes as arguments the **Command** object associated with the soft button and the **Displayable** object on which this action occurred. Line 40 displays a **Form** that **private** method **createServiceAccessForm** (lines 63–145) returns. This **Form** prompts the user to specify whether **BookServiceMIDlet** should access the Book Titles Web service via a servlet or via Enhydra's kSOAP. Lines 68–74 create a **Choice-Group**—a group of items that the user can select in a **Form**—to provide the user with the two options. Note that line 69 declares the **ChoiceGroup** as **EXCLUSIVE**, so the user must specify which item to select by using the center soft button (located in the center of the arrow keys on the MIDP device). **ChoiceGroup**s can be declared either as **EXCLU-SIVE** or **MULTIPLE**. Declaring a **ChoiceGroup** as **INCLUSIVE** results in an **Ille-galArgumentException**.

Lines 77–83 create two **Command** objects—one for selecting the means of accessing the Web service and the other for returning to the **List** of available services. Lines 86–141 register the **Form** as a **CommandListener** to listen for events from the **Command** objects. If the user presses the **Invoke** button, **BookTitleMIDlet** invokes the Book Titles Web service, either by making a *get* request to **BookTitleProxyServlet** or by using Enhydra's kSOAP to send a SOAP request to the Web-service environment. If the user presses the **Back** button, lines 135–136 display the previous screen (**mainScreen**).

When the user presses the **Invoke** button, the Web-service invocation is handled through a reference to a **BookTitles** object (line 109), which is declared on line 96. If the user chose to invoke the service via a servlet, line 101 assigns a **BookTitleServiceViaServlets** object (Fig. 14.10)—which we discuss momentarily—to the **BookTitles** reference. By contrast, if the user chose to invoke the service via Enhydra's kSOAP, line 103 assigns a **BookTitleServiceViaEnhydra** object (Fig. 14.15), which we discuss in Section 14.4, to the **BookTitles** reference.

At this point, the Web service should return a list of book titles. Lines 113–118 instantiate another **List** that displays these titles. Line 121 uses **setDisplay** of the **Display** object to display this **List**. Note that after this method call, the **Display** object no longer will display the **mainScreen List**. At this point, the user can view the book titles by scrolling through the list. If the Web service does not return a list of books, or if **BookTi-tleMIDlet** cannot invoke the Web service, lines 126–130 create an **Alert** that displays an error to the user. The first argument to the **Alert** constructor is the title of the **Alert** page. The second argument is the message that the **Alert** will display to the user. The third argument is an **Image** that the **Alert** can display. We do not display an **Image** in this example, so we pass **null** for this argument. The fourth argument is a constant of class **AlertType**, which indicates the type (i.e., **ALARM**, **CONFIRMATION**, **ERROR**, **INFO** or **WARNING**) of alert.

Figure 14.10 shows the code for **BookTitleServiceViaServlets**, which establishes an HTTP connection with a servlet to invoke the Book Titles Web service. Lines 9–10 import packages **javax.microedition.io** and **java.io**, which are the standard J2ME networking packages that contain classes for establishing network connections from MIDlets.

Method **getBookTitles** (lines 23–46) is the method that **BookTitleMIDlet** calls to invoke the Web service. Lines 29–30 instantiate an **HttpConnection** object of package **javax.microedition.io** to connect to the servlet over HTTP. Line 33 passes a reference to an **HttpConnection** object as an argument to method **getData** (lines 49–71), which is responsible for retrieving the Web-service data from the servlet. Lines 55–56 invoke method **openDataInputStream** of the **HttpConnection** object. This method makes a *get* request to **BookTitleProxyServlet** and returns a reference to an **InputStream** object that receives data from the servlet. Recall that when the servlet receives a *get* request, the servlet uses JAXM to invoke the Book Titles Web service and returns the results to the client. Lines 58–64 use method **read** of the **Input-Stream** object to retrieve the results from **BookTitleProxyServlet**. The results are represented as a **String** that contains several **String**s, delimited by newline character (**'\n'**); each **String** represents a distinct book title. To parse the resulting **String** into an array of **String**s that the MIDlet can display, we use method **parseData** (lines 74–107). This method acts as a **java.util.StringTokenizer** from J2SE; however, because J2ME does not provide a **StringTokenizer**, we must create our own.

After method **parseData** returns the **String** array of book titles, line 35 closes the **HttpConnection**. Method **getBookTitles** then returns the **String** array to the **BookTitleMIDlet** (line 37), which displays the book titles as a **List** to the user.

```
1    // Fig. 14.10: BookTitleServiceViaServlets.java.
2    // BookTitleServiceViaServlets connects to a servlet that
3    // makes a request to the Book Titles Web service.
4    package com.deitel.jws1.j2me.client;
5
6    // import J2ME packages
7    import javax.microedition.midlet.*;
8    import javax.microedition.lcdui.*;
9    import javax.microedition.io.*;
10   import java.io.*;
11
12   // import Deitel packages
13   import com.deitel.jws1.services.BookTitles;
14
15   public class BookTitleServiceViaServlets
16      implements BookTitles {
17
18      // URL of servlet that accesses Book Titles Web service
19      private final static String SERVICE_URL =
20         "http://localhost:8080/j2me/BookTitlesProxy";
21
22      // invoke Book Titles Web service via servlet
23      public String[] getBookTitles()
24      {
25         // invoke Web service and convert result to String array
26         try {
27
28            // establish HTTP connection to servlet
29            HttpConnection httpConnection =
30               ( HttpConnection ) Connector.open( SERVICE_URL );
31
```

Fig. 14.10 **BookTitleServiceViaServlets** uses the J2ME networking packages to invoke the Book Titles Web service via a servlet. (Part 1 of 3.)

```
32           // receive server data
33           String titles[] = getData( httpConnection );
34
35           httpConnection.close(); // close connection
36
37           return titles;
38        }
39
40        // handle exception communicating with HTTP server
41        catch ( IOException ioException ) {
42           ioException.printStackTrace();
43           return null;
44        }
45
46     } // end method getBookTitles
47
48     // open DataInputStream to receive data
49     private String[] getData( HttpConnection httpConnection )
50        throws IOException
51     {
52        StringBuffer data = new StringBuffer();
53
54        // open input stream from connection
55        InputStream inputStream = ( DataInputStream )
56           httpConnection.openDataInputStream();
57
58        int inputCharacter = inputStream.read();
59
60        // read all data
61        while ( inputCharacter != -1 ) {
62           data.append( ( char ) inputCharacter );
63           inputCharacter = inputStream.read();
64        }
65
66        inputStream.close(); // close stream
67
68        // convert data to String array
69        return parseData( data.toString(), '\n' );
70
71     } // end method getData
72
73     // string tokenizer parses String into sub-String array
74     private String[] parseData( String data, char delimiter )
75     {
76        int newLines = 0;
77
78        // determine number of delimiter characters in String
79        for ( int i = 0; i < data.length(); i++ )
80
81           // increase number of delimiters by one
82           if ( data.charAt( i ) == delimiter )
83              newLines++;
```

Fig. 14.10 `BookTitleServiceViaServlets` uses the J2ME networking packages to invoke the Book Titles Web service via a servlet. (Part 2 of 3.)

```
84
85            // create String array to hold String tokens
86            String list[] = new String[ newLines ];
87
88            int oldNewLineIndex = 0;
89            int currentNewLineIndex;
90
91            // store Strings into array based on demiliter
92            for ( int i = 0; i < newLines; i++ ) {
93
94               // determine index where delimiter occurs
95               currentNewLineIndex =
96                  data.indexOf( delimiter, oldNewLineIndex );
97
98               // extract String within delimiter characters
99               list[ i ] = data.substring( oldNewLineIndex,
100                 currentNewLineIndex - 1 );
101
102              oldNewLineIndex = currentNewLineIndex + 1;
103           }
104
105           return list;
106
107      } // end method parseData
108
109 } // end class BookTitleServiceViaServlets
```

Fig. 14.10 `BookTitleServiceViaServlets` uses the J2ME networking packages to invoke the Book Titles Web service via a servlet. (Part 3 of 3.)

14.4 Using J2ME to Access Web Services via Enhydra's kSOAP

In the previous example, we provided a proxy servlet to enable the J2ME client to access the Web service. Now, we use Enhydra's kSOAP to build a client that will create its own SOAP request and send that request to a Web-service environment directly to invoke the service. This approach eliminates the need for a proxy.

We now deploy the Book Titles Web service on the WASP server that we used in Chapter 7. We then use **BookTitleMIDlet** to invoke this Web service directly. We use the WASP toolkit integrated in Forte to generate a Web service from a Java class (**Book-TitlesImpl.java** (Fig. 11.3) from **com/deitel/jws1/services**).

In Forte's **Explorer [Runtime]** window, start the WASP server by right-clicking the name of the WASP server that we created in Section 7.5 and clicking **Start WASP Server**. In Forte's **Explorer [Filesystems]** window, select **BookTitlesImpl**—the name of the Java class for which we are generating the Web service. Then select **Tools>Generate Web Service**. A window will appear that allows the methods from which the toolkit generates Web services to be specified. Make sure that **getBookTitles** (the only method that class **BookTitlesImpl** contains) is selected. Click **Next** to specify the properties for this Web service. We used **urn:com.deitel.jws1.services.BookTitlesImpl** as the **Target Namespace**, **/BookTitlesImpl/** for the **Relative URI**, and **BookTitlesImpl** for the **Service** and **Port** names in the WSDL file that we generate in the next step. Click **Finish** to create the Web service.

To deploy **BookTitlesImpl**, right-click the descriptor item that contains the **BookTitlesImpl** information. Then select **Deploy Web Service** from the pop-up menu. The **Deploy Web Services Wizard** contains four steps:

1. The name of the Web service to deploy (**BookTitlesImpl**) is entered in the **Package Name** screen(Fig. 14.11).

2. The WASP server on which to deploy the Web service is selected in the **WASP Server** screen (Fig. 14.12).

3. Any classes or libraries that the Web service should use are specified in the **Web Service List** screen (Fig.14.13). In our example, **BookTitlesImpl** uses **BookTitles.properties**, which contains the database URL and JDBC driver, and **RmiJdbc.jar** and **cloudclient.jar**, which contain classes for accessing the Cloudscape database. Click **Edit Web Service>Select Classes**; then **Add BookTitles.properties** to the **Chosen content**. Next, click **Select Libraries**, and **Add RmiJdbc.jar** and **cloudclient.jar** to the **Chosen content**.

4. Additional information (e.g., author, version, and time created) about the Web service is includes in the **Package Info** screen (Fig. 14.14).

For creating the SOAP request on the J2ME platform, we use Enhydra's kSOAP and kXML packages. Specifically, kSOAP handles SOAP messaging, and kXML handles XML-document generation and parsing. Enhydra's kSOAP v.0.99 and kXML v.1.2.1 packages are contained in **ksoap.zip** and **kxml.zip**, respectively. They are available for download at

> **ksoap.enhydra.org/software/downloads/index.html**

> **kxml.enhydra.org/software/downloads/index.html**

Remember to place these **zip** files in the class path when compiling J2ME applications. If you are using the Java 2 Micro Edition Wireless Toolkit, place these **zip** files in the **lib** directory of your project.

Fig. 14.11 Web-service creation from a Java class, using the **WASP Developer Advanced** module (step 1). Courtesy of Systinet. Reproduced with permission by Sun Microsystems, Inc.© Copyright 2002. Sun Microsystems, Inc. All Rights Reserved.

Fig. 14.12 Web-service creation from a Java class, using the **WASP Developer Advanced** module (step 2). Courtesy of Systinet. Reproduced with permission by Sun Microsystems, Inc.© Copyright 2002. Sun Microsystems, Inc. All Rights Reserved.

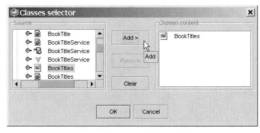

Fig. 14.13 Web-service creation from a Java class, using the **WASP Developer Advanced** module (step 3). Courtesy of Systinet. Reproduced with permission by Sun Microsystems, Inc.© Copyright 2002. Sun Microsystems, Inc. All Rights Reserved. (Part 1 of 2.)

Fig. 14.13 Web-service creation from a Java class, using the **WASP Developer Advanced** module (step 3). Courtesy of Systinet. Reproduced with permission by Sun Microsystems, Inc.© Copyright 2002. Sun Microsystems, Inc. All Rights Reserved. (Part 2 of 2.)

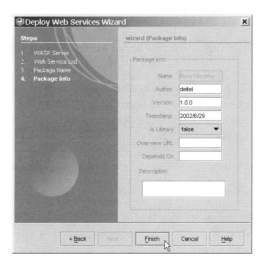

Fig. 14.14 Web-service creation from a Java class, using the **WASP Developer Advanced** module (step 4). Courtesy of Systinet. Reproduced with permission by Sun Microsystems, Inc.© Copyright 2002. Sun Microsystems, Inc. All Rights Reserved.

Figure 14.15 shows the code for **BookTitleServiceViaEnhydra**, which uses kSOAP and kXML to invoke the Book Titles Web service. Lines 10–11 import the kSOAP packages. Note that we did not import the kXML packages; however, kSOAP uses kXML for SOAP message creation, so **kxml.zip** must be present in the class path.

Lines 28–70 define method **getBookTitles**, which is the only method in class **BookTitleServiceViaEnhydra**. Lines 35–36 an **HttpTransport** object, which belongs to package **ksoap.transport**. **HttpTransport** is similar to **HttpConnection** of package **javax.microedition.io**, in that both classes are responsible for establishing a connection and transferring data over HTTP. However, unlike **HttpConnection**, **HttpTransport** deals exclusively with sending SOAP messages. The first argu-

ment to the **HttpTransport** constructor is the URL of the Web service, which we define
in lines 20–21. To determine the value for this URL, open the WSDL document for the Web
service we want the MIDlet to invoke. The URL is located in the **location** attribute of the
address element, which is located in the **port** element of the **service** element. The
second argument in the constructor specifies the SOAP action, which exists in the SOAP
header. Our message does not need to specify a SOAP action, so we specify an empty
String for this argument. The value for the SOAP action is located in the **soapAction**
attribute of the **operation** element, which is located in the **binding** element.

Lines 39–40 create a **SoapObject**, which contains the SOAP request that the client
will send to the Web-service environment. The first argument to the **SoapObject** constructor is the namespace under which the SOAP message is bound. We define this
namespace in lines 24–25. The namespace value is located in the **namespace** attribute of
the **input** element, which is located in the **operation** element of the **binding** element. The second argument is the name of the method that contains the Web service. We
want the Web-service environment to invoke method **getBookTitles** of class
com.deitel.jws1.services.BookTitleImpl, so we specify **"getBookTi-
tles"** as the second argument in the constructor. The method name is located in the **name**
attribute of the **operation** element, which is located in the **binding** element.

Lines 43–44 pass the **SoapObject** as an argument to method **call** of the **Http-
Transport** object. This method invocation invokes the **getBookTitles** Web service,
which returns a **Vector** of **String**s; each **String** represents a distinct book title. Lines
46–53 convert this **Vector** to an array of **String**s and return the array to the client. The
client (**BookTitleMIDlet**) then displays these book titles, using a **List**.

```
1   // Fig. 14.15: BookTitleServiceViaEnhydra.java.
2   // BookTitleServiceViaEnhydra invokes the Book Titles
3   // Web service on behalf of BookTitleMIDlet.
4   package com.deitel.jws1.j2me.client;
5
6   // import J2ME classes
7   import java.util.*;
8
9   // import Enhydra XML and SOAP packages
10  import org.ksoap.*;
11  import org.ksoap.transport.*;
12
13  // import Deitel packages
14  import com.deitel.jws1.services.BookTitles;
15
16  public class BookTitleServiceViaEnhydra
17     implements BookTitles {
18
19     // URL of Book Titles Web service
20     private final static String SERVICE_URL =
21        "http://localhost:6060/BookTitlesImpl/";
22
```

Fig. 14.15 **BookTitleServiceViaEnhydra** uses Enhydra's SOAP and XML
packages to invoke the Book Titles Web service. Reproduced with
permission by Sun Microsystems, Inc.© Copyright 2002. Sun Microsystems,
Inc. All Rights Reserved. (Part 1 of 3.)

```
23      // namespace that Book Titles Web service uses
24      private final static String NAMESPACE =
25         "urn:com.deitel.jws1.services.BookTitlesImpl";
26
27      // invoke Book Titles Web service
28      public String[] getBookTitles()
29      {
30         // invoke Web service and convert result to String array
31         try {
32            String titles[] = null;
33
34            // establish HTTP connection to Web-service URL
35            HttpTransport httpTransport =
36               new HttpTransport( SERVICE_URL, "" );
37
38            // create SOAP request to invoke Book Titles service
39            SoapObject requestMessage =
40               new SoapObject( NAMESPACE, "getBookTitles" );
41
42            // invoke Book Titles Web service
43            Vector response =
44               ( Vector ) httpTransport.call( requestMessage );
45
46            titles = new String[ response.size() ];
47
48            Enumeration iterator = response.elements();
49            int i = 0;
50
51            // convert response to String array
52            while ( iterator.hasMoreElements() )
53               titles[ i++ ] = ( String ) iterator.nextElement();
54
55            return titles;
56         }
57
58         // handle exception in sending or receiving SOAP message
59         catch( java.io.IOException ioException ) {
60            ioException.printStackTrace();
61            return null;
62         }
63
64         // handle exception in populating bookTitles String array
65         catch( ClassCastException exception ) {
66            exception.printStackTrace();
67            return null;
68         }
69
70      } // end method getBookTitles
71
72   } // end class BookTitleServiceViaEnhydra
```

Fig. 14.15 BookTitleServiceViaEnhydra uses Enhydra's SOAP and XML packages to invoke the Book Titles Web service. Reproduced with permission by Sun Microsystems, Inc.© Copyright 2002. Sun Microsystems, Inc. All Rights Reserved. (Part 2 of 3.)

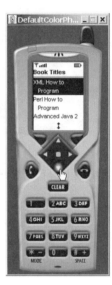

Fig. 14.15 `BookTitleServiceViaEnhydra` uses Enhydra's SOAP and XML packages to invoke the Book Titles Web service. Reproduced with permission by Sun Microsystems, Inc.© Copyright 2002. Sun Microsystems, Inc. All Rights Reserved. (Part 3 of 3.)

In this chapter, we have introduced the Java 2 Micro Edition, Sun's newest addition to the Java platforms. We have discussed the Connected Limited Device Configuration, the Mobile Information Device Protocol and features that are crucial for the execution of a MIDlet. We have also built a MIDlet capable of accessing Web services, using both servlets and Enhydra's kSOAP package. In Chapters 15–17, we present a case study that involves several Web services to retrieve information about Deitel books.

14.5 Summary

Sun introduced J2ME to provide the functionality that the other Java platforms—Java 2 Standard Edition (J2SE™) and Java 2 Enterprise Edition (J2EE™)—do not provide. J2ME enables developers to write applications for other consumer devices, such as Web terminals and embedded systems.

The J2ME platform defines a configuration, which includes both a Java Virtual Machine (JVM) that enables J2ME programs to execute on a J2ME device and a set of APIs that enables developers to create applications that run on devices containing limited resources. The J2ME platform defines a profile, which provides a set of APIs that enables developers to create applications that run on specific devices (e.g., mobile phones), which, in turn, use a configuration.

The Connected Limited Device Configuration (CLDC) is a set of APIs that allows developers to create applications for devices that have limited resources—e.g., limited screen size, memory, power and bandwidth. The J2ME CLDC contains both a virtual machine and a set of classes with which developers can develop and run programs on resource-limited devices.

The *KVM*—the virtual machine offered by the CLDC—runs J2ME applications. The J2ME CLDC contains packages `java.io`, `java.lang` and `java.util`, which developers use to perform such common operations as creating primitive data types, using simple data structures, and sending and receiving data from networks.

The Mobile Information Device Profile (MIDP) is a set of APIs that allows developers to handle mobile-device-specific issues, such as creating user interfaces, permitting local storage and defining the life cycles of MIDP client applications (MIDlets). Devices that use the MIDP to run applications are called MIDP devices. Such devices include cell phones and pagers. MIDP contains packages `javax.microedition.lcdui`, `javax.microedition.io`, `javax.microedition.rms` and `javax.microedition.midlet`.

A MIDlet is a Mobile Information Device application that runs on a MIDP device. MIDP developers store several MIDlets in a JAR file—called a MIDlet suite—on a server. The MIDP device contains a program called the Application Management Software (AMS), which downloads the MIDlet suite from the server, opens the MIDlet suite, and launches the user-specified MIDlet on the MIDP device. The Application Management Software uses an application descriptor file to load MIDlet applications. This file, which has a `.jad` extension, contains certain information on MIDlets. Every MIDlet must extend class `MIDlet` of package `javax.microedition.midlet`. Methods `startApp`, `pauseApp` and `destroyApp` are `abstract` methods of class `MIDlet`.

The low-level user-interface API allows developers to incorporate graphics and shapes at precise pixel locations and to provide animation for applications such as games. The high-level user-interface API allows developers to incorporate text fields, lists, forms and images for programs such as e-commerce applications and basic user interfaces.

Developers can use Enhydra's kSOAP and kXML packages for creating SOAP requests on J2ME platforms. Specifically, kSOAP handles SOAP messaging, and kXML handles XML-document generation and parsing. Developers also can enable a MIDlet to use a servlet for Web-service invocation.

14.6 Internet and World Wide Web Resources

www.java.sun.com/j2me
This site contains Sun's Java 2 Micro Edition, which is available for download.

java.sun.com/products/j2mewtoolkit/download.html
This site contains the Java 2 Micro Edition Wireless Toolkit, which is available free for download.

java.sun.com/j2me/docs/pdf/cldcapi.pdf
This page is a PDF for the Connected Limited Device Configuration API.

java.sun.com/products/midp/midp-wirelessapps-wp.pdf
This page is a PDF for the Mobile Information Device Profile API.

ksoap.enhydra.org/software/downloads/index.html
This is Enhyrda's Web site for downloading kSOAP—a package that enables clients to send and receive SOAP requests to Web services. This site also provides Javadoc documentation for using the kSOAP APIs.

kxml.enhydra.org/software/downloads/index.html
This is Enhyrda's Web site for downloading kXML—a package that enables clients to parse XML documents. This site also provides Javadoc documentation for using the kXML APIs.

www.onjava.com/pub/a/onjava/2001/03/08/J2ME.html
This site contains an article that introduces Java 2 Micro Edition.

www.jguru.com/faq/home.jsp?topic=J2ME
This site lists frequently asked questions regarding J2ME.

www.wirelessdevnet.com/channels/java/features/j2me_http.phtml
This site discusses network programming on J2ME devices.

www.motorola.com/java
This site discusses Motorola's J2ME implementation and integration in Motorola wireless devices.

15

Case Study: Architecture and Web-Service Implementations

Objectives

- To integrate several Web services into a complete application.
- To understand the architecture of the Price Finder Web-services-based application.
- To learn how Web services deployed on disparate Web-service platforms can interoperate.

The great thing about being an architect is you can walk into your dreams.
Harold E. Wagoner

Profits may be obtained either by producing what consumers want or by making consumers want what one is actually producing.
Henry Simons

To serve is beautiful, but only if it is done with joy and a whole heart and a free mind.
Pearl S. Buck

Everything should be made as simple as possible, but not simpler.
Albert Einstein

The art of art, the glory of expression and the sunshine of the light of letters, is simplicity.
Walt Whitman

Outline

15.1 Introduction

Web services enable developers to build integrated applications across businesses. In this case study, we implement and integrate a set of Web services to provide consumers with a means for purchasing Deitel publications at the best prices available from a group of book stores. In this and the following two chapters, we present the architecture and implementation of the Price Finder application, its supporting Web services and the consumer applications that are clients of the Price Finder. This first chapter presents the architecture and the Web-service implementations. Chapter 16 presents three clients that enable consumers to use the Price Finder application from a Web site, a Java 2 Micro Edition application and a Swing-based desktop application. Chapter 17 discusses the process of deploying the Web services, each of which executes on a different Web-services platform.

15.2 Price Finder Application Architecture

The Price Finder application provides a single access point via which consumers can search through the catalogs of three online bookstores to find the best prices on Deitel publications. Consumers can also retrieve detailed information about those books, such as lists of authors, cover images and product descriptions, through the Price Finder application.

By integrating Web services from several fictitious online bookstores and from Deitel & Associates, Inc., the Price Finder application provides its functionality. Figure 15.1 shows the general architecture of the Price Finder application.

Clients access public Web services offered by the Price Finder application to obtain price quotes, place orders for books, and retrieve detailed information about books. Each of these Web services then connects either to the bookstores' Web services or to the Deitel Book Information Web service to compare prices, place orders or obtain information about publications. This simplifies the client implementations: They need only to access the Price Finder's Web services. If the Price Finder application integrates additional bookstores in the future, the clients need not change to take advantage of additional price-quoting or book-ordering services.

Figure 15.2 lists the fictitious organizations in this case study, the Web services they provide, the platforms on which they are deployed and the URLs of the Web-services endpoints.

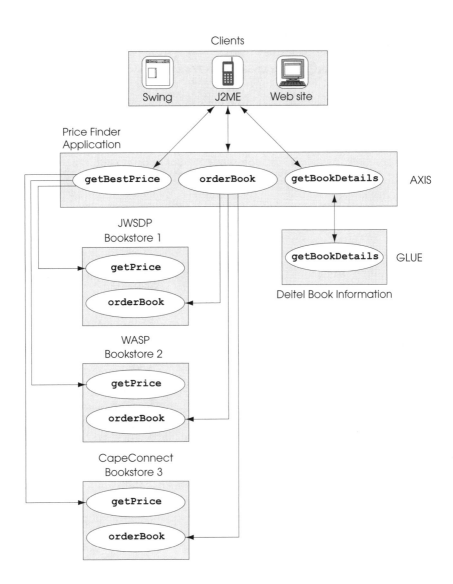

Fig. 15.1   Price Finder application architecture.

Web Service Name	Endpoint URI
Price Finder on Apache Axis	
getBestPrice	localhost:8080/axis/services/BestBookPrice
orderBook	localhost:8080/axis/services/BookPurchase

Fig. 15.2   Service platforms and URLs for case-study Web services. (Part 1 of 2.)

Web Service Name	Endpoint URI
`getBookDetails`	`localhost:8080/axis/services/BookInformation`
Bookstore 1 on JWSDP	
`getPrice`	`localhost:8080/bookstore1/getPrice`
`orderBook`	`localhost:8080/bookstore1/placeOrder`
Bookstore 2 on WASP	
`getPrice`	`localhost:6060/bookstore2/BookPrice/`
`orderBook`	`localhost:6060/bookstore2/BookOrder/`
Bookstore 2 on WASP	
`getPrice`	`localhost:8000/ccx/BookPrice`
`orderBook`	`localhost:8000/ccx/BookOrder`
Deitel & Associates Book Information on GLUE	
`getBookDetails`	`localhost:8004/bookinformation/services/book-information`

Fig. 15.2 Service platforms and URLs for case-study Web services. (Part 2 of 2.)

15.3 Deitel Book Information Web Service

Online and "brick & mortar" bookstores often advertise books to their customers. Many stores also provide descriptions, reviews and background information on the books they sell. To ensure that this information is accurate and up-to-date, we provide the Deitel Book Information Web service, which allows clients to obtain detailed information about various Deitel publications. Clients then can use this information in promotional fliers, catalogs, book descriptions on their Web sites, etc.

The Deitel Book Information Web service obtains information about books from a central database. Figure 15.3 describes the fields of information stored in the database.

Interface **BookInformation** (Fig. 15.4) defines method **getBookDetails** (lines 13–14), which clients invoke to obtain detailed information about a particular Deitel publication.

Field name	Description
`isbn`	International Standard Book Number (primary key)
`title`	Complete book title
`authors`	List of author's last names
`description`	Short description of the book's contents
`coverImageURL`	URL of an image of the book's cover

Fig. 15.3 Fields in the `titles` table of Deitel Book Information Web service database.

```
1   // BookInformation.java
2   // BookInformation defines the public interface for the Deitel
3   // Book Information Web service.
4   package jws1casestudy.deitelbookinformation;
5
6   // Deitel packages
7   import jws1casestudy.pricefinder.common.BookDetails;
8
9   public interface BookInformation {
10
11      // retrieve a BookDetails object with information for the
12      // book with the given ISBN
13      public BookDetails getBookDetails( String ISBN )
14         throws Exception;
15  }
```

Fig. 15.4 **BookInformation** remote interface for the Deitel Book Information Web service.

Class **BookInformationImpl** (Fig. 15.5) is the Deitel Book Information Web-service implementation. The constructor (lines 21–41) establishes a connection to the **deitelbooks** database (lines 26–30) and creates a **PreparedStatement** (lines 33–34) for selecting book information from the **titles** table.

```
1   // BookInformationImpl.java
2   // BookInformationImpl is the implementation of the Deitel
3   // BookInformation Web service, which provides detailed
4   // information for various Deitel publications.
5   package jws1casestudy.deitelbookinformation;
6
7   // Java core packages
8   import java.rmi.RemoteException;
9   import java.sql.*;
10
11  // Deitel packages
12  import jws1casestudy.pricefinder.common.BookDetails;
13
14  public class BookInformationImpl implements BookInformation
15  {
16      // PreparedStatement for obtaining detailed book information
17      private PreparedStatement bookDetailsStatement;
18      private Connection connection;
19
20      // BookInformationImpl constructor
21      public BookInformationImpl()
22      {
23         try {
24
25            // load database driver
26            Class.forName( "COM.cloudscape.core.RmiJdbcDriver" );
```

Fig. 15.5 **BookInformationImpl** implementation of the Deitel Book Information Web service. (Part 1 of 3.)

```
27
28              // connect to database
29              connection = DriverManager.getConnection(
30                 "jdbc:cloudscape:rmi:deitelbooks" );
31
32              // created PreparedStatement for obtaining book details
33              bookDetailsStatement = connection.prepareStatement(
34                 "SELECT * FROM titles WHERE isbn = ?" );
35           }
36
37           // handle exception connecting to database
38           catch ( Exception exception ) {
39              exception.printStackTrace();
40           }
41        }
42
43        // retrieve detailed information about the book with the
44        // given ISBN and return a BookDetails object
45        public BookDetails getBookDetails( String ISBN )
46           throws Exception
47        {
48           try {
49
50              // set the ISBN for the PreparedStatement and execute
51              bookDetailsStatement.setString( 1, ISBN );
52              ResultSet results = bookDetailsStatement.executeQuery();
53
54              // check for empty ResultSet
55              if ( !results.next() )
56                 throw new Exception( "Book Not Found" );
57
58              // populate BookDetails object with data from ResultSet
59              BookDetails details = new BookDetails();
60              details.setIsbn( results.getString( "isbn" ) );
61              details.setTitle( results.getString( "title" ) );
62              details.setAuthors( results.getString( "authors" ) );
63
64              details.setDescription(
65                 results.getString( "description" ) );
66
67              details.setCoverImageURL(
68                 results.getString( "coverImageURL" ) );
69
70              return details;
71
72           } // end try block
73
74           // handle exception retrieving book information
75           catch ( SQLException sqlException ) {
76
77              sqlException.printStackTrace();
78
```

Fig. 15.5 **BookInformationImpl** implementation of the Deitel Book
Information Web service. (Part 2 of 3.)

```
79            // throw exception to remote caller
80            throw new RemoteException(
81               "Error accessing database", sqlException );
82         }
83
84      } // end method getBookDetails
85
86      // close database resources before garbage collection occurs
87      public void finalize()
88      {
89         try {
90
91            if ( bookDetailsStatement != null )
92               bookDetailsStatement.close();
93
94            if ( connection != null )
95               connection.close();
96         }
97
98         // handle exception closing database resources
99         catch ( SQLException sqlException ) {
100           sqlException.printStackTrace();
101        }
102     }
103  }
```

Fig. 15.5 **BookInformationImpl** implementation of the Deitel Book
Information Web service. (Part 3 of 3.)

Method **getBookDetails** (lines 45–84) executes the **bookDetailsState-ment PreparedStatement** to obtain detailed information about the book with the given ISBN. Line 56 throws an exception to the caller if there is no information for the given ISBN. Lines 59–68 create and populate a **BookDetails** object with the ISBN, title, authors, description and cover image URL for the selected book. Method **finalize** (lines 87–102) closes the **PreparedStatement** and database **Connection**. We discuss the deployment of the Deitel Book Information Web service in Chapter 17.

15.4 Bookstore Implementations

In this section, we discuss the roles of the three fictitious bookstores in this case study. Each bookstore exposes two Web services: The Book Price Web service returns a book's price based on that book's ISBN, and the Book Order Web service enables a customer to order a book via that book's ISBN and the customer's information. For simplicity, each bookstore will use the same Web-service implementations—**BookPriceImpl** and **BookOrder-Impl**—but those implementations will be deployed into three separate Web-services platforms. In real bookstores, each bookstore would have its own Web-service implementation. (For example, one bookstore might expose a Book Order Web service via class **BookO-rder** that contains an **orderBook** method, whereas another bookstore might expose a Book Purchase Web service via class **BookPurchase** that contains a **purchaseBook** method—however, each Web service would provide the same functionality.) In our case study, each bookstore exposes a Book Price Web service that contains a **getPrice** method and a Book Order Web service that contains a **placeOrder** method. However, the bookstores differ in that each uses a different technology to deploy its Web services: Bookstore 1 uses JAXM to expose its Web services; Bookstore 2 uses WASP to expose its Web services; Bookstore 3 uses CapeConnect to expose its Web services. By integrating Web services running on different Web-service platforms, we demonstrate the interoperability that SOAP and WSDL provide

Interface **BookPrice** (Fig. 15.6) provides an interface through which clients can access the Book Price Web service. Interface **BookPrice** declares method **getPrice** (lines 15–16), which takes as an argument a **String** that represents a book's ISBN. The method returns a **PriceQuote** that contains the price of that book and information about the bookstore that provided the quote.

Class **BookPriceImpl** (Fig. 15.7) implements interface **BookPrice** and encapsulates the logic for the Book Price Web service. Lines 24–85 define the **BookPrice** constructor. Lines 33–44 open the property files **Database.properties** (Fig. 15.8) and **BookStore.properties** (Fig. 15.9), which contain database and bookstore information, respectively. Lines 47–52 establish a connection to the database that stores the prices. Method **getPrice** (lines 87–146) handles the logic for the Book Price Web service. Lines 102–103 obtain from the database the price associated with the ISBN argument. Lines 112–117 ensure that the price value has two-digit precision. Lines 120–132 create a **PriceQuote** object from the price value and from the values specified in **BookStore.properties**. Lastly, method **finalize** (lines 149–162) closes the database connection.

Class **BookPriceServlet** (Fig. 15.10) is a **JAXMServlet** that uses **BookPriceImpl** to expose the Book Price Web service for Bookstore 1. Method **init** (lines 28–44) creates the **BookPriceImpl** object and obtains the default **MessageFactory** that **BookPriceServlet** uses to create SOAP responses. **BookPriceServlet** invokes method **onMessage** (lines 47–72) upon receiving a SOAP request. Line 53 calls **private** method **getISBN** (lines 75–103) to extract the ISBN from the SOAP request. Line 57 then passes the ISBN value to method **getPrice** of the **BookPriceImpl** object, which returns a **PriceQuote** of the book associated with the ISBN. Line 61 passes this **PriceQuote** reference to **private** method **createResponse** (lines 106–182), which creates a SOAP response that stores the values contained in the **PriceQuote**. Lines 133–135 create the **body** element for this SOAP response. Lines 138–143 create **priceQuoteElement**—a **SOAPElement** that will contain the **PriceQuote** values—and attach it to the SOAP response's **body** element. Lines 146–178 create **SOAPElement**s that contain the **PriceQuote**'s price, ISBN and store ID and description values and attach them to **priceQuoteElement**. Line 180 returns the SOAP response to the client that sent the initial SOAP request.

```
1   // Fig. 15.6: BookPrice.java.
2   // BookPrice provides an interface to the Book Price Web service,
3   // which returns the price of a book, based on a specified ISBN.
4   package jws1casestudy.bookstore1;
5
6   // Java core packages
7   import java.rmi.*;
8
```

Fig. 15.6   **BookPrice** is the interface for the Book Price Web service. (Part 1 of 2.)

```
9    // Deitel packages
10   import jws1casestudy.pricefinder.common.PriceQuote;
11
12   public interface BookPrice extends Remote {
13
14      // service to obtain price of books based on ISBN
15      public PriceQuote getPrice( String ISBN )
16         throws RemoteException;
17
18   } // end interface BookPrice
```

Fig. 15.6 **BookPrice** is the interface for the Book Price Web service. (Part 2 of 2.)

```
1    // Fig. 15.7: BookPriceImpl.java.
2    // Class BookPriceImpl is an implementation of the Book Price Web
3    // service, which returns the price of a book, based on a
4    // specified ISBN.
5    package jws1casestudy.bookstore1;
6
7    // Java core packages
8    import java.io.*;
9    import java.util.*;
10   import java.sql.*;
11   import java.text.NumberFormat;
12   import java.rmi.*;
13
14   // Deitel packages
15   import jws1casestudy.pricefinder.common.PriceQuote;
16
17   public class BookPriceImpl implements BookPrice {
18
19      private Connection connection; // connection to database
20      private Properties databaseProperties;
21      private Properties storeProperties;
22
23      // constructor to initialize database connection
24      public BookPriceImpl() throws Exception
25      {
26         InputStream databasePropertyStream = null;
27         InputStream storePropertyStream = null;
28
29         // load JDBC driver and establish connection to database
30         try {
31
32            // obtain URLs of properties files
33            databasePropertyStream =
34               getClass().getResourceAsStream(
35                  "Database.properties" );
36            storePropertyStream =
37               getClass().getResourceAsStream(
38                  "BookStore.properties" );
```

Fig. 15.7 **BookPriceImpl** handles the logic for the Book Price Web service.
       (Part 1 of 4.)

```
39
40              // load properties files
41              databaseProperties = new Properties();
42              databaseProperties.load( databasePropertyStream );
43              storeProperties = new Properties();
44              storeProperties.load( storePropertyStream );
45
46              // load JDBC driver
47              Class.forName( databaseProperties.getProperty(
48                 "jdbcDriver" ) );
49
50              // establish database connection
51              connection = DriverManager.getConnection(
52                 databaseProperties.getProperty( "databaseURI" ) );
53           }
54
55           // handle exception if database driver does not exist
56           catch ( ClassNotFoundException classNotFoundException ) {
57              classNotFoundException.printStackTrace();
58              throw new Exception( "Unable to initialize service" );
59           }
60
61           // handle exception in making Connection
62           catch ( SQLException sqlException ) {
63              sqlException.printStackTrace();
64              throw new Exception( "Unable to initialize service" );
65           }
66
67           // handle exception in loading properties file
68           catch ( IOException ioException ) {
69              ioException.printStackTrace();
70              throw new Exception( "Unable to initialize service" );
71           }
72
73           // close properties streams
74           finally {
75
76              // close database property stream
77              if ( databasePropertyStream != null )
78                 databasePropertyStream.close();
79
80              // close bookstore property stream
81              if ( storePropertyStream != null )
82                 storePropertyStream.close();
83           }
84        } // end BookPriceImpl constructor
85
86        // service to obtain price of books based on ISBN
87        public PriceQuote getPrice( String ISBN )
88           throws RemoteException
89        {
```

Fig. 15.7 **BookPriceImpl** handles the logic for the Book Price Web service. (Part 2 of 4.)

```
90              // ensure valid database connection
91              if ( connection == null )
92                  throw new RemoteException(
93                      "Unable to establish database connection" );
94
95              // query database for price associated with ISBN
96              try {
97
98                  // SQL query to database
99                  Statement statement = connection.createStatement();
100
101                 // use SQL query to obtain price from database
102                 ResultSet resultSet = statement.executeQuery(
103                     "SELECT price FROM Books WHERE ISBN = " + ISBN );
104
105                 PriceQuote priceQuote = null;
106
107                 // extract price from ResultSet
108                 if ( resultSet != null ) {
109                     resultSet.next();
110
111                     // format price to two decimal places
112                     NumberFormat numberFormat =
113                         NumberFormat.getNumberInstance();
114                     numberFormat.setMaximumFractionDigits( 2 );
115                     double price = Double.parseDouble(
116                         numberFormat.format(
117                             resultSet.getDouble( "price" ) ) );
118
119                     // get store ID from properties file
120                     int storeID = Integer.parseInt(
121                         storeProperties.getProperty( "storeID" ) );
122
123                     // get store description from properties file
124                     String storeDescription =
125                         storeProperties.getProperty( "storeDescription" );
126
127                     // create PriceQuote from ResultSet and properties
128                     priceQuote = new PriceQuote();
129                     priceQuote.setPrice( price );
130                     priceQuote.setIsbn( ISBN );
131                     priceQuote.setStoreID( storeID );
132                     priceQuote.setStoreDescription( storeDescription );
133                 }
134                 statement.close();
135
136                 return priceQuote;
137             }
138
139             // handle exception in executing Statement
140             catch ( SQLException sqlException ) {
141                 sqlException.printStackTrace();
```

Fig. 15.7   **BookPriceImpl** handles the logic for the Book Price Web service.
(Part 3 of 4.)

```
142              throw new RemoteException(
143                  "Error occured in BookPrice Web-service invocation" );
144          }
145
146      } // end method getPrice
147
148      // close database connection
149      public void finalize()
150      {
151          // close database connection
152          try {
153              if ( connection != null )
154                  connection.close();
155          }
156
157          // handle expection in closing database
158          catch ( SQLException sqlException ) {
159              sqlException.printStackTrace();
160          }
161
162      } // end method finalize
163
164  } // end class BookPriceImpl
```

Fig. 15.7   BookPriceImpl handles the logic for the Book Price Web service.
(Part 4 of 4.)

```
1   # Fig. 15.8: Database.properties
2   # Properties file for Bookstore database connectivity
3
4   # property for database URI
5   databaseURI=jdbc:cloudscape:rmi:BookStore1
6
7   # property for database JDBC driver
8   jdbcDriver=COM.cloudscape.core.RmiJdbcDriver
```

Fig. 15.8   Database.properties stores information on **Bookstore 1** database
connectivity.

```
1   # Fig. 15.9: BookStore.properties
2   # Properties file for Bookstore information.
3
4   # property for storeID
5   storeID=1
6
7   # property for store description
8   storeDescription=BookStore1
```

Fig. 15.9   BookStore.properties stores information about Bookstore 1.

```java
1   // Fig. 15.10: BookPriceServlet.java.
2   // Class BookPriceServlet exposes the Book Price Web Service for
3   // Bookstore 1.
4   package jws1casestudy.bookstore1;
5
6   // Java core packages
7   import java.sql.*;
8   import java.util.*;
9
10  // Java extension packages
11  import javax.servlet.*;
12  import javax.xml.messaging.*;
13  import javax.xml.soap.*;
14
15  // Deitel packages
16  import jws1casestudy.pricefinder.common.*;
17
18  public class BookPriceServlet extends JAXMServlet
19     implements ReqRespListener {
20
21     // factory used to create SOAPMessage objects
22     private MessageFactory messageFactory;
23
24     // reference to object that provides Web-Service
25     private BookPrice service;
26
27     // initialize BookPriceServlet
28     public void init( ServletConfig config )
29        throws ServletException
30     {
31        super.init( config );
32
33        // instantiate Web-service object and obtain MessageFactory
34        try {
35           service = new BookPriceImpl();
36           messageFactory = MessageFactory.newInstance();
37        }
38
39        // handle exception in creating MessageFactory
40        catch ( Exception exception ) {
41           exception.printStackTrace();
42        }
43
44     } // end method init
45
46     // container invokes this method upon receiving SOAP message
47     public SOAPMessage onMessage( SOAPMessage message )
48     {
49        // invoke Web service and return results as SOAP message
50        try {
51
```

Fig. 15.10 BookPriceServlet is a JAXMServlet that exposes the Book Price Web service for Bookstore 1. (Part 1 of 4.)

```
52                // extract ISBN from incoming SOAPMessage
53                String isbn = getISBN( message );
54
55                // invoke Book Price Web service
56                if ( service != null && isbn != null ) {
57                   PriceQuote priceQuote = service.getPrice( isbn );
58
59                   // store result as SOAP message and return to client
60                   if ( priceQuote != null )
61                      return createResponse( priceQuote );
62                }
63             }
64
65             // handle exception if unable to create SOAP message
66             catch ( Exception exception ) {
67                exception.printStackTrace();
68             }
69
70             return null;
71
72          } // end method onMessage
73
74          // extract ISBN from SOAP message request
75          private String getISBN( SOAPMessage message )
76             throws SOAPException
77          {
78             // obtain references to envelope and body of message
79             SOAPPart part = message.getSOAPPart();
80             SOAPEnvelope envelope = part.getEnvelope();
81             SOAPBody body = envelope.getBody();
82
83             // get child elements of SOAPBody
84             Iterator childElements = body.getChildElements();
85
86             childElements.next(); // skip first element
87
88             // cast to SOAPBodyElement
89             SOAPBodyElement getPriceElement =
90                ( SOAPBodyElement ) childElements.next();
91
92             // get child elements of SOAPBodyElement
93             Iterator subElements = getPriceElement.getChildElements();
94
95             subElements.next(); // skip first element
96
97             // obtain SOAPElement that contains isbn
98             SOAPElement isbnElement =
99                ( SOAPElement ) subElements.next();
100
101            return isbnElement.getValue();
102
103         } // end method getISBN
```

Fig. 15.10 `BookPriceServlet` is a `JAXMServlet` that exposes the Book Price Web service for Bookstore 1. (Part 2 of 4.)

```
104
105    // store PriceQuote as SOAP message
106    private SOAPMessage createResponse( PriceQuote priceQuote )
107       throws SOAPException
108    {
109       // create empty SOAP message
110       SOAPMessage message = messageFactory.createMessage();
111
112       // obtain references to response message elements
113       SOAPPart part = message.getSOAPPart();
114       SOAPEnvelope envelope = part.getEnvelope();
115       SOAPBody body = envelope.getBody();
116
117       // add namespace declarations
118       envelope.addAttribute( envelope.createName( "xmlns:xsd" ),
119          "http://www.w3.org/2001/XMLSchema" );
120       envelope.addAttribute( envelope.createName( "xmlns:ns1" ),
121          "http://www.deitel.com/BookPrice/type" );
122       envelope.addAttribute( envelope.createName( "xmlns:xsi" ),
123          "http://www.w3.org/2001/XMLSchema-instance" );
124       envelope.addAttribute(
125          envelope.createName( "xmlns:SOAP-ENC" ),
126          "http://schemas.xmlsoap.org/soap/encoding/" );
127
128       // set encoding style for SOAP body
129       body.setEncodingStyle(
130          "http://schemas.xmlsoap.org/soap/encoding/" );
131
132       // create root element
133       SOAPBodyElement returnMessageElement = body.addBodyElement(
134          envelope.createName( "getPriceResponse",
135             "ns2", "http://www.deitel.com/BookPrice.wsdl" ) );
136
137       // create root element
138       SOAPElement priceQuoteElement =
139          returnMessageElement.addChildElement(
140             envelope.createName( "return" ) );
141       priceQuoteElement.addAttribute(
142          envelope.createName( "xsi:type" ),
143             "ns1:PriceQuote" );
144
145       // store price element as priceQuoteElement child
146       SOAPElement priceElement =
147          priceQuoteElement.addChildElement(
148             envelope.createName( "price" ) );
149       priceElement.addTextNode(
150          Double.toString( priceQuote.getPrice() ) );
151       priceElement.addAttribute(
152          envelope.createName( "xsi:type" ), "xsd:double" );
153
```

Fig. 15.10 BookPriceServlet is a JAXMServlet that exposes the Book Price
Web service for Bookstore 1. (Part 3 of 4.)

```
154        // store ISBN element as priceQuoteElement child
155        SOAPElement isbnElement =
156           priceQuoteElement.addChildElement(
157              envelope.createName( "isbn" ) );
158        isbnElement.addTextNode( priceQuote.getIsbn() );
159        isbnElement.addAttribute(
160           envelope.createName( "xsi:type" ), "xsd:string" );
161
162        // store storeID element as priceQuoteElement child
163        SOAPElement storeIdElement =
164           priceQuoteElement.addChildElement(
165              envelope.createName( "storeID" ) );
166        storeIdElement.addTextNode(
167           Integer.toString( priceQuote.getStoreID() ) );
168        storeIdElement.addAttribute(
169           envelope.createName( "xsi:type" ), "xsd:int" );
170
171        // store storeDescription element as priceQuoteElement child
172        SOAPElement storeDescriptionElement =
173           priceQuoteElement.addChildElement(
174              envelope.createName( "storeDescription" ) );
175        storeDescriptionElement.addTextNode(
176           priceQuote.getStoreDescription() );
177        storeDescriptionElement.addAttribute(
178           envelope.createName( "xsi:type" ), "xsd:string" );
179
180        return message;
181
182     } // end method createResponse
183
184 } // end class BookPriceServlet
```

Fig. 15.10 BookPriceServlet is a JAXMServlet that exposes the Book Price Web service for Bookstore 1. (Part 4 of 4.)

Interface **BookOrder** (Fig. 15.11) provides an interface through which clients can access the Book Order Web service. Interface **BookOrder** has a method **placeOrder** (lines 15–16), which takes as arguments a **String** that represents a book's ISBN and a reference to a **Customer** object that contains a customer's information.

```
1  // Fig. 15.11: BookOrder.java.
2  // BookOrder provides an interface to the Book Order Web service,
3  // which enables a client to order a book.
4  package jws1casestudy.bookstore1;
5
6  // Java core packages
7  import java.rmi.*;
8
9  // Deitel packages
10 import jws1casestudy.pricefinder.common.Customer;
11
```

Fig. 15.11 BookOrder is the interface to the Book Order Web service. (Part 1 of 2.)

```
12   public interface BookOrder extends Remote {
13
14       // service to obtain price of books based on ISBN
15       public void placeOrder( String isbn, Customer customer )
16           throws RemoteException;
17
18   } // end interface BookOrder
```

Fig. 15.11 `BookOrder` is the interface to the Book Order Web service. (Part 2 of 2.)

Class **BookOrderImpl** (Fig. 15.12) implements interface **BookOrder** and encapsulates the logic for the Book Order Web service. Lines 26–83 define the **BookOrder** constructor. Lines 35–39 open the property files **Database.properties** (Fig. 15.8) and **Mail.properties** (Fig. 15.13), which contain information on database and e-mail configuration, respectively. Lines 48–53 establishes a connection to the database that stores the prices. Method **placeOrder** (lines 86–153) handles the logic for the Book Order Web service. Lines 101–113 insert into the database's **Customers** table an entry that describes the customer who is placing the order. Upon receiving this entry, the database generates a **customerID** that serves as the primary key for the entry. Lines 116–120 retrieve the **customerID**, and lines 123–124 insert into the database's **Orders** table the **customerID**, as an entry that describes who placed the order. Upon receiving this entry, the database creates an **orderID** that serves as the primary key for the entry. Lines 127–131 retrieve the **orderID**, and lines 134–136 insert into the database's **OrderItems** table the **orderID**, the book's ISBN and the quantity ordered as an entry that describes the ordered item. If the transactions to the database are successful, lines 141–142 call **private** method **mailConfirmation** (lines 156–188) to notify the customer via e-mail of a successful order. If the transactions are unsuccessful, lines 147–148 call method **mailConfirmation** to notify the customer via e-mail of a failed order. Method **mailConfirmation** uses the JavaMail API to send e-mail to the customer's e-mail account. Lines 163–164 create a **Message** object (package **javax.mail**), using the properties file **Mail.properties** (Fig. 15.13). A **Message** object represents the e-mail message that **BookOrderImpl** will send to the customer. For the **Message** object to be instantiated correctly, **Mail.properties** must map the keys **mail.smtp.port** (line 5), **mail.transport.protocol** (line 8) and **mail.smtp.host** (line 11) to the appropriate values associated with the SMTP port, mail protocol and SMTP host on your system. Lines 167–172 specify the message's recipient and sender. Lines 175–177 date the e-mail and include the subject and text content. Line 180 sends the e-mail to the customer's e-mail account.

```
1    // Fig. 15.12: BookOrderImpl.java.
2    // Class BookOrderImpl is an implementation of the Book Order Web
3    // service, which enables a client to order a book.
4    package jws1casestudy.bookstore1;
5
6    // Java core packages
7    import java.io.*;
```

Fig. 15.12 `BookOrderImpl` handles the logic for the Book Order Web service. (Part 1 of 5.)

```java
8   import java.util.*;
9   import java.sql.*;
10  import java.rmi.RemoteException;
11
12  // import Java extension packages
13  import javax.mail.*;
14  import javax.mail.internet.*;
15
16  // Deitel packages
17  import jws1casestudy.pricefinder.common.Customer;
18
19  public class BookOrderImpl implements BookOrder {
20
21      private Connection connection; // connection to database
22      private Properties databaseProperties;
23      private Properties mailProperties;
24
25      // constructor to initialize database connection
26      public BookOrderImpl() throws Exception
27      {
28          InputStream databasePropertyStream = null;
29          InputStream mailPropertyStream = null;
30
31          // load JDBC driver and establish connection to database
32          try {
33
34              // obtain URL of properties file
35              databasePropertyStream = getClass().getResourceAsStream(
36                  "Database.properties" );
37
38              mailPropertyStream =
39                  getClass().getResourceAsStream( "Mail.properties" );
40
41              // load properties file
42              databaseProperties = new Properties();
43              databaseProperties.load( databasePropertyStream );
44              mailProperties = new Properties();
45              mailProperties.load( mailPropertyStream );
46
47              // load JDBC driver
48              Class.forName( databaseProperties.getProperty(
49                  "jdbcDriver" ) );
50
51              // establish database connection
52              connection = DriverManager.getConnection(
53                  databaseProperties.getProperty( "databaseURI" ) );
54          }
55
56          // handle exception if database driver does not exist
57          catch ( ClassNotFoundException classNotFoundException ) {
58              classNotFoundException.printStackTrace();
59          }
```

Fig. 15.12 BookOrderImpl handles the logic for the Book Order Web service.
(Part 2 of 5.)

```
60
61          // handle exception in making Connection
62          catch ( SQLException sqlException ) {
63             sqlException.printStackTrace();
64          }
65
66          // handle exception in loading properties file
67          catch ( IOException ioException ) {
68             ioException.printStackTrace();
69          }
70
71          // close properties streams
72          finally {
73
74             // close database property stream
75             if ( databasePropertyStream != null )
76                databasePropertyStream.close();
77
78             // close mail property stream
79             if ( mailPropertyStream != null )
80                mailPropertyStream.close();
81          }
82
83       } // end BookOrderImpl constructor
84
85       // service to order book
86       public void placeOrder( String isbn, Customer customer )
87          throws RemoteException
88       {
89          // ensure valid database connection
90          if ( connection == null )
91             throw new RemoteException(
92                "Unable to establish database connection." );
93
94          // insert additional entries for Customer and Order
95          try {
96             Statement statement = connection.createStatement(
97                ResultSet.TYPE_SCROLL_INSENSITIVE,
98                ResultSet.CONCUR_READ_ONLY );
99
100            // insert Customer entry in database
101            statement.executeUpdate( "INSERT INTO Customers " +
102               "( firstName, lastName, emailAddress, " +
103               "streetAddress, city, state, zipCode, country, " +
104               "creditCardNumber ) VALUES ('" +
105               customer.getFirstName() + "','" +
106               customer.getLastName() + "','" +
107               customer.getEmailAddress() + "','" +
108               customer.getStreetAddress() + "','" +
109               customer.getCity() + "','" +
110               customer.getState() + "','" +
111               customer.getZipCode() + "','" +
```

Fig. 15.12 BookOrderImpl handles the logic for the Book Order Web service.
(Part 3 of 5.)

```
112                   customer.getCountry() + "','" +
113                   customer.getCreditCardNumber() + "')" );
114
115             // use SQL query to obtain last customerID from database
116             ResultSet resultCustomerID = statement.executeQuery(
117                "VALUES ConnectionInfo.lastAutoincrementValue( " +
118                   "'APP', 'CUSTOMERS', 'CUSTOMERID' )" );
119             resultCustomerID.next();
120             int customerID = resultCustomerID.getInt( 1 );
121
122             // insert Order entry in database
123             statement.executeUpdate( "INSERT INTO Orders " +
124                "( customerID ) VALUES ( " + customerID + ")" );
125
126             // use SQL query to obtain last orderID from database
127             ResultSet resultOrderID = statement.executeQuery(
128                "VALUES ConnectionInfo.lastAutoincrementValue( " +
129                   "'APP', 'ORDERS', 'ORDERID' )" );
130             resultOrderID.next();
131             int orderID = resultOrderID.getInt( 1 );
132
133             // insert OrderItem entry in database
134             statement.executeUpdate( "INSERT INTO OrderItems " +
135                "( ISBN, orderID, quantity ) VALUES ('" +
136                isbn + "'," + orderID + ",1)" );
137
138             statement.close();
139
140             // notify success via email
141             mailConfirmation( customer.getEmailAddress(),
142                "Confirmation", "Your order has been placed." );
143          }
144
145          // handle exception via email notification
146          catch ( Exception exception ) {
147             mailConfirmation( customer.getEmailAddress(),
148                "Failure", "We were unable to complete your order." );
149             throw new RemoteException(
150                "Problem in placeOrder Web-service invocation" );
151          }
152
153       } // end method placeOrder
154
155       // send confirmation email to customer
156       private void mailConfirmation( String email, String subject,
157          String text )
158       {
159          // create email message, then send to customer
160          try {
161
```

Fig. 15.12 **BookOrderImpl** handles the logic for the Book Order Web service.
(Part 4 of 5.)

```
162                // use mail properties to create email message
163                Message message = new MimeMessage(
164                   Session.getInstance( mailProperties, null ) );
165
166                // specify field that indicates who sent the message
167                message.setFrom( new InternetAddress(
168                   mailProperties.getProperty( "senderAddress" ) ) );
169
170                // specify message recipient
171                message.setRecipient( Message.RecipientType.TO,
172                   new InternetAddress( email ) );
173
174                // set message content
175                message.setSentDate( new java.util.Date() );
176                message.setSubject( subject );
177                message.setText( text );
178
179                // send email message to recipient
180                Transport.send( message );
181             }
182
183             // handle exception in sending mail
184             catch ( Exception exception ) {
185                exception.printStackTrace();
186             }
187
188          } // end method mailConfirmation
189
190          // close database connection
191          public void finalize()
192          {
193             // close database connection
194             try {
195                if ( connection != null )
196                   connection.close();
197             }
198
199             // handle expection in closing database
200             catch ( SQLException sqlException ) {
201                sqlException.printStackTrace();
202             }
203
204          } // end method finalize
205
206       } // end class BookOrderImpl
```

Fig. 15.12 BookOrderImpl handles the logic for the Book Order Web service.
(Part 5 of 5.)

```
1    # Mail.properties
2    # Properties file for the Bookstore mail system.
```

Fig. 15.13 Mail.properties stores information on the Bookstore 1 e-mail
configuration. (Part 1 of 2.)

```
 3
 4    # property for mail-server port
 5    mail.smtp.port=25
 6
 7    # property for mail protocol
 8    mail.transport.protocol=smtp
 9
10    # mail server (change this value, based on system's mail host)
11    mail.smtp.host=mail.deitel.net
12
13    # property for sender's email address
14    senderAddress=confirmation@bookstore1.com
```

Fig. 15.13 **Mail.properties** stores information on the Bookstore 1 e-mail configuration. (Part 2 of 2.)

Class **BookOrderServlet** (Fig. 15.14) is a **JAXMServlet** that uses **Book-OrderImpl** to expose the Book Order Web service for Bookstore 1. Method **init** (lines 28–44) creates the **BookOrderImpl** object and obtains the default **MessageFactory** that **BookOrderServlet** uses to create SOAP responses. **BookOrderServlet** invokes method **onMessage** (lines 47–137) upon receiving a SOAP request. Lines 63–75 extract from the SOAP request the ISBN of the book to order, and lines 80–101 extract the information that describes the customer. Lines 104–122 create a **Customer** object from this information. Line 125 passes the ISBN and the **Customer** reference to method **placeOrder** of the **BookOrderImpl** object, which places the order for the book. If the order is successful, line 134 returns an empty SOAP response to the client, indicating success.

```
 1    // Fig. 15.14: BookOrderServlet.java.
 2    // Class BookOrderServlet expose the Book Order Web Service for
 3    // Bookstore 1.
 4    package jws1casestudy.bookstore1;
 5
 6    // Java core packages
 7    import java.util.*;
 8    import java.sql.*;
 9
10    // Java extension packages
11    import javax.servlet.*;
12    import javax.xml.messaging.*;
13    import javax.xml.soap.*;
14
15    // Deitel packages
16    import jws1casestudy.pricefinder.common.*;
17
18    public class BookOrderServlet extends JAXMServlet
19       implements ReqRespListener {
20
21       // factory used to create SOAPMessage objects
22       private MessageFactory messageFactory;
```

Fig. 15.14 **BookOrderServlet** is a **JAXMServlet** that exposes the Book Order Web service for Bookstore 1. (Part 1 of 4.)

```
23
24       // reference to object that provides Web-Service
25       private BookOrder service;
26
27       // initialize BookPriceServlet
28       public void init( ServletConfig config )
29          throws ServletException
30       {
31          super.init( config );
32
33          // instantiate Web-service object and obtain MessageFactory
34          try {
35             service = new BookOrderImpl();
36             messageFactory = MessageFactory.newInstance();
37          }
38
39          // handle exception in creating MessageFactory
40          catch ( Exception exception ) {
41             exception.printStackTrace();
42          }
43
44       } // end method init
45
46       // container invokes this method upon receiving SOAP message
47       public SOAPMessage onMessage( SOAPMessage message )
48       {
49          // call Book Order service and return result to sender
50          try {
51
52             // obtain references to response message elements
53             SOAPPart part = message.getSOAPPart();
54             SOAPEnvelope envelope = part.getEnvelope();
55             SOAPBody body = envelope.getBody();
56
57             // obtain Iterator of all child elements of element Body
58             Iterator bodyChildElements = body.getChildElements();
59
60             bodyChildElements.next(); // skip first element
61
62             // extract element order from SOAP message element Body
63             SOAPBodyElement orderElement =
64                ( SOAPBodyElement ) bodyChildElements.next();
65
66             // get order element's children elements
67             Iterator orderChildren =
68                orderElement.getChildElements();
69
70              orderChildren.next(); // skit first element
71
72             // extract SOAPElement that contains isbn
73             SOAPElement isbnElement =
74                ( SOAPElement ) orderChildren.next();
```

Fig. 15.14 **BookOrderServlet** is a **JAXMServlet** that exposes the Book Order Web service for Bookstore 1. (Part 2 of 4.)

```
75                String isbn = isbnElement.getValue();
76
77                bodyChildElements.next(); // skip third element
78
79                // get customer element's children elements
80                SOAPBodyElement customerElement =
81                   ( SOAPBodyElement ) bodyChildElements.next();
82
83                Iterator customerChildren =
84                   customerElement.getChildElements();
85
86                Hashtable customerValues = new Hashtable();
87                int count = 0;
88
89                // store customer children values in Hashtable
90                while ( customerChildren.hasNext() && count <= 8 ) {
91
92                   customerChildren.next(); // skip TextImpl Element
93                   count++;
94
95                   SOAPElement child =
96                      ( SOAPElement ) customerChildren.next();
97                   String elementName =
98                     child.getElementName().getLocalName();
99                   String elementValue = child.getValue();
100                  customerValues.put( elementName, elementValue );
101               }
102
103               // create Customer from customer element's children
104               Customer customer = new Customer();
105               customer.setFirstName(
106                  ( String ) customerValues.get( "firstName" ) );
107               customer.setLastName(
108                  ( String ) customerValues.get( "lastName" ) );
109               customer.setEmailAddress(
110                  ( String ) customerValues.get( "emailAddress" ) );
111               customer.setStreetAddress(
112                  ( String ) customerValues.get( "streetAddress" ) );
113               customer.setCity(
114                  ( String ) customerValues.get( "city" ) );
115               customer.setState(
116                  ( String ) customerValues.get( "state" ) );
117               customer.setZipCode(
118                  ( String ) customerValues.get( "zipCode" ) );
119               customer.setCountry(
120                  ( String ) customerValues.get( "country" ) );
121               customer.setCreditCardNumber(
122                  ( String ) customerValues.get( "creditCardNumber" ) );
123
124               // invoke Web service
125               service.placeOrder( isbn, customer );
126
```

Fig. 15.14 **BookOrderServlet** is a **JAXMServlet** that exposes the Book Order Web service for Bookstore 1. (Part 3 of 4.)

```
127            // return empty SOAP response
128            return messageFactory.createMessage();
129         }
130
131         // handle exception in invoking Book Order Web service
132         catch ( Exception exception ) {
133            exception.printStackTrace();
134            return null;
135         }
136
137      } // end method onMessage
138
139   } // end class BookOrderServlet
```

Fig. 15.14 **BookOrderServlet** is a **JAXMServlet** that exposes the Book Order Web service for Bookstore 1. (Part 4 of 4.)

15.5 Price Finder Web Services

In this section, we introduce the Price Finder application, which provides three Web services that enable consumers to purchase Deitel books at the best available prices from three fictitious online bookstores. The Web services that the Price Finder application provides provide a central access point through which consumers can access the Web services of each bookstore and the Deitel Book Information Web service. Price Finder Web services Best Book Price and Book Purchase access Web services provided by the three bookstores to obtain pricing information and order books, respectively. Web service Book Information accesses the Deitel Book Information Web service to obtain descriptive information about Deitel publications.

The **jws1casestudy.pricefinder.common** package contains JavaBeans **PriceQuote**, **BookDetails** and **Customer**, which are used by all the Price Finder Web services. Class **PriceQuote** (Fig. 15.15) represents a price quote obtained from a bookstore. Class **BookDetails** (Fig. 15.16) contains the details of a Deitel publication, such as the title, list of authors, ISBN, etc. Class **Customer** (Fig. 15.17) represents billing and shipping information for a customer. These classes follow the JavaBeans design patterns, as required by the JAX-RPC specification. The Price Finder Web services use objects of these classes as arguments and return values to reduce the network traffic required for each Web-service invocation. For example, a consumer can place a book order by passing a **Price-Quote** object and a **Customer** object to the Book Purchase Web service, instead of by passing each piece of information (first name, last name, street address, etc.) individually.

```
1   // PriceQuote.java
2   // PriceQuote maintains price information for one book store.
3   package jws1casestudy.pricefinder.common;
4
5   public class PriceQuote {
6
```

Fig. 15.15 **PriceQuote** JavaBean represents a book price from a book store. (Part 1 of 3.)

```
7      private double price;            // book price
8      private String isbn;             // book ISBN
9      private int storeID;             // store ID
10     private String storeDescription; // store description
11
12     // public default constructor
13     public PriceQuote() {}
14
15     // get book price
16     public double getPrice()
17     {
18        return price;
19     }
20
21     // get book ISBN
22     public String getIsbn()
23     {
24        return isbn;
25     }
26
27     // get store ID
28     public int getStoreID()
29     {
30        return storeID;
31     }
32
33     // get store description
34     public String getStoreDescription()
35     {
36        return storeDescription;
37     }
38
39     // set book price
40     public void setPrice( double price )
41     {
42        if ( price >= 0 )
43           this.price = price;
44        else
45           this.price = 0;
46     }
47
48     // set book ISBN
49     public void setIsbn( String isbn )
50     {
51        this.isbn = isbn;
52     }
53
54     // set book ID
55     public void setStoreID( int storeID )
56     {
57        this.storeID = storeID;
58     }
```

Fig. 15.15 PriceQuote JavaBean represents a book price from a book store.
(Part 2 of 3.)

```
59
60        // set weather description
61        public void setStoreDescription( String storeDescription )
62        {
63           this.storeDescription = storeDescription;
64        }
65
66     } // end class PriceQuote
```

Fig. 15.15 PriceQuote JavaBean represents a book price from a book store. (Part 3 of 3.)

```
1    // BookDetails.java
2    // BookDetails maintains information for one book.
3    package jws1casestudy.pricefinder.common;
4
5    public class BookDetails {
6
7       private String title;          // book title
8       private String isbn;           // book ISBN
9       private String authors;        // store authors
10      private String description;    // store description
11      private String coverImageURL;  // cover image URL
12
13      // public no-arg constructor
14      public BookDetails() {}
15
16      // get book title
17      public String getTitle()
18      {
19         return title;
20      }
21
22      // get book ISBN
23      public String getIsbn()
24      {
25         return isbn;
26      }
27
28      // get authors
29      public String getAuthors()
30      {
31         return authors;
32      }
33
34      // get book description
35      public String getDescription()
36      {
37         return description;
38      }
39
```

Fig. 15.16 BookDetails JavaBean represents information for one book. (Part 1 of 2.)

```
40        // get image URL
41        public String getCoverImageURL()
42        {
43            return coverImageURL;
44        }
45
46        // set book title
47        public void setTitle( String title )
48        {
49            this.title = title;
50        }
51
52        // set book ISBN
53        public void setIsbn( String isbn )
54        {
55            this.isbn = isbn;
56        }
57
58        // set book authors
59        public void setAuthors( String authors )
60        {
61            this.authors = authors;
62        }
63
64        // set book description
65        public void setDescription( String description )
66        {
67            this.description = description;
68        }
69
70        // set image URL
71        public void setCoverImageURL( String coverImageURL )
72        {
73            this.coverImageURL = coverImageURL;
74        }
75
76    } // end class BookDetails
```

Fig. 15.16 BookDetails JavaBean represents information for one book. (Part 2 of 2.)

```
1    // Customer.java
2    // Customer maintains information for one customer.
3    package jws1casestudy.pricefinder.common;
4
5    public class Customer {
6
7        private String firstName;        // first name
8        private String lastName;         // last name
9        private String emailAddress;     // email address
10       private String streetAddress;    // street address
11       private String city;             // city name
```

Fig. 15.17 Customer JavaBean represents a customer. (Part 1 of 4.)

```
12       private String state;          // state name
13       private String zipCode;        // zip code
14       private String country;        // country name
15       private String creditCardNumber;  // credit card number
16
17       // public no-arg constructor
18       public Customer() {}
19
20       // get first name
21       public String getFirstName()
22       {
23          return firstName;
24       }
25
26       // get last name
27       public String getLastName()
28       {
29          return lastName;
30       }
31
32       // get email address
33       public String getEmailAddress()
34       {
35          return emailAddress;
36       }
37
38       // get street address
39       public String getStreetAddress()
40       {
41          return streetAddress;
42       }
43
44       // get city name
45       public String getCity()
46       {
47          return city;
48       }
49
50       // get state name
51       public String getState()
52       {
53          return state;
54       }
55
56       // get zip code
57       public String getZipCode()
58       {
59          return zipCode;
60       }
61
```

Fig. 15.17 Customer JavaBean represents a customer. (Part 2 of 4.)

```
62      // get country name
63      public String getCountry()
64      {
65         return country;
66      }
67
68      // get credit card number
69      public String getCreditCardNumber()
70      {
71         return creditCardNumber;
72      }
73
74      // set first name
75      public void setFirstName( String firstName )
76      {
77         this.firstName = firstName;
78      }
79
80      // set last name
81      public void setLastName( String lastName )
82      {
83         this.lastName = lastName;
84      }
85
86      // set email address
87      public void setEmailAddress( String emailAddress )
88      {
89         this.emailAddress = emailAddress;
90      }
91
92      // set street address
93      public void setStreetAddress( String streetAddress )
94      {
95         this.streetAddress = streetAddress;
96      }
97
98      // set city name
99      public void setCity( String city )
100     {
101        this.city = city;
102     }
103
104     // set state name
105     public void setState( String state )
106     {
107        this.state = state;
108     }
109
110     // set zip code
111     public void setZipCode( String zipCode )
112     {
113        this.zipCode = zipCode;
114     }
```

Fig. 15.17 Customer JavaBean represents a customer. (Part 3 of 4.)

```
115
116     // set country name
117     public void setCountry( String country )
118     {
119        this.country = country;
120     }
121
122     // set credit card number
123     public void setCreditCardNumber( String creditCardNumber )
124     {
125        this.creditCardNumber = creditCardNumber;
126     }
127
128  } // end class Customer
```

Fig. 15.17 **Customer** JavaBean represents a customer. (Part 4 of 4.)

15.5.1 Best Book Price Web Service

The Price Finder application exposes the Best Book Price Web service via class **BestBook-Price** (Fig. 15.18). Method **getBestPrice** (lines 50–86) obtains **PriceQuote**s from the three bookstores and returns the **PriceQuote** with the lowest price. The constructor (lines 22–47) creates **BookPriceProxy** for each book store. Lines 31–38 call each book store's service proxy factory class to get the **BookPriceProxy** (Fig. 15.19). Each bookstore has a service proxy factory—**BookPriceProxyFactory1** (Fig. 15.20), **BookPriceProxyFactory2** (Fig. 15.21) and **BookPriceProxyFactory3** (Fig. 15.22).[1]

In method **getBestPrice** (lines 50–86), lines 58–72 obtain an array of **PriceQuote** objects that contain the book price from each bookstore. Line 75 sorts the array of **PriceQuote** objects. Lines 79–82 check the availability of the book, and line 84 returns the **PriceQuote** that contains the lowest price. For simplicity, all book stores agree on the representation of the **PriceQuote** object, so all Bookstore Book Price Web services return **jws1casestudy.pricefinder.common.PriceQuote** objects when the client requests the book price.

To enable sorting of the **PriceQuote**s, class **PriceComparator** (lines 89–117) implements method **compare** (lines 92–109) of interface **Comparator**. Lines 112–115 implement method **equals** of interface **Comparator** to find out whether two **PriceQuote** objects are equal.

```
1    // BestBookPrice.java
2    // BestBookPrice gets book price from each book store and
3    // find the best price.
4    package jws1casestudy.pricefinder;
```

Fig. 15.18 **BestBookPrice** Web service gets the lowest book price among all book stores. (Part 1 of 4.)

---

1. We create a separate **BookPriceProxyFactory** for each bookstore to simplify the application. A more robust implementation would have a single factory that used method parameters to determine the appropriate proxy object to construct.

```
 5
 6    // Java core packages
 7    import java.util.*;
 8    import java.rmi.RemoteException;
 9
10    // Deitel packages
11    import jws1casestudy.pricefinder.common.*;
12
13    public class BestBookPrice {
14
15       // number of bookstores
16       private static final int BOOKSTORES = 3;
17
18       // contains proxies to different bookstores
19       private BookPriceProxy[] bookPriceProxies;
20
21       // no-argument constructor
22       public BestBookPrice()
23       {
24          // get BookPriceProxy for each book store
25          try {
26
27             // instantiate BookPriceProxy array
28             bookPriceProxies = new BookPriceProxy[ BOOKSTORES ];
29
30             // populate array with BookPriceProxys
31             bookPriceProxies[ 0 ] =
32                BookPriceProxyFactory1.createProxy();
33
34             bookPriceProxies[ 1 ] =
35                BookPriceProxyFactory2.createProxy();
36
37             bookPriceProxies[ 2 ] =
38                BookPriceProxyFactory3.createProxy();
39
40          } // end try
41
42          // handle exception when creating URLs
43          catch( Exception exception ) {
44             exception.printStackTrace();
45          }
46
47       } // end constructor
48
49       // return best price from bookstores for given ISBN
50       public PriceQuote getBestPrice( String isbn )
51          throws RemoteException
52       {
53
54          // contains priceQuotes for given ISBN
55          PriceQuote[] priceQuotes = new PriceQuote[ BOOKSTORES ];
56
```

Fig. 15.18 BestBookPrice Web service gets the lowest book price among all book stores. (Part 2 of 4.)

```
57          // get PriceQuote from each book store
58          for ( int i = 0; i < BOOKSTORES ; i++ ) {
59             PriceQuote quote = null;
60
61             // get book price from service proxy
62             try {
63                quote = bookPriceProxies[ i ].getPrice( isbn );
64             }
65
66             // handle exception in retrieving quote
67             catch ( Exception exception ) {
68                exception.printStackTrace();
69             }
70
71             priceQuotes[ i ] = quote;
72          }
73
74          // sort prices array
75          Arrays.sort( priceQuotes, new PriceComparator());
76
77          // throw exception if book ISBN does not exist
78          if ( priceQuotes[ 0 ] == null ) {
79             throw new RemoteException(
80                "Bookstores do not carry " + isbn );
81          }
82
83          // return lowest price
84          return priceQuotes[ 0 ];
85
86       } // end method getBestPrice
87
88       // utility class used to compare prices
89       private class PriceComparator implements Comparator
90       {
91          // compare two PriceQuote objects
92          public int compare( Object price1, Object price2 )
93          {
94             // base cases
95             if ( price1 == null && price2 == null )
96                return 0;
97
98             if ( price1 == null )
99                return -1;
100
101            if ( price2 == null )
102               return 1;
103
104            PriceQuote priceQuote1 = ( PriceQuote ) price1;
105            PriceQuote priceQuote2 = ( PriceQuote ) price2;
106
```

Fig. 15.18 BestBookPrice Web service gets the lowest book price among all book stores. (Part 3 of 4.)

```
107            return ( int )
108                ( priceQuote1.getPrice() - priceQuote2.getPrice() );
109        }
110
111        // two PriceQuote are equal
112        public boolean equals( Object object )
113        {
114            return object.equals ( this );
115        }
116
117    } // end class PriceComparator
118
119 } // end class BestBookPrice
```

Fig. 15.18 BestBookPrice Web service gets the lowest book price among all book stores. (Part 4 of 4.)

Class **BookPriceProxy** (Fig. 15.19) is a service proxy for each bookstore's Book Price Web service. **BookPriceProxy** uses the Dynamic Invocation Interface (DII) to invoke method **getPrice** of the **BookPrice** service. The **BookPriceProxy** constructor (lines 30–62) takes four arguments—the URL location of the service's WSDL document, the service namespace, the **PriceQuote** namespace and the service's port name.

In this example, the we use the Axis APIs to create DII calls to access the **Book-Price** service. Lines 35–36 create a **Service** object that represents the **BookPrice** service with the service's WSDL document URL and the qualified name of the service. Lines 39–40 specify the qualified service port. Lines 44–45 invoke method **create-Call** of class **Service** to create a **Call** object, which is used later to make the remote procedure call to the service. Method **createCall** takes two arguments—a **QName** that represents the service port and another **QName** that specifies the operation name. Method **createCall** returns a **Call** object used to invoke the Book Price Web service. In our example, the service port is **BookPrice** and the method to call is **get-Price**.

Lines 48–54 construct a **BeanSerializerFactory** and a **BeanDeserializerFactory** for class **PriceQuote**. Both factories take two arguments—a custom **Class** object that follows the JavaBeans design patterns, and a **QName** object that specifies the qualified name of the class. Lines 58–60 invoke method **registerTypeMapping** of the **Call** object to register the type-mapping information for the serializer and deserializer. Method **registerTypeMapping** requires four arguments—the customer **Class**, the qualified name of the class, the serializer factory for the customer class and the deserializer factory for the customer class.

Lines 74–75 of method **getPrice** (lines 65–89) invoke **BookPrice**'s method by calling method **invoke** of the **Call** object. Method **invoke** takes an array of **Object**s that contains input parameters for the remote Web service and returns an **Object** that contains the Web-service invocation's return value. In our example, the return value is an object of type **PriceQuote**, so line 78 casts the return object to a **PriceQuote**.

```
1    // BookPriceProxy.java
2    // BookPriceProxy is a service proxy for each book store's
3    // Book Price Web service.
4    package jws1casestudy.pricefinder;
5
6    // Java core packages
7    import java.net.URL;
8
9    // Java XML packages
10   import javax.xml.namespace.QName;
11   import javax.xml.rpc.ParameterMode;
12   import javax.xml.rpc.ServiceException;
13
14   // Axis packages
15   import org.apache.axis.client.Call;
16   import org.apache.axis.client.Service;
17   import org.apache.axis.encoding.XMLType;
18   import org.apache.axis.encoding.ser.BeanSerializerFactory;
19   import org.apache.axis.encoding.ser.BeanDeserializerFactory;
20
21   // Deitel packages
22   import jws1casestudy.pricefinder.common.PriceQuote;
23
24   public class BookPriceProxy
25   {
26      // Web service invocation object
27      private Call call;
28
29      // constructor
30      public BookPriceProxy( URL serviceWSDL,
31         QName serviceNamespace, QName priceQuoteNamespace,
32         String portName ) throws ServiceException
33      {
34         // construct a service object bases on WSDL
35         Service service =
36            new Service( serviceWSDL, serviceNamespace );
37
38         // create getPrice identifier
39         QName getPriceNamespace =
40            new QName( null, portName );
41
42         // create a Call that specifies the service port and
43         // method to call
44         call = ( Call )service.createCall(
45            getPriceNamespace, "getPrice" );
46
47         // create serializer and deserializer
48         BeanSerializerFactory serializerFactory =
49            new BeanSerializerFactory( PriceQuote.class,
50               priceQuoteNamespace );
51
```

Fig. 15.19 BookPriceProxy is a service proxy for the **BookPrice** Web service of each book store. (Part 1 of 2.)

```
52        BeanDeserializerFactory deserializerFactory =
53           new BeanDeserializerFactory( PriceQuote.class,
54              priceQuoteNamespace );
55
56        // register type mapping for PriceQuote's serializer
57        // and deserializer
58        call.registerTypeMapping( PriceQuote.class,
59           priceQuoteNamespace, serializerFactory,
60           deserializerFactory );
61
62     } // end constructor
63
64     // get price from one book store using DII
65     public PriceQuote getPrice( String isbn )
66     {
67        // response object
68        PriceQuote response = null;
69
70        // invoke Book Price Web service
71        try {
72
73           // invoke Web service method
74           Object responseObj = call.invoke(
75              new Object[] { isbn } );
76
77           // cast return object to PriceQuote
78           response = ( PriceQuote ) responseObj;
79
80        } // end try
81
82        // handle exception in accessing Web service
83        catch ( Exception exception){
84           exception.printStackTrace();
85        }
86
87        return response;
88
89     } // end method getPrice
90
91  } // end class BookPriceProxy
```

Fig. 15.19 BookPriceProxy is a service proxy for the **BookPrice** Web service of each book store. (Part 2 of 2.)

The three **BookPriceProxy** factories (Fig. 15.20, Fig. 15.21, Fig. 15.22) create a **BookPriceProxy** for each book store out of information specified by each bookstore's Book Price Web service. Class **BookPriceProxyFactory1** has a **static** method **createProxy** (lines 16–39) that specifies the URL of the Web service WSDL (lines 20–21), the qualified Web service name (lines 24–26), the qualified custom type **PriceQuote** (lines 29–30) and the service port name (line 33). Lines 36–37 return the **BookPriceProxy** with the specific WSDL URL, qualified service name and qualified **PriceQuote** custom type for Bookstore 1.

```
1    // BookPriceProxyFactory1.java
2    // Service proxy factory for Bookstore 1.
3    package jws1casestudy.pricefinder;
4
5    // Java XML packages
6    import javax.xml.namespace.QName;
7    import javax.xml.rpc.ParameterMode;
8    import javax.xml.rpc.ServiceException;
9
10   // Java core package
11   import java.net.*;
12
13   public class BookPriceProxyFactory1
14   {
15       // create BookPriceProxy instance
16       public static BookPriceProxy createProxy()
17          throws ServiceException, MalformedURLException
18       {
19           // Web service WSDL URL
20           URL wsdlURL = new URL( "http://localhost:8080/" +
21              "bookstore1/WSDL/BookPriceService.wsdl" );
22
23           // Web service namespace
24           QName serviceIdentifier = new QName(
25              "http://www.deitel.com/BookPrice.wsdl",
26              "BookPriceService" );
27
28           // Web service custom type namespace
29           QName priceQuoteIdentifier = new QName(
30              "http://www.deitel.com/BookPrice/type", "PriceQuote" );
31
32           // port name
33           String portName = "BookPricePort";
34
35           // return new book price Web service proxy
36           return new BookPriceProxy( wsdlURL,
37                  serviceIdentifier, priceQuoteIdentifier, portName );
38
39       } // end method createProxy
40
41   } // end class BookPriceProxyFactory1
```

Fig. 15.20 Book Price service-proxy factory for Bookstore 1.

```
1    // BookPriceProxyFactory2.java
2    // Service proxy factory for Bookstore 2.
3    package jws1casestudy.pricefinder;
4
5    // Java XML packages
6    import javax.xml.namespace.QName;
7    import javax.xml.rpc.ParameterMode;
8    import javax.xml.rpc.ServiceException;
```

Fig. 15.21 Book Price service-proxy factory for Bookstore 2. (Part 1 of 2.)

```
9
10     // Java core package
11     import java.net.*;
12
13     public class BookPriceProxyFactory2
14     {
15         // create BookPriceProxy instance
16         public static BookPriceProxy createProxy()
17             throws ServiceException, MalformedURLException
18         {
19             // Web service WSDL URL
20             URL wsdlURL = new URL( "http://localhost:6060/" +
21                 "bookstore2/BookPrice/wsdl" );
22
23             // Web service namespace
24             QName serviceIdentifier = new QName(
25                 "http://systinet.com/wsdl/jws1casestudy/bookstore2/",
26                 "JavaService" );
27
28             // Web service custom type namespace
29             QName priceQuoteIdentifier = new QName(
30                 "http://systinet.com/wsdl/jws1casestudy/" +
31                 "pricefinder/common/", "PriceQuote" );
32
33             // port name
34             String portName = "BookPriceImpl";
35
36             // return new book price Web service proxy
37             return new BookPriceProxy( wsdlURL,
38                 serviceIdentifier, priceQuoteIdentifier, portName );
39
40         } // end method createProxy
41
42     } // end class BookPriceProxyFactory2
```

Fig. 15.21 Book Price service-proxy factory for Bookstore 2. (Part 2 of 2.)

```
1     // BookPriceProxyFactory3.java
2     // Service proxy factory for Bookstore 3.
3     package jws1casestudy.pricefinder;
4
5     // Java XML packages
6     import javax.xml.namespace.QName;
7     import javax.xml.rpc.ParameterMode;
8     import javax.xml.rpc.ServiceException;
9
10     // Java core package
11     import java.net.*;
12
13     public class BookPriceProxyFactory3
14     {
```

Fig. 15.22 Book Price service-proxy factory for Bookstore 3. (Part 1 of 2.)

```
15        // create BookPriceProxy instance
16     public static BookPriceProxy createProxy()
17        throws ServiceException, MalformedURLException
18     {
19           // Web service WSDL URL
20           URL wsdlURL = new URL( "http://localhost:8000/wsdl/" +
21                "BookPrice.wsdl" );
22
23           // Web service namespace
24           QName serviceIdentifier = new QName(
25                "http://www.capeclear.com/BookPrice.wsdl",
26                "BookPrice" );
27
28           // Web service custom type namespace
29           QName priceQuoteIdentifier = new QName(
30                "http://www.capeclear.com/BookPrice.xsd",
31                "PriceQuote" );
32
33           // port name
34           String portName = "BookPriceImpl";
35
36           // return new book price Web service proxy
37           return new BookPriceProxy( wsdlURL,
38                serviceIdentifier, priceQuoteIdentifier, portName );
39
40     } // end method createProxy
41
42  } // end class BookPriceProxyFactory3
```

Fig. 15.22 Book Price service-proxy factory for Bookstore 3. (Part 2 of 2.)

15.5.2 BookInformation Web Service

The Price Finder application exposes the Book Information Web service via class **Book-Information** (Fig. 15.23). Method **getBookDetails** (lines 90–115) returns a **BookDetails** object that contains such book information as the book title, ISBN and authors. Class **BookInformation** also uses Axis DII APIs to make remote calls to the Deitel Book Information Web service. The constructor (lines 30–86) prepares the connection to the Deitel Book Information Web service. Lines 37–38 specify the URL of the service's WSDL. Lines 41–48 specify the qualified service name and create a **Service** object corresponding to the WSDL and service name. Lines 51–57 construct a **Call** object for the operation **getBookDetails** of the service port **BookInformation**. Lines 60–78 specify the qualified name for class **BookDetails**, create **BeanSerializerFactory** and **BeanDeserializerFactory** for **BookDetails** and register type mapping for JavaBean **BookDetails**.

Method **getBookDetails** (lines 90–115) makes the remote procedure call to the remote Book Information Web service (lines 100–101). Line 104 casts the return object from the remote Web service to a **BookDetails** object.

15.5.3 BookPurchase Web Service

The Price Finder application exposes the Book Purchase Web service via class **BookPur-chase** (Fig. 15.24). **BookPurchase** accesses each bookstore's **BookOrder** Web service through a service proxy, **BookOrderProxy** (Fig. 15.25), which is generated by one of the book store's service-proxy factories: **BookOrderProxyFactory1** (Fig. 15.26), **BookOrderProxyFactory2** (Fig. 15.27) or **BookOrderProxyFactory3** (Fig. 15.28).[2]

```java
1   // BookInformation.java
2   // Book Information Web service provides book information.
3   package jws1casestudy.pricefinder;
4
5   // Java core packages
6   import java.rmi.*;
7   import java.net.*;
8
9   // Java XML packages
10  import javax.xml.namespace.QName;
11  import javax.xml.rpc.ParameterMode;
12  import javax.xml.rpc.ServiceException;
13
14  // Axis packages
15  import org.apache.axis.client.Call;
16  import org.apache.axis.client.Service;
17  import org.apache.axis.encoding.XMLType;
18  import org.apache.axis.encoding.ser.BeanSerializerFactory;
19  import org.apache.axis.encoding.ser.BeanDeserializerFactory;
20
21  // Deitel packages
22  import jws1casestudy.pricefinder.common.*;
23
24  public class BookInformation {
25
26     // connection object
27     private Call call;
28
29     // create connection object to Web service
30     public BookInformation() throws ServiceException
31     {
32
33        // connect to Web service and get book info
34        try {
35
36           // specify service WSDL URL
37           URL wsdlURL = new URL( "http://localhost:8004/" +
38              "bookinformation/services/bookinformation.wsdl" );
39
40           // create service identifier
41           QName serviceIdentifier = new QName(
42              "http://www.themindelectric.com" +
```

Fig. 15.23 Book Information Web service obtains book information. (Part 1 of 3.)

2. We create a separate **BookOrderProxyFactory** for each bookstore to simplify the application. A more robust implementation would have a single factory that used method parameters to determine the appropriate proxy object to construct.

```
43                    "/wsdl/BookInformationImpl/",
44                    "BookInformationImpl" );
45
46            // create Service object
47            Service service = new Service( wsdlURL,
48                serviceIdentifier);
49
50            // create method identifier
51            QName getBookDetailsNamespace =
52                new QName( null, "BookInformation" );
53
54            // create Call that specifies service port and
55            // method to call
56            call = ( Call )service.createCall(
57                getBookDetailsNamespace, "getBookDetails" );
58
59            // create QName for BookDetails JavaBean
60            QName bookDetailsIdentifier = new QName(
61                "http://www.themindelectric.com" +
62                "/package/jws1casestudy.pricefinder.common/",
63                "BookDetails" );
64
65            // create serializer and deserializer instances
66            BeanSerializerFactory serializerFactory =
67                new BeanSerializerFactory( BookDetails.class,
68                    bookDetailsIdentifier );
69
70            BeanDeserializerFactory deserializerFactory =
71                new BeanDeserializerFactory( BookDetails.class,
72                    bookDetailsIdentifier );
73
74            // register type mapping for BookDetails serializer
75            // and deserializer
76            call.registerTypeMapping( BookDetails.class,
77                bookDetailsIdentifier, serializerFactory,
78                deserializerFactory );
79
80        } // end try
81
82        catch( MalformedURLException urlException ) {
83            urlException.printStackTrace();
84        }
85
86    } // end constructor
87
88    // implementation for interface BookInformation
89    // method getBookDetails
90    public BookDetails getBookDetails( String isbn )
91        throws RemoteException
92    {
93        // declare response object
94        BookDetails response = null;
95
```

Fig. 15.23 Book Information Web service obtains book information. (Part 2 of 3.)

```
96          // invoke Web service
97          try {
98
99              // invoke method in Book Information Web service
100             Object responseObj = call.invoke(
101                 new Object[] { isbn } );
102
103             // cast return object to BookDetails
104             response = ( BookDetails ) responseObj;
105
106         } // end try
107
108         // handle exception in accessing Web service
109         catch ( Exception exception ) {
110             exception.printStackTrace();
111         }
112
113     return response;
114
115    } // end method getBookDetails
116
117 } // end class BookInformation
```

Fig. 15.23 Book Information Web service obtains book information. (Part 3 of 3.)

BookPurchase exposes one method, **orderBook**, to place the order through the bookstore that offers the best price. The constructor (lines 29–50) creates three **Book-OrderProxy** objects for each book store (lines 36–43) and add the proxies to a **HashMap** (lines 46–48). Method **orderBook** (lines 52–68) takes two arguments—a **PriceQuote** object that contains the best book price and a **Customer** object that contains the customer information. Lines 62–63 get the **BookOrderProxy** corresponding to the bookstore that provides the best book price. Line 66 invokes method **placeOrder** of the **BookOrder-Proxy** to make the order.

```
1  // BookPurchase.java
2  // Book Purchase Web service places orders.
3  package jws1casestudy.pricefinder;
4
5  // Java core packages
6  import java.rmi.*;
7  import java.net.*;
8  import java.util.*;
9
10 // Java XML packages
11 import javax.xml.namespace.QName;
12 import javax.xml.rpc.ParameterMode;
13 import javax.xml.rpc.ServiceException;
14
15 // Axis packages
16 import org.apache.axis.client.Call;
17 import org.apache.axis.client.Service;
```

Fig. 15.24 Book Purchase Web service places orders for a bookstore. (Part 1 of 2.)

```
18   import org.apache.axis.encoding.XMLType;
19
20   // Deitel packages
21   import jws1casestudy.pricefinder.common.*;
22
23   public class BookPurchase {
24
25      // contains BookPurchaseProxy for each bookstore
26      private Map proxies;
27
28      // no-argument constructor
29      public BookPurchase()
30         throws ServiceException, MalformedURLException
31      {
32         // create proxies hashmap
33         proxies = new HashMap();
34
35         // create BookOrder proxies
36         BookOrderProxy bookOrderProxy1 =
37            BookOrderProxyFactory1.createProxy();
38
39         BookOrderProxy bookOrderProxy2 =
40            BookOrderProxyFactory2.createProxy();
41
42         BookOrderProxy bookOrderProxy3 =
43            BookOrderProxyFactory3.createProxy();
44
45         // add proxies to hashmap
46         proxies.put( "1", bookOrderProxy1 );
47         proxies.put( "2", bookOrderProxy2 );
48         proxies.put( "3", bookOrderProxy3 );
49
50      } // end constructor
51
52      public void orderBook( PriceQuote priceQuote,
53         Customer customer ) throws Exception
54      {
55         // get ISBN of book to purchase
56         String isbn = priceQuote.getIsbn();
57
58         // get storeID for bookstore
59         int storeID = priceQuote.getStoreID();
60
61         // order book from corresponding book store
62         BookOrderProxy bookOrderProxy =
63            ( BookOrderProxy ) proxies.get( storeID + "" );
64
65         // place order
66         bookOrderProxy.placeOrder( isbn, customer );
67
68      } // end method orderBook
69
70   } // end class BookPurchase
```

Fig. 15.24 Book Purchase Web service places orders for a bookstore. (Part 2 of 2.)

Class **BookOrderProxy** (Fig. 15.25) is a service proxy for a bookstore's Book Order Web service. The constructor (lines 30–62) creates a **Call** object specific to the Book Order Web service (lines 35–44), creates the serializer and deserializer factories for class **Customer** (lines 47–54) and registers the type mapping for **Customer**'s serializer and deserializer (lines 58–60). Method **placeOrder** (lines 65–81) makes DII calls to the Book Order Web service. The DII call does not return any value.

```
1    // BookOrderProxy.java
2    // BookOrderProxy is a service proxy for Bookstores
3    // Book Order Web service.
4    package jws1casestudy.pricefinder;
5
6    // Java core packages
7    import java.net.URL;
8
9    // Java XML packages
10   import javax.xml.namespace.QName;
11   import javax.xml.rpc.ParameterMode;
12   import javax.xml.rpc.ServiceException;
13
14   // Axis packages
15   import org.apache.axis.client.Call;
16   import org.apache.axis.client.Service;
17   import org.apache.axis.encoding.XMLType;
18   import org.apache.axis.encoding.ser.BeanSerializerFactory;
19   import org.apache.axis.encoding.ser.BeanDeserializerFactory;
20
21   // Deitel packages
22   import jws1casestudy.pricefinder.common.*;
23
24   public class BookOrderProxy
25   {
26      // invocation instance for Web service
27      private Call call;
28
29      // construct BookOrderProxy
30      public BookOrderProxy( URL wsdlURL,
31         QName serviceIdentifier, QName customerNamespace,
32         String portName ) throws ServiceException
33      {
34         // construct service object based on WSDL
35         Service service =
36            new Service( wsdlURL, serviceIdentifier );
37
38         // create method identifier
39         QName methodIdentifier = new QName( null, portName );
40
41         // create Call that specifies service port and
42         // method to call
43         call = ( Call )service.createCall(
44            methodIdentifier , "placeOrder" );
```

Fig. 15.25 BookOrderProxy is a service proxy for Bookstore Book Order Web service. (Part 1 of 2.)

```
45
46          // create serializer factory
47          BeanSerializerFactory serializerFactory =
48             new BeanSerializerFactory( Customer.class,
49                customerNamespace );
50
51          // create deserializer factory
52          BeanDeserializerFactory deserializerFactory =
53             new BeanDeserializerFactory( Customer.class,
54                customerNamespace );
55
56          // register type mapping for Customer serializer
57          // and deserializer
58          call.registerTypeMapping( Customer.class,
59             customerNamespace, serializerFactory,
60             deserializerFactory );
61
62       } // end constructor
63
64       // order book from book store
65       public void placeOrder( String isbn, Customer customer )
66       {
67
68          // create DII call to order book
69          try {
70
71             // invoke Web service
72             call.invoke( new Object[] { isbn, customer } );
73
74          } // end try
75
76          // handle exception in accessing Web service
77          catch( Exception exception ) {
78             exception.printStackTrace();
79          }
80
81       } // end method orderBook
82
83    } // end class BookOrderProxy
```

Fig. 15.25 `BookOrderProxy` is a service proxy for Bookstore Book Order Web service. (Part 2 of 2.)

The **BookOrderProxy** factories create a **BookOrderProxy** for each book store out of each bookstore's WSDL URL, qualified service name and qualified name for the **Customer** class.

```
1    // BookOrderProxyFactory1.java
2    // Service proxy factory for Bookstore 1.
3    package jws1casestudy.pricefinder;
4
```

Fig. 15.26 Book Order service proxy factory for Bookstore 1. (Part 1 of 2.)

```
5   // Java XML packages
6   import javax.xml.namespace.QName;
7   import javax.xml.rpc.ParameterMode;
8   import javax.xml.rpc.ServiceException;
9
10  // Java core package
11  import java.net.*;
12
13  public class BookOrderProxyFactory1
14  {
15     // create BookOrderProxy instance
16     public static BookOrderProxy createProxy()
17        throws ServiceException, MalformedURLException
18     {
19        // Web service WSDL URL
20        URL wsdlURL = new URL( "http://localhost:8080/" +
21           "bookstore1/WSDL/BookOrderService.wsdl" );
22
23        // Web service namespace
24        QName serviceIdentifier = new QName(
25           "http://www.deitel.com/BookOrder.wsdl",
26           "BookOrderService" );
27
28        // Web service custom type namespace
29        QName customerIdentifier = new QName(
30           "http://www.deitel.com/BookOrder/type", "Customer" );
31
32        // port name
33        String portName = "BookOrderPort";
34
35        // return new book price Web service proxy
36        return new BookOrderProxy( wsdlURL,
37           serviceIdentifier, customerIdentifier, portName );
38
39     } // end method createProxy
40
41  } // end class BookOrderProxyFactory1
```

Fig. 15.26 Book Order service proxy factory for Bookstore 1. (Part 2 of 2.)

```
1   // BookOrderProxyFactory2.java
2   // Service proxy factory for Bookstore 2.
3   package jws1casestudy.pricefinder;
4
5   // Java XML packages
6   import javax.xml.namespace.QName;
7   import javax.xml.rpc.ParameterMode;
8   import javax.xml.rpc.ServiceException;
9
10  // Java core package
11  import java.net.*;
12
```

Fig. 15.27 Book Order service proxy factory for Bookstore 2. (Part 1 of 2.)

```
13  public class BookOrderProxyFactory2
14  {
15      // create BookOrderProxy instance
16      public static BookOrderProxy createProxy()
17          throws ServiceException, MalformedURLException
18      {
19          // Web service WSDL URL
20          URL wsdlURL = new URL( "http://localhost:6060/" +
21              "bookstore2/BookOrder/wsdl" );
22
23
24          // Web service namespace
25          QName serviceIdentifier = new QName(
26              "http://systinet.com/wsdl/jws1casestudy/bookstore2/",
27              "JavaService" );
28
29          // Web service custom type namespace
30          QName customerIdentifier = new QName(
31              "http://systinet.com/wsdl/jws1casestudy/pricefinder/" +
32              "common/", "Customer" );
33
34          // port name
35          String portName = "BookOrderImpl";
36
37          // return new book price Web service proxy
38          return new BookOrderProxy( wsdlURL,
39              serviceIdentifier, customerIdentifier, portName );
40
41      } // end method createProxy
42
43  } // end class BookOrderProxyFactory2
```

Fig. 15.27 Book Order service proxy factory for Bookstore 2. (Part 2 of 2.)

```
1   // BookOrderProxyFactory3.java
2   // Service proxy factory for Bookstore 3.
3   package jws1casestudy.pricefinder;
4
5   // Java XML packages
6   import javax.xml.namespace.QName;
7   import javax.xml.rpc.ParameterMode;
8   import javax.xml.rpc.ServiceException;
9
10  // Java core package
11  import java.net.*;
12
13  public class BookOrderProxyFactory3
14  {
15      // create BookOrderProxy instance
16      public static BookOrderProxy createProxy()
17          throws ServiceException, MalformedURLException
18      {
```

Fig. 15.28 Book Order service proxy factory for Bookstore 3. (Part 1 of 2.)

```
19          // Web service WSDL URL
20          URL wsdlURL = new URL( "http://localhost:8000/wsdl/" +
21              "BookOrder.wsdl" );
22
23          // Web service namespace
24          QName serviceIdentifier = new QName(
25              "http://www.capeclear.com/BookOrder.wsdl",
26              "BookOrder" );
27
28          // Web service custom type namespace
29          QName customerIdentifier = new QName(
30              "http://www.capeclear.com/BookOrder.xsd",
31              "Customer" );
32
33          // port name
34          String portName = "BookOrderImpl";
35
36          // return new book price Web service proxy
37          return new BookOrderProxy( wsdlURL,
38              serviceIdentifier, customerIdentifier, portName );
39
40      } // end method createProxy
41
42  } // end class BookOrderProxyFactory3
```

Fig. 15.28 Book Order service proxy factory for Bookstore 3. (Part 2 of 2.)

In this chapter, we presented the overall architecture of the Price Finder application and the implementations of the Price Finder, bookstore, and Deitel & Associates, Inc. Web services. In Chapter 16, we present the three consumer applications that access the Price Finder application. These include a servlet-based Web site, a Java 2 Micro Edition MIDlet and a Swing-based desktop application. In Chapter 17, we complete the case study with a discussion of the steps required to deploy the Price Finder and other associated Web services.

16

Case Study: Client Applications

Objectives

- To understand how clients access the Price Finder Web services.
- To learn how to integrate several clients in a Web-services-based application.

To me, party platforms are contracts with the people.
Harry S. Truman

Advertising is what you do when you can't go see somebody. That's all it is.
Fairfax Cone

Don't overlook the importance of worldwide thinking.
Al Ries

Have thy tools ready.
Charles Kingsley

Outline

16.1 Introduction

In the previous chapter, we presented the overall architecture of the case study and the implementations of the Price Finder, bookstore and Deitel & Associates, Inc., Web services. The Price Finder aggregates book pricing, ordering and description into a suite of Web services for consumers. In this chapter, we implement the consumer applications that communicate with the Price Finder Web services. The first of our consumer applications is a servlet-based Web site, which provides a simple Web-based interface for obtaining price quotes and ordering books. The second application is a desktop application with a Swing-based graphical user interface. The final consumer application is a Java 2 Micro Edition MIDlet that enables consumers to access the Price Finder Web services wirelessly from a cell phone or other mobile device.

16.2 Servlet-Based Web Client

In this section, we introduce a servlet-based Web client that accesses the Price Finder Web services by using JAX-RPC stubs. Numerous components compose the Web-based application. Figure 16.1 lists the components of the Web client. We discuss these components in the following subsections.

File	Description
`FindBook.html`	Provides the initial page that enables users to input a book's ISBN with which to invoke Price Finder's Best Book Price Web service. Users post requests to servlet `FindBestPriceServlet` by clicking button **Find Best Price!**.

Fig. 16.1   Components for the case-study Web client. (Part 1 of 2.)

File	Description
FindBestPriceServlet.java	This servlet (aliased as **findbestprice** in Fig. 16.2) queries Price Finder's Best Book Price Web service to obtain the lowest **PriceQuote** for a given book. The servlet also queries Price Finder's Book Information Web service to obtain information about the book. The information is stored in an **HttpSession** object. Finally, the servlet dispatches the request to **DisplayPrice.jsp**.
DisplayPrice.jsp	This JSP displays price information for a particular book. The resulting page displays button **Buy!**, which, when pressed, forwards the user to **Purchase.html**.
Purchase.html	Displays textfields that enable the user to enter personal information needed for placing an order. This information is sent to servlet **MakeOrderServlet**.
MakeOrderServlet.java	This servlet (aliased as **makeorder** in Fig. 16.2) uses customer information from the **Session** object to invoke the corresponding bookstore's Book Purchase Web service. The servlet then forwards the request to **OrderConfirmation.jsp**.
OrderConfirmation.jsp	This JSP displays confirmation information pertaining to the order servlet **MakeOrderServlet** places.

Fig. 16.1　Components for the case-study Web client. (Part 2 of 2.)

Figure 16.2 shows the Web client's work flow. The work flow illustrates the process by which a user interacts with each Web application component.

Users access **FindBook.html**, which displays a form that enables users to submit an ISBN to **FindBestPriceServlet**. **FindBestPriceServlet** invokes the Price Finder Web service Best Book Price to obtain the best price quote that corresponds to the given ISBN. Then servlet **FindBestPriceServlet** invokes the Price Finder Web service Book Information, which returns the corresponding book information.

After **FindBestPriceServlet** invokes both Web services successfully, it forwards the user to **DisplayPrice.jsp**, which displays the price retrieved by **FindBestPriceServlet**. If the user decides to purchase the displayed book, **DisplayPrice.jsp** forwards the reader to **Purchase.html**. **Purchase.html** displays a form that enables the user to input personal information required for purchasing the book.

When a user submits the form, the form sends the customer information to servlet **MakeOrderServlet**. **MakeOrderServlet** invokes the Price Finder's Book Purchase Web service, which forwards the request to the bookstore specified in the request. **MakeOrderServlet** then dispatches the request to **OrderConfirmation.jsp**, which displays information that confirms the user's purchase request.

16.2.1 Accessing the Web Client

XHTML document **FindBook.html** (Fig. 16.3) is the first page that users access. **FindBook.html** displays a form (lines 16–22) that enables users to specify a book's IS-

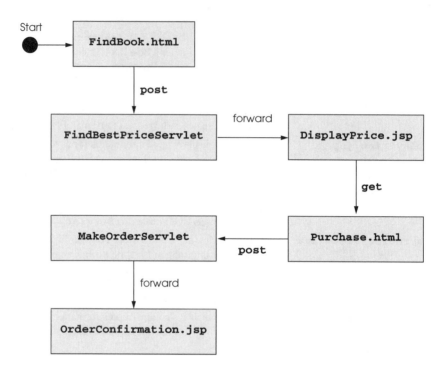

Fig. 16.2   Web-client work flow.

BN. Attribute **action** (line 16) specifies **FindBestPriceServlet** as the target for processing user input. Lines 19–20 display an input field and submit button that enable users to specify and submit an ISBN.

```
1   <!-- Fig. 16.3: FindBook.html
2      Displays a form that enables users to post an ISBN to
3      servlet FindBestPriceServlet (alias findbestprice).
4   -->
5
6   <html xmlns = "http://www.w3.org/1999/xhtml">
7
8      <head>
9         <title>PriceFinder - Find a Book!</title>
10     </head>
11
12     <body>
13
```

Fig. 16.3   **FindBook.html** provides a form that enables users to specify the book ISBN. (Part 1 of 2.)

```
14          <h1>PriceFinder</h1>
15
16          <form action = "/casestudy/findbestprice"
17             method = "post">
18
19             Enter ISBN: <input type="text" size="40" name="isbn">
20             <input type="submit" value="Find Best Price!">
21
22          </form>
23
24       </body>
25
26    </html>
```

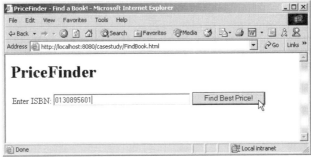

Fig. 16.3   **FindBook.html** provides a form that enables users to specify the book ISBN. (Part 2 of 2.)

16.2.2 Accessing Best Book Price and Book Information

Once a user submits the form displayed by **FindBook.html**, the form values are posted to **FindBestPriceServlet** (Fig. 16.4). **FindBestPriceServlet** invokes the Price Finder Web service Best Book Price to obtain a **PriceQuote** corresponding to the supplied ISBN. **FindBestPriceServlet** also invokes the Price Finder's Book Information Web service to obtain book information corresponding to the supplied ISBN.

```
1    // FindBestPriceServlet.java
2    // Servlet that accesses Best Book Price and Book Informationm Web
3    // services to get best book price and book description.
4    package jws1casestudy.clients.web;
5
6    // Java core packages
7    import java.io.*;
8
9    // Java extension packages
10   import javax.servlet.*;
11   import javax.servlet.http.*;
12
```

Fig. 16.4   **FindBestPriceServlet** accesses the Web services Best Book Price and Book Information to obtain the best book price and book description. (Part 1 of 3.)

```
13   // Deitel packages
14   import jws1casestudy.clients.stubs.bestbookprice.*;
15   import jws1casestudy.clients.stubs.deitelbookinformation.*;
16
17   public class FindBestPriceServlet extends HttpServlet {
18
19      private ServletContext servletContext;
20
21      // obtain servlet context
22      public void init( ServletConfig servletConfig )
23         throws ServletException
24      {
25         servletContext = servletConfig.getServletContext();
26      }
27
28      // display survey form
29      protected void doPost( HttpServletRequest request,
30         HttpServletResponse response )
31         throws ServletException, IOException
32      {
33         // read current user input
34         String isbn = request.getParameter( "isbn" );
35
36         // attempt to access Best Book Price and Book Information
37         // Web services
38         try {
39
40            // create Web service stub factory
41            BestBookPriceService bestBookPriceService =
42               new BestBookPriceService_Impl();
43
44            // obtain reference to Web service stub
45            BestBookPrice bestBookPrice =
46               bestBookPriceService.getBestBookPrice();
47
48            // get best price from Web service
49            PriceQuote priceQuote =
50               bestBookPrice.getBestPrice( isbn );
51
52            // create Web service stub factory
53            BookInformationService bookInformationService =
54               new BookInformationService_Impl();
55
56            // obtain reference to stub
57            BookInformation bookInformation =
58               bookInformationService.getBookInformation();
59
60            // get book info from Web service
61            BookDetails bookDetails =
62               bookInformation.getBookDetails( isbn );
63
```

Fig. 16.4   FindBestPriceServlet accesses the Web services Best Book Price and Book Information to obtain the best book price and book description. (Part 2 of 3.)

```
64              // get user's session object
65              // create a session if one does not exist
66              HttpSession session = request.getSession( true );
67
68              // add PriceQuote contents to session
69              session.setAttribute( "price",
70                 priceQuote.getPrice() + "" );
71
72              session.setAttribute( "isbn",
73                 priceQuote.getIsbn() + "" );
74
75              session.setAttribute( "storeID",
76                 priceQuote.getStoreID() + "" );
77
78              session.setAttribute( "storeDescription",
79                 priceQuote.getStoreDescription() + "" );
80
81              // add BookDetails contents to session
82              session.setAttribute( "title",
83                 bookDetails.getTitle() + "" );
84
85              session.setAttribute( "description",
86                 bookDetails.getDescription() + "" );
87
88              session.setAttribute( "authors",
89                 bookDetails.getAuthors() + "" );
90
91              session.setAttribute( "coverImageURL",
92                 bookDetails.getCoverImageURL() + "" );
93
94              // forward to display JSP
95              RequestDispatcher dispatcher =
96                 servletContext.getRequestDispatcher(
97                     "/DisplayPrice.jsp" );
98
99              dispatcher.forward( request, response );
100         }
101
102      // handle connection exceptions
103      catch ( Exception exception ) {
104          exception.printStackTrace();
105      }
106
107   } // end method doPost
108
109 } // end class FindBestPriceServlet
```

Fig. 16.4 FindBestPriceServlet accesses the Web services Best Book Price
and Book Information to obtain the best book price and book description.
(Part 3 of 3.)

Lines 22–26 overrides method **init** of class **HttpServlet** to obtain the servlet
context. The servlet context enables developers to, among other things, obtain a reference
to a **RequestDispatcher** that forwards requests to alternate Web resources.

Method **doPost** (lines 29–107) processes the user's **post** request. Line 34 invokes **HTTPServletRequest** method **getParameter** to obtain the user-specified ISBN. Lines 38–62 attempt to invoke the Web services Best Book Price and Book Information.

In this example, we use stubs generated by the JWSDP **xrpcc** tool. Section 16.2.7 discusses the process by which to generate the JAX-RPC stubs for the Price Finder's Best Book Price, Book Purchase and Book Information Web services. Lines 41–46 obtain a reference to the **BestBookPrice** Web-service stub. Lines 49–50 invoke the stub method **getBestPrice**, which delegates the invocation to the Web service Best Book Price method **getBestPrice**. Method **getBestPrice** returns an instance of class **Price-Quote** that contains the best price quote for the provided ISBN.

Lines 53–58 obtain a reference to the Web service stub **BookInformation**. Lines 61–62 invoke the stub method **getBookDetails**, which delegates the method invocation to Deitel & Associates' Book Information Web service. Method **getBookDetails** returns an instance of class **BookDetails** that contains the book information.

Line 66 obtains a reference to the user's **Session** object. Lines 69–79 extract the contents of **PriceQuote**, returned by **BestBookPrice** Web service, and store them in the user **Session**. Lines 82–92 extract the contents of **BookDetails**, returned by **BookInformation** Web service, and store them also in the user **Session**.

Note that a more intuitive approach to storing the user's session information would be to store objects **PriceQuote** and **BookDetails** in the **Session** object. This approach is not possible when using JAX-RPC stubs generated by the **xrpcc** tool. Recall, from Chapter 9, that tool **xrpcc** generates implementations of the custom types defined in the WSDL file. In Section 16.3, we show how to generate JAX-RPC stubs for the Best Book Price and Book Purchase Web services. Both Web services use a custom type **PriceQuote**, so the **xrpcc** tool generates two implementations of **Price-Quote**. Both **PriceQuote** implementations expose the same methods, but they belong to two different package structures. To avoid potential conflicts among differing **PriceQuote** implementations, we chose to store **PriceQuote**'s contents in the **Session** and to reconstruct the **PriceQuote** upon invoking the Book Purchase Web service. We use the same approach with **BookDetails**, for consistency. In the Swing-based desktop application we demonstrate the use of fully qualified package names to avoid such conflicts.

Lines 95–99 dispatch the user to **DisplayPrice.jsp** by invoking interface **RequestDispatcher** method **forward**.

16.2.3 Displaying Best Price Quote

FindBestPriceServlet forwards the client requests to the presentation-layer component **DisplayPrice.jsp** (Fig. 16.5). Lines 19–25 obtain **PriceQuote** contents from the **Session**, and lines 28–36 obtain **BookDetails** contents from the **Session**. Lines 41–66 construct a table to display the book price and book details. The form (lines 67–69) enables the user to purchase the book on line. Once the client clicks **Buy!**, **DisplayPrice.jsp** links the client to **Purchase.html**.

16.2.4 Placing Order Requests

XHTML document **Purchase.html** (Fig. 16.6) displays a form (lines 15–77) that enables customers to input such purchase information as the customer's name, e-mail address and credit-card number. Attribute **action** (line 15) specifies **MakeOrderServlet** as the target for processing user input. Lines 16–76 display a table that contains textfields in which users enter information. Line 73 provides a submit button to enable the client to submit the request. **Purchase.html** then posts the user-input information to **MakeOrderServlet**.

```
1   <?xml version ="1.0 "?>
2   <!DOCTYPE html PUBLIC "-//W3C//DTD XHTML 1.0 Strict//EN "
3      "http://www.w3.org/TR/xhtml1/DTD/xhtml1.1-strict.dtd ">
4   <!-- DisplayPrice.jsp -->
5
6   <%-- JSP page settings --%>
7   <%@ page language = "java" session = "true" %>
8
9   <html xmlns = "http://www.w3.org/1999/xhtml">
10
11     <head>
12        <title>PriceFinder - Search Results</title>
13     </head>
14
15     <body>
16
17        <%
18           // get price quote information
19           String price = ( String )session.getAttribute( "price" );
20           String isbn = ( String )session.getAttribute( "isbn" );
21           String storeID =
22              ( String )session.getAttribute( "storeID" );
23
24           String storeDescription =
25              ( String )session.getAttribute( "storeDescription" );
26
27           // get book details information
28           String title = ( String )session.getAttribute( "title" );
29           String description =
30             ( String )session.getAttribute( "description" );
31
32           String authors =
33              ( String )session.getAttribute( "authors" );
34
35           String coverImage =
36              ( String )session.getAttribute( "coverImageURL" );
37        %>
38
39        <center><h1>PriceFinder Results</h1></center>
40
41        <table>
42           <tr>
43              <td width="350" bgColor="#00CC00"> Book </td>
44              <td width="50" bgColor="#00CC00" align="center">
```

Fig. 16.5 **DisplayPrice.jsp** displays the contents of **PriceQuote** and **BookDetails**, which are returned by the Web services Best Book Price and Book Information. (Part 1 of 2.)

```
45                    Price
46              </td>
47              <td width="100" bgColor="#00CC00" align="center">
48                 Store
49              </td>
50              <td width="400" bgColor="#00CC00">
51                 Store Description
52              </td>
53           </tr>
54           <tr>
55              <td>
56                 <img align="center" src=<%= coverImage %>> <p>
57                 <b>Title:</b> <%= title %> <br>
58                 <b>ISBN:</b> <%= isbn %> <br>
59                 <b>Authors:</b> <%= authors %> <br>
60                 <p> <%= description %> </p>
61              </td>
62              <td align="center"> $<%= price %> </td>
63              <td align="center"> <%= storeID %> </td>
64              <td> <%= storeDescription %> </td>
65           </tr>
66        </table>
67        <form action="/casestudy/Purchase.html">
68           <input type="submit" value="Buy!">
69        </form>
70
71     </body>
72  </html>
```

Fig. 16.5 **DisplayPrice.jsp** displays the contents of **PriceQuote** and **BookDetails**, which are returned by the Web services Best Book Price and Book Information. (Part 2 of 2.)

```
1   <!-- Fig. 16.6: Purchase.html
2      Displays a form that enables users to submit purchase
3      information to MakeOrderServlet (alias makeorder).
4   -->
5   <html xmlns = "http://www.w3.org/1999/xhtml">
6
7      <head>
8         <title>PriceFinder - Place Order</title>
9      </head>
10
11     <body>
12
13        <h1>Enter customer information:</h1>
14
15        <form action="/casestudy/makeorder" method="post">
16           <table>
17              <tr>
18                 <td width="100">First Name:</td>
19                 <td>
20                    <input type="text" size="40" name="firstname">
21                 </td>
22              </tr>
23              <tr>
24                 <td width="100">Last Name:</td>
25                 <td>
26                    <input type="text" size="40" name="lastname">
27                 </td>
28              </tr>
29              <tr>
30                 <td width="100">Email:</td>
31                 <td>
32                    <input type="text" size="40" name="email">
33                 </td>
34              </tr>
35              <tr>
36                 <td width="100">Street Address:</td>
37                 <td>
38                    <input type="text" size="40" name="streetaddress">
39                 </td>
40              </tr>
41              <tr>
42                 <td width="100">City:</td>
43                 <td>
44                    <input type="text" size="40" name="city">
45                 </td>
46              </tr>
47              <tr>
48                 <td width="100">State:</td>
49                 <td>
50                    <input type="text" size="40" name="state">
51                 </td>
52              </tr>
```

Fig. 16.6 **Purchase.html** enables customers to enter personal information. (Part 1 of 2.)

```
53                    <tr>
54                      <td width="100">Zip:</td>
55                      <td>
56                         <input type="text" size="40" name="zip">
57                      </td>
58                    </tr>
59                    <tr>
60                      <td width="100">Country:</td>
61                      <td>
62                         <input type="text" size="40" name="country">
63                      </td>
64                    </tr>
65                    <tr>
66                      <td width="100">Credit Card #:</td>
67                      <td>
68                         <input type="text" size="40" name="creditcard">
69                      </td>
70                    </tr>
71                    <tr>
72                      <td>
73                         <input type="submit" size="40" value="Buy!">
74                      </td>
75                    </tr>
76                 </table>
77              </form>
78
79         </body>
80
81    </html>
```

Fig. 16.6   Purchase.html enables customers to enter personal information.
(Part 2 of 2.)

16.2.5 Accessing Price Finder's Book Purchase Web Service

MakeOrderServlet (Fig. 16.7) invokes the Price Finder's Book Purchase Web service to place an order. Lines 23–27 override method **init** of class **HttpServlet** to obtain the servlet context. Method **doPost** (lines 30–132) gets customer information from the client's request and **PriceQuote** contents from the client's **Session** object and places an order via the Price Finder Web service Book Purchase.

```
1   // MakeOrderServlet.java
2   // Retrieves user-input to invoke the Book Purchase Web service
3   // of the specified Book Store.
4   package jws1casestudy.clients.web;
5
6   // Java core packages
7   import java.io.*;
8   import java.util.*;
9
10  // Java extension packages
11  import javax.servlet.*;
12  import javax.servlet.http.*;
13  import javax.xml.rpc.*;
14
15  // Deitel packages
16  import jws1casestudy.clients.stubs.bookpurchase.*;
17
18  public class MakeOrderServlet extends HttpServlet {
19
20     private ServletContext servletContext;
21
22     // obtain servlet context
23     public void init( ServletConfig servletConfig )
24        throws ServletException
25     {
26        servletContext = servletConfig.getServletContext();
27     }
28
29     // invoke Web service Book Purchase with user input
30     protected void doPost( HttpServletRequest request,
31        HttpServletResponse response )
32        throws ServletException, IOException
33     {
34
35        // obtain session if exists
36        HttpSession session = request.getSession( false );
37
38        // if session does not exist, forward to start page
39        if ( session == null ) {
40           RequestDispatcher dispatcher =
41              servletContext.getRequestDispatcher(
42                 "/FindBook.html" );
43
```

Fig. 16.7 **MakeOrderServlet** accesses the Price Finder Web service Book Purchase to place an order for a book. (Part 1 of 3.)

```
44                  dispatcher.forward( null, null );
45            }
46
47         // obtain user input
48         String firstName = request.getParameter( "firstname" );
49         String lastName = request.getParameter( "lastname" );
50         String email = request.getParameter( "email" );
51         String streetAddress =
52            request.getParameter( "streetaddress" );
53
54         String city = request.getParameter( "city" );
55         String state = request.getParameter( "state" );
56         String zip = request.getParameter( "zip" );
57         String country = request.getParameter( "country" );
58         String creditCard = request.getParameter( "creditcard" );
59
60         // instantiate Customer instance
61         Customer customer = new Customer();
62
63         customer.setFirstName( firstName );
64         customer.setLastName( lastName );
65         customer.setEmailAddress( email );
66         customer.setStreetAddress( streetAddress);
67         customer.setCity( city );
68         customer.setState( state );
69         customer.setZipCode( zip );
70         customer.setCountry( country );
71         customer.setCreditCardNumber( creditCard );
72
73         // obtain price quote contents from session
74         String price =
75            ( String )session.getAttribute( "price" );
76
77         String isbn =
78            ( String )session.getAttribute( "isbn" );
79
80         String storeID =
81            ( String )session.getAttribute( "storeID" );
82
83         String storeDescription =
84            ( String )session.getAttribute( "storeDescription" );
85
86         // create PriceQuote from contents in session
87         PriceQuote priceQuote = new PriceQuote();
88
89         priceQuote.setIsbn( isbn );
90         priceQuote.setPrice( Double.parseDouble( price ) );
91         priceQuote.setStoreID( Integer.parseInt( storeID ) );
92         priceQuote.setStoreDescription( storeDescription );
93
```

Fig. 16.7 MakeOrderServlet accesses the Price Finder Web service Book Purchase to place an order for a book. (Part 2 of 3.)

```
94          // attempt to place order
95          try {
96
97             // create Web service stub factory
98             BookPurchaseService bookPurchaseService =
99                new BookPurchaseService_Impl();
100
101            // obtain reference to Web service stub
102            BookPurchase bookPurchase =
103               bookPurchaseService.getBookPurchase();
104
105            // place order
106            bookPurchase.orderBook( priceQuote, customer );
107         }
108
109         // handle Web service exceptions
110         catch ( Exception exception ) {
111            exception.printStackTrace();
112         }
113
114         // store customer information in session
115         session.setAttribute( "firstName", firstName );
116         session.setAttribute( "lastName", lastName );
117         session.setAttribute( "email", email );
118         session.setAttribute( "streetAddress", streetAddress );
119         session.setAttribute( "city", city );
120         session.setAttribute( "state", state );
121         session.setAttribute( "zip", zip );
122         session.setAttribute( "country", country );
123         session.setAttribute( "creditCard", creditCard );
124
125         // dispatch to order confirmation jsp
126         RequestDispatcher dispatcher =
127            servletContext.getRequestDispatcher(
128               "/OrderConfirmation.jsp" );
129
130         dispatcher.forward( request, response );
131
132      } // end method doPost
133
134  } // end class MakeOrderServlet
```

Fig. 16.7 **MakeOrderServlet** accesses the Price Finder Web service Book Purchase to place an order for a book. (Part 3 of 3.)

Line 36 attempts to obtain the user's **Session** object. If the user does not have a **Session** object, lines 40–44 direct the client to **FindBook.html**. Lines 48–58 obtain the user-input purchase information. Lines 61–71 use the purchase information to construct a **Customer** object.

The user's **Session** object contains **PriceQuote** contents set by **FindBest-PriceServlet** (lines 74–84). Lines 87–92 construct a **PriceQuote** object, using the contents extracted from the user's **Session**.

The **try** block (lines 95–107) attempts to place an order via **xrpcc**-generated Book Purchase Web service stubs. Lines 98–103 obtain a reference to the **BookPurchase** service stub from the **xrpcc**-generated class **BookPurchaseService_Impl**. Line 106 invokes method **orderBook** of **BookPurchase**.

OrderConfirmation.jsp (Section 16.2.6) displays a confirmation of the user-input purchase information, so that lines 115–123 can store the purchase information in the user's **Session**. Lines 126–130 dispatch the client to **OrderConfirmation.jsp**, which confirms the user's purchase request.

16.2.6 Displaying Purchase Request Confirmation

OrderConfirmation.jsp (Fig. 16.8) displays the user's purchase request. Line 7 specifies a **page** directive, which specifies that an instance of **HTTPSession** (identified implicitly as **session**) is accessible globally to the JSP. Lines 19–22, lines 25–33 and lines 36–52 extract the **PriceQuote**, **BookDetails** and **Customer** contents stored in the **Session**, respectively. Lines 55–81 display the purchase-request information.

```
1   <?xml version ="1.0 "?>
2   <!DOCTYPE html PUBLIC "-//W3C//DTD XHTML 1.0 Strict//EN "
3      "http://www.w3.org/TR/xhtml1/DTD/xhtml1.1-strict.dtd ">
4   <!-- OrderConfirmation.jsp -->
5
6   <%-- JSP page settings --%>
7   <%@ page language = "java" session = "true" %>
8
9   <html xmlns = "http://www.w3.org/1999/xhtml">
10
11     <head>
12        <title>PriceFinder - Order Confirmation</title>
13     </head>
14
15     <body>
16
17        <%
18        // get price quote contents
19        String price = ( String )session.getAttribute( "price" );
20        String isbn = ( String )session.getAttribute( "isbn" );
21        String storeID =
22           ( String )session.getAttribute( "storeID" );
23
24        // get book details contents
25        String title = ( String )session.getAttribute( "title" );
26        String description =
27           ( String )session.getAttribute( "description" );
28
29        String authors =
30           ( String )session.getAttribute( "authors" );
31
```

Fig. 16.8   OrderConfirmation.jsp displays the customer's purchase request. (Part 1 of 3.)

```
32              String coverImage =
33                 ( String )session.getAttribute( "coverImageURL" );
34
35              // get Customer contents
36              String firstName =
37                 ( String )session.getAttribute( "firstName" );
38              String lastName =
39                 ( String )session.getAttribute( "lastName" );
40
41              String email = ( String )session.getAttribute( "email" );
42              String streetAddress =
43                 ( String )session.getAttribute( "streetAddress" );
44
45              String city = ( String )session.getAttribute( "city" );
46              String state = ( String )session.getAttribute( "state" );
47              String zipCode = ( String )session.getAttribute( "zip" );
48              String country =
49                 ( String )session.getAttribute( "country" );
50
51              String creditCardNumber =
52                 ( String )session.getAttribute( "creditCard" );
53         %>
54
55         <h1>PriceFinder OrderConfirmation</h1>
56
57         <h2>You have requested the following book:</h2>
58         <br><img src=<%= coverImage %>>
59         <br>Title: <%= title %>
60         <br>ISBN: <%= isbn %>
61         <br>Authors: <%= authors %>
62         <br>Description: <%= description %>
63         <br>Price: $<%= price %>
64         <br>StoreID: <%= storeID %>
65
66         <h2>Customer information is:</h2>
67         <br>First Name: <%= firstName %>
68         <br>Last Name: <%= lastName %>
69         <br>Email: <%= email %>
70         <br>Street Address: <%= streetAddress %>
71         <br>City: <%= city %>
72         <br>State: <%= state %>
73         <br>Zip: <%= zipCode %>
74         <br>Country: <%= country %>
75         <br>Credit Card Number: <%= creditCardNumber %>
76
77         <p></p>
78         <h2>
79            An email confirmation of your order has been sent
80            to address <%= email %>.
81         </h2>
82      </body>
83   </html>
```

Fig. 16.8 `OrderConfirmation.jsp` displays the customer's purchase request. (Part 2 of 3.)

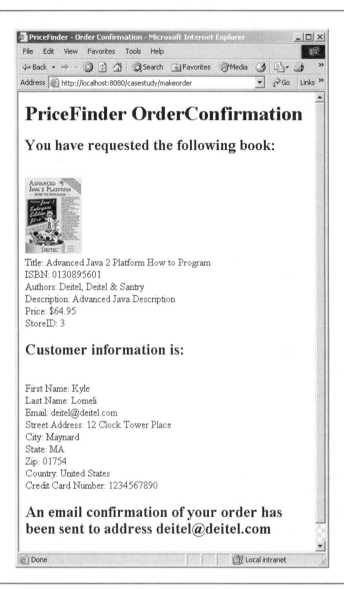

Fig. 16.8 `OrderConfirmation.jsp` displays the customer's purchase request. (Part 3 of 3.)

16.2.7 Deployment

In Appendix A, we discuss the general process for deploying servlets in Apache's Tomcat servlet container. Section 16.3 discusses the process for generating the stubs for the Price Finder Web services Best Book Price, Book Purchase and Book Information. To deploy the Price Finder Web client, create the file and directory structure shown in Fig. 16.9.

File **web.xml** is the deployment descriptor for **FindBestPriceServlet** and **MakeOrderServlet**.

Price Finder Web client directory and file structure

```
casestudy
   FindBook.html
   Purchase.html
   DisplayPrice.jsp
   OrderConfirmation.jsp
   WEB-INF
      web.xml
      classes
         jws1casestudy
            clients
               stubs
                  bestbookprice
                     < xrpcc-generated class files >
                  bookpurchase
                     < xrpcc-generated class files >
                  deitelbookinformation
                     < xrpcc-generated class files >
               web
                  FindBestPriceServlet.class
                  MakeOrderServlet.class
```

Fig. 16.9 Web application directory and file structure for the Price Finder Web client.

```
1   <?xml version="1.0" encoding="UTF-8"?>
2
3   <!-- Fig. 16.10: web.xml
4      Lists configuration settings for the PriceFinder Web client
5      environment.
6   -->
7
8   <!DOCTYPE web-app
9      PUBLIC "-//Sun Microsystems, Inc.//DTD Web Application 2.3//EN"
10      "http://java.sun.com/j2ee/dtds/web-app_2_3.dtd">
11
12  <web-app>
13
14     <!-- Servlet declarations -->
15     <servlet>
16        <servlet-name>findbestprice</servlet-name>
17
18        <servlet-class>
19           jws1casestudy.clients.web.FindBestPriceServlet
20        </servlet-class>
21     </servlet>
22
```

Fig. 16.10 web.xml is the deployment descriptor for the Web client. (Part 1 of 2.)

```
23    <servlet>
24       <servlet-name>makeorder</servlet-name>
25
26       <servlet-class>
27          jws1casestudy.clients.web.MakeOrderServlet
28       </servlet-class>
29    </servlet>
30
31    <!-- Servlet mappings -->
32    <servlet-mapping>
33       <servlet-name>findbestprice</servlet-name>
34       <url-pattern>/findbestprice</url-pattern>
35    </servlet-mapping>
36
37    <servlet-mapping>
38       <servlet-name>makeorder</servlet-name>
39       <url-pattern>/makeorder</url-pattern>
40    </servlet-mapping>
41
42 </web-app>
```

Fig. 16.10 `web.xml` is the deployment descriptor for the Web client. (Part 2 of 2.)

16.3 Swing Desktop Client

The desktop-application client for the Price Finder application provides a simple graphical user interface through which users can obtain price quotes, obtain book information and place orders.

In this example we use JAX-RPC to implement the client, so we must use the **xrpcc** tool to generate stubs and supporting classes for each of the Web services with which the client will communicate.[1] Figure 16.11, Fig. 16.12 and Fig. 16.13 are the **xrpcc** configuration files for generating the JAX-RPC stubs and supporting classes. For each Web service, execute the **xrpcc** tool as follows:

> **xrpcc -classpath . -client -d .** *configuration.xml*

where *configuration.xml* is an appropriate configuration file. Note that the Web services must be deployed and have their WSDL files generated before using **xrpcc** to generate the client-side stubs. We discuss the process of deploying the Web services and generating the WSDL documents in Chapter 17.

```
1    <?xml version="1.0" encoding="UTF-8"?>
2
3    <configuration
4       xmlns = "http://java.sun.com/xml/ns/jax-rpc/ri/config">
5
```

Fig. 16.11 `xrpcc` configuration file for the Best Book Price Web service. (Part 1 of 2.)

---

1. Note that the Price Finder and other Web services must be deployed before you can use **xrpcc** to generate the client-side classes. Please refer to Chapter 17 for complete deployment instructions.

```
 6      <wsdl location =
 7           "http://localhost:8080/axis/services/BestBookPrice?wsdl"
 8        packageName = "jws1casestudy.clients.stubs.bestbookprice">
 9      </wsdl>
10   </configuration>
```

Fig. 16.11 xrpcc configuration file for the Best Book Price Web service. (Part 2 of 2.)

```
 1   <?xml version="1.0" encoding="UTF-8"?>
 2
 3   <configuration
 4      xmlns = "http://java.sun.com/xml/ns/jax-rpc/ri/config">
 5
 6      <wsdl location =
 7           "http://localhost:8080/axis/services/BookPurchase?wsdl"
 8        packageName = "jws1casestudy.clients.stubs.bookpurchase">
 9      </wsdl>
10   </configuration>
```

Fig. 16.12 xrpcc configuration file for Book Purchase Web service.

```
 1   <?xml version="1.0" encoding="UTF-8"?>
 2
 3   <configuration
 4      xmlns = "http://java.sun.com/xml/ns/jax-rpc/ri/config">
 5
 6      <wsdl location =
 7           "http://localhost:8080/axis/services/BookInformation?wsdl"
 8        packageName =
 9           "jws1casestudy.clients.stubs.deitelbookinformation">
10      </wsdl>
11   </configuration>
```

Fig. 16.13 xrpcc configuration file for Book Information Web service.

Class **ServiceAccess** (Fig. 16.14) uses JAX-RPC to communicate with the Price Finder Web services.

```
 1   // ServiceAccess.java
 2   // ServiceAccess provides access to the PriceFinder Web service
 3   // for a Swing-based GUI.
 4   package jws1casestudy.clients.swing;
 5
 6   // JAX-RPC packages
 7   import javax.xml.rpc.*;
 8
 9   // Packages for xrpcc-generated classes
10   import jws1casestudy.clients.stubs.deitelbookinformation.*;
11   import jws1casestudy.clients.stubs.bestbookprice.*;
```

Fig. 16.14 ServiceAccess class for accessing Price Finder Web services through JAX-RPC. (Part 1 of 4.)

```
12   import jws1casestudy.clients.stubs.bookpurchase.*;
13
14   public class ServiceAccess {
15
16      // Stubs for invoking Web services
17      BookInformation_Stub bookInformationService;
18      BestBookPrice_Stub bestBookPriceService;
19      BookPurchase_Stub bookPurchaseService;
20
21      // ServiceAccess constructor
22      public ServiceAccess()
23      {
24         // create Stub for BookInformation Web service
25         bookInformationService = ( BookInformation_Stub )
26            new BookInformationService_Impl().getBookInformation();
27
28         // create Stub for BestBookPrice Web service
29         bestBookPriceService = ( BestBookPrice_Stub )
30            new BestBookPriceService_Impl().getBestBookPrice();
31
32         // create Stub for BookPurchase Web service
33         bookPurchaseService = ( BookPurchase_Stub )
34            new BookPurchaseService_Impl().getBookPurchase();
35
36      } // end ServiceAccess constructor
37
38      // retrieve the best price for the given ISBN from the
39      // BestBookPrice Web service
40      public jws1casestudy.pricefinder.common.PriceQuote
41         getBestPrice( String ISBN ) throws Exception
42      {
43         try {
44            jws1casestudy.clients.stubs.bestbookprice.PriceQuote
45               quote = bestBookPriceService.getBestPrice( ISBN );
46
47            jws1casestudy.pricefinder.common.PriceQuote returnQuote =
48               new jws1casestudy.pricefinder.common.PriceQuote();
49
50            returnQuote.setIsbn( quote.getIsbn() );
51            returnQuote.setPrice( quote.getPrice() );
52            returnQuote.setStoreDescription(
53               quote.getStoreDescription() );
54            returnQuote.setStoreID( quote.getStoreID() );
55
56            return returnQuote;
57         }
58
59         // handle exception retrieving PriceQuote from Web service
60         catch ( Exception exception ) {
61            exception.printStackTrace();
62
```

Fig. 16.14 ServiceAccess class for accessing Price Finder Web services through JAX-RPC. (Part 2 of 4.)

```
63                  throw new Exception( "Error getting price quote." );
64       }
65    } // end method getBestPrice
66
67    // order the book in the give PriceQuote for the given
68    // Customer using the BookPurchase Web service
69    public void orderBook(
70       jws1casestudy.pricefinder.common.PriceQuote quote,
71       jws1casestudy.pricefinder.common.Customer customer )
72       throws Exception
73    {
74       try {
75          jws1casestudy.clients.stubs.bookpurchase.PriceQuote
76             priceQuote = new
77             jws1casestudy.clients.stubs.bookpurchase.PriceQuote();
78
79          priceQuote.setIsbn( quote.getIsbn() );
80          priceQuote.setPrice( quote.getPrice() );
81          priceQuote.setStoreID( quote.getStoreID() );
82          priceQuote.setStoreDescription(
83             quote.getStoreDescription() );
84
85          jws1casestudy.clients.stubs.bookpurchase.Customer
86             remoteCustomer =
87             new jws1casestudy.clients.stubs.bookpurchase.Customer();
88
89          remoteCustomer.setFirstName( customer.getFirstName() );
90          remoteCustomer.setLastName( customer.getLastName() );
91          remoteCustomer.setStreetAddress(
92             customer.getStreetAddress() );
93          remoteCustomer.setCity( customer.getCity() );
94          remoteCustomer.setState( customer.getState() );
95          remoteCustomer.setZipCode( customer.getZipCode() );
96          remoteCustomer.setCountry( customer.getCountry() );
97          remoteCustomer.setEmailAddress(
98             customer.getEmailAddress() );
99          remoteCustomer.setCreditCardNumber(
100            customer.getCreditCardNumber() );
101
102        bookPurchaseService.orderBook( priceQuote, remoteCustomer );
103       }
104
105       // handle exception placing order through Web service
106       catch ( Exception exception ) {
107          exception.printStackTrace();
108
109          throw new Exception( "Error ordering book." );
110       }
111
112    } // end method orderBook
113
```

Fig. 16.14 ServiceAccess class for accessing Price Finder Web services through JAX-RPC. (Part 3 of 4.)

```
114        // retrieve information about the give ISBN from the
115        // BookInformation Web service
116        public jws1casestudy.pricefinder.common.BookDetails
117           getBookDetails( String ISBN ) throws Exception
118        {
119           try {
120
121              // retrieve the BookDetails object
122              jws1casestudy.clients.stubs.deitelbookinformation.BookDe
tails
123                 details = bookInformationService.getBookDetails(
124                    ISBN );
125
126              // package BookDetails information in a common
127              // BookDetails object for returning to the caller
128              jws1casestudy.pricefinder.common.BookDetails
129                 returnDetails =
130                 new jws1casestudy.pricefinder.common.BookDetails();
131
132              returnDetails.setAuthors( details.getAuthors() );
133              returnDetails.setCoverImageURL(
134                 details.getCoverImageURL() );
135
136              returnDetails.setDescription(
137                 details.getDescription() );
138
139              returnDetails.setIsbn( details.getIsbn() );
140              returnDetails.setTitle( details.getTitle() );
141
142              return returnDetails;
143           }
144
145           // handle exception communicating with Web service
146           catch ( Exception exception ) {
147              exception.printStackTrace();
148
149              throw new Exception( "Could not locate information." );
150           }
151
152        } // end method getBookDetails
153
154     } // end class ServiceAccess
```

Fig. 16.14 ServiceAccess class for accessing Price Finder Web services through JAX-RPC. (Part 4 of 4.)

The **ServiceAccess** constructor (lines 22–36) creates stubs for each of the Price Finder Web services. The methods of class **ServiceAccess** use these stubs to invoke the Web-service methods.

Method **getBestPrice** (lines 40–65) takes as a **String** argument the ISBN of a book for which the consumer would like a price quote. Method **getBestPrice** invokes the Best Book Price Web service's **getBestPrice** method to obtain the quote (lines 44–45). Recall that, with JAX-RPC, the **xrpcc** tool generates stubs and other Java classes out of the WSDL description of the Web service. In this case, the **xrpcc** tool has generated class **jws1casestudy.clients.stubs.bestbookprice.PriceQuote**, which represents the return type of the Best Book Price **getBestPrice** method. Although the Book Purchase Web service also uses class **PriceQuote**, the **xrpcc** generates a different implementation (**jws1casestudy.clients.stubs.bookpurchase.PriceQuote**) that is based on the Book Purchase Web service's WSDL document. To prevent the GUI from depending upon one particular implementation, **ServiceAccess** method **getBestPrice** copies the values into a **jws1casestudy.pricefinder.common.PriceQuote** object and returns that object to the caller (lines 47–56).

Method **orderBook** (lines 69–112) uses the Price Finder's Book Purchase Web service to place an order for the book in the given **PriceQuote** for the given **Customer** (both of package **jws1casestudy.pricefinder.common**). The Book Purchase Web service method **orderBook** expects as its first argument an object of class **jws1casestudy.clients.stubs.bookpurchase.PriceQuote**, so lines 75–83 copy the given **jws1casestudy.pricefinder.common.PriceQuote** values into an object of the appropriate type. Lines 89–100 copy the customer information into an object of class **jws1casestudy.clients.stubs.bookpurchase.Customer**. Line 102 invokes the Book Purchase method **orderBook** to place the order.

Method **getBookDetails** (lines 116–152) uses the Price Finder's Book Information Web service method **getBookDetails** to obtain information about the book with the given ISBN. Lines 122–124 invoke the remote method and store the result in an object of class **jws1casestudy.clients.stubs.bookinformation.BookDetails**. Lines 132–140 copy the book information into an object of class **jws1casestudy.pricefinder.common.BookDetails** for use in the GUI.

Class **SwingClient** (Fig. 16.15) provides a simple GUI for invoking the Price Finder's Web services by using an instance of class **ServiceAccess** (line 35). The **SwingClient** constructor (lines 32–119) prompts the user to enter an ISBN (lines 88–89). Lines 94–95 then invoke methods **getBookDetails** and **getBestPrice** of class **ServiceAccess** to obtain the book's detailed information and the best available price, respectively. Lines 98–109 append this information to a **JTextArea** for display to the user. The **ActionListener** for **JButton** instance **orderButton** (lines 47–82) begins the process of ordering the chosen book by prompting the user for address and billing information (lines 50–70). Line 74 invokes **ServiceAccess** method **orderBook** to place the order with the bookstore that offered the lowest price.

```
1   // SwingClient.java
2   // SwingClient provides a graphical user interface for interacting
3   // with the PriceFinder Web service.
4   package jws1casestudy.clients.swing;
5
6   // Java core packages
7   import java.awt.*;
8   import java.awt.event.*;
9   import java.text.NumberFormat;
```

Fig. 16.15 **SwingClient** provides a GUI for accessing the Price Finder Web services. (Part 1 of 4.)

```
10    import java.util.Locale;
11
12    // Java extension packages
13    import javax.swing.*;
14
15    // Deitel packages
16    import jws1casestudy.pricefinder.common.*;
17
18    public class SwingClient extends JFrame {
19
20       private JButton orderButton;
21       private JTextArea bookDetailsArea;
22
23       // ServiceAccess object for invoking Web services
24       private ServiceAccess service;
25
26       // objects for storing price quotes, customer information
27       // and book information
28       private PriceQuote quote;
29       private Customer customer;
30       private BookDetails bookDetails;
31
32       public SwingClient()
33       {
34          // create ServiceAccess object for invoking Web services
35          service = new ServiceAccess();
36
37          bookDetailsArea = new JTextArea( 10, 25 );
38          bookDetailsArea.setEditable( false );
39
40          Container container = getContentPane();
41
42          container.add( bookDetailsArea,
43             BorderLayout.CENTER );
44
45          orderButton = new JButton( "Order Book" );
46          orderButton.addActionListener(
47             new ActionListener() {
48                public void actionPerformed( ActionEvent event )
49                {
50                   customer = new Customer();
51
52                   customer.setFirstName(
53                      getField( "First Name" ) );
54
55                   customer.setLastName(
56                      getField( "Last Name" ) );
57
58                   customer.setStreetAddress(
59                      getField( "Street Address" ) );
60
61                   customer.setCity( getField( "City" ) );
```

Fig. 16.15 **SwingClient** provides a GUI for accessing the Price Finder Web
services. (Part 2 of 4.)

```
62                  customer.setState( getField( "State" ) );
63                  customer.setZipCode( getField( "Zip Code" ) );
64                  customer.setCountry( getField( "Country" ) );
65
66                  customer.setEmailAddress(
67                     getField( "Email Address" ) );
68
69                  customer.setCreditCardNumber(
70                     getField( "Credit Card Number" ) );
71
72                  // place order for best price quote
73                  try {
74                     service.orderBook( quote, customer );
75                  }
76
77                  // handle exceptions placing order
78                  catch ( Exception exception ) {
79                     exception.printStackTrace();
80                  }
81               }
82            }
83         ); // end call to addActionListener
84
85         container.add( orderButton, BorderLayout.SOUTH );
86
87         // prompt user for ISBN
88         String ISBN = JOptionPane.showInputDialog( this,
89            "Enter the ISBN of the book you would like to purchase" );
90
91         // get book information and best price by invoking Web
92         // services through serviceAccess object
93         try {
94            bookDetails = service.getBookDetails( ISBN );
95            quote = service.getBestPrice( ISBN );
96
97            // display book information and price quote
98            bookDetailsArea.append( "\nTitle: " +
99               bookDetails.getTitle() );
100
101            bookDetailsArea.append( "\nAuthors: " +
102               bookDetails.getAuthors() );
103
104            bookDetailsArea.append( "\nDescription: " +
105               bookDetails.getDescription() );
106
107            bookDetailsArea.append( "\nPrice: " +
108               quote.getPrice() + ", from " +
109               quote.getStoreDescription() );
110         }
111
```

Fig. 16.15 **SwingClient** provides a GUI for accessing the Price Finder Web services. (Part 3 of 4.)

```
112        // handle exceptions getting book and price information
113        catch ( Exception exception ) {
114           exception.printStackTrace();
115        }
116
117        setDefaultCloseOperation( EXIT_ON_CLOSE );
118        pack();
119     }
120
121     // get customer information from user
122     private String getField( String fieldName )
123     {
124        return JOptionPane.showInputDialog( this, "Enter " + fieldName
);
125     }
126
127     // launch application
128     public static void main( String args[] )
129     {
130        new SwingClient().show();
131     }
132
133  } // end class SwingClient
```

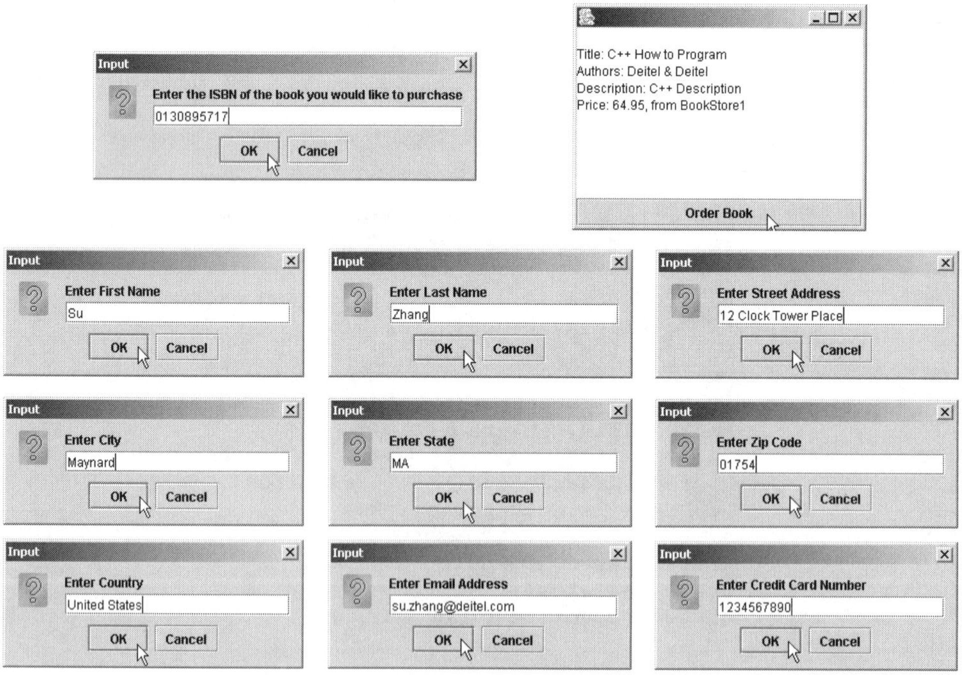

Fig. 16.15 **SwingClient** provides a GUI for accessing the Price Finder Web services. (Part 4 of 4.)

16.4 Java™ 2 Micro Edition Wireless Client

In Chapter 14, Wireless Web Services and Java 2 Micro Edition, we introduced J2ME and showed how to invoke Web services via a wireless client. Now, we use the concepts discussed in Chapter 14 to invoke the Web services that Price Finder exposes. Figure 16.16 presents an overview of how the J2ME client communicates with the Price Finder Web services.

Class **WirelessClient** (Fig. 16.17) is a **MIDlet** subclass that enables a user to select which Price Finder Web service the MIDP device should invoke. Because class **WirelessClient** extends class **MIDlet**, it must implement methods **startApp** (lines 13–19), **pauseApp** (line 22) and **destroyApp** (line 25). When the MIDP device invokes method **startApp**, lines 16–17 initialize the display manager and display a list that contains the available Web services that Price Finder exposes.

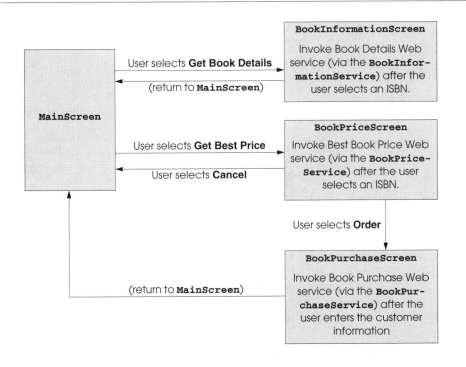

Fig. 16.16 Flowchart for a J2ME client invoking the Web services that Price Finder exposes.

```
1   // Fig. 16.17: WirelessClient.java.
2   // Class WirelessClient invokes the Web services that the
3   // Price Finder company exposes.
```

Fig. 16.17 WirelessClient invokes the Web services that Price Finder exposes. Reproduced with permission by Sun Microsystems, Inc.© Copyright 2002. Sun Microsystems, Inc. All Rights Reserved. (Part 1 of 2.)

```
 4   package jws1casestudy.clients.j2me;
 5
 6   // import J2ME packages
 7   import javax.microedition.midlet.*;
 8   import javax.microedition.lcdui.*;
 9
10   public class WirelessClient extends MIDlet {
11
12       // start MIDlet and enable user input
13       public void startApp()
14       {
15           // get MIDP-device Display manager and display main Screen
16           Display display = Display.getDisplay( this );
17           display.setCurrent( new MainScreen( display ) );
18
19       } // end method startApp
20
21       // pause MIDlet
22       public void pauseApp() {}
23
24       // terminate MIDlet lifecycle
25       public void destroyApp( boolean unconditional ) {}
26
27   } // end class WirelessClient
```

Fig. 16.17 WirelessClient invokes the Web services that Price Finder exposes.
Reproduced with permission by Sun Microsystems, Inc.© Copyright 2002.
Sun Microsystems, Inc. All Rights Reserved. (Part 2 of 2.)

As we construct our wireless client, we create several screens, each of which either enables the user to perform some action or displays information to the user. For example, some screens enable the user to select which Web service to invoke: other screens enable the user to view the results after Web-service invocation. We discuss each of these screens throughout our discussion of this client. For clarity, we create each MIDlet screen as a separate class. For instance, note that line 17 of class **WirelessClient** creates and displays an object of type **MainScreen**. Class **MainScreen** (Fig. 16.18) is a **List** subclass that displays Price Finder's available Web services. The constructor (lines 12–53) creates the **List**. Lines 17–18 append two items that enable the user to invoke either the Book Details Web service or the Best Book Price Web service. Although Price Finder also exposes the Book Purchase Web service, the user cannot invoke this Web service until the user has invoked the Price Finder's Best Book Price Web service. Note that we have hard-coded the available Web services into the MIDlet. A more robust application would download and parse a WSDL document to view Web-service availability; we hard-code the available Web services only for simplicity. Lines 21–51 include soft-button support; the MIDlet invokes a Web service that matches the user's selection from the **List**. If the user selects **Get book details**, lines 38–39 direct the display manager to display a **BookInformationScreen** (Fig. 16.19), which invokes the Book Details Web service and displays details on a specified book. If the user selects **Get best price**, lines 44–45 direct the display manager to display a **BookPriceScreen** (Fig. 16.21), which invokes the Best Book Price Web service and displays a specified book's price.

```
1    // Fig. 16.18: MainScreen.java
2    // MainScreen enables the user to select which Web service the
3    // MIDP device should invoke.
4    package jws1casestudy.clients.j2me;
5
6    // import J2ME packages
7    import javax.microedition.lcdui.*;
8
9    class MainScreen extends List {
10
11       // create list of available Web services
12       MainScreen( final Display display )
13       {
14          super( "Select Web service", List.IMPLICIT );
15
16          // available Web services
17          append( "Get book information", null );
18          append( "Get best price", null );
19
20          // create soft button commands
21          Command selectCommand =
22             new Command( "Select", Command.OK, 0 );
23          addCommand( selectCommand );
24
```

Fig. 16.18 MainScreen provides a list of available Web services that Price Finder exposes. Reproduced with permission by Sun Microsystems, Inc.© Copyright 2002. Sun Microsystems, Inc. All Rights Reserved. (Part 1 of 2.)

```
25          // allow soft button access
26          setCommandListener(
27             new CommandListener() {
28
29                // invoked when user presses soft button
30                public void commandAction(
31                   Command command, Displayable displayable )
32                {
33                   // determine action, based on selected List item
34                   switch( getSelectedIndex() ) {
35
36                      // get book info
37                      case 0:
38                         display.setCurrent(
39                            new BookInformationScreen( display ) );
40                         break;
41
42                      // get best price
43                      case 1:
44                         display.setCurrent(
45                            new BookPriceScreen( display ) );
46                         break;
47                   }
48
49                } // end method commandAction
50             }
51          );
52
53       } // end MainScreen constructor
54
55    } // end class MainScreen
```

Fig. 16.18 MainScreen provides a list of available Web services that Price Finder exposes. Reproduced with permission by Sun Microsystems, Inc.© Copyright 2002. Sun Microsystems, Inc. All Rights Reserved. (Part 2 of 2.)

Class **BookInformationScreen** (Fig. 16.19) is a **Form** subclass that enables the MIDlet to gather the details of a book, using an ISBN that the user specifies. Lines 13–87 define the class constructor, which builds the form that enables the user to select the ISBN. Lines 21–28 create a **ChoiceGroup** that contains possible ISBN values. Once again, we hard-code these values for simplicity; a more robust application might invoke a Web service that retrieves a list of ISBNs for available book titles (e.g., the Book Titles Web service we examined in earlier chapters). Lines 31–37 associate two soft buttons with **BookInformationScreen**. If the user presses **BACK**, line 81 displays the **MainScreen**. If the user presses **OK**, lines 51–60 use a **BookInformationService** object (Fig. 16.20) to invoke the Price Finder's Book Information Web service. **BookInformationService** method **getBookDetails** (lines 27–68) uses Enhydra's kSOAP to invoke this Web service. Lines 37–41 create a SOAP request that contains the ISBN of the book from which the user wants to obtain information, lines 44–45 invoke the Web service and lines 48–58 convert the SOAP response to a **BookDetails** object. If a problem occurred in the Web-service invocation, method **getBookDetails** returns **null**, and **BookInformationScreen** (Fig. 16.19) creates an **Alert** (lines 70–74) that displays the error. If the Web-service invocation was successful, **BookInformationScreen** creates an object of **private** class **ResultScreen** (lines 90–133) to display the results of the Book Information Web service.

```
1   // Fig. 16.19: BookInformationScreen.java
2   // BookInformationScreen is a MIDlet screen that accesses and
3   // displays the results of the BookDetails Web service.
4   package jws1casestudy.clients.j2me;
5
6   // import J2ME packages
7   import javax.microedition.midlet.*;
8   import javax.microedition.lcdui.*;
9
10  // import Deitel packages
11  import jws1casestudy.pricefinder.common.BookDetails;
12
13  class BookInformationScreen extends Form {
14
15      // Form that selects a book on which to obtain information
16      BookInformationScreen( final Display display )
17      {
18          super( "Select book to obtain info" );
19
20          // ChoiceGroup that enables user to choose book
21          final ChoiceGroup choices =
22              new ChoiceGroup( "", ChoiceGroup.EXCLUSIVE );
23          choices.append( "0130895725", null );
24          choices.append( "0130284181", null );
25          choices.append( "0130341517", null );
26          choices.append( "0130293636", null );
```

Fig. 16.19 **BookInformationScreen** enables the user to select a book's ISBN, then uses the ISBN to invoke the Book Information Web service. Reproduced with permission by Sun Microsystems, Inc.© Copyright 2002. Sun Microsystems, Inc. All Rights Reserved. (Part 1 of 4.)

```
27            choices.append( "0130895601", null );
28            append( choices );
29
30            // create soft button commands
31            Command invokeCommand =
32               new Command( "Select", Command.OK, 0 );
33            addCommand( invokeCommand );
34
35            Command backCommand =
36               new Command( "Back", Command.BACK, 1 );
37            addCommand( backCommand );
38
39            // allow soft button access
40            setCommandListener(
41               new CommandListener() {
42
43                  // invoked when user presses soft button
44                  public void commandAction(
45                     Command command, Displayable displayable )
46                  {
47                     // invoke service if user presses Select
48                     if ( command.getCommandType() == Command.OK ) {
49
50                        // create object to invoke Web service
51                        BookInformationService informationService =
52                           new BookInformationService();
53
54                        // obtain isbn of book, based on user selection
55                        int selection = choices.getSelectedIndex();
56                        String isbn = choices.getString( selection );
57
58                        // invoke Book Details Web service
59                        BookDetails bookDetails =
60                           informationService.getBookDetails( isbn );
61
62                        // display book details on success
63                        if ( bookDetails != null )
64                           display.setCurrent( new ResultScreen(
65                              bookDetails, display ) );
66
67                        // display error page on failure
68                        else
69                        {
70                           Alert errorPage = new Alert( "Error",
71                              "Cannot invoke Web Service", null,
72                              AlertType.ERROR );
73                           errorPage.setTimeout( 3000 );
74                           display.setCurrent( errorPage );
75                        }
76                     }
```

Fig. 16.19 **BookInformationScreen** enables the user to select a book's ISBN, then uses the ISBN to invoke the Book Information Web service. Reproduced with permission by Sun Microsystems, Inc.© Copyright 2002. Sun Microsystems, Inc. All Rights Reserved. (Part 2 of 4.)

```
77
78                      // display MainScreen if user presses Back
79                      else if ( command.getCommandType() ==
80                          Command.BACK )
81                          display.setCurrent( new MainScreen( display ) );
82
83                  } // end method commandAction
84              }
85          );
86
87      } // end BookInformationScreen constructor
88
89      // Form to display book details after Web-service invocation
90      private class ResultScreen extends Form {
91          private BookDetails bookDetails;
92
93          ResultScreen( BookDetails info, final Display display )
94          {
95              super( "Book Info" );
96              bookDetails = info;
97
98              // include book title on Form
99              append( new StringItem( "", "Title: " +
100                 bookDetails.getTitle() + '\n' ) );
101
102             // include book ISBN on Form
103             append( new StringItem( "", "ISBN: " +
104                 bookDetails.getIsbn() + '\n'  ) );
105
106             // include book authors on Form
107             append( new StringItem( "", "Author: " +
108                 bookDetails.getAuthors() + '\n'  ) );
109
110             // include book description on Form
111             append( new StringItem( "", "Description: " +
112                 bookDetails.getDescription() + '\n'  ) );
113
114             // create soft button command to view MainScreen
115             Command okCommand = new Command( "OK", Command.OK, 0 );
116             addCommand( okCommand );
117
118             // allow soft button access
119             setCommandListener(
120                 new CommandListener() {
121
122                     // view MainScreen when user presses OK
123                     public void commandAction(
124                         Command command, Displayable displayable )
125                     {
126                         display.setCurrent( new MainScreen( display ) );
```

Fig. 16.19 `BookInformationScreen` enables the user to select a book's ISBN, then uses the ISBN to invoke the Book Information Web service. Reproduced with permission by Sun Microsystems, Inc.© Copyright 2002. Sun Microsystems, Inc. All Rights Reserved. (Part 3 of 4.)

```
127                        }
128                    }
129                );
130
131        } // end ResultSet constructor
132
133    } // end class ResultScreen
134
135 } // end class BookInformationScreen
```

  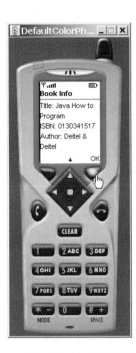

Fig. 16.19 `BookInformationScreen` enables the user to select a book's ISBN, then uses the ISBN to invoke the Book Information Web service. Reproduced with permission by Sun Microsystems, Inc.© Copyright 2002. Sun Microsystems, Inc. All Rights Reserved. (Part 4 of 4.)

```
1   // Fig. 16.20: BookInformationService.java.
2   // BookInformationService invokes the Book Details Web service.
3   package jws1casestudy.clients.j2me;
4
5   // import J2ME classes
6   import java.util.*;
7
8   // import Enhydra XML and SOAP packages
9   import org.ksoap.*;
10  import org.ksoap.transport.*;
```

Fig. 16.20 `BookInformationService` uses Enhydra's kSOAP to invoke the Book Details Web service. (Part 1 of 3.)

```
11   import org.kobjects.serialization.*;
12
13   // import Deitel packages
14   import jws1casestudy.pricefinder.common.BookDetails;
15
16   public class BookInformationService {
17
18      // URL of Book Details Web service
19      private final static String SERVICE_URL =
20         "http://localhost:8080/axis/services/BookInformation";
21
22      // namespace that Book Details Web service uses
23      private final static String NAMESPACE =
24         "http://common.pricefinder.jws1casestudy.BookDetails";
25
26      // Book Details Web service logic
27      public BookDetails getBookDetails( String isbn )
28      {
29         // invoke Web service and store result as BookDetails object
30         try {
31
32            // establish HTTP connection to Web-service URL
33            HttpTransport httpTransport =
34               new HttpTransport( SERVICE_URL, "" );
35
36            // create SOAP request to invoke Book Details service
37            SoapObject request =
38               new SoapObject( NAMESPACE, "getBookDetails" );
39
40            // include isbn as parameter in SOAP request
41            request.addProperty( "isbn", isbn );
42
43            // invoke Book Details Web service
44            SoapObject response = ( SoapObject )
45               httpTransport.call( request );
46
47            // create BookDetails from response values
48            BookDetails bookDetails = new BookDetails();
49            bookDetails.setTitle(
50               ( String ) response.getProperty( "title" ) );
51            bookDetails.setIsbn(
52               ( String ) response.getProperty( "isbn" ) );
53            bookDetails.setDescription(
54               ( String ) response.getProperty( "description" ) );
55            bookDetails.setAuthors(
56               ( String ) response.getProperty( "authors" ) );
57            bookDetails.setCoverImageURL(
58               ( String ) response.getProperty( "coverImageURL" ) );
59
60            return bookDetails;
61         }
62
```

Fig. 16.20 **BookInformationService** uses Enhydra's kSOAP to invoke the Book Details Web service. (Part 2 of 3.)

```
63              // handle exception in Web-service invocation
64              catch ( Exception exception ) {
65                  return null;
66              }
67
68          } // end method getBookDetails
69
70      } // end class BookInformationService
```

Fig. 16.20 `BookInformationService` uses Enhydra's kSOAP to invoke the Book Details Web service. (Part 3 of 3.)

Recall that **MainScreen** also enables the user to invoke the Best Book Price Web service, which requests the Price Finder to locate the bookstore that offers the lowest book price. If the user selects this service, lines 44–45 of class **MainScreen** (Fig. 16.18) create and display an object of class **BookPriceScreen**. Class **BookPriceScreen** (Fig. 16.21) is a **Form** subclass that enables the MIDlet to obtain a **PriceQuote** of a book, given a user-specified ISBN. Lines 13–85 define the class constructor, which builds the user interface that enables the user to select the ISBN. Lines 18–25 create a **Choice-Group** that contains possible ISBN values. Lines 28–34 associate two soft buttons with **BookPriceScreen**. If the user presses **BACK**, line 78 displays the **MainScreen**. If the user presses **OK**, lines 47–56 use a **BookPriceService** object (Fig. 16.22) to invoke the Best Book Price Web service.

BookPriceService (Fig. 16.22) method **getBestPrice** (lines 24–85) uses Enhydra's kSOAP to invoke the Price Finder's Best Book Price Web service. Lines 34–38 create a SOAP request that contains the ISBN of the book for which the user wants to obtain the best possible price. Lines 41–42 invoke the Web service, and lines 45–62 convert the SOAP response to a **PriceQuote** object. Recall that the value stored in the SOAP response's **price** element maps to a floating-point value. However, Java 2 Micro Edition does not support floating-point numbers or operations. For this reason, kSOAP provides class **SoapPrimitive**, which lines 45–46 use to obtain and represent the floating-point value from the **price** element. In addition, our wireless client requires its own "version" of **PriceQuote**—one that does not represent the price as a double. We modify **PriceQuote** (Fig. 16.23) to represent price as a **String**. Note that only the J2ME client uses this class. Also note that **BookPriceService** creates the **Price-Quote** (lines 60–62) by passing the **String** representation of the price **SoapPrimitive** (via method **toString**) to the **PriceQuote** constructor. If a problem occurs anywhere in the Web-service invocation, method **getBestPrice** returns **null**, and **BookPriceScreen** (Fig. 16.21) creates an **Alert** (lines 66–70) that displays the error. If the Web-service invocation was successful, **BookPriceScreen** creates a object of **private** class **ResultScreen** (lines 88–148) to display the results of the Price Finder's Best Book Price Web service. Lines 110–117 enable soft button support for **ResultScreen**. If the user presses **Cancel**, line 139 displays **MainScreen**. If the user presses **Order**, lines 131–132 display an object of class **BookPurchase-Screen**, which enables the user to complete the customer information needed to purchase a book.

Class **BookPurchaseScreen** (Fig. 16.24) is a **Form** subclass that enables the user to enter customer information, then uses that information (along with the **PriceQuote** returned by the Price Finder's Best Book Price Web service) to order a book via the Price Finder's Book Purchase Web service. Lines 18–129 define the class constructor, which builds the form that enables the user to specify the customer information. Lines 24–60 create a series of **TextField**s for the user to input customer information. Class **Text-Field** belongs to package **javax.microedition.lcdui**. The first argument in the **TextField** constructor specifies the **TextField**'s label; the second argument specifies the **TextField**'s initial contents; the third argument specifies the maximum number of characters that the user may input; the fourth argument is a constant that specifies the expected input format.[2] Lines 74–79 associate two soft buttons with **BookPurchase-Screen**. If the user presses **Cancel**, line 123 displays the **MainScreen** without invoking the Price Finder's Book Purchase Web service. If the user presses **OK**, lines 95–109 create a **Customer** object from the **TextField**s' values, then lines 112–113 use a **BookPurchaseService** object (Fig. 16.25) to invoke the Web service.

```
1   // Fig. 16.21: BookPriceScreen.java
2   // BookPriceScreen is a MIDlet screen that invokes the Best Book
3   // Price Web service and displays its results.
4   package jws1casestudy.clients.j2me;
5
6   // import J2ME packages
7   import javax.microedition.midlet.*;
8   import javax.microedition.lcdui.*;
9
10  class BookPriceScreen extends Form {
11
12      // create Form for specifying ISBN of book to obtain price
13      BookPriceScreen( final Display display )
14      {
15          super( "Select book to obtain price" );
16
17          // ChoiceGroup that enables user to specify book ISBN
18          final ChoiceGroup choices =
19              new ChoiceGroup( "", ChoiceGroup.EXCLUSIVE );
20          choices.append( "0130895725", null );
21          choices.append( "0130284181", null );
22          choices.append( "0130341517", null );
23          choices.append( "0130293636", null );
24          choices.append( "0130895601", null );
25          append( choices );
26
```

Fig. 16.21 **BookPriceScreen** enables the user to select a book's ISBN, then uses the ISBN to invoke the Best Book Price Web service. Reproduced with permission by Sun Microsystems, Inc.© Copyright 2002. Sun Microsystems, Inc. All Rights Reserved. (Part 1 of 4.)

2. In this case study, we provide default values for each **TextField**; however, we recommend replacing, at runtime, the value in the e-mail-address **TextField** with a personal e-mail address—this way, the Book Purchase Web service can send you a "confirmation" e-mail regarding the status of the order.

```
27              // create soft button commands
28              Command invokeCommand =
29                 new Command( "Select", Command.OK, 0 );
30              addCommand( invokeCommand );
31
32              Command backCommand =
33                 new Command( "Back", Command.BACK, 1 );
34              addCommand( backCommand );
35
36              // allow soft button access
37              setCommandListener(
38                 new CommandListener() {
39
40                    // invoked when user presses soft button
41                    public void commandAction(
42                       Command command, Displayable displayable )
43                    {
44                       // invoke service if user presses Select
45                       if ( command.getCommandType() == Command.OK ) {
46
47                          BookPriceService priceService =
48                             new BookPriceService();
49
50                          // invoke Web service through interface
51                          int selection = choices.getSelectedIndex();
52                          String isbn = choices.getString( selection );
53
54                          // invoke Best Book Price Web service
55                          PriceQuote quote =
56                             priceService.getBestPrice( isbn );
57
58                          // display PriceQuote results on success
59                          if ( quote != null )
60                             display.setCurrent( new ResultScreen(
61                                quote, display ) );
62
63                          // display error page on failure
64                          else
65                          {
66                             Alert errorPage = new Alert( "Error",
67                                "Cannot invoke Web Service", null,
68                                AlertType.ERROR );
69                             errorPage.setTimeout( 3000 );
70                             display.setCurrent( errorPage );
71                          }
72                       }
73
74                       // display mainScreen if user presses Back
75                       else if ( command.getCommandType() ==
76                          Command.BACK )
```

Fig. 16.21 BookPriceScreen enables the user to select a book's ISBN, then uses the ISBN to invoke the Best Book Price Web service. Reproduced with permission by Sun Microsystems, Inc.© Copyright 2002. Sun Microsystems, Inc. All Rights Reserved. (Part 2 of 4.)

```
77
78                            display.setCurrent( new MainScreen( display ) );
79
80                } // end method commandAction
81
82            } // end anonymous inner class
83        );
84
85    } // end BookPriceScreen constructor
86
87    // create Form to display book information
88    private class ResultScreen extends Form {
89        private PriceQuote priceQuote;
90
91        ResultScreen( PriceQuote quote, final Display display )
92        {
93            super( "Best price" );
94            priceQuote = quote;
95
96            // include book title on Form
97            append( new StringItem( "", "Price: " +
98                priceQuote.getPrice() + '\n' ) );
99
100           // include book ISBN on Form
101           append( new StringItem( "", "ISBN: " +
102               priceQuote.getIsbn() + '\n'  ) );
103
104           // include book authors on Form
105           append( new StringItem( "",
106               "Store Description: " +
107               priceQuote.getStoreDescription() ) );
108
109           // create soft button commands
110           Command okCommand =
111               new Command( "Order", Command.OK, 0 );
112           addCommand( okCommand );
113
114           // create soft button commands
115           Command cancelCommand =
116               new Command( "Cancel", Command.CANCEL, 1 );
117           addCommand( cancelCommand );
118
119           // allow soft button access for this Screen
120           setCommandListener(
121               new CommandListener() {
122
123                   // invoked when user presses soft button
124                   public void commandAction(
125                       Command command, Displayable displayable )
126                   {
```

Fig. 16.21 **BookPriceScreen** enables the user to select a book's ISBN, then uses the ISBN to invoke the Best Book Price Web service. Reproduced with permission by Sun Microsystems, Inc.© Copyright 2002. Sun Microsystems, Inc. All Rights Reserved. (Part 3 of 4.)

```
127                        Screen displayScreen = null;
128
129                        // display order screen if user presses Order
130                        if ( command.getCommandType() == Command.OK ) {
131                            displayScreen = new BookPurchaseScreen(
132                                priceQuote, display );
133                        }
134
135                        // display mainScreen if user presses Cancel
136                        else if ( command.getCommandType() ==
137                            Command.CANCEL )
138
139                            displayScreen = new MainScreen( display );
140
141                            display.setCurrent( displayScreen );
142                    }
143                }
144            );
145
146        } // end ResultScreen constructor
147
148    } // end class ResultScreen
149
150 } // end class BookPriceScreen
```

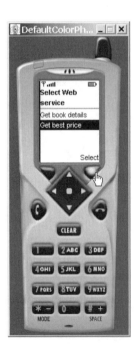
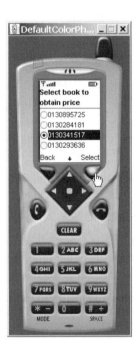
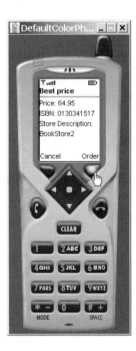

Fig. 16.21 BookPriceScreen enables the user to select a book's ISBN, then uses the ISBN to invoke the Best Book Price Web service. Reproduced with permission by Sun Microsystems, Inc.© Copyright 2002. Sun Microsystems, Inc. All Rights Reserved. (Part 4 of 4.)

```
1    // Fig. 16.22: BookPriceService.java.
2    // Class BookPriceService invokes the Best Book Price Web service.
3    package jws1casestudy.clients.j2me;
4
5    // import J2ME classes
6    import java.util.*;
7
8    // import Enhydra XML and SOAP packages
9    import org.ksoap.*;
10   import org.ksoap.transport.*;
11   import org.kobjects.serialization.*;
12
13   public class BookPriceService {
14
15      // URL of Best Book Price Web service
16      private final static String SERVICE_URL =
17         "http://localhost:8080/axis/services/BestBookPrice";
18
19      // namespace that Best Book Price Web service uses
20      private final static String NAMESPACE =
21         "http://common.pricefinder.jws1casestudy.PriceQuote";
22
23      // invoke Best Book Price Web service
24      public PriceQuote getBestPrice( String isbn )
25      {
26         // invoke Web service and convert result to PriceQuote
27         try {
28
29            // establish HTTP connection to Web-service URL
30            HttpTransport httpTransport =
31               new HttpTransport( SERVICE_URL, "" );
32
33            // create SOAP request to invoke Best Book Price service
34            SoapObject request =
35               new SoapObject( NAMESPACE, "getBestPrice" );
36
37            // include ISBN as parameter in SOAP request
38            request.addProperty( "isbn", isbn );
39
40            // invoke Best Book Price Web service
41            SoapObject response = ( SoapObject )
42               httpTransport.call( request );
43
44            // obtain price from response
45            SoapPrimitive price =
46               ( SoapPrimitive ) response.getProperty( "price" );
47
48            // obtain ISBN from response
49            String ISBN = ( String ) response.getProperty( "isbn" );
50
```

Fig. 16.22 BookPriceService uses Enhydra's kSOAP to invoke the Best Book
Price Web service. (Part 1 of 2.)

```
51              // obtain storeID from response
52              Integer storeID =
53                 ( Integer ) response.getProperty( "storeID" );
54
55              // obtain storeDescription from response
56              String storeDescription =
57                 ( String ) response.getProperty( "storeDescription" );
58
59              // create PriceQuote from response values
60              PriceQuote priceQuote = new PriceQuote(
61                 price.toString(), ISBN, storeID.intValue(),
62                 storeDescription );
63
64              return priceQuote;
65           }
66
67           // handle exception in Web-service invocation
68           catch ( SoapFault fault ) {
69              fault.printStackTrace();
70              return null;
71           }
72
73           // handle exception in sending or receiving SOAP message
74           catch ( java.io.IOException ioException ) {
75              ioException.printStackTrace();
76              return null;
77           }
78
79           // handle exception in PriceQuote cast operation
80           catch ( ClassCastException exception ) {
81              exception.printStackTrace();
82              return null;
83           }
84
85        } // end method getBestPrice
86
87    } // end class BookPriceService
```

Fig. 16.22 BookPriceService uses Enhydra's kSOAP to invoke the Best Book Price Web service. (Part 2 of 2.)

```
1     // Fig. 16.23: PriceQuote.java
2     // J2ME-version of PriceQuote maintains price information for a
3     // book store.
4     package jws1casestudy.clients.j2me;
5
6     public class PriceQuote {
7
8        private String price;              // book price
9        private String isbn;               // book ISBN
10       private int storeID;               // store ID
```

Fig. 16.23 PriceQuote class that a MIDlet can use to circumvent representing a price as a floating-point. (Part 1 of 2.)

```
11      private String storeDescription; // store description
12
13      // public default constructor
14      public PriceQuote() {}
15
16      // PriceQuote constructor
17      public PriceQuote( String bookPrice, String bookIsbn, int ID,
18         String description )
19      {
20         price = bookPrice;
21         isbn = bookIsbn;
22         storeID = ID;
23         storeDescription = description;
24      }
25
26      // obtain book price value
27      public String getPrice()
28      {
29         return price;
30      }
31
32      // obtain book ISBN value
33      public String getIsbn()
34      {
35         return isbn;
36      }
37
38      // obtain store ID value
39      public int getStoreID()
40      {
41         return storeID;
42      }
43
44      // obtain store description value
45      public String getStoreDescription()
46      {
47         return storeDescription;
48      }
49
50   } // end class PriceQuote
```

Fig. 16.23 `PriceQuote` class that a MIDlet can use to circumvent representing a price as a floating-point. (Part 2 of 2.)

```
1    // Fig. 16.24: BookPurchaseScreen.java
2    // BookPurchaseScreen is a MIDlet screen that invokes the Book
3    // Purchase Web service and displays its results.
4    package jws1casestudy.clients.j2me;
```

Fig. 16.24 `BookPurchaseScreen` enables the user to enter customer information, then uses the information and an existing `PriceQuote` to invoke the Price Finder's Book Purchase Web service. Reproduced with permission by Sun Microsystems, Inc.© Copyright 2002. Sun Microsystems, Inc. All Rights Reserved. (Part 1 of 5.)

```
5
6     // import J2ME packages
7     import javax.microedition.midlet.*;
8     import javax.microedition.lcdui.*;
9
10    // import Deitel packages
11    import jws1casestudy.pricefinder.common.Customer;
12
13    class BookPurchaseScreen extends Form {
14
15       PriceQuote priceQuote;
16
17       // create Form for specifying customer information
18       BookPurchaseScreen( PriceQuote quote, final Display display )
19       {
20          super( "Customer info" );
21          priceQuote = quote;
22
23          // create TextField to enter first name
24          final TextField firstNameField = new TextField(
25             "First name:", "Jon", 15, TextField.ANY );
26
27          // create TextField to enter last name
28          final TextField lastNameField = new TextField(
29             "Last name:", "Smith", 15, TextField.ANY );
30
31          // create TextField to enter email address
32          final TextField emailField = new TextField(
33             "Email Address:", "yourName@yourAddress.com", 32,
34             TextField.EMAILADDR );
35
36          // create TextField to enter street address
37          final TextField streetField = new TextField(
38             "Street Address:", "12 Clock Tower Place", 40,
39             TextField.ANY );
40
41          // create TextField to enter city
42          final TextField cityField = new TextField(
43             "City:", "Maynard", 15, TextField.ANY );
44
45          // create TextField to enter state
46          final TextField stateField = new TextField(
47             "State:", "MA", 10, TextField.ANY );
48
49          // create TextField to enter zip code
50          final TextField zipCodeField = new TextField(
51             "Zip code:", "01754", 15, TextField.ANY );
52
```

Fig. 16.24 **BookPurchaseScreen** enables the user to enter customer information, then uses the information and an existing **PriceQuote** to invoke the Price Finder's Book Purchase Web service. Reproduced with permission by Sun Microsystems, Inc.© Copyright 2002. Sun Microsystems, Inc. All Rights Reserved. (Part 2 of 5.)

```
53              // create TextField to enter country
54              final TextField countryField = new TextField(
55                  "Country:", "USA", 15, TextField.ANY );
56
57              // create TextField to enter credit-card number
58              final TextField creditCardField = new TextField(
59                  "Credit card number:", "XXXXXXXXXXXX1234", 24,
60                  TextField.ANY );
61
62              // append TextFields to form
63              append( firstNameField );
64              append( lastNameField );
65              append( emailField );
66              append( streetField );
67              append( cityField );
68              append( stateField );
69              append( zipCodeField );
70              append( countryField );
71              append( creditCardField );
72
73              // create soft button commands
74              Command okCommand = new Command( "OK", Command.OK, 0 );
75              addCommand( okCommand );
76
77              Command cancelCommand =
78                  new Command( "Cancel", Command.CANCEL, 0 );
79              addCommand( cancelCommand );
80
81              // allow soft button access
82              setCommandListener(
83                  new CommandListener() {
84
85                      // invoked when user presses soft button
86                      public void commandAction(
87                          Command command, Displayable displayable )
88                      {
89                          // invoke Book Purchase service if user presses OK
90                          if ( command.getCommandType() == Command.OK ) {
91                              BookPurchaseService purchaseService =
92                                  new BookPurchaseService();
93
94                              // create Customer from TextField info
95                              Customer customer = new Customer();
96                              customer.setFirstName(
97                                  firstNameField.getString() );
98                              customer.setLastName(
99                                  lastNameField.getString() );
100                             customer.setEmailAddress(
101                                 emailField.getString() );
```

Fig. 16.24 BookPurchaseScreen enables the user to enter customer information, then uses the information and an existing **PriceQuote** to invoke the Price Finder's Book Purchase Web service. Reproduced with permission by Sun Microsystems, Inc.© Copyright 2002. Sun Microsystems, Inc. All Rights Reserved. (Part 3 of 5.)

```
102                    customer.setStreetAddress(
103                        streetField.getString() );
104                    customer.setCity( cityField.getString() );
105                    customer.setState( stateField.getString() );
106                    customer.setZipCode( zipCodeField.getString() );
107                    customer.setCountry( countryField.getString() );
108                    customer.setCreditCardNumber(
109                        creditCardField.getString() );
110
111                    // invoke Book Purchase Web service
112                    purchaseService.placeOrder( priceQuote,
113                        customer );
114
115                    // display results
116                    display.setCurrent( new ResultScreen(
117                        display ) );
118                 }
119
120                 // display main screen if user presses Cancel
121                 else if ( command.getCommandType() ==
122                    Command.CANCEL ) {
123                    display.setCurrent( new MainScreen( display ) );
124                 }
125              }
126           }
127        );
128
129     } // end BookPurchaseScreen constructor
130
131     // create Form to display book information
132     private class ResultScreen extends Form {
133
134        ResultScreen( final Display display )
135        {
136           super( "" );
137           append( new StringItem( "", "** Book Ordered **\n" ) );
138           append( new StringItem( "",
139              "Confirmation will be sent via email" ) );
140
141           // create soft button commands
142           Command okCommand = new Command( "OK", Command.OK, 0 );
143           addCommand( okCommand );
144
145           // allow soft button access for this Screen
146           setCommandListener(
147              new CommandListener() {
148
```

Fig. 16.24 BookPurchaseScreen enables the user to enter customer information, then uses the information and an existing PriceQuote to invoke the Price Finder's Book Purchase Web service. Reproduced with permission by Sun Microsystems, Inc.© Copyright 2002. Sun Microsystems, Inc. All Rights Reserved. (Part 4 of 5.)

```
149                    // invoked when user presses soft button
150                    public void commandAction(
151                        Command command, Displayable displayable )
152                    {
153                        // display main screen when user presses button
154                        display.setCurrent( new MainScreen( display ) );
155                    }
156                }
157            );
158
159        } // end ResultScreen constructor
160
161    } // end class ResultScreen
162
163 } // end class BookPurchaseScreen
```

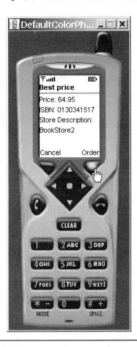
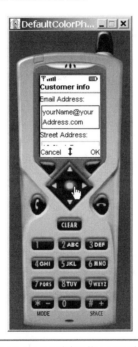

Fig. 16.24 **BookPurchaseScreen** enables the user to enter customer information, then uses the information and an existing **PriceQuote** to invoke the Price Finder's Book Purchase Web service. Reproduced with permission by Sun Microsystems, Inc.© Copyright 2002. Sun Microsystems, Inc. All Rights Reserved. (Part 5 of 5.)

BookPurchaseService (Fig. 16.25) method **placeOrder** (lines 27–96) uses Enhydra's kSOAP to invoke the Book Purchase Web service. Lines 37–38 create a SOAP request to contain the **PriceQuote** and **Customer** data. Lines 42–44 create a **SoapPrimitive** object to represent the price as a **double** in the SOAP request. Lines 47–48 create **SoapObject**s **quoteElement** and **customerElement**, which represent the elements to contain the **PriceQuote** and **Customer** data, respectively. Lines 51–56 include the **PriceQuote** data in **quoteElement**, and lines 59–76 include the

Customer data in **customerElement**. Lines 79–80 include **quoteElement** and **customerElement** as elements to the SOAP request's **body** element. Line 83 then invokes the Price Finder's Book Purchase Web service by sending the SOAP request. If the user specified a valid e-mail, the user will receive an e-mail notification that indicates the order status. When method **placeOrder** returns, lines 116–117 of **BookPurchase-Screen** (Fig. 16.24) display an object of **private** inner class **ResultScreen** (lines 132–161), which informs the user that the MIDlet has placed the order and that the user should expect a confirmation via e-mail.

   In this chapter we presented the consumer applications that access the Price Finder Web services. The final step in our case study is to deploy the Price Finder, bookstore and Deitel & Associates, Inc. Web services in their Web-service environments. We provide detailed instructions for this deployment process in the next chapter.

```java
1   // Fig. 16.25: BookPurchaseService.java.
2   // BookPurchaseService invokes the Book Purchase Web service.
3   package jws1casestudy.clients.j2me;
4
5   // import J2ME classes
6   import java.util.*;
7
8   // import Enhydra XML and SOAP packages
9   import org.ksoap.*;
10  import org.ksoap.transport.*;
11  import org.kobjects.serialization.*;
12
13  // import Deitel packages
14  import jws1casestudy.pricefinder.common.Customer;
15
16  public class BookPurchaseService {
17
18     // URL of Book Purchase Web service
19     private final static String SERVICE_URL =
20        "http://localhost:8080/axis/services/BookPurchase";
21
22     // namespace that Book Purchase Web service uses
23     private final static String NAMESPACE =
24        "http://schemas.xmlsoap.org/soap/envelope/";
25
26     // invoke Book Purchase Web service
27     public void placeOrder( PriceQuote quote, Customer customer )
28     {
29        // invoke Web service and convert result to String array
30        try {
31
32           // establish HTTP connection to Web-service URL
33           HttpTransport httpTransport =
34              new HttpTransport( SERVICE_URL, "" );
35
```

Fig. 16.25 BookPurchaseService uses Enhydra's kSOAP to invoke the Book Purchase Web service. (Part 1 of 3.)

```
36          // create SOAP request to invoke Book Purchase service
37          SoapObject request =
38             new SoapObject( NAMESPACE, "orderBook" );
39
40          // create SoapPrimitive to represent price, because
41          // CLDC does not support floating-point operations
42          SoapPrimitive price = new SoapPrimitive(
43             "http://www.w3.org/2001/XMLSchema", "double",
44             quote.getPrice() );
45
46          // create elements quote and customer
47          SoapObject quoteElement = new SoapObject( "", "" );
48          SoapObject customerElement = new SoapObject( "", "" );
49
50          // include PriceQuote as parameter in SOAP request
51          quoteElement.addProperty( "price", price );
52          quoteElement.addProperty( "isbn", quote.getIsbn() );
53          quoteElement.addProperty( "storeID",
54             new Integer( quote.getStoreID() ) );
55          quoteElement.addProperty( "storeDescription",
56             quote.getStoreDescription() );
57
58          // include Customer as parameter in SOAP request
59          customerElement.addProperty( "firstName",
60             customer.getFirstName() );
61          customerElement.addProperty( "lastName",
62             customer.getLastName() );
63          customerElement.addProperty( "emailAddress",
64             customer.getEmailAddress() );
65          customerElement.addProperty( "streetAddress",
66             customer.getStreetAddress() );
67          customerElement.addProperty( "city",
68             customer.getCity() );
69          customerElement.addProperty( "state",
70             customer.getState() );
71          customerElement.addProperty( "zipCode",
72             customer.getZipCode() );
73          customerElement.addProperty( "country",
74             customer.getCountry() );
75          customerElement.addProperty( "creditCardNumber",
76             customer.getCreditCardNumber() );
77
78          // add elements quote and customer to root element
79          request.addProperty( "quote", quoteElement );
80          request.addProperty( "customer", customerElement );
81
82          // invoke Book Purchase Web service
83          httpTransport.call( request );
84       }
85
```

Fig. 16.25 BookPurchaseService uses Enhydra's kSOAP to invoke the Book
Purchase Web service. (Part 2 of 3.)

```
86              // handle exception in Web-service invocation
87              catch ( SoapFault fault ) {
88                 fault.printStackTrace();
89              }
90
91              // handle exception in sending or receiving SOAP message
92              catch ( java.io.IOException ioException ) {
93                 ioException.printStackTrace();
94              }
95
96         } // end method placeOrder
97
98      } // end class BookPurchaseService
```

Fig. 16.25 BookPurchaseService uses Enhydra's kSOAP to invoke the Book
      Purchase Web service. (Part 3 of 3.)

17

Case Study: Deployment

Objectives

- To learn the deployment process for the Price Finder application.
- To understand the necessary steps for integrating Web services across Web-services platforms.

We provide the music, and you provide the audience.
Leopold Stokowski

Time is the measure of business, as money is of wares.
Francis Bacon

Proper words in proper places, make the true definition of a style.
Jonathan Swift

The message from the moon which we have flashed to the far corners of this planet is that no problem need any longer be considered insoluble.
Norman Cousins

If two laws conflict with each other, the courts must decide on the operation of each.
John Marshall

17.1 Introduction

In Chapters 15 and 16, we presented the implementations of the Price Finder, bookstore, and Deitel & Associates, Inc. Web services, as well as the consumer applications that use those services. In this chapter, we present the deployment instructions and supporting files for each of the Web services. We use a variety of Web-services platforms and technologies to more closely emulate the range of technologies in use for real-world Web services.

17.2 Deploying the Bookstore Web Services

The following sections discuss the deployment of the Web services of the three fictitious bookstores. We deploy the first bookstore's Web services via the Java API for XML Messaging. We deploy the second bookstore's Web services on Systinet's WASP Web-services platform. We deploy the third bookstore's Web services on CapeClear's CapeConnect Web-services platform.

17.2.1 Generating Bookstore1's WSDL files

Chapter 9 discussed the process by which developers can generate WSDL files from class files, using the **xrpcc** tool. **BookPrice.xml** (Fig. 17.1) and **BookOrder.xml** (Fig. 17.2) are the configuration files that the **xrpcc** tool uses to generate the WSDL files for Web services Book Price and Book Order, respectively.

```
1   <?xml version="1.0" encoding="UTF-8"?>
2
3   <!--Fig. 17.1: BookPrice.xml
4      Configuration file tool xrpcc uses to generate stubs and WSDL
5      documents.
6   -->
7
8   <configuration
9      xmlns="http://java.sun.com/xml/ns/jax-rpc/ri/config">
10
```

Fig. 17.1 **BookPrice.xml** is the configuration file that **xrpcc** uses to generate stubs and a WSDL document for the Book Price Web service. (Part 1 of 2.)

```
11      <service name="BookPrice"
12         targetNamespace="http://www.deitel.com/BookPrice.wsdl"
13         typeNamespace="http://www.deitel.com/BookPrice/type">
14         packageName="jws1casestudy.bookstore1">
15
16         <interface name="jws1casestudy.bookstore1.BookPrice"
17                 servantName="jws1casestudy.bookstore1.BookPriceImpl"/>
18
19      </service>
20   </configuration>
```

Fig. 17.1 **BookPrice.xml** is the configuration file that **xrpcc** uses to generate stubs and a WSDL document for the Book Price Web service. (Part 2 of 2.)

```
1    <?xml version="1.0" encoding="UTF-8"?>
2
3    <!--Fig. 17.2: BookOrder.xml
4       Configuration file tool xrpcc uses to generate stubs and WSDL
5       documents.
6    -->
7
8    <configuration
9       xmlns="http://java.sun.com/xml/ns/jax-rpc/ri/config">
10
11      <service name="BookOrderService"
12         targetNamespace="http://www.deitel.com/BookOrder.wsdl"
13         typeNamespace="http://www.deitel.com/BookOrder/type">
14         packageName="jws1casestudy.bookstore1">
15
16         <interface name="jws1casestudy.bookstore1.BookOrder"
17                 servantName="jws1casestudy.bookstore1.BookOrderImpl"/>
18
19      </service>
20   </configuration>
```

Fig. 17.2 **BookOrder.xml** is the configuration file that **xrpcc** uses to generate stubs and a WSDL document for the Book Order Web service.

The **xrpcc** tool initializes the service's target endpoint address to **REPLACE_WITH_ACTUAL_URL**. To enable clients to access Web service Book Price, replace value **REPLACE_WITH_ACTUAL_URL** with **http://localhost:8080/bookstore1/getPrice**. To enable clients to access Web service Book Order, replace value **REPLACE_WITH_ACTUAL_URL** with **http://localhost:8080/bookstore1/placeOrder**.

17.2.2 Bookstore1 Deployment Instructions

In this section, we deploy the Web services for Bookstore 1, using the Java API for XML Messaging reference implementation, which is part of the Java Web Services Developer Pack (JWSDP). We provide detailed instructions for deploying JAXM Web services in Chapter 11. To deploy the Bookstore1 Web service, create the directory structure of Fig. 17.3 in the **%TOMCAT_HOME%\webapps** directory (Windows) or the **$TOMCAT_HOME/webapps** directory (UNIX).

Bookstore 1 Web application directory and file structure

```
bookstore1
   WSDL
      BookPriceService.wsdl
      BookOrderService.wsdl
   WEB-INF
      web.xml
      classes
         jws1casestudy
            bookstore1
               BookPrice.class
               BookPriceImpl.class
               BookOrder.class
               BookOrderImpl.class
               BookPriceServlet.class
               BookOrderServlet.class
               BookStore.properties
               Database.properties
               Mail.properties
            pricefinder
               common
                  BookDetails.class
                  Customer.class
                  PriceQuote.class
      lib
         cloudclient.jar
         RmiJdbc.jar
         mail.jar
         activation.jar
```

Fig. 17.3   Web application directory and file structure for Bookstore1.

Create directory **bookstore1** as a subdirectory of **webapps**. Subdirectories of **webapps** represent independent Web-application contexts. Directory **bookstore1** therefore represents the Web-application context in which clients access Bookstore 1's Web services, including their WSDL files.

Bookstore 1's **WEB-INF** subdirectory **classes** contains the class files that implement Bookstore 1's Web services. The **classes** subdirectory contains the root of the package structure for the Web-service implementation classes. Within subdirectory **classes**, create the complete package structure for Bookstore 1's Web-services class files. Place the class files and the property files within their respective directories.

Bookstore 1's Book Price and Book Order Web services establish connections to a local instance of the Cloudscape database, so they require access to the JAR files that contain the database drivers and support classes. The J2EE 1.3 SDK includes the class files that the Web services use to connect to the database. To obtain the installation file for Sun's J2EE, visit **java.sun.com/j2ee**.

Directory **%J2EE_HOME%\lib\cloudscape** contains the JAR files required for the Cloudscape database. Copy **RmiJdbc.jar** and **cloudclient.jar** to Bookstore 1's **WEB-INF\lib** directory.

BookOrderImpl uses the JavaMail API to send e-mail confirmations for book orders. The JWSDP contains an implementation of the JavaMail API. Directory **%JWSDP_HOME%\common\lib** contains the JavaMail API implementation **mail.jar**, which depends on **activation.jar**. Copy **mail.jar** and **activation.jar** to Bookstore 1's **WEB-INF\lib** directory.

Tomcat requires a deployment descriptor for the Web application's servlets. Figure 17.4 is the deployment descriptor for Bookstore 1's servlets.

Clients must have access to the WSDL files for the Web services. Section 17.2.1 discusses how to generate WSDL files **BookPrice.wsdl** and **BookOrder.wsdl** for Web services Book Price and Book Order, respectively. To enable clients to access these files, place the WSDL files in subdirectory WSDL of the Bookstore 1 context root. Recall that in our case study, the client for the bookstores' Web services is the Price Finder.

Figure 17.5 lists the URLs for accessing Bookstore 1's Web services and supporting WSDL documents.

```
1    <?xml version="1.0" encoding="ISO-8859-1"?>
2
3    <!-- Fig. 17.4: web.xml
4       Lists configuration settings for the Bookstore1 Web application
5       environment.
6    -->
7
8    <!DOCTYPE web-app
9       PUBLIC "-//Sun Microsystems, Inc.//DTD Web Application 2.2//EN"
10      "http://java.sun.com/j2ee/dtds/web-app_2_2.dtd">
11
12   <web-app>
13
14      <!-- servlet definitions -->
15      <servlet>
16         <servlet-name>BookPriceServlet</servlet-name>
17
18         <servlet-class>
19            jws1casestudy.bookstore1.BookPriceServlet
20         </servlet-class>
21      </servlet>
22
23      <servlet>
24         <servlet-name>BookOrderServlet</servlet-name>
25
26         <servlet-class>
27            jws1casestudy.bookstore1.BookOrderServlet
28         </servlet-class>
29      </servlet>
30
```

Fig. 17.4 Bookstore1 Web application configuration file **web.xml**. (Part 1 of 2.)

```
31      <!-- servlet mappings -->
32      <servlet-mapping>
33          <servlet-name>BookPriceServlet</servlet-name>
34          <url-pattern>/getPrice</url-pattern>
35      </servlet-mapping>
36
37      <servlet-mapping>
38          <servlet-name>BookOrderServlet</servlet-name>
39          <url-pattern>/placeOrder</url-pattern>
40      </servlet-mapping>
41
42  </web-app>
```

Fig. 17.4   Bookstore1 Web application configuration file **web.xml**. (Part 2 of 2.)

URL	Description
`http://localhost:8080/bookstore1/getPrice`	Book Price Web service target endpoint.
`http://localhost:8080/bookstore1/placeOrder`	Book Order Web service target endpoint.
`http://localhost:8080/bookstore1/WSDL/` `    BookPriceService.wsdl`	Book Price WSDL file.
`http://localhost:8080/bookstore1/WSDL/` `    BookOrderService.wsdl`	Book Order WSDL file.

Fig. 17.5   Bookstore1 URLs.

17.2.3 Bookstore2 Deployment Instructions

Bookstore2 provides Web services Book Price and Book Order, which we deploy on Systinet's WASP server, version 4.0. Chapter 6 discusses the deployment process for the WASP server.

Before deploying, create the JAR file **BookStore2.jar**, which contains the class files and property files for Bookstore 2's Book Price and Book Order Web services. To begin, start the WASP server. [*Note*: Five JAR files—**cloudscape.jar**, **RmiJdbc.jar**, **BookStore2.jar**, **activation.jar** and **mail.jar**—should be included in the classpath before starting the WASP server.] The deployment process involves creating a Web service package, then deploying the Web service package to the WASP server, using **DeployTool**.

The **WaspPackager** tool enables developers to package Web-service implementation classes and supporting files for deployment to the WASP server. To create a Web service package for Bookstore 2's Book Price Web service, execute the following command-line instruction:

```
WaspPackager -p BookPrice -o BookPriceWASP.jar -n BookPrice
    -u /BookPrice/ -c jws1casestudy.bookstore2.BookPriceImpl
    --sbs rpc -l %J2EE_HOME%\lib\cloudscape\cloudclient.jar;
    %J2EE_HOME%\lib\cloudscape\RmiJdbc.jar;BookStore2.jar
```

Option **-p** specifies the name of the package as **BookPrice**. Option **-o** specifies the output file name as **BookPriceWASP.jar**. Option **-n** specifies the name of the Web service as **BookPrice**. Option **-u** specifies the Web service's path on the server as **/BookPrice/**. Option **-c** specifies class **BookPriceImpl** as the Web service to deploy. Option **--sbs** sets the service binding style to **rpc** (Remote Procedure Call). Option **-l** specifies the database libraries **cloudclient.jar** and **RmiJdbc.jar**, in addition to **BookStore2.jar**.

To deploy the Book Price Web service, deploy **BookPriceWASP.jar** to the WASP server by executing the following command:

```
DeployTool --deploy -t http://localhost:6060
    -j BookPriceWASP.jar -C bookstore2
```

Option **-t** specifies the local system's URL as the deployment target. Option **-j** specifies **BookPriceWASP.jar** as the name of the Web services package. Option **-C** specifies **bookstore2** as the context to which Web service Book Price belongs.

The process for packaging and deploying the Book Order Web service is similar to the process for packaging and deploying the Book Price Web service. The following command packages Web service Book Order:

```
WaspPackager -p BookOrder -o BookOrderWASP.jar -n BookOrder
    -u /BookOrder/ -c jws1casestudy.bookstore2.BookOrderImpl
    --sbs rpc -l %J2EE_HOME%\lib\cloudscape\cloudclient.jar;
    %J2EE_HOME%\lib\cloudscape\RmiJdbc.jar;BookStore2.jar;
    %JWSDP_HOME%\common\lib\activation.jar;
    %JWSDP_HOME%\common\lib\mail.jar
```

Deploy the Book Order Web service to the WASP server with the following command:

```
DeployTool --deploy -t http://localhost:6060
    -j BookOrderWASP.jar -C bookstore2
```

Figure 17.6 lists the URLs for accessing Bookstore 2's Web services and supporting WSDL documents.

URL	Description
`http://localhost:6060/bookstore2/BookPrice/`	Book Price Web service target endpoint.
`http://localhost:6060/bookstore2/BookOrder/`	Book Order Web service target endpoint.

Fig. 17.6   Bookstore2 URLs. (Part 1 of 2.)

URL	Description
`http://localhost:6060/bookstore2/BookPrice/wsdl`	Book Price WSDL file.
`http://localhost:6060/bookstore2/BookOrder/wsdl`	Book Order WSDL file.

Fig. 17.6 Bookstore2 URLs. (Part 2 of 2.)

17.2.4 Bookstore3 Deployment Instructions

Bookstore 3 exposes Web services Book Price and Book Order, which we deploy on Cape-Clear's CapeConnect, version 3.5. Chapter 6 discusses the deployment process for Cape-Connect 3.5 in detail.

To begin, create the JAR file **BookStore3.jar**, which contains the class files and property files for Bookstore 3's Book Price and Book Order Web services. We also use the CapeStudio Developer Center to deploy the Web services contained in **BookStore3.jar**.

Next, open the CapeStudio Developer Center. Select **Project > New...** to create a project. Enter **BookPrice** as the name of the project, and click **OK**. Select **Design > Generate WSDL from Java/J2EE/CORBA....** Select **Java** in the **Component Type** radio-button group. Click **Add** to select **BookStore3.jar**. Add **RmiJdbc.jar** and **cloudclient.jar** to enable communication with the Cloudscape database. [*Note*: **BookStore3.jar** must be added first.]

In the Book Price tree node, select **BookStore3.jar**. In the left contents pane, select **jws1casestudy.bookstore3.BookPriceImpl** and click **Finish**. Close the verbose window.

Select **Deploy > Package...** to package the Web service files. In the **Package in a Web Service (WSAR) file** window, click **Create**. Select **Deploy > Deploy Service** to deploy the package.

Deploy Web service Book Order, using the same process. In addition, include **mail.jar** and **activation.jar** in the **Components** list of window **Generate WSDL from Java/J2EE/CORBA**.

CapeConnect applies its own security settings to Web services. File **server.policy** contains CapeConnect's security settings and is located in directory **%CAPECONNECT_HOME%\xmlengine\conf**. Classes **BookPriceImpl** and **BookOrderImpl** require file read privileges that are not granted by **server.policy**. To grant file read privileges to CapeConnect Web services, append the following text to the end of **server.policy**:

```
grant {
    permission java.io.FilePermission "<<ALL FILES>>", "read";
};
```

To restrict file access privileges, replace the **server.policy** modification with more restrictive settings.

Figure 17.7 lists the URLs for accessing Bookstore 3's Web services and supporting WSDL documents.

URL	Description
`http://localhost:8000/ccx/BookPrice`	Book Price Web service target endpoint.
`http://localhost:8000/ccx/BookOrder`	Book Order Web service target endpoint.
`http://localhost:8000/wsdl/BookPrice.wsdl`	Book Price WSDL file.
`http://localhost:8000/wsdl/BookOrder.wsdl`	Book Order WSDL file.

Fig. 17.7   Bookstore3 URLs.

17.3 Book Information Web Service Deployment Instructions

In this section, we deploy the Deitel & Associates, Inc., Book Information Web service to the GLUE Standard 3.0 Web-services platform. Chapter 6 discusses in detail the installation and deployment process using GLUE Standard 3.0. To begin, create application template **bookinformation** by executing the following command:

> **newapp bookinformation**

Directory **bookinformation** represents the Book Information Web-service application structure and contains a set of default files. Rename file **sample.xml** located in **bookinformation\WEB-INF\services** as **bookinformation.xml**. Add the Book Information Web service's class files and package structure to directory **bookinformation\WEB-INF\classes**. Deitel & Associates, Inc.'s Book Information Web service establishes a connection to a local Cloudscape database instance, so add files **cloudclient.jar** and **RmiJdbc.jar** to directory **bookinformation\WEB-INF\lib**. The resulting package structure for Web service Book Information is shown in Fig. 17.8.

Figure 17.9 is Web service Book Information's configuration file. Replace the default values in **bookinformation.xml** with those shown in Fig. 17.9.

The following command starts the GLUE server that will host application **bookinformation**:

> **runapp bookinformation**

Figure 17.10 lists the target endpoint and WSDL URLs for the Book Information Web service.

17.4 PriceFinder Deployment Instructions

In this section, we discuss the deployment of the Price Finder application Web services on the Apache Axis Web-services platform. Chapter 6 discusses in detail the process by which to deploy Web services using Axis.[1]

---

1. The beta 2 release of Apache's Axis was not compatible with JWSDP 1.0. For the purposes of this case study, we used the nightly build of Axis from June 25, 2002.

Unlike the examples provided in Chapter 6, Price Finder's Web services define Java-Bean custom types as parameter arguments and return types. Axis provides a set of pre-defined XML-to-Java mappings. These predefined mappings enable developers to focus on building a Web service without having to provide code that processes SOAP messages directly. Axis provides a JavaBean-mapping algorithm that enables Web services to specify custom JavaBean types as method parameters and return types. Developers specify the JavaBean types to which Axis applies the JavaBean mappings in the Web-services deployment descriptor. Figure 17.11 is the deployment descriptor for Price Finder's Best Book Price, Book Purchase and Book InformationWeb services.

Book Information Web service application directory and file structure

```
bookinformation
   WEB-INF
      config.xml
      web.xml
      classes
         jws1casestudy
            deitelbookinformation
               BookInformation.class
               BookInformationImpl.class
            pricefinder
               common
                  BookDetails.class
      lib
         cloudclient.jar
         RmiJdbc.jar
      maps
         standard.map
      services
         bookinformation.xml
         system
            admin.xml
            deployment.xml
```

Fig. 17.8 Web service Book Information application directory structure.

```
1   <!-- Fig. 17.9: bookinformation.xml
2      Web service configuration file specifies the deployment
3      settings for Web service Book Information.
4   -->
5   <service>
6
7      <!--name of service class-->
8      <constructor>
9         <class>
```

Fig. 17.9 Web service configuration file specifies deployment settings for the Web service Book Information. (Part 1 of 2.)

```
10                jws1casestudy.deitelbookinformation.BookInformationImpl
11          </class>
12      </constructor>
13
14      <!--name of interface(s) to publish
15          (default is all public methods)-->
16      <interface>
17          jws1casestudy.deitelbookinformation.BookInformation
18      </interface>
19
20      <!--message style, rpc (default) or document-->
21      <style>rpc</style>
22
23      <!--activation mode, application (default), session,
24          or request-->
25      <activation>application</activation>
26
27      <!--if yes (default), create and publish the service-->
28      <publish>yes</publish>
29
30      <!--description of service, used during WSDL generation-->
31      <description>Deitel Book Information Web service</description>
32
33      <!--interceptor for inbound SOAP requests-->
34      <inboundSoapRequestInterceptor/>
35
36      <!--interceptor for outbound SOAP responses-->
37      <outboundSoapResponseInterceptor/>
38
39      <!--target namespace (default is
40          http://www.themindelectric.com/wsdl/<name>/)-->
41      <targetNamespace/>
42
43      <!--namespace (default is http://tempuri.org/<class name>)-->
44      <namespace>http://deitel.com/BookInformation/</namespace>
45
46      <!--manually add named class and its closure to WSDL file-->
47      <xmlInclude/>
48
49      <!--soapAction (default is operation name)-->
50      <soapAction/>
51
52      <!--directory for FileDataHandlers to store attachments-->
53      <dataDirectory/>
54
55      <!--handler for inbound attachments of specified content type-->
56      <dataHandler>
57          <type>*/*</type>
58          <class>electric.util.mime.MemoryDataHandler</class>
59      </dataHandler>
60
61  </service>
```

Fig. 17.9　Web service configuration file specifies deployment settings for the Web service Book Information. (Part 2 of 2.)

URL	Description
`http://localhost:8004/bookinformation/services/` `bookinformation`	Book Information Web service target endpoint.
`http://localhost:8004/bookinformation/services/` `bookinformation.wsdl`	Book Information WSDL file.

Fig. 17.10 Web service Book Information URLs.

```
1   <!-- Fig. 17.11: PriceFinder.wsdd
2      Deployment Descriptor for Web services Best Book Price,
3      Book Purchase and Book Information that defines custom-type
4      mappings and namespaces and methods to expose.
5   -->
6   <deployment xmlns="http://xml.apache.org/axis/wsdd/"
7      xmlns:java="http://xml.apache.org/axis/wsdd/providers/java">
8
9      <!-- deployment settings for Web service Best Book Price -->
10     <service name="BestBookPrice" provider="java:RPC">
11
12        <parameter name="className"
13           value="jws1casestudy.pricefinder.BestBookPrice"/>
14
15        <parameter name="allowedMethods" value="*"/>
16
17        <beanMapping qname="deitelNS:PriceQuote"
18           xmlns:deitelNS="http://common.pricefinder.jws1casestudy"
19           languageSpecificType="java:jws1casestudy.pricefinder.com-
mon.PriceQuote"/>
20
21     </service>
22
23     <!-- deployment settings for Web service Book Purchase -->
24     <service name="BookPurchase" provider="java:RPC">
25
26        <parameter name="className"
27           value="jws1casestudy.pricefinder.BookPurchase"/>
28
29        <parameter name="allowedMethods" value="*"/>
30
31        <beanMapping qname="deitelNS:Customer"
32           xmlns:deitelNS="http://common.pricefinder.jws1casestudy"
33           languageSpecificType="java:jws1casestudy.pricefinder.com-
mon.Customer"/>
34
35        <beanMapping qname="deitelNS:PriceQuote"
36           xmlns:deitelNS="http://common.pricefinder.jws1casestudy"
37           languageSpecificType="java:jws1casestudy.pricefinder.com-
mon.PriceQuote"/>
```

Fig. 17.11 PriceFinder Web-Service deployment descriptor. (Part 1 of 2.)

```
38
39        </service>
40
41        <!-- deployment settings for Web service Book Information -->
42        <service name="BookInformation" provider="java:RPC">
43
44            <parameter name="className"
45                value="jws1casestudy.pricefinder.BookInformation"/>
46
47            <parameter name="allowedMethods" value="*"/>
48
49            <beanMapping qname="deitelNS:BookDetails"
50                xmlns:deitelNS="http://common.pricefinder.jws1casestudy"
51                languageSpecificType="java:jws1casestudy.pricefinder.com-
mon.BookDetails"/>
52
53        </service>
54
55    </deployment>
```

Fig. 17.11 PriceFinder Web-Service deployment descriptor. (Part 2 of 2.)

Lines 10–21 define the deployment settings for the Web service Best Book Price. Lines 12–13 specify the class that implements the Web service. Line 15 instructs the Axis deployment tool to expose all methods in class **BestBookPrice** as Web services. Lines 17–19 define the JavaBean-mapping configuration that the Axis environment uses to serialize and deserialize custom types that SOAP messages contain. Element **beanMapping** contains three attributes that set the mappings—**qname**, **xmlns** and **languageSpecificType**.

Attribute **qname** (line 17) specifies the namespace. Axis uses the **qname** value to identify any custom types to deserialize. Likewise, attribute **qname** identifies the SOAP-representation type after serialization. The **qname** value is in the form *namespace:type*. We use namespace **http://common.pricefinder.jws1casestudy** in this example.

Attribute **xmlns** (line 18) specifies the namespace identifier and its associated value. Attribute **xmlns** must be in the format **xmlns:***namespaceIdentifier***="***namespace value***"**. The namespace identifier is a name that maps to the namespace value. The namespace identifier must match the specified value for attribute **qname**.

Attribute **languageSpecificType** specifies the JavaBean for the deserialization and serialization processes, respectively. The attribute value must be a fully-qualified class name that is prefixed by the language type. Axis currently specifies **java** as the prefix for Java types.

Lines 24–39 and lines 42–53 define the deployment settings for the Book Purchase and Book Information Web services, respectively.

Copy the package structure and Web service class files to the Axis classes directory to deploy the Web services Best Book Price, Book Purchase and Book Information. Start Tomcat by executing **startup.bat** (Windows) or **startup.sh** (UNIX), and execute the following command line:

```
java -classpath
   %AXIS_HOME%\lib\axis.jar;%AXIS_HOME%\lib\jaxrpc.jar;
   %AXIS_HOME%\lib\commons-logging.jar;
   %JWSDP_HOME%\common\lib\jaxrpc-api.jar
   %JWSDP_HOME%\common\lib\jaxrpc-ri.jar;
   %JWSDP_HOME%\common\endorsed\dom.jar;
   %JWSDP_HOME%\common\endorsed\sax.jar;
   %JWSDP_HOME%\common\lib\jaxp-api.jar;
   %JWSDP_HOME%\common\endorsed\xercesImpl.jar
   %JWSDP_HOME%\common\lib\saaj-api.jar
   %JWSDP_HOME%\common\lib\saaj-ri.jar
   org.apache.axis.client.AdminClient PriceFinder.wsdd
```

Figure 17.12 lists the URLs for accessing the Price Finder application's Web services and supporting WSDL documents.

URL	Description
`http://localhost:8080/axis/services/` `BestBookPrice`	Best Book Price Web service target endpoint.
`http://localhost:8080/axis/services/` `BookPurchase`	Book Purchase Web service target endpoint.
`http://localhost:8080/axis/services/` `BookInformation`	Book Information Web service target endpoint.
`http://localhost:8080/axis/services/` `BestBookPrice?wsdl`	Best Book Price WSDL file.
`http://localhost:8080/axis/services/` `BookPurchase?wsdl`	Book Purchase WSDL file.
`http://localhost:8080/axis/services/` `BookInformation?wsdl`	Book Information WSDL file.

Fig. 17.12 PriceFinder URLs.

Servlets

Objectives

- To execute servlets with the Apache Tomcat server.
- To be able to respond to HTTP requests from an **HttpServlet**.
- To be able to redirect requests to static and dynamic Web resources.
- To be able to maintain session information with cookies and **HttpSession** objects.
- To be able to access a database from a servlet.

A fair request should be followed by the deed in silence.
Dante Alighieri

The longest part of the journey is said to be the passing of the gate.
Marcus Terentius Varro

If nominated, I will not accept; if elected, I will not serve.
General William T. Sherman

Me want cookie!
The Cookie Monster, *Sesame Street*

When to the sessions of sweet silent thought
I summon up remembrance of things past, …
William Shakespeare

Friends share all things.
Pythagoras

Outline

A.1 Introduction

There is much excitement over the Internet and the World Wide Web. The Internet ties the "information world" together. The World Wide Web makes the Internet easy to use and gives it the flair and sizzle of multimedia. Organizations see the Internet and the Web as crucial to their information systems strategies. Java provides a number of built-in networking capabilities that make it easy to develop Internet-based and Web-based applications. Not only can Java specify parallelism through multithreading, but it can enable programs to search the world for information and to collaborate with programs running on other computers internationally, nationally or just within an organization. Java can even enable applets and applications running on the same computer to communicate with one another, subject to security constraints.

Networking is a massive and complex topic. Computer science and computer engineering students typically take a full-semester, upper-level course in computer networking and continue with further study at the graduate level. Java provides a rich complement of networking capabilities and will likely be used as an implementation vehicle in computer networking courses.

Java's networking capabilities are grouped into several packages. The fundamental networking capabilities are defined by classes and interfaces of package *java.net*, through which Java offers *socket-based communications* that enable applications to view networking as streams of data—a program can read from a *socket* or write to a socket as simply as reading from a file or writing to a file. The classes and interfaces of package **java.net** also offer *packet-based communications* that enable individual *packets* of information to be transmitted—commonly used to transmit audio and video over the Internet. Our book *Java How to Program, Fourth Edition* shows how to create and manipulate sockets and how to communicate with packets of data.

Higher-level views of networking are provided by classes and interfaces in the **java.rmi** packages (five packages) for *Remote Method Invocation (RMI)* and **org.omg** packages (seven packages) for *Common Object Request Broker Architecture (CORBA)* that are part of the Java 2 API. The RMI packages allow Java objects running on separate Java Virtual Machines (normally on separate computers) to communicate via remote method calls. Such method calls appear to be to an object in the same program, but actually have built-in networking (based on the capabilities of package **java.net**) that communicates the method calls to another object on a separate computer. The CORBA packages provide similar functionality to the RMI packages. A key difference between RMI and CORBA is that RMI can only be used between Java objects, whereas CORBA can be used between any two applications that understand CORBA—including applications written in other programming languages. In Chapter 13 of our book *Advanced Java 2 Platform How to Program*, we present Java's RMI capabilities. Chapters 26–27 of *Advanced Java 2 Platform How to Program* discuss the basic CORBA concepts and present a case study that implements a distributed system in CORBA.

Our discussion of networking in these appendices focuses on both sides of a *client-server relationship*. The *client* requests that some action be performed and the *server* performs the action and responds to the client. This request-response model of communication is the foundation for the highest-level views of networking in Java—*servlets* and *JavaServer Pages (JSP)*. A servlet extends the functionality of a server. Packages **javax.servlet** and **javax.servlet.http** provide the classes and interfaces to define servlets. Packages **javax.servlet.jsp** and **javax.servlet.jsp.tagext** provide the classes and interfaces that extend the servlet capabilities for JavaServer Pages. Using special syntax, JSP allows Web-page implementors to create pages that use encapsulated Java functionality and even to write *scriptlets* of actual Java code directly in the page.

A common implementation of the request-response model is between World Wide Web browsers and World Wide Web servers. When a user selects a Web site to browse through their browser (the client application), a request is sent to the appropriate Web server (the server application). The server normally responds to the client by sending the appropriate XHTML Web page. Servlets are effective for developing Web-based solutions that help provide secure access to a Web site, interact with databases on behalf of a client, dynamically generate custom XHTML documents to be displayed by browsers and maintain unique session information for each client.

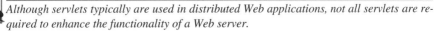

Software Engineering Observation A.1

Although servlets typically are used in distributed Web applications, not all servlets are required to enhance the functionality of a Web server.

This appendix discusses servlets, which enhance the functionality of World Wide Web servers—the most common form of servlet today. Appendix B discusses JSPs, which are translated into servlets. JSPs are a convenient and powerful way to implement the request/ response mechanism of the Web without getting into the lower-level details of servlets. Together, servlets and JSPs form the Web tier of the Java 2 Enterprise Edition (J2EE).

Many developers feel that servlets are the right solution for database-intensive applications that communicate with so-called *thin clients*—applications that require minimal client-side support. The server is responsible for database access. Clients connect to the server using standard protocols available on most client platforms. Thus, the presentation-logic code for generating dynamic content can be written once and reside on the server for access by clients, to allow programmers to create efficient thin clients.

In this appendix, our servlet examples demonstrate the Web's request/response mechanism (primarily with **get** and **post** requests), session-tracking capabilities, redirecting requests to other resources and interacting with databases through JDBC.

Sun Microsystems, through the *Java Community Process*, is responsible for the development of the servlet and JavaServer Pages specifications. The reference implementation of both these standards is under development by the *Apache Software Foundation* (**www.apache.org**) as part of the *Jakarta Project* (**jakarta.apache.org**). As stated on the Jakarta Project's home page, "The goal of the Jakarta Project is to provide commercial-quality server solutions based on the Java Platform that are developed in an open and cooperative fashion." There are many subprojects under the Jakarta project to help commercial server-side developers. The servlet and JSP part of the Jakarta Project is called *Tomcat*. This is the official reference implementation of the JSP and servlet standards. Tomcat is included as part of the Java Web Services Developer Pack, so we use it to demonstrate the servlets in this appendix. We discuss the set up and configuration of Tomcat in Section A.3.1 and Section A.3.2 after we introduce our first example.

In our directions for testing each of the examples in this appendix, we indicate that you should copy files into specific Tomcat directories. All the example files for this appendix downloadable from our Web site **www.deitel.com**.

[*Note*: At the end of Section A.11, we provide a list of Internet specifications (as discussed in the Servlet 2.2 Specification) for technologies related to servlet development. Each is listed with its RFC (Request for Comments) number. We provide the URL of a Web site that allows you to locate each specification for your review.]

A.2 Servlet Overview and Architecture

In this section, we overview Java servlet technology. We discuss at a high level the servlet-related classes, methods and exceptions. The next several sections present live-code examples in which we build multi-tier client–server systems using servlet and JDBC technology.

The Internet offers many protocols. The HTTP (*Hypertext Transfer Protocol*) that forms the basis of the World Wide Web uses *URIs* (*Uniform Resource Identifiers*— sometimes called *Universal Resource Locators* or *URLs*) to locate resources on the Internet. Common URIs represent files or directories and can represent complex tasks such as database lookups and Internet searches. For more information on URL formats, visit

    www.w3.org/Addressing

For more information on the HTTP protocol, visit

    www.w3.org/Protocols/HTTP

For information on a variety of World Wide Web topics, visit

www.w3.org

JavaServer Pages technology is an extension of servlet technology. Normally, JSPs are used primarily when most of the content sent to the client is static text and markup, and only a small portion of the content is generated dynamically with Java code. Normally, servlets are used when a small portion of the content sent to the client is static text or markup. In fact, some servlets do not produce content. Rather, they perform a task on behalf of the client, then invoke other servlets or JSPs to provide a response. Note that in most cases servlet and JSP technologies are interchangeable. The server that executes a servlet often is referred to as the *servlet container* or *servlet engine*.

Servlets and JavaServer Pages have become so popular that they are now supported directly or with third-party plug-ins by most major Web servers and application servers, including the Netscape iPlanet Application Server, Microsoft's Internet Information Server (IIS), the Apache HTTP Server, BEA's WebLogic application server, IBM's WebSphere application server, the World Wide Web Consortium's Jigsaw Web server, and many more.

The servlets in this appendix demonstrate communication between clients and servers via the HTTP protocol. A client sends an HTTP request to the server or servlet container. The server or servlet container receives the request and directs it to be processed by the appropriate servlet. The servlet does its processing, which may include interacting with a database or other server-side components such as other servlets, JSPs or Enterprise Java-Beans. The servlet returns its results to the client—normally in the form of an HTML, XHTML or XML document to display in a browser, but other data formats, such as images and binary data, can be returned.

A.2.1 Interface **Servlet** and the Servlet Life Cycle

Architecturally, all servlets must implement the **Servlet** interface. As with many key applet methods, the methods of interface **Servlet** are invoked automatically (by the server on which the servlet is installed, also known as the servlet container). This interface defines five methods described in Fig. A.1.

 Software Engineering Observation A.2

*All servlets must implement the **Servlet** interface of package **javax.servlet**.*

Method	Description

void init(ServletConfig config)

This method is automatically called once during a servlet's execution cycle to initialize the servlet. The **ServletConfig** argument is supplied by the servlet container that executes the servlet.

Fig. A.1   Methods of interface **Servlet** (package **javax.servlet**). (Part 1 of 2.)

Method	Description

ServletConfig getServletConfig()

This method returns a reference to an object that implements interface **ServletConfig**. This object provides access to the servlet's configuration information such as servlet initialization parameters and the servlet's **ServletContext**, which provides the servlet with access to its environment (i.e., the servlet container in which the servlet executes).

String getServletInfo()

This method is defined by a servlet programmer to return a **String** containing servlet information such as the servlet's author and version.

void service(ServletRequest request, ServletResponse response)

The servlet container calls this method to respond to a client request to the servlet.

void destroy()

This "cleanup" method is called when a servlet is terminated by its servlet container. Resources used by the servlet, such as an open file or an open database connection, should be deallocated here.

Fig. A.1   Methods of interface **Servlet** (package **javax.servlet**).
(Part 2 of 2.)

A servlet's life cycle begins when the servlet container loads the servlet into memory—normally, in response to the first request that the servlet receives. Before the servlet can handle that request, the servlet container invokes the servlet's *init* method. After **init** completes execution, the servlet can respond to its first request. All requests are handled by a servlet's *service* method, which receives the request, processes the request and sends a response to the client. During a servlet's life cycle, method **service** is called once per request. Each new request typically results in a new thread of execution (created by the servlet container) in which method **service** executes. When the servlet container terminates the servlet, the servlet's **destroy** method is called to release servlet resources.

Performance Tip A.1

Starting a new thread for each request is more efficient than starting an entirely new process, as is the case in some other server-side technologies such as CGI. [Note: Like servlets, Fast CGI eliminates the overhead of starting a new process for each request.]

The servlet packages define two **abstract** classes that implement the interface **Servlet**—class *GenericServlet* (from the package **javax.servlet**) and class *HttpServlet* (from the package **javax.servlet.http**). These classes provide default implementations of all the **Servlet** methods. Most servlets extend either **GenericServlet** or **HttpServlet** and override some or all of their methods.

The examples in this appendix all extend class **HttpServlet**, which defines enhanced processing capabilities for servlets that extend the functionality of a Web server. The key method in every servlet is **service**, which receives both a *Serv-*

letRequest object and a ***ServletResponse*** object. These objects provide access to input and output streams that allow the servlet to read data from the client and send data to the client. These streams can be either byte based or character based. If problems occur during the execution of a servlet, either **ServletException**s or **IOException**s are thrown to indicate the problem.

Software Engineering Observation A.3

Servlets can implement tagging interface ***javax.servlet.SingleThreadModel*** *to indicate that only one thread of execution may enter method* ***service*** *on a particular servlet instance at a time. When a servlet implements* ***SingleThreadModel***, *the servlet container can create multiple instances of the servlet to handle multiple requests to the servlet in parallel. In this case, you may need to provide synchronized access to shared resources used by method* ***service***.

A.2.2 `HttpServlet` Class

Web-based servlets typically extend class **HttpServlet**. Class **HttpServlet** overrides method **service** to distinguish between the typical requests received from a client Web browser. The two most common *HTTP request types* (also known as *request methods*) are **get** and **post**. A **get** request *gets* (or *retrieves*) information from a server. Common uses of **get** requests are to retrieve an HTML document or an image. A **post** request *posts* (or *sends*) data to a server. Common uses of **post** requests typically send information, such as authentication information or data from a *form* that obtains user input, to a server.

Class **HttpServlet** defines methods *doGet* and *doPost* to respond to **get** and **post** requests from a client, respectively. These methods are called by the **service** method, which is called when a request arrives at the server. Method **service** first determines the request type, then calls the appropriate method for handling such a request. Other less common request types are beyond the scope of this book. Methods of class **HttpServlet** that respond to the other request types are shown in Fig. A.2. They all receive parameters of type **HttpServletRequest** and **HttpServletResponse** and return **void**. The methods of Fig. A.2 are not frequently used. For more information on the HTTP protocol, visit

`www.w3.org/Protocols.`

Software Engineering Observation A.4

Do not override method service in an ***HttpServlet*** *subclass. Doing so prevents the servlet from distinguishing between request types.*

Methods **doGet** and **doPost** receive as arguments an **HttpServletRequest** object and an **HttpServletResponse** object that enable interaction between the client and the server. The methods of **HttpServletRequest** make it easy to access the data supplied as part of the request. The **HttpServletResponse** methods make it easy to return the servlet's results to the Web client. Interfaces **HttpServletRequest** and **HttpServletResponse** are discussed in the next two sections.

Method	Description
doDelete	Called in response to an HTTP *delete* request. Such a request is normally used to delete a file from a server. This may not be available on some servers, because of its inherent security risks (i.e., the client could delete a file that is critical to the execution of the server or an application).
doOptions	Called in response to an HTTP *options* request. This returns information to the client indicating the HTTP options supported by the server, such as the version of HTTP (1.0 or 1.1) and the request methods the server supports.
doPut	Called in response to an HTTP *put* request. Such a request is normally used to store a file on the server. This may not be available on some servers, because of its inherent security risks (i.e., the client could place an executable application on the server, which, if executed, could damage the server—perhaps by deleting critical files or occupying resources).
doTrace	Called in response to an HTTP *trace* request. Such a request is normally used for debugging. The implementation of this method automatically returns a\n HTML document to the client containing the request header information (data sent by the browser as part of the request).

Fig. A.2   Other methods of class **HttpServlet**.

A.2.3 HttpServletRequest Interface

Every call to **doGet** or **doPost** for an **HttpServlet** receives an object that implements interface **HttpServletRequest**. The Web server that executes the servlet creates an **HttpServletRequest** object and passes this to the servlet's **service** method (which, in turn, passes it to **doGet** or **doPost**). This object contains the request from the client. A variety of methods are provided to enable the servlet to process the client's request. Some of these methods are from interface *ServletRequest*—the interface that **HttpServletRequest** extends. A few key methods used in this appendix are presented in Fig. A.3. You can view a complete list of **HttpServletRequest** methods online at

> **java.sun.com/j2ee/j2sdkee/techdocs/api/javax/servlet/http/**
> **HttpServletRequest.html**

or you can download and install Tomcat (discussed in Section A.3.1) and view the documentation on your local computer.

Method	Description
String getParameter(String name)	Obtains the value of a parameter sent to the servlet as part of a **get** or **post** request. The **name** argument represents the parameter name.

Fig. A.3   Some methods of interface **HttpServletRequest**. (Part 1 of 2.)

Method	Description

Enumeration getParameterNames()

Returns the names of all the parameters sent to the servlet as part of a **post** request.

String[] getParameterValues(String name)

For a parameter with multiple values, this method returns an array of **String**s containing the values for a specified servlet parameter.

Cookie[] getCookies()

Returns an array of **Cookie** objects stored on the client by the server. **Cookie**s can be used to uniquely identify clients to the servlet.

HttpSession getSession(boolean create)

Returns an **HttpSession** object associated with the client's current browsing session. An **HttpSession** object can be created by this method (**true** argument) if an **HttpSession** object does not already exist for the client. **HttpSession** objects can be used in similar ways to **Cookie**s for uniquely identifying clients.

Fig. A.3   Some methods of interface **HttpServletRequest**. (Part 2 of 2.)

A.2.4 HttpServletResponse Interface

Every call to **doGet** or **doPost** for an **HttpServlet** receives an object that implements interface **HttpServletResponse**. The Web server that executes the servlet creates an **HttpServletResponse** object and passes it to the servlet's **service** method (which, in turn, passes it to **doGet** or **doPost**). This object provides a variety of methods that enable the servlet to formulate the response to the client. Some of these methods are from interface *ServletResponse*—the interface that **HttpServletResponse** extends. A few key methods used in this appendix are presented in Fig. A.4. You can view a complete list of **HttpServletResponse** methods online at

```
java.sun.com/j2ee/j2sdkee/techdocs/api/javax/servlet/http/
HttpServletResponse.html
```

or you can download and install Tomcat (discussed in Section A.3.1) and view the documentation on your local computer.

Method	Description

void addCookie(Cookie cookie)

Used to add a **Cookie** to the header of the response to the client. The **Cookie**'s maximum age and whether **Cookie**s are enabled on the client determine if **Cookie**s are stored on the client.

Fig. A.4   Some methods of interface **HttpServletResponse**. (Part 1 of 2.)

Method	Description

ServletOutputStream getOutputStream()

Obtains a byte-based output stream for sending binary data to the client.

PrintWriter getWriter()

Obtains a character-based output stream for sending text data to the client.

void setContentType(String type)

Specifies the MIME type of the response to the browser. The MIME type helps the browser determine how to display the data (or possibly what other application to execute to process the data). For example, MIME type **"text/html"** indicates that the response is an HTML document, so the browser displays the HTML page. For more information on

Fig. A.4   Some methods of interface **HttpServletResponse**. (Part 2 of 2.)

A.3 Handling HTTP get Requests

The primary purpose of an HTTP **get** request is to retrieve the content of a specified URL—normally the content is an HTML or XHTML document (i.e., a Web page). The servlet of Fig. A.5 and the XHTML document of Fig. A.6 demonstrate a servlet that handles HTTP **get** requests. When the user clicks the **Get HTML Document** button (Fig. A.6), a **get** request is sent to the servlet **WelcomeServlet** (Fig. A.5). The servlet responds to the request by generating dynamically an XHTML document for the client that displays "**Welcome to Servlets!**". Figure A.5 shows the **WelcomeServlet** source code. Figure A.6 shows the XHTML document the client loads to access the servlet and shows screen captures of the client's browser window before and after the interaction with the servlet. [*Note*: Section A.3.1 discusses how to set up and configure Tomcat to execute this example.]

```
1   // Fig. A.5: WelcomeServlet.java
2   // A simple servlet to process get requests.
3   package com.deitel.jws.servlets;
4
5   import javax.servlet.*;
6   import javax.servlet.http.*;
7   import java.io.*;
8
9   public class WelcomeServlet extends HttpServlet {
10
11      // process "get" requests from clients
12      protected void doGet( HttpServletRequest request,
13         HttpServletResponse response )
14            throws ServletException, IOException
15      {
```

Fig. A.5   **WelcomeServlet** that responds to a simple HTTP **get** request. (Part 1 of 2.)

```
16          response.setContentType( "text/html" );
17          PrintWriter out = response.getWriter();
18
19          // send XHTML page to client
20
21          // start XHTML document
22          out.println( "<?xml version = \"1.0\"?>" );
23
24          out.println( "<!DOCTYPE html PUBLIC \"-//W3C//DTD " +
25             "XHTML 1.0 Strict//EN\" \"http://www.w3.org" +
26             "/TR/xhtml1/DTD/xhtml1-strict.dtd\">" );
27
28          out.println(
29             "<html xmlns = \"http://www.w3.org/1999/xhtml\">" );
30
31          // head section of document
32          out.println( "<head>" );
33          out.println( "<title>A Simple Servlet Example</title>" );
34          out.println( "</head>" );
35
36          // body section of document
37          out.println( "<body>" );
38          out.println( "<h1>Welcome to Servlets!</h1>" );
39          out.println( "</body>" );
40
41          // end XHTML document
42          out.println( "</html>" );
43          out.close();  // close stream to complete the page
44       }
45  }
```

Fig. A.5   **WelcomeServlet** that responds to a simple HTTP **get** request.
(Part 2 of 2.)

Lines 5 and 6 import the **javax.servlet** and **javax.servlet.http** packages. We use several data types from these packages in the example.

Package **javax.servlet.http** provides superclass **HttpServlet** for servlets that handle HTTP **get** requests and HTTP **post** requests. This class implements interface **javax.servlet.Servlet** and adds methods that support HTTP protocol requests. Class **WelcomeServlet** extends **HttpServlet** (line 9) for this reason.

Superclass **HttpServlet** provides method *doGet* to respond to **get** requests. Its default functionality is to indicate a "Method not allowed" error. Typically, this error is indicated in Internet Explorer with a Web page that states "This page cannot be displayed" and in Netscape Navigator with a Web page that states "Error: 405." Lines 12–44 override method **doGet** to provide custom **get** request processing. Method **doGet** receives two arguments—an **HttpServletRequest** object and an **HttpServletResponse** object (both from package **javax.servlet.http**). The **HttpServletRequest** object represents the client's request, and the **HttpServletResponse** object represents the server's response to the client. If method **doGet** is unable to handle a client's request, it throws an exception of type *javax.servlet.ServletException*. If **doGet** encounters an error during stream processing (reading from the client or writing to the client), it throws a *java.io.IOException*.

To demonstrate a response to a **get** request, our servlet creates an XHTML document containing the text "**Welcome to Servlets!**". The text of the XHTML document is the response to the client. The response is sent to the client through the **PrintWriter** object obtained from the **HttpServletResponse** object.

Line 16 uses the **response** object's *setContentType* method to specify the content type of the data to be sent as the response to the client. This enables the client browser to understand and handle the content. The content type also is known as the *MIME* type (*Multipurpose Internet Mail Extension*) of the data. In this example, the content type is *text/html* to indicate to the browser that the response is an XHTML document. The browser knows that it must read the XHTML tags in the document, format the document according to the tags and display the document in the browser window. For more information on MIME types visit **www.irvine.com/~mime**.

Line 17 uses the **response** object's *getWriter* method to obtain a reference to the **PrintWriter** object that enables the servlet to send content to the client. [*Note*: If the response is binary data, such as an image, method *getOutputStream* is used to obtain a reference to a **ServletOutputStream** object.]

Lines 22–42 create the XHTML document by writing strings with the **out** object's *println* method. This method outputs a newline character after its **String** argument. When rendering the Web page, the browser does not use the newline character. Rather, the newline character appears in the XHTML source that you can see by selecting **Source** from the **View** menu in Internet Explorer or **Page Source** from the **View** menu in Netscape Navigator. Line 43 closes the output stream, flushes the output buffer and sends the information to the client. This commits the response to the client.

The XHTML document in Fig. A.6 provides a **form** that invokes the servlet defined in Fig. A.5. The **form**'s **action** (**/jws/welcome**) specifies the URL path that invokes the servlet, and the **form**'s **method** indicates that the browser sends a **get** request to the server, which results in a call to the servlet's **doGet** method. The URL specified as the **action** in this example is discussed in detail in Section A.3.2 after we show how to set up and configure the *Apache Tomcat server* to execute the servlet in Fig. A.5.

```
1   <?xml version = "1.0"?>
2   <!DOCTYPE html PUBLIC "-//W3C//DTD XHTML 1.0 Strict//EN"
3      "http://www.w3.org/TR/xhtml1/DTD/xhtml1-strict.dtd">
4
5   <!-- Fig. A.6: WelcomeServlet.html -->
6
7   <html xmlns = "http://www.w3.org/1999/xhtml">
8   <head>
9      <title>Handling an HTTP Get Request</title>
10  </head>
11
12  <body>
13     <form action = "/jws/welcome1" method = "get">
14
```

Fig. A.6   HTML document in which the **form**'s **action** invokes **WelcomeServlet** through the alias **welcome1** specified in **web.xml** (Part 1 of 2.).

```
15              <p><label>Click the button to invoke the servlet<br/><br/>
16                 <input type = "submit" value = "Get HTML Document" />
17              </label></p>
18
19         </form>
20     </body>
21     </html>
```

Fig. A.6   HTML document in which the **form**'s **action** invokes
                WelcomeServlet through the alias **welcome1** specified in **web.xml**
                (Part 2 of 2.).

Note that the sample screen captures show a URL containing the server name **local-host**—a well-known server *host name* on most computers that support TCP/IP-based networking protocols such as HTTP. We often use **localhost** to demonstrate networking programs on the local computer, so that readers without a network connection can still learn network programming concepts. In this example, **localhost** indicates that the server on which the servlet is installed is running on the local machine. The server host name is followed by **:8080**, specifying the TCP port number at which the Tomcat server awaits requests from clients. Web browsers assume TCP port 80 by default as the server port at which clients make requests, but the Tomcat server awaits client requests at TCP port 8080. This allows Tomcat to execute on the same computer as a standard Web server application without affecting the Web server application's ability to handle requests. If we do not explicitly specify the port number in the URL, the servlet never will receive our request and an error message will be displayed in the browser.

Software Engineering Observation A.5

The Tomcat documentation specifies how to integrate Tomcat with popular Web server applications such as the Apache HTTP Server and Microsoft's IIS.

Ports in this case are not physical hardware ports to which you attach cables; rather, they are logical locations named with integer values that allow clients to request different services on the same server. The port number specifies the logical location where a server waits for and receives connections from clients—this is also called the *handshake point*. When a client connects to a server to request a service, the client must specify the port number for that service; otherwise, the client request cannot be processed. Port numbers are positive integers with values up to 65,535, and there are separate sets of these port numbers for both the TCP and UDP protocols. Many operating systems reserve port numbers below 1024 for system services (such as email and World Wide Web servers). Generally, these ports should not be specified as connection ports in your own server programs. In fact, some operating systems require special access privileges to use port numbers below 1024.

With so many ports from which to choose, how does a client know which port to use when requesting a service? The term *well-known port number* often is used when describing popular services on the Internet such as Web servers and email servers. For example, a Web server waits for clients to make requests at port 80 by default. All Web browsers know this number as the well-known port on a Web server where requests for HTML documents are made. So when you type a URL into a Web browser, the browser normally connects to port 80 on the server. Similarly, the Tomcat server uses port 8080 as its port number. Thus, requests to Tomcat for Web pages or to invoke servlets and Java-Server Pages must specify that the Tomcat server waiting for requests on port 8080.

The client can access the servlet only if the servlet is installed on a server that can respond to servlet requests. In some cases, servlet support is built directly into the Web server, and no special configuration is required to handle servlet requests. In other cases, it is necessary to integrate a servlet container with a Web server (as can be done with Tomcat and the Apache or IIS Web servers). Web servers that support servlets normally have an installation procedure for servlets. If you intend to execute your servlet as part of a Web server, please refer to your Web server's documentation on how to install a servlet. For our examples, we demonstrate servlets with the Apache Tomcat server. Section A.3.1 discusses the setup and configuration of Tomcat for use with this appendix. Section A.3.2 discusses the deployment of the servlet in Fig. A.5.

A.3.1 Setting Up the Apache Tomcat Server

Tomcat is a fully functional implementation of the JSP and servlet standards. It includes a Web server, so it can be used as a standalone test container for JSPs and servlets. Tomcat also can be specified as the handler for JSP and servlet requests received by popular Web servers such as the Apache Software Foundation's Apache Web server or Microsoft's Internet Information Server (IIS). Tomcat is integrated into the Java 2 Enterprise Edition reference implementation from Sun Microsystems.

The Java Web Services Developer Pack includes the most recent release of Tomcat (version 4). Installation of the JWSDP will install Tomcat. For Tomcat to work correctly, you must define environment variables **JAVA_HOME**, **CATALINA_HOME** and **TOMCAT_HOME**. Environment variable **JAVA_HOME** should point to the directory containing your Java installation (ours is **d:\jdk1.3.1**), and both **CATALINA_HOME** and **TOMCAT_HOME** should point to **%JWSDP_HOME%/bin**.

Testing and Debugging Tip A.1

On some platforms you may need to restart your computer for the new environment variables to take effect.

After setting the environment variables, you can start the Tomcat server. Open a command prompt (or shell) and change directories to **TOMCAT_HOME**. In this directory are the files *startup.bat* and *startup.sh*, for starting the Tomcat server on Windows and UNIX (Linux or Solaris), respectively. The Tomcat server executes on TCP port 8080 to prevent conflicts with standard Web servers that typically execute on TCP port 80. To prove that Tomcat is executing and can respond to requests, open your Web browser and enter the URL

```
http://localhost:8080/
```

This should display the Tomcat documentation home page. The host **localhost** indicates to the Web browser that it should request the home page from the Tomcat server on the local computer.

If the Tomcat documentation home page does not display, try the URL

```
http://127.0.0.1:8080/
```

The host **localhost** translates to the IP address **127.0.0.1**.

Testing and Debugging Tip A.2

*If the host name **localhost** does not work on your computer, substitute the IP address **127.0.0.1** instead.*

Note that the **TOMCAT_HOME** directory also contains the files *shutdown.bat* and *shutdown.sh*, which are used to stop the Tomcat server on Windows and UNIX (Linux or Solaris), respectively.

A.3.2 Deploying a Web Application

JSPs, servlets and their supporting files are deployed as part of *Web applications*. Normally, Web applications are deployed in the **webapps** subdirectory of the **%JWSDP_HOME%** directory. A Web application has a well-known directory structure in which all the files that are part of the application reside. This directory structure can be created by the server administrator in the **webapps** directory, or the entire directory structure can be archived in a *Web application archive file*. Such an archive is known as a *WAR file* and ends with the *.war* file extension. If a WAR file is placed in the **webapps** directory, then, when the Tomcat server begins execution, it extracts the contents of the WAR file into the appropriate **webapps** subdirectory structure. For simplicity as we teach servlets and JavaServer Pages, we create the already expanded directory structure for all the examples in this appendix and Appendix B.

The Web application directory structure contains a *context root*—the top-level directory for an entire Web application—and several subdirectories. These are described in Fig. A.7.

Common Programming Error A.1

Using "servlet" or "servlets" as a context root may prevent a servlet from working correctly on some servers.

Directory	Description
context root	This is the root directory for the Web application. The name of this directory is chosen by the Web application developer. All the JSPs, HTML documents, servlets and supporting files such as images and class files reside in this directory or its subdirectories. The name of this directory is specified by the Web application creator. To provide structure in a Web application, subdirectories can be placed in the context root. For example, if your application uses many images, you might place an images subdirectory in this directory. The examples of this appendix and Appendix B use **jws** as the context root.
WEB-INF	This directory contains the Web application *deployment descriptor* (**web.xml**).
WEB-INF/classes	This directory contains the servlet class files and other supporting class files used in a Web application. If the classes are part of a package, the complete package directory structure would begin here.
WEB-INF/lib	This directory contains Java archive (JAR) files. The JAR files can contain servlet class files and other supporting class files used in a Web application.

Fig. A.7   Web application standard directories.

Configuring the context root for a Web application in Tomcat simply requires creating a subdirectory in the **webapps** directory. When Tomcat begins execution, it creates a context root for each subdirectory of **webapps**, using each subdirectory's name as a context root name. To test the examples in this appendix and Appendix B, create the directory **jws** in Tomcat's **webapps** directory.

After configuring the context root, we must configure our Web application to handle the requests. This configuration occurs in a *deployment descriptor*, which is stored in a file called **web.xml**. The deployment descriptor specifies various configuration parameters such as the name used to invoke the servlet (i.e., its *alias*), a description of the servlet, the servlet's fully qualified class name and a *servlet mapping* (i.e., the path or paths that cause the servlet container to invoke the servlet). You must create the **web.xml** file for this example. Many Java Web-application deployment tools create the **web.xml** file for you. The **web.xml** file for the first example in this appendix is shown in Fig. A.8. We enhance this file as we add other servlets to the Web application throughout this appendix.

```
1   <!DOCTYPE web-app PUBLIC
2       "-//Sun Microsystems, Inc.//DTD Web Application 2.2//EN"
3       "http://java.sun.com/j2ee/dtds/web-app_2_2.dtd">
4
5   <web-app>
6
```

Fig. A.8   Deployment descriptor (**web.xml**) for the **jws** Web application. (Part 1 of 2.)

```
7        <!-- General description of your Web application -->
8        <display-name>
9            Java Web Services for Experienced Programmers JSP
10           and Servlet Examples
11       </display-name>
12
13       <description>
14           This is the Web application in which we
15           demonstrate our JSP and Servlet examples.
16       </description>
17
18       <!-- Servlet definitions -->
19       <servlet>
20           <servlet-name>welcome1</servlet-name>
21
22           <description>
23               A simple servlet that handles an HTTP get request.
24           </description>
25
26           <servlet-class>
27               com.deitel.jws.servlets.WelcomeServlet
28           </servlet-class>
29       </servlet>
30
31       <!-- Servlet mappings -->
32       <servlet-mapping>
33           <servlet-name>welcome1</servlet-name>
34           <url-pattern>/welcome1</url-pattern>
35       </servlet-mapping>
36
37   </web-app>
```

Fig. A.8   Deployment descriptor (**web.xml**) for the **jws** Web application.
(Part 2 of 2.)

Lines 1–3 specify the document type for the Web application deployment descriptor and the location of the DTD for this XML file. Element **web-app** (lines 5–37) defines the configuration of each servlet in the Web application and the servlet mapping for each servlet. Element **display-name** (lines 8–11) specifies a name that can be displayed to the administrator of the server on which the Web application is installed. Element **description** (lines 13–16) specifies a description of the Web application that might be displayed to the administrator of the server.

Element **servlet** (lines 19–29) describes a servlet. Element **servlet-name** (line 20) is the name we chose for the servlet (**welcome1**). Element **description** (lines 22–24) specifies a description for this particular servlet. Again, this can be displayed to the administrator of the Web server. Element **servlet-class** (lines 26–28) specifies compiled servlet's fully qualified class name. Thus, the servlet **welcome1** is defined by class **com.deitel.jws.servlets.WelcomeServlet**.

Element **servlet-mapping** (lines 32–35) specifies **servlet-name** and **url-pattern** elements. The *URL pattern* helps the server determine which requests are sent to the servlet (**welcome1**). Our Web application will be installed as part of the **jws** context root discussed in Section A.3.2. Thus, the URL we supply to the browser to invoke the servlet in this example is

```
/jws/welcome1
```

where **/jws** specifies the context root that helps the server determine which Web application handles the request and **/welcome1** specifies the URL pattern that is mapped to servlet **welcome1** to handle the request. Note that the server on which the servlet resides is not specified here, although it is possible to do so as follows:

```
http://localhost:8080/jws/welcome1
```

If the explicit server and port number are not specified as part of the URL, the browser assumes that the form handler (i.e., the servlet specified in the **action** property of the **form** element) resides at the same server and port number from which the browser downloaded the Web page containing the **form**.

There are several URL pattern formats that can be used. The **/welcome1** URL pattern requires an exact match of the pattern. You can also specify *path mappings*, extension mappings and a *default servlet* for a Web application. A path mapping begins with a **/** and ends with a **/***. For example, the URL pattern

```
/jws/example/*
```

indicates that any URL path beginning with **/jws/example/** will be sent to the servlet that has the preceding URL pattern. An extension mapping begins with ***.** and ends with a file name extension. For example, the URL pattern

```
*.jsp
```

indicates that any request for a file with the extension **.jsp** will be sent to the servlet that handles JSP requests. In fact, servers with JSP containers have an implicit mapping of the **.jsp** extension to a servlet that handles JSP requests. The URL pattern **/** represents the default servlet for the Web application. This is similar to the default document of a Web server. For example, if you type the URL **www.deitel.com** into your Web browser, the document you receive from our Web server is the default document **index.html**. If the URL pattern matches the default servlet for a Web application, that servlet is invoked to return a default response to the client. This can be useful for personalizing Web content to specific users. We discuss personalization in Section A.7, Session Tracking.

Finally, we are ready to place our files into the appropriate directories to complete the deployment of our first servlet, so we can test it. There are three files we must place in the appropriate directories—**WelcomeServlet.html**, **WelcomeServlet.class** and **web.xml**. In the **webapps** subdirectory of your **jakarta-tomcat-3.2.3** directory, create the **jws** subdirectory that represents the context root for our Web application. In this directory, create subdirectories named **servlets** and **WEB-INF**. We place our HTML files for this servlets appendix in the **servlets** directory. Copy the **WelcomeServlet.html** file into the **servlets** directory. In the **WEB-INF** directory, create the subdirectory **classes**, then copy the **web.xml** file into the **WEB-INF** directory, and copy the **WelcomeServlet.class** file, including all its package name directories, into the **classes** directory. Thus, the directory and file structure under the **webapps** directory should be as shown in Fig. A.9 (file names are in italics).

WelcomeServlet Web application directory and file structure

```
jws
   servlets
      WelcomeServlet.html
   WEB-INF
      web.xml
      classes
         com
            deitel
               jws
                  servlets
                     WelcomeServlet.class
```

Fig. A.9   Web application directory and file structure for **WelcomeServlet**.

Testing and Debugging Tip A.3

*Restart the Tomcat server after modifying the **web.xml** deployment descriptor file. Otherwise, Tomcat will not recognize your new Web application.*

After the files are placed in the proper directories, start the Tomcat server, open your browser and type the following URL—

http://localhost:8080/jws/servlets/WelcomeServlet.html

—to load **WelcomeServlet.html** into the Web browser. Then, click the **Get HTML Document** button to invoke the servlet. You should see the results shown in Fig. A.6. You can try this servlet from several different Web browsers to demonstrate that the results are the same across Web browsers.

Common Programming Error A.2

Not placing servlet or other class files in the appropriate package directory structure prevents the server from locating those classes properly. This, in turn, results in an error response to the client Web browser. This error response normally is "Not Found (404)" in Netscape Navigator and "The page cannot be found" plus an explanation in Microsoft Internet Explorer.

Actually, the HTML file in Fig. A.6 was not necessary to invoke this servlet. A **get** request can be sent to a server simply by typing the URL in the Web browser. In fact, that is exactly what you are doing when you request a Web page in the browser. In this example, you can type

http://localhost:8080/jws/welcome1

in the **Address** or **Location** field of your browser to invoke the servlet directly.

Testing and Debugging Tip A.4

*You can test a servlet that handles HTTP **get** requests by typing the URL that invokes the servlet directly into your browser's **Address** or **Location** field.*

A.4 Handling HTTP get Requests Containing Data

When requesting a document or resource from a Web server, it is possible to supply data as part of the request. The servlet **WelcomeServlet2** of Fig. A.10 responds to an HTTP **get** request that contains a name supplied by the user. The servlet uses the name as part of the response to the client.

```java
1   // Fig. A.10: WelcomeServlet2.java
2   // Processing HTTP get requests containing data.
3   package com.deitel.jws.servlets;
4
5   import javax.servlet.*;
6   import javax.servlet.http.*;
7   import java.io.*;
8
9   public class WelcomeServlet2 extends HttpServlet {
10
11      // process "get" request from client
12      protected void doGet( HttpServletRequest request,
13         HttpServletResponse response )
14            throws ServletException, IOException
15      {
16         String firstName = request.getParameter( "firstname" );
17
18         response.setContentType( "text/html" );
19         PrintWriter out = response.getWriter();
20
21         // send XHTML document to client
22
23         // start XHTML document
24         out.println( "<?xml version = \"1.0\"?>" );
25
26         out.println( "<!DOCTYPE html PUBLIC \"-//W3C//DTD " +
27            "XHTML 1.0 Strict//EN\" \"http://www.w3.org" +
28            "/TR/xhtml11/DTD/xhtml11-strict.dtd\">" );
29
30         out.println(
31            "<html xmlns = \"http://www.w3.org/1999/xhtml\">" );
32
33         // head section of document
34         out.println( "<head>" );
35         out.println(
36            "<title>Processing get requests with data</title>" );
37         out.println( "</head>" );
38
39         // body section of document
40         out.println( "<body>" );
41         out.println( "<h1>Hello " + firstName + ",<br />" );
42         out.println( "Welcome to Servlets!</h1>" );
43         out.println( "</body>" );
44
```

Fig. A.10 **WelcomeServlet2** responds to a **get** request that contains data. (Part 1 of 2.)

```
45          // end XHTML document
46          out.println( "</html>" );
47          out.close();  // close stream to complete the page
48      }
49  }
```

Fig. A.10 `WelcomeServlet2` responds to a **get** request that contains data. (Part 2 of 2.)

Parameters are passed as name/value pairs in a **get** request. Line 16 demonstrates how to obtain information that was passed to the servlet as part of the client request. The **request** object's *getParameter* method receives the parameter name as an argument and returns the corresponding **String** value, or **null** if the parameter is not part of the request. Line 41 uses the result of line 16 as part of the response to the client.

The **WelcomeServlet2.html** document (Fig. A.11) provides a **form** in which the user can input a name in the text **input** element **firstname** (line 17) and click the **Submit** button to invoke **WelcomeServlet2**. When the user presses the **Submit** button, the values of the **input** elements are placed in name/value pairs as part of the request to the server. In the second screen capture of Fig. A.11, notice that the browser appended

    ?firstname=Paul

to the end of the **action** URL. The **?** separates the *query string* (i.e., the data passed as part of the **get** request) from the rest of the URL in a **get** request. The name/value pairs are passed with the name and the value separated by **=**. If there is more than one name/value pair, each name/value pair is separated by **&**.

```
1   <?xml version = "1.0"?>
2   <!DOCTYPE html PUBLIC "-//W3C//DTD XHTML 1.0 Strict//EN"
3      "http://www.w3.org/TR/xhtml1/DTD/xhtml1-strict.dtd">
4
5   <!-- Fig. A.11: WelcomeServlet2.html -->
6
7   <html xmlns = "http://www.w3.org/1999/xhtml">
8   <head>
9      <title>Processing get requests with data</title>
10  </head>
11
12  <body>
13     <form action = "/jws/welcome2" method = "get">
14
15        <p><label>
16           Type your first name and press the Submit button
17           <br /><input type = "text" name = "firstname" />
18           <input type = "submit" value = "Submit" />
19        </p></label>
```

Fig. A.11 HTML document in which the **form**'s **action** invokes **WelcomeServlet2** through the alias **welcome2** specified in **web.xml**. (Part 1 of 2.)

```
20
21      </form>
22    </body>
23    </html>
```

Fig. A.11   HTML document in which the **form**'s **action** invokes
WelcomeServlet2 through the alias **welcome2** specified in
web.xml. (Part 2 of 2.)

Once again, we use our **jws** context root to demonstrate the servlet of Fig. A.10. Place
WelcomeServlet2.html in the **servlets** directory created in Section A.3.2. Place
WelcomeServlet2.class in the **classes** subdirectory of **WEB-INF** in the **jws**
context root. Remember that classes in a package must be placed in the appropriate package
directory structure. Then, edit the **web.xml** deployment descriptor in the **WEB-INF** directory to include the information specified in Fig. A.12. This table contains the information
for the **servlet** and **servlet-mapping** elements that you will add to the **web.xml**
deployment descriptor. You should not type the italic text into the deployment descriptor.
Restart Tomcat and type the following URL in your Web browser:

> **http://localhost:8080/jws/servlets/WelcomeServlet2.html**

Type your name in the text field of the Web page, then click **Submit** to invoke the servlet.
Once again, note that the **get** request could have been typed directly into the
browser's **Address** or **Location** field as follows:

> **http://localhost:8080/jws/welcome2?firstname=Paul**

Try it with your own name.

Descriptor element	Value
servlet element	
servlet-name	welcome2
description	Handling HTTP get requests with data.
servlet-class	com.deitel.jws.servlets.WelcomeServlet2
servlet-mapping element	
servlet-name	welcome2
url-pattern	/welcome2

Fig. A.12 Deployment descriptor information for servlet **WelcomeServlet2**.

A.5 Handling HTTP post Requests

An HTTP **post** request is often used to post data from an HTML form to a server-side form handler that processes the data. For example, when you respond to a Web-based survey, a **post** request normally supplies the information you specify in the HTML form to the Web server.

Browsers often *cache* (save on disk) Web pages so they can quickly reload the pages. If there are no changes between the last version stored in the cache and the current version on the Web, this helps speed up your browsing experience. The browser first asks the server if the document has changed or expired since the date the file was cached. If not, the browser loads the document from the cache. Thus, the browser minimizes the amount of data that must be downloaded for you to view a Web page. Browsers typically do not cache the server's response to a **post** request, because the next **post** might not return the same result. For example, in a survey, many users could visit the same Web page and respond to a question. The survey results could then be displayed for the user. Each new response changes the overall results of the survey.

When you use a Web-based search engine, the browser normally supplies the information you specify in an HTML form to the search engine with a **get** request. The search engine performs the search, then returns the results to you as a Web page. Such pages are often cached by the browser in case you perform the same search again. As with **post** requests, **get** requests can supply parameters as part of the request to the Web server.

The **WelcomeServlet3** servlet of Fig. A.13 is identical to the servlet of Fig. A.10, except that it defines a **doPost** method (line 12) to respond to **post** requests rather than a **doGet** method. The default functionality of **doPost** is to indicate a "Method not allowed" error. We override this method to provide custom **post** request processing. Method **doPost** receives the same two arguments as **doGet**—an object that implements interface **HttpServletRequest** to represent the client's request and an object that implements interface **HttpServletResponse** to represent the servlet's response. As with **doGet**, method **doPost** throws a **ServletException** if it is unable to handle a client's request and throws an **IOException** if a problem occurs during stream processing.

```
1    // Fig. A.13: WelcomeServlet3.java
2    // Processing post requests containing data.
3    package com.deitel.jws.servlets;
4
5    import javax.servlet.*;
6    import javax.servlet.http.*;
7    import java.io.*;
8
9    public class WelcomeServlet3 extends HttpServlet {
10
11       // process "post" request from client
12       protected void doPost( HttpServletRequest request,
13          HttpServletResponse response )
14             throws ServletException, IOException
15       {
16          String firstName = request.getParameter( "firstname" );
17
18          response.setContentType( "text/html" );
19          PrintWriter out = response.getWriter();
20
21          // send XHTML page to client
22
23          // start XHTML document
24          out.println( "<?xml version = \"1.0\"?>" );
25
26          out.println( "<!DOCTYPE html PUBLIC \"-//W3C//DTD " +
27             "XHTML 1.0 Strict//EN\" \"http://www.w3.org" +
28             "/TR/xhtml1/DTD/xhtml1-strict.dtd\">" );
29
30          out.println(
31             "<html xmlns = \"http://www.w3.org/1999/xhtml\">" );
32
33          // head section of document
34          out.println( "<head>" );
35          out.println(
36             "<title>Processing post requests with data</title>" );
37          out.println( "</head>" );
38
39          // body section of document
40          out.println( "<body>" );
41          out.println( "<h1>Hello " + firstName + ",<br />" );
42          out.println( "Welcome to Servlets!</h1>" );
43          out.println( "</body>" );
44
45          // end XHTML document
46          out.println( "</html>" );
47          out.close();  // close stream to complete the page
48       }
49    }
```

Fig. A.13 **WelcomeServlet3** responds to a **post** request that contains data.

WelcomeServlet3.html (Fig. A.14) provides a **form** (lines 13–21) in which the user can input a name in the text **input** element **firstname** (line 17), then click the **Submit** button to invoke **WelcomeServlet3**. When the user presses the **Submit** button, the values of the **input** elements are sent to the server as part of the request. However, note that the values are not appended to the request URL. Note that the form's **method** in this example is **post**. Also, note that a **post** request cannot be typed into the browser's **Address** or **Location** field and users cannot bookmark **post** requests in their browsers.

```
1   <?xml version = "1.0"?>
2   <!DOCTYPE html PUBLIC "-//W3C//DTD XHTML 1.0 Strict//EN"
3       "http://www.w3.org/TR/xhtml1/DTD/xhtml1-strict.dtd">
4
5   <!-- Fig. A.14: WelcomeServlet3.html -->
6
7   <html xmlns = "http://www.w3.org/1999/xhtml">
8   <head>
9       <title>Handling an HTTP Post Request with Data</title>
10  </head>
11
12  <body>
13      <form action = "/jws/welcome3" method = "post">
14
15          <p><label>
16              Type your first name and press the Submit button
17              <br /><input type = "text" name = "firstname" />
18              <input type = "submit" value = "Submit" />
19          </label></p>
20
21      </form>
22  </body>
23  </html>
```

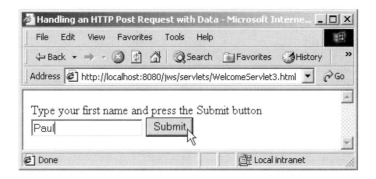

Fig. A.14 HTML document in which the **form**'s **action** invokes
WelcomeServlet3 through the alias **welcome3** specified in
web.xml. (Part 1 of 2.)

Fig. A.14 HTML document in which the **form**'s **action** invokes
WelcomeServlet3 through the alias **welcome3** specified in
web.xml. (Part 2 of 2.)

We use our **jws** context root to demonstrate the servlet of Fig. A.13. Place
WelcomeServlet3.html in the **servlets** directory created in Section A.3.2. Place
WelcomeServlet3.class in the **classes** subdirectory of **WEB-INF** in the **jws**
context root. Then, edit the **web.xml** deployment descriptor in the **WEB-INF** directory to
include the information specified in Fig. A.15. Restart Tomcat and type the following URL
in your Web browser:

```
http://localhost:8080/jws/servlets/WelcomeServlet3.html
```

Type your name in the text field of the Web page, then click **Submit** to invoke the servlet.

A.6 Redirecting Requests to Other Resources

Sometimes it is useful to redirect a request to a different resource. For example, a servlet
could determine the type of the client browser and redirect the request to a Web page that
was designed specifically for that browser. The **RedirectServlet** of Fig. A.16 receives a page parameter as part of a **get** request, then uses that parameter to redirect the
request to a different resource.

Descriptor element	Value
servlet *element*	
servlet-name	welcome3
description	Handling HTTP post requests with data.
servlet-class	com.deitel.jws.servlets.WelcomeServlet3
servlet-mapping *element*	
servlet-name	welcome3
url-pattern	/welcome3

Fig. A.15 Deployment descriptor information for servlet **WelcomeServlet3**.

```
1    // Fig. A.16: RedirectServlet.java
2    // Redirecting a user to a different Web page.
3    package com.deitel.jws.servlets;
4
5    import javax.servlet.*;
6    import javax.servlet.http.*;
7    import java.io.*;
8
9    public class RedirectServlet extends HttpServlet {
10
11       // process "get" request from client
12       protected void doGet( HttpServletRequest request,
13          HttpServletResponse response )
14             throws ServletException, IOException
15       {
16          String location = request.getParameter( "page" );
17
18          if ( location != null )
19
20             if ( location.equals( "deitel" ) )
21                response.sendRedirect( "http://www.deitel.com" );
22             else
23                if ( location.equals( "welcome1" ) )
24                   response.sendRedirect( "welcome1" );
25
26          // code that executes only if this servlet
27          // does not redirect the user to another page
28
29          response.setContentType( "text/html" );
30          PrintWriter out = response.getWriter();
31
32          // start XHTML document
33          out.println( "<?xml version = \"1.0\"?>" );
34
35          out.println( "<!DOCTYPE html PUBLIC \"-//W3C//DTD " +
36             "XHTML 1.0 Strict//EN\" \"http://www.w3.org" +
37             "/TR/xhtml1/DTD/xhtml1-strict.dtd\">" );
38
39          out.println(
40             "<html xmlns = \"http://www.w3.org/1999/xhtml\">" );
41
42          // head section of document
43          out.println( "<head>" );
44          out.println( "<title>Invalid page</title>" );
45          out.println( "</head>" );
46
47          // body section of document
48          out.println( "<body>" );
49          out.println( "<h1>Invalid page requested</h1>" );
50          out.println( "<p><a href = " +
51             "\"servlets/RedirectServlet.html\">" );
52          out.println( "Click here to choose again</a></p>" );
```

Fig. A.16 Redirecting requests to other resources. (Part 1 of 2.)

```
53          out.println( "</body>" );
54
55          // end XHTML document
56          out.println( "</html>" );
57          out.close();  // close stream to complete the page
58      }
59  }
```

Fig. A.16 Redirecting requests to other resources. (Part 2 of 2.)

Line 16 obtains the **page** parameter from the request. If the value returned is not **null**, the **if/else** structure at lines 20–24 determines if the value is either "**deitel**" or "**welcome1**." If the value is "**deitel**," the **response** object's *sendRedirect* method (line 21) redirects the request to **www.deitel.com**. If the value is "**welcome1**," line 24 redirect the request to the servlet of Fig. A.5. Note that line 24 does not explicitly specify the **jws** context root for our Web application. When a servlet uses a relative path to reference another static or dynamic resource, the servlet assumes the same base URL and context root as the one that invoked the servlet—unless a complete URL is specified for the resource. So, line 24 actually is requesting the resource located at

> **http://localhost:8080/jws/welcome1**

Similarly, line 51 actually is requesting the resource located at

> **http://localhost:8080/jws/servlets/RedirectServlet.html**

Software Engineering Observation A.6

Using relative paths to reference resources in the same context root makes your Web application more flexible. For example, you can change the context root without making changes to the static and dynamic resources in the application.

Once method **sendRedirect** executes, processing of the original request by the **RedirectServlet** terminates. If method **sendRedirect** is not called, the remainder of method **doPost** outputs a Web page indicating that an invalid request was made. The page allows the user to try again by returning to the XHTML document of Fig. A.17. Note that one of the redirects is sent to a static XHTML Web page and the other is sent to a servlet.

The **RedirectServlet.html** document (Fig. A.17) provides two hyperlinks (lines 15–16 and 17–18) that allow the user to invoke the servlet **RedirectServlet**. Note that each hyperlink specifies a **page** parameter as part of the URL. To demonstrate passing an invalid page, you can type the URL into your browser with no value for the **page** parameter.

```
1   <?xml version = "1.0"?>
2   <!DOCTYPE html PUBLIC "-//W3C//DTD XHTML 1.0 Strict//EN"
3       "http://www.w3.org/TR/xhtml1/DTD/xhtml1-strict.dtd">
4
```

Fig. A.17 **RedirectServlet.html** document to demonstrate redirecting requests to other resources. (Part 1 of 2.)

```
5    <!-- Fig. A.17: RedirectServlet.html -->
6
7    <html xmlns = "http://www.w3.org/1999/xhtml">
8    <head>
9       <title>Redirecting a Request to Another Site</title>
10   </head>
11
12   <body>
13      <p>Click a link to be redirected to the appropriate page</p>
14      <p>
15      <a href = "/jws/redirect?page=deitel">
16         www.deitel.com</a><br />
17      <a href = "/jws/redirect?page=welcome1">
18         Welcome servlet</a>
19      </p>
20   </body>
21   </html>
```

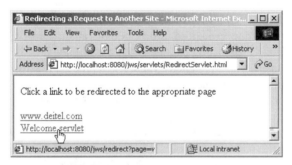

Fig. A.17 **RedirectServlet.html** document to demonstrate redirecting requests to other resources. (Part 2 of 2.)

We use our **jws** context root to demonstrate the servlet of Fig. A.16. Place **RedirectServlet.html** in the **servlets** directory created in Section A.3.2. Place **RedirectServlet.class** in the **classes** subdirectory of **WEB-INF** in the **jws** context root. Then, edit the **web.xml** deployment descriptor in the **WEB-INF** directory to include the information specified in Fig. A.18. Restart Tomcat, and type the following URL in your Web browser:

http://localhost:8080/jws/servlets/RedirectServlet.html

Click a hyperlink in the Web page to invoke the servlet.

Descriptor element	Value
servlet element	
servlet-name	redirect
description	Redirecting to static Web pages and other serv-lets.
servlet-class	com.deitel.jws.servlets.RedirectServlet
servlet-mapping element	
servlet-name	redirect
url-pattern	/redirect

Fig. A.18 Deployment descriptor information for servlet **RedirectServlet**.

When redirecting requests, the request parameters from the original request are passed as parameters to the new request. Additional request parameters also can be passed. For example, the URL passed to **sendRedirect** could contain name/value pairs. Any new parameters are added to the existing parameters. If a new parameter has the same name as an existing parameter, the new parameter value takes precedence over the original value. However, all the values are still passed. In this case, the complete set of values for a given parameter name can be obtained by calling method *getParameterValues* from interface **HttpServletRequest**. This method receives the parameter name as an argument and returns an array of **String**s containing the parameter values in order from most recent to least recent.

A.7 Session Tracking

Many e-businesses can personalize users' browsing experiences, tailoring Web pages to their users' individual preferences and letting users bypass irrelevant content. This is done by tracking the consumer's movement through the Internet and combining that data with information provided by the consumer, which could include billing information, interests and hobbies, among other things. *Personalization* is making it easier and more pleasant for many people to surf the Internet and find what they want. Consumers and companies can benefit from the unique treatment resulting from personalization. Providing content of special interest to your visitor can help establish a relationship that you can build upon each time that person returns to your site. Targeting consumers with personal offers, advertisements, promotions and services may lead to more customer loyalty—many customers enjoy the individual attention that a customized site provides. Originally, the Internet lacked personal assistance when compared with the individual service often experienced in bricks-and-mortar stores. Sophisticated technology helps many Web sites offer a personal touch to their visitors. For example, Web sites such as MSN.com and CNN.com allow you to customize their home page to suit your needs. Online shopping sites often customize their Web pages to individuals, and such sites must distinguish between clients so the company can determine the proper items and charge the proper amount for each client. Personalization is important for Internet marketing and for managing customer relationships to increase customer loyalty.

Hand in hand with the promise of personalization, however, comes the problem of *privacy invasion*. What if the e-business to which you give your personal data sells or gives those data to another organization without your knowledge? What if you do not want your movements on the Internet to be tracked by unknown parties? What if an unauthorized party gains access to your private data, such as credit-card numbers or medical history? These are some of the many questions that must be addressed by consumers, e-businesses and lawmakers alike.

As we have discussed, the request/response mechanism of the Web is based on HTTP. Unfortunately, HTTP is a *stateless protocol*—it does not support persistent information that could help a Web server determine that a request is from a particular client. As far as a Web server is concerned, every request could be from the same client or every request could be from a different client. Thus, sites like MSN.com and CNN.com need a mechanism to identify individual clients. To help the server distinguish between clients, each client must identify itself to the server. There are a number of popular techniques for distinguishing between clients. We introduce two techniques to track clients individually—*cookies* (Section A.7.1) and *session tracking* (Section A.7.2). Two other techniques not discussed in this appendix are using **input** form elements of type **"hidden"** and *URL rewriting*. With "hidden" form elements, the servlet can write session-tracking data into a **form** in the Web page it returns to the client to satisfy a prior request. When the user submits the form in the new Web page, all the form data, including the "hidden" fields, are sent to the form handler on the server. With URL rewriting, the servlet embeds session-tracking information as **get** parameters directly in the URLs of hyperlinks that the user might click to make the next request to the Web server.

A.7.1 Cookies

A popular way to customize Web pages is via *cookies*. Browsers can store cookies on the user's computer for retrieval later in the same browsing session or in future browsing sessions. For example, cookies could be used in a shopping application to store unique identifiers for the users. When users add items to their online shopping carts or perform other tasks resulting in a request to the Web server, the server receives cookies containing unique identifiers for each user. The server then uses the unique identifier to locate the shopping carts and perform the necessary processing. Cookies could also be used to indicate the client's shopping preferences. When the servlet receives the client's next communication, the servlet can examine the cookie(s) it sent to the client in a previous communication, identify the client's preferences and immediately display products of interest to the client.

Cookies are text-based data that are sent by servlets (or other similar server-side technologies) as part of responses to clients. Every HTTP-based interaction between a client and a server includes a *header* containing information about the request (when the communication is from the client to the server) or information about the response (when the communication is from the server to the client). When an **HttpServlet** receives a request, the header includes information such as the request type (e.g., **get** or **post**) and the cookies that are sent by the server to be stored on the client machine. When the server formulates its response, the header information includes any cookies the server wants to store on the client computer and other information such as the MIME type of the response.

Depending on the *maximum age* of a cookie, the Web browser either maintains the cookie for the duration of the browsing session (i.e., until the user closes the Web browser) or stores the cookie on the client computer for future use. When the browser requests a resource from a server, cookies previously sent to the client by that server are returned to the server as part of the request formulated by the browser. Cookies are deleted automatically when they *expire* (i.e., reach their maximum age).

Testing and Debugging Tip A.5

Some clients do not accept cookies. When a client declines a cookie, the Web site or the browser application can inform the client that the site may not function correctly without cookies enabled.

Figure A.19 demonstrates cookies. The example allows the user to select a favorite programming language and **post** the choice to the server. The response is a Web page in which the user can select another favorite language or click a link to view a list of book recommendations. When the user selects the list of book recommendations, a **get** request is sent to the server. The cookies previously stored on the client are read by the servlet and used to form a Web page containing the book recommendations.

CookieServlet (Fig. A.19) handles both the **get** and the **post** requests. The **CookieSelectLanguage.html** document of Fig. A.20 contains four radio buttons (**C**, **C++**, **Java** and **VB 6**) and a **Submit** button. When the user presses **Submit**, the **CookieServlet** is invoked with a **post** request. The servlet adds a cookie containing the selected language to the response header and sends an XHTML document to the client. Each time the user clicks **Submit**, a cookie is sent to the client.

Line 11 defines **Map books** as a **HashMap** (package **java.util**) in which we store key/value pairs that use the programming language as the key and the ISBN number of the recommended book as the value. The **CookieServlet init** method (line 14–20) populates books with four key/value pairs of books. Method **doPost** (lines 24–69) is invoked in response to the **post** request from the XHTML document of Fig. A.20. Line 28 uses method **getParameter** to obtain the user's **language** selection (the value of the selected radio button on the Web page). Line 29 obtains the ISBN number for the selected language from **books**.

Line 30 creates a new *Cookie* object (package *javax.servlet.http*), using the **language** and **isbn** values as the *cookie name* and *cookie value*, respectively. The cookie name identifies the cookie; the cookie value is the information associated with the cookie. Browsers that support cookies must be able to store a minimum of 20 cookies per Web site and 300 cookies per user. Browsers may limit the cookie size to 4K (4096 bytes). Each cookie stored on the client includes a domain. The browser sends a cookie only to the domain stored in the cookie.

```
1   // Fig. A.19: CookieServlet.java
2   // Using cookies to store data on the client computer.
3   package com.deitel.jws.servlets;
4
5   import javax.servlet.*;
6   import javax.servlet.http.*;
7   import java.io.*;
8   import java.util.*;
```

Fig. A.19 Storing user data on the client computer with cookies. (Part 1 of 4.)

```
9
10   public class CookieServlet extends HttpServlet {
11      private final Map books = new HashMap();
12
13      // initialize Map books
14      public void init()
15      {
16         books.put( "C", "0130895725" );
17         books.put( "C++", "0130895717" );
18         books.put( "Java", "0130125075" );
19         books.put( "VB6", "0134569555" );
20      }
21
22      // receive language selection and send cookie containing
23      // recommended book to the client
24      protected void doPost( HttpServletRequest request,
25         HttpServletResponse response )
26            throws ServletException, IOException
27      {
28         String language = request.getParameter( "language" );
29         String isbn = books.get( language ).toString();
30         Cookie cookie = new Cookie( language, isbn );
31
32         response.addCookie( cookie );  // must precede getWriter
33         response.setContentType( "text/html" );
34         PrintWriter out = response.getWriter();
35
36         // send XHTML page to client
37
38         // start XHTML document
39         out.println( "<?xml version = \"1.0\"?>" );
40
41         out.println( "<!DOCTYPE html PUBLIC \"-//W3C//DTD " +
42            "XHTML 1.0 Strict//EN\" \"http://www.w3.org" +
43            "/TR/xhtml1/DTD/xhtml11-strict.dtd\">" );
44
45         out.println(
46            "<html xmlns = \"http://www.w3.org/1999/xhtml\">" );
47
48         // head section of document
49         out.println( "<head>" );
50         out.println( "<title>Welcome to Cookies</title>" );
51         out.println( "</head>" );
52
53         // body section of document
54         out.println( "<body>" );
55         out.println( "<p>Welcome to Cookies! You selected " +
56            language + "</p>" );
57
58         out.println( "<p><a href = " +
59            "\"/jws/servlets/CookieSelectLanguage.html\">" +
60            "Click here to choose another language</a></p>" );
61
```

Fig. A.19 Storing user data on the client computer with cookies. (Part 2 of 4.)

```
62         out.println( "<p><a href = \"/jws/cookies\">" +
63            "Click here to get book recommendations</a></p>" );
64         out.println( "</body>" );
65
66         // end XHTML document
67         out.println( "</html>" );
68         out.close();    // close stream
69      }
70
71      // read cookies from client and create XHTML document
72      // containing recommended books
73      protected void doGet( HttpServletRequest request,
74         HttpServletResponse response )
75            throws ServletException, IOException
76      {
77         Cookie cookies[] = request.getCookies();  // get cookies
78
79         response.setContentType( "text/html" );
80         PrintWriter out = response.getWriter();
81
82         // start XHTML document
83         out.println( "<?xml version = \"1.0\"?>" );
84
85         out.println( "<!DOCTYPE html PUBLIC \"-//W3C//DTD " +
86            "XHTML 1.0 Strict//EN\" \"http://www.w3.org" +
87            "/TR/xhtml1/DTD/xhtml1-strict.dtd\">" );
88
89         out.println(
90            "<html xmlns = \"http://www.w3.org/1999/xhtml\">" );
91
92         // head section of document
93         out.println( "<head>" );
94         out.println( "<title>Recommendations</title>" );
95         out.println( "</head>" );
96
97         // body section of document
98         out.println( "<body>" );
99
100        // if there are any cookies, recommend a book for each ISBN
101        if ( cookies != null && cookies.length != 0 ) {
102           out.println( "<h1>Recommendations</h1>" );
103           out.println( "<p>" );
104
105           // get the name of each cookie
106           for ( int i = 0; i < cookies.length; i++ )
107              out.println( cookies[ i ].getName() +
108                 " How to Program. ISBN#: " +
109                 cookies[ i ].getValue() + "<br />" );
110
111           out.println( "</p>" );
112        }
```

Fig. A.19 Storing user data on the client computer with cookies. (Part 3 of 4.)

```
113          else {    // there were no cookies
114             out.println( "<h1>No Recommendations</h1>" );
115             out.println( "<p>You did not select a language.</p>" );
116          }
117
118          out.println( "</body>" );
119
120          // end XHTML document
121          out.println( "</html>" );
122          out.close();    // close stream
123       }
124  }
```

Fig. A.19   Storing user data on the client computer with cookies. (Part 4 of 4.)

Software Engineering Observation A.7

Browser users can disable cookies, so Web applications that use cookies may not function properly for clients with cookies disabled.

Software Engineering Observation A.8

*By default, cookies exist only for the current browsing session (until the user closes the browser). To make cookies persist beyond the current session, call **Cookie** method **set-MaxAge** to indicate the number of seconds until the cookie expires.*

Line 32 adds the cookie to the **response** with method **addCookie** of interface **HttpServletResponse**. Cookies are sent to the client as part of the HTTP header. The header information is always provided to the client first, so the cookies should be added to the **response** with **addCookie** before any data is written as part of the response. After the cookie is added, the servlet sends an XHTML document to the client (see the second screen capture of Fig. A.20).

Common Programming Error A.3

*Writing response data to the client before calling method **addCookie** to add a cookie to the response is a logic error. Cookies must be added to the header first.*

The XHTML document sent to the client in response to a **post** request includes a hyperlink that invokes method **doGet** (lines 73–123). The method reads any **Cookie**s that were written to the client in **doPost**. For each **Cookie** written, the servlet recommends a Deitel book on the subject. Up to four books are displayed on the Web page created by the servlet.

Line 77 retrieves the cookies from the client using **HttpServletRequest** method **getCookies**, which returns an array of **Cookie** objects. When a **get** or **post** operation is performed to invoke a servlet, the cookies associated with that server's domain are automatically sent to the servlet.

If method **getCookies** does not return **null** (i.e., there were no cookies), lines 106–109 retrieve the name of each **Cookie** using **Cookie** method **getName**, retrieve the value of each **Cookie** using **Cookie** method **getValue** and write a line to the client indicating the name of a recommended book and its ISBN number.

Software Engineering Observation A.9

*Normally, each servlet class handles one request type (e.g., **get** or **post**, but not both).*

Figure A.20 shows the XHTML document the user loads to select a language. When the user presses **Submit**, the value of the currently selected radio button is sent to the server as part of the **post** request to the **CookieServlet**, which we refer to as **cookies** in this example.

We use our **jws** context root to demonstrate the servlet of Fig. A.19. Place **Cookie-SelectLanguage.html** in the **servlets** directory created previously. Place **CookieServlet.class** in the **classes** subdirectory of **WEB-INF** in the **jws** context root. Then, edit the **web.xml** deployment descriptor in the **WEB-INF** directory to include the information specified in Fig. A.21. Restart Tomcat and type the following URL in your Web browser:

```
http://localhost:8080/jws/servlets/
CookieSelectLanguage.html
```

Select a language, and press the **Submit** button in the Web page to invoke the servlet.

```xml
1   <?xml version = "1.0"?>
2   <!DOCTYPE html PUBLIC "-//W3C//DTD XHTML 1.0 Strict//EN"
3      "http://www.w3.org/TR/xhtml11/DTD/xhtml11-strict.dtd">
4
5   <!-- Fig. A.20: CookieSelectLanguage.html -->
6
7   <html xmlns = "http://www.w3.org/1999/xhtml">
8   <head>
9      <title>Using Cookies</title>
10  </head>
11
12  <body>
13     <form action = "/jws/cookies" method = "post">
14
15        <p>Select a programming language:</p>
16        <p>
17           <input type = "radio" name = "language"
18              value = "C" />C <br />
19
20           <input type = "radio" name = "language"
21              value = "C++" />C++ <br />
22
23           <!-- this radio button checked by default -->
24           <input type = "radio" name = "language"
25              value = "Java" checked = "checked" />Java<br />
26
27           <input type = "radio" name = "language"
28              value = "VB6" />VB 6
29        </p>
30
31        <p><input type = "submit" value = "Submit" /></p>
32
33     </form>
```

Fig. A.20   **CookieSelectLanguage.html** document for selecting a programming language and posting the data to the **CookieServlet**. (Part 1 of 3.)

```
34    </body>
35    </html>
```

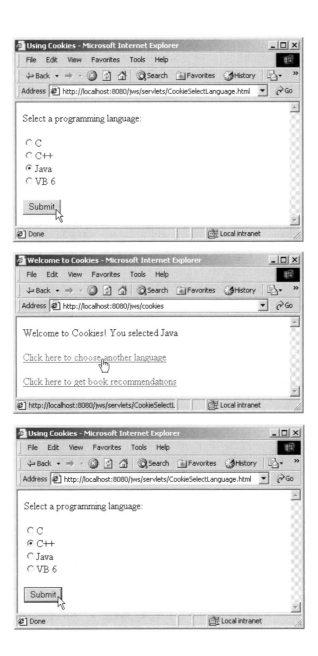

Fig. A.20 `CookieSelectLanguage.html` document for selecting a programming language and posting the data to the `CookieServlet`. (Part 2 of 3.)

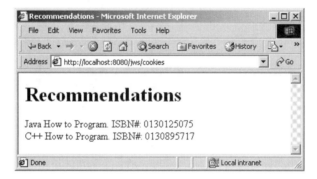

Fig. A.20 `CookieSelectLanguage.html` document for selecting a programming language and posting the data to the `CookieServlet`. (Part 3 of 3.)

Various **Cookie** methods are provided to manipulate the members of a **Cookie**. Some of these methods are listed in Fig. A.22.

Descriptor element	Value
servlet element	
servlet-name	cookies
description	Using cookies to maintain state information.
servlet-class	com.deitel.jws.servlets.CookieServlet
servlet-mapping element	
servlet-name	cookies
url-pattern	/cookies

Fig. A.21 Deployment descriptor information for servlet `CookieServlet`.

A.7.2 Session Tracking with `HttpSession`

Java provides enhanced session tracking support with the servlet API's *HttpSession* interface. To demonstrate basic session-tracking techniques, we modified the servlet from Fig. A.19 to use *HttpSession* objects (Fig. A.23). Once again, the servlet handles both **get** and **post** requests. The document **SessionSelectLanguage.html** of Fig. A.24 contains four radio buttons (**C**, **C++**, **Java** and **VB 6**) and a **Submit** button. When the user presses **Submit**, **SessionServlet** is invoked with a **post** request. The servlet responds by creating an object of type **HttpSession** for the client (or using an existing session for the client) and adds the selected language and an ISBN number for the recommended book to the **HttpSession** object. Then, the servlet sends an XHTML page to the client. Each time the user clicks **Submit**, a new language/ISBN pair is added to the **HttpSession** object.

Method	Description
`getComment()`	Returns a **String** describing the purpose of the cookie (**null** if no comment has been set with **setComment**).
`getDomain()`	Returns a **String** containing the cookie's domain. This determines which servers can receive the cookie. By default, cookies are sent to the server that originally sent the cookie to the client.
`getMaxAge()`	Returns an **int** representing the maximum age of the cookie in seconds.
`getName()`	Returns a **String** containing the name of the cookie as set by the constructor.
`getPath()`	Returns a **String** containing the URL prefix for the cookie. Cookies can be "targeted" to specific URLs that include directories on the Web server. By default, a cookie is returned to services operating in the same directory as the service that sent the cookie or a subdirectory of that directory.
`getSecure()`	Returns a **boolean** value indicating if the cookie should be transmitted using a secure protocol (**true**).
`getValue()`	Returns a **String** containing the value of the cookie as set with **setValue** or the constructor.
`getVersion()`	Returns an **int** containing the version of the cookie protocol used to create the cookie. A value of 0 (the default) indicates the original cookie protocol as defined by Netscape. A value of 1 indicates the current version, which is based on *Request for Comments (RFC) 2109*.
`setComment( String )`	The comment describing the purpose of the cookie that is presented by the browser to the user. (Some browsers allow the user to accept cookies on a per-cookie basis.)

Fig. A.22 Important methods of class **Cookie**. (Part 1 of 2.)

Method	Description
setDomain(String)	This determines which servers can receive the cookie. By default, cookies are sent to the server that originally sent the cookie to the client. The domain is specified in the form ".deitel.com", indicating that all servers ending with .deitel.com can receive this cookie.
setMaxAge(int)	Sets the maximum age of the cookie in seconds.
setPath(String)	Sets the "target" URL prefix indicating the directories on the server that lead to the services that can receive this cookie.
setSecure(boolean)	A true value indicates that the cookie should only be sent using a secure protocol.
setValue(String)	Sets the value of a cookie.
setVersion(int)	Sets the cookie protocol for this cookie.

Fig. A.22 Important methods of class **Cookie**. (Part 2 of 2.)

Software Engineering Observation A.10

*A servlet should not use instance variables to maintain client state information, because clients accessing that servlet in parallel might overwrite the shared instance variables. Servlets should maintain client state information in **HttpSession** objects.*

Most of class **SessionServlet** is identical to **CookieServlet** (Fig. A.19), so we concentrate on only the new features here. When the user selects a language from the document **SessionSelectLanguage.html** (Fig. A.24) and presses **Submit**, method **doPost** (lines 24–90) is invoked. Line 28 gets the user's **language** selection. Then, line 32 uses method *getSession* of interface **HttpServletRequest** to obtain the **HttpSession** object for the client. If the server has an existing **HttpSession** object for the client from a previous request, method **getSession** returns that **HttpSession** object. Otherwise, the **true** argument to method **getSession** indicates that the servlet should create a unique new **HttpSession** object for the client. A **false** argument would cause method **getSession** to return **null** if the **HttpSession** object for the client did not already exist. Using a **false** argument could help determine whether a client has logged into a Web application.

```
1   // Fig. A.23: SessionServlet.java
2   // Using HttpSession to maintain client state information.
3   package com.deitel.jws.servlets;
4
5   import javax.servlet.*;
6   import javax.servlet.http.*;
7   import java.io.*;
8   import java.util.*;
9
```

Fig. A.23 Maintaining state information with **HttpSession** objects. (Part 1 of 4.)

```
10   public class SessionServlet extends HttpServlet {
11      private final Map books = new HashMap();
12
13      // initialize Map books
14      public void init()
15      {
16         books.put( "C", "0130895725" );
17         books.put( "C++", "0130895717" );
18         books.put( "Java", "0130125075" );
19         books.put( "VB6", "0134569555" );
20      }
21
22      // receive language selection and create HttpSession object
23      // containing recommended book for the client
24      protected void doPost( HttpServletRequest request,
25         HttpServletResponse response )
26            throws ServletException, IOException
27      {
28         String language = request.getParameter( "language" );
29
30         // Get the user's session object.
31         // Create a session (true) if one does not exist.
32         HttpSession session = request.getSession( true );
33
34         // add a value for user's choice to session
35         session.setAttribute( language, books.get( language ) );
36
37         response.setContentType( "text/html" );
38         PrintWriter out = response.getWriter();
39
40         // send XHTML page to client
41
42         // start XHTML document
43         out.println( "<?xml version = \"1.0\"?>" );
44
45         out.println( "<!DOCTYPE html PUBLIC \"-//W3C//DTD " +
46            "XHTML 1.0 Strict//EN\" \"http://www.w3.org" +
47            "/TR/xhtml1/DTD/xhtml1-strict.dtd\">" );
48
49         out.println(
50            "<html xmlns = \"http://www.w3.org/1999/xhtml\">" );
51
52         // head section of document
53         out.println( "<head>" );
54         out.println( "<title>Welcome to Sessions</title>" );
55         out.println( "</head>" );
56
57         // body section of document
58         out.println( "<body>" );
59         out.println( "<p>Welcome to Sessions! You selected " +
60            language + ".</p>" );
61
```

Fig. A.23 Maintaining state information with `HttpSession` objects. (Part 2 of 4.)

```
62              // display information about the session
63              out.println( "<p>Your unique session ID is: " +
64                 session.getId() + "<br />" );
65
66              out.println(
67                 "This " + ( session.isNew() ? "is" : "is not" ) +
68                 " a new session<br />" );
69
70              out.println( "The session was created at: " +
71                 new Date( session.getCreationTime() ) + "<br />" );
72
73              out.println( "You last accessed the session at: " +
74                 new Date( session.getLastAccessedTime() ) + "<br />" );
75
76              out.println( "The maximum inactive interval is: " +
77                 session.getMaxInactiveInterval() + " seconds</p>" );
78
79              out.println( "<p><a href = " +
80                 "\"servlets/SessionSelectLanguage.html\">" +
81                 "Click here to choose another language</a></p>" );
82
83              out.println( "<p><a href = \"sessions\">" +
84                 "Click here to get book recommendations</a></p>" );
85              out.println( "</body>" );
86
87              // end XHTML document
88              out.println( "</html>" );
89              out.close();     // close stream
90           }
91
92        // read session attributes and create XHTML document
93        // containing recommended books
94        protected void doGet( HttpServletRequest request,
95           HttpServletResponse response )
96              throws ServletException, IOException
97        {
98           // Get the user's session object.
99           // Do not create a session (false) if one does not exist.
100          HttpSession session = request.getSession( false );
101
102          // get names of session object's values
103          Enumeration valueNames;
104
105          if ( session != null )
106             valueNames = session.getAttributeNames();
107          else
108             valueNames = null;
109
110          PrintWriter out = response.getWriter();
111          response.setContentType( "text/html" );
112
113          // start XHTML document
114          out.println( "<?xml version = \"1.0\"?>" );
```

Fig. A.23 Maintaining state information with **HttpSession** objects. (Part 3 of 4.)

```
115
116             out.println( "<!DOCTYPE html PUBLIC \"-//W3C//DTD " +
117                "XHTML 1.0 Strict//EN\" \"http://www.w3.org" +
118                "/TR/xhtml1/DTD/xhtml1-strict.dtd\">" );
119
120             out.println(
121                "<html xmlns = \"http://www.w3.org/1999/xhtml\">" );
122
123             // head section of document
124             out.println( "<head>" );
125             out.println( "<title>Recommendations</title>" );
126             out.println( "</head>" );
127
128             // body section of document
129             out.println( "<body>" );
130
131             if ( valueNames != null &&
132                  valueNames.hasMoreElements() ) {
133                out.println( "<h1>Recommendations</h1>" );
134                out.println( "<p>" );
135
136                String name, value;
137
138                // get value for each name in valueNames
139                while ( valueNames.hasMoreElements() ) {
140                   name = valueNames.nextElement().toString();
141                   value = session.getAttribute( name ).toString();
142
143                   out.println( name + " How to Program. " +
144                      "ISBN#: " + value + "<br />" );
145                }
146
147                out.println( "</p>" );
148             }
149             else {
150                out.println( "<h1>No Recommendations</h1>" );
151                out.println( "<p>You did not select a language.</p>" );
152             }
153
154             out.println( "</body>" );
155
156             // end XHTML document
157             out.println( "</html>" );
158             out.close();    // close stream
159      }
160 }
```

Fig. A.23 Maintaining state information with **HttpSession** objects. (Part 4 of 4.)

Like a cookie, an **HttpSession** object can store name/value pairs. In session terminology, these are called *attributes*, and they are placed into an **HttpSession** object with
method **setAttribute**. Line 35 uses **setAttribute** to put the language and the corresponding recommended book's ISBN number into the **HttpSession** object. One of
the primary benefits of using **HttpSession** objects rather than cookies is that **Http-**

Session objects can store any object (not just **String**s) as the value of an attribute. This allows Java programmers flexibility in determining the type of state information they wish to maintain for clients of their Web applications. If an attribute with a particular name already exists when **setAttribute** is called, the object associated with that attribute name is replaced.

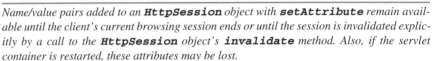

Software Engineering Observation A.11

*Name/value pairs added to an **HttpSession** object with **setAttribute** remain avail-able until the client's current browsing session ends or until the session is invalidated explic-itly by a call to the **HttpSession** object's **invalidate** method. Also, if the servlet container is restarted, these attributes may be lost.*

After the values are added to the **HttpSession** object, the servlet sends an XHTML document to the client (see the second screen capture of Fig. A.24). In this example, the document contains various information about the **HttpSession** object for the current client. Line 64 uses **HttpSession** method *getID* to obtain the session's unique ID number. Line 67 determines whether the session is new or already exists with method *isNew*, which returns **true** or **false**. Line 71 obtains the time at which the session was created with method *getCreationTime*. Line 74 obtains the time at which the session was last accessed with method *getLastAccessedTime*. Line 77 uses method *get-MaxInactiveInterval* to obtain the maximum amount of time that an **HttpSession** object can be inactive before the servlet container discards it.

The XHTML document sent to the client in response to a **post** request includes a hyperlink that invokes method **doGet** (lines 94–159). The method obtains the **HttpSession** object for the client with method **getSession** (line 100). We do not want to make any recommendations if the client does not have an existing **HttpSession** object. So, this call to **getSession** uses a **false** argument. Thus, **getSession** returns an **HttpSession** object only if one already exists for the client.

If method **getSession** does not return **null**, line 106 uses **HttpSession** method *getAttributeNames* to retrieve an **Enumeration** of the attribute names (i.e., the names used as the first argument to **HttpSession** method **setAttribute**). Each name is passed as an argument to **HttpSession** method *getAttribute* (line 141) to retrieve the ISBN of a book from the **HttpSession** object. Method **getAttribute** receives the name and returns an **Object** reference to the corresponding value. Next, a line is written in the response to the client containing the title and ISBN number of the rec-ommended book.

Figure A.24 shows the XHTML document the user loads to select a language. When the user presses **Submit**, the value of the currently selected radio button is sent to the server as part of the **post** request to the **SessionServlet**, which we refer to as **ses-sions** in this example.

```
1    <?xml version = "1.0"?>
2    <!DOCTYPE html PUBLIC "-//W3C//DTD XHTML 1.0 Strict//EN"
3        "http://www.w3.org/TR/xhtml1/DTD/xhtml1-strict.dtd">
```

Fig. A.24 **SessionSelectLanguage.html** document for selecting a programming language and posting the data to the **SessionServlet**. (Part 1 of 4.)

```
4
5   <!-- Fig. A.24: SessionSelectLanguage.html -->
6
7   <html xmlns = "http://www.w3.org/1999/xhtml">
8   <head>
9      <title>Using Sessions</title>
10  </head>
11
12  <body>
13     <form action = "/jws/sessions" method = "post">
14
15        <p>Select a programming language:</p>
16        <p>
17           <input type = "radio" name = "language"
18              value = "C" />C <br />
19
20           <input type = "radio" name = "language"
21              value = "C++" />C++ <br />
22
23           <!-- this radio button checked by default -->
24           <input type = "radio" name = "language"
25              value = "Java" checked = "checked" />Java<br />
26
27           <input type = "radio" name = "language"
28              value = "VB6" />VB 6
29        </p>
30
31        <p><input type = "submit" value = "Submit" /></p>
32
33     </form>
34  </body>
35  </html>
```

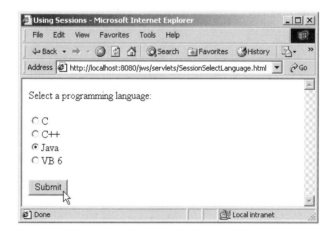

Fig. A.24 **SessionSelectLanguage.html** document for selecting a
programming language and posting the data to the **SessionServlet**.
(Part 2 of 4.)

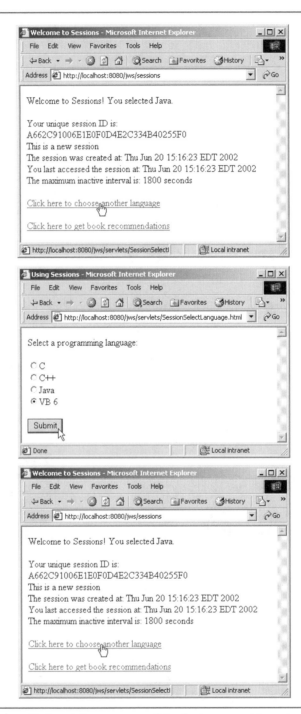

Fig. A.24 **SessionSelectLanguage.html** document for selecting a programming language and posting the data to the **SessionServlet**. (Part 3 of 4.)

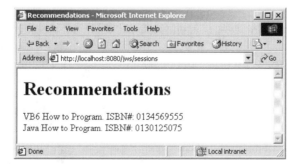

Fig. A.24 `SessionSelectLanguage.html` document for selecting a programming language and posting the data to the `SessionServlet`. (Part 4 of 4.)

We use our **jws** context root to demonstrate the servlet of Fig. A.23. Place **SessionSelectLanguage.html** in the **servlets** directory created previously. Place **SessionServlet.class** in the **classes** subdirectory of **WEB-INF** in the **jws** context root. Then, edit the **web.xml** deployment descriptor in the **WEB-INF** directory to include the information specified in Fig. A.25. Restart Tomcat and type the following URL in your Web browser:

```
http://localhost:8080/jws/servlets/
SessionSelectLanguage.html
```

Select a language, and press the **Submit** button in the Web page to invoke the servlet.

A.8 Multi-Tier Applications: Using JDBC from a Servlet

Servlets can communicate with databases via JDBC (Java Database Connectivity). JDBC provides a uniform way for a Java program to connect with a variety of databases in a general manner without having to deal with the specifics of those database systems.

Many of today's applications are *three-tier distributed applications*, consisting of a *user interface*, *business logic* and *database access*. The user interface in such an application is often created using HTML, XHTML (as shown in this appendix) or Dynamic HTML. In some cases, Java applets are also used for this tier. HTML and XHTML are the preferred mechanisms for representing the user interface in systems where portability is a concern. Because HTML is supported by all browsers, designing the user interface to be accessed through a Web browser guarantees portability across all platforms that have browsers. Using the networking provided automatically by the browser, the user interface can communicate with the middle-tier business logic. The middle tier can then access the database to manipulate the data. The three tiers can reside on separate computers that are connected to a network.

In multi-tier architectures, Web servers often represent the middle tier. They provide the business logic that manipulates data from databases and that communicates with client Web browsers. Servlets, through JDBC, can interact with popular database systems. Developers do not need to be familiar with the specifics of each database system. Rather, developers use SQL-based queries and the JDBC driver handles the specifics of interacting with each database system.

The **SurveyServlet** of Fig. A.26 and the **Survey.html** document of Fig. A.27 demonstrate a three-tier distributed application that displays the user interface in a browser using XHTML. The middle tier is a Java servlet that handles requests from the client browser and provides access to the third tier—a Cloudscape database accessed via JDBC. The servlet in this example is a survey servlet that allows users to vote for their favorite animal. When the servlet receives a **post** request from the **Survey.html** document, the servlet updates the total number of votes for that animal in the database and returns a dynamically generated XHTML document containing the survey results to the client.

Descriptor element	Value
servlet *element*	
servlet-name	**sessions**

Fig. A.25 Deployment descriptor information for servlet **WelcomeServlet2**. (Part 1 of 2.)

Descriptor element	Value
description	Using sessions to maintain state information.
servlet-class	com.deitel.jws.servlets.SessionServlet
servlet-mapping element	
servlet-name	sessions
url-pattern	/sessions

Fig. A.25 Deployment descriptor information for servlet `WelcomeServlet2`. (Part 2 of 2.)

Lines 12 and 13 begin by declaring a **Connection** reference to manage the database connection and three **PreparedStatement** references for updating the vote count for an animal, totalling all the votes and obtaining the complete survey results.

```
1   // Fig. A.26: SurveyServlet.java
2   // A Web-based survey that uses JDBC from a servlet.
3   package com.deitel.jws.servlets;
4
5   import java.io.*;
6   import java.text.*;
7   import java.sql.*;
8   import javax.servlet.*;
9   import javax.servlet.http.*;
10
11  public class SurveyServlet extends HttpServlet {
12     private Connection connection;
13     private PreparedStatement updateVotes, totalVotes, results;
14
15     // set up database connection and prepare SQL statements
16     public void init( ServletConfig config )
17        throws ServletException
18     {
19        // attempt database connection and create PreparedStatements
20        try {
21           Class.forName( "COM.cloudscape.core.RmiJdbcDriver" );
22           connection = DriverManager.getConnection(
23              "jdbc:rmi:jdbc:cloudscape:animalsurvey" );
24
25           // PreparedStatement to add one to vote total for a
26           // specific animal
27           updateVotes =
28              connection.prepareStatement(
29                 "UPDATE surveyresults SET votes = votes + 1 " +
30                 "WHERE id = ?"
31              );
32
```

Fig. A.26 Multi-tier Web-based survey using XHTML, servlets and JDBC. (Part 1 of 4.)

```
33              // PreparedStatement to sum the votes
34              totalVotes =
35                 connection.prepareStatement(
36                    "SELECT sum( votes ) FROM surveyresults"
37                 );
38
39              // PreparedStatement to obtain surveyoption table's data
40              results =
41                 connection.prepareStatement(
42                    "SELECT surveyoption, votes, id " +
43                    "FROM surveyresults ORDER BY id"
44                 );
45           }
46
47           // for any exception throw an UnavailableException to
48           // indicate that the servlet is not currently available
49           catch ( Exception exception ) {
50              exception.printStackTrace();
51              throw new UnavailableException(exception.getMessage());
52           }
53
54     }  // end of init method
55
56     // process survey response
57     protected void doPost( HttpServletRequest request,
58        HttpServletResponse response )
59           throws ServletException, IOException
60     {
61        // set up response to client
62        response.setContentType( "text/html" );
63        PrintWriter out = response.getWriter();
64        DecimalFormat twoDigits = new DecimalFormat( "0.00" );
65
66        // start XHTML document
67        out.println( "<?xml version = \"1.0\"?>" );
68
69        out.println( "<!DOCTYPE html PUBLIC \"-//W3C//DTD " +
70           "XHTML 1.0 Strict//EN\" \"http://www.w3.org" +
71           "/TR/xhtml1/DTD/xhtml1-strict.dtd\">" );
72
73        out.println(
74           "<html xmlns = \"http://www.w3.org/1999/xhtml\">" );
75
76        // head section of document
77        out.println( "<head>" );
78
79        // read current survey response
80        int value =
81           Integer.parseInt( request.getParameter( "animal" ) );
82
83        // attempt to process a vote and display current results
84        try {
85
```

Fig. A.26 Multi-tier Web-based survey using XHTML, servlets and JDBC. (Part 2 of 4.)

```
86              // update total for current surevy response
87              updateVotes.setInt( 1, value );
88              updateVotes.executeUpdate();
89
90              // get total of all survey responses
91              ResultSet totalRS = totalVotes.executeQuery();
92              totalRS.next();
93              int total = totalRS.getInt( 1 );
94
95              // get results
96              ResultSet resultsRS = results.executeQuery();
97              out.println( "<title>Thank you!</title>" );
98              out.println( "</head>" );
99
100             out.println( "<body>" );
101             out.println( "<p>Thank you for participating." );
102             out.println( "<br />Results:</p><pre>" );
103
104             // process results
105             int votes;
106
107             while ( resultsRS.next() ) {
108                out.print( resultsRS.getString( 1 ) );
109                out.print( ": " );
110                votes = resultsRS.getInt( 2 );
111                out.print( twoDigits.format(
112                   ( double ) votes / total * 100 ) );
113                out.print( "%  responses: " );
114                out.println( votes );
115             }
116
117             resultsRS.close();
118
119             out.print( "Total responses: " );
120             out.print( total );
121
122             // end XHTML document
123             out.println( "</pre></body></html>" );
124             out.close();
125          }
126
127       // if database exception occurs, return error page
128       catch ( SQLException sqlException ) {
129          sqlException.printStackTrace();
130          out.println( "<title>Error</title>" );
131          out.println( "</head>" );
132          out.println( "<body><p>Database error occurred. " );
133          out.println( "Try again later.</p></body></html>" );
134          out.close();
135       }
136
137    }  // end of doPost method
138
```

Fig. A.26 Multi-tier Web-based survey using XHTML, servlets and JDBC. (Part 3 of 4.)

```
139     // close SQL statements and database when servlet terminates
140     public void destroy()
141     {
142        // attempt to close statements and database connection
143        try {
144           updateVotes.close();
145           totalVotes.close();
146           results.close();
147           connection.close();
148        }
149
150        // handle database exceptions by returning error to client
151        catch( SQLException sqlException ) {
152           sqlException.printStackTrace();
153        }
154     }  // end of destroy method
155  }
```

Fig. A.26   Multi-tier Web-based survey using XHTML, servlets and JDBC. (Part 4 of 4.)

Servlets are initialized by overriding method **init** (lines 16–54). Method **init** is called exactly once in a servlet's lifetime, before any client requests are accepted. Method **init** takes a **ServletConfig** argument and throws a **ServletException**. The argument provides the servlet with information about its *initialization parameters* (i.e., parameters not associated with a request, but passed to the servlet for initializing servlet variables). These parameters are specified in the **web.xml** deployment descriptor file as part of a **servlet** element. Each parameter appears in an **init-param** element of the following form:

```
<init-param>
   <param-name>parameter name goes here</param-name>
   <param-value>parameter value goes here</param-value>
</init-param>
```

Servlets can obtain initialization parameter values by invoking **ServletConfig** method **getInitParameter**, which receives a string representing the name of the parameter.

In this example, the servlet's **init** method (lines 16–54) performs the connection to the Cloudscape database. Line 21 loads the driver (**COM.cloudscape.core.Rmi-JdbcDriver**). Lines 22–23 attempt to open a connection to the **animalsurvey** database. The database contains one table (**surveyresults**) that consists of three fields—a unique integer to identify each record called **id**, a string representing the survey option called **surveyoption** and an integer representing the number of votes for a survey option called **votes**. [*Note*: The examples folder for this appendix contains an SQL script (**animalsurvey.sql**) that you can use to create the **animalsurvey** database for this example. For information on starting the Cloudscape server and executing the SQL script, please refer back to Chapter 1.]

Lines 27–44 create **PreparedStatement** objects called **updateVotes**, **totalVotes** and **results**. The **updateVotes** statement adds one to the **votes** value for the record with the specified ID. The **totalVotes** statement uses SQL's built-in *sum* capability to total all the **votes** in the **surveyresults** table. The results statement returns all the data in the **surveyresults** table.

When a user submits a survey response, method **doPost** (lines 57–137) handles the request. Lines 80–81 obtain the survey response, then the **try** block (lines 84–125) attempts to process the response. Lines 87–88 set the first parameter of **Prepared-Statement updateVotes** to the survey response and update the database. Lines 91–93 execute **PreparedStatement totalVotes** to retrieve the total number of votes received. Then, lines 96–123 execute **PreparedStatement results** and process the **ResultSet** to create the survey summary for the client. When the servlet container terminates the servlet, method *destroy* (lines 140–154) closes each **Prepared-Statement**, then closes the database connection. Figure A.27 shoes survey.html, which invokes **SurveyServlet** with the alias **animalsurvey** when the user submits the form.

We use our **jws** context root to demonstrate the servlet of Fig. A.26. Place **Survey.html** in the **servlets** directory created previously. Place **SurveyServlet.class** in the **classes** subdirectory of **WEB-INF** in the **jws** context root. Then, edit the **web.xml** deployment descriptor in the **WEB-INF** directory to include the information specified in Fig. A.28. Also, this program cannot execute in Tomcat unless the Web application is aware of the JAR files **cloudscape.jar** and **RmiJdbc.jar** that contain the Cloudscape database driver and its supporting classes. The **cloudscape.jar** file is located in your Cloudscape installation's **lib** directory. The **RmiJdbc.jar** file is located in your Cloudscape installation's **frameworks\RmiJdbc\classes** directory. Place *copies* of these files in the **WEB-INF** subdirectory **lib** to make them available to the Web application. Please refer to Chapter 1 for more information on the setup and configuration of Cloudscape.

A copy of these files should be placed in the **jws** context root's **WEB-INF** subdirectory called **lib**. After copying these files, restart Tomcat and type the following URL in your Web browser:

http://localhost:8080/jws/servlets/Survey.html

Select a survey response, and press the **Submit** button in the Web page to invoke the servlet.

```
1    <?xml version = "1.0"?>
2    <!DOCTYPE html PUBLIC "-//W3C//DTD XHTML 1.0 Strict//EN"
3       "http://www.w3.org/TR/xhtml1/DTD/xhtml1-strict.dtd">
4
5    <!-- Fig. A.27: Survey.html -->
6
7    <html xmlns = "http://www.w3.org/1999/xhtml">
8    <head>
9       <title>Survey</title>
10   </head>
11
12   <body>
13   <form method = "post" action = "/jws/animalsurvey">
14
15      <p>What is your favorite pet?</p>
16
```

Fig. A.27 Survey.html document that allows users to submit survey responses to **SurveyServlet**. (Part 1 of 2.)

```
17          <p>
18             <input type = "radio" name = "animal"
19                value = "1" />Dog<br />
20             <input type = "radio" name = "animal"
21                value = "2" />Cat<br />
22             <input type = "radio" name = "animal"
23                value = "3" />Bird<br />
24             <input type = "radio" name = "animal"
25                value = "4" />Snake<br />
26             <input type = "radio" name = "animal"
27                value = "5" checked = "checked" />None
28          </p>
29
30          <p><input type = "submit" value = "Submit" /></p>
31
32      </form>
33      </body>
34      </html>
```

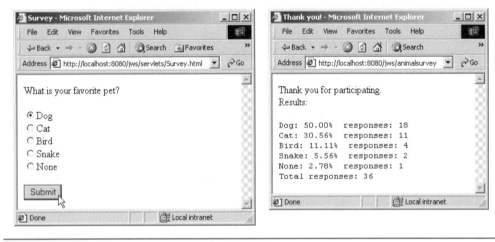

Fig. A.27 **Survey.html** document that allows users to submit survey responses to **SurveyServlet**. (Part 2 of 2.)

Descriptor element	Value
servlet element	
servlet-name	animalsurvey
description	Connecting to a database from a servlet.
servlet-class	com.deitel.jws.servlets.SurveyServlet
servlet-mapping element	

Fig. A.28 Deployment descriptor information for servlet **SurveyServlet**. (Part 1 of 2.)

Descriptor element	Value
servlet-name	animalsurvey
url-pattern	/animalsurvey

Fig. A.28 Deployment descriptor information for servlet **SurveyServlet**. (Part 2 of 2.)

A.9 **HttpUtils** Class

Class **HttpUtils** provides three **static** utility methods to simplify servlet programming. These methods are discussed in Fig. A.29.

A.10 Summary

The classes and interfaces used to define servlets are found in packages **javax.servlet** and **javax.servlet.http**. The Internet offers many protocols. The HTTP protocol (Hypertext Transfer Protocol) that forms the basis of the World Wide Web uses URIs (Uniform Resource Identifiers) to locate resources on the Internet. Common URLs represent files or directories and can represent complex tasks such as database lookups and Internet searches.

JavaServer Pages technology is an extension of servlet technology. Servlets are normally executed as part of a Web server (also known as the servlet container). Servlets and JavaServer Pages have become so popular that they are now supported by most major Web servers and application servers. All servlets must implement the **Servlet** interface. The methods of interface **Servlet** are invoked automatically by the servlet container.

Method	Description
getRequestURL	This method takes the **HttpServletRequest** object as an argument and returns a **StringBuffer** containing the original URL that initiated the request.
parsePostData	This method receives an integer and **ServletInputStream** as arguments. The integer represents the number of bytes in the **ServletInputStream**. The **ServletInputStream** contains the key/value pairs **post**ed to the servlet from a **form**. The method returns a **Hashtable** containing the key/value pairs.
parseQueryString	This method receives a **String** representing the query string in a **get** request as an argument and returns a **Hashtable** containing the key/value pairs in the query string. The value of each key is an array of **String**s. The query string can be obtained with **HttpServletRequest** method **getQueryString**.

Fig. A.29 **HttpUtils** class methods.

A servlet's life cycle begins when the servlet container loads the servlet into memory—normally in response to the first request to that servlet. Before the servlet can handle the first request, the servlet container invokes the servlet's **init** method. After **init** completes execution, the servlet can respond to its first request. All requests are handled by a servlet's **service** method, which may be called many times during the life cycle of a servlet. When the servlet container terminates the servlet, the servlet's **destroy** method is called to release servlet resources.

The servlet packages define two **abstract** classes that implement the interface **Servlet**—class **GenericServlet** and class **HttpServlet**. Most servlets extend one of these classes and override some or all of their methods with appropriate customized behaviors.

The key method in every servlet is method **service**, which receives both a **ServletRequest** object and a **ServletResponse** object. These objects provide access to input and output streams that allow the servlet to read data from the client and send data to the client.

Web-based servlets typically extend class **HttpServlet**. Class **HttpServlet** overrides method **service** to distinguish between the typical requests received from a client Web browser. The two most common HTTP request types (also known as request methods) are **get** and **post**.

Class **HttpServlet** defines methods **doGet** and **doPost** to respond to **get** and **post** requests from a client, respectively. These methods are called by the **HttpServlet** class's **service** method, which is called when a request arrives at the server.

Methods **doGet** and **doPost** receive as arguments an **HttpServletRequest** object and an **HttpServletResponse** object that enable interaction between the client and the server. A response is sent to the client through a **PrintWriter** object returned by the **getWriter** method of the **HttpServletResponse** object. The **HttpServletResponse** object's **setContentType** method specifies the MIME type of the response to the client. This enables the client browser to understand and handle the content.

The server **localhost** (IP address **127.0.0.1**) is a well-known server host name on most computers that support TCP/IP-based networking protocols such as HTTP. This host name can be used to test TCP/IP applications on the local computer. The Tomcat server awaits requests from clients on port 8080. This port number must be specified as part of the URL to request a servlet running in Tomcat.

The client can access a servlet only if that servlet is installed on a server that can respond to servlet requests. Web servers that support servlets normally have an installation procedure for servlets. Tomcat is a fully functional implementation of the JSP and servlet standards. It includes a Web server, so it can be used as a stand-alone test container for JSPs and servlets. Tomcat can be specified as the handler for JSP and servlet requests received by popular Web servers such as Apache and IIS. Tomcat also is integrated into the Java 2 Enterprise Edition reference implementation from Sun Microsystems.

JSPs, servlets and their supporting files are deployed as part of Web applications. In Tomcat, Web applications are deployed in the **webapps** subdirectory of the Tomcat installation. A Web application has a well-known directory structure in which all the files that are part of the application reside. This directory structure can be set up by the Tomcat server administrator in the **webapps** directory, or the entire directory structure can be archived in a Web application archive file. Such an archive is known as a WAR file and ends with the **.war** file extension. If a WAR file is placed in the **webapps** directory, when the Tomcat server starts up it extracts the contents of the WAR file into the appropriate **webapps** subdirectory structure.

The Web application directory structure is separated into a context root—the top-level directory for an entire Web application—and several subdirectories. The context root is the root directory for the Web application. All the JSPs, HTML documents, servlets and supporting files such as images and class files reside in this directory or its subdirectories. The **WEB-INF** directory contains the Web application deployment descriptor (**web.xml**). The **WEB-INF/classes** directory contains the servlet class files and other supporting class files used in a Web application. The **WEB-INF/lib** directory contains Java archive (JAR) files that may include servlet class files and other supporting class files used in a Web application.

Before deploying a Web application, the servlet container must be made aware of the context root for the Web application. In Tomcat, this can be done simply by placing a directory in the **webapps** subdirectory. Tomcat uses the directory name as the context name. Deploying a Web application requires the creation of a deployment descriptor (**web.xml**).

HTTP **get** requests can be typed directly into your browser's **Address** or **Location** field. Parameters are passed as name/value pairs in a **get** request. A **?** separates the URL from the data passed as part of a **get** request. Name/value pairs are passed with the name and the value separated by **=**. If there is more than one name/value pair, each name/value pair is separated by **&**. Method **getParameter** of interface **HttpServletRequest** receives the parameter name as an argument and returns the corresponding **String** value, or **null** if the parameter is not part of the request.

An HTTP **post** request is often used to post data from an Web-page form to a server-side form handler that processes the data. Browsers often cache (save on disk) Web pages so they can quickly reload the pages. Browsers do not cache the server's response to a **post** request. Method **doPost** receives the same two arguments as **doGet**—an object that implements interface **HttpServletRequest** to represent the client's request and an object that implements interface **HttpServletResponse** to represent the servlet's response.

Method **sendRedirect** of **HttpServletResponse** redirects a request to the specified URL. When a servlet uses a relative path to reference another static or dynamic resource, the servlet assumes the same context root unless a complete URL is specified for the resource. Once method **sendRedirect** executes, processing of the request by the servlet that called **sendRedirect** terminates. When redirecting requests, the request parameters from the original request are passed as parameters to the new request. Additional request parameters also can be passed.

New parameters are added to the existing request parameters. If a new parameter has the same name as an existing parameter, the new parameter value takes precedence over the original value. However, all the values are still passed. The complete set of values for a given request-parameter name can be obtained by calling method **getParameter-Values** from interface **HttpServletRequest**, which receives the parameter name as an argument and returns an array of **String**s containing the parameter values in order from the most recently added value for that parameter to the least recently added.

Many Web sites today provide custom Web pages and/or functionality on a client-by-client basis. HTTP is a stateless protocol—it does not support persistent information that could help a Web server determine that a request is from a particular client. Cookies can store information on the user's computer for retrieval later in the same or in future browsing sessions. Cookies are text-based data that are sent by servlets (or other similar technologies) as part of responses to clients.

Every HTTP-based interaction between a client and a server includes a header containing information about the request (when the communication is from the client to the server) or information about the response (when the communication is from the server to the client). When the server receives a request, the header includes information such as the request type (e.g., **get** or **post**) and the cookies stored on the client machine by the server.

When the server formulates its response, the header information includes any cookies the server wants to store on the client computer and other information such as the MIME type of the response. Depending on the maximum age of a cookie, the Web browser either maintains the cookie for the duration of the browsing session or stores the cookie on the client computer for future use. When the browser requests a resource from a server, cookies previously sent to the client by that server are returned to the server as part of the request formulated by the browser. Cookies are deleted automatically when they expire.

By default, cookies only exist for the current browsing session (until the user closes the browser). To make cookies persist beyond the current session, call **Cookie** method **setMaxAge** to indicate the number of seconds until the cookie expires. Method **addCookie** of interface **HttpServletResponse** adds a cookie to the response. Cookies are sent to the client as part of the HTTP header. The header information is always provided to the client first, so the cookies should be added before the response is output.

HttpServletRequest method **getCookies** returns an array of **Cookie** objects. Method **getCookies** returns **null** if there are no cookies in the request.

Cookie method **getName** retrieves the name of a cookie. **Cookie** method **getValue** retrieves the value of a cookie.

An alternative approach to cookies is to track a session with **HttpSession**s, which eliminate the problems associated with clients disabling cookies in their browsers by making the session-tracking mechanism transparent to the programmer.

Method **getSession** of interface **HttpServletRequest** obtains an **HttpSession** object for the client. Like a cookie, an **HttpSession** object can store name/value pairs. In sessions, these are called attributes, and they are stored with **setAttribute** and retrieved with **getAttribute**. Name/value pairs added to an **HttpSession** object with **setAttribute** remain available until the client's current browsing session ends or until the session is explicitly invalidated by a call to the **HttpSession** object's **invalidate** method. **HttpSession** method **getID** obtains the session's unique ID number. **HttpSession** method **isNew** determines whether a session is new or already exists. Method **getCreationTime** obtains the time at which the session was created. **HttpSession** method **getLastAccessedTime** obtains the time at which the session was last accessed. **HttpSession** method **getMaxInactiveInterval** obtains the maximum amount of time that an **HttpSession** object can be inactive before the servlet container discards it.

Many of today's applications are three-tier distributed applications, consisting of a user interface, business logic and database access. In multi-tier architectures, Web servers often represent the middle tier. They provide the business logic that manipulates data from databases and that communicates with client Web browsers.

Servlet method **init** takes a **ServletConfig** argument and throws a **ServletException**. The argument provides the servlet with information about its initialization parameters that are specified in a **servlet** element in the deployment descriptor. Each parameter appears in an **init-param** element with child elements **param-name** and **param-value**.

A.11 Internet and World Wide Web Resources

This section lists a variety of servlet resources available on the Internet and provides a brief description of each.

java.sun.com/products/servlet/index.html
The servlet page at the Sun Microsystems, Inc., Java Web site provides access to the latest servlet information and servlet resources.

jakarta.apache.org
This is the Apache Project's home page for the *Jakarta Project. Tomcat*—the servlets and JavaServer Pages reference implementation— is one of many subprojects of the Jakarta Project.

jakarta.apache.org/tomcat/index.html
Home page for the Tomcat servlets and JavaServer Pages reference implementation.

java.apache.org
This is the Apache Project's home page for all Java-related technologies. This site provides access to many Java packages useful to servlet and JSP developers.

www.servlets.com
This is the Web site for the book *Java Servlet Programming* published by O'Reilly. The book provides a variety of resources. This book is an excellent resource for programmers who are learning servlets.

theserverside.com
TheServerSide.com is dedicated to information and resources for Enterprise Java.

www.servletsource.com
ServletSource.com is a general servlet resource site containing code, tips, tutorials and links to many other Web sites with information on servlets.

www.cookiecentral.com
A good all-around resource site for cookies.

developer.netscape.com/docs/manuals/communicator/jsguide4/cookies.htm
A description of Netscape cookies.

www.javacorporate.com
Home of the open-source *Expresso Framework*, which includes a library of extensible servlet components to help speed Web application development.

www.servlet.com/srvdev.jhtml
ServletInc's Servlet Developers Forum provides resources for server-side Java developers and information about Web servers that support servlet technologies.

www.servletforum.com
ServletForum.com is a newsgroup where you can post questions and have them answered by your peers.

www.coolservlets.com
Provides free open-source Java servlets.

www.cetus-links.org/oo_java_servlets.html
Provides a list of links to resources on servlets and other technologies.

www.javaskyline.com
Java Skyline is an online magazine for servlet developers.

www.rfc-editor.org
The RFC Editor provides a search engine for RFCs (Request for Comments). Many of these RFCs provide details of Web-related technologies. RFCs of interest to servlet developers include *URIs* (RFC 1630), *URLs* (RFC 1738)URL, *Relative URLs* (RFC 1808), *HTTP/1.0* (RFC 1945), *MIME* (RFCs 2045–2049), *HTTP State Management Mechanism* (RFC 2109), *Use and Interpretation of HTTP Version Numbers* (RFC 2145), *Hypertext Coffee Pot Control Protocol* (RFC 2324), HTTP/1.1 (RFC 2616) and *HTTP Authentication: Basic and Digest Authentication* (RFC 2617).

www.irvine.com/~mime
The *Multipurpose Internet Mail Extensions FAQ* provides information on MIME and a list of many registered MIME types, as well as links to other MIME resources.

JavaServer Pages (JSP)

Objectives

- To be able to create and deploy JavaServer Pages.
- To use JSP's implicit objects and Java to create dynamic Web pages.
- To specify global JSP information with directives.
- To use actions to manipulate JavaBeans in a JSP, to include resources dynamically and to forward requests to other JSPs.
- To create custom tag libraries that encapsulate complex functionality in new tags that can be reused by JSP programmers and Web-page designers.

A tomato does not communicate with a tomato, we believe. We could be wrong.
Gustav Eckstein

A donkey appears to me like a horse translated into Dutch.
Georg Christoph Licthtenberg

Talent is a question of quantity. Talent does not write one page: it writes three hundred.
Jules Renard

Every action must be due to one or other of seven causes: chance, nature, compulsion, habit, reasoning, anger, or appetite.
Aristotle

Outline

B.1 Introduction

Our discussion of fundamental Web technologies continues in this appendix with *JavaServer Pages (JSP)*—an extension of servlet technology. JavaServer Pages simplify the delivery of dynamic Web content. They enable Web application programmers to create dynamic content by reusing predefined components and by interacting with components using server-side scripting. JavaServer Page programmers can reuse JavaBeans and create custom tag libraries that encapsulate complex, dynamic functionality. Custom-tag libraries even enable Web-page designers who are not familiar with Java to enhance Web pages with powerful dynamic content and processing capabilities.

In addition to the classes and interfaces for programming servlets (from packages **javax.servlet** and **javax.servlet.http**), classes and interfaces specific to JavaServer Pages programming are located in packages **javax.servlet.jsp** and **javax.servlet.jsp.tagext**. We discuss many of these classes and interfaces throughout this appendix as we present JavaServer Pages fundamentals. For a complete description of JavaServer Pages, see the JavaServer Pages 1.1 specification, which can be downloaded from **java.sun.com/products/jsp/download.html**. We also include other JSP resources in Section B.10. [*Note:* The source code and images for all the examples in this appendix can be found on our Web site **www.deitel.com.**]

B.2 JavaServer Pages Overview

There are four key components to JSPs: *directives*, *actions*, *scriptlets* and *tag libraries*. Directives are messages to the JSP container that enable the programmer to specify page settings, to include content from other resources and to specify custom tag libraries for use in a JSP. Actions encapsulate functionality in predefined tags that programmers can embed in a JSP. Actions often are performed based on the information sent to the server as part of a particular client request. They also can create Java objects for use in JSP scriptlets. Scriptlets, or *scripting elements*, enable programmers to insert Java code that interacts with components in a JSP (and possibly other Web application components) to perform request processing. Tag libraries are part of the *tag extension mechanism* that enables programmers to create custom tags. Such tags enable programmers to manipulate JSP content. These JSP component types are discussed in detail in subsequent sections.

In many ways, Java Server Pages look like standard XHTML or XML documents. In fact, JSPs normally include XHTML or XML markup. Such markup is known as *fixed-template data* or *fixed-template text*. Fixed-template data often help a programmer decide whether to use a servlet or a JSP. Programmers tend to use JSPs when most of the content sent to the client is fixed template data and only a small portion of the content is generated dynamically with Java code. Programmers use servlets when only a small portion of the content sent to the client is fixed-template data. In fact, some servlets do not produce content. Rather, they perform a task on behalf of the client, then invoke other servlets or JSPs to provide a response. Note that in most cases, servlet and JSP technologies are interchangeable. As with servlets, JSPs normally execute as part of a Web server. The server often is referred to as the *JSP container*.

Software Engineering Observation B.1

Literal text in a JSP becomes string literals in the servlet that represents the translated JSP.

When a JSP-enabled server receives the first request for a JSP, the JSP container translates that JSP into a Java servlet that handles the current request and future requests to the JSP. If there are any errors compiling the new servlet, these errors result in *translation-time errors*. The JSP container places the Java statements that implement the JSP's response in method **_jspService** at translation time. If the new servlet compiles properly, the JSP container invokes method **_jspService** to process the request. The JSP may respond directly to the request or may invoke other Web application components to assist in processing the request. Any errors that occur during request processing are known as *request-time errors*.

Performance Tip B.1

Some JSP containers translate JSPs to servlets at installation time. This eliminates the translation overhead for the first client that requests each JSP.

Overall, the request/response mechanism and life cycle of a JSP is the same as that of a servlet. JSPs can define methods **jspInit** and **jspDestroy** (similar to servlet methods **init** and **destroy**), which the JSP container invokes when initializing a JSP and terminating a JSP, respectively. JSP programmers can define these methods using JSP *declarations*—part of the JSP scripting mechanism.

B.3 A First JavaServer Page Example

We begin our introduction to JavaServer Pages with a simple example (Fig. B.1) in which the current date and time are inserted into a Web page using a JSP expression.

As you can see, most of **clock.jsp** consists of XHTML markup. In cases like this, JSPs are easier to implement than servlets. In a servlet that performs the same task as this JSP, each line of XHTML markup typically is a separate Java statement that outputs the string representing the markup as part of the response to the client. Writing code to output markup can often lead to errors. Most JSP editors provide syntax coloring to help programmers check that their markup follows proper syntax.

```
1   <?xml version = "1.0"?>
2   <!DOCTYPE html PUBLIC "-//W3C//DTD XHTML 1.0 Strict//EN"
3      "http://www.w3.org/TR/xhtml1/DTD/xhtml1-strict.dtd">
4
5   <!-- Fig. B.1: clock.jsp -->
6
7   <html xmlns = "http://www.w3.org/1999/xhtml">
8
9      <head>
10         <meta http-equiv = "refresh" content = "60" />
11
12         <title>A Simple JSP Example</title>
13
14         <style type = "text/css">
15            .big { font-family: helvetica, arial, sans-serif;
16                   font-weight: bold;
17                   font-size: 2em; }
18         </style>
19      </head>
20
21      <body>
22         <p class = "big">Simple JSP Example</p>
23
24         <table style = "border: 6px outset;">
25            <tr>
26               <td style = "background-color: black;">
27                  <p class = "big" style = "color: cyan;">
28
29                     <!-- JSP expression to insert date/time -->
30                     <%= new java.util.Date() %>
31
32                  </p>
33               </td>
34            </tr>
35         </table>
36      </body>
```

Fig. B.1   Using a JSP expression to insert the date and time in a Web page.
(Part 1 of 2.)

```
37
38    </html>
```

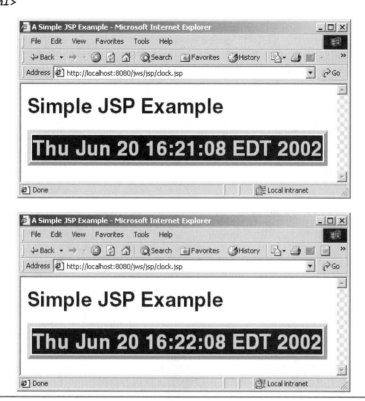

Fig. B.1   Using a JSP expression to insert the date and time in a Web page. (Part 2 of 2.)

 Software Engineering Observation B.2

JavaServer Pages are easier to implement than servlets when the response to a client request consists primarily of markup that remains constant between requests.

The JSP of Fig. B.1 generates an XHTML document that displays the current date and time. The key line in this JSP (line 30) is the expression

```
<%= new java.util.Date() %>
```

JSP expressions are delimited by **<%=** and **%>**. This particular expression creates a new instance of class **Date** from package **java.util**. When the client requests this JSP, the preceding expression inserts the **String** representation of the date and time in the response to the client. [Note: Proper internationalization requires that the JSP return the date in the client locale's format. In this example, the server's local determines the **String** representation of the **Date**. In Fig. B.9, **clock2.jsp** demonstrates how to determine the client's locale and uses a **DateFormat** (package **java.text**) object to format the date using that locale.]

Software Engineering Observation B.3

*The JSP container converts the result of every JSP expression into a **String** that is output as part of the response to the client.*

Note that we use the XHTML **meta** *element* on line 10 to set a *refresh interval* of 60 seconds for the document. This causes the browser to request **clock.jsp** every 60 seconds. For each request to **clock.jsp**, the JSP container reevaluates the expression on line 30, creating a new **Date** object with the server's current date and time.

As in Appendix A, we use Apache Tomcat to test our JSPs in the **jws** Web application we created previously. For details on creating and configuring the **jws** Web application, review Section A.3.1 and Section A.3.2. To test **clock.jsp**, create a new directory called **jsp** in the **jws** subdirectory of Tomcat's **webapps** directory. Next, copy **clock.jsp** into the **jsp** directory. Open your Web browser and enter the following URL to test **clock.jsp**:

> `http://localhost:8080/jws/jsp/clock.jsp`

When you first invoke the JSP, notice the delay as Tomcat translates the JSP into a servlet and invokes the servlet to respond to your request. [*Note:* It is not necessary to create a directory named **jsp** in a Web application. We use this directory to separate the examples in this appendix from the servlet examples in Appendix A.]

B.4 Implicit Objects

Implicit objects provide programmers with access to many servlet capabilities in the context of a JavaServer Page. Implicit objects have four scopes: *application*, *page*, *request* and *session*. The JSP and servlet container application owns objects with *application scope*. Any servlet or JSP can manipulate such objects. Objects with *page scope* exist only in the page that defines them. Each page has its own instances of the page-scope implicit objects. Objects with *request scope* exist for the duration of the request. For example, a JSP can partially process a request, then forward the request to another servlet or JSP for further processing. Request-scope objects go out of scope when request processing completes with a response to the client. Objects with *session scope* exist for the client's entire browsing session. Figure B.2 describes the JSP implicit objects and their scopes. This appendix demonstrates several of these objects.

Implicit Object	Description
Application Scope	
application	This **javax.servlet.ServletContext** object represents the container in which the JSP executes.
Page Scope	
config	This **javax.servlet.ServletConfig** object represents the JSP configuration options. As with servlets, configuration options can be specified in a Web application descriptor.

Fig. B.2   JSP implicit objects. (Part 1 of 2.)

Implicit Object	Description
exception	This **java.lang.Throwable** object represents the exception that is passed to the JSP error page. This object is available only in a JSP error page.
out	This **javax.servlet.jsp.JspWriter** object writes text as part of the response to a request. This object is used implicitly with JSP expressions and actions that insert string content in a response.
page	This **java.lang.Object** object represents the **this** reference for the current JSP instance.
pageContext	This **javax.servlet.jsp.PageContext** object hides the implementation details of the underlying servlet and JSP container and provides JSP programmers with access to the implicit objects discussed in this table.
response	This object represents the response to the client. The object normally is an instance of a class that implements **HttpServletResponse** (package **javax.servlet.http**). If a protocol other than HTTP is used, this object is an instance of a class that implements **javax.servlet.ServletResponse**.
Request Scope	
request	This object represents the client request. The object normally is an instance of a class that implements **HttpServletRequest** (package **javax.servlet.http**). If a protocol other than HTTP is used, this object is an instance of a subclass of **javax.servlet.ServletRequest**.
Session Scope	
session	This **javax.servlet.http.HttpSession** object represents the client session information if such a session has been created. This object is available only in pages that participate in a session.

Fig. B.2   JSP implicit objects. (Part 2 of 2.)

Note that many of the implicit objects extend classes or implement interfaces discussed in Appendix A. Thus, JSPs can use the same methods that servlets use to interact with such objects, as described in Appendix A. Most of the examples in this appendix use one or more of the implicit objects in Fig. B.2.

B.5 Scripting

JavaServer Pages often present dynamically generated content as part of an XHTML document sent to the client in response to a request. In some cases, the content is static, but is output only if certain conditions are met during a request (such as providing values in a **form** that submits a request). JSP programmers can insert Java code and logic in a JSP using scripting.

 Software Engineering Observation B.4

JavaServer Pages currently support scripting only with Java. Future JSP versions may support other scripting languages.

B.5.1 Scripting Components

JSP scripting components include scriptlets, comments, expressions, declarations and escape sequences. This section describes each of these scripting components. Many of these scripting components are demonstrated in Fig. B.4 at the end of Section B.5.2.

Scriptlets are blocks of code delimited by `<%` and `%>`. They contain Java statements that the container places in method `_jspService` at translation time.

JSPs support three comment styles: JSP comments, XHTML comments and comments from the scripting language. *JSP comments* are delimited by `<%--` and `--%>`. Such comments can be placed throughout a JSP, but not inside scriptlets. *XHTML comments* are delimited with `<!--` and `-->`. These comments can be placed throughout a JSP, but not inside scriptlets. Scripting language comments are currently Java comments, because Java is the only JSP scripting language at the present time. Scriptlets can use Java's single-line comments (delimited by `/` and `/`) and multiline comments (delimited by `/*` and `*/`).

Common Programming Error B.1

Placing a JSP comment or XHTML comment inside a scriptlet is a translation-time syntax error that prevents the JSP from being translated properly.

JSP comments and scripting-language comments are ignored and do not appear in the response to a client. When clients view the source code of a JSP response, they will see only the XHTML comments in the source code. The different comment styles are useful for separating comments that the user should be able to see from comments that document logic processed on the server.

A JSP expression, delimited by `<%=` and `%>`, contains a Java expression that is evaluated when a client requests the JSP containing the expression. The container converts the result of a JSP expression to a **String** object, then outputs the **String** as part of the response to the client.

Declarations (delimited by `<%!` and `%>`) enable a JSP programmer to define variables and methods. Variables become instance variables of the servlet class that represents the translated JSP. Similarly, methods become members of the class that represents the translated JSP. Declarations of variables and methods in a JSP use Java syntax. Thus, a variable declaration must end in a semicolon, as in

```
<%! int counter = 0; %>
```

Common Programming Error B.2

Declaring a variable without using a terminating semicolon is a syntax error.

Software Engineering Observation B.5

Variables and methods declared in JSP declarations are initialized when the JSP is initialized and are available for use in all scriptlets and expressions in that JSP. Variables declared in this manner become instance variables of the servlet class that represents the translated JSP.

Software Engineering Observation B.6

*As with servlets, JSPs should not store client state information in instance variables. Rather, JSPs should use the JSP implicit **session** object.*

Special characters or character sequences that the JSP container normally uses to delimit JSP code can be included in a JSP as literal characters in scripting elements, fixed template data and attribute values using *escape sequences*. Figure B.3 shows the literal character or characters and the corresponding escape sequences and discusses where to use the escape sequences.

B.5.2 Scripting Example

The JSP of Fig. B.4 demonstrates basic scripting capabilities by responding to **get** requests. The JSP enables the user to input a first name, then outputs that name as part of the response. Using scripting, the JSP determines whether a **firstName** parameter was passed to the JSP as part of the request; if not, the JSP returns an XHTML document containing a **form** through which the user can input a first name. Otherwise, the JSP obtains the **firstName** value and uses it as part of an XHTML document that welcomes the user to JavaServer Pages.

Literal	Escape sequence	Description
<%	<\%	The character sequence <% normally indicates the beginning of a scriptlet. The <\% escape sequence places the literal characters <% in the response to the client.
%>	%\>	The character sequence %> normally indicates the end of a scriptlet. The %\> escape sequence places the literal characters %> in the response to the client.
' " \	\' \" \\	As with string literals in a Java program, the escape sequences for characters ', " and \ allow these characters to appear in attribute values. Remember that the literal text in a JSP becomes string literals in the servlet that represents the translated JSP.

Fig. B.3   JSP escape sequences.

```
1   <?xml version = "1.0"?>
2   <!DOCTYPE html PUBLIC "-//W3C//DTD XHTML 1.0 Strict//EN"
3      "http://www.w3.org/TR/xhtml1/DTD/xhtml1-strict.dtd">
4
5   <!-- Fig. B.4: welcome.jsp -->
6   <!-- JSP that processes a "get" request containing data. -->
7
8   <html xmlns = "http://www.w3.org/1999/xhtml">
9
10     <!-- head section of document -->
11     <head>
12        <title>Processing "get" requests with data</title>
13     </head>
```

Fig. B.4   Scripting a JavaServer Page—**welcome.jsp**. (Part 1 of 3.)

```
14
15       <!-- body section of document -->
16       <body>
17          <% // begin scriptlet
18
19             String name = request.getParameter( "firstName" );
20
21             if ( name != null ) {
22
23          %> <%-- end scriptlet to insert fixed template data --%>
24
25             <h1>
26                Hello <%= name %>, <br />
27                Welcome to JavaServer Pages!
28             </h1>
29
30          <% // continue scriptlet
31
32             }  // end if
33             else {
34
35          %> <%-- end scriptlet to insert fixed template data --%>
36
37             <form action = "welcome.jsp" method = "get">
38                <p>Type your first name and press Submit</p>
39
40                <p><input type = "text" name = "firstName" />
41                   <input type = "submit" value = "Submit" />
42                </p>
43             </form>
44
45          <% // continue scriptlet
46
47             }  // end else
48
49          %> <%-- end scriptlet --%>
50       </body>
51
52    </html>  <!-- end XHTML document -->
```

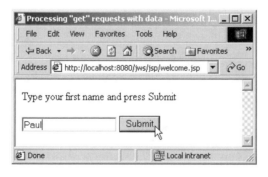

Fig. B.4   Scripting a JavaServer Page—**welcome.jsp**. (Part 2 of 3.)

Fig. B.4   Scripting a JavaServer Page—**welcome.jsp**. (Part 3 of 3.)

Notice that the majority of the code in Fig. B.4 is XHTML markup (i.e., fixed template data). Throughout the **body** element are several scriptlets (lines 17–23, 30–35 and 45–49) and a JSP expression (line 26). Note that three comment styles appear in this JSP.

The scriptlets define an **if/else** structure that determines whether the JSP received a value for the first name as part of the request. Line 19 uses method **getParameter** of JSP implicit object **request** (an **HttpServletRequest** object) to obtain the value for parameter **firstName** and assigns the result to variable **name**. Line 21 determines if **name** is not **null**, (i.e., a value for the first name was passed to the JSP as part of the request). If this condition is **true**, the scriptlet terminates temporarily so the fixed template data at lines 25–28 can be output. The JSP expression in line 26 outputs the value of variable **name** (i.e., the first name passed to the JSP as a request parameter). The scriptlet continues at lines 30–35 with the closing curly brace of the **if** structure's body and the beginning of the **else** part of the **if/else** structure. If the condition at line 21 is **false**, lines 25–28 are not output. Instead, lines 37–43 output a **form** element. The user can type a first name in the **form** and press the **Submit** button to request the JSP again and execute the **if** structure's body (lines 25–28).

Software Engineering Observation B.7

Scriptlets, expressions and fixed template data can be intermixed in a JSP to create different responses based on information in a request to a JSP.

Testing and Debugging Tip B.1

It is sometimes difficult to debug errors in a JSP, because the line numbers reported by a JSP container normally refer to the servlet that represents the translated JSP, not the original JSP line numbers. Program development environments such as Sun Microsystems, Inc.'s Forte for Java Community Edition enable JSPs to be compiled in the environment, so you can see syntax error messages. These messages include the statement in the servlet that represents the translated JSP, which can be helpful in determining the error.

Testing and Debugging Tip B.2

*Many JSP containers store the servlets representing the translated JSPs. For example, the Tomcat installation directory contains a subdirectory called **work** in which you can find the source code for the servlets translated by Tomcat.*

To test Fig. B.4 in Tomcat, copy **welcome.jsp** into the **jsp** directory created in Section B.3. Open your Web browser and enter the following URL to test **welcome.jsp**:

http://localhost:8080/jws/jsp/welcome.jsp

When you first execute the JSP, it displays the **form** in which you can enter your first name, because the preceding URL does not pass a **firstName** parameter to the JSP. After you submit your first name, your browser should appear as shown in the second screen capture of Fig. B.4. *Note*: As with servlets, it is possible to pass **get** request arguments as part of the URL. The following URL supplies the **firstName** parameter to **welcome.jsp**:

http://localhost:8080/jws/jsp/welcome.jsp?firstName=Paul

B.6 Standard Actions

We continue our JSP discussion with the *JSP standard actions* (Fig. B.5). These actions provide JSP implementors with access to several of the most common tasks performed in a JSP, such as including content from other resources, forwarding requests to other resources and interacting with JavaBeans. JSP containers process actions at request time. Actions are delimited by **<jsp:***action***>** and **</jsp:***action***>**, where *action* is the standard action name. In cases where nothing appears between the starting and ending tags, the XML empty element syntax **<jsp:***action* **/>** can be used. Figure B.5 summarizes the JSP standard actions. We use the actions in the next several subsections.

Action	Description
<jsp:include>	Dynamically includes another resource in a JSP. As the JSP executes, the referenced resource is included and processed.
<jsp:forward>	Forwards request processing to another JSP, servlet or static page. This action terminates the current JSP's execution.
<jsp:plugin>	Allows a plug-in component to be added to a page in the form of a browser-specific **object** or **embed** HTML element. In the case of a Java applet, this action enables the downloading and installation of the *Java Plug-in*, if it is not already installed on the client computer.
<jsp:param>	Used with the **include**, **forward** and **plugin** actions to specify additional name/value pairs of information for use by these actions.
JavaBean Manipulation	
<jsp:useBean>	Specifies that the JSP uses a JavaBean instance. This action specifies the scope of the bean and assigns it an ID that scripting components can use to manipulate the bean.

Fig. B.5   JSP standard actions. (Part 1 of 2.)

Action	Description
`<jsp:setProperty>`	Sets a property in the specified JavaBean instance. A special feature of this action is automatic matching of request parameters to bean properties of the same name.
`<jsp:getProperty>`	Gets a property in the specified JavaBean instance and converts the result to a string for output in the response.

Fig. B.5   JSP standard actions. (Part 2 of 2.)

B.6.1 `<jsp:include>` Action

JavaServer Pages support two include mechanisms—the *`<jsp:include>`* *action* and the *`include`* *directive*. Action **`<jsp:include>`** enables dynamic content to be included in a JavaServer Page. If the included resource changes between requests, the next request to the JSP containing the **`<jsp:include>`** action includes the new content of the resource. On the other hand, the **`include`** directive copies the content into the JSP once, at JSP translation time. If the included resource changes, the new content will not be reflected in the JSP that used the **`include`** directive unless that JSP is recompiled. Figure B.6 describes the attributes of action **`<jsp:include>`**.

Software Engineering Observation B.8

*According to the JavaServer Pages 1.1 specification, a JSP container is allowed to determine whether a resource included with the **include** directive has changed. If so, the container can recompile the JSP that included the resource. However, the specification does not provide a mechanism to indicate a change in an included resource to the container.*

Performance Tip B.2

*The **`<jsp:include>`** action is more flexible than the **include** directive, but requires more overhead when page contents change frequently. Use the **`<jsp:include>`** action only when dynamic content is necessary.*

Common Programming Error B.3

*Setting the **`<jsp:include>`** action's **flush** attribute to **false** is a translation-time error. Currently, the **flush** attribute supports only **true** values.*

Attribute	Description
`page`	Specifies the relative URI path of the resource to include. The resource must be part of the same Web application.
`flush`	Specifies whether the buffer should be flushed after the **include** is performed. In JSP 1.1, this attribute is required to be **true**.

Fig. B.6   Action `<jsp:include>` attributes.

Common Programming Error B.4

Not specifying the **<jsp:include>** *action's* **flush** *attribute is a translation-time error. Specifying this attribute is mandatory.*

Common Programming Error B.5

Specifying in a **<jsp:include>** *action a page that is not part of the same Web application is a request-time error. In such a case, the* **<jsp:include>** *action does not include any content.*

The next example demonstrates action **<jsp:include>** using four XHTML and JSP resources that represent both static and dynamic content. JavaServer Page **include.jsp** (Fig. B.10) includes three other resources: **banner.html** (Fig. B.7), **toc.html** (Fig. B.8) and **clock2.jsp** (Fig. B.9). JavaServer Page **include.jsp** creates an XHTML document containing a **table** in which **banner.html** spans two columns across the top of the **table**, **toc.html** is the left column of the second row and **clock2.jsp** (a simplified version of Fig. B.1) is the right column of the second row. Figure B.10 uses three **<jsp:include>** actions (lines 38–39, 48 and 55–56) as the content in **td** elements of the **table**. Using two XHTML documents and a JSP in Fig. B.10 demonstrates that JSPs can include both static and dynamic content. The output windows in Fig. B.10 demonstrate the results of two separate requests to **include.jsp**.

Figure B.9 (**clock2.jsp**) demonstrates how to determine the client's **Locale** (package **java.util**) and uses that **Locale** to format a **Date** with a *DateFormat* (package **java.text**) object. Line 14 invokes the **request** object's **getLocale** method, which returns the client's **Locale**. Lines 17–20 invoke **DateFormat static** method **getDateTimeInstance** to obtain a **DateFormat** object. The first two arguments indicate that the date and time formats should each be **LONG** format (other options are **FULL, MEDIUM, SHORT** and **DEFAULT**). The third argument specifies the **Locale** for which the **DateFormat** object should format the date. Line 25 invokes the **DateFormat** object's **format** method to produce a **String** representation of the **Date**. The **DateFormat** object formats this **String** for the **Locale** specified on lines 17–20. [*Note*: This example works for Western languages that use the ISO-8859-1 character set. However, for languages that do not use this character set, the JSP must specify the proper character set using the JSP **page** directive (Section B.7.1). At the site **java.sun.com/ j2se/1.3/docs/guide/intl/encoding.doc.html**, Sun provides a list of character encodings. The response's content type defines the character set to use in the response. The content type has the form: *"mimeType;* **charset=***encoding"* (e.g., **"text/html;charset=ISO-8859-1"**.]

To test Fig. B.10 in Tomcat, copy **banner.html**, **toc.html**, **clock2.jsp**, **include.jsp** and the **images** directory into the **jsp** directory created in Section B.3. Open your Web browser and enter the following URL to test **welcome.jsp**:

        http://localhost:8080/jws/jsp/include.jsp

```
1   <!-- Fig. B.7: banner.html                    -->
2   <!-- banner to include in another document -->
```

Fig. B.7   Banner (**banner.html**) to include across the top of the XHTML document created by Fig. B.10. (Part 1 of 2.)

```
 3    <div style = "width: 580px">
 4       <p>
 5          Java(TM), C, C++, Visual Basic(R),
 6          Object Technology, and <br /> Internet and
 7          World Wide Web Programming Training <br />
 8          On-Site Seminars Delivered Worldwide
 9       </p>
10
11       <p>
12          <a href = "mailto:deitel@deitel.com">
13             deitel@deitel.com</a><br />
14
15          978.579.9911<br />
16          490B Boston Post Road, Suite 200,
17          Sudbury, MA 01776
18       </p>
19    </div>
```

Fig. B.7 Banner (**banner.html**) to include across the top of the XHTML document created by Fig. B.10. (Part 2 of 2.)

```
 1    <!-- Fig. B.8: toc.html                          -->
 2    <!-- contents to include in another document -->
 3
 4    <p><a href = "http://www.deitel.com/books/index.html">
 5       Publications/BookStore
 6    </a></p>
 7
 8    <p><a href = "http://www.deitel.com/whatsnew.html">
 9       What's New
10    </a></p>
11
12    <p><a href = "http://www.deitel.com/books/downloads.html">
13       Downloads/Resources
14    </a></p>
15
16    <p><a href = "http://www.deitel.com/faq/index.html">
17       FAQ (Frequently Asked Questions)
18    </a></p>
19
20    <p><a href = "http://www.deitel.com/intro.html">
21       Who we are
22    </a></p>
23
24    <p><a href = "http://www.deitel.com/index.html">
25       Home Page
26    </a></p>
27
28    <p>Send questions or comments about this site to
29       <a href = "mailto:deitel@deitel.com">
30          deitel@deitel.com
```

Fig. B.8 Table of contents (**toc.html**) to include down the left side of the XHTML document created by Fig. B.10. (Part 1 of 2.)

```
31        </a><br />
32        Copyright 1995-2002 by Deitel &amp; Associates, Inc.
33        All Rights Reserved.
34     </p>
```

Fig. B.8   Table of contents (**toc.html**) to include down the left side of the XHTML document created by Fig. B.10. (Part 2 of 2.)

```
1   <!-- Fig. B.9: clock2.jsp                          -->
2   <!-- date and time to include in another document -->
3
4   <table>
5      <tr>
6         <td style = "background-color: black;">
7            <p class = "big" style = "color: cyan; font-size: 3em;
8               font-weight: bold;">
9
10              <%-- script to determine client local and --%>
11              <%-- format date accordingly             --%>
12              <%
13                 // get client locale
14                 java.util.Locale locale = request.getLocale();
15
16                 // get DateFormat for client's Locale
17                 java.text.DateFormat dateFormat =
18                    java.text.DateFormat.getDateTimeInstance(
19                       java.text.DateFormat.LONG,
20                       java.text.DateFormat.LONG, locale );
21
22              %>  <%-- end script --%>
23
24              <%-- output date --%>
25              <%= dateFormat.format( new java.util.Date() ) %>
26           </p>
27        </td>
28     </tr>
29  </table>
```

Fig. B.9   JSP **clock2.jsp** to include as the main content in the XHTML document created by Fig. B.10.

```
1   <?xml version = "1.0"?>
2   <!DOCTYPE html PUBLIC "-//W3C//DTD XHTML 1.0 Strict//EN"
3      "http://www.w3.org/TR/xhtml1/DTD/xhtml1-strict.dtd">
4
5   <!-- Fig. B.7: include.jsp -->
6
7   <html xmlns = "http://www.w3.org/1999/xhtml">
8
9      <head>
10        <title>Using jsp:include</title>
```

Fig. B.10   JSP **include.jsp** Includes resources with **<jsp:include>**. (Part 1 of 3.)

```
11
12          <style type = "text/css">
13             body {
14                font-family: tahoma, helvetica, arial, sans-serif;
15             }
16
17             table, tr, td {
18                font-size: .9em;
19                border: 3px groove;
20                padding: 5px;
21                background-color: #dddddd;
22             }
23          </style>
24      </head>
25
26      <body>
27         <table>
28            <tr>
29               <td style = "width: 160px; text-align: center">
30                  <img src = "images/logotiny.png"
31                     width = "140" height = "93"
32                     alt = "Deitel & Associates, Inc. Logo" />
33               </td>
34
35               <td>
36
37                  <%-- include banner.html in this JSP --%>
38                  <jsp:include page = "banner.html"
39                     flush = "true" />
40
41               </td>
42            </tr>
43
44            <tr>
45               <td style = "width: 160px">
46
47                  <%-- include toc.html in this JSP --%>
48                  <jsp:include page = "toc.html" flush = "true" />
49
50               </td>
51
52               <td style = "vertical-align: top">
53
54                  <%-- include clock2.jsp in this JSP --%>
55                  <jsp:include page = "clock2.jsp"
56                     flush = "true" />
57
58               </td>
59            </tr>
60         </table>
61      </body>
62   </html>
```

Fig. B.10   JSP `include.jsp` Includes resources with `<jsp:include>`.
(Part 2 of 3.)

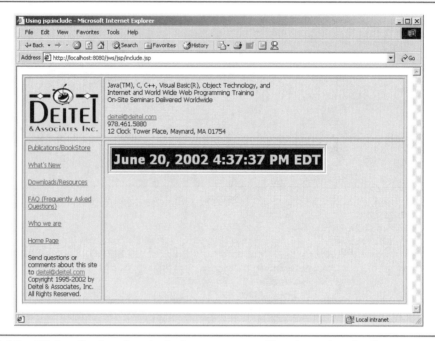

Fig. B.10   JSP `include.jsp` Includes resources with `<jsp:include>`.
(Part 3 of 3.)

B.6.2 `<jsp:forward>` Action

Action `<jsp:forward>` enables a JSP to forward request processing to a different resource. Request processing by the original JSP terminates as soon as the JSP forwards the request. Action `<jsp:forward>` has only a **page** attribute that specifies the relative URI of the resource (in the same Web application) to which the request should be forwarded.

 Software Engineering Observation B.9

When using the `<jsp:forward>` action, the resource to which the request will be forwarded must be in the same context (Web application) as the JSP that originally received the request.

JavaServer Page **forward1.jsp** (Fig. B.11) is a modified version of **welcome.jsp** (Fig. B.4). The primary difference is in lines 22–25 in which JavaServer Page **forward1.jsp** forwards the request to JavaServer Page **forward2.jsp** (Fig. B.12). Notice the `<jsp:param>` action in lines 23–24. This action adds a request parameter representing the date and time at which the initial request was received to the request object that is forwarded to **forward2.jsp**.

The `<jsp:param>` action specifies name/value pairs of information that are passed to the `<jsp:include>`, `<jsp:forward>` and `<jsp:plugin>` actions. Every `<jsp:param>` action has two required attributes: **name** and **value**. If a `<jsp:param>` action specifies a parameter that already exists in the request, the new value for the parameter takes precedence over the original value. All values for that parameter can be obtained by using the JSP implicit object **request**'s **getParameterValues** method, which returns an array of **String**s.

JSP **forward2.jsp** uses the **name** specified in the **<jsp:param>** action
(**"date"**) to obtain the date and time. It also uses the **firstName** parameter originally
passed to **forward1.jsp** to obtain the user's first name. JSP expressions in Fig. B.12
(lines 23 and 31) insert the request parameter values in the response to the client. The screen
capture in Fig. B.11 shows the initial interaction with the client. The screen capture in
Fig. B.12 shows the results returned to the client after the request was forwarded to
forward2.jsp.

To test Fig. B.11 and Fig. B.12 in Tomcat, copy **forward1.jsp** and
forward2.jsp into the **jsp** directory created in Section B.3. Open your Web browser
and enter the following URL to test **welcome.jsp**:

> `http://localhost:8080/jws/jsp/forward1.jsp`

```
1   <?xml version = "1.0"?>
2   <!DOCTYPE html PUBLIC "-//W3C//DTD XHTML 1.0 Strict//EN"
3      "http://www.w3.org/TR/xhtml1/DTD/xhtml1-strict.dtd">
4
5   <!-- Fig. B.11: forward1.jsp -->
6
7   <html xmlns = "http://www.w3.org/1999/xhtml">
8
9   <head>
10     <title>Forward request to another JSP</title>
11  </head>
12
13  <body>
14     <% // begin scriptlet
15
16        String name = request.getParameter( "firstName" );
17
18        if ( name != null ) {
19
20     %> <%-- end scriptlet to insert fixed template data --%>
21
22           <jsp:forward page = "forward2.jsp">
23              <jsp:param name = "date"
24                 value = "<%= new java.util.Date() %>" />
25           </jsp:forward>
26
27     <% // continue scriptlet
28
29        }  // end if
30        else {
31
32     %> <%-- end scriptlet to insert fixed template data --%>
33
34           <form action = "forward1.jsp" method = "get">
35              <p>Type your first name and press Submit</p>
36
```

Fig. B.11   JSP **forward1.jsp** receives a **firstName** parameter, adds a date to
the request parameters and forwards the request to **forward2.jsp** for
further processing. (Part 1 of 2.)

```
37                    <p><input type = "text" name = "firstName" />
38                        <input type = "submit" value = "Submit" />
39                    </p>
40                </form>
41
42        <%  // continue scriptlet
43
44            }  // end else
45
46        %> <%-- end scriptlet --%>
47    </body>
48
49    </html>   <!-- end XHTML document -->
```

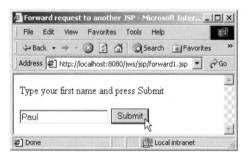

Fig. B.11   JSP **forward1.jsp** receives a **firstName** parameter, adds a date to
the request parameters and forwards the request to **forward2.jsp** for
further processing. (Part 2 of 2.)

```
1    <?xml version = "1.0"?>
2    <!DOCTYPE html PUBLIC "-//W3C//DTD XHTML 1.0 Strict//EN"
3        "http://www.w3.org/TR/xhtml1/DTD/xhtml1-strict.dtd">
4
5    <!-- forward2.jsp -->
6
7    <html xmlns = "http://www.w3.org/1999/xhtml"v
8
9    <head>
10       <title>Processing a forwarded request</title>
11
12       <style type = "text/css">
13          .big {
14             font-family: tahoma, helvetica, arial, sans-serif;
15             font-weight: bold;
16             font-size: 2em;
17          }
18       </style>
19    </head>
20
```

Fig. B.12   JSP **forward2.jsp** receives a request (from **forward1.jsp** in this
example) and uses the request parameters as part of the response to the
client. (Part 1 of 2.)

```
21    <body>
22       <p class = "big">
23          Hello <%= request.getParameter( "firstName" ) %>, <br />
24          Your request was received <br /> and forwarded at
25       </p>
26
27       <table style = "border: 6px outset;">
28          <tr>
29             <td style = "background-color: black;">
30                <p class = "big" style = "color: cyan;">
31                   <%= request.getParameter( "date" ) %>
32                </p>
33             </td>
34          </tr>
35       </table>
36    </body>
37
38    </html>
```

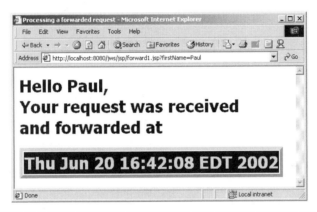

Fig. B.12   JSP **forward2.jsp** receives a request (from **forward1.jsp** in this example) and uses the request parameters as part of the response to the client. (Part 2 of 2.)

B.6.3 <jsp:plugin> Action

Action **<jsp:plugin>** adds an applet or JavaBean to a Web page in the form of a browser-specific **object** or **embed** XHTML element. This action also enables the client to download and install the *Java Plug-in* if it is not already installed. Figure B.13 describes the attributes of action **<jsp:plugin>**.

Attribute	Description
type	Component type—bean or applet.
code	Class that represents the component.

Fig. B.13   Attributes of the **<jsp:plugin>** action. (Part 1 of 2.)

Attribute	Description
codebase	Location of the class specified in the **code** attribute and the archives specified in the **archive** attribute.
align	Alignment of the component.
archive	A space-separated list of archive files that contain resources used by the component. Such an archive may include the class specified by the **code** attribute.
height	Component height in the page specified in pixels or percentage.
hspace	Number of pixels of space that appear to the left and to the right of the component.
jreversion	Version of the Java Runtime Environment and plug-in required to execute the component. The default value is 1.1.
name	Name of the component.
vspace	Number of pixels of space that appear above and below the component.
title	Text that describes the component.
width	Component width in the page specified in pixels or percentage.
nspluginurl	Location for download of the Java Plug-in for Netscape Navigator.
iepluginurl	Location for download of the Java Plug-in for Internet Explorer.

Fig. B.13 Attributes of the **<jsp:plugin>** action. (Part 2 of 2.)

Figure B.14 defines an applet that draws a picture using the Java2D API. The applet has three parameters that enable the JSP implementor to specify the background color for the drawing. The parameters represent the **red**, **green** and **blue** portions of an RGB color with values in the range 0–255. The applet obtains the parameter values in lines 21–23. If any exceptions occur while processing the parameters, the exceptions are caught at line 32 and ignored, leaving the applet with its default white background color.

```
1   // Fig. B.14: ShapesApplet.java
2   // Applet that demonstrates a Java2D GeneralPath.
3   package com.deitel.jws.jsp.applet;
4
5   // Java core packages
6   import java.applet.*;
7   import java.awt.event.*;
8   import java.awt.*;
9   import java.awt.geom.*;
10
11  // Java extension packages
12  import javax.swing.*;
13
14  public class ShapesApplet extends JApplet {
15
```

Fig. B.14 An applet to demonstrate **<jsp:plugin>** in Fig. B.15. (Part 1 of 3.)

```
16        // initialize the applet
17        public void init()
18        {
19           // obtain color parameters from XHTML file
20           try {
21              int red = Integer.parseInt( getParameter( "red" ) );
22              int green = Integer.parseInt( getParameter( "green" ) );
23              int blue = Integer.parseInt( getParameter( "blue" ) );
24
25              Color backgroundColor = new Color( red, green, blue );
26
27              setBackground( backgroundColor );
28           }
29
30           // if there is an exception while processing the color
31           // parameters, catch it and ignore it
32           catch ( Exception exception ) {
33              // do nothing
34           }
35        }
36
37        public void paint( Graphics g )
38        {
39           // create arrays of x and y coordinates
40           int xPoints[] =
41              { 55, 67, 109, 73, 83, 55, 27, 37, 1, 43 };
42           int yPoints[] =
43              { 0, 36, 36, 54, 96, 72, 96, 54, 36, 36 };
44
45           // obtain reference to a Graphics2D object
46           Graphics2D g2d = ( Graphics2D ) g;
47
48           // create a star from a series of points
49           GeneralPath star = new GeneralPath();
50
51           // set the initial coordinate of the GeneralPath
52           star.moveTo( xPoints[ 0 ], yPoints[ 0 ] );
53
54           // create the star--this does not draw the star
55           for ( int k = 1; k < xPoints.length; k++ )
56              star.lineTo( xPoints[ k ], yPoints[ k ] );
57
58           // close the shape
59           star.closePath();
60
61           // translate the origin to (200, 200)
62           g2d.translate( 200, 200 );
63
64           // rotate around origin and draw stars in random colors
65           for ( int j = 1; j <= 20; j++ ) {
66              g2d.rotate( Math.PI / 10.0 );
67
```

Fig. B.14 An applet to demonstrate `<jsp:plugin>` in Fig. B.15. (Part 2 of 3.)

```
68              g2d.setColor(
69                  new Color( ( int ) ( Math.random() * 256 ),
70                              ( int ) ( Math.random() * 256 ),
71                              ( int ) ( Math.random() * 256 ) ) );
72
73              g2d.fill( star );    // draw a filled star
74          }
75      }
76  }
```

Fig. B.14   An applet to demonstrate `<jsp:plugin>` in Fig. B.15. (Part 3 of 3.)

Most Web browsers in use today do not support applets written for the Java 2 platform. Executing such applets in most of today's browsers requires the Java Plug-in. Figure B.15 uses the `<jsp:plugin>` action (lines 10–22) to embed the Java Plug-in. Line 11 indicates the package name and class name of the applet class. Line 12 indicates the **code-base** from which the applet should be downloaded. Line 13 indicates that the applet should be 400 pixels wide and line 14 indicates that the applet should be 400 pixels tall. Lines 16–20 specify the applet parameters. You can change the background color in the applet by changing the red, green and blue values. Note that the `<jsp:plugin>` action requires any `<jsp:param>` actions to appear in a `<jsp:params>` action.

To test the `<jsp:plugin>` action in Tomcat, copy `plugin.jsp` and `ShapesApplet.class` into the `jsp` directory created in Section B.3. [*Note:* `ShapesApplet` is defined in package `com.deitel.jws.jsp.applet`. This example will work only if the proper package directory structure is defined in the `jsp` directory.] Open your Web browser and enter the following URL to test `plugin.jsp`:

```
http://localhost:8080/jws/jsp/plugin.jsp
```

The screen captures in Fig. B.15 show the applet executing in Microsoft Internet Explorer 5.5 and Netscape Navigator 6.0.

```
1   <!-- Fig. B.15: plugin.jsp -->
2
3   <html>
4
5      <head>
6         <title>Using jsp:plugin to load an applet</title>
7      </head>
8
9      <body>
10        <jsp:plugin type = "applet"
11           code = "com.deitel.jws.jsp.applet.ShapesApplet"
12           codebase = "/jws/jsp"
13           width = "400"
14           height = "400">
15
16           <jsp:params>
17              <jsp:param name = "red" value = "255" />
```

Fig. B.15   Using `<jsp:plugin>` to embed a Java 2 applet in a JSP. (Part 1 of 2.)

```
18                    <jsp:param name = "green" value = "255" />
19                    <jsp:param name = "blue" value = "0" />
20             </jsp:params>
21
22          </jsp:plugin>
23      </body>
24  </html>
```

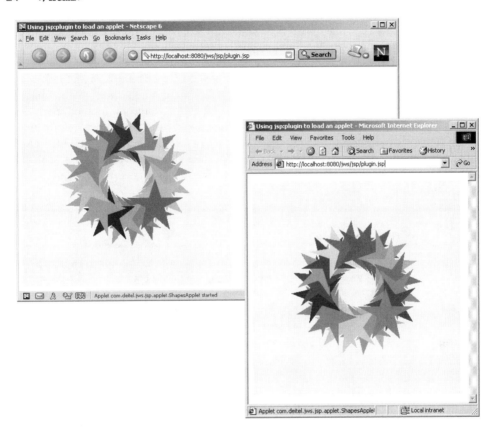

Fig. B.15 Using **<jsp:plugin>** to embed a Java 2 applet in a JSP. (Part 2 of 2.)

B.6.4 **<jsp:useBean>** Action

Action **<jsp:useBean>** enables a JSP to manipulate a Java object. This action creates a Java object or locates an existing object for use in the JSP. Figure B.16 summarizes action **<jsp:useBean>**'s attributes. If attributes **class** and **beanName** are not specified, the JSP container attempts to locate an existing object of the type specified in attribute **type**. Like JSP implicit objects, objects specified with action **<jsp:useBean>** have **page**, **request**, **session** or **application** scope that indicates where they can be used in a Web application. Objects with **page** scope are accessible only to the page in which they are defined. Multiple JSP pages potentially can access objects with other scopes. For example, all JSPs that process a single request can access an object with **request** scope.

Common Programming Error B.6

One or both of the `<jsp:useBean>` *attributes* `class` *and* `type` *must be specified; otherwise, a translation-time error occurs.*

Many Web sites today place rotating advertisements on their Web pages. Each visit to one of these pages typically results in a different advertisement being displayed in the user's Web browser. Typically, clicking an advertisement takes you to the Web site of the company that placed the advertisement. Our first example of `<jsp:useBean>` demonstrates a simple advertisement rotator bean that cycles through a list of five advertisements. In this example, the advertisements are covers for some of our books. Clicking a cover takes you to the Amazon.com Web site where you can read about and possibly order the book.

The **Rotator** bean (Fig. B.17) has three methods: **getImage**, **getLink** and **nextAd**. Method **getImage** returns the image file name for the book cover image. Method **getLink** returns the hyperlink to the book at Amazon.com. Method **nextAd** updates the **Rotator** so the next calls to **getImage** and **getLink** return information for a different advertisement. Methods **getImage** and **getLink** each represent a read-only JavaBean property—**image** and **link**, respectively. **Rotator** keeps track of the current advertisement with its **selectedIndex** variable, which is updated by invoking method **nextAd**.

Attribute	Description
id	The name used to manipulate the Java object with actions `<jsp:setProperty>` and `<jsp:getProperty>`. A variable of this name is also declared for use in JSP scripting elements. The name specified here is case sensitive.
scope	The scope in which the Java object is accessible—**page**, **request**, **session** or **application**. The default scope is **page**.
class	The fully qualified class name of the Java object.
beanName	The name of a bean that can be used with method **instantiate** of class **java.beans.Beans** to load a JavaBean into memory.
type	The type of the JavaBean. This can be the same type as the **class** attribute, a superclass of that type or an interface implemented by that type. The default value is the same as for attribute **class**. A **ClassCastException** occurs if the Java object is not of the type specified with attribute **type**.

Fig. B.16 Attributes of the `<jsp:useBean>` action.

```
1    // Fig. B.17: Rotator.java
2    // A JavaBean that rotates advertisements.
3    package com.deitel.jws.jsp.beans;
4
5    public class Rotator {
6       private String images[] = { "images/jhtp3.jpg",
7          "images/xmlhtp1.jpg", "images/ebechtp1.jpg",
8          "images/iw3htp1.jpg", "images/cpphtp3.jpg" };
9
```

Fig. B.17 **Rotator** bean that maintains a set of advertisements. (Part 1 of 2.)

```
10      private String links[] = {
11         "http://www.amazon.com/exec/obidos/ASIN/0130125075/" +
12            "deitelassociatin",
13         "http://www.amazon.com/exec/obidos/ASIN/0130284173/" +
14            "deitelassociatin",
15         "http://www.amazon.com/exec/obidos/ASIN/013028419X/" +
16            "deitelassociatin",
17         "http://www.amazon.com/exec/obidos/ASIN/0130161438/" +
18            "deitelassociatin",
19         "http://www.amazon.com/exec/obidos/ASIN/0130895717/" +
20            "deitelassociatin" };
21
22      private int selectedIndex = 0;
23
24      // returns image file name for current ad
25      public String getImage()
26      {
27         return images[ selectedIndex ];
28      }
29
30      // returns the URL for ad's corresponding Web site
31      public String getLink()
32      {
33         return links[ selectedIndex ];
34      }
35
36      // update selectedIndex so next calls to getImage and
37      // getLink return a different advertisement
38      public void nextAd()
39      {
40         selectedIndex = ( selectedIndex + 1 ) % images.length;
41      }
42   }
```

Fig. B.17 **Rotator** bean that maintains a set of advertisements. (Part 2 of 2.)

Lines 7–8 of JavaServer Page **adrotator.jsp** (Fig. B.18) obtain a reference to an instance of class **Rotator**. The **id** for the bean is **rotator**. The JSP uses this name to manipulate the bean. The scope of the object is **session**, so that each individual client will see the same sequence of ads during their browsing session. When **adrotator.jsp** receives a request from a new client, the JSP container creates the bean and stores it in JSP that client's **session** (an **HttpSession** object). In each request to this JSP, line 22 uses the **rotator** reference created in line 7 to invoke the **Rotator** bean's **nextAd** method. Thus, each request will receive the next advertisement maintained by the **Rotator** bean. Lines 29–34 define a hyperlink to the Amazon.com site for a particular book. Lines 29–30 introduce action **<jsp:getProperty>** to obtain the value of the **Rotator** bean's **link** property. Action **<jsp:getProperty>** has two attributes—**name** and **property**—that specify the bean object to manipulate and the property to get. If the JavaBean object uses standard JavaBean naming conventions, the method used to obtain the **link** property value from the bean should be **getLink**. Action **<jsp:getProperty>** invokes **getLink** on the bean referenced with **rotator**, converts the return value into a **String** and outputs the **String** as part of the response to the client. The **link** property becomes the value of the hyperlink's **href** attribute. The hyperlink is represented in the resulting Web page as the book cover image. Lines 32–33 create an **img** element and use another **<jsp:getProperty>** action to obtain the **Rotator** bean's **image** property value.

The link and image properties also can be obtained with JSP expressions. For example, the **<jsp:getProperty>** action in lines 29–30 can be replaced with the expression

```
<%= rotator.getLink() %>
```

Similarly, the **<jsp:getProperty>** action in lines 32–33 can be replaced with the expression

```
<%= rotator.getImage() %>
```

```
1   <?xml version = "1.0"?>
2   <!DOCTYPE html PUBLIC "-//W3C//DTD XHTML 1.0 Strict//EN"
3      "http://www.w3.org/TR/xhtml1/DTD/xhtml1-strict.dtd">
4
5   <!-- Fig. B.18: adrotator.jsp -->
6
7   <jsp:useBean id = "rotator" scope = "application"
8      class = "com.deitel.jws.jsp.beans.Rotator" />
9
10  <html xmlns = "http://www.w3.org/1999/xhtml">
11
12     <head>
13        <title>AdRotator Example</title>
14
15        <style type = "text/css">
16           .big { font-family: helvetica, arial, sans-serif;
17                  font-weight: bold;
18                  font-size: 2em }
19        </style>
20
21        <%-- update advertisement --%>
22        <% rotator.nextAd(); %>
23     </head>
24
25     <body>
26        <p class = "big">AdRotator Example</p>
27
28        <p>
29           <a href = "<jsp:getProperty name = "rotator"
30              property = "link" />">
31
32              <img src = "<jsp:getProperty name = "rotator"
33                 property = "image" />" alt = "advertisement" />
34           </a>
35        </p>
36     </body>
37  </html>
```

Fig. B.18   JSP **adrotator.jsp** uses a **Rotator** bean to display a different advertisement on each request to the page. (Courtesy of Prentice Hall.) (Part 1 of 2.)

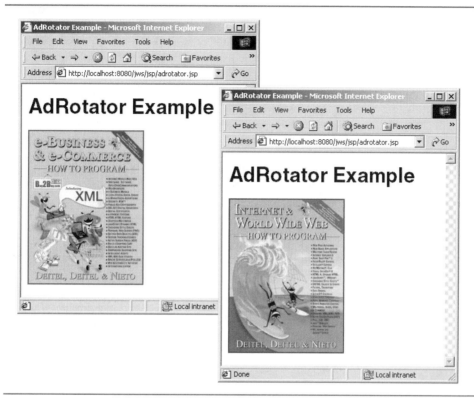

Fig. B.18 JSP `adrotator.jsp` uses a `Rotator` bean to display a different advertisement on each request to the page. (Courtesy of Prentice Hall.) (Part 2 of 2.)

To test **adrotator.jsp** in Tomcat, copy **adrotator.jsp** into the **jsp** directory created in Section B.3. You should have copied the **images** directory into the **jsp** directory when you tested Fig. B.10. If not, you must copy the **images** directory there now. Copy **Rotator.class** into the **jws** Web application's **WEB-INF\classes** directory in Tomcat. [*Note:* This example will work only if the proper package directory structure for **Rotator** is defined in the **classes** directory. **Rotator** is defined in package **com.deitel.jws.jsp.beans**.] Open your Web browser and enter the following URL to test **adrotator.jsp**:

> **http://localhost:8080/jws/jsp/adrotator.jsp**

Try reloading this JSP several times in your browser to see the advertisement change with each request.

Action **<jsp:setProperty>** can set JavaBean property values. This action is particularly useful for mapping request parameter values to JavaBean properties. Request parameters can be used to set properties of primitive types **boolean**, **byte**, **char**, **int**, **long**, **float** and **double** and **java.lang** types **String**, **Boolean**, **Byte**, **Character**, **Integer**, **Long**, **Float** and **Double**. Figure B.19 summarizes the **<jsp:setProperty>** attributes.

Attribute	Description
name	The ID of the JavaBean for which a property (or properties) will be set.
property	The name of the property to set. Specifying **"*"** for this attribute causes the JSP to match the request parameters to the properties of the bean. For each request parameter that matches (i.e., the name of the request parameter is identical to the bean's property name), the corresponding property in the bean is set to the value of the parameter. If the value of the request parameter is **""**, the property value in the bean remains unchanged.
param	If request parameter names do not match bean property names, this attribute can be used to specify which request parameter should be used to obtain the value for a specific bean property. This attribute is optional. If this attribute is omitted, the request parameter names must match bean property names.
value	The value to assign to a bean property. The value typically is the result of a JSP expression. This attribute is particularly useful for setting bean properties that cannot be set using request parameters. This attribute is optional. If this attribute is omitted, the JavaBean property must be of a data type that can be set using request parameters.

Fig. B.19   Attributes of the **<jsp:setProperty>** action.

Common Programming Error B.7

*Use action **<jsp:setProperty>**'s **value** attribute to set JavaBean property types that cannot be set with request parameters; otherwise, conversion errors occur.*

Software Engineering Observation B.10

*Action **<jsp:setProperty>** can use request-parameter values to set JavaBean properties only for properties of the following types: **String**s, primitive types (**boolean**, **byte**, **char**, **short**, **int**, **long**, **float** and **double**) and type wrapper classes (**Boolean**, **Byte**, **Character**, **Short**, **Integer**, **Long**, **Float** and **Double**).*

Our next example is a guest book that enables users to place their first name, last name and e-mail address into a guest book database. After submitting their information, users see a Web page containing all the users in the guest book. Each person's e-mail address is displayed as a hyperlink that allows the user to send an e-mail message to the person. The example demonstrates action **<jsp:setProperty>**. In addition, the example introduces the JSP *page directive* and *JSP error pages*.

The guest book example consists of JavaBeans **GuestBean** (Fig. B.20) and **Guest-DataBean** (Fig. B.21), and JSPs **guestBookLogin.jsp** (Fig. B.22), **guestBookView.jsp** (Fig. B.23) and **guestBookErrorPage.jsp** (Fig. B.24). Sample outputs from this example are shown in Fig. B.25.

JavaBean **GuestBean** (Fig. B.20) defines three guest properties: **firstName**, **lastName** and **email**. Each is a read/write property with *set* and *get* methods to manipulate the property.

```
1   // Fig. B.20: GuestBean.java
2   // JavaBean to store data for a guest in the guest book.
3   package com.deitel.jws.jsp.beans;
4
5   public class GuestBean {
6      private String firstName, lastName, email;
7
8      // set the guest's first name
9      public void setFirstName( String name )
10     {
11        firstName = name;
12     }
13
14     // get the guest's first name
15     public String getFirstName()
16     {
17        return firstName;
18     }
19
20     // set the guest's last name
21     public void setLastName( String name )
22     {
23        lastName = name;
24     }
25
26     // get the guest's last name
27     public String getLastName()
28     {
29        return lastName;
30     }
31
32     // set the guest's email address
33     public void setEmail( String address )
34     {
35        email = address;
36     }
37
38     // get the guest's email address
39     public String getEmail()
40     {
41        return email;
42     }
43  }
```

Fig. B.20 **GuestBean** stores information for one guest.

JavaBean **GuestDataBean** (Fig. B.21) connects to the **guestbook** database and provides methods **getGuestList** and **addGuest** to manipulate the database. The guestbook database has a single table (**guests**) containing three columns (**firstName**, **lastName** and **email**). We provide an SQL script (**guestbook.sql**) with this example that can be used with the Cloudscape DBMS to create the **guestbook** database. For further details on creating a database with Cloudscape, refer to Chapter 1.

```
1   // Fig. B.21: GuestDataBean.java
2   // Class GuestDataBean makes a database connection and supports
3   // inserting and retrieving data from the database.
4   package com.deitel.jws.jsp.beans;
5
6   // Java core packages
7   import java.io.*;
8   import java.sql.*;
9   import java.util.*;
10
11  public class GuestDataBean {
12     private Connection connection;
13     private PreparedStatement addRecord, getRecords;
14
15     // construct TitlesBean object
16     public GuestDataBean() throws Exception
17     {
18        // load the Cloudscape driver
19        Class.forName( "COM.cloudscape.core.RmiJdbcDriver" );
20
21        // connect to the database
22        connection = DriverManager.getConnection(
23           "jdbc:rmi:jdbc:cloudscape:guestbook" );
24
25        getRecords =
26           connection.prepareStatement(
27              "SELECT firstName, lastName, email FROM guests"
28           );
29
30        addRecord =
31           connection.prepareStatement(
32              "INSERT INTO guests ( " +
33                 "firstName, lastName, email ) " +
34              "VALUES ( ?, ?, ? )"
35           );
36     }
37
38     // return an ArrayList of GuestBeans
39     public ArrayList getGuestList() throws SQLException
40     {
41        ArrayList guestList = new ArrayList();
42
43        // obtain list of titles
44        ResultSet results = getRecords.executeQuery();
45
46        // get row data
47        while ( results.next() ) {
48           GuestBean guest = new GuestBean();
49
50           guest.setFirstName( results.getString( 1 ) );
51           guest.setLastName( results.getString( 2 ) );
52           guest.setEmail( results.getString( 3 ) );
```

Fig. B.21 **GuestDataBean** performs database access on behalf of **guestBookLogin.jsp**. (Part 1 of 2.)

```
53
54              guestList.add( guest );
55          }
56
57          return guestList;
58      }
59
60      // insert a guest in guestbook database
61      public void addGuest( GuestBean guest ) throws SQLException
62      {
63          addRecord.setString( 1, guest.getFirstName() );
64          addRecord.setString( 2, guest.getLastName() );
65          addRecord.setString( 3, guest.getEmail() );
66
67          addRecord.executeUpdate();
68      }
69
70      // close statements and terminate database connection
71      protected void finalize()
72      {
73          // attempt to close database connection
74          try {
75              getRecords.close();
76              addRecord.close();
77              connection.close();
78          }
79
80          // process SQLException on close operation
81          catch ( SQLException sqlException ) {
82              sqlException.printStackTrace();
83          }
84      }
85  }
```

Fig. B.21   `GuestDataBean` performs database access on behalf of
`guestBookLogin.jsp`. (Part 2 of 2.)

GuestDataBean method getGuestList (lines 39–58) returns an ArrayList
of GuestBean objects representing the guests in the database. Method getGuestList
creates the GuestBean objects from the ResultSet returned by PreparedStatement getRecords (defined at lines 25–28 and executed at line 44).

GuestDataBean method addGuest (lines 61–68) receives a GuestBean as an
argument and uses the GuestBean's properties as the arguments to PreparedStatement addRecord (defined at lines 30–35). This PreparedStatement (executed at
line 67) inserts a new guest in the database.

Note that the GuestDataBean's constructor, getGuestList and addGuest
methods do not process potential exceptions. In the constructor, line 19 can throw a
ClassNotFoundException, and the other statements can throw SQLExceptions.
Similarly, SQLExceptions can be thrown from the bodies of methods getGuestList
and addGuest. In this example, we purposely let any exceptions that occur get passed

back to the JSP that invokes the **GuestDataBean**'s constructor or methods. This enables us to demonstrate JSP error pages. When a JSP performs an operation that causes an exception, the JSP can include scriptlets that catch the exception and process it. Exceptions that are not caught can be forwarded to a JSP error page for handling.

JavaServer Page **guestBookLogin.jsp** (Fig. B.22) is a modified version of **forward1.jsp** (Fig. B.11) that displays a **form** in which users can enter their first name, last name and e-mail address. When the user submits the **form**, **guestBook-Login.jsp** is requested again, so it can ensure that all the data values were entered. If not, the **guestBookLogin.jsp** responds with the **form** again, so the user can fill in missing field(s). If the user supplies all three pieces of information, **guestBook-Login.jsp** forwards the request to **guestBookView.jsp**, which displays the guest book contents.

```
1   <?xml version = "1.0"?>
2   <!DOCTYPE html PUBLIC "-//W3C//DTD XHTML 1.0 Strict//EN"
3      "http://www.w3.org/TR/xhtml1/DTD/xhtml1-strict.dtd">
4
5   <!-- Fig. B.22: guestBookLogin.jsp -->
6
7   <%-- page settings --%>
8   <%@ page errorPage = "guestBookErrorPage.jsp" %>
9
10  <%-- beans used in this JSP --%>
11  <jsp:useBean id = "guest" scope = "page"
12     class = "com.deitel.jws.jsp.beans.GuestBean" />
13  <jsp:useBean id = "guestData" scope = "request"
14     class = "com.deitel.jws.jsp.beans.GuestDataBean" />
15
16  <html xmlns = "http://www.w3.org/1999/xhtml">
17
18  <head>
19     <title>Guest Book Login</title>
20
21     <style type = "text/css">
22        body {
23           font-family: tahoma, helvetica, arial, sans-serif;
24        }
25
26        table, tr, td {
27           font-size: .9em;
28           border: 3px groove;
29           padding: 5px;
30           background-color: #dddddd;
31        }
32     </style>
33  </head>
34
```

Fig. B.22   JavaServer page **guestBookLogin.jsp** enables the user to submit a first name, a last name and an e-mail address to be placed in the guest book. (Part 1 of 3.)

```
35    <body>
36       <jsp:setProperty name = "guest" property = "*" />
37
38       <% // start scriptlet
39
40          if ( guest.getFirstName() == null ||
41              guest.getLastName() == null ||
42              guest.getEmail() == null ) {
43
44       %> <%-- end scriptlet to insert fixed template data --%>
45
46             <form method = "post" action = "guestBookLogin.jsp">
47                <p>Enter your first name, last name and email
48                   address to register in our guest book.</p>
49
50                <table>
51                   <tr>
52                      <td>First name</td>
53
54                      <td>
55                         <input type = "text" name = "firstName" />
56                      </td>
57                   </tr>
58
59                   <tr>
60                      <td>Last name</td>
61
62                      <td>
63                         <input type = "text" name = "lastName" />
64                      </td>
65                   </tr>
66
67                   <tr>
68                      <td>Email</td>
69
70                      <td>
71                         <input type = "text" name = "email" />
72                      </td>
73                   </tr>
74
75                   <tr>
76                      <td colspan = "2">
77                         <input type = "submit"
78                            value = "Submit" />
79                      </td>
80                   </tr>
81                </table>
82             </form>
83
```

Fig. B.22 JavaServer page **guestBookLogin.jsp** enables the user to submit a first name, a last name and an e-mail address to be placed in the guest book. (Part 2 of 3.)

```
84      <% // continue scriptlet
85
86         } // end if
87         else {
88            guestData.addGuest( guest );
89
90      %> <%-- end scriptlet to insert jsp:forward action --%>
91
92            <%-- forward to display guest book contents --%>
93            <jsp:forward page = "guestBookView.jsp" />
94
95      <% // continue scriptlet
96
97         } // end else
98
99      %> <%-- end scriptlet --%>
100 </body>
101
102 </html>
```

Fig. B.22 JavaServer page **guestBookLogin.jsp** enables the user to submit a first name, a last name and an e-mail address to be placed in the guest book. (Part 3 of 3.)

Line 8 of **guestBookLogin.jsp** introduces the **page** *directive*, which defines information that is globally available in a JSP. Directives are delimited by **<%@** and **%>**. In this case, the **page** directive's *errorPage attribute* is set to **guestBookErrorPage.jsp** (Fig. B.24), indicating that all uncaught exceptions are forwarded to **guestBookErrorPage.jsp** for processing. A complete description of the **page** directive appears in Section B.7.

Lines 11–14 define two **<jsp:useBean>** actions. Lines 11–12 create an instance of **GuestBean** called **guest**. This bean has **page** scope—it exists for use only in this page. Lines 14–14 create an instance of **GuestDataBean** called **guestData**. This bean has **request** scope—it exists for use in this page and any other page that helps process a single client request. Thus, when **guestBookLogin.jsp** forwards a request to **guestBookView.jsp**, the **GuestDataBean** is still available for use in **guestBookView.jsp**.

Line 36 demonstrates setting properties of the **GuestBean** called **guest** with request parameter values. The **input** elements on lines 55, 63 and 71 have the same names as the **GuestBean** properties. So, we use action **<jsp:setProperty>**'s ability to match request parameters to properties by specifying **"*"** for attribute **property**. Line 36 also can set the properties individually with the following lines:

```
<jsp:setProperty name = "guest" property = "firstName"
   param = "firstName" />

<jsp:setProperty name = "guest" property = "lastName"
   param = "lastName" />

<jsp:setProperty name = "guest" property = "email"
   param = "email" />
```

If the request parameters had names that differed from **GuestBean**'s properties, the **param** attribute in each of the preceding **<jsp:setProperty>** actions could be changed to the appropriate request parameter name.

JavaServer Page **guestBookView.jsp** (Fig. B.23) outputs an XHTML document containing the guest book entries in tabular format. Lines 8–10 define three **page** directives. Line 8 specifies that the error page for this JSP is **guestBookErrorPage.jsp**. Lines 9–10 introduce attribute ***import*** of the **page** directive. Attribute ***import*** enables programmers to specify Java classes and packages that are used in the context of the JSP. Line 9 indicates that classes from package **java.util** are used in this JSP, and line 10 indicates that classes from our package **com.deitel.jws.jsp.beans** also are used.

Lines 13–14 specify a **<jsp:useBean>** action that obtains a reference to a **GuestDataBean** object. If a **GuestDataBean** object already exists, the action returns a reference to the existing object. Otherwise, the action creates a **GuestDataBean** for use in this JSP. Lines 50–59 define a scriptlet that gets the guest list from the **GuestDataBean** and begin a loop to output the entries. Lines 61–70 combine fixed template text with JSP expressions to create rows in the table of guest book data that will be displayed on the client. The scriptlet at lines 72–76 terminates the loop.

```
1   <?xml version = "1.0"?>
2   <!DOCTYPE html PUBLIC "-//W3C//DTD XHTML 1.0 Strict//EN"
3      "http://www.w3.org/TR/xhtml1/DTD/xhtml1-strict.dtd">
4
5   <!-- Fig. B.23: guestBookView.jsp -->
6
7   <%-- page settings --%>
8   <%@ page errorPage = "guestBookErrorPage.jsp" %>
9   <%@ page import = "java.util.*" %>
10  <%@ page import = "com.deitel.jws.jsp.beans.*" %>
11
12  <%-- GuestDataBean to obtain guest list --%>
13  <jsp:useBean id = "guestData" scope = "request"
14     class = "com.deitel.jws.jsp.beans.GuestDataBean" />
15
16  <html xmlns = "http://www.w3.org/1999/xhtml">
17
18     <head>
19        <title>Guest List</title>
20
21        <style type = "text/css">
22           body {
23              font-family: tahoma, helvetica, arial, sans-serif;
24           }
25
26           table, tr, td, th {
27              text-align: center;
28              font-size: .9em;
29              border: 3px groove;
30              padding: 5px;
```

Fig. B.23   JavaServer page **guestBookView.jsp** displays the contents of the guest book. (Part 1 of 2.)

```
31                 background-color: #dddddd;
32              }
33          </style>
34      </head>
35
36      <body>
37          <p style = "font-size: 2em;">Guest List</p>
38
39          <table>
40              <thead>
41                  <tr>
42                      <th style = "width: 100px;">Last name</th>
43                      <th style = "width: 100px;">First name</th>
44                      <th style = "width: 200px;">Email</th>
45                  </tr>
46              </thead>
47
48              <tbody>
49
50          <% // start scriptlet
51
52              List guestList = guestData.getGuestList();
53              Iterator guestListIterator = guestList.iterator();
54              GuestBean guest;
55
56              while ( guestListIterator.hasNext() ) {
57                  guest = ( GuestBean ) guestListIterator.next();
58
59          %> <%-- end scriptlet; insert fixed template data --%>
60
61                  <tr>
62                      <td><%= guest.getLastName() %></td>
63
64                      <td><%= guest.getFirstName() %></td>
65
66                      <td>
67                          <a href = "mailto:<%= guest.getEmail() %>">
68                              <%= guest.getEmail() %></a>
69                      </td>
70                  </tr>
71
72          <% // continue scriptlet
73
74              } // end while
75
76          %> <%-- end scriptlet --%>
77
78              </tbody>
79          </table>
80      </body>
81
82  </html>
```

Fig. B.23   JavaServer page **guestBookView.jsp** displays the contents of the guest book. (Part 2 of 2.)

JavaServer Page **guestBookErrorPage.jsp** (Fig. B.24) outputs an XHTML document containing an error message based on the type of exception that causes this error page to be invoked. Lines 8–10 define several **page** directives. Line 8 introduces **page** directive attribute *isErrorPage*. Setting this attribute to **true** makes the JSP an error page and enables access to the JSP implicit object **exception** that refers to an exception object indicating the problem that occurred.

Common Programming Error B.8

*JSP implicit object **exception** can be used only in error pages. Using this object in other JSPs results in a translation-time error.*

Lines 29–46 define scriptlets that determine the type of exception that occurred and begin outputting an appropriate error message with fixed template data. The actual error message from the exception is output at line 56.

```
1    <?xml version = "1.0"?>
2    <!DOCTYPE html PUBLIC "-//W3C//DTD XHTML 1.0 Strict//EN"
3       "http://www.w3.org/TR/xhtml1/DTD/xhtml1-strict.dtd">
4
5    <!-- Fig. B.24: guestBookErrorPage.jsp -->
6
7    <%-- page settings --%>
8    <%@ page isErrorPage = "true" %>
9    <%@ page import = "java.util.*" %>
10   <%@ page import = "java.sql.*" %>
11
12   <html xmlns = "http://www.w3.org/1999/xhtml">
13
14      <head>
15         <title>Error!</title>
16
17         <style type = "text/css">
18            .bigRed {
19               font-size: 2em;
20               color: red;
21               font-weight: bold;
22            }
23         </style>
24      </head>
25
26      <body>
27         <p class = "bigRed">
28
29            <% // scriptlet to determine exception type
30               // and output beginning of error message
31               if ( exception instanceof SQLException )
32            %>
33
34               An SQLException
35
```

Fig. B.24   JavaServer page **guestBookErrorPage.jsp** responds to exceptions in **guestBookLogin.jsp** and **guestBookView.jsp**. (Part 1 of 2.)

```
36        <%
37            else if ( exception instanceof ClassNotFoundException )
38        %>
39
40            A ClassNotFoundException
41
42        <%
43          else
44        %>
45
46            An exception
47
48        <%-- end scriptlet to insert fixed template data --%>
49
50          <%-- continue error message output --%>
51          occurred while interacting with the guestbook database.
52        </p>
53
54        <p class = "bigRed">
55          The error message was:<br />
56          <%= exception.getMessage() %>
57        </p>
58
59        <p class = "bigRed">Please try again later</p>
60      </body>
61
62    </html>
```

Fig. B.24   JavaServer page **guestBookErrorPage.jsp** responds to exceptions in **guestBookLogin.jsp** and **guestBookView.jsp**. (Part 2 of 2.)

Figure B.25 shows sample interactions between the user and the JSPs in the guest book example. In the first two rows of output, separate users entered their first name, last name and e-mail. In each case, the current contents of the guest book are returned and displayed for the user. In the final interaction, a third user specified an e-mail address that already existed in the database. The e-mail address is the primary key in the **guests** table of the **guestbook** database, so its values must be unique. Thus, the database prevents the new record from being inserted, and an exception occurs. The exception is forwarded to **guestBookErrorPage.jsp** for processing, which results in the last screen capture.

To test the guest book in Tomcat, copy **guestBookLogin.jsp**, **guestBook-View.jsp** and **guestBookErrorPage.jsp** into the **jsp** directory created in Section B.3. Copy **GuestBean.class** and **GuestDataBean.class** into the **jws** Web application's **WEB-INF\classes** directory in Tomcat. [*Note:* This example will work only if the proper package directory structure for **GuestBean** and **Guest-DataBean** is defined in the **classes** directory. These classes are defined in package **com.deitel.jws.jsp.beans**.] Open your Web browser and enter the following URL to test **guestBookLogin.jsp**:

```
http://localhost:8080/jws/jsp/guestBookLogin.jsp
```

Fig. B.25 JSP guest book sample output windows. (Part 1 of 2.)

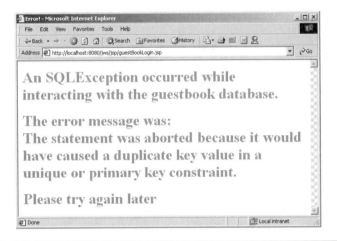

Fig. B.25   JSP guest book sample output windows. (Part 2 of 2.)

B.7 Directives

Directives are messages to the JSP container that enable the programmer to specify page settings (such as the error page), to include content from other resources and to specify custom-tag libraries for use in a JSP. Directives (delimited by `<%@` and `%>`) are processed at translation time. Thus, directives do not produce any immediate output, because they are processed before the JSP accepts any requests. Figure B.26 summarizes the three directive types. These directives are discussed in the next several subsections.

B.7.1 page Directive

The **page** *directive* specifies global settings for the JSP in the JSP container. There can be many **page** directives, provided that there is only one occurrence of each attribute. The only exception to this rule is the **import** attribute, which can be used repeatedly to import Java packages used in the JSP. Figure B.27 summarizes the attributes of the **page** directive.

Directive	Description
page	Defines page settings for the JSP container to process.
include	Causes the JSP container to perform a translation-time insertion of another resource's content. As the JSP is translated into a servlet and compiled, the referenced file replaces the **include** directive and is translated as if it were originally part of the JSP.
taglib	Allows programmers to include their own new tags in the form of *tag libraries*. These libraries can be used to encapsulate functionality and simplify the coding of a JSP.

Fig. B.26   JSP directives.

Common Programming Error B.9

*Providing multiple **page** directives with one or more attributes in common is a JSP translation-time error.*

Common Programming Error B.10

*Providing a **page** directive with an attribute or value that is not recognized is a JSP translation-time error.*

Attribute	Description
language	The scripting language used in the JSP. Currently, the only valid value for this attribute is **java**.
extends	Specifies the class from which the translated JSP will be inherited. This attribute must be a fully qualified package and class name.
import	Specifies a comma-separated list of fully qualified class names and/or packages that will be used in the current JSP. When the scripting language is **java**, the default import list is **java.lang.***, **javax.servlet.***, **javax.servlet.jsp.*** and **javax.servlet.http.***. If multiple **import** properties are specified, the package names are placed in a list by the container.
session	Specifies whether the page participates in a session. The values for this attribute are **true** (participates in a session—the default) or **false** (does not participate in a session). When the page is part of a session, the JSP implicit object **session** is available for use in the page. Otherwise, **session** is not available. In the latter case, using **session** in the scripting code results in a translation-time error.
buffer	Specifies the size of the output buffer used with the implicit object **out**. The value of this attribute can be **none** for no buffering, or a value such as **8kb** (the default buffer size). The JSP specification indicates that the buffer used must be at least the size specified.
autoFlush	When set to **true** (the default value), this attribute indicates that the output buffer used with implicit object **out** should be flushed automatically when the buffer fills. If set to **false**, an exception occurs if the buffer overflows. This attribute's value must be **true** if the buffer attribute is set to **none**.
isThreadSafe	Specifies if the page is thread safe. If **true** (the default), the page is considered to be thread safe, and it can process multiple requests at the same time. If **false**, the servlet that represents the page implements interface **java.lang.SingleThreadModel** and only one request can be processed by that JSP at a time. The JSP standard allows multiple instances of a JSP to exists for JSPs that are not thread safe. This enables the container to handle requests more efficiently. However, this does not guarantee that resources shared across JSP instances are accessed in a thread-safe manner.
info	Specifies an information string that describes the page. This string is returned by the **getServletInfo** method of the servlet that represents the translated JSP. This method can be invoked through the JSP's implicit **page** object.

Fig. B.27   Attributes of the **page** directive. (Part 1 of 2.)

Attribute	Description
errorPage	Any exceptions in the current page that are not caught are sent to the error page for processing. The error page implicit object **exception** references the original exception.
isErrorPage	Specifies if the current page is an error page that will be invoked in response to an error on another page. If the attribute value is **true**, the implicit object **exception** is created and references the original exception that occurred. If **false** (the default), any use of the **exception** object in the page results in a translation-time error.
contentType	Specifies the MIME type of the data in the response to the client. The default type is **text/html**.

Fig. B.27   Attributes of the **page** directive. (Part 2 of 2.)

Software Engineering Observation B.11

*According to the JSP specification section 2.7.1, the **extends** attribute "should not be used without careful consideration as it restricts the ability of the JSP container to provide specialized superclasses that may improve on the quality of rendered service." Remember that a Java class can extend exactly one other class. If your JSP specifies an explicit superclass, the JSP container cannot translate your JSP into a subclass of one of the container application's own enhanced servlet classes.*

Common Programming Error B.11

*Using JSP implicit object **session** in a JSP that does not have its **page** directive attribute **session** set to **true** is a translation-time error.*

B.7.2 **include** Directive

The ***include*** *directive* includes the content of another resource once, at JSP translation time. The **include** directive has only one attribute—**file**—that specifies the URL of the page to include. The difference between directive **include** and action **<jsp:include>** is noticeable only if the included content changes. For example, if the definition of an XHTML document changes after it is included with directive **include**, future invocations of the JSP will show the original content of the XHTML document, not the new content. In contrast, action **<jsp:include>** is processed in each request to the JSP. Therefore, changes to included content would be apparent in the next request to the JSP that uses action **<jsp:include>**.

Software Engineering Observation B.12

*The JavaServer Pages 1.1 specification does not provide a mechanism for updating text included in a JSP with the **include** directive. Version 1.2 of the JSP specification allows the container to provide such a mechanism, but the specification does not provide for this directly.*

JavaServer Page **includeDirective.jsp** (Fig. B.28) reimplements JavaServer Page **include.jsp** (Fig. B.10) using **include** directives. To test **includeDirective.jsp** in Tomcat, copy **includeDirective.jsp** into the **jsp** directory created in Section B.3. Open your Web browser and enter the following URL to test **include-Directive.jsp**:

> `http://localhost:8080/jws/jsp/includeDirective.jsp`

```
1   <?xml version = "1.0"?>
2   <!DOCTYPE html PUBLIC "-//W3C//DTD XHTML 1.0 Strict//EN"
3      "http://www.w3.org/TR/xhtml1/DTD/xhtml1-strict.dtd">
4
5   <!-- Fig. B.28: includeDirective.jsp -->
6
7   <html xmlns = "http://www.w3.org/1999/xhtml">
8
9      <head>
10        <title>Using the include directive</title>
11
12        <style type = "text/css">
13           body {
14              font-family: tahoma, helvetica, arial, sans-serif;
15           }
16
17           table, tr, td {
18              font-size: .9em;
19              border: 3px groove;
20              padding: 5px;
21              background-color: #dddddd;
22           }
23        </style>
24     </head>
25
26     <body>
27        <table>
28           <tr>
29              <td style = "width: 160px; text-align: center">
30                 <img src = "images/logotiny.png"
31                    width = "140" height = "93"
32                    alt = "Deitel & Associates, Inc. Logo" />
33              </td>
34
35              <td>
36
37                 <%-- include banner.html in this JSP --%>
38                 <%@ include file = "banner.html" %>
39
40              </td>
41           </tr>
42
43           <tr>
44              <td style = "width: 160px">
45
46                 <%-- include toc.html in this JSP --%>
47                 <%@ include file = "toc.html" %>
```

Fig. B.28 JSP **includeDirective.jsp** demonstrates including content at translation-time with directive **include**. (Part 1 of 2.)

```
48
49                </td>
50
51                <td style = "vertical-align: top">
52
53                    <%-- include clock2.jsp in this JSP --%>
54                    <%@ include file = "clock2.jsp" %>
55
56                </td>
57            </tr>
58        </table>
59    </body>
60 </html>
```

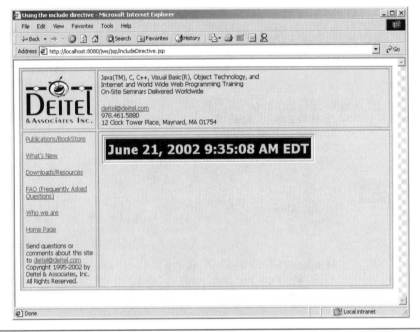

Fig. B.28   JSP `includeDirective.jsp` demonstrates including content at translation-time with directive `include`. (Part 2 of 2.)

B.8 Custom Tag Libraries

Throughout this appendix, you have seen how JavaServer Pages can simplify the delivery of dynamic Web content. Our discussion continues with JSP *custom tag libraries*, which provide another mechanism for encapsulating complex functionality for use in JSPs. Custom tag libraries define one or more *custom tags* that JSP implementors can use to create dynamic content. The functionality of these custom tags is defined in Java classes that implement interface **Tag** (package **javax.servlet.jsp.tagext**), normally by extending class **TagSupport** or **BodyTagSupport**. This mechanism enables Java programmers to create complex functionality for Web page designers who have no Java programming knowledge.

Previously, we introduced action **<jsp:useBean>** and JavaBeans to incorporate complex, encapsulated functionality in a JSP. In many cases, action **<jsp:useBean>** and JavaBeans can perform the same tasks as custom tags can. However, action **<jsp:useBean>** and JavaBeans have disadvantages—JavaBeans cannot manipulate JSP content and Web page designers must have some Java knowledge to use JavaBeans in a page. With custom tags, it is possible for Web page designers to use complex functionality without knowing any Java.

In this section, we present three examples of custom tags. Each tag is part of a single custom tag library that we refer to as **jws**. A JSP includes a custom tag library with the *taglib directive*. Figure B.29 summarizes the **taglib** directive's attributes.

Each of the examples in this section uses directive **taglib**. There are several types of custom tags that have different levels of complexity. We demonstrate simple tags, simple tags with attributes and tags that can process their body elements. For complete details on custom tag libraries, see the resources in Section B.10.

B.8.1 Simple Custom Tag

Our first custom tag example implements a simple custom tag that inserts the string "**Welcome to JSP Tag Libraries**" in a JSP. When implementing custom tags, you must define a tag-handler class for each tag that implements the tag's functionality, a *tag library descriptor* that provides information about the tag library and its custom tags to the JSP container and a JSP that uses the custom tag. Figure B.30 (**customTagWelcome.jsp**) demonstrates our first custom tag. At the end of this section, we discuss how to configure this example for testing on Tomcat.

Attribute	Description
uri	Specifies the relative or absolute URI of the tag library descriptor.
tagPrefix	Specifies the required prefix that distinguishes custom tags from built-in tags. The prefix names **jsp**, **jspx**, **java**, **javax**, **servlet**, **sun** and **sunw** are reserved.

Fig. B.29   Attributes of the **taglib** directive.

```
1   <?xml version = "1.0"?>
2   <!DOCTYPE html PUBLIC "-//W3C//DTD XHTML 1.0 Strict//EN"
3      "http://www.w3.org/TR/xhtml1/DTD/xhtml1-strict.dtd">
4
5   <!-- Fig. B.30: customTagWelcome.jsp           -->
6   <!-- JSP that uses a custom tag to output content. -->
7
8   <%-- taglib directive --%>
9   <%@ taglib uri = "jws-taglib.tld" prefix = "jws" %>
10
11  <html xmlns = "http://www.w3.org/1999/xhtml">
```

Fig. B.30   JSP **customTagWelcome.jsp** uses a simple custom tag. (Part 1 of 2.)

```
12
13       <head>
14          <title>Simple Custom Tag Example</title>
15       </head>
16
17       <body>
18          <p>The following text demonstrates a custom tag:</p>
19          <h1>
20             <jws:welcome />
21          </h1>
22       </body>
23
24    </html>
```

Fig. B.30 JSP `customTagWelcome.jsp` uses a simple custom tag. (Part 2 of 2.)

The **taglib** directive at line 9 enables the JSP to use the tags in our tag library. The directive specifies the **uri** of the tag library descriptor file (**jws-taglib.tld**; Fig. B.32) that provides information about our tag library to the JSP container and the **prefix** for each tag (**jws**). JSP programmers use the tag library **prefix** when referring to tags in a specific tag library. Line 20 uses a custom tag called **welcome** to insert text in the JSP. Note that the prefix **jws:** precedes the tag name. This enables the JSP container to interpret the meaning of the tag and invoke the appropriate *tag handler*. Also note that line 20 can be written with start and end tags as follows:

> `<jws:welcome> </jws:welcome>`

Figure B.31 defines class **WelcomeTagHandler**—the tag handler that implements the functionality of our custom tag **welcome**. Every tag handler must implement interface **Tag**, which defines the methods a JSP container invokes to incorporate a tag's functionality in a JSP. Most tag handler classes implement interface **Tag** by extending either class **TagSupport** or class **BodyTagSupport**.

Software Engineering Observation B.13

*Classes that define custom tag handlers must implement interface **Tag** from package **jav-ax.servlet.jsp.tagext**.*

Software Engineering Observation B.14

*A custom tag handler class should extend class **TagSupport** if the body of the tag is ignored or simply output during custom tag processing.*

Software Engineering Observation B.15

A custom tag handler class should extend class BodyTagSupport if the handler interacts with the tag's body content.

Software Engineering Observation B.16

Custom tag handlers must be defined in Java packages.

Class **WelcomeTagHandler** implements interface **Tag** by extending class **Tag-Support** (both from package **java.servlet.jsp.tagext**). The most important methods of interface **Tag** are *doStartTag* and *doEndTag*. The JSP container invokes these methods when it encounters the starting custom tag and the ending custom tag, respectively. These methods throw **JspException**s if problems are encountered during custom-tag processing.

```
1   // Fig. B.31: WelcomeTagHandler.java
2   // Custom tag handler that handles a simple tag.
3   package com.deitel.jws.jsp.taglibrary;
4
5   // Java core packages
6   import java.io.*;
7
8   // Java extension packages
9   import javax.servlet.jsp.*;
10  import javax.servlet.jsp.tagext.*;
11
12  public class WelcomeTagHandler extends TagSupport {
13
14     // Method called to begin tag processing
15     public int doStartTag() throws JspException
16     {
17        // attempt tag processing
18        try {
19           // obtain JspWriter to output content
20           JspWriter out = pageContext.getOut();
21
22           // output content
23           out.print( "Welcome to JSP Tag Libraries!" );
24        }
25
26        // rethrow IOException to JSP container as JspException
27        catch( IOException ioException ) {
28           throw new JspException( ioException.getMessage() );
29        }
30
31        return SKIP_BODY;  // ignore the tag's body
32     }
33  }
```

Fig. B.31 **WelcomeTagHandler** custom tag handler.

Software Engineering Observation B.17

*If exceptions other than **JspException**s occur in a custom tag handler class, the exceptions should be caught and processed. If such exceptions would prevent proper tag processing, the exceptions should be rethrown as **JspException**s.*

In this example, class **WelcomeTagHandler** overrides method **doStartTag** to output text that becomes part of the JSP's response. Line 20 uses the custom tag handler's **pageContext** object (inherited from class **TagSupport**) to obtain the JSP's **JspWriter** object that method **doStartTag** uses to output text. Line 23 uses the **JspWriter** to output a string. Line 31 returns the **static** integer constant ***SKIP_BODY*** (defined in interface **Tag**) to indicate that the JSP container should ignore any text or other elements that appear in the tag's body. To include the body content as part of the response, specify **static** integer constant ***EVAL_BODY_INCLUDE*** as the return value. This example does not require any processing when the ending tag is encountered by the JSP container, so we did not override **doEndTag**.

Figure B.32 defines the custom tag library descriptor file. This XML document specifies information required by the JSP container such as the version number of the tag library (element **tlibversion**), the JSP version number (element **jspversion**), information about the library (element **info**) and information about the tags in the library (one **tag** element for each tag). In this tag library descriptor, the **tag** element at lines 18–30 describes our **welcome** tag. Line 19 specifies the tag's ***name***—used by JSP programmers to access the custom functionality in a JSP. Lines 21–23 specify the ***tagclass***—the custom tag handler class. This element associates the tag name with a specific tag handler class. Element ***bodycontent*** (line 25) specifies that our custom tag has an ***empty*** body. This value can also be ***tagdependent*** or ***JSP***. Lines 27–29 specify information about the tag with an **info** element. [*Note:* We introduce other elements of the tag library descriptor as necessary. For a complete description of the tag library descriptor, see the JavaServer Pages 1.1 specification, which can be downloaded from **java.sun.com/ products/jsp/download.html**.]

Software Engineering Observation B.18

*The custom tag handler class must be specified with its full package name in the **tagclass** element of the tag library descriptor.*

```
1   <?xml version = "1.0" encoding = "ISO-8859-1" ?>
2   <!DOCTYPE taglib PUBLIC
3      "-//Sun Microsystems, Inc.//DTD JSP Tag Library 1.1//EN"
4      "http://java.sun.com/j2ee/dtds/web-jsptaglibrary_1_1.dtd">
5
6   <!-- a tag library descriptor -->
7
8   <taglib>
9      <tlibversion>1.0</tlibversion>
10     <jspversion>1.1</jspversion>
11     <shortname>jws</shortname>
12
```

Fig. B.32   Custom tag library descriptor file **jws-taglib.tld**. (Part 1 of 2.)

```
13        <info>
14           A simple tab library for the examples
15        </info>
16
17        <!-- A simple tag that outputs content -->
18        <tag>
19           <name>welcome</name>
20
21           <tagclass>
22              com.deitel.jws.jsp.taglibrary.WelcomeTagHandler
23           </tagclass>
24
25           <bodycontent>empty</bodycontent>
26
27           <info>
28              Inserts content welcoming user to tag libraries
29           </info>
30        </tag>
31  </taglib>
```

Fig. B.32 Custom tag library descriptor file **jws-taglib.tld**. (Part 2 of 2.)

To test **customTagWelcome.jsp** in Tomcat, copy **customTagWelcome.jsp** and **jws-taglib.tld** into the **jsp** directory created in Section B.3. Copy **WelcomeTagHandler.class** into the **jws** Web application's **WEB-INF\classes** directory in Tomcat. [*Note*: Class **WelcomeTagHandler** must appear in its proper package director structure in **classes** directory. **WelcomeTagHandler** is defined in package **com.deitel.jws.jsp.taglibrary**.] Open your Web browser and enter the following URL to test **customTagWelcome.jsp**:

```
http://localhost:8080/jws/jsp/customTagWelcome.jsp
```

B.8.2 Custom Tag with Attributes

Many XHTML and JSP elements use attributes to customize functionality. For example, an XHTML element can specify a **style** attribute that indicates how the element should be formatted in a client's Web browser. Similarly, the JSP action elements have attributes that help customize their behavior in a JSP. Our next example demonstrates how to specify attributes for your custom tags.

Figure B.33 (**customTagAttribute.jsp**) is similar to Fig. B.30. This example uses a new tag called, **welcome2**, to insert text in the JSP that is customized based on the value of attribute **firstName**. The screen capture shows the results of the **welcome2** tags on lines 20 and 30. The tag at line 20 specifies the value **"Paul"** for attribute **firstName**. Lines 26–28 define a scriptlet that obtains the value of request parameter **name** and assign it to **String** reference **name**. Line 30 uses the **name** in a JSP expression as the value for the **firstName** attribute. In the sample screen capture, this JSP was invoked with the following URL:

```
http://localhost:8080/jws/jsp/
customTagAttribute.jsp?firstName=Sean
```

```
1   <?xml version = "1.0"?>
2   <!DOCTYPE html PUBLIC "-//W3C//DTD XHTML 1.0 Strict//EN"
3      "http://www.w3.org/TR/xhtml1/DTD/xhtml1-strict.dtd">
4
5   <!-- Fig. B.33: customTagAttribute.jsp                -->
6   <!-- JSP that uses a custom tag to output content. -->
7
8   <%-- taglib directive --%>
9   <%@ taglib uri = "jws-taglib.tld" prefix = "jws" %>
10
11  <html xmlns = "http://www.w3.org/1999/xhtml">
12
13     <head>
14        <title>Specifying Custom Tag Attributes</title>
15     </head>
16
17     <body>
18        <p>Demonstrating an attribute with a string value</p>
19        <h1>
20           <jws:welcome2 firstName = "Paul" />
21        </h1>
22
23        <p>Demonstrating an attribute with an expression value</p>
24        <h1>
25           <%-- scriptlet to obtain "name" request parameter --%>
26           <%
27              String name = request.getParameter( "name" );
28           %>
29
30           <jws:welcome2 firstName = "<%= name %>" />
31        </h1>
32     </body>
33
34  </html>
```

Fig. B.33   Specifying attributes for a custom tag.

When defining the custom tag handler for a tag with attributes, you must provide methods that enable the JSP container to set the attribute values in the tag handler. Methods that manipulate attributes follow the same *set-* and *get-*method naming conventions as do JavaBean properties. Thus, the custom tag's **firstName** attribute is set with method **setFirstName**. Similarly, the method to obtain the **firstName** attribute's value would be **getFirstName** (we did not define this method for this example). Class **Welcome2TagHandler** (Fig. B.34) defines its **firstName** variable at line 13 and a corresponding *set* method **setFirstName** (lines 37–40). When the JSP container encounters a **welcome2** tag in a JSP, it creates a new **Welcome2TagHandler** object to process the tag and sets the tag's attributes. Next, the container invokes method **doStartTag** (lines 16–34) to perform the custom tag processing. Lines 24–25 use the **firstName** attribute value as part of the text output by the custom tag.

```
1   // Fig. B.34: Welcome2TagHandler.java
2   // Custom tag handler that handles a simple tag.
3   package com.deitel.jws.jsp.taglibrary;
4
5   // Java core packages
6   import java.io.*;
7
8   // Java extension packages
9   import javax.servlet.jsp.*;
10  import javax.servlet.jsp.tagext.*;
11
12  public class Welcome2TagHandler extends TagSupport {
13     private String firstName = "";
14
15     // Method called to begin tag processing
16     public int doStartTag() throws JspException
17     {
18        // attempt tag processing
19        try {
20           // obtain JspWriter to output content
21           JspWriter out = pageContext.getOut();
22
23           // output content
24           out.print( "Hello " + firstName +
25              ", <br />Welcome to JSP Tag Libraries!" );
26        }
27
28        // rethrow IOException to JSP container as JspException
29        catch( IOException ioException ) {
30           throw new JspException( ioException.getMessage() );
31        }
32
33        return SKIP_BODY;  // ignore the tag's body
34     }
35
```

Fig. B.34 **Welcome2TagHandler** custom tag handler for a tag with an attribute. (Part 1 of 2.)

```
36        // set firstName attribute to the users first name
37        public void setFirstName( String username )
38        {
39            firstName = username;
40        }
41    }
```

Fig. B.34   `Welcome2TagHandler` custom tag handler for a tag with an attribute. (Part 2 of 2.)

Before the **welcome2** tag can be used in a JSP, we must make the JSP container aware of the tag by adding it to a tag library. To do this, add the tag element of Fig. B.35 as a child of element **taglib** in the tag library descriptor **jws-taglib.tld**. As in the previous example, element **tag** contains elements **name**, **tagclass**, **bodycontent** and **info**. Lines 16–20 introduce element ***attribute*** for specifying the characteristics of a tag's attributes. Each attribute must have a separate attribute element that contains the **name**, ***required*** and ***rtexprvalue*** elements. Element **name** (line 17) specifies the attribute's name. Element **required** specifies whether the attribute is required (**true**) or optional (**false**). Element **rtexprvalue** specifies whether the value of the attribute can be the result of a JSP expression evaluated at runtime (**true**) or whether it must be a string literal (**false**).

To test **customTagAttribute.jsp** in Tomcat, copy **customTagAttribute.jsp** and the updated **jws-taglib.tld** into the **jsp** directory created in Section B.3. Copy **Welcome2TagHandler.class** into the **jws** Web application's **WEB-INF\classes** directory in Tomcat. [*Note:* This example will work only if the proper package-directory structure for **Welcome2TagHandler** is defined in the **classes** directory.] Open your Web browser and enter the following URL to test **customTagAttribute.jsp**:

> http://localhost:8080/jws/jsp/
> customTagAttribute.jsp?firstName=Sean

The text **?firstName=Sean** in the preceding URL specifies the value for request parameter **name** that is used by the custom tag **welcome2** at line 30 in Fig. B.33.

```
1    <!-- A tag with an attribute -->
2    <tag>
3        <name>welcome2</name>
4
5        <tagclass>
6            com.deitel.jws.jsp.taglibrary.Welcome2TagHandler
7        </tagclass>
8
9        <bodycontent>empty</bodycontent>
10
11       <info>
12           Inserts content welcoming user to tag libraries. Uses
13           attribute "name" to insert the user's name.
14       </info>
```

Fig. B.35   Element **tag** for the **welcome2** custom tag. (Part 1 of 2.)

```
15
16      <attribute>
17         <name>firstName</name>
18         <required>true</required>
19         <rtexprvalue>true</rtexprvalue>
20      </attribute>
21   </tag>
```

Fig. B.35 Element **tag** for the **welcome2** custom tag. (Part 2 of 2.)

B.8.3 Evaluating the Body of a Custom Tag

Custom tags are particularly powerful for processing the element body. When a custom tag interacts with the element body, additional methods are required to perform those interactions. The methods are defined in class **BodyTagSupport**. In our next example, we reimplement **guestBookView.jsp** (Fig. B.23) and replace the JavaBean processing performed in the JSP with a custom **guestlist** tag.

Figure B.36 (**customTagBody.jsp**) uses the custom **guestlist** tag at lines 41–52. Note that the JSP expressions in the body of element **guestlist** use variable names that are not defined in the JSP. These variables are defined by the custom tag handler when the custom tag is encountered. The custom tag handler places the variables in the JSP's **PageContext**, so the variables can be used throughout the page. Although no repetition is defined in the JSP, the custom tag handler is defined to iterate over all the guests in the **guestbook** database. This action results in the creation of a table row in the resulting Web page for each guest in the database.

```
1    <?xml version = "1.0"?>
2    <!DOCTYPE html PUBLIC "-//W3C//DTD XHTML 1.0 Strict//EN"
3       "http://www.w3.org/TR/xhtml1/DTD/xhtml1-strict.dtd">
4
5    <!-- customTagBody.jsp -->
6
7    <%-- taglib directive --%>
8    <%@ taglib uri = "jws-taglib.tld" prefix = "jws" %>
9
10   <html xmlns = "http://www.w3.org/1999/xhtml">
11
12      <head>
13         <title>Guest List</title>
14
15         <style type = "text/css">
16            body {
17               font-family: tahoma, helvetica, arial, sans-serif
18            }
19
20            table, tr, td, th {
21               text-align: center;
22               font-size: .9em;
23               border: 3px groove;
```

Fig. B.36 Using a custom tag that interacts with its body. (Part 1 of 2.)

```
24                    padding: 5px;
25                    background-color: #dddddd
26                 }
27           </style>
28        </head>
29
30        <body>
31           <p style = "font-size: 2em">Guest List</p>
32
33           <table>
34              <thead>
35                 <th style = "width: 100px">Last name</th>
36                 <th style = "width: 100px">First name</th>
37                 <th style = "width: 200px">Email</th>
38              </thead>
39
40              <%-- guestlist custom tag --%>
41              <jws:guestlist>
42                 <tr>
43                    <td><%= lastName %></td>
44
45                    <td><%= firstName %></td>
46
47                    <td>
48                       <a href = "mailto:<%= email %>">
49                          <%= email %></a>
50                    </td>
51                 </tr>
52              </jws:guestlist>
53           </table>
54        </body>
55
56     </html>
```

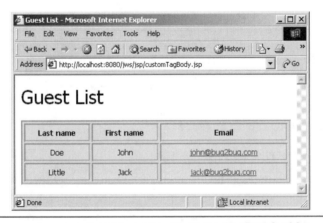

Fig. B.36   Using a custom tag that interacts with its body. (Part 2 of 2.)

As in **guestBookView.jsp**, the custom tag handler **GuestBookTag** (Fig. B.37) creates a **GuestDataBean** to access the **guestbook** database. Class **GuestBookTag** extends **BodyTagSupport**, which contains several new methods including *doInit-*

Body and *doAfterBody* (from interface *BodyTag*). Method **doInitBody** is called once, after **doStartTag** and before **doAfterBody**. Method **doAfterBody** can be called many times to process the body of a custom tag.

Software Engineering Observation B.19

*Method **doInitBody** typically performs one-time processing before method **doAfter-Body** processes the body of a custom tag. If method **doStartTag** returns Tag.SKIP_BODY, method **doInitBody** will not be called.*

```
1    // Fig. B.37: GuestBookTag.java
2    // Custom tag handler that reads information from the guestbook
3    // database and makes that data available in a JSP.
4    package com.deitel.jws.jsp.taglibrary;
5
6    // Java core packages
7    import java.io.*;
8    import java.util.*;
9
10   // Java extension packages
11   import javax.servlet.jsp.*;
12   import javax.servlet.jsp.tagext.*;
13
14   // Deitel packages
15   import com.deitel.jws.jsp.beans.*;
16
17   public class GuestBookTag extends BodyTagSupport {
18      private String firstName;
19      private String lastName;
20      private String email;
21
22      private GuestDataBean guestData;
23      private GuestBean guest;
24      private Iterator iterator;
25
26      // Method called to begin tag processing
27      public int doStartTag() throws JspException
28      {
29         // attempt tag processing
30         try {
31            guestData = new GuestDataBean();
32
33            List list = guestData.getGuestList();
34            iterator = list.iterator();
35
36            if ( iterator.hasNext() ) {
37               processNextGuest();
38
39               return EVAL_BODY_BUFFERED; // continue body processing
40            }
41            else
42               return SKIP_BODY;           // terminate body processing
43         }
```

Fig. B.37 **GuestBookTag** custom tag handler. (Part 1 of 2.)

```
44
45         // if any exceptions occur, do not continue processing
46         // tag's body
47         catch( Exception exception ) {
48            exception.printStackTrace();
49            return SKIP_BODY;   // ignore the tag's body
50         }
51      }
52
53      // process body and determine if body processing
54      // should continue
55      public int doAfterBody()
56      {
57         // attempt to output body data
58         try {
59            bodyContent.writeOut( getPreviousOut() );
60         }
61
62         // if exception occurs, terminate body processing
63         catch ( IOException ioException ) {
64            ioException.printStackTrace();
65            return SKIP_BODY;            // terminate body processing
66         }
67
68         bodyContent.clearBody();
69
70         if ( iterator.hasNext() ) {
71            processNextGuest();
72
73            return EVAL_BODY_BUFFERED; // continue body processing
74         }
75         else
76            return SKIP_BODY;            // terminate body processing
77      }
78
79      // obtains the next GuestBean and extracts its data
80      private void processNextGuest()
81      {
82         // get next guest
83         guest = ( GuestBean ) iterator.next();
84
85         pageContext.setAttribute(
86            "firstName", guest.getFirstName() );
87
88         pageContext.setAttribute(
89            "lastName", guest.getLastName() );
90
91         pageContext.setAttribute(
92            "email", guest.getEmail() );
93      }
94   }
```

Fig. B.37   GuestBookTag custom tag handler. (Part 2 of 2.)

The JSP container invokes method **doStartTag** (lines 27–51) when it encounters the custom **guestlist** tag in a JSP. Lines 31–34 create a new **GuestDataBean**, obtain a **List** of **GuestBean**s from the **GuestDataBean** and create an **Iterator** for manipulating the **ArrayList** contents. If there are no elements in the list (tested at line 36), line 42 returns **SKIP_BODY** to indicate that the container should perform no further processing of the **guestlist** tag's body. Otherwise, line 37 invokes **private** method **processNextGuest** (lines 80–93) to extract the information for the first guest and create variables containing that information in the JSP's **PageContext** (represented with variable **pageContext** that was inherited from **BodyTagSupport**). Method **processNextGuest** uses **PageContext** method *setAttribute* to specify each variable's name and value. The container is responsible for creating the actual variables used in the JSP. This is accomplished with the help of class **GuestBookTagExtraInfo** (Fig. B.38).

Method **doAfterBody** (lines 55–77)performs the repetitive processing of the **guestlist** tag's body. The JSP container determines whether method **doAfterBody** should be called again, based on the method's return value. If **doAfterBody** returns **EVAL_BODY_BUFFERED**, the container calls method **doAfterBody** again. If **doAfterBody** returns **SKIP_BODY**, the container stops processing the body and invokes the custom tag handler's **doEndTag** method to complete the custom processing. Line 59 invokes **writeOut** on variable **bodyContent** (inherited from **BodyTagSupport**) to process the first client's data (stored when **doStartTag** was called). Variable **bodyContent** refers to an object of class **BodyContent** from package **javax.servlet.jsp.tagext**. The argument to method **writeOut** is the result of method **getPreviousOut** (inherited from class **BodyTagSupport**), which returns the **JspWriter** object for the JSP that invokes the custom tag. This enables the custom tag to continue building the response to the client using the same output stream as the JSP. Next, line 68 invokes **bodyContent**'s method **clearBody** to ensure that the body content that was just output does not get processed as part of the next call to **doAfterBody**. Lines 70–76 determine whether there are more guests to process. If so, **doAfterBody** invokes **private** method **processNextGuest** to obtain the data for the next guest and returns **EVAL_BODY_BUFFERED** to indicate that the container should call **doAfterBody** again. Otherwise, **doAfterBody** returns **SKIP_BODY** to terminate processing of the body.

The JSP container cannot create variables in the **PageContext** unless the container knows the names and types of those variables. This information is specified by a class with the same name as the custom tag handler and that ends with **ExtraInfo** (**GuestBookTagExtraInfo** in Fig. B.38). **ExtraInfo** classes extend class *TagExtraInfo* (package **javax.servlet.jsp.tagext**). The container uses the information specified by a subclass of **TagExtraInfo** to determine what variables it should create (or use) in the **PageContext**. To specify variable information, override method *getVariableInfo*. This method returns an array of **VariableInfo** objects that the container uses either to create new variables in the **PageContext** or to enable a custom tag to use existing variables in the **PageContext**. The **VariableInfo** constructor receives four arguments—a **String** representing the name of the variable, a **String** representing the variable's class name, a **boolean** indicating whether or not the variable should be created by the container (**true** if so) and a **static** integer constant representing the variable's scope in the JSP. The constants in class **VariableInfo** are **NESTED**, **AT_BEGIN** and **AT_END**. **NESTED** indicates that the variable can be used only in the custom tag's body.

AT_BEGIN indicates that the variable can be used anywhere in the JSP after the starting tag of the custom tag is encountered. **AT_END** indicates that the variable can be used anywhere in the JSP after the ending tag of the custom tag.

Before the **guestlist** tag can be used in a JSP, we must make the JSP container aware of the tag by adding it to a tag library. To do this, add the **tag** element of Fig. B.39 as a child of element **taglib** in the tag library descriptor **jws-taglib.tld**. As in the previous example, element **tag** contains elements **name**, **tagclass**, **bodycontent** and **info**. Lines 10–12 introduce element *teiclass* for specifying the custom tag's **ExtraInfo** class.

To test **customTagBody.jsp** in Tomcat, copy **customTagBody.jsp** and the updated **jws-taglib.tld** into the **jsp** directory created in Section B.3. Copy **Guest-BookTag.class** and **GuestBookTagExtraInfo.class** into the **jws** Web application's **WEB-INF\classes** directory in Tomcat. [*Note*: This example will work only if the proper package directory structure for **GuestBookTag** and **GuestBookTagExtraInfo** is defined in the **classes** directory.] Open your Web browser and enter the following URL to test **customTagBody.jsp**:

```
http://localhost:8080/jws/jsp/customTagBody.jsp
```

```
1   // Fig. B.38: GuestBookTagExtraInfo.java
2   // Class that defines the variable names and types created by
3   // custom tag handler GuestBookTag.
4   package com.deitel.jws.jsp.taglibrary;
5
6   // Java core packages
7   import javax.servlet.jsp.tagext.*;
8
9   public class GuestBookTagExtraInfo extends TagExtraInfo {
10
11      // method that returns information about the variables
12      // GuestBookTag creates for use in a JSP
13      public VariableInfo [] getVariableInfo( TagData tagData )
14      {
15         VariableInfo firstName = new VariableInfo( "firstName",
16            "String", true, VariableInfo.NESTED );
17
18         VariableInfo lastName = new VariableInfo( "lastName",
19            "String", true, VariableInfo.NESTED );
20
21         VariableInfo email = new VariableInfo( "email",
22            "String", true, VariableInfo.NESTED );
23
24         VariableInfo varableInfo [] =
25            { firstName, lastName, email };
26
27         return varableInfo;
28      }
29   }
```

Fig. B.38   **GuestBookTagExtraInfo** used by the container to define scripting variables in a JSP that uses the **guestlist** custom tag.

```
1   <!-- A tag that iterates over an ArrayList of GuestBean -->
2   <!-- objects, so they can be output in a JSP            -->
3   <tag>
4      <name>guestlist</name>
5
6      <tagclass>
7         com.deitel.jws.jsp.taglibrary.GuestBookTag
8      </tagclass>
9
10     <teiclass>
11        com.deitel.jws.jsp.taglibrary.GuestBookTagExtraInfo
12     </teiclass>
13
14     <bodycontent>JSP</bodycontent>
15
16     <info>
17        Iterates over a list of GuestBean objects
18     </info>
19  </tag>
```

Fig. B.39 Element **tag** for the **guestlist** custom tag.

This appendix has presented many JSP capabilities. However, there are additional features that are beyond the scope of this book. For a complete description of JavaServer Pages, see the JavaServer Pages 1.1 specification, which can be downloaded from **java.sun.com/products/jsp/download.html**. Other JSP resources are listed in Section B.10.

B.9 Summary

JavaServer Pages (JSPs) are an extension of servlet technology. JavaServer Pages enable Web application programmers to create dynamic content by reusing pre-defined components and by interacting with components using server-side scripting.

JSP programmers can create custom tag libraries that enable Web-page designers who are not familiar with Java programming to enhance their Web pages with powerful dynamic content and processing capabilities.

Classes and interfaces specific to JavaServer Pages programming are located in packages **javax.servlet.jsp** and **javax.servlet.jsp.tagext**. The JavaServer Pages 1.1 specification can be downloaded from **java.sun.com/products/jsp/download.html**.

There are four key components to JSPs—directives, actions, scriptlets and tag libraries. Directives specify global information that is not associated with a particular JSP request. Actions encapsulate functionality in predefined tags that programmers can embed in a JSP. Scriptlets, or scripting elements, enable programmers to insert Java code that interacts with components in a JSP (and possibly other Web application components) to perform request processing. Tag libraries are part of the tag extension mechanism that enables programmers to create new tags that encapsulate complex Java functionality.

JSPs normally include XHTML or XML markup. Such markup is known as fixed template data or fixed template text. Programmers tend to use JSPs when most of the content sent to the client is fixed template data and only a small portion of the content is generated dynamically with Java code. Programmers use servlets when a small portion of the content is fixed template data.

JSPs normally execute as part of a Web server. The server often is referred to as the JSP container. When a JSP-enabled server receives the first request for a JSP, the JSP container translates that JSP into a Java servlet that handles the current request and future requests to the JSP. The JSP container places the Java statements that implement a JSP's response in method **_jspService** at translation time. The request/response mechanism and life cycle of a JSP are the same as those of a servlet. JSPs can define methods **jspInit** and **jspDestroy** that are invoked when the container initializes a JSP and when the container terminates a JSP, respectively.

When you first invoke a JSP in Tomcat, there is a delay as Tomcat translates the JSP into a servlet and invokes the servlet to respond to your request.

Implicit objects provide programmers with servlet capabilities in the context of a JavaServer Page. Implicit objects have four scopes—application, page, request and session. Objects with application scope are part of the JSP and servlet container application. Objects with page scope exist only as part of the page in which they are used. Each page has its own instances of the page-scope implicit objects. Objects with request scope exist for the duration of the request. Request-scope objects go out of scope when request processing completes with a response to the client. Objects with session scope exist for the client's entire browsing session.

JSP scripting components include scriptlets, comments, expressions, declarations and escape sequences. Scriptlets are blocks of code delimited by **<%** and **%>**. They contain Java statements that are placed in method **_jspService** when the container translates a JSP into a servlet. JSP comments are delimited by **<%--** and **--%>**. XHTML comments are delimited by **<!--** and **-->**. Java's single-line comments (**//**) and multiline comments (delimited by **/*** and ***/**) can be used inside scriptlets. JSP comments and scripting language comments are ignored and do not appear in the response. A JSP expression, delimited by **<%=** and **%>**, contains a Java expression that is evaluated when a client requests the JSP containing the expression. The container converts the result of a JSP expression to a **String** object, then outputs the **String** as part of the response to the client. Declarations, delimited by **<%!** and **%>**, enable a JSP programmer to define variables and methods. Variables become instance variables of the class that represents the translated JSP. Similarly, methods become members of the class that represents the translated JSP. Special characters or character sequences that the JSP container normally uses to delimit JSP code can be included in a JSP as literal characters in scripting elements, fixed template data and attribute values by using escape sequences.

JSP standard actions provide JSP implementors with access to several of the most common tasks performed in a JSP. JSP containers process actions at request time. JavaServer Pages support two include mechanisms—the **<jsp:include>** action and the **include** directive. Action **<jsp:include>** enables dynamic content to be included in a JavaServer Page. If the included resource changes between requests, the next request to the JSP containing the **<jsp:include>** action includes the new content of the resource.

The **include** directive is processed once, at JSP translation time, and causes the content to be copied into the JSP. If the included resource changes, the new content will not be reflected in the JSP that used the include directive unless that JSP is recompiled.

Action **<jsp:forward>** enables a JSP to forward the processing of a request to a different resource. Processing of the request by the original JSP terminates as soon as the request is forwarded.

Action **<jsp:param>** specifies name/value pairs of information that are passed to the **include**, **forward** and **plugin** actions. Every **<jsp:param>** action has two required attributes—**name** and **value**. If a **param** action specifies a parameter that already exists in the request, the new value for the parameter takes precedence over the original value. All values for that parameter can be obtained with the JSP implicit object **request**'s **getParameterValues** method, which returns an array of **String**s.

JSP action **<jsp:plugin>** enables an applet or JavaBean to be added to a Web page in the form of a browser-specific **object** or **embed** XHTML element. This action also enables the downloading and installation of the Java Plug-in if it is not already installed on the client computer.

Action **<jsp:useBean>** enables a JSP to manipulate a Java object. This action can be used to create a Java object for use in the JSP or to locate an existing object. Like JSP implicit objects, objects specified with action **<jsp:useBean>** have **page**, **request**, **session** or **application** scope that indicates where they can be used in a Web application. Action **<jsp:getProperty>** obtains the value of JavaBean's property. Action **<jsp:get-Property>** has two attributes—**name** and **property**—that specify the bean object to manipulate and the property to get. JavaBean property values can be set with action **<jsp:setProperty>**. This action is particularly useful for mapping request parameter values to JavaBean properties. Request parameters can be used to set properties of primitive types **boolean**, **byte**, **char**, **int**, **long**, **float** and **double** and **java.lang** types **String**, **Boolean**, **Byte**, **Character**, **Integer**, **Long**, **Float** and **Double**.

The **page** directive defines information that is globally available in a JSP. Directives are delimited by **<%@** and **%>**. The **page** directive's **errorPage** attribute indicates where all uncaught exceptions are forwarded for processing. Action **<jsp:setProperty>** has the ability to match request parameters to properties of the same name in a bean by specifying **"*"** for attribute **property**.

Attribute **import** of the **page** directive enables programmers to specify Java classes and packages that are used in the context of a JSP. If the attribute **isErrorPage** of the **page** directive is set to **true**, the JSP is an error page. This condition enables access to the JSP implicit object **exception** that refers to an exception object indicating the problem that occurred.

Directives are messages to the JSP container that enable the programmer to specify page settings (such as the error page), to include content from other resources and to specify custom tag libraries that can be used in a JSP. Directives are processed at the time a JSP is translated into a servlet and compiled. Thus, directives do not produce any immediate output.

The **page** directive specifies global settings for a JSP in the JSP container. There can be many **page** directives, provided that there is only one occurrence of each attribute. The exception to this rule is the **import** attribute, which can be used repeatedly to import Java packages.

Custom tag libraries define one or more custom tags that JSP implementors can use to create dynamic content. The functionality of these custom tags is defined in Java classes that implement interface **Tag** (package **javax.servlet.jsp.tagext**), normally by extending class **TagSupport** or **BodyTagSupport**. A JSP can include a custom tag library with the **taglib** directive.

When implementing custom tags, you must define a tag handler class for each tag that provides the tag's functionality, a tag library descriptor that provides information about the tag library and its custom tags to the JSP container and a JSP that uses the custom tag.

The most important methods of interface **Tag** are **doStartTag** and **doEndTag**. The JSP container invokes these methods when it encounters the starting custom tag and the ending custom tag, respectively. A custom tag library descriptor file is an XML document that specifies information about the tag library that is required by the JSP container.

Class **BodyTagSupport** contains several methods for interacting with the body of a custom tag, including **doInitBody** and **doAfterBody** (from interface **BodyTag**). Method **doInitBody** is called once after **doStartTag** and once before **doAfterBody**. Method **doAfterBody** can be called many times to process the body of a custom tag.

B.10 Internet and World Wide Web Resources

java.sun.com/products/jsp
The home page for information about JavaServer Pages at the Sun Microsystems Java site.

java.sun.com/products/servlet
The home page for information about servlets at the Sun Microsystems Java site.

java.sun.com/j2ee
The home page for the Java 2 Enterprise Edition at the Sun Microsystems Java site.

www.w3.org
The World Wide Web Consortium home page. This site provides information about current and developing Internet and Web standards, such as XHTML, XML and CSS.

jsptags.com
This site includes tutorials, tag libraries, software and other resources for JSP programmers.

jspinsider.com
This Web programming site concentrates on resources for JSP programmers. It includes software, tutorials, articles, sample code, references and links to other JSP and Web programming resources.

Index

The DEITEL™
Suite of Products...

Web Services:
A Technical Introduction

© 2003, 400 pp., paper (0-13-046135-0)

Web Services: A Technical Introduction from the DEITEL™ Developer Series familiarizes programmers, technical managers and project managers with key Web services concepts, including what Web services are and why they are revolutionary. The book covers the business case for Web services—the underlying technologies, ways in which Web services can provide competitive advantages and opportunities for Web services-related lines of business. Readers learn the latest Web-services standards, including XML, SOAP, WSDL and UDDI; learn about Web services implementations in .NET and Java; benefit from an extensive comparison of Web services products and vendors; and read about Web services security options. Although this is not a programming book, the appendices show .NET and Java code examples to demonstrate the structure of Web services applications and documents. In addition, the book includes numerous case studies describing ways in which organizations are implementing Web services to increase efficiency, simplify business processes, create new revenue streams and interact better with partners and customers.

Java™ Web Services
for Experienced Programmers

© 2003, 700 pp., paper (0-13-046134-2)

Java™ Web Services for Experienced Programmers from the DEITEL™ Developer Series provides the experienced Java programmer with 103 LIVE-CODE™ examples and covers industry standards including XML, SOAP, WSDL and UDDI. Learn how to build and integrate Web services using the Java API for XML RPC, the Java API for XML Messaging, Apache Axis and the Java Web Services Developer Pack. Develop and deploy Web services on several major Web services platforms. Register and discover Web services through public registries and the Java API for XML Registries. Build Web Services clients for several platforms, including J2ME. Significant Web Services case studies also are included.

Visual Basic® .NET
for Experienced Programmers

©2003, paper, approximately 1150 pp., (0-13-046131-8)

Visual Basic .NET for Experienced Programmers from the DEITEL™ Developer Series presents experienced programmers with a concise introduction to programming fundamentals before delving into more sophisticated topics. Learn how to create reusable software components with assemblies, modules and dynamic link libraries. Learn Visual Basic .NET through LIVE-CODE™ examples of ASP.NET, multi-threading, object-oriented programming, XML processing, mobile application development and Web services.

Visual C++ .NET
for Experienced Programmers:
A Managed Code Approach

© 2003, 1500 pp., paper (0-13-045821-X)

Visual C++ .NET for Experienced Programmers: A Managed Code Approach from the DEITEL™ Developer Series teaches programmers with C++ programming experience how to develop Visual C++ applications for Microsoft's new .NET Framework. The book begins with a condensed introduction to Visual C++ programming fundamentals, then covers more sophistcated .NET application-development topics in detail. Key topics include: creating reusable software components with assemblies, modules and dynamic link libraries; using classes from the Framework Class Library (FCL); building graphical user interfaces (GUIs) with the FCL; implementing multithreaded applications; building networked applications; manipulating databases with ADO .NET and creating XML Web services. In addition, the book provides several chapters on unmanaged code in Visual C++ .NET. These chapters demonstrate how to use "attributed programming" to simplify common tasks (such as connecting to a database) and improve code readability; how to integrate managed- and unmanaged-code software components; and how to use ATL Server to create Web-based applications and Web services with unmanaged code. The book features detailed LIVE-CODE™ examples that highlight crucial .NET-programming concepts and demonstrate Web services at work. A substantial introduction to XML also is included.

Java™ How to Program
Fourth Edition

BOOK / CD-ROM

©2002, 1546 pp., paper
(0-13-034151-7)

The world's best-selling Java text is now even better! The Fourth Edition of *Java How to Program* includes a new focus on object-oriented design with the UML, design patterns, full-color program listings and figures and the most up-to-date Java coverage available.

Readers will discover key topics in Java programming, such as graphical user interface components, exception handling, multithreading, multimedia, files and streams, networking, data structures and more. In addition, a new chapter on design patterns explains frequently recurring architectural patterns—information that can help save designers considerable time when building large systems.

The highly detailed optional case study focuses on object-oriented design with the UML and presents fully implemented working Java code.

Updated throughout, the text includes new and revised discussions on topics such as Swing, graphics and socket- and packet-based networking. Three introductory chapters heavily emphasize problem solving and programming skills. The chapters on RMI, JDBC™, servlets and JavaBeans have been moved to *Advanced Java 2 Platform How to Program*, where they are now covered in much greater depth. (See *Advanced Java 2 Platform How to Program* below.)

Advanced Java™ 2 Platform How to Program

BOOK / CD-ROM

©2002, 1811 pp., paper
(0-13-089560-1)

Expanding on the world's best-selling Java textbook—*Java How to Program*—*Advanced Java 2 Platform How To Program* presents advanced Java topics for developing sophisticated, user-friendly GUIs; significant, scalable enterprise applications; wireless applications and distributed systems. Primarily based on Java 2 Enterprise Edition (J2EE), this textbook integrates technologies such as XML, JavaBeans, security, Java Database Connectivity (JDBC), JavaServer Pages (JSP), servlets, Remote Method Invocation (RMI), Enterprise JavaBeans™ (EJB) and design patterns into a production-quality system that allows developers to benefit from the leverage and platform independence Java 2 Enterprise Edition provides. The book also features the development of a complete, end-to-end e-business solution using advanced Java technologies. Additional topics include Swing, Java 2D and 3D, XML, design patterns, CORBA, Jini™, JavaSpaces™, Jiro™, Java Management Extensions (JMX) and Peer-to-Peer networking with an introduction to JXTA. This textbook also introduces the Java 2 Micro Edition (J2ME™) for building applications for handheld and wireless devices using MIDP and MIDlets. Wireless technologies covered include WAP, WML and i-mode.

C# How to Program

BOOK / CD-ROM

©2002, 1568 pp., paper
(0-13-062221-4)

An exciting new addition to the How to Program series, *C# How to Program* provides a comprehensive introduction to Microsoft's new object-oriented language. C# builds on the skills already mastered by countless C++ and Java programmers, enabling them to create powerful Web applications and components—ranging from XML-based Web services on Microsoft's .NET platform to middle-tier business objects and system-level applications. *C# How to Program* begins with a strong foundation in the introductory and intermediate programming principles students will need in industry. It then explores such essential topics as object-oriented programming and exception handling. Graphical user interfaces are extensively covered, giving readers the tools to build compelling and fully interactive programs. Internet technologies such as XML, ADO .NET and Web services are also covered as well as topics including regular expressions, multithreading, networking, databases, files and data structures.

Also coming soon in the Deitels' .NET Series:

• *Visual C++ .NET How to Program*

Sign up now for the new *DEITEL™ Buzz Online* newsletter at:

programming concepts that yield visible or audible results in Web pages and Web-based applications. This book discusses effective Web-based design, server- and client-side scripting, multitier Web-based applications development, ActiveX® controls and electronic commerce essentials. This book offers an alternative to traditional programming courses using markup languages (such as XHTML, Dynamic HTML and XML) and scripting languages (such as JavaScript, VBScript, Perl/CGI, Python and PHP) to teach the fundamentals of programming "wrapped in the metaphor of the Web."

Updated material on **www.deitel.com** and **www.prenhall.com/deitel** provides additional resources for instructors who want to cover Microsoft® or non-Microsoft technologies. The Web site includes an extensive treatment of Netscape® 6 and alternate versions of the code from the Dynamic HTML chapters that will work with non-Microsoft environments as well.

i-mode, Bluetooth, MIDP, MIDlets, ASP, Microsoft .NET Mobile Framework, BREW™, multimedia, Flash™ and VBScript.

Python How to Program

BOOK / CD-ROM

©2002, 1376 pp., paper
(0-13-092361-3)

This exciting new book provides a comprehensive introduction to Python— a powerful object-oriented programming language with clear syntax and the ability to bring together various technologies quickly and easily. This book covers introductory-programming techniques and more advanced topics such as graphical user interfaces, databases, wireless Internet programming, networking, security, process management, multithreading, XHTML, CSS, PSP and multimedia. Readers will learn principles that are applicable to both systems development and Web programming. The book features the consistent and applied pedagogy that the *How to Program Series* is known for, including the Deitels' signature LIVE-CODE™ Approach, with thousands of lines of code in hundreds of working programs; hundreds of valuable programming tips identified with icons throughout the text; an extensive set of exercises, projects and case studies; two-color four-way syntax coloring and much more.

Wireless Internet & Mobile Business How to Program

©2002, 1292 pp., paper
(0-13-062226-5)

While the rapid expansion of wireless technologies, such as cell phones, pagers and personal digital assistants (PDAs), offers many new opportunities for businesses and programmers, it also presents numerous challenges related to issues such as security and standardization. This book offers a thorough treatment of both the management and technical aspects of this growing area, including coverage of current practices and future trends. The first half explores the business issues surrounding wireless technology and mobile business, including an overview of existing and developing communication technologies and the application of business principles to wireless devices. It also discusses location-based services and location-identifying technologies, a topic that is revisited throughout the book. Wireless payment, security, legal and social issues, international communications and more are also discussed. The book then turns to programming for the wireless Internet, exploring topics such as WAP (including 2.0), WML, WMLScript, XML, XHTML™, wireless Java programming (J2ME)™, Web Clipping and more. Other topics covered include career resources, wireless marketing, accessibility, Palm™, PocketPC, Windows CE,

e-Business & e-Commerce for Managers

©2001, 794 pp., cloth
(0-13-032364-0)

This comprehensive overview of building and managing e-businesses explores topics such as the decision to bring a business online, choosing a business model, accepting payments, marketing strategies and security, as well as many other important issues (such as career resources). The book features Web resources and online demonstrations that supplement the text and direct readers to additional materials. The book also includes an appendix that develops a complete Web-based shopping-cart application using HTML, JavaScript, VBScript, Active Server Pages, ADO, SQL, HTTP, XML and XSL. Plus, company-specific sections provide "real-world" examples of the concepts presented in the book.

XML How to Program

BOOK / CD-ROM

©2001, 934 pp., paper (0-13-028417-3)

This book is a comprehensive guide to programming in XML. It teaches how to use XML to create customized tags and includes chapters that address standard custom-markup languages for science and technology, multimedia, commerce and many other fields. Concise introductions to Java, JavaServer Pages, VBScript, Active Server Pages and Perl/CGI provide readers with the essentials of these programming languages and server-side development technologies to enable them to work effectively with XML. The book also covers cutting-edge topics such as XSL, DOM™ and SAX, plus a real-world e-commerce case study and a complete chapter on Web accessibility that addresses Voice XML. It includes tips such as Common Programming Errors, Software Engineering Observations, Portability Tips and Debugging Hints. Other topics covered include XHTML, CSS, DTD, schema, parsers, XPath, XLink, namespaces, XBase, XInclude, XPointer, XSLT, XSL Formatting Objects, JavaServer Pages, XForms, topic maps, X3D, MathML, OpenMath, CML, BML, CDF, RDF, SVG, Cocoon, WML, XBRL and BizTalk™ and SOAP™ Web resources.

Perl How to Program

BOOK / CD-ROM

©2001, 1057 pp., paper (0-13-028418-1)

This comprehensive guide to Perl programming emphasizes the use of the Common Gateway Interface (CGI) with Perl to create powerful, dynamic multi-tier Web-based client/server applications. The book begins with a clear and careful introduction to programming concepts at a level suitable for beginners, and proceeds through advanced topics such as references and complex data structures. Key Perl topics such as regular expressions and string manipulation are covered in detail. The authors address important and topical issues such as object-oriented programming, the Perl database interface (DBI), graphics and security. Also included is a treatment of XML, a bonus chapter introducing the Python programming language, supplemental material on career resources and a complete chapter on Web accessibility. The text includes tips such as Common Programming Errors, Software Engineering Observations, Portability Tips and Debugging Hints.

e-Business & e-Commerce How to Program

BOOK / CD-ROM

©2001, 1254 pp., paper (0-13-028419-X)

This innovative book explores programming technologies for developing Web-based e-business and e-commerce solutions, and covers e-business and e-commerce models and business issues. Readers learn a full range of options, from "build-your-own" to turnkey solutions. The book examines scores of the top e-businesses (examples include Amazon, eBay, Priceline, Travelocity, etc.), explaining the technical details of building successful e-business and e-commerce sites and their underlying business premises. Learn how to implement the dominant e-commerce models—shopping carts, auctions, name-your-own-price, comparison shopping and bots/ intelligent agents—by using markup languages (HTML, Dynamic HTML and XML), scripting languages (JavaScript, VBScript and Perl), server-side technologies (Active Server Pages and Perl/CGI) and database (SQL and ADO), security and online payment technologies. Updates are regularly posted to www.deitel.com and the book includes a CD-ROM with software tools, source code and live links.

www.deitel.com/newsletter/subscribe.html

ORDER INFORMATION

SINGLE COPY SALES:
Visa, Master Card, American Express, Checks, or Money Orders only
Toll-Free: 800-643-5506; Fax: 800-835-5327

GOVERNMENT AGENCIES:
Prentice Hall Customer Service
(#GS-02F-8023A)
Phone: 201-767-5994; Fax: 800-445-6991

COLLEGE PROFESSORS:
For desk or review copies, please visit us on the World Wide Web at www.prenhall.com

CORPORATE ACCOUNTS:
Quantity, Bulk Orders totaling 10 or more books. Purchase orders only — No credit cards.
Tel: 201-236-7156; Fax: 201-236-7141
Toll-Free: 800-382-3419

CANADA:
Pearson Technology Group Canada
10 Alcorn Avenue, suite #300
Toronto, Ontario, Canada M4V 3B2
Tel.: 416-925-2249; Fax: 416-925-0068
E-mail: phcinfo.pubcanada@pearsoned.com

UK/IRELAND:
Pearson Education
Edinburgh Gate
Harlow, Essex CM20 2JE UK
Tel: 01279 623928; Fax: 01279 414130
E-mail: enq.orders@pearsoned-ema.com

EUROPE, MIDDLE EAST & AFRICA:
Pearson Education
P.O. Box 75598
1070 AN Amsterdam, The Netherlands
Tel: 31 20 5755 800; Fax: 31 20 664 5334
E-mail: amsterdam@pearsoned-ema.com

ASIA:
Pearson Education Asia
317 Alexandra Road #04-01
IKEA Building
Singapore 159965
Tel: 65 476 4688; Fax: 65 378 0370

JAPAN:
Pearson Education
Nishi-Shinjuku, KF Building 101
8-14-24 Nishi-Shinjuku, Shinjuku-ku
Tokyo, Japan 160-0023
Tel: 81 3 3365 9001; Fax: 81 3 3365 9009

INDIA:
Pearson Education Indian Liaison Office
90 New Raidhani Enclave, Ground Floor
Delhi 110 092, India
Tel: 91 11 2059850 & 2059851
Fax: 91 11 2059852

AUSTRALIA:
Pearson Education Australia
Unit 4, Level 2
14 Aquatic Drive
Frenchs Forest, NSW 2086, Australia
Tel: 61 2 9454 2200; Fax: 61 2 9453 0089
E-mail: marketing@pearsoned.com.au

NEW ZEALAND/FIJI:
Pearson Education
46 Hillside Road
Auckland 10, New Zealand
Tel: 649 444 4968; Fax: 649 444 4957
E-mail: sales@pearsoned.co.nz

SOUTH AFRICA:
Pearson Education
P.O. Box 12122
Mill Street
Cape Town 8010 South Africa
Tel: 27 21 686 6356; Fax: 27 21 686 4590

LATIN AMERICA:
Pearson Education Latinoamerica
815 NW 57th Street Suite 484
Miami, FL 33158
Tel: 305 264 8344; Fax: 305 264 7933

Complete Training Courses

Each complete package includes the corresponding *How to Program Series* book and interactive multimedia CD-ROM Cyber Classroom. *Complete Training Courses* are perfect for anyone interested Web and e-commerce programming. They are affordable resources for college students and professionals learning programming for the first time or reinforcing their knowledge.

Each *Complete Training Course* is compatible with Windows 95, Windows 98, Windows NT and Windows 2000 and includes the following features:

Intuitive Browser-Based Interface

You'll love the *Complete Training Courses'* new browser-based interface, designed to be easy and accessible to anyone who's ever used a Web browser. Every *Complete Training Course* features the full text, illustrations and program listings of its corresponding *How to Program* book—all in full color—with full-text searching and hyperlinking.

Further Enhancements to the Deitels' Signature LIVE-CODE™ Approach

Every code sample from the main text can be found in the interactive, multimedia, CD-ROM-based *Cyber Classrooms* included in the *Complete Training Courses*. Syntax coloring of code is included for the *How to Program* books that are published in full color. Even the recent two-color and one-color books use effective multi-way syntax shading. The *Cyber Classroom* products always are in full color.

Audio Annotations

Hours of detailed, expert audio descriptions of thousands of lines of code help reinforce concepts.

Easily Executable Code

With one click of the mouse, you can execute the code or save it to your hard drive to manipulate using the programming environment of your choice. With selected *Complete Training Courses*, you can also load all of the code into a development environment such as Microsoft® Visual C++™, enabling you to modify and execute the programs with ease.

Abundant Self-Assessment Material

Practice exams test your understanding with hundreds of test questions and answers in addition to those found in the main text. Hundreds of self-review questions, all with answers, are drawn from the text; as are hundreds of programming exercises, half with answers.

www.phptr.com/phptrinteractive

Sign up now for the new *DEITEL™ Buzz Online* newsletter at:

Future Publications

Here are some new titles we are considering for 2002/2003 release:

Computer Science Series: *Operating Systems 3/e, Data Structures in C++, Data Structures in Java, Theory and Principles of Database Systems.*

Database Series: *Oracle, SQL Server, MySQL.*

Internet and Web Programming Series: *Open Source Software Development: Apache, Linux, MySQL and PHP.*

Programming Series: *Flash™.*

.NET Programming Series: *ADO .NET with Visual Basic .NET, ASP .NET with Visual Basic .NET, ADO .NET with C#, ASP .NET with C#.*

Object Technology Series: *OOAD with the UML, Design Patterns, Java™ and XML.*

Advanced Java™ Series: *JDBC, Java 2 Enterprise Edition, Java Media Framework (JMF), Java Security and Java Cryptography (JCE), Java Servlets, Java2D and Java3D, JavaServer Pages™ (JSP), JINI and Java 2 Micro Edition™ (J2ME).*

DEITEL™ BUZZ ONLINE Newsletter

The Deitel and Associates, Inc. free opt-in newsletter includes:

- Updates and commentary on industry trends and developments
- Resources and links to articles from our published books and upcoming publications.
- Information on the Deitel publishing plans, including future publications and product-release schedules
- Support for instructors
- Resources for students
- Information on Deitel Corporate Training

To sign up for the Deitel™ Buzz Online newsletter, visit `www.deitel.com /newsletter/subscribe.html`.

E-Books

We are committed to providing our content in traditional print formats and in emerging electronic formats, such as e-books, to fulfill our customers' needs. Our R&D teams are currently exploring many leading-edge solutions.

Visit `www.deitel.com` and read the DEITEL™ BUZZ ONLINE for periodic updates.

Turn the page to find out more about Deitel & Associates!

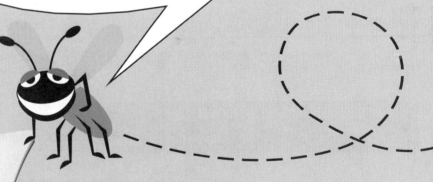